IUS COMMUNE CASEE
FOR THE COMMON LAW C

CASES, MATERIALS AND TEXT ON EUROPEAN LAW AND PRIVATE LAW

Cases, Materials and Text on European Law and Private Law

Edited by

Arthur Hartkamp, Carla Sieburgh, Wouter Devroe

·H A R T·
PUBLISHING
OXFORD AND PORTLAND, OREGON
2017

Hart Publishing

An imprint of Bloomsbury Publishing Plc

Hart Publishing Ltd
Kemp House
Chawley Park
Cumnor Hill
Oxford OX2 9PH
UK

Bloomsbury Publishing Plc
50 Bedford Square
London
WC1B 3DP
UK

www.hartpub.co.uk
www.bloomsbury.com

Published in North America (US and Canada) by
Hart Publishing
c/o International Specialized Book Services
920 NE 58th Avenue, Suite 300
Portland, OR 97213-3786
USA

www.isbs.com

HART PUBLISHING, the Hart/Stag logo, BLOOMSBURY and the
Diana logo are trademarks of Bloomsbury Publishing Plc

First published 2017

© The Editors 2017

British Library Cataloguing-in-Publication Data
A catalogue record for this book is available from the British Library.

ISBN: HB: 978-1-50991-187-5
ePDF: 978-1-50991-189-9
ePub: 978-1-50991-188-2

Library of Congress Cataloging-in-Publication Data

Names: Hartkamp, A. S., editor. | Sieburgh, C. H., editor. | Devroe, W., editor.

Title: Cases, materials, and text on European law and private law / edited by Arthur Hartkamp,
Carla Sieburgh & Wouter Devroe.

Description: Oxford [UK] ; Portland, Oregon : Hart Publishing, 2017. | Series: IUS commune casebooks for the common
law of Europe | Includes bibliographical references and index.

Identifiers: LCCN 2017001276 (print) | LCCN 2017002146 (ebook) | ISBN 9781509911875
(pbk. :alk. paper) | ISBN 9781509911882 (Epub)

Subjects: LCSH: Law—European Union countries. | Law—European Union countries—Cases. | Treaty Establishing the
European Economic Community (1957 March 25) | Civil law—European Union countries. | Antitrust law—European
Union countries. | Constitutional law—European Union countries. | Civil rights—European Union countries. |
Court of Justice of the European Union. | LCGFT: Casebooks

Classification: LCC KJE945 .C373 2017 (print) | LCC KJE945 (ebook) | DDC 349.24—dc23

LC record available at https://lccn.loc.gov/2017001276

Typeset by Compuscript Ltd, Shannon
Printed and bound in Great Britain by CPI Group (UK) Ltd, Croydon CR0 4YY

To find out more about our authors and books visit www.hartpublishing.co.uk. Here you will find extracts, author information,
details of forthcoming events and the option to sign up for our newsletters.

ACKNOWLEDGEMENTS

The editors and publisher gratefully acknowledge the authors and publishers of extracted material which appears in this book and in particular the following:

R van den Bergh, 'Private Enforcement of European Competition Law and the Persisting Collective Action Problem' (2013) 20(1) *Maastricht Journal of European and Comparative Law* 12.

G Blanke and P Landolt, *EU and US Antitrust Arbitration: A Handbook for Practitioners, Volume 1* (Alphen aan den Rijn, Kluwer Law International, 2011).

C Cauffman, 'The Impact of Voidness for Infringements of Article 101 TFEU on Related Contracts' (2012) 12(1) *European Competition Journal* 122.

P Craig and G de Búrca, *EU Law: Text, Cases, and Materials*, 6th ed (Oxford, Oxford University Press, 2015).

T Eilmansberger, 'Zur Nichtigkeit kartellrechtswidriger Vereinbarungen und ihren Konsequenzen (2. Teil)' (2009) 131(7) *Juristische Blätter* 434.

X Groussot, *General Principles of Community Law* (Groningen, Europa Law Publishing, 2006).

AS Hartkamp, *European Law and National Private Law. Effect of EU Law and European Human Rights Law on Legal Relationships between Individuals*, 2nd ed (Cambridge, Intersentia, 2016).

LAD Keus, 'The Principle of Legal Certainty' in AS Hartkamp, CH Sieburgh, LAD Keus, JS Kortmann & MH Wissink (eds), *The Influence of EU Law on National Private Law*, Serie Onderneming en Recht Volume 81-1 | General Part (Deventer, Kluwer, 2014).

AP Komninos, '"Transient" and "Transitional" Voidness of Anti-competitive Agreements: A Non-issue and an Issue' (2007) 28(8) *European Competition Law Review* 445.

AP Komninos, 'Private Antitrust Enforcement in the National Courts—Second Generation Questions' in 'Special Issue—Private Enforcement: An Overview of EU and National Case Law', *e-Competitions*, March 2012.

K Lenaerts and P van Nuffel, *European Union Law*, 3rd ed (London, Sweet & Maxwell, 2011).

S Peyer, 'Injunctive Relief and Private Antitrust Enforcement' (2011) *CCP Working Papers* (Centre for Competition Policy, University of East Anglia) 11-7.

S Prechal, *Directives in EC Law* (Oxford, Oxford University Press, 2005).

S Prechal and R Widdershoven, 'Redefining the Relationship between "Rewe-Effectiveness" and Effective Judicial Protection' (2011) 4(2) *Review of European Administrative Law* 46.

V Rose and D Baily (eds), *Bellamy & Child, European Union Law of Competition*, 7th ed (Oxford, Oxford University Press, 2013).

K Schmidt, 'Art 101 Abs 2 AEUV', in U Immenga, E-J Mestmäcker and T Körber, *Immenga/Mestmäcker Wettbewerbsrecht. Band 1: EU/ Teil 1 Kommentar zum Europäischen Kartellrecht* (München, Verlag C.H. Beck, 2012).

T Tridimas, *The General Principles of EU Law*, 2nd ed (Oxford, Oxford University Press, 2006).

R Whish and D Bailey, *Competition Law*, 8th ed (Oxford, Oxford University Press, 2015).

B de Witte, 'Direct Effect, Primacy and the Nature of the legal order' in P Craig and G De Búrca (eds) *The Evolution of EU Law* (Oxford, Oxford University Press, 2011).

While every care has been taken to establish and acknowledge copyright, and to contact copyright owners, the publishers apologise for any accidental infringement and would be pleased to come to a suitable agreement with the rightful copyright owners in each case.

PREFACE

This Casebook deals with the horizontal effects of EU law, viz. its effects on relationships between individuals. To a large extent, these effects have been created by the Court of Justice of the European Union (CJEU) on the basis of the European Treaties. Whereas the impact of directives on private law has become more or less well-known by now, until recently the developments relating to primary EU law were hardly noted by private lawyers due to their inexperience in the field of EU law; and those developments were perhaps not sufficiently explained by scholars of EU law due to their inexperience with private law.[1]

For these reasons, the editors of this Casebook believe that the time has come to devote serious attention to the relevance of the case law of the Court of Justice (CJ) for private law in the Member States of the EU, as applied by the courts in those Member States. Guidance must be provided to national private lawyers, including judges, who increasingly have to deal with these cases. On the other hand, EU lawyers need to become more familiar with the ways in which EU law interacts with private law.

Although the focus of this Casebook is on the effects of developments in primary EU law (in particular TFEU provisions, general principles and Charter provisions), secondary EU law must not remain out of sight. The CJ case law relating to (non-)implementation

---

[1] Important exceptions can be found in particular in German literature, notably E Steindorff, *EG-Vertrag und Privatrecht* (Baden-Baden, Nomos, 1996); I Klauer, *Die Europäisierung des Privatrechts* (Baden-Baden, Nomos, 1998); O Remien, *Zwingendes Vetragsrecht und Grundfreiheiten des EG-Vertrages* (Tübingen, Mohr Siebeck, 2003); M Gebauer and T Wiedmann, *Zivilrecht unter europäischem Einfluss*, 2nd ed (Stuttgart, Boorberg, 2010).
In recent years academic discussion has intensified. See the following collections of essays:

- AS Hartkamp, CH Sieburgh and LAD Keus (eds), *De invloed van het Europese recht op het Nederlandse privaatrecht*, Deel I Algemeen Deel, Deel II Bijzonder Deel Serie Onderneming en Recht delen 42-I en 42-II (Deventer, Kluwer, 2007).
- I Samoy, V Sagaert and E Terryn (eds), *Invloed van het Europese recht op het Belgisch Privaatrecht* (Antwerpen, Intersentia, 2012).
- D Leczykiewicz and S Weatherill (eds), *The Involvement of EU Law in Private Law Relationships* (Oxford, Oxford University Press, 2013).
- U Bernitz, X Groussot and F Shulyok et al (eds), *General Principles of EU Law and European Private law*, European Monographs series (Alphen aan den Rijn, Kluwer Law International, 2013).
- AS Hartkamp, CH Sieburgh, LAD Keus, JS Kortmann & MH Wissink (eds), *The Influence of EU Law on National Private Law*, Serie Onderneming en Recht Volume 81-I General Part, Volume 81-II Bijzonder Deel (Deventer, Kluwer, 2014).
- H-W Micklitz (ed), *Constitutionalization of European Private Law* (Oxford, Oxford University Press, 2014).

Some recent monographs:

- AS Hartkamp, *European Law and National Private Law. Effect of EU Law and European Human Rights Law on Legal relationships between Individuals*, 2nd ed (Cambridge, Intersentia, 2016).
- N Reich, *General Principles of EU Civil Law* (Cambridge, Intersentia, 2014).
- H-W Micklitz, P Rott and K Tonner, *European Consumer Law*, 2nd ed (Cambridge, Intersentia, 2014).

of directives (including harmonious interpretation of national law and *Francovich* liability of Member States) is interesting in theory and important in the practice of the Member States. The same is true for the *ex officio* application of provisions of consumer law directives imposed by CJ case law relating to this subject.[2] It is not the intention to enter into the details of secondary law, eg the way in which individual directives are interpreted by the CJ or transposed in specific Member States or how the transposing legislation is interpreted in Member States.

So the thrust of the Casebook is the influence of primary EU law on general private law, including the interaction with national private law, as applied by Member States courts. For that purpose it is necessary to define which provisions and principles of EU law do have an impact (or a potential for having an impact) on private law. Against that background the research focuses on national private law in a number of Member States with the aim of discovering if and to what extent (and in which sense) EU primary law has already directly or indirectly exercised its influence on the case law in those jurisdictions.

For practical and financial reasons it has not been possible to include the jurisdictions of all Member States in our research. The group consisted of members from Belgium, England, France, Germany, Hungary, Italy, the Netherlands, Poland, Portugal and Sweden. Several members were able to search for relevant case law in more than one jurisdiction. The members of the group were:

Jean-Sylvestre Bergé (*Université Jean Moulin Lyon 3*)
Ulf Bernitz (*University of Stockholm*)
José Caramelo Gomes (*Universidade Portucalense)*
Wouter Devroe (*KU Leuven*)
Balász Fekete (*Hungarian Academy of Sciences, Eötvös Loránd University Budapest*)
Arthur Hartkamp (*Radboud University Nijmegen*, chair)
Roel van Leuken (*Radboud University Nijmegen*, secretary)
Anna Maria Mancaleoni (*University of Cagliari*)
Jerzy Pisulinski (*Jagiellonian University Cracow*)
Jeremias Prassl (*St. John's College, Oxford University)*
Oliver Remien (*Universität Würzburg*)
Ilse Samoy (*KU Leuven*)
Carla Sieburgh (*Radboud University Nijmegen*)

Chapters have been written by the group members and the following persons:

Caroline Cauffman (*Maastricht University*)
Blandine de Clavière (*Université Jean Moulin Lyon 3*)

---

[2] Although the Casebook in general restricts itself to substantive private law and therefore leaves aside procedural law and private international law, *ex officio* application is dealt with (in Ch 7) for several reasons. First, the subject is closely related to both substantive and procedural law. Secondly, *ex officio* application is relevant both in primary law and in secondary law; however, for directives it works differently, because—unlike a rule of primary law or a regulation—a directive, in the absence of direct horizontal effect, cannot itself be applied *ex officio* in a horizontal relationship. Consequently, the CJ has held that EU law requires the *ex officio* application of the national implementing legislation and not of the directive.

Sander Van Loock (*KU Leuven*)
Marloes van de Moosdijk (*Radboud University Nijmegen*)

Against the background of the state of affairs in EU law, the Casebook intends to explore national case law in order to assess to what extent national practice in the civil courts of Member States has already been dealing with the influence of primary EU law on general private law. The authors of the chapters in principle based their research on national case law reported by the other group members, who have all agreed to act as national reporters.

The results of our research can be the basis for a more profound academic exchange between EU law and private law. They can also stimulate judges and other practitioners in Member States to familiarise themselves with the problems involved and to plead relevant cases in court.

Moreover, from the point of view of comparative private law this has been an interesting research, both as regards the subjects that have come to the fore and the ways in which they have been solved by the national courts in the various Member States. Some experience in this regard had been gained in Belgium and the Netherlands. The 'Association for the Comparative Study of the Law in Belgium and the Netherlands', which every year invites comparative studies of the law in these two countries in the fields of constitutional law, criminal law and private law, devoted the 2011 endeavours of the private law section to studies of the influence of primary EU law on the case law in the two jurisdictions.[3]

It is the intention of the editors to continue to follow the developments in national private law. Users of this Casebook are invited to get into contact with us, either directly or through the website of the Casebook Project (see below), to share with us developments in the case law of their national jurisdictions which might be interesting for a second edition of this book.

Against the background of the considerations presented in Chapter 1, the Casebook deals with the following subjects. The authors primarily responsible for the chapter are indicated in italics.

Chapter 1. Introduction: Effects of EU law on relationships between individuals (*Hartkamp*).
Chapter 2. Competition law *(Devroe, Cauffman, Bernitz)*.
Chapter 3. Fundamental freedoms (TFEU provisions on free movement) (*Van Leuken, De Clavière, Bergé, Remien*).
Chapter 4. Non-discrimination provisions in the TFEU (*i.e.* other than the provisions on fundamental freedoms) (*Sieburgh*).
Chapter 5. General Principles of EU law.

    — General principles of a public-law nature *(Van Leuken, Gomes)*.
    — Prohibition of discrimination (*Sieburgh*).

---

[3] The two studies were presented to and discussed in the meeting of November 2011: W Devroe and J Stuyck, 'De horizontale werking van het (primaire) recht van de Europese Unie en het Belgische vermogensrecht'; AS Hartkamp, 'De horizontale werking van het (primaire) recht van de Europese Unie en het Nederlandse vermogensrecht' in *Preadviezen voor de Vereniging voor de vergelijkende studie van het recht in Nederland en België* (Den Haag, Boom Juridische uitgevers, 2011) p 241–304 and p 305–361 respectively.

— Abuse of right (*Prassl*).
— Unjust enrichment (*Van de Moosdijk*).

Chapter 6. Directives (*Van Loock, Samoy, Pisulinski*).
Chapter 7. Application of primary and secondary EU law on the national courts' own motion (*Fekete, Mancaleoni*).

The group has operated within the framework of the *Ius Commune* Casebooks, founded by professor Walter van Gerven. His intellectual influence on the project has been great. Many of the editors and contributors were inspired by the way he combined broad expertise, profound knowledge of both private law and EU law and their mutual interaction and a contagious creativeness to discover deep rooted justice.

For further information on the *Ius Commune* Casebooks we refer to its website (www. casebooks.eu). The coordinator of this project, *Dimitri Droshout* (Leuven), has been a valuable adviser of our research group.

The work of the group has been made possible by a grant of Ammodo, a Dutch foundation for the advancement of science, humanities and the arts (www.ammodo.org).

The Hague/Nijmegen/Leuven, 18 July 2016
Arthur Hartkamp
Carla Sieburgh
Wouter Devroe

CONTENTS

TABLE OF ABBREVIATIONS

List of abbreviations used in this Casebook

Art., Arts.	Article(s)
ABGB	Allgemeines Bürgerliches Gesetzbuch *(Austrian Civil Code)*
AC	Law Reports, Appeal Cases, House of Lords and Privy Council (since 1980)
AG	Advocate General
AcP	Archiv für die civilistische Praxis
ACPCP	Act on Commercial Practices and Consumer Protection
AM	Actualiteiten Mededingingsrecht
ArbG	Arbeitsgericht *(Employment Tribunal)*
Arr Cass	Arresten van het Hof van Cassatie België
Arr.GwH	Arresten Grondwettelijk Hof
BFR	Bank- en financieel recht *(Financial forum)*
BGB	Bürgerliches Gesetzbuch *(German Code Civil)*
BGH	Bundesgerichtshof *(Federal Supreme Court of Germany)*
BW	Burgerlijk Wetboek *(Dutch Civil Code)*
Cass it.	Corte di Cassazione *(Italian Court of Cassation)*
Cour de cassation (Ch. Soc.)	Court de Cassation, Chambre Social *(French Court of Cassation, Social Chamber)*
CCC	Contrats Concurrence Consommation
CCP Working Papers	Centre for Competition Policy Working Papers
CDE	Cahiers de Droit Europeen
Cf	compare *(in Latin: confer)*
Charter (of Fundamental Rights (EU))	Charter of Fundamental Rights of the European Union
CJEU	Court of Justice of the European Union
CJ	Court of Justice
CMLR	Common Market Law Review

CPC	Code de Procédure Civile *(French Code of Civil Procedure)*
D.	Recueil Dalloz
DCCR	Droit de la Consommation
DCFR	Draft Common Frame of Reference
Dz.U.	Dziennik Ustaw *(Journal of Laws)*
EBLR	European Business Law Review
EC	European Commission/Community
ECHR	European Convention of Human Rights
ECLI	European Case Law Identifier
ECLR	European Competition Law Reporter
ECN	European Competition Network
ECR	European Court Reports
EEA	European Economic Area
ed, eds	editor(s)
ed	edition
eg	for example
E.L. Rev.	European Law Review
EPL	European Public Law
et al	and others *(in Latin: et alii)*
etc	et cetera
ERPL	European Review of Private Law
EU	European Union
EuR	EuropaRecht
Eur.Vervoerr.	Europees Vervoersrecht *(European transport law)*
EuZW	Europäische Zeitschrift für Wirtschaftsrecht
EWS	Europäisches Wirtschafts- und Steuerrecht
f,ff	following 1 more page, 2 or more following pages
Foro it.	Foro italiano
GC	General Court of the European Union
GRUR	Gewerblicher Rechtsschutz und Urheberrecht
ICCPR	International Covenant on Civil and Political Rights
I.C.R.	Industrial Cases Reports
i.e.	that is *(in Latin: id est)*
IIC	International Review of Industrial Property and Copyright Law

infra	below
HR	Hoge Raad der Nederlanden *(Supreme Court of the Netherlands)*
JB	Juristische Blätter
JCP. G	Juris-Classeur Périodique, Édition Générale
JCP	Juris-Classeur Périodique
J.L.M.B.	Jurisprudence de Liege, Mons et Bruxelles
JORF	Journal Officiel de la République française
JT	Journal des Tribunaux
JuS	Juristische Schulung
JZ	Juristenzeitung
MJ	Maastricht Journal of European and Comparative Law
MvT	Memorie van Toelichting
NCAs	National competition authorities
NJ	Nederlandse Jurisprudentie
NJF	Nederlandse Jurisprudentie Feitenrechtspraak
NJW	Nieuw Juridisch Weekblad / Neue Juristische Wochenschrift
no, nos	number(s)
n.y.r.	not yet reported
LEC	Ley de Enjuiciamiento Civil *(Spanish Code of Civil Procedure)*
LJN	Landelijk Jurisprudentie Nummer
LQR	The Law Quarterly Review
OLG	Higher Regional Court
op. cit.	in the work cited *(in Latin: opere citato)*
OSNAPiUS	Jurisprudence of Supreme Court Administration, Employment and Social Security Chamber
OSNC	Jurisprudence of Supreme Court Civil Chamber
para, paras	paragraph(s)
Pas.	Pasicrisie belge
Parl. St. Kamer	Parliamentary Proceedings Chamber of Representatives
p, pp	page(s)
PECL	Principles of European Contract Law
PICC	Principles of International Commercial Contracts
PJ	Pensioen Jurisprudentie

RabelsZ	Rabels Zeitschrift für ausländisches und internationales Privatrecht
R.D.C.	Référence Revue de droit commercial belge
RGAR	Revue générale des assurances et des responsabilités
R.C.J.B.	Revue critique de jurisprudence belge
RTD. civ	Revue trimestrielle de droit civil
RTD. Com.	Revue trimestrielle de droit commercial et de droit économique
R.W.	Rechtskundig Weekblad
supra	above
TBBR	Tijdschrift voor Belgisch burgerlijk recht
T.B.H.	Tijdschrift voor Belgisch Handelsrecht *(Revue de Droit Commercial Belge)*
TBM-RCB	Tijdschrift voor Belgische Mededinging / Revue de la Concurrence Belge
TEU	Treaty on the European Union
TFEU	Treaty on the Functioning of the European Union
TPR	Tijdschrift voor Privaatrecht
TzBfG	Act on Part-Time Work and Fixed-Term Employment Contracts
UKHL	United Kingdom House of Lords Decisions
UKSC	United Kingdom Supreme Court
viz.	videlicet / namely
vol	volume
WiB	Wirtschaftsrechtliche Beratung
W.L.R.	Weekly Law Reports
WM	Zeitschrift für Wirtschafts- und Bankrecht
WPNR	Weekblad voor Privaatrecht, Notariaat en Registratie
WuW/E BGH	Wirtschaft und Wettbewerb-Entscheidungen des Bundesgerichtshofs
ZEuP	Zeitschrift für Europäisches Privatrecht
ZIP	Zeitschrift für Wirtschaftsrecht
ZPO	Zivilprozessordung *(German Code of Civil Procedure)*

LIST OF SHORT TITLES

This list of short titles contains the most important literature used by the authors when writing this Casebook.

BOOKS

Bernitz/Groussot/Schulyok (eds) 2013

U Bernitz, X Groussot and F Schulyok (eds), *General Principles of EU Law and European Private law*, European Monographs (Alphen aan den Rijn, Kluwer Law International, 2013).

Craig and De Búrca 2015

P Craig and G de Búrca, *EU Law: Text, Case and Materials*, 6th ed (Oxford, Oxford University Press, 2015).

Dashwood/Dougan/Rodger/Spaventa/Wyatt 2011

A Dashwoord, M Dougan, B Rodger, E Spaventa and D Wyatt, *Wyatt and Dashwood's European Union Law*, 6th ed (Oxford, Hart Publishing, 2011).

De la Feria and Vogenauer (eds) 2011

R de la Feria and S Vogenauer, *Prohibition of Abuse of Law: A New General Principle of EU Law?* (Oxford, Hart Publishing, 2011).

Gullifer and Vogenauer (eds) 2014

L Gullifer and S Vogenauer, *English and European Perspectives on Contract and Commercial Law. Essays in Honour of Hugh Beale* (Oxford, Hart Publishing, 2014).

Inmmenga/Mestmäcker 2012

U Immenga and E-J Mestmäcker, *Wettbewerbsrecht*, Band 1 EU/Teil 1 Kommentar zum Europäischen Kartelrecht 5. Auflage (Munich, Verlag C.H. Beck München, 2012).

Hartkamp 2016

AS Hartkamp, *European Law and National Private Law. Effect of EU Law and European Human Rights Law on Legal Relationships between Individuals*, 2nd ed (Cambridge, Intersentia, 2016).

Hartkamp/Sieburgh/Keus/Kortmann/Wissink (eds) 2014

AS Hartkamp, CH Sieburgh, LAD Keus, JS Kortmann & MH Wissink (eds), *The Influence of EU Law on National Private Law*, Serie Onderneming en Recht Volume 81-1 | General Part (Deventer, Kluwer, 2014).

Hartley 2010

TC Hartley, *The Foundations of European Union Law* (Oxford, Oxford University Press, 2010).

Komninos 2008

AP Komninos, EC Private Antitrust Enforcement. Decentralised Application of EC Competition Law by National Courts (Oxford, Hart Publishing, 2007).

Lenaerts and Van Nuffel 2011

K Lenaerts and P van Nuffel, *European Union Law*, 3rd ed (London, Sweet & Maxwell, 2011).

Loewenheim/Meessen/Riesenkamp (eds) 2009
U Loewenheim, KM Meessen and A Riesenkamp (eds), *Kartellrecht – Kommentar*, 2. Auflage (Munich, Verlag C.H. Beck München, 2009).

Prechal 2005
S Prechal, *Directives in EC Law* (Oxford, Oxford University Press, 2005).

Rose and Baily (eds) 2013
V Rose and D Baily (eds), *Bellamy & Child, European Union Law of Competition*, 7th ed (Oxford, Oxford University Press, 2013).

Tridimas 2006
T Tridimas, *The General Principles of EU Law*, 2nd ed (Oxford, Oxford University Press, 2006).

JOURNAL TITLES

Cauffman 2012
C Cauffman, 'The impact of voidness for Infringement of Article 101 Tfeu on Related Contracts' (2012) *European Competition Journal* vol 12 no 1 p 95–121.

Ebers 2010
M Ebers 'ECJ (First Chamber) 6 October 2009, Case C-40/08, Asturcom Telecomunicaciones SL v. Cristina Rodríguez Nogueira. From Océono to Asturcom: Mandatory Consumer Law, *Ex Officio* Application of European Union Law and Res Judicata' (2010) *ERPL* vol 18 no 4 p 823–846.

Gebauer 2010
M Gebauer, 'Europäische Auslegung des Zivilrechts. Methodik – Auslegung und Direktwirkung des europäischen Rechts – Richtlinienkonforme Auslegung und Fortbildung des nationalen Rechts', Kapitel 3 in M Gebauer and T Wiedmann (eds), *Zivilrecht unter europäischem Einfluss* (Stuttgart, Richard Boorberg, 2010) p 111–139.

Van Gerven 2011
W van Gerven, 'A Common Law for Europe: The Future Meeting the Past?' (2011) *ERPL* vol 9 no 4 p 485–503.

Habersack and Mayer 2010
M Habersack and C Mayer, '§15 Die Problematik der überschießenden Umsetzung' in K Riesenhuber (ed), *Europäische Methodenlehre* (Berlin, De Gruyter, 2010) p 334–365.

Hartkamp 2011
AS Hartkamp, 'The General Principles of EU Law and Private Law' (2011) *RabelsZ* vol 75 no 2 p 241-259.

Hartkamp 2014
AS Hartkamp, '*Ex officio* Application in Case of Unenforceable Contracts or Contract Clauses: EU Law and National Laws Confronted' in L Gullifer and S Vogenauer *Englisch and European Perspectives on Contract and Commercial Law*, Essays in Honour of Hugh Beale 1th ed (Oxford, Hart Publishing, 2014) p 467-484.

Hartkamp 2014 (I)

AS Hartkamp, 'Unjust enrichment and *condictio indebiti* in European Union law' in Hartkamp/Sieburgh/Keus/Kortmann/Wissink (eds) 2014 p 567–588.

Kapteyn 2008

P Kapteyn, 'Chapter VII The Application and Enforcement of Community Law in the National Legal Systems' in P Kapteyn, A McDonnell, K Mortelmans, C Timmermans and L Geelhoed (eds), *The Law of the European Union and the European Communities* (Alphen aan den Rijn, Kluwer Law International, 2008) p 511–574.

Komninos 2007

AP Komninos, *'Transient" and "transitional" voidness of anti-competitive agreements: a non-issue and an issue'* (2007) *ECLR* vol 28 no 8 p 445–450.

Loos 2007

M Loos, 'The Influence of European Consumer Law on General Contract Law and the Need for Spontaneous Harmonization' (2007) *ERPL* vol 15 no 4 p 515–531.

Miravalls 2011

JM Miravalls, 'Contract annulment due to minimum price-fixing: the bad application of private enforcement of competition law' in LA Velasco San Pedro et al (eds), *Private enforcement of competition law*, 1th ed (Valladolid, Lex Nova S.A.U., 2011) p 337–347.

Prechal 1998

S Prechal, 'Community Law in National Courts: The Lessons from Van Schijndel' (1998) *CMLR* vol 35 no 3 p 681–706.

Roth 2010

W-H Roth, '§14 Die Richtlinienkonforme Auslegung' in K Riesenhuber (ed), *Europäische Methodenlehre* (Berlin, De Gruyter, 2010) p 308–333.

Schebesta 2010

H Schebesta, 'Does the National Court Know European Law? A Note on *Ex Officio* Application after Asturcom' (2010) *ERPL* vol 18 no 4 p 847–880.

TABLE OF CASES

Cases are ordered by date except where otherwise indicated. Citations and page numbers in bold indicate verbatim quotations from court reports. For the convenience of the reader, the instruments and provisions have been listed in the same language in which they appear in this work and have been ordered alphabetically.

EU CASE LAW

COURT OF JUSTICE (CJ)

Alphabetically by name

Ordered by case number

GENERAL COURT (GC)

NATIONAL CASE LAW

AUSTRIA

Oberste Gerichtshof *(Supreme Court)*

DENMARK

Sø- Og Handelsretten *(Danish Maritime and Commercial Court)*

FRANCE

Cour de Cassation *(French Court of Cassation)*

Tribunal d'instance *(First Instance Court)*

FINLAND

Helsingin hovioikeus *(Helsinki Court of Appeal)*

GERMANY

Bundesverfassungsgericht *(Federal Constitutional Court of Germany)*

Bundesgerichtshof *(Federal Supreme Court of Germany)*

OLG *(Higher Regional Court)*

Bundesarbeitsgericht *(Federal Labour Court)*

Landesarbeidsgericht *(Labour Court of Appeal)*

Corte di cassazione *(Court of Cassation)*

Tribunale *(First Instance Courts)*

THE NETHERLANDS

Hoge Raad der Nederlanden *(Supreme Court)*

UNITED KINGDOM

Alphabetically by name

House of Lords/Supreme Court of the United Kingdom

High Court

Court of Appeal

Employment Appeal Tribunal

TABLE OF LEGISLATION

Citations and page numbers in bold indicate verbatim quotations from the instrument/provision in question.

INTERNATIONAL

EUROPEAN UNION *(subdivided by category of instrument)*

OTHER

DECISIONS

DIRECTIVES *(chronological order)*

EC NOTES, GUIDELINES AND PAPERS

REGULATIONS

NATIONAL

AUSTRIA

BELGIUM

FRANCE

GERMANY

NORDIC COUNTRIES

SPAIN

SLOVENIA

SWITZERLAND

UNITED KINGDOM

INTRODUCTION
EFFECTS OF EU LAW ON RELATIONSHIPS BETWEEN INDIVIDUALS

*Arthur Hartkamp**

I. EU LAW AND PRIVATE LAW: INTRODUCTORY REMARKS

Like its predecessor the EC Treaty (1957), the Treaty on the Functioning of the European Union (TFEU, 2007) nearly exclusively contains rules of a public law nature. To a considerable extent, the system created by the Treaty consists of rules of conduct for the national governments in the form of instructions or prohibitions. Rules of conduct for enterprises are found among the provisions for a common competition policy.[1] Only a few provisions are of a private law nature. For example, the provision that agreements between undertakings which have as their object or effect the prevention, restriction or distortion of competition within the internal market are automatically void (Article 101(2) TFEU) and that in the case of non-contractual liability, the EU shall, in accordance with the general

---

* This chapter builds on previous publications of the author, in particular Hartkamp 2016 and AS Hartkamp, 'Horizontal Effects (or "Effects in Relationships between Individuals") of EU Law' in Hartkamp/Sieburgh/Keus/Kortmann/Wissink (eds) 2014 57–71.

[1] See PJG Kapteyn, AM McDonnell, KJM Mortelmans and CWA Timmermans, *The Law of the European Union and the European Communities* (Deventer, Kluwer Law International, 2008) 66.

principles common to the laws of the Member States, make good any damage caused by its institutions or by its servants in the performance of their duties (Article 340(2) TFEU).[2] And Article 345 TFEU provides that the Treaties shall in no way prejudice the rules in Member States governing the system of property ownership.

Against this background, it is remarkable that the Treaty has acquired a much greater significance in private law than would correspond with those few provisions. EU law has exercised its influence through both legislation and judgments of the CJ.

According to Articles 114 and 115 TFEU, the EU legislature may issue measures for the approximation of such laws and regulations of the Member States which directly affect or have as their object the establishment or functioning of the internal market. Other articles provide more specific bases for legislative competence, such as Article 169 TFEU on consumer protection. These Treaty provisions have enabled a substantive legislative activity consisting of both directives and regulations covering topics of general private law such as product liability, consumer sales law, general conditions, doorstep selling and distance selling by electronic means, as well as topics in the fields of labour law, company law, transport law and private international law. In general, this legislation does not pose many problems to legal practice, at least as long as the national legislatures faithfully implement the directives into national legislation. Sometimes problems of interpretation do arise, as with all legislation. Where implementation is late or incorrect, the national courts are faced with the sometimes arduous task of interpreting their national law as being in conformity with the directive or of deciding if and to what extent individuals may rely directly on the directive against their national authorities.[3]

Broadly speaking, the CJ has intervened in private law along two lines (apart from its case law relating to directives and regulations). On the one hand, it has interpreted some central Treaty provisions in such a way that they have become directly applicable to relationships between individuals, in the sense that they create subjective rights and obligations between them. In other words, these provisions now produce a direct effect in private law relationships. EU law may also have indirect effects on private law relationships. These effects will be dealt with in section II below.

On the other hand, private law is affected by the general principles of EU law, which the CJ has developed on the basis of Article 19(1) of the Treaty on European Union (TEU).[4] Like the Treaty itself, the general principles of EU law predominantly appertain to the realm of public law in its various ramifications of institutional law, constitutional law and administrative law. To a large extent, they serve to review the legality of acts (legislative and administrative) of the organs of the EU and of Member States acting within the scope of EU law. However, they are also significant for private law. Of particular importance is the principle of effectiveness, which was at the root of important private

---

[2] In some jurisdictions, liability of public bodies for damages (eg, in case of unlawful acts) belongs to private law, while in others, it is a part of public (administrative) law.

[3] See Ch 6.

[4] 'The Court of Justice ... shall ensure that in the interpretation and application of this Treaty the law is observed.'

law developments such as the creation of a number of legal remedies in order to enforce EU rights, the control exercised by the CJ over national statutory provisions that unduly restrict the exercise of such rights, and the creation of liability of Member States for acts violating EU law.[5] The case law relating to direct horizontal effect was inspired by the principle of effectiveness as well.

II. DIRECT HORIZONTAL EFFECT AND INDIRECT HORIZONTAL EFFECTS OF EU LAW RULES: TERMINOLOGY AS USED IN THIS CASEBOOK

Private law enters the picture of EU law because EU law may affect relationships between individuals. Private law is essentially concerned with legal relationships consisting of rights and obligations between individuals. They may be called 'horizontal relationships' as opposed to 'vertical relationships' between individuals and public authorities. EU law rules may affect those horizontal relationships directly or indirectly.

Direct effect exists when a rule of EU law directly influences the substance of legal relationships between individuals; in other words, when it creates, modifies or extinguishes rights and obligations between the parties. This may have the result, for example, that a contract concluded between parties is supplemented by a rule not agreed on between the parties, that a contract conflicting with a rule of EU law is null and void, that one citizen's act constitutes an unlawful act vis-a-vis another citizen because the act conflicts with a rule of EU law or that a right of recovery (*condictio indebiti*) arises.

Indirect effect exists if a rule of EU law affects a legal relationship between individuals in a manner different from the direct manner defined above. This can happen in a number of different ways, some of which will be described elsewhere. At this point I will just mention two examples. EU law may impose a duty on national courts to interpret national law in such a way that it conforms to a rule of EU law (eg, a directive which has not been implemented or has been implemented incorrectly into the national legal system). Alternatively, a rule of national law may be reviewed against a rule of EU law and found to be incompatible with it, so that it must be disapplied. This may have consequences for the validity of contracts concluded under the national rule; however, it is easy to see that such consequences may differ from the situation where the nullity is based on incompatibility of the national rule with an EU law rule which itself prohibits the conclusion of the contract.

II.A DIRECT HORIZONTAL EFFECT

The concept of direct horizontal effect will be explained on the basis of some provisions of the TFEU. Such effect may also be accorded to other rules and principles of EU law, a matter to be discussed in section II.C below.

---

[5] See Tridimas 2006 418 ff and 498 ff; Hartkamp 2016 nos 105 ff. See also section I in Ch 5.

Article 101(2) TFEU (discussed in Chapter 2) expressly provides for direct horizontal effect by imposing the sanction of voidness in the case elaborated by the first paragraph of that Article. In other cases, where there is no such specific text in the Treaty, it has been the CJ that accorded direct horizontal effect to a Treaty provision. This happened, for example, with respect to Article 157 TFEU (discussed in Chapter 4), which provides that each Member State shall ensure the application of the principle of equal pay for male and female workers for equal work or work of equal value. The CJ (*Defrenne I*) ruled that the provision is:

> [M]andatory in nature so that the prohibition on discrimination between men and women applies not only to the action of public authorities, but also extends to all agreements which are intended to regulate paid labour collectively, as well as to contracts between individuals.[6]

The same happened with respect to the freedom of movement of persons and of services. A groundbreaking judgment on this issue was that in *Walrave and Koch* (discussed in Chapter 3)[7] concerning a rule of the International Cycling Union (UCI), which was held to be contrary to the free movement of persons. The CJ ruled in paras 18 and 19:

> The abolition as between Member States of obstacles to freedom of movement for persons and to freedom to provide services, which are fundamental objectives of the [EU] contained in Article 3(c) of the Treaty would be compromised if the abolition of barriers of national origin could be neutralized by obstacles resulting from the exercise of their legal autonomy by associations or organizations which do not come under public law.
>
> Since, moreover, working conditions in the various Member States are governed sometimes by means of provisions laid down by law or regulation and sometimes by agreements and other acts concluded or adopted by private persons, to limit the prohibitions in question to acts of a public authority would risk creating inequality in their application.

Consequently, the applicability of Article 45 TFEU extends to agreements and rules that do not emanate from public authorities, which, as the CJ stated in the operative part ('all legal relationships'), include both collective and non-collective agreements between individuals.

If a rule of EU law has direct horizontal effect but does not itself provide for the resulting legal consequences (as is done in Article 101(2) TFEU), it is the responsibility of the CJ to do so. The CJ may determine the legal consequences itself or leave this to national law.

Direct horizontal effect can also result in acts of individuals being unlawful, as is shown in the first place by the judgment given in *Courage v Crehan*,[8] which concerned infringement of Article 101(2) TFEU: a brewery imposed a beer tie on an 'affiliated'

---

[6] CJ 8 April 1976 Case C-43/75 *Defrenne v Sabena (Defrenne I)* [1976] I-0455 ECLI:EU:C:1976:56, para 39.

[7] CJ 12 December 1974 Case C-36/74 *BNO Walrave and LJN Koch v Association Union cycliste internationale, Koninklijke Nederlandsche Wielren Unie and Federación Española Ciclismo* [1974] I-01495 ECLI:EU:C:1974:140.

[8] CJ 20 September 2001 Case C-453/99 *Courage v Crehan* [2001] I-06297 ECLI:EU:C:2001:465.

tenant. In its judgment, the CJ recognised the tenant's claim for damages against the brewery because the purchase price charged by the latter was higher than the market price. The CJ based the brewer's liability on the principle of effectiveness. The full effectiveness of what is now Article 101 TFEU and, in particular, its practical effect would be put at risk if:

> [I]t were not open to any individual to claim damages for loss caused to him by a contract or by conduct liable to restrict or distort competition.

The CJ pointed out that the national courts must ensure that the provisions of EU law take full effect and protect the rights which they confer on individuals.

Individuals may also be liable in damages for infringement of Treaty provisions and other rules having direct horizontal effect that fall outside the scope of competition law. This inference can be drawn from the judgments given in *Viking* and *Laval*[9] relating to disputes between undertakings and trade unions about the lawfulness of collective actions. The undertakings argued that these actions were unlawful because they infringed Articles 49 and 56 TFEU relating to the freedoms of services and establishment, and they based claims for a prohibitory injunction and for damages on these articles. The CJ ruled that these Treaty provisions also apply to collective actions by trade unions and that such an action may constitute a restriction of the freedoms; however, such a restriction may be justified if it serves a legitimate interest and satisfies the requirement of proportionality.

Direct horizontal effect may furthermore have other private law consequences than nullity or liability in damages. A Treaty provision may result in a claim arising from undue payment or unjust enrichment, or it may restrict individuals in the exercise of unqualified (absolute) rights they have under national private law.

Once a provision has been recognised to have direct horizontal effect, it may in principle result in a variety of private law effects. For example, once the CJ has accorded direct horizontal effect to a Treaty provision in a judgment concerning an agreement that infringes the provision, it is in principle an established fact that an act contrary to the provision may constitute an unlawful act, so that it can serve as a basis for a claim for compensation or a prohibitory injunction. The *Courage v Crehan* case[10] is an apt illustration of this.

After it has been established that a provision of EU law has direct horizontal effect, 'follow-up questions' arise. One important example is a procedural aspect, known as the *ex officio* or 'automatic' application of the provision. When a Treaty provision, for example, the prohibition on cartels (Article 101 TFEU), a prohibition of discrimination or the freedom of movement for workers, has direct horizontal effect, does that mean that the national courts must also apply the provision in cases brought before them if the parties have not invoked it, ie, must they apply it *ex officio*?

---

[9] CJ 11 December 2007 Case C-438/05 *ITWF v Viking* [2007] I-10779 ECLI:EU:C:2007:772; and CJ 18 December 2007 Case C-341/05 *Laval v Unions* [2007] I-11767 ECLI:EU:C:2007:809. These cases, as well as the national follow-up case in *Laval*, are discussed in Ch 3.

[10] *Courage v Crehan* (n 8).

II.B INDIRECT HORIZONTAL EFFECTS

As set out in section II.A, the term 'direct horizontal effect' as used in this case-book refers to the situation where EU law directly influences the substance of legal relationships between individuals; in other words, where it creates, modifies or extinguishes rights and obligations between the parties. All other cases where EU law influences relationships between individuals in more indirect or incidental ways may be subsumed under the label 'indirect horizontal effects', even though they differ widely. The following paragraphs describe some of those effects. The examples are restricted to relationships between individuals, meaning that, for example, the *Francovich* doctrine (liability of Member States on account of infringement of EU law) is not mentioned here, even though in some jurisdictions such liability is part of private law. However, state liability for damages in relation to the late or incorrect implementation of directives is discussed in Chapter 6.

II.B.i. HARMONIOUS INTERPRETATION OF NATIONAL LAW BY NATIONAL COURTS IMPOSED BY EU LAW

The first example of an indirect horizontal effect is the situation where a rule of EU law is given effect in private law relationships through the interpretation of a rule of national law. This is particularly important if the relevant EU rule itself does not have direct horizontal effect, for if it has, then strictly speaking it is unnecessary to make the detour of harmonious interpretation of a national rule. However, a national court will usually be inclined to try to achieve the aim required by EU law by the harmonious interpretation of national law; it is only if it is impossible for the court to do so that it will, if possible, proceed to directly apply the EU law provision.[11] This explains why courts sometimes do not make clear whether they interpret the national rule in conformity with an EU rule or disapply the national rule because it is incompatible with the EU rule.[12] It also explains why the method has flourished primarily for dealing with EU rules that 'by definition' have no direct horizontal effect, such as provisions of EU directives (see section II.C.iv below) and of the European Convention on Human Rights (ECHR), which cannot be relied on in horizontal relationships.

With respect to non-implemented or incorrectly implemented EU directives, the method is often called 'harmonious interpretation', a term which also lends itself to being used in other cases where national law is interpreted in conformity with EU law. However, in the case of directives, some special characteristics are involved because the Member States are obliged to implement directives. In the first place, the case law of the CJ shows that the national courts are obliged to apply this method of interpretation

---

[11] This also seems to be favoured by the CJ; compare the judgments in, eg, CJ 5 October 2004 Joined Cases C-397/01–C-403/01 *Pfeiffer et al v Deutsches Rotes Kreuz* [2004] I-08835 ECLI:EU:C:2004:584 and CJ 24 January 2012 Case C-282/10 *Maribel Dominguez v Centre informatique du Centre Ouest Atlantique and Préfet de la region Centre* ECLI:EU:C:2012:33.

[12] For an example, see section IV.A.iii in Ch 4.

whenever they can possibly do so. In the second place, although it is true that the obligation to use harmonious interpretation extends to all national legal rules, in practice it will often be applied to national legislation implementing the directive in question and therefore to more or less specific provisions of the law.

II.B.ii. HARMONIOUS INTERPRETATION OF NATIONAL LAW BY NATIONAL COURTS NOT IMPOSED BY EU LAW

Harmonious interpretation can also be used in cases where it is not imposed by EU law, but applied voluntarily by the national courts.[13] In those cases, it will normally take the form of influence exerted by the EU law provision, eg, a free movement provision of the TFEU, through open-ended principles of national private law (reasonableness and fairness, generally accepted conduct, public order/public policy, public morals etc). In the ambit of the ECHR (and also of national constitutions), this is a well-known process. The fundamental or human right is one of the factors considered in assessing whether a contract touching upon a party's constitutional rights is void on account of a violation of public order/public policy or public morals, or cannot be relied on because reliance on such a contract is unacceptable according to the standards of reasonableness and fairness, or whether an action constitutes an unlawful act, or whether the dismissal of an employee is manifestly unreasonable and so on and so forth. So far, this variant of indirect horizontal effect has not been frequently used in connection with the provisions of the TFEU or in any case not in the materials studied in preparing this casebook. The method can also be used with regard to other provisions of EU law, such as provisions of the Charter or provisions of directives (outside the reach of the obligation of harmonious interpretation mentioned in the previous section).[14]

II.B.iii. REVIEW OF THE COMPATIBILITY OF NATIONAL RULES WITH EU LAW IN PROCEEDINGS BETWEEN INDIVIDUALS

Member States must act in conformity with EU law, which implies among other things that they cannot issue and maintain legislation in contravention of EU law. If there is a dispute as to whether a legislative act is contrary to a provision or general principle of EU law, individuals may submit the dispute to the courts for assessment. This often happens in disputes between an individual and the state (a 'vertical relationship'), but it may also happen in disputes between two individuals (a 'horizontal relationship'). In EU legal doctrine, this is often referred to as (or subsumed under the heading of) direct horizontal effect (see section III.C below). The preceding sections will have made clear why this terminology is not followed in this casebook.

---

[13] However, the CJ may stimulate national courts to resort to this type of indirect effect, as it has done in connection with unlawful state aid in CJ 11 July 1996 Case C-39/94 *Syndicat francais de l'Express international (SFEI) et al v La Poste et al* [1996] I-03547 ECLI:EU:C1996:285, para 75. See Hartkamp 2016 no 94.
[14] For the Charter, see C Mak, 'Unchart(er)ed Territory EU Fundamental Rights and National Private Law' in Hartkamp/Sieburgh/Keus/Kortmann/Wissink (eds) 2014 p 323–56. For directives, see the examples in section IV in Ch 6 and in Hartkamp 2016 no 158.

If the national rule is found to be contrary to a provision (or general principle) of EU law, the consequence is that it cannot be applied. What happens next depends on the nature of the EU law provision. If it creates rights and obligations between the parties, it is a case of direct horizontal effect of that provision. If it does not, the relationship between the parties will be determined by another rule, in some cases another EU law rule which does have direct horizontal effect, but more often a rule of national law or a valid agreement between the parties. The *Delhaize* judgment is a good example.[15] A Spanish seller of wine invoked force majeure against his Belgian buyer because national (Spanish) legislation prohibited him from exporting the wine. The buyer sued the seller, claiming performance of the agreement and arguing that the Spanish legislation contravened what is now Article 35 TFEU. This position turned out to be correct, so that the legislation could not be applied. As a result, the seller was bound to deliver the wine pursuant to the agreement. It is true that in this case, the non-applicability of the national law on account of contravention of the Treaty provision did have consequences for the legal relationship between the parties (horizontal effect), but since the substance of the contract was not directly affected by the EU rule, this is considered to be an example of indirect horizontal effect.

Delhaize was about reviewing the compatibility of a rule of economic administrative law with a Treaty provision. The above remarks also apply in the case of review against EU law rules of a different nature (a general principle of EU law, a provision of a regulation, a provision of the Charter), subject to the proviso that in principle, individuals cannot rely on the incompatibility of national legislation with a directive (see section II.C.iv below). But in case of exceptions, they apply to directives as well. A case in point is the judgment in *CIA Security v Securitel*,[16] in which the CJ ruled that national standards and technical regulations that, in violation of the notification directive,[17] had not been notified to the European Commission were non-binding. This may have the result of changing the substance of a contractual relationship. An example is *Unilever v Central Food*.[18] A buyer refused payment of a consignment of olive oil on the grounds that the oil did not satisfy an Italian labelling regulation. The CJ ruled that the regulation was inapplicable because it infringed the procedures to be followed pursuant to the aforementioned directive (although in this case the regulation had been notified, Italy had not observed the standstill period). As a result, the goods were found to conform to the contract and the buyer was bound to pay. This case law will be discussed in section V.A in Chapter 6.

As was stated above, in proceedings between individuals, a national measure may not be reviewed against a directive, but it may be reviewed against a general principle

---

[15] CJ 9 June 1992 Case C-47/90 *Delhaize v Promalvin SA and AGE Bodegas Unidas SA* [1992] I-03669 ECLI:EU:C:1992:250.

[16] CJ 30 April 1996 Case C-194/94 *CIA Security International v Signalson and Securitel* [1996] I-02201 ECLI:EU:C:1996:172.

[17] Directive 83/189/EEC, subsequently superseded by Directive 98/34/EC, supplemented by Directive 98/48/EC.

[18] CJ 26 September 2000 Case C-443/98 *Unilever Italia SpA v Central Food SpA* [2000] I-07535 ECLI:EU:C:2000:496.

of EU law. In several well-known cases, the CJ reviewed national measures against the general principle prohibiting age discrimination, which has found expression in Directive 2000/78.[19] This case law has been considered a 'disguised' exception to the absence of the horizontal effect of directives, but that view seems to be incorrect. In a subsequent judgment,[20] the CJ made clear in relation to the judgment in *Kücükdeveci*[21] 'that the principle of non-discrimination on grounds of age at issue in that case, laid down in Article 21(1) of the Charter, is sufficient in itself to confer on individuals an individual right which they may invoke as such'. This case law will be discussed in section II in Chapter 5 and section V.B in Chapter 6 of this casebook.

II.B.iv. POSITIVE OBLIGATIONS

The EU Treaties can be construed to imply an obligation for the Member States to protect the rights deriving from the free movement provisions and the prohibitions on discrimination, and to safeguard these rights vis-a-vis their citizens, also in horizontal relationships. This construct is well known in the sphere of fundamental rights, both at the national level and in the context of the ECHR. It means that the national constitution or the ECHR, as the case may be, must be interpreted to mean that the state does not only have a 'negative' obligation to refrain from infringing the citizens' fundamental rights, but under certain circumstances also has a 'positive' obligation to safeguard the exercise of those rights both towards the state and towards other citizens by means of legislative or other action. Failure to comply with the positive obligation may make the Member State liable in damages.

In EU law, such an obligation can be based among other things on Article 4(3) TEU, under which the Member States are committed to 'sincere cooperation': they must take any appropriate measure, whether general or particular, to ensure the fulfilment of the Treaty. Examples can be found in the judgments given in *Commission v France ('Spanish Strawberries')* and *Schmidberger*:[22] where the free movement of goods is hampered by road blockades or (other) disturbances of public order, the state may under certain circumstances be obliged to take measures to put an end to such actions.

In principle, national courts, as part of the national public authorities, may also have such a positive obligation. However, it is not exactly clear what that means. Probably it means something different in EU law from what it means in ECHR law. This thorny

---

[19] CJ 22 November 2005 Case C-144/04 *Werner Magnold v Rüdiger Helm* [2005] I-09981 ECLI:EU:C:2005:709; CJ 19 January 2010 Case C-555/07 *Kücükdevci v Swedex & Co* [2010] I-00365 ECLI:EU:C:2010:21; Council Directive 2000/78/EC of the European Council of 27 November 2000 establishing a general framework for equal treatment in employment and occupation [2000] OJ L303/16.

[20] CJ 15 January 2014 Case C-176/12 *Association de Médiation Sociale v Union locale des syndicats (CGT), Hichem Laboubi et al* ECLI:EU:C:2014:2.

[21] *Kücükdevci* (n 19).

[22] CJ 9 December 2009 Case C-265/95 *Commission v France* [1997] I-06959 ECLI:EU:C:1997:595; CJ 12 June 2003 Case C-112/00 *Schmidberger, Internationale Transporte und Planzüge v Republik Österreich* [2003] I-06569 ECLI:EU:C:2003:33.

question will not be pursued here. In this book, the concept of positive obligation will not be used in relation to the application of EU law by national courts.[23]

II.C DIRECT AND INDIRECT HORIZONTAL EFFECTS AND THE SOURCES OF EU LAW

II.C.i. INTRODUCTORY REMARKS

The sources of EU law that are relevant for the perspective of this casebook are the Treaties, the general principles of EU law, directives and regulations, as well as the case law of the CJEU. These sources may be further divided into primary law and secondary law or into written law and unwritten law, but these subdivisions are not relevant for the present purpose.

This section briefly surveys which (types of) EU law rules or general principles may have direct horizontal effect in the sense explained in section II.A. Since the TEU is not relevant in this respect, attention will be paid first to the TFEU, then to regulations and directives, and, finally, leaving the firm ground of settled CJ case law, to general principles of EU law and the Charter.

Subject to the exception mentioned below (see section II.C.iv), all EU law rules and general principles may, in principle, have indirect effects on horizontal relationships, such as the effects mentioned in section II.B above. This topic will not be dealt with in this section, but examples will be provided in the following chapters.

II.C.ii. THE TFEU

Attention must be directed in the first place towards the TFEU. The direct horizontal effect of Article 101 TFEU follows from the Treaty itself and must be extended to its sister provisions, such as Article 102 TFEU. The same effect has been accorded by the CJ to most of the fundamental freedoms[24] (in fact, after *Fra.bo*,[25] there only remains uncertainty as to the free movement of capital)[26] and to the prohibitions of discrimination.[27] All these instances will be discussed in Chapters 2, 3 and 4 on competition law, fundamental freedoms and non-discrimination.

II.C.iii. REGULATIONS

A large part of EU law (including private law) is embodied in secondary EU legislation, that is, in directives and regulations. A regulation 'shall be binding in its entirety and

---

[23] See Hartkamp 2016 no 20. For directives, see section IV in Ch 6.

[24] Free movement of goods (arts 34 and 35 TFEU), workers (art 45 TFEU), freedom of establishment (art 49 TFEU), and freedom to provide and receive services (art 56 TFEU).

[25] CJ 12 July 2012 Case C-171/11 *Fra.bo v Deutsche Vereinigung des Gas- und Wasserfaches* [2012] ECLI:EU:C:2012:453 relating to the free movement of goods (art 34 TFEU).

[26] Article 63 TFEU.

[27] Viz (apart from the freedoms) arts 18 (nationality) and 157 TFEU (equal pay for men and women).

directly applicable in all Member States' (Article 288(2) TFEU). As such, it has direct effect with respect to anyone to whom it is addressed, regardless of whether this is a public body or an individual. In the wording of the CJ (*Prosciutto di Parma*, paras 87–89):

> [A] regulation … creates not only rights but also obligations for individuals, on which they may rely against other individuals before national courts. Nevertheless, the requirement of legal certainty means that [EU] rules must enable those concerned to know precisely the extent of the obligations which they impose on them'.[28]

If the direct effect leads to individuals being bound by (or deriving rights from) regulations vis-a-vis other individuals, this is referred to in this casebook as direct horizontal effect.

As has been made clear in section II.A, the direct horizontal effect of regulations means that non-observance of a regulation can lead to, for example, the nullity of a contractual provision (*Safety Hi-Tech*)[29] or the unlawfulness of factual conduct (*Muñoz*).[30]

II.C.iv. DIRECTIVES

A directive 'shall be binding, as to the result to be achieved, upon each Member State to which it is addressed, but shall leave to the national authorities the choice of form and methods' (Article 288(3) TFEU). On the basis of this text, the CJ has decided that directives do not have 'direct horizontal effect' within the meaning given to this term in this casebook (see section II.A above), so that a directive cannot create rights or obligations between individuals. As the CJ has ruled numerous times, eg, in *Marshall*,[31] 'a directive may not of itself impose obligations on an individual'. It follows that a directive cannot confer rights on an individual against another individual. In *Faccini Dori*,[32] for example, the CJ ruled that given that Italy had not transposed the directive protecting the consumer in respect of contracts negotiated away from business premises within the prescribed time limit, consumers could not derive from the directive itself a right to repudiate contracts thus negotiated.

In *Marshall* and also in many subsequent judgments, the CJ further held that 'a provision of a directive may not be relied upon as such against an individual'.[33] This passage in the wording of the CJ means more than that an individual cannot derive any rights from a directive against another individual. The ruling that a provision of a directive may

---

[28] CJ 20 May 2003 Case C-108/01 *Prosciutto di Parma v Asda Stores Ltd and Hygrade Foods Ltd.* [2003] I-05121 ECLI:EU:C:2003:296.

[29] CJ 14 July 1998 Case C-284/95 *Safety Hi-Tech Sri v S.& T Sri* [1998] I-04301 ECLI:EU:C:1998:352.

[30] CJ 17 September 2002 Case C-253/00 *Muñoz v Frumar* [2002] I-7289 ECLI:EU:C:2002:497.

[31] CJ 11 November 1997 Case C-409/950 *Hellmut Marshall v Land Nordrhein-Westfalen* [1997] I-06363 ECLI:EU:C:1997:533.

[32] CJ 14 July 1994 Case C-91/92 *Faccini Dori v Recreb Srl* [1994] I-03325 ECLI:EU:C:1994:292.

[33] See also, eg, *Pfeiffer* (n 11) para 108; *Kücükdeveci* (n 19) para 46; and *Maribel Dominguez* (n 11) para 37. The conclusion drawn from these two statements is that: 'It follows that even a clear, precise and unconditional provision of a directive seeking to confer rights or impose obligations on individuals cannot of itself apply in proceedings exclusively between private parties' (see *Pfeiffer* (n 11) para 109). Sometimes only this conclusion is provided in the judgment (eg, in *Association de Médiation Sociale* (n 20) para 36).

not be relied upon against individuals also implies that an individual cannot invoke a directive against another individual to bring about a declaration of non-applicability of a provision of national law that is incompatible with the directive. Such a declaration might likewise have the consequence of changing a party's or the parties' legal positions under national law or under a contract, which the CJ has held to be contrary to Article 288(3) TFEU. Hence, directives are not only incapable of exercising direct horizontal effect, but also of exercising the type of indirect horizontal effect as set out in section II.B.iii (review of compatibility with EU law in proceedings between individuals). However, directives may well have other indirect horizontal effects, as discussed in section II.B.[34]

In vertical relationships, however, the CJ has allowed direct effect. In order to prevent a Member State from being better off by not implementing a directive which imposes obligations on it vis-a-vis its citizens, the CJ has recognised that after the transposition period has expired, individuals may rely against the authorities on provisions of a directive whose substance is unconditional and sufficiently precise. It is irrelevant whether the provisions are of a public law or a private law nature (eg, a labour contract between a government body and an employee). The effect of this doctrine is enhanced by the fact that the terms 'authorities' and 'government' include legal persons governed by private law which perform public duties.

The subjects mentioned in this section will be further pursued in Chapter 6.

II.C.v. GENERAL PRINCIPLES OF EU LAW

The law of the EU comprises general principles of EU law. They embody fundamental principles of the EU and of its Member States, and constitute deeply rooted principles without which a civilised society would not exist.[35] According to the case law of the CJ, they have constitutional status.[36] They include fundamental rights which are now codified in the Charter. They also include a number of principles which have their origin in private law, eg, good faith, the principle of compensation for damage caused by violation of EU law, abuse of rights, force majeure, causal link as a prerequisite for liability, the obligation to pay interest as a part of compensation, *pacta sunt servanda*, *rebus sic stantibus*, *venire contra factum proprium*, the right of property, redress of unjust enrichment etc.[37]

---

[34] See, in particular, sections II.B.i and II.B.ii.

[35] AG Tristenjak Opinion 30 June 2009 in Case C-101/08 *Audiolux SA v Groupe Bruxelles Lambert SA (GBL) et al and Bertelsmann AG et al* [2009] I-09823 ECLI:EU:C:2009:140, para 70.

[36] CJ 15 October 2009 Case C-108/08 *Audiolux SA v Groupe Bruxelles Lambert SA (GBL) et al and Bertelsmann AG et al* [2009] I-09823 ECLI:EU:C2009:626; CJ 29 October 2009 Case C-174/08 *NNC Construction Danmark A/s v Skatteministeriet* [2009] I-10567 ECLI:EU:C:2009:669.

[37] See AS Hartkamp, 'The General Principles of EU Law and Private Law' (2011) 75(2) *RabelsZ* 241; Hartkamp 2016 nos 87 ff.

It is probable that the general principles of EU law may have direct horizontal effect, depending on the nature of the principle concerned and the circumstances of the case. This is true in particular for those principles which have a private law background, such as good faith and other principles related to the notion of proportionality,[38] but it may equally apply to other general principles, such as non-discrimination.[39]

II.C.vi. THE CHARTER OF FUNDAMENTAL RIGHTS

Contrary to the prevailing opinion in a number of Member States regarding provisions of national Constitutions,[40] it is clear that provisions of the Charter may have direct horizontal effect. This is true in particular for Article 15(2) of the Charter, which repeats three fundamental freedoms (freedoms of movement, establishment and services) that have been accorded such effect by the CJ, and for Articles 16 (freedom to conduct a business) and 17 (right to property), which in recent cases seem to have been recognised as grounds on which a claim or a defence in litigation between private parties may be based.[41] It may be equally true for other provisions. In this respect, there would seem to be no difference between the Charter and those general provisions of EU law that have been transposed into Charter provisions.[42]

---

[38] See Hartkamp 2016 no 132.

[39] Some CJ judgments point in that direction. In CJ 13 October 2005 Case C-458/03 *Parking Brixen v Gemeinde Brixen and Stadtwerkte Brixen* [2005] I-08585 ECLI:EU:C:2005:605, paras 52 and 62, the possibility was accepted of a legal act (the award of a public service concession) being contrary to the principles of equal treatment, non-discrimination and transparency. In CJ 23 September 2008 Case C-427/06 *Birgit Bartsch v Bosch und Siemens Hausgeräte (BSH) Altersfürsorg* [2008] I-07245 ECLI:EU:C:2008:517, it seems that the CJ considered the possibility of reviewing the guidelines of a pension fund against that same principle, but for the fact that the case at issue did not fall within the scope of EU law. In CJ 27 March 2014 Case C-314/12 *UPC Telekabel Wien v Constantin Film Verleih and Wega Filmproduktionsgesellschaft* ECLI:EU:C:2014:192, the CJ came very close to according direct horizontal effect to fundamental rights in analysing whether an injunction might be awarded. The remark in *Association de Médiation Sociale* (n 20) that 'the principle of non-discrimination on grounds of age ... is sufficient in itself to confer on individuals an individual right which they may invoke as such' would seem to include the possibility of a direct review of a legal relationship between individuals against that principle.

[40] See the literature mentioned in Hartkamp 2016 no 227.

[41] In *UPC Telekabel* (n 39), the CJ came very close to according direct horizontal effect to these fundamental rights in analysing whether an injunction might be awarded. See AS Hartkamp, Fundamental Rights—Constitutionalising European Contract Law? in Secola Conference 2014 no 3.2 (forthcoming). See in Dutch AS Hartkamp, 'De invloed van het EU Handvest van de grondrechten op het privaatrecht' *WPNR* (2014) 145(7035) 961 ff.

[42] The opinion of AG Trstenjak 8 September 2011 in Case C-282/10 *Maribel Dominguez* ECLI:EU:C:2011:559, according to which art 51(1) excludes direct horizontal effect of Charter provisions, has not been favourably received by commentators; see AG Villalon Opinion 18 July 2013 in Case C-176/12 *Association de Médiation Sociale* ECLI:EU:C:2013:491 paras 28 ff; T Tridimas, 'Horizontal Effect of General Principles: Bold Rulings and Fine Distinctions' in Bernitz/Groussot/Shulyok et al (eds) 2013 213 ff; A Ward, 'Remedies under the EU Charter in the Context of Disputes Arising in Private Law' in Bernitz/Groussot/Shulyok et al (eds) 2013 327, 331 ff; R Barents, *Het Verdrag van Lissabon. Achtergronden en commentaar* (Deventer, Kluwer, 2008) 549 no 1120, which argues that the CJ's case law on the horizontal effect of the fundamental freedoms lends itself to being smoothly carried over to the Charter; Hartkamp (n 41).

III. DIRECT AND INDIRECT HORIZONTAL EFFECTS: THE TERMINOLOGY OF EU LAW SCHOLARS AND OF PRIVATE LAW SCHOLARS COMPARED AND THE SOURCES OF EU LAW

III.A. INTRODUCTORY REMARKS

The terminology described above corresponds with the private lawyer's approach to the way in which public law influences private law. It is also used for the way in which national fundamental rights affect private law relationships. If a fundamental rights provision in a national constitution directly affects a private law relationship in the sense that it creates rights or obligations which can be relied on by the parties, such effect is called a direct horizontal effect (in German law, it is also called 'Drittwirkung'). Other influences are called indirect.[43] As stated above, the reason for this is that private law is essentially concerned with legal relationships consisting of rights and obligations between individuals. A private lawyer looks at the law in order to see what it means for such relationships. He is interested to know whether norms of public law directly influence the validity, substance (content) or interpretation of legal relationships between individuals; in other words, whether they create, modify or extinguish rights and obligations between the parties. Constitutional law doctrine follows a similar approach. The focus is on the body of law (legal rules, measures, horizontal relationships) that gets influenced by the constitutional standard. If a legal rule is reviewed against a fundamental right and the legal relationship governed by the rule under review is a horizontal relationship, the influence of the fundamental right on that relationship is characterised as an indirect horizontal effect. Only if the contents of the horizontal relationship itself are directly determined by the fundamental right in the sense that it creates rights or obligations which can be relied on by the parties is such effect called a direct horizontal effect.

The approach of scholars of EU law is different, as is their terminology. EU law is traditionally public law and for a large part institutional law. One of the most important questions in EU law is whether it has primacy over national law and, if so, how this can be effected in practice. Against this background, the EU law concept of direct (vertical) effect has been developed.

III.B DIRECT EFFECT IN EU LAW TERMINOLOGY

In EU law terminology, 'direct effect' means that a norm of EU law can be invoked by a party in a national court. The focus is on the situation, typical for EU law, that individuals invoke EU law against a Member State or public authority (or a private law legal

---

[43] See, eg, LFM Besselink, 'The Protection of Fundamental Rights Post-Lisbon: The Interaction between the EU Charter of Fundamental Rights, the European Convention on Human Rights (ECHR) and National Constitutions' in Reports of the XV FIDE Congress, *The Protection of the Fundamental Post-Lisbon* (Tartu: TUP 2012) Volume 1. Besselink also uses this terminology in relation to EU law.

person which exercises public power).[44] Normally, EU law is invoked against a national measure of public law, in particular a statutory provision or an administrative practice. Direct effect is not in the first place connected with invoking subjective rights. As Bruno de Witte puts it:

> Originally, direct effect was often defined, not least by the Court of Justice itself, as the creation of rights for individuals which the national courts must protect. That expression was gradually superseded by what the French call *invocabilité*, namely the capacity of the norm to be invoked by individuals in national courts which are bound to apply them. The reason for this shift was the gradual realization that many norms of [EU] law, particularly norms contained in directives, though not having as their object the attribution of a benefit to individuals, may very well serve as a standard for reviewing the legality of Member State action when individuals can show a sufficient interest in the outcome of such a review.[45]

He goes on to state:

> Therefore, direct effect really boils down, as far as courts are concerned, to a test of justiciability: is the norm 'sufficiently operational in itself to be applied by a court' in a given case.[46]

In a similar vein, Prechal offers the following definition:

> Direct effect is the obligation of a court or another authority to apply the relevant provision of [EU] law, either as a norm which governs the case or as a standard for legal review.[47]

III.C HORIZONTAL EFFECTS IN EU LAW PARLANCE

The concepts of horizontal effect and direct horizontal effect are used in different ways by EU scholars. Peter Oliver and Wulf-Henning Roth[48] correctly propose that a distinction must be made between the 'question whether private parties are or should be considered addressees of, and therefore directly bound by, the four freedoms' and the case where national regulations are reviewed for their compatibility with EU law in proceedings between private parties. However, they seem to catch the two situations under the same concept of 'horizontal application' or 'direct application of the freedoms to private persons'.[49]

Bruno de Witte at first seems to restrict the concept of 'horizontal direct effect (in relationships between private parties)' to the situation where private persons are directly bound by an EU norm. He also calls that 'horizontal application' or 'the (EU norm) may be relied upon against private parties' (at 334). However, speaking of

---

[44] The latter case is labelled 'administrative direct effect': see Craig and De Búrca 2015 207.

[45] B de Witte, 'Direct Effect, Primacy and the Nature of the legal order' in Craig and De Búrca (eds) 2011 323 ff, at 323 and 330. See in the same vein the leading Dutch experts R Barents and LJ Brinkhorst, *Grondlijnen van Europees recht*, 13th edn (Deventer, Kluwer, 2012) no 102.

[46] In this sense, see AG Van Gerven Opinion 27 October in Case C-128/92 *Banks & Co v British Coal Corporation* [1994] I-01209 ECLI:EU:C:1993:860, para 27.

[47] Prechal 2005 241.

[48] P Oliver and W-H Roth, 'The Internal Market and the Four Freedoms' (2004) 41(2) *CMLR* 407 ff.

[49] See ibid 426.

directives (at 335), he—and the same is true for Prechal (at 255)—refers to the settled case law since *Marshall*[50] on the absence of horizontal effect of directives,[51] which he describes as 'absence of horizontal direct effect', meaning that he includes in this term the absence of legal review of national regulations in proceedings between individuals. When discussing the words 'of itself', he mentions several exceptions,[52] which he brings under the heading of 'indirect' or 'triangular' horizontal effect, to conclude (referring to Dashwood) with the denomination 'indirect horizontal effect cases'.[53]

For Craig and De Búrca, 'horizontal direct effect' means imposing obligations on individuals.[54] Treaty provisions may have such effect, as well as regulations, but not directives, since they cannot of themselves impose obligations on individuals. Where a directive may exceptionally be invoked by an individual for the purpose of legal review of a national legislative measure, they speak of 'incidental horizontal effect'.[55] For harmonious interpretation, they use the term 'indirect effect'.[56] Sometimes these authors seem to classify both situations in *Marshall* under the absence of direct horizontal effect, while sometimes they seem to call the second situation 'absence of incidental effect'.[57]

Instead of 'horizontal effect', we also find expressions such as third-party effect, *Drittwirkung*, effects between private persons, direct application of EU law to acts of private persons etc.

III.D THE APPROACHES COMPARED

It is clear that for EU law scholars, the concept of 'direct effect' is of primordial importance. In fact, the tandem 'primacy' and 'direct effect' belong to the core of EU law. Direct effect is one of the most important vehicles for the realisation of primacy, because

---

[50] *Marshall* (n 31).

[51] 'According to settled case-law, a directive cannot of itself impose obligations on an individual and cannot therefore be relied upon as such against an individual.' As pointed out before (see section II.C.iv), this formulation includes: (1) that a directive cannot create rights and obligations in a relationship between individuals vis-a-vis each other; and (2) that it cannot be relied upon by an individual in proceedings against another individual in order to have a national measure reviewed for its compatibility with a directive.

[52] *CIA Security v Securitel* (n 16); CJ 7 January 2004 Case C-201/02 *Delena Wells v Secretary of State for Transport* [2004] I-00723 ECLI:EU:C:2004:12.

[53] De Witte, 'Direct Effect, Primacy and the Nature of the legal order' (n 45) 335 and fn 45.

[54] Craig and De Búrca 2015 184 and 192. As an example of horizontal direct effect, they mention (at 193) *ITWF v Viking* (n 9). Regulations, too, have direct effect (at 198).

[55] '[A] directive can in certain cases be legally invoked in proceedings between private parties (incidental effect) so long as the directive does not in itself impose a legal obligation on one of the parties' (p 185), and p 186–173 sub 6: "incidental horizontal effects', whereby a directive can preclude reliance on a provision of national law that is inconsistent with the provisions of the directive even in an action between private parties.' See also at 217, where the same situation is called 'indirect horizontal reliance'. It is an 'exclusionary' rather than 'substitutionary effect' (at 219).

[56] ibid 186 and 209.

[57] This corresponds with an inherent ambiguity in the CJ's formulation, since the second situation according to its literal meaning covers both the case where one party invokes an obligation against the other party (the first situation) and the case where the provision of a directive is invoked for the purposes of legal review of a national provision.

it enables national courts at the request of interested individuals to resolve the conflict between EU law and national law in favour of the former.

However, primacy and direct effect are not inextricably linked. Primacy also operates through ways other than by means of individuals invoking (the direct effect of) norms before the courts in proceedings against a state authority. For instance, it also operates through the intermediary of an obligation imposed on administrative bodies and through the intermediary of an obligation of harmonious interpretation imposed on the courts. Direct effect originated in vertical relationships with conflicting EU and national norms (and, as such, was linked to the notion of primacy), but gradually it also came to play a role in horizontal relationships without conflicting EU and national norms.

Primacy does not play a big role in a private lawyer's conceptual thinking. Of course, a private lawyer acknowledges that a contract may be at variance with mandatory provisions of law, but he would not call that 'primacy of mandatory law over a private contract'. The concept of primacy is concerned with several layers of public regulations and, as such, is a constitutional principle.

For the same reason, a private lawyer would not normally use the term 'review' or the expressions 'substitution effect' and 'exclusion effect' for, on the one hand, a legality review of national regulations and, on the other, an assessment of the consequences of EU law in private law relationships (eg, assessing the validity of a contract or the legality of factual conduct in the light of a free movement provision).[58]

For a scholar of public law, the difference between the two situations repeatedly alluded to above—that is, on the one hand, relying on a EU norm which serves to review the compatibility of a national regulation with EU law and, on the other hand, relying on a norm of EU law which creates a right for the party concerned—seems not to be very large. He will often put them under the same heading. For him, the first situation (legality review) seems to be the most important one; the concept of conferring rights and obligations is a corollary. Legality review was originally phrased in terms of the conferment of rights and obligations on private persons, even if it was unclear what kind of rights were involved (certainly not always subjective rights; perhaps not more than the right to invoke the EU norm).

A private law scholar looks at matters from the opposite side. Reviewing national measures against higher-ranking EU legislation is not a normal part of his activity. He will associate direct effect in the first place with the contents of a legal relationship, not with the review of legality of a national measure. He will be interested to know whether the norms of EU law directly influence the validity, substance or interpretation of legal relationships between individuals; in other words, whether they create, modify or extinguish rights and obligations between the parties.

Only occasionally will the answer to this question be influenced by a legal review of national norms against norms of EU law. National norms of private law are only rarely

---

[58] However, see in that sense M de Mol, 'The Novel Approach of the CJEU on the Horizontal Direct Effect of the EU Principle of Non-discrimination: (Unbridled) Expansionism of EU Law?' (2011) 18(1–2) *MJ* 109, 110–11.

reviewed against EU law.[59] National norms of public law are often reviewed against EU law, but usually not in a private law context.[60] And even if the context is a private law relationship, the outcome will usually not be that the national norm that is 'excluded' due to its incompatibility with a EU norm will be 'substituted' by the latter norm in the sense that it creates rights or obligations between the parties. More often, the exclusion of the conflicting national regulation will lead to re-applicability of the contractual norm or the national norm (eg, a norm of general private law in the Civil Code) that was applicable between the parties in the first place.

III.E CONCLUDING REMARKS

In order to understand what EU laws means for private law—that is, for relationships covered by private law—a private lawyer needs more conceptual 'grip' than is offered to him in EU law doctrine. That is why this casebook uses the terminology set out in section II above. This terminology will give private lawyers greater clarity, while it differs from settled EU law doctrine on only a few points. The most important one is that what is called 'direct effect' in EU law is in this casebook split into two:

— If an individual may rely on a rule (including a general principle) of EU law in order to assert a subjective right against another individual, the rule is conceived as producing 'direct horizontal effect'.
— If an individual may, as against another individual, rely on a rule (including a general principle) of EU law in order to have a national statutory provision or administrative practice reviewed for its compatibility with EU law, that rule is conceived as having 'indirect horizontal effect'.[61]

The latter term does not say anything specific about the nature of the effect that a finding of incompatibility may have on the legal relationship. Nor is the concept of 'indirect horizontal effect' specific for this situation, because there are many other ways in which an EU law rule may influence private law relationships. In EU law doctrine, there is no uniform 'nomenclature' for all these different types of horizontal effect. This casebook does not attempt to create one for private law purposes. It is suggested that for the time being, clarity must be pursued by precisely indicating what type of indirect horizontal effect is being referred to. Section II.B offers a survey of examples that is not exhaustive.

---

[59] Examples are CJ 24 January 1991 Case C/339-89 *Alsthom Atlantique SA v Compagnie de construction mécanique Sulzer* [1991] I-00107 ECLI:EU:C:1991:28; and CJ 13 October 1993 Case C/93–92 *CMC Motorradcenter GmbH v Pelin Baskiciogullari* [1993] I-05009 ECLI:EU:C:1993:838. The situation may be different in specialised parts of private law, such as labour law. See section II.B.iii.
[60] Examples of the latter are *Delhaize* (n 15); and *Unilever Italia SpA* (n 18), which are both discussed in section II.B.iii.
[61] Being the consequence of 'direct effect' in the EU law sense.

III.F DIRECT HORIZONTAL EFFECT AND INDIRECT HORIZONTAL EFFECTS: CHART ILLUSTRATING THE TERMINOLOGY USED IN THIS CASEBOOK WITH SOME WELL-KNOWN CJ CASES

Type of horizontal effect	Definition	Well-known examples (CJ cases)
Direct horizontal effect	A rule or principle of EU law creates, modifies or extinguishes rights and obligations in relationships between individuals (section II.A). Infringement may lead to private law consequences such as nullity, unlawful act or injunction	1. Article 101 TFEU: *Courage v Crehan*; *Manfredi* 2. Article 157 TFEU: *Defrenne v Sabena* 3. Free movement provisions of TFEU: *Walrave*; *Angonese*; *Viking*; *Laval*; *Fra.bo* 4. Regulation: *Muñoz*
Indirect horizontal effects (not exhaustive list)		
1.	Harmonious interpretation of national law by national courts, imposed by EU law (section II.B.i)	*Pfeiffer*; *Adeneler*; *Dominguez*
2.	Harmonious interpretation of national law by national courts, not imposed by EU law (section II.B.ii)	*SFEI*
3.	Review of compatibility of national rules with EU law in proceedings between individuals (section II.B.iii): either rules of private law or rules of public law (if review has private law consequences)	1. Rules of private law: *Alsthom*; *Motorradcenter*; *Krantz*; *Mangold*; *Kücükdeveci* 2. Rules of public law: *Delhaize*; *Rüffert v Niedersachsen*; *Unilever v Central Food*
4.	Positive obligation (obligation for Member State(s) to protect rights of individuals)	*Commission v France*; *Schmidberger*

IV. SPILLOVER EFFECTS

IV.A. INTRODUCTORY REMARKS

To be distinguished from the 'indirect horizontal effects' discussed in section II.B, which relate to the effects of EU rules on specific legal relationships between individuals, are situations where EU law may have (what is here tentatively called)[62] broader 'spillover effects' on the national laws (including private law) of Member States. Examples are:

1. broader harmonisation than is envisaged by a directive;
2. aligning national systems in a stage later than at the implementation of a directive;
3. the principle of equality demanding an equal treatment of internal and external (EU) situations.

IV.B A VOLUNTARILY BROADER (OR 'SPONTANEOUS') HARMONISATION

Directives unfold their operation primarily through transposition (also known as 'implementation') into national law (Article 288(3) TFEU). When transposing a directive, the legislator may, by practising 'spontaneous harmonisation', adjust its national law further than the directive requires. For example, when the German legislator implemented the directive on the sale of consumer goods, it seized the opportunity to bring the German general law of obligations into line with, *inter alia*, the system of non-performance chosen in that directive.[63]

'Spontaneous harmonisation' must be distinguished from taking further-reaching measures, for example, measures aimed at consumer protection going beyond the level of 'minimum harmonisation' which the directive seeks to achieve.[64] In the case of spontaneous harmonisation, the national courts may in principle refer questions to the CJ for a preliminary ruling on the meaning of concepts used in a directive, even if the dispute

---

[62] For an extensive discussion of spillover effects, see A Johnston, '"Spillovers" from EU Law into National Law: (Un)intended Consequences for Private Law Relationships' in D Leczykiewicz and S Weatherill (eds), *The Involvement of EU Law in Private Law Relationships*, (Oxford, Hart Publishing, 2013) 357 ff. Johnston chooses the following definition: 'true "spillover" involves an effect from EU law upon national law which does not occur by virtue of EU law's claim to normative force, of itself, in the national legal order. Rather, spillover effects concern the impact of EU law by virtue merely of its *presence* within the national legal system, requiring the rules and structures of that system to react to EU law, albeit in areas not (intended to be) covered by EU law itself'. The elaborate categorisation subsequently proposed by the author cannot be reflected in this chapter.

[63] See R Zimmermann, *The New German Law of Obligations: Historical and Comparative Law of Obligations* (Oxford, Oxford University Press, 2005). See in Dutch MBM Loos, *Spontane harmonisatie in het contracten- en consumentenrecht. Over de verstoring en herstel van de coherentie van het nationale contracten—en consumentenrecht onder invloed van het Europese recht*, (The Hague, Boom Juridische uitgevers, 2006).

[64] In Germany, both are subsumed under the same term 'Überschiessendes nationales Recht'; see M Gebauer and T Wiedmann (eds), *Zivilrecht unter europäischem Einfluss*, 2nd edn (Stuttgart, Richard Boorberg Verlag, 2012) Kap 4 Rn 22.

relates to a provision of law that is the product of spontaneous harmonisation; in the other case (going beyond the minimum level of harmonisation), this is different, at any rate insofar as the 'added' measure lies beyond the conceptual framework of the directive.

In both cases, there is no obligation of harmonious interpretation, although this will in fact be desirable from the perspective of the coherence of the national legal system. When a directive seeks to achieve 'maximum harmonisation', further reaching measures are not allowed. This topic will—to a limited extent—be taken up in section IV in Chapter 6 on directives.

IV.C ALIGNING NATIONAL SYSTEMS AT A STAGE LATER THAN AT THE IMPLEMENTATION OF A DIRECTIVE

Aligning a national legal system to a directive may also occur after the implementation of the directive has been completed. In the course of time, the difference between the regime instituted by the directive and the rest of the national system may be felt to be too large—and unjustifiably so. The result may be—apart from judicial interpretation in the sense indicated in section II.B.i—that the legislator interferes and extends the rules imposed by the directive to the remaining private law. A topic often mentioned in this respect is Directive 2004/48. The regime instituted by Directive 2004/48 imposing full reimbursement of (reasonable) legal costs in the area of intellectual property procedures, has in legal systems where such full reimbursement does not exist been extended to other areas of procedural law. This subject will not be pursued in this casebook.

IV.D INTERNAL AND EXTERNAL SITUATIONS

EU law only applies to situations covered by it. In the absence of a harmonisation measure based on the Treaties, it does not apply in 'purely internal situations', that is, in situations which do not show any relationship with other Member States apart from the one in which the facts occur. Whether such an internal situation exists is often difficult to ascertain. No general answer is possible. The answer will depend on the specific part of EU law concerned. In competition law or fundamental freedoms law, it may very well be answered differently from procurement law or state aid law. It depends to a considerable extent on whether the CJ requires that an inter-Member State interaction is established or deems it sufficient that it is merely probable or even possible.

That a case is purely internal is often pleaded in a litigation pending before the CJ on the basis of a preliminary reference. The CJ will normally not declare the question inadmissible on this ground, because it assumes that if the national court refers a case, it will need an answer and that it is up to the referring court to judge whether the case is governed by EU law. The CJ will only decide otherwise if it is clear—and for some reason necessary to state explicitly—that the case is not governed by EU law (or is a merely fictitious case).

This situation may lead to the result that a national case is decided in a way which is less favourable to an individual than if his case would have been covered by EU law. This result is undesirable but, from an EU law point of view, inevitable (and irrelevant).

EU law can only oppose discrimination existing in national law to the detriment of rights provided by EU law; the CJ does so in particular by applying the principle of equivalence in reviewing national legislation for its compatibility with EU law. A reverse discrimination by a Member State of its own citizens in internal situations can only be countered by the law of that Member State declaring in a general fashion (eg, in the national constitution or by a decision of its constitutional court) that such a result creates a discrimination which is forbidden by national law. Examples will be found elsewhere in this casebook in section III.B.ii in Chapter 3, (case 3.11 (BE)) and in section IV.A in Chapter 4 (cases 4.9 (FR), 4.11 (NL) and 4.14 (IT)).

The spillover effects of directives will be discussed in Chapter 6.

2

COMPETITION LAW

W Devroe, C Cauffman and U Bernitz

I. GENERAL PART

I.A GENERAL APPROACH

This chapter aims to be different from, and bring added value to, the dozens of textbooks on competition law that already exist. It is different in that it focuses as much as possible on national case law. Excellent works exist on: (a) EU competition regulation and case law; and (b) national regulation, sometimes in combination with national case law on competition in individual Member States. However, this chapter aims to study national case law throughout a range of Member States, searching not only for differences and common features between national legal systems but also for characteristics of interaction between national and EU competition laws.

Moreover, the chapter may gain added value by its incorporation in a casebook which transcends competition law, so that links with other areas of law become visible. At the same time, this forces us to be focused and brief. Some choices had to be made.

First, and from a competition law perspective, the chapter focuses on restrictive practices and abuse of dominance, ie, on traditional 'cartel law'. However, it should be stressed that instances of the impact of EU competition law on national private law also occur in other branches of competition law, in particular in merger law (concentration control) and in state aid matters. For example, violation of the obligation not to implement a concentration before it has been notified or declared compatible with the internal market, may have important private law consequences. Individual transactions and contracts, including securities transactions, may be invalidated.[1] Similarly, in state aid matters, proceedings to recover illegal or incompatible state aid after the European Commission (EC) has ordered a Member State to do so, are national private law proceedings. One also begins to find private enforcement cases in state aid matters in national jurisdictions, even though the private enforcement of cartel law remains much more common.

---

[1] See art 7(4) of Council Regulation (EC) No 139/2004 of 20 January 2004 on the control of concentrations between undertakings [2004] OJ L24/1 (hereinafter 'the EC Merger Regulation').

Second, in line with the remainder of this casebook, we excerpt (national and exceptionally EU) case law rather than administrative decisions. This means that the decisions of national competition authorities (NCAs) and of the EC are not excerpted. Indirectly, however, these decisions are to some extent part of the analysis because some of the judgments concern appeals against administrative decisions.

Third, even within the case law as a legal source, we had to be selective. Most of the judgments in cases between private parties that deal with private law instruments are not taken into consideration because they do not add to the existing knowledge on the relationship between EU law and national law. An example can clarify this. A case where one private undertaking claims, before a national court, the nullity of its private law contract with another private undertaking on the grounds of breach of Article 102 TFEU will *not* be excerpted if the judgment exclusively focuses on the existence of a dominant position on the basis of EU competition law criteria. However, we would consider to excerpt that same case if the undertaking argues that on the basis of EU law a new type of remedy has to be introduced at the national level.

Finally, and most importantly, it should also be recognised that much of the impact of EU competition law on national private law does not appear from case law. To start with, many cases in this field are settled out of court. More fundamentally, one should in all modesty recognise that while competition law (eg, EU Block Exemption Regulations) dictates the formation and wording of hundreds of contracts (eg, the duration, the content and even the enforcement of the contracts) on a daily basis, this only exceptionally leads to court cases. For example, competition law can determine the decision to enter or not to enter into a contract, or it can be used or abused to elegantly escape from contractual obligations, even when compliance with competition law is not the sole or primary objective (common lawyers refer to this growing phenomenon as the 'Euro-defence' or the 'Euro-tort', but one finds few judgments to illustrate this).

One can only conclude that the influence of European competition law on national private law is (much) larger even than will appear from the analysis below.

I.B SOURCES OF EU COMPETITION LAW

The main substantive provisions of EU competition are included in the TFEU. Most relevant from a private law perspective are the principled prohibitions of anticompetitive agreements (Article 101 TFEU) and of abuse of dominance (Article 102 TFEU), and a specific provision on public undertakings and undertakings to which Member States grant special or exclusive rights (Article 106 TFEU). As already indicated, this chapter will not deal with concentration control or with state aid.

I.B.i ARTICLE 101 TFEU AND THE NOTION OF 'AGREEMENT'

Article 101 TFEU   **2.1 (EU)**

1. The following shall be prohibited as incompatible with the internal market: all agreements between undertakings, decisions by associations of undertakings and concerted practices which may affect trade between Member States and which have as their object or effect the prevention, restriction or distortion of competition within the internal market …

2. Any agreements or decisions prohibited pursuant to this Article shall be automatically void.

3. The provisions of paragraph 1 may, however, be declared inapplicable in the case of:

— any agreement or category of agreements between undertakings,

— any decision or category of decisions by associations of undertakings,

— any concerted practice or category of concerted practices,

which contributes to improving the production or distribution of goods or to promoting technical or economic progress, while allowing consumers a fair share of the resulting benefit, and which does not:

(a) impose on the undertakings concerned restrictions which are not indispensable to the attainment of these objectives;

(b) afford such undertakings the possibility of eliminating competition in respect of a substantial part of the products in question.

The notion 'agreement' under Article 101 TFEU is not identical to that same notion under private law. This appears, for example, from a comparison with the Draft Common Frame of Reference (DCFR).

DCFR Book II Chapter 1: General provisions   **2.2 (EU)**

Article II.–1:101: Meaning of 'contract' and 'juridical act'

(1) A contract is an agreement which is intended to give rise to a binding legal relationship or to have some other legal effect. It is a bilateral or multilateral juridical act.

(2) A juridical act is any statement or agreement, whether express or implied from conduct, which is intended to have legal effect as such. It may be unilateral, bilateral or multilateral.

An agreement under Article 101(1) TFEU is not necessarily intended to give rise to a binding legal relationship, whereas this is required under the DCFR.

General Court of the European Union (GC), 20 March 2002[2]   **2.3 (EU)**

HFB Holding für Fernwärmetechnik Beteiligungsgesellschaft mbH & Co KG and others v EC

NOTION OF 'AGREEMENT'

The cartelising gentlemen

Also gentlemen's agreements which are not formally binding can come under the scope of Article 101 TFEU

Facts: On 21 October 1998, the EC adopted Decision 1999/60/EC relating to a proceeding under (now) Article 101 TFEU finding that various undertakings and, in particular, certain of the applicants had participated in a series of agreements and concerted practices within the meaning of (now) Article 101(1) TFEU (hereinafter the cartel).

The applicants seek the annulment of the EC decision. They claim that a gentlemen's agreement is not an agreement. The conduct of the undertakings could at most be characterised as an attempt to agree, which is not punishable by a fine in competition law.

[2] GC 20 March 2002 Case T-9/99 *HFB Holding für Fernwärmetechnik Beteiligungsgesellschaft et al v Commission of the European Communities* [2002] II-01487 ECLI:EU:T:2002:70, para 201.

Held: The GC rejects the claim.

Judgment: 199 It is settled case-law that in order for there to be an agreement within the meaning of [now Article 101(1) TFEU] it is sufficient that the undertakings in question should have expressed their joint intention to conduct themselves on the market in a specific way …

200 That is the case where there is a gentlemen's agreement between a number of undertakings representing the faithful expression of such a joint intention concerning a restriction of competition … In those circumstances, the question whether the undertakings in question considered themselves bound—in law, in fact or morally—to adopt the agreed conduct is therefore irrelevant …

201 Contrary to what the applicants allege, the opposite conclusion cannot be inferred from the provision in [now Article 101(2) TFEU] that any agreement referred to in [now Article 101(1) TFEU] is automatically void, which is intended for cases where a legal obligation is actually in issue. The fact that only binding agreements can, by their nature, be rendered void does not mean that non-binding agreements must escape the prohibition laid down in [now Article 101(1) TFEU].

R Whish and D Bailey, Competition Law[3]   **2.4 (EU)**

A legal contract of course qualifies as an agreement, including a compromise of litigation such as a trade mark delimitation agreement or the settlement of a patent action. 'Gentleman's agreements' and simple understandings have been held to be agreements, though neither is legally binding; there is no requirement that an agreement should be supported by enforcement procedures. A 'protocol' which reflects a genuine concurrence of will between the parties constitutes an agreement within the meaning of Article 101(1). Connected agreements may be treated as a single one. An agreement may be oral. The EC will treat the contractual terms and conditions in a standard-form contract as an agreement within Article 101(1).

An agreement which has expired by effluxion of time but the effects of which continue to be felt can be caught by Article 101(1). … There may be 'inchoate understandings and conditional or partial agreement' during a bargaining process sufficient to amount to an agreement in the sense of Article 101(1). Guidelines issued by one person that are adhered to by another can amount to an agreement; and circulars and warnings sent by a manufacturer to its dealers may be treated as part of the general agreement that exists between them, although the Commission lost a case of this kind in *Volkswagen*. …

The fact that an undertaking was forced into an agreement by other undertakings does not affect the existence of an agreement. Where an agreement is entered into unwillingly, this may be significant in influencing the Commission to mitigate a fine, not to impose a fine or not to institute proceedings at all. An agreement may exist even if it is never implemented …

The fact that the natural person who entered into the agreement did not have authority to do so does not mean that the undertaking that employs him or her is not liable.

I.B.ii ARTICLE 102 TFEU   **2.5 (EU)**

Any abuse by one or more undertakings of a dominant position within the internal market or in a substantial part of it shall be prohibited as incompatible with the internal market in so far as it may affect trade between Member States …

[3] R Whish and D Bailey, *Competition Law*, 8th edn (Oxford, Oxford University Press, 2015) 104–06, footnotes omitted.

I.B.iii ARTICLE 106 TFEU   **2.6 (EU)**

1. In the case of public undertakings and undertakings to which Member States grant special or exclusive rights, Member States shall neither enact nor maintain in force any measure contrary to the rules contained in the Treaties, in particular to those rules provided for in Article 18 and Articles 101 to 109.

2. Undertakings entrusted with the operation of services of general economic interest or having the character of a revenue-producing monopoly shall be subject to the rules contained in the Treaties, in particular to the rules on competition, in so far as the application of such rules does not obstruct the performance, in law or in fact, of the particular tasks assigned to them. The development of trade must not be affected to such an extent as would be contrary to the interests of the Union.

3. The EC shall ensure the application of the provisions of this Article and shall, where necessary, address appropriate directives or decisions to Member States.

I.B.iv BLOCK EXEMPTION REGULATIONS

Block Exemption Regulations are adopted by the EC under Article 103 TFEU and set out the conditions under which certain types of agreements (for example vertical agreements or research and development agreements) are held to satisfy the conditions of Article 101(3) TFEU and thus not to be prohibited by Article 101(1) TFEU.

They typically feature one or more Articles containing definitions and delimiting the scope of application of the Block Exemption, as well as a list of hard core restrictions whose inclusion deprives an agreement of the benefit of the Block Exemption, a list of other clauses whose inclusion does not deprive the entire agreement of the benefit of the Block Exemption but which need to be assessed individually under Article 101(1) TFEU, and a number of other provisions. The fact that an agreement does not satisfy the conditions of a Block Exemption does not mean that it is void, but that it needs to be assessed individually under Article 101 TFEU.

Hof van Cassatie België (Belgian Court of Cassation),
15 May 2009[4]   **2.7 (BE)**

Brouwerij Haacht NV v BM

NON-COMPLIANCE WITH A BLOCK EXEMPTION

The exclusive brewery contract

A vertical agreement falling outside the scope of the Block Exemption Regulation is not a priori illegal

Facts: A contract between a brewer and a pub tenant contained an exclusive purchase clause with a duration of 10 years. The clause was excluded from the then applicable vertical agreements block exemption.[5]

---

[4] Belgian Court of Cassation, 15 May 2009 no C.08.0029.N *Brouwerij Haacht NV v BM*.
[5] Article 5 of Commission Regulation (EC) No 2790/1999 of 22 December 1999 on the application of Article 81(3) of the Treaty to categories of vertical agreements and concerted practices [1999] OJ L336/12.

Held: A vertical agreement that is not covered by the Block Exemption Regulation is not a priori illegal. It should be assessed separately under (now) Article 101(1) and (3) TFEU on the basis of all the available data and in the light of the economic and legal context of the agreement.

Judgment: It follows from the Guidelines on vertical restraints ... and from the case law of the Court of Justice ... in particular from the judgments of 30 April 1998, *Cabour SA*, C-230/90 and of 13 July 2006, *Manfredi*, joint cases C-295/04–C-298/04, that the part of the vertical agreement which is not covered by the block exemption regulation is not a priori considered illegal, but needs to be individually examined on the basis of all the available data and in the light of the economic and legal context of the agreement. In such a case, the term in question will only be void to the extent that it has as its object or effect to significantly restrict competition within the internal market and to significantly affect trade between the Member States and to the extent that it cannot be (individually) exempted under [now Article 101(3) TFEU].

Notes:

(1) The judgment makes clear that the excessive duration of an agreement does not entail the loss of the benefit of the Block Exemption for the entire agreement. This may be different in the case of a breach of other provisions of the Block Exemption.

(2) The decision of the Court of Appeal had held that the clause in question was prohibited under (now) Article 101(1) TFEU and therefore void under (now) Article 101(2) TFEU. This aspect of the decision was not criticized. Before the appellate court the brewer had not argued that the agreement satisfied the requirements of (now) Article 101(3) TFEU. The brewer then appealed to the Belgian Court of Cassation, requesting the decision of the Court of Appeal to be quashed because it failed to apply (now) Article 101(3) TFEU *ex officio*. On this issue, see Chapter 7 and section II.B below.

I.B.v OTHER SECONDARY LEGISLATION

In competition law, considerably less use is made of directives than in other areas of law. Recently, however, the so-called 'Damages Directive'[6] concerning private enforcement of the law on restrictive practices was adopted. It will be analysed separately below.

Of utmost importance in practice are individual decisions which may serve as precedents for other cases. As these decisions concern the relationship between an enforcement authority and an individual, they fall outside the scope of this chapter.

I.B.vi EC NOTICES AND GUIDELINES

The EC regularly publishes Notices and Guidelines providing guidance on the application of the EU competition rules and setting out its practices in this respect. A well-known example is the so-called 'De Minimis Notice'.[7]

---

[6] Directive 2014/104/EU of the European Parliament and of the Council of 26 November 2014 on certain rules governing actions for damages under national law for infringements of the competition law provisions of the Member States and of the European Union [2014] OJ L349/1 (hereinafter 'the Damages Directive').

[7] Commission Notice on agreements of minor importance which do not appreciably restrict competition under Article 101(1) of the Treaty on the Functioning of the European Union [2014] OJ C291/1 (hereinafter 'the De Minimis Notice').

These Notices and Guidelines are binding on the EC, but not on the EU courts, NCAs or national courts.[8] This was confirmed by the CJ in *Expedia*: 'in order to determine whether or not a restriction of competition is appreciable, the competition authority of a Member State may take into account the thresholds established in paragraph 7 of the de minimis notice but is not required to do so'.[9]

The more recently adopted 'Communication on quantifying harm in actions for damages based on breaches of [now Articles 101 or 102 TFEU]'[10] is different from others in that it is not meant to be applied by the EC itself, but only to give guidance to national courts.

I.B.vii CASE LAW OF THE GC AND THE CJ

This source, which is at the heart of this casebook, will be extensively analysed below.

I.C LEGISLATIVE VS ENFORCEMENT POWERS IN EU COMPETITION LAW

I.C.i LEGISLATIVE POWERS IN EU COMPETITION LAW

Based on the sources mentioned above, the *legislative competence* in the field of competition law relating to behaviour which may affect trade between Member States has all the signs of being an exclusive EU competence: Member States may only adopt rules to the extent that they are empowered to do so by the EU. Since the Lisbon Treaty, the exclusive character of the EU's legislative competence has been confirmed in Article 3(1)(b) TFEU.

I.C.ii ENFORCEMENT POWERS IN EU COMPETITION LAW

I.C.ii.a The Position of the Treaties

Article 103 TFEU confers on the Council the power to lay down, on a proposal from the EC and after consulting the European Parliament: 'The appropriate regulations or directives to give effect to the principles set out in Articles 101 and 102.'

Article 105 TFEU confers on the EC the power to ensure the application of the EU competition rules in particular by allowing the EC to investigate cases of suspected infringements and, where an infringement is found, to propose appropriate measures to bring it to an end. If the infringement is not brought to an end, the EC shall record the infringement in a reasoned decision. The EC may publish its decision and may authorise Member States to take the measures, the conditions and details of which it shall determine, needed to remedy the situation.

---

[8] See, eg, A Jones and B Sufrin, *EU Competition Law, Text, Cases, and Materials* (Oxford, Oxford University Press, 2014) 188.
[9] CJ 13 December 2012 Case C-226/11 *Expedia Inc v Autorité de la concurrence et al* nyr ECLI:EU:C:2012:795.
[10] Communication from the EC on quantifying harm in actions for damages based on breaches of Article 101 or 102 of the Treaty on the Functioning of the European Union [2013] OJ C167/19.

I.C.ii.b The CJEU and the Development of an EU Doctrine of Private Enforcement of Competition Law

In 1974, the CJ recognised in *BRT I* that the provisions of (now) Articles 101 and 102 TFEU create direct rights for individuals, which the national courts must safeguard. At the time, the power to award exemptions under (now) Article 101(3) TFEU was exclusively reserved to the EC. In *BRT I*, the CJ distinguished between: (a) '[administrative] authorities of the Member States' 'including in certain Member States courts especially entrusted with the task of applying domestic legislation on competition or that of ensuring the legality of that application by the administrative authorities'; and (b) 'courts before which the direct effect of [now Article 102 TFEU] is pleaded'.[11] Without using the words, the CJ thus distinguished between: (a) public enforcement of competition law, by public authorities and in the public interest; and (b) private enforcement of competition law by national courts protecting subjective rights which physical or legal persons derive from EU law. In the same vein, the GC in *Automec* distinguished between 'civil courts, whose task [it] is to safeguard the individual rights of private persons in their relations inter se' and 'an administrative authority [which] must act in the public interest'.[12]

Private enforcement of competition law has been given a new boost since the CJ adopted its seminal judgment in *Courage v Crehan* in 2001, recognising the right of 'any individual to claim damages for loss caused to him by a contract or by conduct liable to restrict or distort competition'.[13] This type of private enforcement through damages actions will be dealt with separately in section II.A.vi below.

I.C.ii.c An Increased Role for National Judges

The role of national judges in competition law enforcement has gradually increased. This is in part due to the so-called 'modernisation of enforcement' of the law on restrictive practices, which began by the end of the previous century and which culminated in the adoption of Regulation 1/2003.[14] 'Modernisation' entails a decentralisation of enforcement by attributing a larger role in competition law enforcement to NCAs and national courts. Regulation 1/2003 abolished the notification system, making now Article 101 TFEU applicable in its entirety by NCAs and national courts. It also lays down rules for the cooperation between the EC and national courts. In order to ensure the uniform application of EU competition law, Article 16(1) Regulation 1/2003 provides that: 'When national courts rule on agreements, decisions or practices under [now Article 101 or Article 102 TFEU] which are already the subject of an EC decision, they cannot take decisions running counter to the decision adopted by the EC. They must also avoid giving decisions which would conflict with a decision contemplated by the EC in proceedings it

---

[11] CJ 30 January 1974 Case C-127/73 *BRT v SV SABAM and NV Fonior (BRT I)* [1974] I-00051 ECLI:EU:1974:6, para 19.

[12] GC 18 September 1992 Case T-24/90 *Automec Srl v Commission of the European Communities* [1992] II-02223 ECLI:EU:T:1992:97, para 85.

[13] CJ 20 September 2001 Case C-453/99 *Courage v Crehan* [2001] I-06297 ECLI:EU:C:2001:465, para 26.

[14] Council Regulation (EC) No 1/2003 of 16 December 2002 on the implementation of the rules on competition laid down in Articles 81 and 82 of the Treaty [2003] OJ L1/1.

has initiated. To that effect, the national court may assess whether it is necessary to stay its proceedings. This obligation is without prejudice to the rights and obligations under Article 234 of the Treaty.'

The rules on cooperation between the EC and national courts were further developed in the 2005 EC Notice on the cooperation with national courts.[15] In this Notice, the EC sets out which rules, in its opinion, national courts have to apply in civil proceedings involving now Articles 101 TFEU and/or 102 TFEU.

> *2005 EC Notice on the co-operation between the Commission*
> *and the national courts*[16]   **2.8 (EU)**

These [EU] law provisions prevail over national rules. Therefore, national courts have to set aside national rules which, if applied, would conflict with these [EU] law provisions. Where such [EU] law provisions are directly applicable, they are a direct source of rights and duties for all those affected, and must be fully and uniformly applied in all the Member States from the date of their entry into force. In the absence of [EU] law provisions on procedures and sanctions related to the enforcement of [EU] competition rules by national courts, the latter apply national procedural law and impose sanctions provided for under national law. However, the application of these national provisions must be compatible with the general principles of [EU] law.

The extent to which there are EU law rules on private law remedies and how they interact with national rules on remedies will be analysed below.

II. REMEDIES FOR INFRINGEMENTS OF THE COMPETITION PROVISIONS

II.A NULLITY AS A SANCTION FOR INFRINGEMENT OF ARTICLE 101(1) TFEU

II.A.i NULLITY AS A SANCTION OF EU LAW

Now Article 101(2) TFEU is the only provision of the TFEU dealing directly with the private law consequences of competition law infringements.

> *Article 101(2) TFEU*   **2.9 (EU)**

Any agreements or decisions prohibited pursuant to [now Article 101(1)] shall be automatically void.

As a remedy, the nullity (or voidness—we use the terms as synonyms here) of agreements between undertakings or of decisions by associations of undertakings which infringe

---

[15] Commission Notice on the co-operation between the Commission and the courts of the EU Member States in the application of Articles 81 and 82 EC [2004] OJ C101/54.

[16] ibid, paras 9 and 10, footnotes omitted.

Article 101(1) TFEU is a matter of EU law itself.[17] The remedy is obtained without there being any need to apply national rules holding contracts or legal acts contrary to law void, such as Article 3:40 of the Dutch Civil Code (BW) or §139 of the German Civil Code (BGB).[18]

The nullity of agreements or decisions under Article 101(2) does not affect the powers of the EC or the NCAs to impose positive or negative injunctions ordering the undertakings or associations of undertakings to cease the infringement of the competition rules or to modify the agreements or decisions.[19]

Article 101(2) TFEU only mentions nullity as a sanction for anticompetitive agreements and decisions. It does not mention nullity of concerted practices. Only in 2013 did the President of the CJEU decide that there is no such nullity of concerted practices. Positions in national case law vary.

Swedish Supreme Court (Högsta Domstolen),
23 December 2004[20]   **2.10 (SE)**

Boliden Mineral Aktiebolag v AB Fortum Värme samägt med Stockholms stad

CONCERTED PRACTICES CANNOT BE VOID

The concerted standard terms

Concerted practices cannot be void and cannot in principle give rise to nullity of a 'follow-on' agreement

Facts: Boliden (a mining facility) contracted with Korsnäs (a supplier of electricity). According to a standard form agreement that was attached to the contract, the price of electricity could be modified due to taxes, fees or legislation. Fortum (supplier of electricity) later replaced Korsnäs under the contract and raised electricity prices. Boliden refused to pay the increased price and requested the price adjustment clause in the standard form agreement to be declared void for a breach of section 7 of the Swedish Competition Act and of (now) Article 101(2) TFEU.

Held: Concerted practices cannot be void and cannot in principle give rise to nullity of a 'follow-on' agreement.

Judgment: The question, as asserted by Boliden, is whether the price adjustment clause at hand should be treated as prohibited and regarded as null because it has been incorporated in an agreement between a participating undertaking and a third party which is a direct consequence or part of an alleged prohibited price cooperation.

It does not seem possible to give a general answer since [the validity of the follow-on contract] will depend for instance on the connection between the prohibited agreement

---

[17] K Schmidt, 'Art 101 Abs 2 Rn 6', in Immenga/Mestmäcker, *Wettbewerbsrecht. Kommentar zum Europäischen Kartellrecht*, Verlag C.H. Beck 2012 (hereafter 'Immenga/Mestmäcker').

[18] K Schmidt, 'Art 101 Abs 2 Rn 2', in Immenga/Mestmäcker.

[19] K Schmidt, 'Art 101 Abs 2 Rn 4', in Immenga/Mestmäcker.

[20] Swedish Supreme Court 23 December 2004 case no T 2280-02 *Boliden Mineral Aktiebolag and AB Fortum Värme samägt med Stockholms stad*. See also C Wetter and CJ Sundqvist, 'The Swedish Supreme Court Declares that a Concerted Practice Cannot Be Subject to Nullity under Section 7 of the [Former] Swedish Competition Act (Boliden Mineral Aktiebolag and AB Fortum Värme samägt med Stockholms stad)' (2004) *e-Competitions Bulletin December*, art no 21213; M Gustafsson, 'Private Enforcement of EC Competition Law: Swedish Supreme Court Judgment on the Validity of "Follow-on" Contracts' (2006) 27(1) *ECLR* 5.

and the follow-on agreement, as well as on the importance in each case of protecting the public interest of a well-functioning competition in the marketplace.

Cooperation such as that resulting in the standard form agreement does not as such give rise to a valid agreement or binding decision between the participants [in the concerted practice], and does therefore not result in legal effects that can lead to nullity under section 7 of the Swedish Competition Act. The possible competition law sanctions for those participating in a prohibited concerted practice are infringement fines and damages or, under national law, in any case a court order to stop the cooperation.

Notes:

(1) The case does not concern the act of concertation between the cartelists themselves, but agreements and decisions implementing the 'implicit agreement' between the cartelists in their relationship with third parties. In this sense, the agreements based on concerted practices are similar to agreements following on to cartel agreements (*cf* note (5) below).

(2) In November 2008, in his *Artisjus* decision, the President of the CJEU made clear that (now) Article 101(2) TFEU does not apply to prohibited 'concerted practices'.[21] The case concerned a request from a Hungarian association for the collective management of copyright (*Artisjus*) to suspend the operation of the EC's CISAC Decision.[22] The EC's decision was addressed to 24 collecting societies which are members of CISAC and established in the EEA,[23] and which manage the rights held by the authors (lyricists and composers) in the musical works of their creation. In the said decision, the EC had *inter alia* found that the EU collecting societies had infringed (now) Article 101 TFEU by imposing identical territorial limitations in each of the representation agreements which they concluded between themselves and in which they entrusted each other, on a reciprocal basis, with the management of their repertoire in their respective operating territories. The EC had also ordered the infringement to be brought to an end. Artisjus claimed *inter alia* the suspension of this part of the decision, arguing that it was unclear whether it should extend the mandates it had granted to the other collecting societies or whether the territorial clauses in its reciprocal representation agreements were void under (now) Article 101(2) TFEU. The President held that 'it suffices to note that [now Article 101(2) TFEU] makes void only "agreements [between undertakings] or decisions [by associations of undertakings]" prohibited by [now Article 101(1) TFEU], whereas that civil-law sanction does not apply to prohibited "concerted practices" … the EC limits itself to stating that the collecting societies mentioned have infringed [now Article 101 TFEU] "by coordinating the territorial delineations" … The unlawfulness of the concerted practice referred to in the contested decision cannot therefore make void the alleged result of that practice, namely the reciprocal representation agreements.'[24]

---

[21] Order of the President of the CJEU 14 November 2008 Case T-411/08 R *Artisjus Magyar Szerzői Jogvédő Iroda Egyesület v Commission of the European Communities* [2008] II-00270 ECLI:EU:T:2008:503, paras 46–47.
[22] International Confederation of Societies of Authors and Composers.
[23] European Economic Area.
[24] *Artisjus* (n 21) paras 46–47.

(3) The reason why concerted practices are not mentioned in now Article 101(2) TFEU seems to be that an act of concertation which does not amount to an actual agreement is not a binding legal contract or act in civil law terms so that there is no need to declare it void.

(4) As we will see later, long-standing case law of the CJEU holds that the contracts concluded with third parties following-on to an actual anticompetitive agreement between undertakings are not automatically void as a matter of EU law. It is consistent with this case law to not automatically hold agreements or decisions following-on to the 'implicit agreement' between the concerting undertakings void as a matter of EU law. However, it must be admitted that, given the absence of an actual agreement between the concerting parties, the distinction between (a) the act of concertation itself and (b) the agreements concluded with, or the decisions directed towards, third parties, is less clear.

(5) It is interesting to note that in a case where four Slovenian domestic banks with a market share of about 80 per cent introduced an ATM fee[25] in the same amount on the same day, the Slovenian competition authority classified this behaviour as a concerted practice and declared the decisions introducing the ATM fees null and void pursuant to Article 5 of the Slovenian Competition Act, the national equivalent of Article 101 TFEU.[26] The case was appealed. The appellate decision confirmed the existence of a concerted practice, but did not address the voidness. As a result of media pressure, however, the Slovenian banks made reimbursements to their clients.

II.A.ii NULLITY AS A DEFENCE OR AN ACTION

Nullity under Article 101(2) TFEU is most often invoked as a defence against an action for performance of a contract or against an action for damages for breach of contract.[27]

Court of Appeal, 21 December 1995[28]   **2.11 (UK)**

Dr Andrew James Higgins v Marchant & Eliot Underwriting Ltd

EURODEFENCE

The ingenious insurer

Invoking an infringement of competition law as a defence against a claim for payment of a debt is considered a lawyer's ingenuity

Facts: Dr Higgins, a Lloyd's Name, appointed Marchant & Eliot Underwriting as his managing agent on the terms of a standard agency agreement in respect of his participation in a syndicate. The standard agency

---

[25] Automatic Teller Machine fee: the fee you pay the bank when taking out money from a cash machine.
[26] Slovenian Competition Protection Office 26 February 2007 arrest no 306-14/2006-100 *Nova Ljubljanska banka, Banka Celje, Nova KBM, Abaka Vipa*. See also A Fatur, 'The Slovenian Competition Authority Declares Null and Void Decisions of Four Major Banks Introducing a New ATM Fee (Nova Ljubljanska banka, Banka Celje, Nova KBM, Abaka Vipa)' (2007) *e-Competitions Bulletin February*, art no 14069.
[27] Apart from the cases mentioned later on in this section, see also French Court of Cassation, Commercial Division 2 July 2002 no 00-14939 *Intercaves v Mlle X* (case 2.18 (FR)) discussed in section II.A.iii below.
[28] *Dr Andrew James Higgins v Marchant & Eliot Underwriting Ltd* [1996] 3 CMLR 349.

agreement (SAA) contained a 'pay now, sue later' provision by which Higgins became liable to make the payments requested by the managing agent in order to satisfy insurance claims without raising any initial objections. The managing agent called upon Higgins for a total of £6,000. When Higgins failed to make this payment, the managing agent sought summary judgment. Higgins contended that he had an arguable defence based on (now) Article 101 TFEU which raised triable issues, so that summary judgment was not appropriate. The High Court gave summary judgment on behalf of the managing agent and Higgins appealed.

Held: The Court of Appeal confirmed the judgment holding that clause 7 did not infringe (now) Article 101 TFEU.

Judgment: As a Name at Lloyd's, Dr Higgins promised to pay calls without question. Calls were made to him for the total sum of £6,000. But he and others like him have decided not to pay until they have to, and to leave Lloyd's to take care of itself. Dr Higgins proffers no defence to his managing agents' claim, except under (now) Article 101 TFEU. It is of course fanciful to suppose that he has ever thought of the SAA which he entered into with his managing agents, or of the Byelaw under which it was made, as affecting trade between Member States. But now through the ingenuity of his lawyers he relies upon the Article to evade payment of his debts. It is our task to see whether that ingenuity has been well directed and will avail him.

Notes:

(1) English courts especially are sceptical towards the invocation of the so-called 'Eurodefence' by a contracting party wishing to escape carefully negotiated clauses on grounds of infringement of the EU competition rules. However, in *Eco Swiss China Time Ltd v Benetton*,[29] the CJ confirmed the importance of the nullity sanction for the effectiveness of Article 101 TFEU: 'However, according to Article 3(g) of the EC Treaty [now Protocol No 27 attached to the TEU and TFEU], [now Article 101 TFEU] of the Treaty constitutes a fundamental provision which is essential for the accomplishment of the tasks entrusted to the Union and, in particular, for the functioning of the internal market. The importance of such a provision led the framers of the Treaty to provide expressly, in [now Article 101(2) TFEU] of the Treaty, that any agreements or decisions prohibited pursuant to that article are to be automatically void.'[30]

(2) Legal scholars are divided about the value of nullity as a defence against anticompetitive infringements; see and compare the two following excerpts:

R Whish and D Bailey, Competition Law[31]   **2.12 (EU)**

It will be noted … that the sanction of voidness, as a general proposition, impacts not on serious infringements of the competition rules, such as the operation of cartels, but on more innocuous agreements where the harm to competition is much less obvious; this is a powerful reason for urging competition authorities to adopt a 'realistic' approach to the application of Article 101(1) and its progeny in the Member States to agreements.

---

[29] CJ 1 June 1999 Case-126/97 *Eco Swiss China Time Ltd v Benetton International NV* [1999] I-03055 ECLI:EU:C:1999:296.
[30] See ibid, para 36.
[31] Whish and Bailey (n 3) 344, footnotes omitted.

AP Komninos, '"Transient" and "Transitional" Voidness of Anti-competitive Agreements: A Non-issue and an Issue '[32]   **2.13 (EU)**

It would be a mistake to consider that the raising of the nullity sanction, in other words what is known to English lawyers as 'shield litigation', does not constitute a form of private antitrust enforcement that enhances the effectiveness of the competition law prohibitions.

Occasionally, an action is brought in order to obtain a declaration of nullity.

Danish Maritime and Commercial High Court (Sø- og Handelsretten), 29 April 2010[33]   **2.14 (DK)**

Pandora Production Co Ltd and WIPEC Holding Aps v Lise Aagaard Copenhagen A/S

ACTION FOR NULLITY

The glass pearls

A Danish court annulled an unlawful provision of a licence agreement (royalty fees)

Facts: Pandora, a producer of jewellery, entered into a licence agreement with LAC: LAC designed a special series of glass pearls for Pandora and Pandora paid a royalty of 12.5 per cent. No problem occurred when LAC was the sole supplier, but when Pandora started buying glass pearls from other suppliers as well, LAC insisted that royalty payments were to be paid for all glass pearl sales, irrespective of the supplier and design. Pandora filed a complaint with the Danish Competition Authority (refused owing to lack of general interest) and then with the Commercial Court, claiming nullity of the royalty provision.

Held: The Commercial Court in Copenhagen assessed the agreement under both Danish and EU law and found it contrary to both. The Court found the agreement to have as its object the partial regulation of the selling price. The royalty fee provision was declared null and void pursuant to Article 101(2) TFEU and section 6(5) cf (1) of the Danish Competition Act. The rest of the contract was held valid (partial annulment).

Judgment: In this case, two competing enterprises have agreed on conditions of a so-called hardcore character. It should be presumed that the object of the conditions is to limit competition—irrespective of the parties' explanations about the background and purposes of the conditions. This is the case irrespective of whether or not it can be demonstrated that the conditions have actually caused an effect on competition. Thus, the conditions are null and void pursuant to section 6(5) of the Danish Competition Act and Article 101(2) TFEU.

Notes:

(1) In this case the party who intended to rely on the nullity (Pandora) did not wait until the other party claimed performance of the anticompetitive clause, but proactively

---

[32] AP Komninos, '"Transient" and "Transitional" Voidness of Anti-competitive Agreements: A Non-issue and an Issue' (2007) 28(8) *European Competition Law Review* 445.

[33] Danish Maritime and Commercial Court 29 April 2010 Case No U-3-08 *Pandora Production Co Ltd v Lise Aagaard Copenhagen A/S*. See also: http://domstol.fe1.tangora.com/media/-300011/files/U-0003-08ber.pdf.

took the initiative to start proceedings in order to have the anticompetitive clause declared void.[34]

(2) The Danish Supreme Court reversed the decision. It did not regard the contract provision according to which Pandora also had to pay LAC royalties on pearls purchased from other producers as contravening Article 101 TFEU or its Danish counterpart. The Supreme Court found that the royalty fee constituted a very small part of the costs of the pearl production and that it was not established that the object or effect of the royalty agreement was to restrict competition.

(3) The case illustrates how private parties try to invoke competition law on nullity of restrictive clauses in a private law dispute of a typically commercial character.

The invocation of nullity as a defence against an action for performance of a null contract can also be combined with an action for damages based on the fact that the void agreement (or clause) causes damage to one of the parties. This occurred in *Courage v Crehan*, which led to the seminal CJ case recognising a right to claim damages for infringements of the EU competition rules. This case will be dealt with in the next section and in section III below.

II.A.iii CHARACTERISTICS OF EU COMPETITION LAW NULLITY

Nullity under Article 101(2) TFEU is absolute, which means that it is effective *erga omnes*.[35] It is also *ex tunc*[36] and *automatic*.[37] The CJ nicely summed up these characteristics in its *Courage v Crehan* judgment: 'That principle of automatic nullity can be relied on by anyone, and the courts are bound by it once the conditions for the application of [now Article 101(1) TFEU] are met … Since the nullity referred to in [now Article 101(2) TFEU] is absolute, an agreement which is null and void by virtue of this provision has no effect as between the contracting parties and cannot be set up against third parties … Moreover, it is capable of having a bearing on all the effects, either past or future, of the agreement or decision concerned.'[38] The confirmation of the absolute character of the nullity dates back to case law of the CJEU from as early as 1971 (*Béguelin*).[39]

The *erga omnes* character of the nullity set out in Article 101(2) TFEU means that it can be relied on by anyone, whether they are party to the anticompetitive agreement or not.

---

[34] See also section II.B below: *English, Welsh and Scottish Railway Ltd v E.ON UK plc* [2007] EWHC 599 (Comm).

[35] CJ 25 November 1971 Case C-22/71 *Béguelin Import Co v SAGL Import Export* [1971] I-00949 ECLI:EU:C:1971:113, para 29.

[36] CJ 6 February 1973 Case C-48/72 *Brasserie de Haecht v Wilkin-Janssen (Haecht II)* [1973] I-00077 ECLI:EU:C:1973:11, paras 26–27.

[37] ibid, para 25.

[38] *Courage v Crehan* (n 13) para 22. This statement has been reproduced almost word by word in CJ 13 July 2006 Joined Cases C-295–98/04 *Manfredi et al v Lloyd Adriatico Assicurazioni SpA et al* [2006] I-06619 ECLI:EU:C:2006:461, para 57. See also CJ 11 September 2008 Case C-279/06 *CEPSA Estaciones de Servicio SA v LV Tobar e Hijos SL* [2008] I-06681 ECLI:EU:C:2008:485, para 74.

[39] *Béguelin* (n 35) para 29: 'Since the nullity referred to in [now Article 101(2) TFEU] is absolute, an agreement which is null and void by virtue of this provision has no effect as between the contracting parties and cannot be set up against third parties.'

Cour de Cassation, chambre commerciale (Court of Cassation,
Commercial Division), 25 March 1991[40]   **2.15 (FR)**

Optilas and others v Quantel

ERGA OMNES EFFECT OF NULLITY

The unfaithful cartelist and his contractual partner

*Commercialising products in an area reserved to another company by means of an illegal
market sharing agreement does not result in manifestely illegal nuisance*

Facts: In July 1985, a previous subsidiary of Quantel had concluded with another company (X) a market
sharing agreement relating *inter alia* to France. In breach of this agreement, X had appointed Optilas as its
distributor for France. Quantel then claimed claimed interim measures against both X and Optilas, alleging
that these companies caused Quantel manifestly illegal nuisance by commercialising their products on the
market reserved to it (ie, Quantel). The Court of Appeal gave judgment for Quantel. X and Optilas appealed
to the French Supreme Court.

Held: The French Court of Cassation quashed the decision of the Court of Appeal.

Judgment: In so deciding while it had noted that the agreement contained a market sharing clause concerning sales promotion and after sales services relating to specified goods
and in particular by reserving Western Europe to Quantel contrary to [EU] and national
competition law ... which may lead to the voidness of the contract, the Court of Appeal
has not drawn the legal consequences of its findings, which showed in the case at hand
the absence of manifestly illegal nuisance.

Notes:

(1) Article 873 of the new French Code of Civil Procedure allows the President of the
court in urgent cases to order interim measures in order to terminate manifestly illegal
nuisance or to prevent imminent damage. This is even possible if the case is seriously
disputed.

(2) The case excerpted above shows that illustrates the *erga omnes* effect of voidness
of Article 101 TFEU and its French national counterpart. The infringement of an agreement that contravenes Article 101 TFEU by a party to that agreement does not result in
manifestly illegal nuisance to the other party to the anticompetitive agreement. Likewise,
when a party to an anticompetitive agreement concludes a contract with a third party in
breach of the anticompetitive agreement, that third party cannot be held to cause manifestly illegal nuisance to the other party to the anticompetitive agreement.

---

[40] French Court of Cassation Commercial Division 25 March 1991 nos 89-10.800 and 89-11.124 *Bulletin
IV* 1991 no 120, 84 *Optilas et al v Quantel.*

High Court of England and Wales Chancery Division,
26 June 2003[41]   **2.16 (UK)**

Bernard Crehan v Inntrepreneur Pub Company (CPC)
and Brewman Group Ltd

DAMAGES CLAIMS

A landmark case but no money

Parties to anticompetitive and void agreements can claim damages on the basis of these agreements

Facts: Mr Crehan leased a pub from Inntrepreneur. The agreement contained a beer tie providing that Crehan was to purchase all his beers from Courage at certain prices. Crehan got into financial difficulties. When sued by Courage for payment for the beers, Crehan invoked the nullity of the agreement and counter-claimed for damages, arguing that the beer tie was anticompetitive and that as a consequence of this anticompetitive agreement, he had suffered loss. However, under English law, a party to an illegal agreement cannot claim damages for loss suffered as a result of the illegality of the agreement to which he himself is a party. Asked about the conformity of the English rule with EU law, the CJ held that 'any individual can rely on a breach of [now Article 101(1) TFEU] before a national court even where he is a party to a contract that is liable to restrict or distort competition within the meaning of that provision'.[42]

Held: The court which had to decide the case after the CJEU had answered the preliminary ruling questions rejected Crehan's claim, holding that in the circumstances of the case, there was no infringement of (now) Article 101 TFEU.

Judgment: 129. The questions to the [CJEU] as formulated by the Court of Appeal were as follows:

> '(1) Is [Article 101 TFEU] to be interpreted as meaning that a party to a prohibited tied house agreement may rely on that article to seek relief from the courts from the other contracting party?
> (2) If the answer to question (1) is 'yes', is the party claiming relief entitled to recover damages alleged to arise as a result of his adherence to the clause in the agreement which is prohibited under [now Article 101 TFEU]?
> (3) Should a rule of national law which provides that courts should not allow a person to plead and/or rely on his own illegal actions as a necessary step to recovery of damages be allowed as consistent with [EU] law?
> (4) If the answer to question 3 is that in some circumstances such a rule may be inconsistent with [EU] law, what circumstances should the national court take into consideration?'

130. [The CJEU] concluded that a party to a contract which infringes [now Article 101 TFEU] is in principle entitled to damages under [EU] law for any loss which the contract causes to him. As regards whether he could lose his right to damages after all on the ground that he is attempting to rely on his own illegality, the court held that rules of national law could permissibly have such an effect, but only if the claimant had significant responsibility for the distortion of competition. In that connection it was necessary to take into account the economic and legal context in which the parties found themselves, and

---

[41] *Bernard Crehan v Inntrepreneur Pub Company (CPC) and Brewman Group Ltd* [2003] EWHC 1510 (Ch).
[42] *Courage v Crehan* (n 13) para 24.

their respective bargaining power and conduct. The court wrapped up together the four questions which had been posed by the Court of Appeal, and answered them as follows:

> A party to a contract liable to restrict or distort competition within the meaning of [now Article 101 TFEU] can rely on the breach of that article to obtain relief from the other contracting party. [now Article 101 TFEU] precludes a rule of national law under which a party to a contract liable to restrict or distort competition within the meaning of that provision is barred from claiming damages for loss caused by performance of the contract on the sole ground that the claimant is a party to that contract. [EU] law does not preclude a rule of national law barring a party to a contract liable to restrict or distort competition from relying on his own unlawful actions to obtain damages where it is established that that party bears significant responsibility for the distortion of competition.

131. The [CJEU] judgment was obviously a positive development in the case from Mr Crehan's point of view, and he was in a better position after it than he was after the decision of Carnwath J. However, before I move on I comment that the judgment does not attempt to answer the question of whether the beer ties of which Mr Crehan made complaint were in breach of [now Article 101 TFEU]. The questions referred by the Court of Appeal invited the [CJEU] to proceed on the assumption that the 'tied house agreement' which it was considering was prohibited. The [CJEU] proceeded on that hypothetical basis. Neither the form of the questions nor the answers which the court gave can be read as implying that tied house agreements are necessarily prohibited. They may or may not be, and all that the [CJEU] was deciding was that, if a particular tied house agreement was prohibited by [now Article 101 TFEU], the lessee might have a claim for damages; further, the lessee would not lose his claim for damages on the ground that he was himself a party to the agreement, unless he had a significant responsibility himself for the infringement of the Article.

132. So the matter reverted to the English courts. In November 2001 the Court of Appeal refused an invitation by Inntrepreneur to direct the determination of another preliminary issue. Instead it directed that the case should proceed to trial. Pursuant to that direction it came before me in February and March of this year, 2003.

...

297. So at last I have reached the end of this very long judgment. I will not attempt to summarise here the many points with which I have attempted to deal. On most of the issues which have been debated I agree with the case advanced on behalf of Mr Crehan. However, for him to succeed it is critical that the Inntrepreneur beer ties were in breach of [now Article 101 TFEU] ... For that to be the case both of the Delimitis conditions needed to be satisfied. For the reasons which I have given, which have nothing to do with Mr Crehan's personal activities as the tenant and occupier of *The Cock Inn* and *The Phoenix*, I conclude that Delimitis condition 1 was certainly not satisfied, and that condition 2 may not have been satisfied either. In those circumstances and for that reason I must dismiss Mr Crehan's damages claim.

Notes:

(1) The two *Delimitis* conditions to which the court refers and which determine whether a beer supply agreement is prohibited by Article 101 TFEU are: (1) 'Having regard to the economic and legal context of the agreement at issue, it is difficult for competitors who could enter the market or increase their market share to gain access to the national market for the distribution of beer in premises for the sale and consumption

of drinks. The fact that, in that market, the agreement in issue is one of a number of similar agreements having a cumulative effect on competition constitutes only one factor amongst others in assessing whether access to that market is indeed difficult'; and (2) 'The agreement in issue [makes] a significant contribution to the sealing-off effect brought about by the totality of those agreements in their economic and legal context. The extent of the contribution made by the individual agreement depends on the position of the contracting parties in the relevant market and on the duration of the agreement.' These conditions are cumulative.[43]

(2) The above case was reversed by a decision of the Court of Appeal dated 21 May 2004,[44] but it was later reinstated by the House of Lords, which quashed the appeal judgment.[45]

(3) Neither of the parties to an anticompetitive agreement can successfully claim performance of the void agreement or clause, and neither of the parties will have a remedy for non-performance of the void clause.[46]

(4) However, the voidness of a clause for infringement of Article 101(1) TFEU does not prevent either of the contracting parties from invoking the voidness of that clause.[47] The voidness even has to be invoked by the national court *ex officio*, unless the national procedural rules do not allow this.[48]

(5) As *Courage v Crehan* has made clear, the voidness of a contract or clause for breach of Article 101 TFEU (and probably Article 102 TFEU; see below) does not prevent either of the contracting parties from claiming damages for loss caused to them by the infringement of competition law consisting in the integration of an anticompetitive clause in a contract. Here, antitrust liability takes the form of a precontractual liability or liability for *culpa in contrahendo*. It must be stressed that the damages do not serve to compensate loss caused by non-performance of the anticompetitive clause. Since the clause is null, it does not bind the parties and non-performance of the clause does not give rise to compensation. On the contrary, compensation is due to the party who to his detriment abided by the void clause.

(6) However, in *Courage v Crehan*, the CJ does allow Member States to prevent unjust enrichment (*cf* below).[49] Similarly, following the principle that 'a litigant should not profit from his own unlawful conduct, where this is proven', Member States may deny a party who is found to bear significant responsibility for the distortion of competition the

---

[43] CJ 29 February 1991 Case C-234/89 *Stergios Delimitis v Henninger Bräu AG* [1991] I-00935 ECLI:EU:C:1991:91 operative part.

[44] *Brenard Crehan v Inntrepreneur Pub Company CPC* [2004] EWCA Civ 637.

[45] *Inntrepreneur Pub Company (CPC) and others v Crehan* [2007] AC 333; [2006] UKHL 38; [2006] ICR 1344; [2007] 1 AC 333; [2006] 30 EGCS 103; [2006] 30 EG 103; [2006] 3 WLR 148; [2006] NPC 85; [2006] 4 All ER 465.

[46] K Schmidt, 'Art 101 Abs 2 Rn 13', in Immenga/Mestmäcker (*supra*, footnote 17).

[47] See *Courage v Crehan* (n 13) paras 22 ('that principle of automatic nullity can be relied on by anyone') and 24: 'It follows ... that any individual can rely on a breach of [now Article 101(1) TFEU] before a national court even where he is a party to a contract that is liable to restrict or distort competition within the meaning of that provision.'

[48] CJ 14 December 1995 Joined Cases C-430/93 to C-431/93 *Jeroen van Schijndel and Johannes Nicolaas Cornelis van Veen v Stichting Pensioenfonds voor Fysiotherapeuten* [1995] I-04705 ECLI:EU:C:1995:44, para 15.

[49] ibid, para 30.

right to obtain damages from the other contracting party, provided that the principles of equivalence and effectiveness are respected.[50] This is in line with the case law of the US Supreme Court. In its *Perma Life Mufflers Inc v International Parts Corp.* decision,[51] referred to by the Court of Appeal in *Courage*, the US Supreme Court indeed held that where a party to an anticompetitive agreement is in an economically weaker position, he may sue the other contracting party for damages.

Hof van Beroep Brussel (Court of Appeal of Brussels),
28 September 2004[52]   **2.17 (BE)**

Lodiso v MONDE

ANTICOMPETITIVE DECISIONS BY ASSOCIATIONS PRODUCE
NO EFFECT AGAINST THIRD PARTIES

The colluding architect

A decision by an association of undertakings that infringes Article 101(1) TFEU is null and void. It cannot be invoked against third parties and it produces no future or past effects against them

Facts: A contract concluded between a client and an architect referred to a decision by the professional association of Belgian architects concerning minimum tariffs and provided that in case the architect could not accomplish his tasks for reasons not imputable to him, he would still be entitled to half of the contract price. After the contract was concluded, the professional association adopted a decision stating that the former decision only contained indicative tariffs. The client terminated the agreement and the architect claimed payment of half the contract price. The client invoked nullity of the contract because it referred to an anticompetitive decision by an association of undertakings. While the case was pending, the EC fined the association of Belgian architects, holding that its guidance on minimum tariffs breached EU competition law.

Held: Since the EC had found the decision of the association of architects to be contrary to [now Article 101(1) TFEU], the decision was null and void, could not be invoked against third parties and did not produce any past or future effects.

Judgment: The decision of the national Order of Belgian Architects ... which has been considered by the EC as a decision by an association of undertakings which is prohibited under [now Article 101(1) TFEU] is therefore automatically void under [now Article 101(2) TFEU].

As the voidness is absolute, the decision cannot be invoked against third parties. Moreover, it is capable of affecting all consequences whether past or future of the concerned decision ... The application of national competition law may not lead to a different result.

Notes:

(1) The dispute between the parties concerned a so-called follow-on agreement, a contract concluded with a third party according to the terms agreed on by the cartelists or,

[50] ibid, para 3.
[51] *Perma Life Mufflers Inc. v International Parts Corp* [1968] 392 US 134.
[52] Court of Appeal of Brussels 28 September 2004 *Jaarboek Handelspraktijken & Mededinging* 2004, 925 *Lodiso v MONDE*. Under the applicable national competition law, the national court seised of the case had to make a preliminary reference to the Court of Appeal of Brussels, which specialises in competition matters.

in this case, imposed or suggested by an association of undertakings. This issue is dealt with extensively in section II.A.vi below.

(2) In the case excerpted above, the Court of Appeal of Brussels was only asked to decide whether the decision adopted by the professional association of architects infringed the competition rules. It was not asked to decide on the impact of the potential voidness of this agreement on the contract between the parties to the dispute: an individual architect and his client. On this issue, *cf* section II.A.vi below.

Under CJEU case law, Article 101(2) TFEU nullity is 'capable of having a bearing on all the effects, either past or future, of the agreement or decision [and] consequently, the nullity provided for in [now Article 101(2) TFEU] is of retroactive effect'.[53]

Cour de Cassation, chambre commerciale (Court of Cassation, Commercial Division), 2 July 2002[54] **2.18 (FR)**

Intercaves v Mlle X

VOIDNESS *AB INITIO*

A complex of exclusive liquors contracts

Even if the lower court erred as to the order and autonomy of contracts, its decision to declare all contracts void should be upheld where all contracts were void ab initio

Facts: Intercaves concluded four successive exclusive franchising contracts for liquors with a franchisee. The fourth 'partnership contract' replaced the previous contracts and contained in essence the same provisions, except for a resale price maintenance clause. When Intercaves sued the franchisee for unpaid deliveries, the franchisee invoked the nullity of the agreement for infringement of the French equivalent of Article 101 TFEU. The defence was successful. Intercaves appealed to the French Court of Cassation arguing *inter alia* that the Court of Appeal had infringed the principle of the binding force of contracts by deciding that the fourth contract constituted only a prolongation of the previous ones on the grounds that all contracts had the same object and that the main provisions remained in essence the same, without specifying why these elements would deprive the fourth contract of its autonomy. Intercaves also objected to the finding that the first three contracts were void and that the fourth contract could not remedy this as it re-affirmed the void clauses and the parties still considered themselves bound by the first contracts.

Held: The appeal is rejected because, irrespective of the correctness of the Court of Appeal's judgment as to the absence of autonomy of the fourth contract, the conclusion that the four contracts were void *ab initio* was correct, even if some of them had in the meantime been terminated.

Judgment: Whereas it results from the attacked judgment that the company Intercaves, having as its object the distribution of wines and spirits, concluded with Miss X … four successive franchising contracts … the fourth on 26 May 1994, bearing the title 'partnership contract', replacing and annulling any previous agreement and taking over the essentials of the previous terms with the exception of the resale price maintenance clause; that the company Intercaves notified Miss X … of the suspension of deliveries on 31 May 1995 because of non-payment; that Miss X brought an action for annulment of the contracts for infringement of Articles 7 and 9 Ordonnance of 1 December 1986.

  …

---

[53] *Haecht II* (n 36). See also *CEPSA* (n 38); and *Manfredi* (n 38).
[54] French Court of Cassation Commercial Division 2 July 2002 no 00-14939 *Intercaves v Mlle X*.

But whereas, even if it was wrong to annul the four contracts and to set aside the arguments of the company Intercaves which alleged that only the partnership contract was to be taken into account, even if the Court of Appeal decided contrary to the clear terms of the contract which specified that it replaced and annulled any previous contract, that it was only an extension of the previous contracts from which it was not autonomous, and that it could not cover the voidness affecting these contracts, the decision is nevertheless justified since the nullity of the litigious contracts deprived them retroactively of all effects, whether or not they had in the meantime been terminated.

Notes:

(1) This decision of the French Court of Cassation given under the previous French Competition Act and dealing with the French national equivalent of Article 101 TFEU is in line with the EU case law proclaiming the retroactive effect of the nullity set out in Article 101(2) TFEU.[55]

(2) However, according to the 'theory of transient nullity', which is sometimes applied (but not in France), 'absolute' nullity does not necessarily imply that the agreement or decision infringing Article 101(1) TFEU is void as from the moment when it came into effect.

*English Court of Appeal Civil Division,
2 February 1999*[56]   **2.19 (UK)**

David John Passmore v Morland and others

TRANSIENT NULLITY

The validated beer tie

Automatic nullity only applies for so long as an agreement is affected by the cartel prohibition

Facts: The claimant, Passmore, was the tenant of a pub under a 20 year tenancy granted by IPCL, which had concluded similar contracts with a large number of other pub tenants. The lease contains a tie requiring the lessee to purchase exclusively from IPCL, its successors, assigns or nominees. On 1 July 1992, IPCL notified its standard form lease to the EC seeking an individual exemption. It subsequently withdrew notification as it expected not to obtain an exemption, and transferred its interest in the premises to Morland, a smaller operator.

Five years later, Passmore wrote to Morland that because of the failure to obtain the individual exemption, the beer tie was void ab initio regardless of the identity of the current owner. Thereafter, Passmore no longer lived up to the terms of the contract and started proceedings for damages and restitution of the sums alleged to have been unlawfully charged. Morland invoked as a defence that the number of tied premises it owned was so small that there was neither a material effect on trade within the internal market nor a breach of EU competition law.

Held: Since its transfer from a large to a smaller operator, the lease agreement is no longer affected by the EU cartel law prohibition, and is therefore no longer null and void.

Judgment: [28] [Now Article 101(2) TFEU] has to be construed in conjunction with [now Article 101(1) TFEU]. In particular [now Article 101(2) TFEU] has to be construed in the

---

[55] *Haecht II* (n 36). See also *CEPSA* (n 38); and *Manfredi* (n 38).
[56] *David John Passmore v Morland et al* [1999] 3 All ER 1005; [1999] 1 CMLR 1129.

light of an appreciation that the prohibition in [now Article 101(1) TFEU] is not an absolute prohibition, but rather a prohibition which arises when, and continues for so long as (and only for so long as), it is needed in order to promote the freedom of competition within the [internal market] which is the stated objective of [now Article 101(1) TFEU]. The prohibition is temporaneous (or transient) rather than absolute; in the sense that it endures for a finite period of time—the period of time for which it is needed—rather than for all time. With this in mind the question of construction to which the language used in [now Article 101(2) TFEU] gives rise may be stated in these terms: does [now Article 101(2) TFEU] mean that 'any agreements or decisions *while* prohibited pursuant to [now Article 101(1) TFEU] shall be automatically void'; or does it mean that 'any agreements or decisions *once* prohibited pursuant to [now Article 101(1) TFEU] shall therefore be automatically void'?

[29] In support of the contention that [now Article 101(2) TFEU] should be given a meaning which limits its effect to the period during which the prohibition imposed by [now Article 101(1) TFEU] is in force, we were referred to two decisions of the Court of Justice on the question whether the effect of [now Article 101(2) TFEU] is to make void the whole of an agreement which contains a provision which is prohibited by [now Article 101(1) TFEU]; that is to say, whether the effect of [now Article 101(2) TFEU] is to make void other provisions in the agreement which, if they stood alone, would not themselves be prohibited by [now Article 101(1) TFEU] …

[31] … The judgment (in Case 56/65, *Société Technique Minière v Maschinenbau Ulm GmbH*, 9) contains the following passage, at page 250:

> [Now Article 101(2) TFEU] provides that 'Any agreements or decisions prohibited pursuant to the Article shall be automatically void.' This provision, which is intended to ensure compliance with the Treaty, can only be interpreted with reference to its purpose in [EU] law, and it must be limited to this context. The automatic nullity in question only applies to those parts of the agreement affected by the prohibition, or to the agreement as a whole if it appears that those parts are not severable from the agreement itself. Consequently any other contractual provisions which are not affected by the prohibition, and which therefore do not involve the application of the Treaty, fall outside [EU] law.

[32] The analogy, it is submitted, is that automatic nullity only applies to the relevant provision in the agreement for so long as it is affected by the prohibition. During any period that the relevant provision is not affected by the prohibition—because the circumstances during that period are such that the provision does not then have as its effect the prevention, restriction or distortion of competition within the [internal market]—the provision calls for no application of the Treaty and falls outside [EU] law.

[33] The Court of Justice reached a similar conclusion in Case 319/82 *Société de Vente de Ciments et Betons de L'Est SA v Kerpen & Kerpen GmbH & Co KG* …

[11] It also follows from previous judgments of the Court … that the automatic nullity decreed in [now Article 101(2) TFEU] applies only to those contractual provisions which are incompatible with [now Article 101(1) TFEU]. The consequences of such nullity for other parts of the agreement are not a matter for [EU] law …

[34] It is clear from the Court's reference to the decision in the *Société Technique Minière* case that it was affirming that the automatic nullity applied to the provisions of the agreement only in so far as they were prohibited by [now Article 101(1) TFEU]. On a proper reading of the passage which I have set out, the observation does, I think, support the view that, as a matter of [EU] law, the nullity imposed by [Article now 101(2) TFEU] is

an exact reflection of the prohibition imposed by [now Article 101(1) TFEU]. If the prohibition is temporaneous (or transient) then so is the nullity.

Notes:

(1) The theory of transient nullity is supported by UK[57] legal scholarship, Belgian case law[58] and German legal scholarship.[59] According to the Federal Supreme Court of Germany, however, only a confirmation within the meaning of §141 BGB, provided by the parties after the situation causing the voidness of the agreement or clause, may render the agreement valid for the future.[60]

(2) However, the theory of transient nullity also has opponents, for example, in German scholarship. It has been strongly opposed by Komninos in 2007.

AP Komninos, '"Transient" and "Transitional" Voidness of Anti-competitive Agreements: A Non-issue and an Issue'[61] **2.20 (EU)**

Ever since *Passmore*, English courts and commentators have taken as granted this theory. This is remarkable, since this is a national theory that refers to a [EU] law concept and it has never been confirmed by the European Court of Justice, which remains the only competent court to interpret [EU] law in an authoritative manner. It is even more remarkable that English courts and commentators have never wondered why this is and still remains largely an English issue and why national courts and commentators in other Member States have not considered this an issue.

In our view, the English theory of 'transient voidness' violates the [EU] law meaning of the [now Article 101(2) TFEU] nullity and, in any event, a preliminary reference to the European Court of Justice was called for before the Court of Appeal could come to such a finding. According to the Court of Justice's case law the [now Article 101(2) TFEU] nullity 'is ... capable of having a bearing on all the effects, either past or future, of the agreement or decision [in question]'. While it is true that certain conduct might cease to fall under the prohibition of [now Article 101 TFEU], the absolute and automatic character of the nullity sanction cannot be affected. Any other result would not be compatible with the *effet utile* of that provision and would not facilitate enforcement of aggrieved parties' rights under the doctrine of direct effect of [now Article101 TFEU]. In all cases of 'transient prohibition', the contract, as initially concluded, will be void, although the conduct involved may no longer be prohibited.

In short, although there is indeed a possibility that a contract might be caught by the prohibition of [now Article 101 TFEU] only for a specific period while thereafter changed circumstances may have taken the contract outside the ambit of illegality, the civil validity of that contract is a totally different issue. The automatic, retrospective and prospective nature of the [now Article 101(2) TFEU] civil sanction of nullity makes it clear that such a contract will be null and void. It is quite another issue whether a *new* valid contract

[57] *David John Passmore v Morland et al* [1999] 3 All ER 1005; BJ Rodger, 'The Interface between Competition Law and Private Law: Article 81, Illegality and Unjustified Enrichment' (2002) 6(2) *Edinburgh Law Review* 233.
[58] Court of Appeal of Brussels 23 June 2005 *TBM-RCB* 2006/2, 107 *Edmond Laurent v Brasserie Haacht*.
[59] K Schmidt, 'Art 101 Abs 2 Rn 16 and 17', in Immenga/Mestmäcker (*supra*, footnote 17).
[60] BGH 11 December 2001 Az *KZR* 13/00 *Sabet v Massa*; BGH 05 July 2005 X ZR 14/03 *Abgasreinigungsvorrichtung*; MünchKommEUWettbR/Säcker/Jaecks 2007 art 81 EG Rn 800, 723.
[61] Komninos (n 32) 447–49 (footnotes omitted).

(possibly implied) can be considered to exist between the same parties, which will be operable ever since the prohibition of [now Article 101 TFEU] has ceased to apply. However, in such a case the validity of the new contract will operate *ex nunc* and will affect neither the effects of the voidness of the initial contract, nor any possible claims for damages referring to the crucial period of the contract's voidness.'

Some support for the theory of transient nullity could however be found in the CJ's judgment in *Cepsa* where it was held that: 'It follows from settled case-law that, once the conditions for the application of [now Article 101(1) TFEU] are met and *so long as* the agreement concerned does not justify the grant of an exemption under [now Article 101(3) TFEU], the nullity referred to in [now Article 101(2) TFEU] can be relied on by anyone. Since that nullity is absolute, it is capable of having a bearing on all the effects, either past or future, of the agreement concerned.'[62] It follows from the wording 'so long as' that the Court considers that an agreement which was prohibited and null during a certain period of time can later on qualify for an exemption. Once it is exempted, it will no longer be null until it loses the benefit of the exemption.

The nullity for infringement of Article 101(1) TFEU is *automatic*. This means that it is a consequence of the law itself (voidness *ex lege*).[63] No prior decision of the EC, an NCA or a Court is required.[64] The decision whereby the national court finds an agreement to be null for infringement of Article 101(1) TFEU has a declaratory rather than a constitutive character.[65] As already mentioned, the CJ stated in *Courage* that the courts are bound by the principle of automatic nullity, once the conditions for the application of Article 101(1) TFEU are met. This gives rise to the question whether courts are bound to apply the nullity *ex officio*.

Hof van Cassatie België (Belgian Court of Cassation), 15 May 2009[66]   **2.21 (BE)**

Brouwerij Haacht NV v BM

EX OFFICIO APPLICATION OF ARTICLE 101(2)

Exemptio, but not *ex officio*

The national court may complete the arguments of the parties by applying Article 101(2) ex officio, but it must not change the subject matter of the claim either by expanding it, or by substituting it for another

Facts: In a brewery contract, a relationship of exclusivity was set up for a period of 10 years. The Court of Appeal had held that the clause in question was prohibited under (now) Article 101(1) of the Treaty and therefore void under (now) Article 101(2) TFEU. This part of the court's judgment was not criticised. Before the appellate court, the brewer had not argued that the agreement satisfied the requirements of (now)

---

[62] *CEPSA* (n 38) para 74, emphasis added. *cf* section II.A.iv.

[63] K Schmidt, 'Art 101 Abs 2 Rn 14', in Immenga/Mestmäcker (*supra*, footnote 17).

[64] *Haecht II* (n 36); AP Komninos, *EC Private Antitrust Enforcement. Decentralised Application of EC Competition Law by National Courts* (Oxford, Hart Publishing, 2008) 151–52.

[65] Komninos (n 64) 15; M Libertini and MR Maugeri, 'Infringement of Competition Law and Invalidity of Contracts' (2005) 1(2) *European Review of Contract Law* 256.

[66] Belgian Court of Cassation 15 May 2009 C.08.0029.N *Brouwerij Haacht NV v BM*.

Article 101(3) TFEU. The brewer appealed to the Court of Cassation requesting the decision of the Court of Appeal to be quashed because it had failed to apply (now) Article 101(3) TFEU *ex officio*.

Held: The Belgian Court of Cassation upheld the appellate decision.

Judgment: Given the passive role assigned to him, the judge must not modify on his own motion the object of the request, either by extending it or by substituting it for another. The judge may, it is true, complete on his own motion the arguments made by the parties in support of their request, provided, however, that he does not raise an issue that the parties have excluded by their written pleadings and that he only builds on the elements that have been brought before him regularly and that he does not modify either the object or the cause of the request. In its decision of 10 December 1995, *Van Schijndel*, Joined cases C-430/93 and C-431/93, the Court of Justice … has underlined that [EU] law does not compel the national jurisdictions to invoke on their own motion any issue concerning the breach of [EU] law where examination of that issue would oblige them to abandon the passive role assigned to them by going beyond the ambit of the dispute defined by the parties and relying on facts and circumstances other than those on which the party with an interest in application of those provisions bases his claim. Therefore, the appellate judges could legally decide that the agreements concluded are void [now Article 101(2) TFEU] to the extent they provide that the exclusive purchase obligations apply for a duration of more than five years.

Notes:

(1) The Belgian Court of Cassation refused to quash an appellate decision that had failed to invoke Article 101(3) TFEU *ex officio* in a case where it could decide on the basis of the facts presented to it that the requirements of Article 101(1) were satisfied, but not that the requirements of Article 101(3) were satisfied.

(2) The Court of Cassation referred to Article 2 of Regulation 1/2003, last sentence, which provides that: 'The undertaking or association of undertakings claiming the benefit of [now Article 101(3) of the Treaty] shall bear the burden of proving that the conditions of that paragraph are fulfilled.' In addition, the Court of Cassation referred to *Van Schijndel*. In this case the CJ held that national courts are under a duty to apply Article 101 TFEU *ex officio* where domestic law allows such application (para 15), but that they are not required to do so where it 'would oblige them to abandon the passive role assigned to them by going beyond the ambit of the dispute defined by the parties themselves and relying on facts and circumstances other than those on which the party with an interest in application of those provisions bases his claim' (para 22).

(3) The decision of the Court of Cassation is compatible with *Van Schijndel*. Nevertheless, it was met with criticism from certain scholars. It was questioned whether the decision was to be interpreted as meaning that the judge would not be under a duty to raise Article 101(3) TFEU *ex officio*, while he would be under a duty to raise Article 101(1) TFEU *ex officio*, and whether this did not create an artificial distinction between the two paragraphs of Article 101 TFEU. Furthermore, the question was raised whether Article 101 TFEU should not be considered to be of public order in its entirety since the reasons underlying all its paragraphs equally affect the public economic order and this interpretation would be in line with the aim pursued by Regulation 1/2003.[67]

---

[67] A Lamote and P L'Ecluse, 'Noot: art. 101, VWEU—Van openbare orde in Luxemburg maar niet in Brussel? Enkele bedenkingen bij het "Haacht" arrest van het Hof van Cassatie' (2010) 3 *TBM-RBC* 40–41.

(4) The abovementioned decision of the Court of Cassation can be compared with a case decided by the Austrian Supreme Court on the duties of a first instance in relation to Article 101(1) and (2) TFEU. The Austrian Supreme Court decided that the absolute nullity set out in Article 101(2) TFEU does not mean that the factual preconditions of Article 101(1) TFEU are to be investigated *ex officio*. It only means that a formal assertion of nullity is not required. The factual preconditions, however, need to be asserted in the first instance or at least need to appear clearly from the case file. Since that was not the case, the Court did not need to apply the nullity sanction.[68]

It is interesting to compare the CJ's decision in *Van Schijndel* with its case law in relation to the Unfair Terms Directive.[69] In *Pannon*, the CJ still held that: 'The national court is required to examine, of its own motion, the unfairness of a contractual term where it has available to it the legal and factual elements necessary for that task.'[70] This decision did not make clear whether the national court may or must also examine the unfairness of a contractual term of its own motion where it does not have the legal and factual elements necessary for that task at its disposal; in other words, whether it is also required to establish of its own motion the facts and the law necessary for that examination. In *Pénzügyi*, the CJ was asked to clarify this issue in relation to a jurisdiction clause in a consumer contract. The CJ's answer was that 'the national court must investigate of its own motion whether a term conferring exclusive territorial jurisdiction in a contract concluded between a seller or supplier and a consumer, which is the subject of a dispute before it, falls within the scope of the Directive and, if it does, assess of its own motion whether such a term is unfair'.[71] Investigating whether a term in a B2C contract falls within the scope of the Directive implies investigating whether it has been individually negotiated (Article 3(1) of the Unfair Terms Directive). The CJ made clear that its decision in *Pénzügyi* was motivated by the fact that the Unfair Terms Directive aims to protect the consumer who is in a weak position vis-a-vis the seller or supplier, as regards both his bargaining power and his level of knowledge. The CJ added that the provision of the Directive holding unfair terms non-binding on the consumer 'is a mandatory provision which aims to replace the formal balance which the contract establishes between the rights and obligations of the parties with an effective balance which re-establishes equality between them … In order to guarantee the protection intended by the Directive,

---

[68] Austrian Supreme Court 11 December 2013 no 7Ob210/13b RdW 2014/370 S 336—*RdW* 2014, 336.

[69] Council Directive 93/13/EEC of 5 April 1993 on unfair terms in consumer contracts [1993] OJ L95/29.

[70] CJ 4 June 2009 Case C-243/08 *Pannon GSM Zrt v Erzsébet Sustikné Győrfi* [2009] I-04713 ECLI:EU:C:2009:350.

[71] CJ 9 November 2010 Case C-137/08 *VB Pénzügyi Lízing Zrt. v Ferenc Schneider* [2010] I-10847 ECLI:EU:C:2010:659, para 56 and operative part 3. Confirmed in CJ 14 June 2012 Case C-618/10 *Banco Español de Crédito SA v Joaquin Calderón Camino* nyr ECLI:EU:C:2012:349 para 44; CJ 21 February 2013 Case C-472/11 *Banif Plus Bank Zrt v Csaba Csipai and Viktória Csipai* nyr ECLI:EU:C:2013:88 para 24; CJ 14 March 2013 Case C-415/11 *Mohamed Aziz v Caixa d'Estalvis de Catalunya, Tarragona i Manresa (Catalunyacaixa)* nyr ECLI:EU:C:2013:164 para 47. It should be noted that in later case law on the Unfair Terms Directive, the CJ no longer used the phrase from *Pénzügyi* referring to an investigation into the fact of whether a contract term had been individually negotiated, but limited itself to the wording used in or very similar to that used in *Pannon*: the CJ's duty to examine of its own motion the possible unfairness of a term exists 'where it has available to it the legal and factual elements necessary for that task', 'as soon as it has available to it the legal or factual elements necessary for that task'. See CJ 30 May 2013 Case C-488/11 *Dirk Frederik Asbeek Brusse and Katarina de Man Garabito v Jahani BV* nyr ECLI:EU:C:2013:341; CJ 30 May 2013 Case C-397/11 *Erika Jőrös v Aegon Magyarország Hitel Zrt* nyr ECLI:EU:C:2013:340, para 27.

the CJ has also stated that the imbalance which exists between the consumer and the seller or supplier may be corrected only by positive action unconnected with the actual parties to the contract'.[72] One could argue that competition law applies mostly between professional parties and that the financial value of the disputes is generally higher than in consumer cases, which means that the parties are more likely to invest in sound legal advice. This might justify a different treatment of national courts' obligations to carry out of their own motion an investigation into the facts of a dispute. However, particularly in vertical agreements between undertakings, there may also be significant differences in the economic and bargaining power as well as in the legal expertise of the parties to the dispute. Furthermore, in *Pannon* and *Banif*, the CJ ruled that the national court, although it has a duty to disregard a non-binding term, may nevertheless apply it, if the consumer, after having been informed of the term's non-binding status, opposes its non-application.[73] This exception can be explained by the fact that the non-bindingness of an unfair term serves to protect the interests of the consumer. A similar exception is not appropriate in competition cases since here the nullity serves to protect the public interest.

Finally, it was implied in *Pannon* and made explicit in *Banif* that 'the principle of *audi alteram partem*, as a general rule, requires the national court which has found of its own motion that a contractual term is unfair to inform the parties to the dispute of that fact and to invite each of them to set out its views on that matter, with the opportunity to challenge the views of the other party, in accordance with the formal requirements laid down in that regard by the national rules of procedure'.[74] This seems to apply in cases of private enforcement of competition law as well, even though in these cases the claimant cannot prevent the application of the nullity in the case that the conditions of Article 101 TFEU are fulfilled.

The automatic nature of the nullity also gives rise to the question whether the right to avail oneself of the nullity can be subject to prescription. Some scholars answer in the negative, arguing that the nullity is not the result of an 'action for nullity', so that there is no action that can be time barred.[75] Komninos, however, argues that this opinion would lead to an unacceptable level of legal uncertainty, which would be incompatible with EU law. He therefore argues that the national rules on prescription need to be applied, taking into account the principles of effectiveness and equivalence. Given the public policy nature of EU competition rules, the national rules on prescription that apply in cases of nullity for infringement of rules of public policy would need to be applied. Where such rules do not exist, the general national regime applicable to civil law actions would apply, subject to the principles of effectiveness and equivalence.[76]

---

[72] *Pénzügyi* (n 71) paras 46–48.

[73] *Pannon* (n 70) para 33 and operative part 2; *Banif* (n 71) paras 27 and 35.

[74] *Banif* (n 71).

[75] O Blažo, 'What Do Limitation Periods for Sanctions in Antitrust Matters Really Limit?', *Yearbook of Antitrust and Regulatory Studies* (Warsaw, University of Warsaw), 2012, (79), 85; M Cienfuegos Mateo, 'L'application de la nullité de l'article 85, § 2, du Traité C.E.E. par les juridictions nationales (avec un examen particulier du domaine des transports aériens) conséquences dans l'ordre juridique interne' (1991) *CDE* 322–23; A Frignani and M Waelbroeck, *European Competition Law* (New York, Transnational Publishers, 1999) 524.

[76] Komninos (n 64) 154.

II.A.iv IMPACT OF NULLITY ON THE NON-INFRINGING PARTS OF THE AGREEMENT

The CJEU's case law on the impact of the nullity of a specific clause for infringement of Article 101 TFEU on the remainder of the agreement dates back to *Société Technique Minière*[77] and *Consten and Grundig*,[78] which were both decided in 1966. In these cases, the CJ stated in almost identical words that the automatic nullity provided by Article 101(2) TFEU applies only to those parts of the agreement affected by the prohibition, or to the agreement as a whole if those parts are not severable from the agreement itself. Any other contractual provisions which are not affected by the prohibition fall outside the scope of EU law.

In later cases the CJ changed its wording a little, stating that: 'The automatic nullity decreed by [now Article 101(2) TFEU] applies only to those contractual provisions which are incompatible with [now Article 101(1) TFEU]. The consequences of such nullity for other parts of the agreement … are not a matter for [EU] law. Those consequences are to be determined by the national court according to its own law.'[79]

This wording could be interpreted as implying that the automatic nullity provided by Article 101(2) TFEU applies only to the clauses actually infringing Article 101(1) TFEU, the consequences for the remainder of the agreement being left to the national law to decide.

In *Cepsa*, however, the CJ reverted to the wording used in *Société Technique Minière* and *Consten*, ruling that: 'The automatic nullity provided for in [now Article 101(2) TFEU] affects a contract in its entirety only if the clauses which are incompatible with [now Article 101(1) TFEU] are not severable from the contract itself. Otherwise, the consequences of the nullity, in respect of all the other parts of the contract, are not a matter for [EU] law.'[80]

The case law of the CJEU has not laid down a criterion for severability itself. In *Cepsa*, the CJ was asked whether the voidness of a clause fixing retail prices affected the contract as a whole. It had the opportunity to formulate a criterion for severability. However, instead of determining whether such a clause was severable from the remainder of the contract, the CJ limited itself to the general statement referred to above.[81] This could be read as a confirmation of the fact that the criterion for severability is to be determined by national law. Yet, this is difficult to reconcile with the CJ's statement that the consequences of the voidness of the anticompetitive clause for the remainder of the agreement

---

[77] CJ 30 June 1966 Case C-56/65 *La Société Technique Minière (LTM) v Maschinenbau Ulm GmbH (MBU)* [1966] I-00235 ECLI:EU:C:1966:38.

[78] CJ 13 July 1966 Joined Cases C-56 and C-58/64 *Établissements Consten SàRL and Grundig-Verkaufs-GmbH v Commission of the European Economic Community* [1996] I-0299 ECLI:EU:C:1966:41.

[79] CJ 30 April 1998 Case C-230/96 *Cabour SA and Nord Distribution Automobile SA v Arnor 'SOCO' SARL* [1998] I-02055 ECLI:EU:C:1998:181, para 51; CJ 18 December 1986 Case C-10/86 *VAG France v Établissements Magne SA* [1986] I-04071 ECLI:EU:C:1986:502, paras 14 and 15; CJ 30 November 2006 Joined Cases C-376/05 and C-377/05 *Brünsteiner and Autohaus Hilgert v Bayerische Motorenwerke AG* [2006] I-11383 ECLI:EU:C:2006:753, para 48.

[80] *Cespa* (n 38).

[81] ibid, paras 78–79.

is a matter of national law only where this clause is severable from the remainder of the agreement.

The way in which national legal systems deal with this obscurity in the CJEU's case law differs.

§139 of the German Civil Code (BGB): Partial nullity   **2.22 (GERM)**

If part of a legal transaction is null and void, the entire legal transaction is void unless it is to be assumed that it would have been undertaken even without the void part.

K Schmidt in Immenga/Mestmäcker, Wettbewerbsrecht[82]   **2.23 (GERM)**

3. Application of §139 BGB

23 Insofar as clauses in the light of Art. 101 can be severed from the invalid agreement, the legal effects of the partial annulment with regard to these severable agreements or decisions are subject to rules of national law …

a) [Precondition of §139 BGB …]

24 First of all §139 BGB *presupposes* the *severability* of prohibited and permitted parts of the contract (because without such severability Art. 101 par. 2 immediately applies to the entire contract …), as well as that the contract can objectively exist without the cartelized clauses. Full nullity occurs when numerous contractual clauses are null and void and without them the contract would receive a substantially different content, not intended by the parties. *In distribution systems* (distributor systems, franchise systems, commercial agency systems) the voidness of cartelized agreements leads to the nullity of the entire agreement if the void agreement has such a central role in the contracts that its voidness triggers the voidness of the entire agreement. Therefore the voidness of a clause providing territorial protection, exclusivity or an export or re-import prohibition does not necessarily extend to the entire agreement.

b) [… no specific legal or contractual rules …]

25 Subsequently, the application of §139 BGB requires that no specific legal or contractual rules, in particular no severability clause, exist …

c) [… hypothetical intention of the parties …]

26 Finally, §139 BGB takes the *hypothetical intention* of the parties into account: if—in view of business customs and good faith (§157 BGB)—it can be assumed that the contract (or decision) would also have been concluded without the invalid part, it remains effective insofar. The hypothetical intention of the parties must be determined while considering? both parties—not only the party whom the void clause should serve—and in case law related to competition law it will largely be typecast as mere severability … In particular, when assuming mere severability would remove the economic purpose pursued by the parties from the entire contract, the nullity of the entire contract will be assumed, subject to possible renegotiation obligations … Conversely, objections to side issues in a contract concerning a distribution system do not lead to its complete nullity. Equally, the invalidity of a mere default clause will generally not entail the voidness of the entire agreement.

---

[82] K Schmidt, 'Art 101 Abs 2 Rn 23, 25 and 26', in Immenga/Mestmäcker (*supra*, footnote 17).

Notes:

(1) It should be noted that §139 BGB is not used to determine *whether* an anticompetitive clause can be severed from the remainder of the agreement. It is argued that §139 BGB comes into play only *if* a clause that infringes Article 101(1) TFEU can be severed from the remainder of the agreement.[83]

(2) Whether a clause is severable from the remainder of the contract is to be determined solely in view of the purpose of the cartel prohibition. The fairness of the contract is not relevant in this regard.[84]

(3) If the clause infringing Article 101 TFEU is inseverable from the remainder of the agreement, the voidness of the entire agreement follows from Article 101(2) TFEU.

(4) If the clause is severable according to this definition, §139 BGB is to be applied. §139 BGB contains a presumption that the voidness of a particular clause extends to the entire contract. The party that wants to maintain the remainder of the contract bears the burden of proving that the parties would have concluded the contract even without the void clause, but this is to be judged taking into account common practice and good faith.

(5) If the anticompetitive clause is a standard clause, §306 BGB is considered to prevail over §139 BGB. §306 BGB provides that if standard clauses are ineffective, the remainder of the contract remains in effect. The ineffective clauses are supplemented by statutory default rules. If the contract would amount to unreasonable hardship for one party even after this supplementation, the entire contract is ineffective. §306 BGB is applied in *The Body Shop* (discussed below).

Oberster Gerichtshof (Austrian Supreme Court),
22 February 2001[85]   **2.24 (AT)**

M AG v August S

SEVERABILITY

The Austrian filling station

When assessing severability, the intention of the parties is not decisive. Severability must rather be assessed in view of the function of the sanction of voidness. The point of reference is not the idea of contractual justice, but the restoration of the economic freedom of the bound parties

Facts: The claimant is a wholesaler of mineral oils. She and the mother of the defendant concluded an agreement for the exploitation of a filling station on a plot of land owned by the mother. The contract was concluded for an undetermined duration, but could be terminated by either party with a notification period of three months. However, the mother waived her right of termination until 31 December 1995 and agreed that if she did not use her right of termination at the first possible occasion, the waiver would be extended by five years. The defendant succeeded his mother as a contracting party and tried to terminate the agreement in 1995. He

[83] K Schmidt, 'Art 101 Abs 2 Rn 22 and 23', in Immenga/Mestmäcker (*supra*, footnote 17).
[84] ibid.
[85] Austrian Supreme Court 22 February 2001 no 6Ob322/00x *M AG v August S.* See also: https://www.ris.bka.gv.at/Dokument.wxe?Abfrage=Justiz&Dokumentnummer=JJT_20010222_OGH0002_0060OB00322_00X0000_000.

sent a first notification and his lawyer sent a second notification on 22 December 1995 indicating an intention to terminate per 31 March 1996. The claimant argued that the notification was ineffective given the waiver and brought several claims. The defendant argued that the waiver infringed (now) Article 101(1) TFEU. The first instance court considered (now) Article 101 TFEU to be inapplicable, but considered the waiver clause to be void and immoral under §879 of the Austrian Civil Code. It considered the agreement terminated not on 31 December 1995, but on 31 March 1996. The defendant had to pay the damages provided for in the contract for not operating the filling station during the first three months of 1996. Both parties appealed. The Court of Appeal rejected both appeals. Both parties claimed the revision of the decision by the Austrian Supreme Court.

Held: If the defendant were a distributor and not a commercial agent, the principled prohibition of (now) Article 101 TFEU would apply and the agreement would not benefit from the relevant block exemption Regulation because its duration exceeded 10 years. Whether the agreement is void then depends on fulfilment of the conditions of (now) Article 101(1) TFEU. The voidness would in any case be limited to the degree to which the agreement's duration exceeds 10 years because of the waiver of termination for five additional years. The clause providing the possibility to terminate upon three months' notification is not void under competition law. The application of §879 of the Austrian Civil Code leads to the same result. It is therefore not necessary to determine whether the requirements for the application of (now) Article 101(1) TFEU are in fact satisfied.

Judgment: With regard to the scope of the nullity the Supreme Court holds, in accordance with legal scholarship, the opinion that the directly applicable nullity for infringement of the [EU] cartel prohibition is indeed absolute and essentially leads to ineffectiveness *ex tunc* ... however, according to the case law of the [CJEU] this does not apply to the entire agreement, but only to those parts which either themselves infringe the prohibition of [now Article 101 TFEU] or cannot reasonably be severed from the parts that are void ... Only when a clause which infringes [EU] law cannot be severed from the remainder of the agreement will the entire agreement be void. When assessing the severability it is not the intention of the parties that is determinative. Severance must rather be assessed in view of the function of the sanction of voidness. The point of reference is not the idea of contractual justice, but the restoration of the economic freedom of the bound parties ... The scope of the nullity follows from the protective scope of the prohibition ... The elimination of the entire agreement with retroactive effect followed by a lengthy reversed transaction under the law of unjustified enrichment cannot have any impact on the restriction of competition that has already taken place. The block exemption allows contractual agreements with duration of a maximum of 10 years. Only the further restriction through the waiver of the right to terminate for five more years is void; the power awarded by the contract to terminate upon three months notification is not. It follows that the contract is valid for the past and can be severed from the anticompetitive clauses. The three month notification term is compatible with the competition rules. The voidness of the entire contract would only be a sanction in addition to the penalties and periodic penalties provided for by [EU] competition law, for which there is in the light of the protective scope of [now Article 101(1) TFEU] no discernible objective ground. Whether the remaining parts of the contracts are valid under Austrian law is still to be dealt with. The consideration that for the purposes of competition law the relevance of an exclusive purchase agreement for multiple years lies in the parts of the contract that limit the freedom of decision power of the exclusive purchaser and the intrusion of a competitor in the market pleads in favour of a reduction of the excessive restriction under [EU] law. A long term contract that can at any time be terminated is neutral for the purposes of competition law. Therefore, only the fact that the exclusive purchaser is bound during the eleventh year of the contract and the waiver of termination for an additional period of five years are void under [now Article 101(2) TFEU].

Notes:

(1) Article 101 TFEU applies to acts of collusion between independent undertakings. Commercial agents who negotiate and conclude contracts on behalf of their principal, who do not purchase the goods from the principal and who do not bear any commercial risk are not considered as independent undertakings, but as forming part of the undertaking of their principal. Consequently, Article 101 TFEU does not apply to agreements between such commercial agents and their principal.[86]

(2) In the annotated judgment, the Austrian Supreme Court advocates an objective approach to determining the severability of an anticompetitive clause for the purposes of Article 101(2) TFEU.

(3) An Austrian scholar who conducted extensive research into the issue of voidness for infringement of the competition rules agrees that it is in the first place the objective of the infringed rule (*Normzweck*) that is determinative. However, in his opinion, the purpose of the competition rules is generally 'colourless' (*farblos*), when they are not aimed at protecting undertakings from abuse. If the objective of the rule is colourless, severability would need to be determined by the hypothetical intention of the parties. Only when this hypothetical intention cannot be determined would severability need to be accepted, so that the contract would need to be held valid except for the anticompetitive clause.[87]

*Tribunal Supremo. Sala de lo Civil (Supreme Court of Spain
Civil Section), 30 July 2009*[88]   **2.25 (ES)**

Sveyn SA and Svenson International SA v Hair National Center SL and others

INSEVERABILITY

Minimum resale prices, void contracts

A franchising agreement containing a minimum resale price maintenance clause is void in its entirety

Facts: The parties had concluded two franchising contracts. The franchisor brought a claim for non-performance against the franchisee. He claimed compensation from the franchisee and his joint guarantors. The franchisee invoked as a defence and counter-claim the nullity of the agreements because they infringed both EU and national competition law by imposing minimum resale prices.

---

[86] Whish and Bailey (n 3) 658. See also the EC Guidelines on vertical restraints [2010] OJ C130/1, paras 12–21.

[87] T Eilmansberger, 'Zur Nichtigkeit kartellrechtswidriger Vereinbarungen und ihren Konsequenzen (1. Teil)' (2009) 131(6) *JB* 345.

[88] Supreme Court of Spain Civil Section 30 July 2010 ECLI:ES:TS:2009:5933 *Sveyn SA and Svenson International SA v Hair national Center SL et al.* See also: www.poderjudicial.es/search/doAction?action =contentpdf&databasematch=TS&reference=4740030&links=&optimize=20091022&publicinterface=true. Summarised and translated by JM Miravalls, 'Contract Annulment Due to Minimum Price-Fixing: The Bad Application of Private Enforcement of Competition Law' in LA Velasco San Pedro et al (eds), *Private Enforcement of Competition Law* (Valladolid, Lex Nova SAU, 2011) 337–47. The author further notes that this decision is followed almost word for word in a number of lower court decisions, more particularly Court of Appeal Madrid 12 July 2004, Court of Appeal Firona 10 July 2004; First Instance Court Madrid 27 July 2009; Commercial Court Barcelona 27 October 2009; Commercial Court Madrid 29 July 2005; Commercial Court Madrid 15 April 2005.

Held: The Supreme Court of Spain upheld the judgment on appeal which held the entire contract void.

Judgment: In this case total nullity must be upheld because the considerations presented in the judgment being appealed against are a reasonable and consistent legal response fully in accordance with the law given that the suppression of the restrictive clause not only affects the franchisee's freedom to set the price, but also indirectly and consequentially affects the fee payable to the franchisor by the franchisee which is an essential consideration in the contract and therefore obviously affects a structural element and the economics of the business. It is not possible therefore to find that the fixed price can be maintained in relation to free market pricing because that requires mutual agreement between the two parties.

Notes:

(1) The decision excerpted above is an illustration of the doctrine developed by the Supreme Court of Spain, according to which the presence of resale price maintenance clauses in vertical agreements leads to the voidness of the entire agreement. This doctrine is based on the one hand on the essential nature of the clauses concerned and on the other hand on respect for the parties' intentions.[89]

(2) While the doctrine is supported by certain Spanish scholars,[90] it has also been subject to criticism. According to the critics, severability is to be assessed using a normative criterion. This would entail that 'the purpose and underlying principles of the imperative norm whose infringement is the reason for the nullity of the prohibited clause must be examined and assessed to decide whether the effects of the nullity are limited to the clause in question or whether the entire agreement is void'.[91] When the norm voiding the agreement does not mention whether it leads to total or partial voidness, the underlying purpose of the rule establishing the prohibition is to be taken into account and it is to be assessed how that purpose is best achieved while ignoring the parties' intentions.[92] Indeed, the purpose of the competition rules is to promote the public interest by ensuring free competition on the market. They do not serve to protect the parties to the agreement by determining hypothetical fair contract terms. The purpose of competition law would be best achieved by adjusting the contract to the limits set by law.[93] The counter-argument that total nullity is preferable because of its preventive aim is refuted

---

[89] Miravalls (n 88) 346.

[90] A Arroyo Aparicio, 'Applicación de la normativa protectora de la libra competencia: la STS (Sala 1. &) de 2 de junio de 2000' (2001) 3 *Aranzadi civil: revista doctrinal* 2201; and F Mercadal Vidal, 'Sentencia de 2de junio de 2000, Derecho europeo de la competencia. Nulidad de pleno derecho par violación de Tratado de Roma y del Reglamento de exención por categorías apreciadoa por el juez español' (2001) 55 *Cuadernos Civitas de jurispudencia civil* 87, referred to by Miravalls (n 88) 342.

[91] Miravalls (n 88) 342, with reference.

[92] Miravalls (n 88) 342, also referring to MA Parra Lucán, 'Sentencia de 3de octubre de 2007: Nulidad de pleno derecho de contrato de abanderamiento por *infr*acción de Reglamento comunitario' (2008) 77 *Cuadernos Civitas de jurisprudencia civil* 761.

[93] Miravalls (n 88) 343. The author points out that certain lower case law relating in particular to exclusive supply clauses supports this position. In particular, he refers to Vizcaya Provincial court (section 4) 23 April 2010; Court of Appeal Madrid (section 28) 13 October 2008, 6 February 2007 and 27 October 2006; Commercial court Palma de Mallorca 3 March 2009.

on the basis that nullity does not serve a preventive aim. Prevention and deterrence would be achieved through the public enforcement rules.[94]

Hof van Beroep Brussel (Court of Appeal of Brussels),
23 November 1995[95]   **2.26 (BE)**

Nina Ricci NV and others v Parfums Christian Dior SA and others

VOIDNESS EXTENDED TO ENTIRE CONTRACTS

The cosmetics distribution contracts

In the absence of legal and contractual provisions, the court must investigate whether the void clause is severable from the remainder of the agreement

Facts: A number of selective distribution contracts contained clauses infringing (now) Article 101 TFEU. The question arose whether the voidness was limited to these clauses or affected the agreements in their entirety.

Held: Given that the contracts formed part of a network of similar agreements forming a selective distribution network, the closed nature of which was guaranteed by the void clauses which rendered the network more anticompetitive than necessary for the products concerned, the Court extended the voidness to the contracts in their entirety. The Court did not want to turn a prohibited system of selective distribution into a permitted one *post factum.*

Judgment: [I]t also appears that NV Belgilux ... and the NV Impro-Lux and NV Copardis have set up a system of selective distribution based on agreements with selected distributors in Belgium which are incompatible with [now Article 101 TFEU] and cannot be exempted;

Whereas the nullity provided for by [now Article 101(2) TFEU] is absolute, so that the void agreement cannot have any effect between the contracting parties and cannot be invoked against third parties ... and the nullity has effect *ex tunc, id est* affects all past consequences ...;

Whereas it first has to be determined what the parties have agreed thereon in their contract;

It is perfectly possible that they agree specifically, whether explicitly or implicitly, that the voidness of a specific part entails or does not entail the voidness of the entire agreement;

this is *in casu* not the case ...;

this also entails that the voidness of certain clauses can affect the entire agreement if they constitute an indissoluble unity ...,

but the question whether this is indeed the case has to be determined by the national law ...

Whereas in case of silence of the law and the contract, the judge has to determine whether the void clause constitutes an indissoluble part of the entire contract and therefore constitutes an inseverable part of it;

Only when this is the case will the voidness of one or more clauses entail the voidness of the entire agreement;

---

[94] Miravalls (n 88) 343.
[95] Court of Appeal of Brussels 23 November 1995 *Jaarboek Handelspraktijken & Mededinging* 1995, 645 *Nina Ricci NV and others v Parfums Christian Dior SA et al.*

to determine the existence of such an indissoluble link the judge in the first place needs to verify what the intention of the parties has been, id est whether the concerned clause was decisive for the consensus of the parties;

subsequently, he needs to take the structure itself of the agreement into account and assess how the void clause relates to the other clauses individually and as a whole;

the voidness of the clause can indeed entail the loss of the consistency of the contract and obstruct the normal performance of the contract;

Whereas in this case it may not be forgotten that the concerned contracts form part of a network of similar agreements which together constitute one system of selective distribution, from which the producer and the main supplier as well as the selected distributors hope to benefit;

the distinct clauses which have been held above to be contrary to [now Article 101 TFEU] and which are therefore void are meant to render this system as closed and watertight as possible, as a consequence whereof it limits competition more than strictly necessary for the type of the distributed products.

Such clauses are inherent to the contracts of which they form part and to the distribution system that is based thereon;

therefore ... the nullity cannot be limited to the clauses concerned with the effect that a system of selective distribution that is void in the light of [now Article 101 TFEU] would be transformed *post factum* in a legal system.

Notes:

(1) Neither the Belgian competition legislation nor the Belgian Civil Code contain rules specifying the consequences of the nullity of a specific clause for the remainder of the contract. Such a rule does exist with regard to unfair terms.[96]

(2) The Belgian Court of Cassation did to some extent develop a theory under which the voidness of a clause can only entail the voidness of the entire agreement when that clause is inseverable from (indissolubly connected to) the remainder of the agreement.[97] Belgian scholarship is divided on the question whether the severability is to be determined based on subjective standards (the intention of the parties) and/or objective standards (the structure of the agreement, the purpose of the rule whose infringement is sanctioned by voidness).[98]

(3) In the annotated judgment, the Appeal Court offers a detailed overview of the steps which are to be followed to determine whether a clause that infringes Article 101 TFEU is severable from the remainder of the agreement. In the first place account is to be taken of any severance clauses and any legal provisions. In the second place, the court will look at the intention of the parties: was the clause decisive for their agreement? Next, it will look at the structure of the agreement, at how the void clause relates to the other clauses, at the coherence of the contract and whether normal performance will be

---

[96] ArticleVI.84 §1 of the Code of Economic Law (*Wetboek Economisch Recht*).

[97] Belgian Court of Cassation 27 February 1959 *Pas.* 1959 vol I 653; Belgian Court of Cassation 13 October 1960 *Arr Cass* 1961, 160 and *Pas.* 1961 vol I 160. See further C Cauffman, 'Vers un endiguement du pouvoir modérateur du juge en cas de nullité?' (2007) *RCJB* 432–33.

[98] On this issue, see Cauffman (n 97) 433.

affected. Finally, it looks at the entire distribution system of which the contract containing the void clauses forms part. In the absence of legal provisions dealing with severance, the court thus starts from a subjective approach, focusing on the intention of the parties. It only turns to an objective approach afterwards, taking into account the structure of the contract and the distribution network of which the clauses form part. It is interesting to note that where the subjective approach would lead to the voidness being limited to particular clauses, the court could nevertheless hold the entire agreement void on the basis of the function of the clauses within the contracts and the distribution network, and the purpose of the sanction of voidness in Article 101 TFEU.

(4) Not all Belgian judgments are as carefully motivated. In *Fiat*, the Court of Appeal of Brussels extended the nullity of a clause to the entire agreement based on the fact that the supplier, who had imposed the void clause, would not have consented to the distribution contract without the said clause. The Court thus seemed to have adopted a uniquely subjective approach to the issue of severance. In this particular case, this turned out well for the distributor, who was sued by Fiat for breach of the distribution contract and who invoked the voidness of the contract as a defence.[99] As illustrated by the Cosmetics distribution case discussed above, a purely subjective approach does not necessarily lead to a result that suits the purposes of Article 101.

(5) Regulation no 2016-131 reforming the French law of contract, the general rules and the rules on proof of obligations[100] introduced a provision into the French Civil Code that explicitly deals with the impact of one or more null clause on the remainder of the contract. The new French Article 1184(1) of the Civil Code (applicable as of 1 October 2016) provides that when the cause of nullity only affects one or more contract clauses, it only entails the nullity of the entire agreement when the clause(s) in question was (were) decisive for one or both parties to enter into the agreement. The party invoking the decisive character of the clause bears the burden of proof thereof.[101] The nullity will in any case be limited to the affected clause(s) when the law considers it (them) non-written (*réputée(s) non-écrite(s)*) or when the purpose of the rule requires the maintenance of the remainder of the contract (Article 1184(2)). It follows that a combined subjective-objective approach is taken when determining the impact of the nullity of a specific clause on the remainder of the agreement. The criterion used is subjective: the intention of one or both parties, However, the intention of the parties will not be taken into account when the legislator indicated by the terminology used (*réputé non écrit*) that he wants the nullity to be limited to a specific clause, or when this follows from the purpose of the infringed rule. The rule confirms (and clarifies) earlier case law.[102]

---

[99] Court of Appeal of Brussels 28 April 2010 *TBH* 2011 vol 8 p 814–17 annotated by P Kileste and C Staudt. An appeal to the Belgian Court of Cassation relating to the application of the effect on trade criterion failed: Belgian Court of Cassation 24 February 2012 C.11.0032.F.

[100] L'ordonnance no 2016-131 du 10 février 2016 portant réforme du droit des contrats, du régime général et de la preuve des obligations' *JORF* 11 Febuary 2016 no 0035 text no 26.

[101] ibid, text no 25.

[102] ibid.

Hoge Raad der Nederlanden (Supreme Court of the Netherlands),
20 December 2013[103]   **2.27 (NL)**

BP Europa Se v X and Y

VOIDNESS LIMITED TO THE VOID CLAUSE

The partially void filling station agreement

An exploitation agreement shall remain valid insofar as it is not inextricably linked to an exclusive purchase clause which infringes competition law and is void as a consequence thereof

Facts: An exploitation agreement for a filling station contained an exclusive purchase clause which infringed the Dutch Competition Act. The question arose whether the entire contract was null or only the clause. The Court of Appeal held that only the clause was void. The supplier appealed to the Dutch Supreme Court.

Held: The Supreme Court confirms that the Court of Appeal correctly ruled that only the infringing clause was void.

Judgment: The fourth part of the grief is directed against [the paragraph] where the Court [of Appeal] investigated whether the nullity of Article 6(2) of the Dutch Competition Act only affects the exclusive purchase clause or the [entire] exploitation agreement between BP and [defendant 1].

...

In evaluating these complaints, the following is to be taken into account. Article 3:41 [of the Dutch Civil Code provides that] if a cause of nullity only affects part of a judicial act, this judicial act shall remain in place insofar as it is not indissolubly connected with the null part. This is to be judged taking into account the content and the purpose of the juridical act. The question whether there is such a connection is a matter of interpretation of the juridical act. In that regard the following elements may be relevant: the nature, content and purpose of the juridical act, the extent to which the parts are related and what the parties intended to achieve with the juridical act. In the light thereof the judge is to decide whether, taking into account the circumstances of the case and the interests of all interested parties, there is a sufficient justification for the partial maintenance of the juridical act.

Notes:

(1) The Supreme Court of the Netherlands accepted the application of Article 3:41 of the Dutch Civil Code *(BW)* to a contract containing a clause that infringes the Dutch Competition Act. According to Article 3:41 of the Dutch Civil Code (BW), the voidness of a clause only affects the remainder of the contract to the extent that it is indissolubly linked to the void clause.

(2) According to the Supreme Court, it is a matter of interpretation whether there is an indissoluble connection between the void clause and other parts of the contract and, in that regard, both subjective and objective elements can be taken into account. Taking this criterion into account, the Supreme Court held that the Court of Appeal correctly applied the law.

---

[103] HR 20 December 2013 *NJ* 2014, 347 annotated by MR Mok and Jac Hijma ECLI:NL:HR:2013:2123 *BP Europa Se v X and Y.*

(3) The Court of Appeal had held that extending the nullity to the remainder of the contract would mean that the operators of the filling station would lose all rights the exploitation agreements conferred on them. This would not do justice to the purpose of the sanction of nullity and it would undermine the effective sanctioning of agreements restricting competition since it would discourage tenants from invoking the nullity of exclusive purchase obligations. Moreover, even without the exclusive purchase obligation, the contract remained useful for both parties.

(4) The Advocate General considered the Court of Appeal's reasoning insufficiently clear. In his opinion, it would at least require further reasoning as to why the supplier would have allowed the claimant or anybody else to run the filling stations it had built on leased land without being sure that the station would sell at least predominantly the supplier's products. The AG did not see why the purchaser would require more protection than the supplier. The clause was agreed between commercial parties at a moment when it was permitted. When the new block exemption Regulation on vertical restraints entered into force, the purchaser should have taken the initiative to modify the contract. In addition, the AG general pointed out that partial nullity does not always serve the purpose of combating anticompetitive clauses. Partial nullity can contribute to a party accepting a clause that is essential for the other party because the former party knows that he can later invoke the partial nullity of that clause.[104] As seen above, the Supreme Court did not follow the opinion of its AG.

(5) Given the need for consistent application of EU and national competition law, it seems that the Dutch courts would need to apply the reasoning of the case excerpted above when a contract contains a clause that infringes the European competition rules.

(6) Compare the method used for the application of conversion (Article 3:42 of the Dutch Civil Code (BW)); see section II.A.v below).

Bundesgerichtshof (Federal Supreme Court of Germany),
24 September 2002[105]   **2.28 (GERM)**

X v Y

SEVERANCE CLAUSE

Tennishallenpacht

A severance clause only shifts the burden of proof

Facts: The claimants rented out an indoor tennis and badminton court to the defendant. The lease contained a clause stating that the landlords would inform the tenant before the start of each season of the prices to be applied. The tenant was not allowed to grant reductions on the subscriptions without prior written consent of the landlord. These clauses were considered to infringe German national competition law. The contract

---

[104] AG Keus Opinion 20 September 2013 in Case 12/04752 *BP Europa Se v X and Y* ECLI:NL:PHR:2013:875, paras 2.39–2.43. Prior to Keus' opinion, a Dutch scholar had already raised doubts regarding the desirability partial nullity in cases of anticompetitieve clauses; see JF Appeldoorn, *Eenheid in verscheidenheid: de gespreide toepassing van artikel 81 EG* (The Hague, Boom Juridische uitgevers, 2011) 230–32. See also EJ Zippro, 'Privaatrechtelijke handhaving van mededingingsrecht' (2008) 6838 *WPNR* 64–65, 67 and 71.
[105] BGH 24 September 2002 *NJW* 2003, 347 (Tennishallenprecht).

furthermore contained a clause providing that when one or more of the clauses were without effect or void, this would not affect the other clauses (ie, a severance clause). The parties were bound to replace ineffective or void clauses by valid ones that achieved as closely as possible the economic effects desired by the pre-existing clauses (ie, a replacement clause).

The claimants terminated the contract without notice after non-payment by the defendant. They claimed payment of sums due. The tenants claimed that the sums due were to be set off against their claim for damages based on fraudulent misrepresentation about the profitability of the tennis and badminton court.

Held: A severance clause only shifts the burden of proof. In the absence of a severance clause, the party who wants to maintain the partially void contract bears the burden of proving that the remainder of the contract still contains a meaningful and balanced deal for both parties and therefore should persist, according to the common intention of the parties, without the void clause. If the contract contains a severance clause, the party that wants the entire contract to be removed from the legal order needs to prove that the contract without the void clause no longer contains a meaningful and balanced deal for both parties so that their common intention is that the contract would no longer persist.

Judgment: Contrary to the view of the appeal court, the widespread and generally standardised severance and replacement clauses (salvatorischen Erhaltens- und Ersetzungsklauseln) do not entail that the parts of the transaction that are not directly covered by the ground for nullity have to be treated as effective under all circumstances—limited only by the public policy. Rather, they only contain a provision on the distribution of the burden of proof in the context of §139 BGB, and are always subject to proof as to whether the parties would have discarded the partly void business as a whole or would have accepted the rest. Whereas in the absence of a severance clause the party who wants to maintain the partially void transaction bears the burden of proof, the party who wants to reject the entire contract bears this burden if a severance clause has been agreed, as in this case. Only this understanding of severance clauses duly recognises that it depends on the meaning of the invalid provision for the entire contract whether the contract would still contain a sensible and balanced regulation of the respective interests and whether it can be presumed that the contract should be valid according to the corresponding will of both parties even without the void provision.

This assessment of severance clauses does not only correspond to the jurisdiction of other civil divisions of the Federal Court of Justice … it also prevails in legal scholarship … Thorough reasons for allowing exceptions to this rule in case of application of the [national competition act] do not exist.

Notes:

(1) This judgment marks an important change in German law regarding the impact of severance and replacement clauses on anticompetitive agreements. Previous judgments of the Competition Division of the Federal Supreme Court of Germany[106] had inferred from the inclusion of a severance clause that the nullity of a certain clause for infringement of the EU competition rules did not affect the remainder of the contract. The *Tennishallenpacht* judgment aligned the opinion of the Competition Division to that of other civil divisions of the Federal Supreme Court: a severance clause only shifts the burden of proof in relation to §139 BGB.[107]

---

[106] See BGH 8 February 1994 KZR 2/93, *NJW* 1994, 1651 (Pronuptia II).

[107] See further HJ Bunte, 'Die Bedeutung salvatorischer Klauseln in kartellrechtswidrigen Verträgen' (2014) *GRUR* 301–04; V Emmerich, 'Bedeutung einer salvatorischen Klausel' (2003) *JuS* 497–98; F Endter, 'Federal Supreme Court (Bundesgerichtshof), Decision vom September 24, 2002—Case No. KZR 10/01

(2) If the severance clause forms part of standard terms, account is to be taken of §307 BGB: it will be ineffective if, contrary to the requirement of good faith, it unreasonably disadvantages the other party to the contract. If the standard clause is ineffective, the remainder of the contract as supplemented by default rules remains in effect unless it would result in unreasonable hardship for the other party (§306 BGB).

(3) It has been argued that if a contract contains a severance clause and a replacement clause, the severance clause should only be tested under §139 BGB after replacement according to the replacement clause has taken place.[108]

Hof van Cassatie België (Belgian Court of Cassation),
28 June 2012[109]

2.29 (BE)

Bauer Kompressoren GmbH v Dubraco sa

SEVERANCE CLAUSE

Prohibiting passive sales and the essential purpose of the contract

A court can legally decide that the nullity of an anticompetitive clause does not entail the nullity of the entire agreement where the contract so provided and the essential purpose of the contract can still be achieved without the anticompetitive clause

Facts: A German producer of industrial compressors provided Dubraco with the exclusive right of distribution in Belgium and Luxembourg. After a few years, Dubraco found out that another undertaking was distributing the same compressors within its exclusive territory. Dubraco therefore sued the producer for damages. Bauer claimed that Dubraco had first committed a breach of contract itself. The first instance court *ex officio* declared the contract void because it contained a prohibition for the distributor to engage in passive sales outside its territory. On appeal, the nullity was limited to the terms prohibiting passive sales. Bauer lodged an appeal with the Belgian Supreme Court.

Held: Cassation was denied. The Court of Appeal had legally justified its decision stating that the essential purpose of the contract could still be achieved without the anticompetitive clause and pointing out that the contract contained a severance clause.

Judgment: 3. With regard to the scope of the absolute nullity for infringement of [now Article 101(2) TFEU], the agreement is only entirely void when the clauses that are irreconcilable with [now Article 101(1) TFEU] cannot be severed from the agreement itself. In the opposite case, the consequences of the voidness of all other parts of the agreement are not determined by [EU] Law. Under the applicable national law, the national judge has to determine the scope and the consequences for the whole of the contractual relationship if certain terms of the agreement are void for infringement of [now Article 101(2) TFEU].

4. With regard to the question whether the nullity under national law entails the partial or total nullity of the agreement, the appellate judge has found that:

— the essence of the agreement is the exclusive distribution for which the claimant has committed himself as a supplier to not sell the products to the defendant with a

---

"Leasing of a Tennis Court" (Tennishallenpacht)' (2004) *IIC* 997–1000; J Hennrichs, 'Bedeutung einer salvatorischen Erhaltensklausel bei Nichtigkeit eines Vertragsteils' (2003) *LMK- Kommentierte BGH Rechtsprechung* 19–20.

[108] HJ Bunte, 'Die Bedeutung salvatorischer Klauseln in kartellrechtswidrigen Verträgen'(2014) *GRUR* 303–04.

[109] Belgian Court of Cassation 28 June 2012 no C.10.0433.N *Bauer Kompressoren GmbH v Dubraco sa.*

view to their resale in a specific sector while the claimant has committed himself as an exclusive reseller to purchase exclusively from the claimant;
— the parties have agreed in Article 18.2 of the agreement that the nullity of one or more articles does not automatically entail the nullity of the entire agreement.

The appellate judge has decided that the agreement is only null to the extent that it concerns the prohibition of passive sales, as follows from the Articles 3.1 and 6.5 of the convention.

5. In so ruling, the appellate judge has legally justified his decision.

Notes:

The Belgian Court of Cassation accepted that a severance clause is an element that a court can take into account when deciding whether an anticompetitive clause is severable from the remainder of the agreement. However, it must be noted that the presence of the severance clause was not the only element that the Court of Cassation had taken into account to reach its decision on severance. It had also found that the essential purpose of the contract could still be achieved without the anticompetitive clause. Therefore, it cannot be derived from *Bauer* that the presence of a severance clause would automatically justify severance.

Comparative overview

General rules

It follows from the case law of the CJEU that the nullity set out in Article 101(2) TFEU may extend not only to the contractual clause that infringes Article 101(1) TFEU, but also to the entire agreement. This will apply when the anticompetitive clause is inseverable from the remainder of the agreement. The consequences of the nullity of a severable anticompetitive clause for the remainder of the agreement are to be determined under national law. The case law of the CJEU does not specify a criterion for severability. The way in which national legal systems deal with the issue of severability varies.

The criteria used to determine severability may be objective (the structure of the agreement, the purpose of the rule whose infringement is sanctioned by voidness), subjective (the intention of the parties) or mixed. Some Member States start from an objective approach. This is the case for Austria and Germany. The Austrian Supreme Court clearly applies an objective criterion: it is not the intention of the parties that is determinative, but rather the function of the sanction of voidness and the restoration of the economic freedom of the bound parties. However, although agreeing with this starting point, an Austrian scholar has argued that the purpose of Article 101(1) is often indifferent as to the further existence of the remainder of the contract. In that case, the hypothetical intention of the parties would need to be used as a criterion to determine severability and when this hypothetical intention cannot be determined, the remainder of the contract needs to be held valid.

In Germany, a two-tier test is applied. The first step is regarded as a matter of EU law. In view of the purpose of Article 101(1) TFEU, it is to be determined whether the voidness of a clause infringing Article 101(1) TFEU extends to the entire agreement or remains limited to the anticompetitive clause or part thereof. Furthermore, partial nullity of course requires that the remainder of the agreement remains objectively viable on its own. Only when the clause is severable under these criteria is it to be investigated whether the remainder of the contract is valid under German law. In the second stage of the analysis, §139 BGB comes into play. In the first part of its two-tier analysis, Germany clearly uses objective elements: the purpose of Article 101 TFEU and the objective viability of the remainder of the contract. However, the second part of the analysis in principle brings in a subjective element. §139 BGB contains a presumption that the voidness of the particular clause extends to the entire contract. The party that wants to maintain the remainder of the contract needs to rebut this presumption, proving that the parties would have concluded the contract even without the void clause. However, this is to be judged taking into account common practice and good faith. This means that a mixed subjective-objective criterion is applied. Yet, if the anticompetitive clause is a standard clause, the objectively criterion of §306 BGB prevails over §139 BGB: the remainder of the contract as supplemented by default rules remains in effect unless it would result in unreasonable hardship for the other party.

In other Member States, objective and subjective criteria may be taken into account altogether as from the start. This is the case for the Netherlands, the UK and Spain. In the Netherlands, however, there seems to be some freedom in the criteria that can be taken into account. In the UK, the criteria to be used are specifically described. In Spain, the objective criterion that was used by the Supreme Court in a case concerning a resale maintenance clause is that clauses infringing the EU competition rules cannot be held to be of secondary importance to the entire contract and that the elimination of such clauses would completely alter the economics of the contract. The subjective criterion is the intention of the parties. The objective criterion used by the Supreme Court applies to other types of clauses infringing EU competition law as well. It would seem that only strong evidence of the parties' intention to keep the contract in place without the anti-competitive clause could save any contract containing an anticompetitive clause from being null in its entirety. However, it is exactly the sole use of another objective criterion that is put forward by scholars who advocate the possibility of partial nullity in cases of resale price maintenance clauses: severability would need to be determined in view of the purpose and underlying principles of the infringed rule.

Belgian case law attaches great importance to the intention of the parties. In one case, dealing with an anticompetitive clause and decided by a lower court, the intention of the parties appeared to be used as the sole criterion. Another judgment decided by a lower court made a combined use of the intention of the parties and objective elements. This is also the approach chosen by the Belgian Court of Cassation when dealing with a severance clause and in a case dealing with judicial modification (which did, however, not concern an infringement of the competition rules). In fact, there always seems to be some objective element involved in a severability analysis, since in practice it is always required that the remainder of the contract can exist on its own.

Some legal systems are more prone to extending the nullity of an anticompetitive clause to the remainder of the contract than others. As mentioned above, the Spanish Supreme Court extended the nullity of resale price maintenance clauses to the remainder of the contract and its reasoning is easily transposable to other contracts. §139 BGB contains a presumption that the voidness of a particular clause extends to the entire contract.

By contrast, under Dutch law, partial nullity is the starting point: Article 3:41 of the Dutch Civil Code (BW) provides that the voidness of a particular clause only affects other parts of the agreement insofar as it is indissolubly linked to them. Also under the new Article 1184 of the French Civil Code, the nullity that affects only one or more clauses of an agreement remains limited to that (those) clause(s) unless one of the parties proves that the clause was decisive in making one or both parties enter into the agreement.

The impact of severance clauses

Severance clauses are only relevant to the extent that the intention of the parties is taken into account when determining severability. The Belgian Court of Cassation held that a severance clause is an element that the Court may take into account when deciding on severability. In Germany, a severance clause only shifts the burden of proof under §139 BGB; in the presence of a severance clause, it is the party that wants to obtain the voidness of the entire contact that bears the burden of proving that without the anticompetitive clause, the contract would no longer contain a sensible and balanced regulation of the respective interests of the parties and that according to the corresponding will of the parties, it should not be held valid.

II.A.v MODIFICATION OF A VOID AGREEMENT OR CLAUSE?

Hof van Beroep Brussel (Court of Appeal of Brussels),
7 March 2006[110] **2.30 (BE)**

DDD Invest v Power Oil

JUDICIAL CONVERSION

***Power Oil* forever**

National law not opposed to the judicial mitigation of a contractual clause

Facts: By way of preliminary referral, the Court of Appeal of Brussels was asked to determine whether an exclusive purchase obligation for fuels and related products for a period of ten years was valid and, if not, whether it could be reduced to five years or whether the clause was void and this would lead to the voidness of the entire contract.

Held: Given the factual circumstances submitted to the Court, the clause could not significantly affect competition on a significant part of the relevant market, but it is the first instance court itself that had to decide on this. If the clause were held to infringe (now) Article 101 TFEU and the counterpart in national competition law, it could be limited in time. If the clause was not to have any legal effect, it would follow from the nature of the contract and the non-severability of the clause that the entire contract was void.

Judgment: 29. The question whether the judge may limit the effect of a clause in time is to be assessed according to the general principles that determine his jurisdiction regarding the content of contracts.

---

[110] Court of Appeal of Brussels 7 March 2006 *Jaarboek Handelspraktijken & Mededinging* 2006, 773 *Power Oil NV v DDD Invest NV*.

Under Belgian law there does not seem to be a fundamental objection to the mitigation of the effects of a contractual clause.

Notes:

(1) Referring to *Société Technique Minière*[111] and *Ciments*,[112] the CJ confirmed in *VAG France*[113] that the consequences of the automatic voidness of contractual provisions which are incompatible with Article 101(1) TFEU for all other parts of the agreement or for other obligations flowing from it are not a matter for EU law, but for national law. It specified that it is therefore up to the national law to determine whether the parties may amend their contract in order to prevent it from being void, for example, by replacing the void clause by one that is exempted under a Block Exemption Regulation. In the same vein, the CJ held in *Cepsa* that: 'It is for the referring court to ascertain whether, under national law, the contractual clause relating to [fixed resale prices] can be amended by unilateral authorisation of the supplier … and whether a contract which is automatically void may become valid following an amendment of that contractual clause which has the effect of bringing that clause into line with [now Article 101(1) TFEU].'[114] Following the reasoning behind the CJ's judgments, it would also seem up to the national law to determine whether the Court has the power to replace the void clause by one that is valid (*cf* below).

(2) In the case excerpted above, the Court of Appeal of Brussels held that under Belgian law, there did not seem to be a fundamental objection to the mitigation of the effects of a contractual clause. At the time, this decision was rather exceptional. Standing case law was that non-competition clauses that were not sufficiently limited in time, geographical scope and/or type of activities were contrary to the freedom of trade and industry and absolutely void, without possibility of mitigation.[115] The decision is, however, in line with the current case law of the Belgian Supreme Court. Indeed, in a judgment of 23 January 2015, the Belgian Court of Cassation held that: 'If a contract or a clause infringes a provision of public order and is therefore void, the Court may, if a partial voidness is possible, and unless the law so forbids, limit the voidness to the infringing part of the contract or clause provided that the persistence of the partly nullified contract or clause is in conformity with the parties' intention.' The Court of Cassation thus formulates three conditions for the availability of partial voidness: (1) partial voidness must be possible; (2) the law must not forbid partial voidness; (3) the persistence of the partially

---

[111] *Société Technique Minière* (n 77).

[112] CJ 14 December 1983 Case C-319/82 *Société de Vente de Ciments et Bétons de l'Est SA v Kerpen & Kerpen GmbH und Co KG* [1983] I-04173 ECLI:EU:C:1983:374.

[113] *VAG France SA* (n 79) para 14; *Cabour SA* (n 79) para 51; *Brünsteiner* (n 79) para 48.

[114] *Cespa* (n 38) para 79.

[115] Belgian Court of Cassation 3 February 1971 *Pas* 1972 vol I, 511 and *Arr Cass* 1971.538; Belgian Court of Cassation 12 July 1894 *Pas* 1894 vol I, 263; Court of Appeal Ghent 17 December 2012 no 2012/AR/ 1102. See also: www.go-dis.eu; Court of Appeal Ghent 25 May 2005 *D.A.O.R* 2005, 334; Court of Appeal Antwerp 25 May 2009 *Jaarboek Handelspraktijken & Mededinging* 2009, 998–1028; Com Hasselt 30 January 2008 *JDSC* 2013, 78 annotated by M Coipel *TRV* 2011 no 4, 313 annotated by B Bellen; Com Hasselt 5 May 2004 *Limburgs Rechtseven* 2007 no 2, 144, annotated by H van Gompel; M Vansteenbeeck, 'Concurrentieclausules' in GL Ballon et al (eds), *Gemeenrechtelijke clausules*, vol I (Antwerp, Intersentia, 2013) 916 with further references.

voided contract must be in conformity with the parties' intention. Therefore, the Court uses a combination of objective and subjective elements to determine the possibility of partial nullity. It is also interesting that in its general formulation of the possibility of partial nullity, the Court speaks of the *possibility* for it to hold a contract partially void, but where it applies this rule to the facts of the case, it switches from a possibility to an obligation, quashing a judgment where the Court of Appeal chose to hold the clause void in its entirety.[116]

(3) What the Court of Cassation calls partial nullity (*partiële nietigheid*) is in fact what is known in Germany as reduction (*Reduktion*), ie, bringing an excessive clause within legal boundaries.

Hoge Raad der Nederlanden (Supreme Court of the Netherlands),
18 December 2009[117]   **2.31 (NL)**

Prisma Vastgoed BV and Prisma Food Retail BV v anonymised defendants

NO CONVERSION

The inconvertible option clause

Conversion is incompatible with the aim of the Dutch equivalent of Article 101(2) TFEU

Facts: Slager was a franchisee of Prisma and bought his shop from Prisma. The sale was part of a cooperation agreement between the parties which imposed limitations on the use of the shop and contained an option for Prisma to repurchase the shop at a given price if Slager ended his cooperation with Prisma, or if he would sell or mortgage the shop or have it used by a third party. When Slager terminated the cooperation with Prisma, Prisma decided to make use of its option right. Slager then invoked the nullity of the cooperation agreement, alleging that it contained anticompetitive clauses. The contract contained a severance clause providing that in case of illegality or voidness of one or more clauses of the agreement, the parties would enter into negotiations in order to replace the void clause with a clause that would reach the same result insofar as possible. The Court of Appeal held the option clause void and refused the conversion. It held that the absolute voidness imposed by the Dutch Competition Act intended to prevent illegal restrictions of competition and that this aim would be undermined if conversion were allowed. The Court of Appeal thus took no account of the severance clause and considered the void clause to be indissolubly linked to the remainder of the agreement. Prisma brought the case before the Supreme Court of the Netherlands.

Held: The decision refusing conversion was confirmed, but the appeal judgment was quashed on other grounds.

Judgment: [T]he Court of Appeal has rightly held that the application of Art. 3:42 BW is incompatible with the absolute voidness provided for by Art. 6(2) of the Competition Act, which aims to ban agreements restricting competition which are prohibited by law.

Notes:

(1) The statement that Article 6(2) of the Dutch Competition Act (*Mededingingswet*) is sanctioned with absolute voidness may look surprising since the Supreme Court of the

---

[116] Belgian Court of Cassation 23 January 2014 C.13.0579.N., as confirmed by the Belgian Court of Cassation 25 June 2015 C.14.0008.F *JT* 2015, 6620, 727, *JLMB* 2015, 1305; *JTT* 2015, 1232, 483; M Wantiez *NJW* 2015, 914.
[117] HR 18 December 2009 *NJ* 2010, 140 (Prisma) annotated by MR Mok ECLI:NL:HR:2009:BJ9439.

Netherlands held in a case of 16 January 2009[118] that Article 6 of the said Act does not contain rules of public order which the Court would have to apply *ex officio*, even if it had to exceed the limits of the dispute between the parties. However, in Dutch law, the concept of 'absolute voidness' is not restricted to cases where a contract or a contract clause is null and void because it violates public order. Only a nullity on account of the violation of public order must be applied *ex officio*. See on this point Chapter 7 (case 7.12 (NL) note (2)).

(2) The case excerpted above ended a long-standing dispute in the Netherlands as to whether conversion of anticompetitive clauses is permissible. Article 3:42 BW provides that: 'When the necessary implications of an invalid juridical act are in conformity with those of another—valid—juridical act and this in such a degree that it is presumable that this other juridical act would have been chosen instead of the invalid one if the acting party or parties would have been aware of the invalidity of the latter act, then this invalid juridical act shall be converted by operation of law into that other valid juridical act with all its normal legal effects, unless such a conversion would be unreasonable towards an interested person who has not participated as a party in the involved juridical act.' According to the majority opinion, this article could not apply in cases of voidness for infringement of Article 101 TFEU. Two reasons were given to support this opinion: first, voidness for infringement of Article 101 TFEU is an autonomous concept of EU law and therefore the rules of the BW do not apply to the consequences of such voidness; second, Article 3:42 BW was considered inapplicable in cases of infringement of Article 101 TFEU because it would undermine the preventive effect of that provision. If parties including anticompetitive clauses into their contracts would merely run the risk of having these clauses converted into a permissible clause, this would reduce their efforts to comply with Article 101 TFEU.[119] A minority view doubted this reasoning, drawing a parallel with partial voidness (limitation of the consequences of the voidness to the particular part of the contract infringing Article 101 TFEU), which has long been recognised by the CJEU, although partial nullity too might reduce the preventive effect of the sanction of nullity. In his conclusion before *Prisma*, the AG referred to these two conflicting opinions in Dutch legal scholarship and pointed out that in the past, he had supported the minority view. In *Prisma*, the Supreme Court of the Netherlands nevertheless followed the majority view, rejecting the application of Article 3:42 BW. It has confirmed this view in a later case, indicating that conversion is excluded both in cases where the nullity sanctions infringements which have as their object to restrict competition, as in cases where the nullity sanctions infringements which have as their effect to restrict competition.[120]

(3) The case law of the CJEU is not opposed to the amendment of terms infringing the EU competition rules. It ruled in *VAG France* that: 'It is for the national court to determine in accordance with the relevant national law the extent and consequences, for the contractual relations as a whole, of the nullity of certain contractual provisions by virtue of [now Article 101(2) TFEU]. It is on the basis of national law that it is necessary in particular to determine whether such incompatibility may have the effect of obliging the

---

[118] HR 16 January 2009 *NJ* 2009, 54 ECLI:NL:HR:2009:BG3582.
[119] HR 18 December 2009 annotated by MR Mok no 4 (see n 117).
[120] HR 20 December 2013 *NJ* 2014, 347 annotated by MR Mok and Jac Hijma ECLI:NL:HR:2013:2123.

contracting parties to amend the content of their agreement in order to prevent it from being void.'[121]

(4) It is interesting to compare this case with the case law of the CJEU on unfair terms. In *Banco Español*, the CJ held that national courts may only hold the unfair clause non-binding on the consumer. The remainder of the contract 'must continue in existence in so far as this is legally possible in accordance with the rules of domestic law ... National legislation may not allow the court to modify the contract by revising the content of the unfair term'.[122] In the same vein, the CJ decided in *Asbeek Brusse* that national law may not allow national courts to reduce unfair penalty clauses. Instead, the national court must exclude the application of that clause in its entirety with regard to the consumer.[123] This line of case law aims to ensure the preventive character of the Directive. The CJ reasons that the power of national courts to 'revise the content of unfair terms ... would weaken the dissuasive effect on sellers or suppliers of the straightforward non-application of those unfair terms with regard to the consumer'.[124] In *Kásler*, however, the CJ nuanced its earlier case law, specifying that if 'a contract concluded between a seller or supplier and a consumer cannot continue in existence after an unfair term has been deleted, that provision does not preclude a rule of national law enabling the national court to cure the invalidity of that term by substituting for it a supplementary provision of national law'.[125] It must be noted that *Kásler*, does not empower national courts to modify unfair terms when and as they like. The power to modify the contract only exists when the contract cannot continue to exist without the unfair term and the modification may only consist in the substitution of the term by a supplementary provision of national law. In *Unicaja Banco and Caixabank*, the CJ more addressed the power of national judges to modify contractual terms in accordance with national legislation. The case concerned a Spanish national provision under which the national court hearing mortgage enforcement proceedings is required to adjust the amounts due under a term in a mortgage-loan contract providing for default interest at a rate more than three times greater than the statutory rate in order that the amount of that interest may not exceed that threshold. The CJEU held that the Unfair Terms Directive does not preclude such a provision, provided that 'the application of that national provision is without prejudice to the assessment by that national court of the unfairness of such a term and does not prevent that court removing that term if it were to find the latter to be 'unfair', within the meaning of Article 3(1) of that directive'.[126] The judgment seems to confirm the Court's earlier case law that once a national court has identified a term in a consumer contract as unfair, it has to declare it

---

[121] *VAG France SA* (n 79) para 15.
[122] CJ *Banco Español* (n 71) paras 65, 73 and 89.
[123] CJ *Asbeek Brusse* (n 71) paras 60 and 61.
[124] CJ *Banco Español* (n 71) paras 66–69; ibid para 58.
[125] CJ 30 April 2014 Case C-26/13 *Árpád Kásler, Hajnalka Káslerné Rábai v OTP Jelzálogbank Zrt* nyr ECLI:EU:C:2014.282, paras 85 and 86.
[126] CJ 21 January 2015 Joined Cases C-482/13, C-484/13, C-485/13 and C-487/13 *Unicaja Banco, SA v José Hidalgo Rueda et al and Caixabank SA v Manuel Maria Rueda Ledesma et al* ECLI:EU:C:2015:21, para 42 and dispositive part. See also CJ 11 June 2015 Case C-602/13 *Banco Bilbao Vizcaya Argentaria SA v Fernando Quintano Ujeta and María-Isabel Sánchez García* nyr ECLI:EU:C:2015:397; CJ 8 July 2015 Case C-90/14 *Banco Grupo Cajatres SA v María Mercedes Manjón Pinilla and Comunidad Hereditaria formada al fallecimiento de DMA Viana Gordejuela* nyr ECLI:EU:C:2015:465.

inapplicable, except where the conditions of *Kásler* are satisfied. Outside the application of *Kásler*, national courts may only apply national legislation requiring modification of contractual insofar as these terms are not unfair within the meaning of the Unfair Terms Directive.

Article 36 of the Nordic
Contracts Act   2.32 (SE, DK, FI, IS, NO)

A contract term may be adjusted or held unenforceable if the term is unreasonable with respect to the contract's contents, circumstances at the formation of the contract, subsequent events or other circumstances. If the term is of such significance for the contract that the remaining part of the contract cannot reasonably be upheld in its original form, the contract may be adjusted in other respects or held unenforceable in its entirety.

Notes:

(1) All the Nordic countries have a Contracts Act in force which is practically identical in the five countries. Article 36 of each of these Acts contains a similarly worded so-called general clause, which makes it possible for the courts to set aside or adjust unreasonable contract terms.

(2) In Nordic law, this article deals with the issue of severability. If a contract contains a restrictive clause which is unenforceable according to EU or national competition law, the court can either uphold the rest of the contract as it is, find the contract unenforceable in its entirety or adjust the terms of the remaining parts of the contract. Thus, the court can adjust an excessive price by lowering it to a level considered reasonable. It is also possible for the court to mitigate a restrictive covenant, for example, by holding it valid for two or three years and invalid thereafter, or by restricting its scope.

(3) No application of the rule to cases of nullity for infringement of the competition rules has been found.

Oberlandesgericht Düsseldorf (Higher Regional
Court Düsseldorf), 14 April 2007[127]   2.33 (GERM)

X v Y

IMPOSED CONSENSUAL CONVERSION

The Body Shop version 2.0

A German court modifies a provision of a standard franchise agreement (exclusive purchase clause)

Facts: By means of a clause in a standard contract, the Body Shop, a cosmetics chain, obliged its franchisees to purchase their entire demand from the Body Shop and prohibited them from selling competing products.

---

[127] OLG Düsseldorf 14 April 2007 VI-U (Kart) 13/06 *BeckRS* 2007, 08367 *X v Y*. See also M Klasse, 'A German Court Finds an Exclusive Purchase Obligation in Breach of Art. 81 EC and Replaces a Void Non-Compete Obligation in a Franchise Agreement (The Body Shop)' (2007) *e-Competitions Bulletin April*, no 13965.

This obligation was found to be in breach of (now) Article 101 TFEU, under explicit reference to CJEU case law. The contract contained a replacement clause.

Held: The court declared the exclusive purchase clause null and void under national law and EU law. The contract as a whole remained valid due to the replacement clause and due to the German law rule that nullity of the entire contract would only follow if fulfilment of the contract would amount to 'unreasonable hardship'. The court ordered the parties to consent to a new contract provision which replaced the annulled clause and limited exclusivity to 80 per cent instead of 100 per cent.

Judgment: In §25 number 25.2 the franchising contract contains ... a replacement clause. Under this clause the contracting parties are held to replace an ineffective or unenforceable clause by a valid or enforceable one which corresponds to the economic and ideological provisions as much as possible.

...

bb) §306 I BGB provides that in the case of invalid standard clauses the remainder of the contract remains in place. The allegation of the defendant that he would not have concluded the franchising contract without the concerned exclusive purchase clause is irrelevant. Only if the persistence of the contract would result in unreasonable hardship for one party, does the law provide for the voidness of the entire agreement (§306 III BGB). In determining unreasonable hardship, account is to be taken of the content of the agreement as it is after completion of the lacunae by default rules or by means of interpretation (*ergänzender Vertragsauslegung*). The defendant does not invoke this hardship clause in the present case.

2. In application of the replacement clause in ... the franchise contract, the gap resulting from Paragraph 11.1 is to be filled with a provision holding that the claimant has to purchase in principle from the defendant ... or from another authorized supplier, but is entitled to purchase from and distribute to third parties up to 20% of its total purchases of contract goods and additional products ...

Only to this extent is a purchasing obligation for more than 5 years in fact harmless from a competition law perspective. This follows from ... the block exemption for vertical agreements. According to this provision, purchasing obligations that are agreed for more than 5 years are considered as restraints of trade ... only if they bind a maximum of 80% of the buyers' product purchases.

Notes:

(1) The case concerns a standard contract within the meaning of §305 BGB. This is a contract that has been drafted by one of the parties in order to be used multiple times and that is submitted to the other party with the request to adhere to it. The mere fact that one party makes objections against certain clauses during the negotiations and even obtains a modification of one or more clauses does not mean that the contract becomes an individually negotiated contract. Standard contract terms only become a part of a contract if the user (the party who formulated the terms), when entering into the contract: (1) explicitly refers the other party to the contract to these terms or, where explicit reference is possible only with disproportionate difficulty due to the way in which the contract is entered into, posts a clearly visible notice at the place where the contract is entered into; (2) gives the other party to the contract the opportunity to take notice of these terms' contents in an acceptable manner which also takes into reasonable account any physical handicap of the other party to the contract that is discernible to the user; and (3) if the other party to the contract agrees to their applying (§305 II BGB).

(2) When the anticompetitive clause is objectively severable from the remainder of the agreement, its impact on the remainder of the contract is dealt with by §139 BGB or, if the anticompetitive clause is a standard contract clause, by §306 BGB. In the case excerpted above, the anticompetitive clause is a standard clause and its impact on the remainder of the contract is therefore to be determined under §306 BGB. In this respect, the case differs from the *Tennishallenpacht* case (*cf* above), where the anticompetitive clause was an individually negotiated clause subject to §139 BGB.

(3) If a standard clause is ineffective, the remainder of the contract as supplemented by default rules remains in effect unless it would result in unreasonable hardship for the other party (§306 BGB). In the case excerpted above, the defendant did not invoke unreasonable hardship and the conditions were therefore not fulfilled. The voidness was therefore limited to the anticompetitive clause. However, the Higher Regional Court proceeded to the application of the replacement clause and modified the clause to bring it within the boundaries of what is permitted.

(4) The Higher Regional Court first applied §306 III BGB to determine whether keeping the contract in place without the void clause would result in unreasonable hardship for the defendant. Only after a negative answer to this question, did the Court proceed to the application of the replacement clause. It did this instead of first performing the replacement and then deciding whether there was unreasonable hardship.

(5) Even if §139 BGB applies, clauses which provide for the replacement of a void, ineffective or unenforceable term by a specific other term are considered not to be affected by the *Tennishallenpacht* case. For this type of situation, however, it has been argued that the replacement should take place before §139 is applied, so that it is to be judged if the contract with the replaced clause would contain a sensible and balanced regulation of the respective interests and could be presumed valid according to the corresponding will of both parties (*cf* above).

(6) Although the 'reduction' of the content of a clause to what is permitted by law (*Reduktion*) is generally regarded as an application of §139 BGB (partial nullity),[128] occasionally §140 BGB (conversion) has been applied instead.[129]

(7) It has been alleged that the *effet utile* of Article 101 TFEU prohibits clauses which would save any anticompetitive clause from voidness under Article 101(2) TFEU by an undetermined correction of the voidness.[130]

Comparative overview

The extent to which national legal systems allow courts to replace void terms by valid ones (conversion), to reduce a clause in order to bring it within legal limits (reduction) or to allow parties to do so varies between European legal systems. Equally, the degree to which national legal systems distinguish between these mechanisms varies. Moreover,

---

[128] BGH WuW/E BGH 1600, 1603 (Frischbeton); NJW 1991, 699, 700; OLG Hamburg WuW/E OLG 3249, 3251 (Castrol); OLG Frankfurt WuW/E OLG 2811 (Zum Engel); OLG München WuW/E OLG 3118, 3120.

[129] OLG Stuttgart WuW/E OLG 3492 (Tanzschule). See on this point *Schmidt* in Immenga/Mestmäcker 2012 AEUV Art 101 Abs 2 Rn 29.

[130] K Schmidt, 'Art 101 Abs 2 Rn 32', in Immenga/Mestmäcker (*supra*, footnote 17).

even if these techniques are known in general contract law, this does not automatically mean that their use is permitted in cases of infringement of EU or national competition rules.

The Supreme Court of the Netherlands excludes judicial modification (conversion) of anticompetitive clauses.[131] For a long time, Belgian case law and legal scholarship were also opposed to judicial modification of anticompetitive clauses. In a recent judgment that did not deal with clauses infringing competition law, the Belgian Court of Cassation accepted judicial modification (in the form of reduction) of clauses infringing rules of public order under certain conditions. German case law also generally appears to reject the power of courts to reduce the ambit of anticompetitive clauses in order to bring them within legal limits (*Reduktion*),[132] which is generally regarded as an application of §139 BGB.[133] However, the application of replacement clauses is accepted.

Moreover, in the absence of a replacement clause, the disappearance of an anticompetitive clause from a contract may lead to obligations for the parties to renegotiate a contract based on 'Wirtschaftsklauseln', interpretation (*ergänzender Vertragsauslegung*) or frustration.[134]

The aversion to the modification of anticompetitive clauses (in the Netherlands) and reduction (in Germany) is motivated by the aim and purpose of Article 101 TFEU. While these legal systems have specific rules of civil law, they are generally considered not to apply to anticompetitive clauses. Allowing judicial modification of such clauses would undermine the preventive aim of Article 101 TFEU. In Belgium, the Civil Code does not contain any rules on judicial modification of void clauses and case law considered such modification in general irreconcilable with the all-or-nothing character of civil law nullity.[135] As mentioned above, the Belgian Court of Cassation has recently changed its view on this point—albeit not in relation to an infringement of Article 101 TFEU. In the Netherlands and Germany,[136] the rejection of judicial modification of anticompetitive clauses has been criticised by certain legal scholars. The Nordic countries have a general civil law rule on judicial modification of void clauses, but we did not find any applications thereof to anticompetitive clauses.

---

[131] ibid, 'Art 101 Abs 2 Rn 29'.

[132] OLG Frankfurt 11 December 2007 Az. 11 U 44/07 (Kart). This decision is criticised in the authoritative literature: ibid, 'Art 101 Abs 2 Rn 29'.

[133] Although sometimes this is seen as an application of §140 of the German Civil Code (BGB). ibid, with further references.

[134] ibid, 'Art 101 Abs 2 Rn 31'.

[135] But see Court of Appeal Brussels 7 March 2006 *Jaarboek Handelspraktijken & Mededinging* 2006, 773 *Power Oil NV v DDD Invest N.*

[136] K Schmidt, 'Art 101 Abs 2 Rn 29', in Immenga/Mestmäcker (*supra*, footnote 17).

II.A.vi IMPACT OF NULLITY ON FOLLOW-ON AGREEMENTS

II.A.vi.a Introduction: The Position of the EU Courts

CJ, 14 December 1983[137]   **2.34 (EU)**

Société de Vente de Ciments et Bétons de l'Est SA v Kerpen & Kerpen GmbH und Co KG

IMPACT OF NULLITY ON RELATED AGREEMENTS

Cement

National law determines what the consequences are of the nullity of an agreement under Article 101(2) TFEU on related (follow-on) agreements

Facts: The claimant had concluded with the defendant a contract for the annual delivery of approximately 40,000 tonnes of cement for a period of five years. After the defendant had taken delivery of and paid for part of the quantity agreed for 1978, it received but failed to pay for a further 6,051.29 tonnes of cement, to the value of DM 392,224.42, between August and October 1978. On 31 October 1978, the claimant terminated the contract and claimed the sum of DM 392,244.42. In addition to pleading a set off in respect of certain sums arising from the contract, the defendant contended that the contract was void for infringement of (now) Article 101 TFEU.

The national court referred to the CJ the question whether if the abovementioned agreement is to be regarded as a basic contract and if it is void under (now) Article 101(2) TFEU, individual contracts of sale made in performance of that contract are likewise to be regarded as void.

Held: The CJ answered that the consequences of such nullity for any orders and deliveries made on the basis of the agreement are left to the national law.

Judgment: [T]he automatic nullity decreed by [now Article 101(2) TFEU] applies only to those contractual provisions which are incompatible with [now Article 101(1) TFEU]. The consequences of such nullity ... for any orders and deliveries made on the basis of the agreement, and the resulting financial obligations are not a matter for [EU] law. Those consequences are to be determined by the national court according to its own law.

Notes:

(1) Follow-on agreements can be described as agreements which are concluded between an infringing party and a third party and whose terms are based on the collusive act that infringes Article 101 TFEU. *Kerpen and Kerpen*, also known as *Ciments*, is the seminal case on the impact of infringements of Article 101(1) TFEU on follow-on agreements. The CJEU confirmed its ruling in *Ciments* in later case law.[138]

(2) In *Allianz Hungaria*, however, the CJ seems to have changed or at least nuanced its views on the matter, ruling that 'if there was a horizontal agreement or a concerted practice between those two companies designed to partition the market, such an agreement or practice would have to be treated as a restriction by object and would also result in the unlawfulness of the vertical agreements concluded in order to implement that agreement

---

[137] CJ *Ciments* (n 112) para 12.
[138] *VAG France SA* (n 79) para 14; CJ *Cabour* (n 79) para 51; CJ *Brünsteiner* (n 79) para 48.).

or practice'.[139] According to Faull and Nikpay, this judgment may have far-reaching consequences for national contract law as it could, for example, mean that as a matter of EU law, sales contracts between cartel members and their customers could be automatically void under Article 101(2) TFEU.[140] Future case law of the CJEU will have to make clear whether this is indeed what the CJEU had in mind.

(3) As will appear from the following, the current situation is that the status of follow-on contracts is often uncertain and that there are wide varieties between the Member States.

(4) Since *Courage v Crehan*, it has been clear that parties who suffer damage as a result of an infringement of Article 101 TFEU, including those who have contracted with cartelists, can derive rights from that article. It can equally be argued that the effective enforcement of Article 101 TFEU requires that contracts on cartelised terms be void, at least to the extent of the overcharge, or that they be entirely or partially voidable at the request of the customer. A clear statement by the CJEU that follow-on contracts are void to the extent of the overcharge or the otherwise cartelised term or are voidable at the initiative of the innocent party would be welcome.[141]

II.A.vi.b Starting Position of National Courts: No Impact on Follow-on Agreements

In general, national courts start from the position that the nullity set out in Article 101(2) TFEU does not affect other contracts that are related to the void contract or the contract containing the void clause.[142] This is in particular the case when the related contracts are concluded between a cartelist and a third party.

High Court Queen's Bench Division, Commercial Court
20 September 2013[143]   **2.35 (UK)**

Deutsche Bank and others v Unitech Global and others

VALIDITY OF FOLLOW-ON CONTRACTS WITH THIRD PARTIES

LIBOR-based contracts

Although a number of banks infringed competition rules in the process of setting the London Interbank Offered Rate (LIBOR), this does not affect the validity of contracts which those banks concluded with their clients

Facts: A number of banks were alleged to have manipulated the London Interbank Offered Rate (LIBOR) in breach of Article 101 of the TFEU and section 2 of the Competition Act 1998. One of the banks alleged to

---

[139] CJ 14 March 2013 Case C-32/11 *Allianz Hungária Biztosító Zrt et al v Gazdasági Versenyhivatal* nyr ECLI:EU:C:2013:160, para 45.

[140] J Faull and A Nikay, *The EU Law of Competition*, 3rd edn (Oxford, Oxford University Press, 2014) no 3.444.

[141] C Cauffman, 'The Impact of Voidness for Infringements of Article 101 TFEU on Related Contracts' (2012) 12(1) *European Competition Journal* 122.

[142] In this sense, see also A Lamadrid de Pablo and L Ortiz Blanco, 'Nullity/Voidness: An Overview of EU and National Case Law' (2012) *e-Competitions Bulletin November*, no 49199. See also: https://antitrustlair. files.wordpress.com/2012/11/foreword-ecompetitions.pdf.

[143] *Deutsche Bank et al v Unitech Global et al* [2013] EWHC 2793 (Comm). The decision was reversed, but on grounds unrelated to the excerpt above. See also on this case V Rose and D Baily (eds), *Bellamy & Child, European Union Law of Competition*, 7th edn (Oxford, Oxford University Press, 2013) no 16.054.

be involved in this competition law infringement sued the defendants for non-performance of a number of contracts based on LIBOR. The defendants argued that these contracts were void due to the alleged infringement of the competition rules.

Held: Even if there has been a breach of Article 101 of the TFEU and section 2 of the Competition Act 1998 in the process by which LIBOR was set, and the offending agreements between the banks are void, the validity of the credit and swap agreements between one of those banks and its clients will not affected, although they are based upon LIBOR.

Judgment: 24. It is common ground that the implications of an illegal and void agreement between undertakings as a result of a breach of Article 101 are a matter for the national law. The suggestion that the vertical agreements between the Claimants and the Defendants are so closely connected to and/or spring from the horizontal agreements between the banks that they too should be considered void picks up the language of the Court of Appeal in *Courage Limited v Crehan* [1999] ECC 455 which in turn appears to have picked up the language in *Fisher v Bridges* (1854) 3 E & B 642 (Ex Ch). In *Courage Limited v Crehan* the tenants of tied public houses argued (i) that their tied house agreements were illegal and void under (what is now) Article 101 (Article 85 at the time) and (ii) that their individual beer supply contracts with their landlord were likewise illegal and void. The landlord conceded that it was arguable that the tied house agreements were contrary to (what was then) Article 85. The Court of Appeal held at paragraph 60 that the beer supply contract could not be considered 'so closely connected with the breach of [now Article 101 TFEU] so that it should be regarded as springing from or founded on the agreement rendered illegal by [now Article 101 TFEU]'.

25. There is no doubt that any LIBOR agreement between the banks (the 'horizontal agreement') and the credit and swap agreements between the Claimants and the Defendants (the 'vertical agreements') are connected. The latter make use of the former and are based upon it. But what is the suggested legal basis for saying that because of that connection the vertical agreement must also be void? Mr Sharpe's written and oral submissions suggest three. The first is that the horizontal and vertical agreements must be regarded as 'indissolubly linked' so that all must fail (leaving aside the possibility that the illegal parts may be severed). The second is that such conclusion is right in policy terms because it ensures that the Claimants do not benefit from their illegal conduct. The third is that once void a term cannot be resurrected by it being included in a vertical agreement which is subsidiary to the horizontal agreement.

26. I am not persuaded that any of these arguments leads to the conclusion that the credit and swap agreements between the Claimants and the Defendants are void (subject to the possible effect of severance).

27. As to the first of the arguments (that the horizontal and vertical agreements are indissolubly linked), the agreement between the banks and the agreements between the Claimants and the Defendants are separate and distinct agreements. There is a link or a connection between the two but it does not follow that if one is void so must the others be. The one is void because it breaches (or is assumed to have breached) competition law. The others do not breach competition law.

28. Similarly, as to the third of Mr Sharpe's arguments (that a void term cannot be resurrected), any LIBOR agreement between the banks may be void but the provisions in the credit and swap agreements, albeit based upon or derived from any LIBOR agreement between the banks, are legally separate and distinct. It is, in my judgment, misleading to refer to any LIBOR agreement between the banks as having been 'resurrected' in the loan and swap agreements. The vertical agreements are separate and distinct from the horizontal agreements, are between different parties and contain their own terms.

29. I am therefore unable to accept that either the first or third arguments advanced by Mr Sharpe lead to the conclusion that if the horizontal agreement is void so must the vertical agreements be void.

30. My conclusions with regard to the first and third arguments are consistent with the decision of the Court of Appeal in *Courage Limited v Crehan*. In that case the tied house agreements obliged the tenants to purchase their beer from Courage. Thus there was the clearest possible linkage and connection between the beer supply contracts and tied house agreements and yet the fact that the latter were void did not result in the former being void. In *Fisher v Bridges* it was held that a guarantee of a contract which was void on the grounds of illegality was also void. But the connection between the banks' LIBOR agreement and the credit and swap agreements are not comparable to the connection between a principal contract and a contract guaranteeing obligations arising under the principal agreement as in *Fisher v Bridges*.

31. Mr Sharpe's second argument is based upon public policy. I accept that the policy of English law is to prevent wrongdoers from benefitting from their own wrong. However, the policy of English law is also to respect and enforce agreements. Effect can be given to both policies by enforcing the credit and swap agreement and by granting customers of the banks a cause of action in damages where a bank has engaged in anti-competitive practices. The same point was made by Morgan J in *Bookmakers' Afternoon Greyhound Services Limited v Amalgamated Racing UK Limited* [2008] EWHC 1978 (Ch) at paragraph 409 where he said:

> If the consumer under the vertical agreement wishes to complain that the price charged by the price fixer was excessive tchen the consumer will have a claim for damages for breach of [now Article 101(1) TFEU]. It is not necessary, in order to protect the position of the consumer, for the law to enable the consumer to say that the contract was from the outset void.

32. I am mindful that questions of public policy can be heavily dependent upon the facts of the individual case and therefore will usually be inappropriate to determine at an interlocutory stage. However, in the context of this case (which involves loan and swap agreements no doubt typical of many in the market involving very large sums) I am persuaded that there is no real prospect that the agreements between the Claimants and the Defendants will be held to be void on public policy grounds.

33. I have therefore concluded that there is no real prospect that the Credit Agreement and Swap Agreement will be void on account of the alleged (and for this purpose assumed) breach of competition law. Permission to amend must therefore be refused.

Notes:

However, there are many ways in which the related contracts may after all turn out to be void or voidable. The voidness/voidability of the related contracts may result from a rule of national competition law, a national rule of general contract law which extends the consequences of the voidness of a certain contract to linked contracts, or national rules of general contract law relating to the validity of the linked contract itself. These possibilities will be investigated below.

II.A.vi.c Extension of Nullity Based on a Specific Provision

A specific provision of national law may extend the nullity of an agreement or decision infringing the competition rules to contracts or other legal acts related to that agreement or decision.

Article L.420-3 of the Consumer Code   **2.36 (FR)**

Any undertaking, agreement or contractual clause referring to a practice prohibited by Articles L. 420-1, L. 420-2 and L. 420-2–1 shall be invalid.

Cour de Cassation, chambre commerciale (Court of Cassation, Commercial Division), 24 October 2000[144]   **2.37 (FR)**

MX v Société Carrières de Sainte-Marthe (CSM)

VOIDNESS OF A FOLLOW-ON CONTRACT WITH A THIRD PARTY

The stone pit

A follow-on contract between a cartelist and a third party is void. However, the notification of a contract with a third party as a result of a cartel agreement is not void

Facts: When the tenancy contract of a stone pit approached its end, the landlord conducted negotiations with his sitting tenant and in parallel with a group of competing undertakings which intended to obtain a lease on the stone pit and a neighbouring parcel for a subsidiary in order to finalise an agreement to share markets. This intention was unknown to the landlord. The landlord notified the sitting tenant and concluded a contract with the subsidiary of one of the members of the group of competing undertakings. Subsequently, this contract was transferred to a new company, established by the group of competing undertakings. The French competition authority found the group of competing undertakings guilty of a cartel having as its object to jointly obtain a production unit operated by a competitor in order to finalise a market sharing agreement. This decision was confirmed on appeal. The original tenant then brought a claim before the civil court in order to have the notification of his contract as well as the tenancy contract with the subsidiary of his competitors and the transfer of this contract to a new company declared void. The Court of Appeal declared the tenancy agreement with the subsidiary of one of the members of the group of competing undertakings void as far as it concerned the stone pit which was originally operated by the original tenant. However, it declared the tenant's claim inadmissible as far as it concerned the neighbouring parcel. The Court of Appeal also refused to declare the notification of the original tenant void.

Held: The French Court of Cassation confirmed the voidness of the contract concluded between the landlord and the subsidiary, stating that the fact that one of the parties did not participate in the anticompetitive practice or was not aware of it is irrelevant for the decision as to the voidness of the contract. It annulled the Court of Appeal's decision that the tenant's claim was not admissible where it concerned the neighbouring parcel which had never been rented out to the tenant. Finally, it confirmed the Court of Appeal's decision where it refused to declare the notification of the original tenant void, stressing that Article 9 of the previous French Competition Act does not allow the Court to order the conclusion of a contract or its renewal.

Judgment: On the first branch of the main ground of appeal:

...

But, whereas according to Article 9 of the Ordonnace 'any engagement, agreement or contractual clause relating to (a prohibited anticompetitive) practice' is void, this text does not provide the possibility for the judge to order the conclusion or renewal of a contract; hence, the Court of Appeal has not misapplied the said text by refusing to annul the notification given to the company CSM; ...

---

[144] French Court of Cassation, Commercial Division 24 October 2000 no98-14.382 *Bulletin IV* no163, 145 annotated by A Marmontel *D* 2000, 429; A Marmontel *RTD civ* 2001, 140; J Mestre and B Fages *RTD civ* 2001, 163; P-Y Gautier *RTD com* 2001, 427.

But on the second branch of the main ground of appeal:

Given Article 9 of the Ordonnance of 1 December 1986 and Article 125 of the New Code of Civil Procedure; Whereas in order to pronounce inadmissible the request by the company CSM to annul the rental contract relating to plot B 49 and concluded between M. X and the competitors of the company, the decision states that the latter has never held any right on this plot.

Whereas by holding on these grounds, but after having held that company CSM was a candidate for renting plot B 49 and without investigating whether it did not have an interest in putting an end to the anticompetitive practice committed by the members of GIE BGP and if the rent of plot B 49 was not for them an element of these practices, the Court of Appeal has not given a legal basis to its decision. On these grounds, Quashes and annuls, but only where it has denied the admissibility of the request of the company Carrières de Sainte-Marthe aiming at the annulment of the rental contract agreed to SOMET on plot B 49 and to the cession of this rental agreement to the company Granulats de Provence, the decision given on 19 February 1998, between the parties, by the Court of Appeal of Aix-en-Provence ...

Notes:

(1) The case was decided under Article 9 of the previous French Competition Act (Regulation no 86-12431 December 1986 on freedom of prices and competition) *(Ordonnance no 86-12431 December 1986 relative à la liberté des prix et de la concurrence)*. However, this article is repeated word for word in the current Article L.420-3 of the French Commercial Code. The nullity imposed by this article is one of 'ordre public économique'[145] and is therefore absolute. This means that it can be requested by all interested parties, including the contracting party that deliberately included the element of voidness in the contract. If the parties do not invoke the nullity themselves, the Court is obliged to invoke it of its own motion.[146]

(2) It is not entirely clear what is meant by *'relating to'* ('se rapportant') in the above-cited Article 9 of the previous French Competition Act or the current Article L.420-3 of the French Commercial Code (*Code de commerce*). However, it is certain that the provision can be applied even if one of the parties to the agreement was not aware of the anticompetitive purpose.[147]

(3) Legal scholars rarely analyse Article L.420-3 of the French Commercial Code (*Code de commerce*) or its predecessors in detail. It has been argued that Article L.420-3 could not be applied to contracts concluded with third parties under conditions which were previously agreed upon by competitors.[148]

(4) In a communication on civil actions for damages for anticompetitive practices published in April 2008, the *Direction générale de la concurrence, de la consommation et de la repression des fraudes* stated that a public authority that has been the victim of

---

[145] ibid.

[146] In this sense, see French Court of Cassation Commercial Division 24 October 2000 (n 144); Cauffman 2012 p 98 (n 141).

[147] ibid.

[148] TMJ Möllers and A Heinemann (eds), *The Enforcement of Competition Law in Europe* (Cambridge, Cambridge University Press, 2010) 586–87.

bid-rigging can have the contract concluded on the basis of rigged bids declared void on the ground of Article L.420-3.[149]

II.A.vi.d Theories Developed by National Courts and Legal Scholarship

C Cauffman, 'The Impact of Voidness for Infringements of Article 101 TFEU on Related Contracts'[150]   **2.38 (EU)**

In Germany, the prevailing opinion in the current literature is that a distinction is to be made between, on the one hand, contracts that are not only the consequence of a contract prohibited by Article 101(1) TFEU but also a means to bring about the agreement prohibited by Article 101(1) TFEU (*Ausführungsverträge*) and, on the other hand, contracts with third parties that are merely the consequence of a contract that is prohibited by Article 101(1) TFEU (*Folgeverträge*).[151] The majority opinion holds that only contracts concluded between the same parties as the cartel agreement can qualify as *Ausführungsverträge*.[152] A minority opinion considers that contracts with third parties can also constitute a means to bring about the agreement prohibited by Article 101(1) TFEU and can then be qualified as *Ausführungsverträge*.[153]

Ausführungsverträge are considered indissoluble from the agreement that infringes Article 101(1) TFEU and are therefore considered void on the ground of Article 101(1) TFEU itself.[154]

Folgeverträge are in principle considered valid.[155] This is even the case if such a contract is the purpose for which the prohibited agreement was concluded and if the party with whom it is concluded is a party that is protected by the cartel prohibition. Even the fact that such party knows of the infringement of Article 101(1) TFEU does not render the *Folgevertrag* void under Article 101(2) TFEU.[156] However, *Folgeverträge* will be void when they themselves infringe Article 101(1) TFEU or when they are affected by another ground of voidness or voidability.[157]

---

[149] Cauffman (n 141) 100.

[150] ibid 100–01. See also on this case Rose and Baily (n 143) no 16.054.

[151] See eg W Jaeger, 'Art 81 Abs 2 Rn 22 and 24–25', in Loewenheim/Meessen/Riesenkampff, *Kartellrecht. Europäisches und Deutsches Recht. Kommentar*, Verlag C.H. Beck 2009 (hereafter Loewenheim/Meessen/Riesenkampff); OLG Düsseldorf 30 July 1987 Az Kart U 29/86, WuW/E OLG 4182. See also OLG Brandenburg 18 April 2006 Az Kart U 4/05; K Schmidt, 'Art 101 Abs 2 Rn 34-36', in Immenga/Mestmäcker (*supra*, footnote 17).

[152] ibid.

[153] K Paul, *Gesetzesverstoß und Vertrag im Wettbewerbs- und Regulierungsrecht. Eine Untersuchung der Schutz- und Verbotsgesetzeigenschaft wettbewerbsschützender Normen sowie deren Auswirkungen auf Folgeverträge* (Baden-Baden, Nomos, 2010) 23–24.

[154] K Schmidt, 'Art 101 Abs 2 Rn 35', in Immenga/Mestmäcker (*supra*, footnote 17); W Jaeger, 'Art 81 Abs 2 EGV Rn 22' in Loewenheim/Meessen/Riesenkampff (*supra*, footnote 151).

[155] See eg W Jaeger, 'Art 81 Abs 2 EGV Rn 22 and 24-25' in Loewenheim/Meessen/Riesenkampff; K Schmidt, 'Art 101 Abs 2 Rn 36', in Immenga/Mestmäcker; BGH 21 January 1965 III ZR 217/1963 *NJW* 1965, 2001; OLG Düsseldorf 30 July 1987 WuW/E OLG 4182.

[156] OLG 15 February 1963 WuW/E OLG 559.

[157] K Schmidt, 'Art 101 Abs 2 Rn 36', in Immenga/Mestmäcker.

*Bundesgerichtshof (Federal Supreme Court
of Germany), 4 May 1956*[158]   **2.39 (GERM)**

X v Y

A CARTEL DOES NOT AFFECT THE VALIDITY OF FOLLOW-ON
CONTRACTS WITH THIRD PARTIES

Spediteurbedingungen

*The validity of a contract referring to contract terms agreed by a professional association
is not affected by the fact that the terms referred to might be cartelised*

Facts: Several German industrial organisations together drafted a set of general terms and conditions that were recommended for use in relation to transportation contracts. The German Supreme Court had to decide whether individual agreements which were subjected to these terms and conditions were void for infringement of the competition rules.

Held: Even if the general terms and conditions were cartelised, this would not affect the validity of the individual contracts that were subjected to these terms and conditions.

Judgment: The agreement on the General Terms of Haulage Contractors (GTHC) for the individual haulage contract, of which only the §§7 and 32 are applied, does not conflict with competition law (AmMRG 56, BrMRVO 78, FrMRVO 96). Even if this were the case, it would not follow that the single haulage contract under the GTHC between haulier and customer, or even the single contract between the opposing parties to this lawsuit, is void due to violation of the competition law. This agreement does not contain provisions that would as such bring about a significant restriction of free competition, irrespective of by whom and under what circumstances they are applied. An agreement based on the GTHC only falls under the cartel prohibition, when the hauliers amongst themselves would have agreed upon a general use in commercial transactions (§134 BGB). By contrast, there is no sufficient reason to also consider the individual haulage contracts between the haulier and his customers to fall under the prohibition of cartels when they are based on the GTHC. Given the widespread habit in the German economy to use general terms which were previously defined by the economic sectors concerned a general extension of the cartel prohibition to all individual contracts concluded on such terms would entail indefinite and almost uncontrollable legal consequences and disorders of economic life. The competition laws therefore cannot be interpreted in this way.

Notes:

   This case does not concern the compatibility of the contract terms referred to with EU competition law, but with German Competition Acts that are no longer in force. Nevertheless, the case is still cited as one of the main precedents confirming that the voidness of a cartel agreement does not entail the voidness of agreements between one of the cartelists and a third party.[159] This principle has later been confirmed in the Federal

---

[158] BGH 4 May 1956 I ZR 194/54 (KG) *NJW* 1956, 1201 *X v Y*.
[159] See also the earlier case RG 22 May 1931 *RGZ* 133, 51, 58 ff.

Supreme Court's case law[160] and is largely followed by lower case law[161] and legal scholarship. It also applies when the initial cartel agreement infringes EU competition law.[162]

II.A.vi.e Extension Based on General Contract Law Provisions

Article 6:229 BW	**2.40 (NL)**

Agreement based on a non-existent legal relationship

An agreement which necessarily implicates an elaboration on an already existing legal relationship between parties is voidable if this legal relationship does not exist, unless the nature of the agreement, the general principles of society or the circumstances of the case imply that the non-existence of that legal relationship should remain for account of the person who appeals to its non-existence.

Notes:

(1) Article 6:229 BW concerns building-on agreements. It is typical of building-on agreements that they build on a pre-existing legal relationship between the same parties. Building-on agreements usually aim to modify, supplement, specify, perform or extinguish a pre-existing relationship between the parties.[163] Article 6:229 BW could, for example, be used to avoid a contract for the supply of beer which builds on a beer tie which infringes Article 101(1) TFEU.[164]

(2) Article 6:229 BW is normally only available if both contracts are concluded between the same parties. However, a Dutch scholar suggests extending the application of Article 6:229 BW at least by way of analogy to subsequent contracts concluded with 'related third parties'. 'Related third parties' are parties that, although possessing a separate legal personality, form part of the same economic unit as one of the parties to the cartel agreement.[165]

---

[160] BGH 9 July 1984 *NJW* 1984, 2372, 2373 (using the concept *Folgeverträge*).

[161] OLG Frankfurt 30 July 1996 *WiB* 1996, 1068 (also concerning an infringement of EU competition law); OLG Düsseldorf 30 July 1987 WuW/E OLG 4182, 4184; OLG München 19 February 2002 *NJW-RR* 2002, 886, 887 ff.

[162] *cf* footnotes 137–140 above.

[163] Asser/Hartkamp & Sieburgh 6-III* 2010 no 301; CJ van Zeben and JW Du Pon, *Parlementaire geschiedenis van het nieuwe burgerlijk wetboek* (Deventer, Kluwer, 1981) 913; IPM Ligteringen, 'Privaatrechtelijke rechtsgevolgen van het Europese kartelverbod voor voortbordurende rechtshandelingen' (2009) 6784 *WPNR* 79.

[164] Cauffman (n 141) 103–04.

[165] Ligteringen (n 163) 84; Cauffman (n 141) 104.

II.A.vi.f The Follow-on Contract is Itself Affected by a Ground of Voidness or
Voidability

C Cauffman, 'The Impact of Voidness for Infringements of
Article 101 TFEU on Related Contracts'[166]   **2.41 (EU)**

The question whether the existence of a cartel agreement affects the validity requirements
of subsequent agreements cannot be answered unequivocally. According to the currently
prevailing opinions in England, Germany and the Netherlands, the existence of the cartel agreement will, in general, not render the subsequent agreement with a third party
contrary to statute law, public order or good morals. In Belgium, however, there was a
case that was decided otherwise. French and German scholars have argued in the same
vein and the same idea may have been the underlying reason why a Dutch court without
further argumentation extended the voidness of a cartel agreement to a contract with a
third party concluded on cartelized terms. A German court has also held that a contract
between a procurer and a winning bid-rigger is void where it infringes a specific provision
of the German criminal code …

When a contract concluded between a cartelist and a third party is not held to be void
on the ground that it is contrary to a statutory provision, public order or good morals, it
can still be voidable because of a defect of consent. Whether the cartel agreement results
in a defect of consent on the side of the innocent party who contracted with a cartelist
is unclear. Concluding a cartel agreement is fraudulent in common parlance, but does it
also amount to fraud as a defect of consent? In Belgium and France it will generally only
amount to incidental fraud, because without the fraud the innocent party would still have
concluded the contract, albeit perhaps on different terms. This type of fraud will only lead
to an action for damages. In Germany, bid-rigging will amount to fraud as a defect of
consent, but other types of cartels generally will not. In England, an action for fraudulent
misrepresentation will only lie where the cartelist explicitly stated not to have participated
in a cartel. The cartel agreement will generally not render the subsequent contract with a
third party voidable for mistake in any of the legal systems studied. The cartel agreement
is also unlikely to amount to coercion. The same will generally apply for abuse of circumstances. What prevents the avoidance of the subsequent agreement on the basis of a
defect of consent is usually the fact that the impact of the cartel on the contract is not
sufficiently serious. In cases of public procurement, avoidance for defects of consent may
be more readily available because it seems more feasible that in such cases, the cartel had
a serious impact on the contractual terms and conditions.

Notes:

   The sort of follow-on contracts under Italian law have been studied by Libertini and
Maugeri. With many references to Italian case law, the authors point out that Italian courts
generally do not consider follow-on contracts void, although there are some exceptions
to this. Certain Italian scholars, such as Mirone,[167] have advocated the extension of the
voidness for infringement of the competition rules to follow-on contracts. However, after

---

[166] Cauffman (n 141) 120–21.
[167] A Mirone, *Standardizzazione dei contratti bancari e tutela della concorrenza* (Turin, Giappichelli,
2003) 72.

reviewing various grounds that have been advanced or could be advanced to justify such extension, Libertini and Maugeri conclude that follow-on contracts can only be held void for infringement of the competition rules when their own object or cause infringes these rules.[168]

Hoge Raad der Nederland (Supreme Court of the Netherlands),
16 September 2011[169] **2.42 (NL)**

Batavus v Vriend

UNILATERAL TERMINATION OF A DISTRIBUTION CONTRACT

Batavus my friend

The termination by a manufacturer of an agreement with a client as a result of pressure exerted by competitors of that client infringes the Dutch Competition Act

Facts: Batavus (the claimant), a bicycle manufacturer, cancelled an agreement with its online distributor Vriend (the defendant) as a result of pressure exerted by bricks-and-mortar competitors of that distributor. Later on, the claimant refused to permit the defendant to take part in its selective distribution system set up in 2004.

Held: Cancellation of the agreement is contrary to the Dutch Competition Act and therefore null and void pursuant to that Act.

Judgment: 3.12 There are no grounds to exclude unilateral acts such as notifications from the sanction of voidness under Article 6(2) Dutch Competition Act, when they follow from, are part of or relate sufficiently to a concerted practice that is prohibited under Article 6(1) Dutch Competition Act.

Notes:

(1) Legal scholars have argued that it would have been better to hold the unilateral termination void or inapplicable on the ground of illegality (Article 3:40(2) BW) or reasonableness and fairness (Article 6:248(2) BW).[170]

(2) It is interesting to compare this case with the French case relating to the stone pit. Contrary to the French Court of Cassation, the Supreme Court of the Netherlands does not see any objections to holding a notification contrary to the competition rules, thereby de facto ordering the contract to remain in place.

In a Belgian case, the fact that a contract was concluded on the basis of a prohibited tariff agreement was considered to result in a mistake which rendered the contract voidable.

---

[168] M Libertini and MR Maugeri, 'Infringement of Competition Law and Invalidity of Contracts' (2005) 1(2) *European Review of Contract Law* 250.
[169] HR 16 September 2011 *NJ* 2011,572 ECLI:NL:HR:2011:BQ2213 *Batavus BV v Vriend's Tweewieler-centrum Blokker VOF.*
[170] HR 16 September 2011 ECLI:NL:HR:BQ:2213, note by K van Haastrecht and JMM van de Hell *AM* 2012, 214–22.

Hof van Beroep Gent (Court of Appeal of Ghent),
15 February 2008[171]   **2.43 (BE)**

Review Toepassingen van Communicatie bvba
v De Schepper J and Competition Council

MISTAKE

The colluding interior designer

A consumer's consent is affected by mistake if at the time the contract was concluded, he was not aware of the illegality of the deontological rule on which the fee was based

Facts: A consumer agreed orally to pay an interior designer a fee of 12 per cent of the price for carrying out his design as provided by a deontological rule, not knowing that this rule infringed (now) Article 101 TFEU. The architect claimed payment of the 12 per cent fee. The consumer brought a counter-claim for avoidance of the contract on the ground of mistake as at the time the contract was concluded, he was not aware of the illegality of the deontological rule on which the fee was based.

Held: The agreement to pay a 12 per cent fee is void on the ground of mistake. Nevertheless, the architect, who had delivered his part of the agreement, is entitled to payment for the work done. Therefore, the consumer is ordered to pay a certain sum (less than the 12 per cent fee) determined by the Court.

Judgment: These circumstances were such that the claimant believed that this was the rule and contained an obligation (hence his mention under nr. 37 of his last briefs: '... was he forced to agree to a percentage of 12% ...') and did not know that this was illegal. The conclusion regarding the deontological rule of interior designers cannot be different from the EC's decision of 24.6.04 with regard to deontological rule nr. 2 of the architects. The Court therefore assumes that only the mentioned circumstances in which the claimant on appeal gave her consent, and her ignorance, relating to the illegality of the deontological rule have been determining for her consent. This consent was therefore given under the influence of a false impression of things.

Claimant on appeal has therefore erred and this error is excusable as it may be assumed that the entire context regarding the consent and more particularly the presentation of the deontological rule as an obligation would have pushed a normally careful and diligent person with the same qualities and placed in the same circumstances to consent ...

The oral agreement relating to a fee of 12% is therefore void. This does not entail however that the defendant is not entitled to a fee. It is clear that the parties intended that the defendant would be paid for his services.

The defendant has performed his tasks correctly ... Therefore he is entitled to his fee.

In order to determine this fee the scope and the type of the works carried out have to be taken into account. Given the description of the works (...) mentioned in the non-signed agreement—it is not contested that these mentions describe the task as it has been carried out—and the price of the construction works (...) + the costs of the engineer (...), the compensation to which the defendant is entitled is fixed at ....

Notes:

(1) In Belgium (as in France), a mistake will only render a contract voidable if it relates to the substance of the subject matter and if it is excusable. That the mistake must

---

[171] Court of Appeal of Ghent 15 February 2008 *Jaarboek Handelspraktijken & Mededinging* 2008, 814, annotated by K Baekelandt *Review Toepassingen van Communicatie bvba v De Schepper J and Raad voor de Mededinging.*

relate to the substance of the subject matter means that the mistake needs to relate to a characteristic of the subject matter of the contract which is of such importance to the mistaken party that he would not have concluded the contract but for that characteristic.[172] It can be questioned whether the Court of Appeal of Ghent was right to consider a mistake as to the fact that the contract was concluded at competitive conditions as a mistake concerning the substance of the subject matter.[173]

(2) The Court of Appeal is not clear on the legal basis of its decision to award the architect a fee, although the agreement to pay a 12 per cent fee was held void. Technically, such award could only be based on unjust enrichment, a source of obligations not mentioned in the Civil Code, but recognised by the French Court of Cassation.[174] The amount payable should then be based on the lesser of the following two amounts: the impoverishment of the architect or the enrichment of the client.[175]

(3) The consumer had also complained about these facts to the Belgian Competition Authority. About five months after the decision of the Court of Appeal was given, the Belgian Competition Authority held that the individual architect had not infringed Article 2 of the Belgian Competition Act, but the association of interior designers had.[176]

T Eilmansberger on nullity of follow-on agreements[177]   **2.44 (AT)**

A follow-on agreement, which is an implementing act of a hard-core competition law infringement and whose content is therefore (e.g. in case of a price cartel) directly affected by the agreement, or (e.g. in a market sharing cartel) which owes its existence to this agreement, is void under §879 ABGB.

Notes:

The author rightly points out that the issue has not been widely researched in Austrian law before, and that, to the extent that it has been discussed, the majority opinion follows the German position holding *Folgeverträge* valid in principle. This position is justified on the basis of the argument that the content of these contracts is not as such illegal, and that their voidness would lead to legal uncertainty and to incalculable consequences and

---

[172] Belgium: Court of Cassation 31 October 1966 *Arr Cass* 1967.301; Court of Cassation 3 March 1967 *Arr Cass* 1967.829; Court of Cassation 24 September 2007 *TBBR* 2009 vol 4, 216, note by D Philippe *TBBR* 2009 vol 4, 218–23; L Cornelis, *Algemene theorie van de verbintenis* (Antwerp, Intersentia Rechtswetenschappen, 2000) no 35, 46; P Wéry, *Droit des obligation, Volume 1 Théorie générále du contract*, 2nd edn (Brussels, Larcier, 2010) no 231, 215. See already Belgian Court of Cassation 8 May 1905 *Pas* 1905 vol I, 214. France: Court of Cassation 28 January 1913 *S* 1913,487 note by J Flour; J-L Aubert and E Savaux, *Droit civil, Les obligations, Volume 1 L'acte juridique* (Paris, Armand Colin, 2004) nos 197 ff and 138 ff. See also French Court of Cassation 20 October 1970 *JCP* 1971 II-16916, annotated by J Ghestin *RTD civ* 1971, 13.

[173] W Devroe and J Stuyck, 'De horizontale werking van het (primaire) recht van de Europese Unie en het Belgische vermogensrecht' in *Preadviezen voor de Vereniging voor de vergelijkende studie van het recht in Nederland en België* (The Hague, Boom Juridische uitgevers, 2011) 272.

[174] Belgian Court of Cassation 27 May 1909 *Pas* 1909 vol 1, 272, with the opinion of AG Terlinden.

[175] P Maes, 'Ongegronde vermogensverschuivingen en driepartijenverhoudingen' (2010) *TPR* 210; W van Gerven, *Verbintenissenrecht*, 3th edn (Leuven, ACCO Uitgeverij, 2010) 291; P van Ommeslaghe, *Droit des obligations*, vol II (Brussels, Bruylant, 2010) no 792.

[176] Belgian Competition Authority 25 July 2008 Decision No 2008-P/K-45 *Review BVBA v Associatie van Interieurarchitecten van België*.

[177] T Eilmansberger, 'Zur Nichtigkeit kartellrechtswidriger Vereinbarungen und ihren Konsequenzen (2. Teil)' (2009) 131(7) *Juristische Blätter* 434.

disruptions of trade. Specifically for Austrian law, it is added that §879 of the Austrian Civil Code (ABGB) only concerns the content of contracts, not the way in which they have been concluded.

According to Eilmansberger, these arguments do not apply to the contracts concluded between a cartelist and a third party (first-degree *Folgeverträge*), but only to subsequent contracts concluded further on in the supply chain (second- and further-degree *Folgeverträge*). The number of contracts concluded directly with the cartelists is normally not incalculable and legal uncertainty is only a problem insofar as it affects the cartelist's counter-party. The cartelist himself is unworthy of protection.

With regard to §879 ABGB, Eilmansberger points out that a cartel directly affects the content of a first-degree *Folgevertrag*: without the cartel agreement, the *Folgevertrag* would not have been concluded on the same terms. The link between the cartel and second- or further-degree *Folgevertrage* contracts would, however, not be close enough to consider the content of these 'second- and further-degree' contracts to be affected by the cartel.

Where long-term contracts or contracts that are infrequently concluded are concerned, the purpose and effective enforcement of the cartel prohibition would, moreover, require their voidness. With regard to other contracts, this would be less so, but the purpose and effective enforcement of the cartel prohibition would in any case not be opposed to their voidness.

First-degree *Folgeverträge*, however, whose content is directly affected by the cartel would therefore be void under §879 ABGB. However, the voidness would only be a relative voidness, meaning that it cannot be invoked by the cartelist and the court cannot invoke it *ex officio*; it can only be invoked by the cartelists' counter-party. Furthermore, the voidness would not affect the entire contract. The cartelised prices or conditions would only need to be reduced to the competitive level. The voidness would, however, have effect *ex tunc*.[178]

II.A.vii REIMBURSEMENT DUTIES

Oberster Gerichtshof (Austrian Supreme Court),
13 March 2012[179]   **2.45 (AT)**

B* AG v G* OG and others

UNJUST ENRICHMENT

A brewer in good faith

The rules on unjust enrichment require both parties to an anticompetitive agreement to restitute the benefits and payments which they had exchanged on the basis of a void agreement, unless a party had been aware of illegality at the time of conclusion of the agreement

Facts: A contract between a brewer and a restaurant obliged the restaurant to obtain all its beer from that brewer for a period 10 ten years (non-compete obligation). The brewer paid a large sum of money to the

---

[178] See ibid, 432–35.
[179] Austrian Supreme Court 13 March 2012 no 10 Ob 10/12m ECLI:AT:OGH0002:2012:0100OB00010. 12M.0313.000 *B* AG v G* OG et al.*

restaurant upfront as remuneration for its exclusive right of supply. The restaurant did not purchase the minimum quantity and after some time informed the brewer that it would no longer purchase beer at all. The brewer claimed back part of its upfront payment, whereas the restaurant claimed nullity of the exclusive purchase obligation for breach of competition law.

Held: Even if the agreement were void pursuant to Article 101(2) TFEU, the brewer was entitled to claim back part of the upfront payment. The rules on unjust enrichment require both parties to restitute the benefits and payments which they had exchanged on the basis of a void agreement.

Judgment: 2. Related to the question of the scope of the consequences of nullity is the problem of restitution.

In the course of the implementation and completion of cartel agreements performances are often exchanged between the parties. When an agreement infringes [now Article 101 TFEU] and is entirely or partly null, the question arises whether the exchanged performances need to be restituted. In the absence of a clear European rule this question is to be answered under national law ... The restitution of performances made under prohibited contracts or contracts *contra bonos mores* is determined by §877 ABGB ... Content and scope of the claim are determined following general principles of the law of restitution ... Pursuant to §877 ABGB the party who claims restitution of a legal transaction on the ground of nullity also has to return everything he received from the contract to his benefit ...

2.1 Applied to agreements that are void for infringement of the cartel prohibition of [now Article 101 TFEU] this means that the performances that have already been received by all sides need to be returned. This is in these cases also the most appropriate solution, because the protection of the rights guaranteed by EU law should not, also according to the case law of the ECJ, lead to unjustified enrichment of the claimant (ECJ, 20. 9. 2001, C-453/99, *Courage/Crehan*, ECR 2001, I-6297 nr. 30). This is in accordance with the fact that the aim of [now Article 101 TFEU] is to restore the freedom of action of the parties involved and not to shift property in favour of one of the parties involved ...

2.2. However, the claim for restitution by the party who has pushed the other party to bring about a cooperation that is prohibited by cartel law or who has provided assets in return for a promise that infringes cartel law is limited in two respects.

2.2.1. In the first place, the claim for restitution is limited by and insofar as the performing party (e.g. the supplier, who provided the purchaser money or goods in return for an exclusive purchase clause) has already obtained the counterperformance (the exclusive purchasing or the purchase of a certain amount) that infringes cartel law ... This limitation was in the present case taken into account by the claimant by the fact that she only claims the not yet 'amortised' part of her counterperformance.

2.2.2. In the second place ... restitution is not possible of what has knowingly been given in order to obtain an impossible or prohibited act. However, a party only performs 'knowingly' if he knows or should have known of the prohibition or in case of acts *contra bonos mores* ... [This] docs not hamper restitution because the claimant at the time of the conclusion of the exclusive purchase agreement in 1998 could by no means have known of the prohibition of an agreement with a duration exceeding 5 years that was only introduced by block exemption Reg No 2790/1999.

Notes:

(1) The question arises whether the application of national rules prohibiting a party from claiming reimbursement of what has been performed (for example based on the principle *in pari causa turpitudinis cessat repetitio*) under a contract that is void for

infringement of the competition rules is compatible with Articles 101 and 102 TFEU and the principle of effectiveness.

(2) In *Courage v Crehan*, the CJ held that Article 101 TFEU precludes a rule of national law under which a party to a contract liable to restrict or distort competition is barred from claiming damages for loss caused by performance of that contract on the sole ground that the claimant is a party to that contract, but that EU law does not preclude a rule of national law barring a party to a contract liable to restrict or distort competition from relying on his own unlawful actions to obtain damages where it is established that that party bears significant responsibility for the distortion of competition (*cf* below).

(3) Is the ruling in *Courage v Crehan* to be extended to national rules concerning reimbursement of what has been performed under a void contract? Not necessarily. It is possible that the CJEU will allow the application of the normal national rules concerning reimbursement after termination to the extent that these are based on another legal basis than the right to claim damages for infringements of the EU competition rules. The parties to the terminated agreement will, however, maintain the right to claim damages according to the rules established by the CJEU and Directive 2014/104[180] (*cf* below).

II.B NULLITY AS A SANCTION FOR INFRINGEMENT OF ARTICLE 102 TFEU

As Article 102 TFEU does not contain an equivalent of Article 101(2) TFEU, the question arises whether agreements or unilateral legal acts infringing Article 102 TFEU will nevertheless be void as a matter of EU law. Certain scholars appear to answer in the affirmative.

G Blanke and P Landolt, EU and US
Antitrust Arbitration[181]   **2.46 (EU)**

The EU courts have also determined that, despite the absence of equivalent wording in the text of Article 102 TFEU, practices in violation of Article 102 TFEU are also automatically void and subject to the same treatment as agreements in violation of EU competition law are under Article 101 TFEU. This is an expression of the direct effect of Article 102 TFEU under EU law.

Careful analysis of the case law of the CJEU warrants a cautious position. In *BRT v Sabam*, the CJ recognized that (now) Article 102 TFEU has direct effect, stating that: 'If abusive practices are exposed, it is … for the [national] court to decide whether and to what extent they affect the interests of authors or third parties concerned, with a view to deciding the consequences with regard to the validity and effect of the contracts in dispute or certain of their provisions.'[182] This does not automatically imply that agreements infringing Article 102 TFEU are affected by an EU law nullity.

---

[180] [2014] OJ L349/1 (n 6).

[181] G Blanke and P Landolt, *EU and US Antitrust Arbitration: A Handbook for Practitioners, Volume 1* (Alphen aan den Rhijn, Kluwer Law International, 2011) 630.

[182] CJ 27 March 1974 Case C-127/73 *BRT v SV SABAM and NV Fornoir (BRT II)* [1974] I-00313 ECLI:EU:C:1974:25, para 14.

The CJ's later decision in *Ahmed Saeed Flugreisen* leaves it to national law to determine the consequences of a breach of Article 102 TFEU 'If it is found that an undertaking has abused its dominant position on the market and that trade between Member States may be affected, the conduct of the undertaking concerned falls under the prohibition laid down in [now Article 102 TFEU]. In the absence of action by the EC … the competent national administrative or judicial authorities must draw the inferences from the applicability of the prohibition and, where appropriate, rule that the agreement in question is void on the basis, in the absence of relevant [EU] rules, of their national legislation.'[183]

Göta Hovrätt (Swedish Court of Appeal),
27 April 2001[184]   **2.47 (SE)**

Scandinavian Airlines System (SAS) v Swedish Board
of Civil Aviation (BCA)

PARTIAL NULLITY

Terminal 2

To the extent they contravene the prohibition of abuse of a dominant position under EU and national competition law, the contract terms are void; the rest of the parties' contractual relations remain in place

Facts: BCA managed Arlanda Airport, the major airport in Stockholm. BCA had a special terminal (Terminal 2) built at the airport for the needs of the domestic air traffic run by SAS. After some years, SAS found Terminal 2 to be unsuitable and moved out of it. BCA required SAS to pay not only the general landing charges applicable to all airlines, but also substantial payments for the abandoned Terminal 2. In a civil case, SAS sued BCA, claiming that BCA's pricing amounted to price discrimination prohibited under what is now Article 102 TFEU and its counterpart in the Swedish Competition Act.

The Court of Appeal found the competition rules applicable and clearly spelt out that these rules were mandatory and could not be derogated from by way of agreement between the parties. Thus, the Court set aside the argument that SAS had agreed to the payment arrangement. The Court found that BCA was applying dissimilar conditions to equivalent transactions and that this was clearly done to the disadvantage of SAS. It found BCA unable to prove objective justification for its price differentiation.

Held: The pricing conditions applied to SAS constitute an abuse of dominant position contrary to Article 102 TFEU and its Swedish counterpart. The contract terms at issue are void to the extent that they are in breach of EU and national competition law. The remainder of the parties' contractual relations remain in place. SAS must only pay BCA charges in accordance with the same principles as other aviation companies; excess amounts are to be refunded to SAS.

Judgment: EU law demands efficient implementation and efficient protection of rights conferred to private parties and requires equal treatment of claims based on national law and EU law (cf Art. 4(3) TEU and elated case law). This strongly indicates that contract terms involving an abuse of dominant position according to national law and [EU] law are to be considered as inoperative, given the direct effect of Article 102 in the Member States.

---

[183] CJ 11 April 1989 Case C-66/86 *Ahmed Saeed Flugreisen v Zentrale zur Bekämpfung unlauteren Wetbewerbs eV* [1989] I-00803 ECLI:EU:C:1989:140, para 45.
[184] Swedish Court of Appeal 27 April 2001 Case No T 33-00 *Scandinavian Airlines System (SAS) v Swedish Board of Civil Aviation (BCA)*. On this case, see U Bernitz, 'The Arlanda Terminal 2 Case: Substantial Damages for Breach of Article 82' [2003] *Competition Law Journal* 195.

...

Referring to the principle that rights conferred by [EU] law should not be virtually impossible or excessively difficult to exercise, the [CJEU] requires that there shall be entitlement to repayment of charges levied by a Member State or a public undertaking in breach of [EU] law.

Notes:

(1) In support of its statement that contract terms involving an abuse of a dominant position are to be considered inoperative, the Swedish Court of Appeal referred to *BRT II*.[185] It thus bases the ineffectiveness of the clause infringing Article 102 TFEU on the direct effect of this provision.

(2) The same approach can be found in English case law.

High Court of Justice Queen's Bench Division,
23 March 2007[186]   **2.48 (UK)**

English, Welsh and Scottish Railway Ltd v E.ON UK plc

LEGAL BASIS OF NULLITY

Abusive railway haulage contracts

Given the direct effect of Article 102 TFEU, clauses contrary to this provision are null and void

Facts: The claimant (EWS) was an operator of bulk rail freight services. The defendant (E.ON) was in the business of electricity generation. The claimant and the defendant entered into a Coal Carriage Agreement (CCA). Under the CCA, E.ON was obliged to use EWS to carry all coal which E.ON required to be moved to one of a number of specified power stations from one of a number of specified 'Supply Points', subject to certain exclusions (clauses 4.2 and 4.3). The first exclusion allowed E.ON under certain circumstances to use another haulier for carriage from new supply points. The second is an 'English' clause that entitled E.ON to use another coal haulier if EWS did not match that haulier's quote (clause 4.3(d)). The third allowed E.ON to use other hauliers for up to eight per cent of its remaining coal (clause 4.3(f)). Additional power stations and Supply Points can be added to those already specified if a notification procedure is complied with and the parties reach agreement, thereby extending the reach of clause 4.2 (clauses 5.4 and 6.1). Clauses 4.2, 4.3, 5.4 and 6.1 are referred to hereafter as 'the exclusionary terms'.

In 2006, the Office of Rail Regulation (ORR) found that EWS had infringed (now) Article 102 TFEU and its national equivalent (the Chapter II prohibition contained in section 18 of the Competition Act 1998), *inter alia* by entering into and maintaining the exclusionary terms of the CCA. The ORR required the contracting parties to remove or modify certain offending contractual provisions in the CCA, which they did not do.

Since the CCA was financially unfavourable to EWS, it asked a court to rule that the CCA was void and unenforceable. However, E.ON claimed that neither the breach of (now) Article 102 TFEU nor the ORR's decision had the automatic effect of voiding the CCA. The ORR submitted that the relevant terms of the CCA were illegal and void 'as a matter of public law', because of the direct effect of Article 102 and by reason of Article 1(3) of Regulation 1/2003.

Held: The exclusionary terms of the agreement are void.

---

[185] *cf* CJ *BRT II* (n 182) 51.

[186] *English, Welsh and Scottish Railway* (n 34). See also A Jones, 'The UK High Court of Justice Rules that, Although Art. 82 EC Does Not Contain a Declaration of Nullity Equivalent to Art. 81 EC, the Effect is the Same (English Welsh & Scottish Railway/E.ON)' (2007) *e-Competitions Bulletin March*, no 13379.

Judgment: 26. I agree with Mr Turner's submission that given: (i) the ORR's findings; (ii) Article 1.3 of Council Regulation 1/2003; and (iii) the direct effect of [now Article 102 TFEU], the exclusionary terms were illegal as a matter of public law from the moment the CCA was executed. And from 1 March 2000, when Chapter II of the Act came into effect, the exclusionary terms were doubly illegal for being in breach of the Chapter II prohibition. The consequence is that from the time the CCA was executed the exclusionary terms have been void. The Directions to remove the terms are an administrative measure to ensure that the CCA is brought within the law.

Notes:

(1) E.ON appealed to the Competition Appeal Tribunal (CAT), but the proceedings were stayed and no judgment was given.

(2) The decision seems to contradict the CJ's decision in *Ahmed Saeed Flugreisen*.[187] However, it must be admitted that *Ahmed Saeed* preceded the entry into force of Regulation 1/2003 which provides in its Article 1(3): 'The abuse of a dominant position referred to in [now Article 102 TFEU] shall be prohibited, no prior decision to that effect being required.' Yet, this article does not explicitly provide that legal acts which infringe Article 102 are void.

(3) The UK High Court held in a later case: 'The EWS case is no doubt an important decision as to the consequences of a breach of [now Article 102 TFEU] where the infringing action consists of the party with the dominant position entering into a contract with a third party. The decision did not, however, involve the court in construing words such as those that appear in [now Article 101(2) TFEU], because no such words appear in [now Article 102 TFEU]. Further, the [CJ] said in *Ciments et Bétons* that the consequences of automatic voidness of a contract which infringes [now Article 101(1) TFEU] for any orders or deliveries made on the basis of that agreement is not a matter for [EU] law but is a matter for national law.'[188]

Helsingin hovioikeus (Helsinki Court of Appeal),
30 June 2011[189]   **2.49 (FI)**

Teosto v Imatran Kylpylä Oy and others

LEGAL BASIS OF NULLITY

Price increases by the Finnish collection society

A clause infringing Article 102 TFEU and its national equivalent is void because a specific provision of the (old) Finnish Competition Act declares clauses infringing the national equivalent of Article 102 TFEU to be void

Facts: Teosto was the Finnish copyright organisation for composers, lyric writers, arrangers and music publishers. It had a factual monopoly in providing licences to perform and reproduce copyrighted music. In 2006,

---

[187] CJ *Ahmed Saeed Flugreisen* (n 183).

[188] *Bookmakers Afternoon Greyhound Services Ltd and others v Amalgamated Racing Ltd and others* [2008] EWHC 1978 (Ch). See also: http://judgmental.org.uk/judgments/EWHC-Ch/2008/[2008]_EWHC_1978_(Ch).html.

[189] Helsinki Court of Appeal 30 June 2011 no S 08/2682 *Teosto v Imatran Kylpylä Oy et al.* See also: http://ec.europa.eu/competition/antitrust/national_courts/1356744.pdf.

it introduced a new more uniform pricing model which resulted in a significant price increase for restaurants. A number of hotels and restaurants filed a claim seeking a declaratory judgment that they owed money to Teosto only according to a lower self-determined rate. Teosto filed a counter-claim seeking a declaratory judgment that it was entitled to payments in accordance with its new pricing model. The District Court rejected both claims. The hotels' and restaurants' claim was rejected because the court did not want to declare the rate they proposed to be correct. Teosto's counter-claim was rejected because the court found that the new pricing model amounted to an abuse of dominant market position under Finnish competition law and that the grounds for the payments Teosto demanded from the restaurants were null and void. Both the restaurants and Teosto appealed.

Held: The Helsinki Court of Appeal upheld the District Court's judgment adding that Article 102 TFEU was also breached.

Judgment: The payments from Imatran Kylpylä Oy and its co-parties ... referred to in the claim of Teosto are, as to their grounds and amounts, null and void on the basis of §18 of the Finnish Act on Competition Restrictions.

Notes:

(1) According to the Court of Appeal, Teosto abused its dominant position in applying the new uniform royalty system to firms falling within the previous restaurant category. Therefore, Teosto was precluded from implementing its new royalty system and from recovering the additional royalties resulting therefrom.

(2) While there was a breach of the national and EU prohibition of abuse of a dominant position, the voidness is only based on an infringement of the then applicable national competition act.[190]

(3) The case did not comprise any claims for refund of money paid to Teosto or for damages.

Article L.420-3 of the Consumer Code   **2.50 (FR)**

Any undertaking, agreement or contractual clause referring to a practice prohibited by Articles L. 420-1, L. 420-2 and L. 420-2-1 shall be invalid.

Notes:

(1) Under French competition law, the sanction of nullity thus relates both to prohibited agreements and to abuse of dominance. Given the need for the consistent application of EU and national competition law, French courts would have to apply this rule mutatis mutandis to agreements, contracts or contractual clauses infringing Article 102 TFEU if they were to find that the nullity of agreements or decisions infringing this Article would not automatically follow from the direct effect of the Article itself.

(2) If courts in other Member States held the opinion that the nullity of agreements or decisions infringing Article 102 TFEU does not follow from the Article itself, they would generally conclude that such agreements or decisions are void anyway based on the general rules of contract law or of legal acts. The rules of civil law of the Member States do indeed contain in general a provision holding that contracts and/or other legal acts infringing statute law and/or public order are void. See, eg, Article 3:40 BW.

---

[190] See on this case N Fagerlund case no 2215; S 08/2682 OCL 126 (FI 2011).

High Court of Justice Queen's Bench Division,
23 March 2007[191]   **2.51 (UK)**

English, Welsh and Scottish Railway Ltd v E.ON UK plc

IMPACT OF NULLITY AS A CONSEQUENCE OF INFRINGEMENT OF
ARTICLE 102 TFEU ON THE REMAINDER OF THE AGREEMENT

Abusive railway haulage contracts (repeated)

*The impact of nullity of a contract clause on the remainder of the contract is similar under
Articles 101 and 102 TFEU*

Facts: See case 2.48 (UK) above. In 2006, the Office of Rail Regulation (ORR) found that, contrary to (now) Article 102 TFEU and its national equivalent (the Chapter II prohibition contained in section 18 of the Competition Act 1998), EWS had abused its dominant position, *inter alia* by entering into and maintaining the exclusionary terms of the CCA.

Held: The effect of the ORR's decision issued on 17 November 2006 was that the exclusionary terms were void and since those clauses cannot be severed, the whole of the CCA is void and unenforceable.

Judgment: 27. Where terms are void at common law for being in restraint of trade or by reason of [now Article 102 TFEU] and the Chapter I prohibition, the courts apply the doctrine of severance to determine if the offending terms can be severed from the contract leaving the residue to continue to operate as an enforceable contract; see eg *Crehan v Courage Limited; Byrne v Inntreprenneur Beer Supply Co Ltd* [1999] EuLR 834 at 896E–901A. In my judgement, exactly the same approach applies where a term or terms of a contract are void by reason of being in breach of [now Article 102 TFEU] and the Chapter II prohibition. It is thus not a question of whether the contract is frustrated but whether the test for severance as formulated in the cases has been satisfied.

28. The Court of Appeal in *Crehan v Courage* rehearsed various formulations of the severance test propounded over the years without identifying which, if any, was to be preferred. These included: (i) whether the invalid restraint formed the whole or substantially the whole consideration for the promise; (ii) whether the contract would be so changed in its character as not to be the sort of contract that the parties intended to enter at all; (iii) whether what was unenforceable was part of the main purpose and substance, or whether the deletion altered entirely the scope and intention of the agreement or, on the contrary, left the rest of the agreement a reasonable arrangement between the parties; (iv) whether it would disappoint the main purposes of one of the main parties; and (v) whether the agreement was in substance an agreement for an invalid restraint.

29. Mr Sharpe conceded that if the doctrine of severance applied, the CCA without the exclusionary terms would be of a fundamentally different nature. In my judgement this concession was well made. Accordingly, subject to the true effect of clause 34 of the CCA, there can be no severance of the exclusionary terms and the whole contract is void and unenforceable. As to this latter point, the Court of Appeal in *Richard Ground Ltd v (GB) Ltd* [1997] EuLR 277 upheld the finding of the first instance judge that a clause in substantially similar words to clause 34 was ineffective to allow severance where the resulting contract would not be the sort of contract that the parties intended to enter at all. Unsurprisingly, Mr Sharpe accepted that in the light of this decision clause 34 did not allow for severance where the common law test was not satisfied.

---

[191] *English, Welsh and Scottish Railway* (n 34). See also Jones (n 186).

Conclusion

30. For the reasons given above, EWS is entitled to a declaration the substance of which is that the effect of the ORR's Decision issued on 17 November 2006 and the Directions contained therein is that clauses 4.2, 4.3, 5.4 and 6.1 of the CCA have from the inception of the contract been void and since those clauses cannot be severed the whole of the CCA is void and unenforceable.

II.C INJUNCTIONS AND INTERIM RELIEF

II.C.i GENERAL OVERVIEW

Private enforcement is all too often assimilated these days with actions, launched under national law, for damages for infringement of national or EU competition law. Damages actions are what Directive 2014/104/EU[192] currently aims to promote, and they will be analysed in section II.D below. However, whereas the 2004 Ashurst Report which started the EC's drive for promotion of damages actions found the EU to be in a position of 'astonishing diversity and total underdevelopment' in relation to such damages actions,[193] Europe has a much longer tradition of injunctive relief in competition matters.

There is no harmonisation at the EU level of injunctive relief. This may make for 'astonishing diversity', but there is certainly no 'total underdevelopment' of this remedy.

Under the principle of procedural 'autonomy' (procedural competence), national legal systems will determine whether a private party can claim injunctive relief and, if so, in what form and under which conditions,[194] subject to the conditions of equivalence and effectiveness. The conditions as to both the substance and the procedure laid down by national law may not be less favourable than those relating to similar domestic claims (equivalence), and Member States have to ensure that the conditions to obtain remedies do not render it virtually impossible or overly difficult to exercise the rights that are granted under EU law (effectiveness).

Injunctions can be negative (prohibitory) or positive. They can be permanent or are granted by way of interim relief, which is more common. There is indeed a strong link between injunctive relief and interim relief, which is one of four EU law remedies (next to the remedies of setting aside, restitution and compensation).[195]

Bellamy & Child, European Union Law of Competition[196]

Injunctive relief. The EU courts have had little opportunity to assess the conditions for the grant of injunctions to bring to an end, and prevent, infringements of Articles 101(1)

---

[192] [2014] OJ L349/1 (n 6).

[193] D Waelbroek, D Slater and G Even-Shoshan, *Study on the Conditions of Claims for Damages in Case of Infringement of EC Competition Rules* (Brussels, Ashurst, 31 August 2004). See also: ec.europa.eu/competition/antitrust/actionsdamages/comparative_report_clean_en.pdf.

[194] For an overview, see C Cauffman, 'Injunctions at the Request of Third Parties in EU Competition Law' (2010) *MJ* 58.

[195] W van Gerven, 'Of Rights, Remedies and Procedures' (2000) 37(30) *CMLR* 501.

[196] Rose and Baily (n 143) nos 16.058, 16.059 and 16.061, footnotes omitted.

and/or 102. However, in the light of the requirement for effective private enforcement confirmed in *Courage v Crehan*, injunctive relief should as a matter of EU law be available to anyone suffering loss—or threatened with such loss—as a consequence of anticompetitive conduct. Such relief may be more relevant and effective on an interim basis than on a final determination.

Test for interim injunction is a matter for national law. In *Pharma Lab v Glaxosmithkline*, the French Cour de Cassation considered the question whether, in a claim for interim measures, the test to be applied was the test which the EU Commission applies in deciding whether to grant interim measures under Article 8 of Regulation 1/2003 or whether French case law applied … The Cour de Cassation … held that … the national authorities should apply their own national procedural rules unless that would make it impossible or more difficult to implement EU competition law …

Mandatory injunctions. Mandatory interim injunctions carry a risk of injustice in that they require the respondent to take a positive step rather than to refrain from doing something. … Applications for mandatory injunctions often arise in cases where the alleged infringement of Article 102 is a refusal to supply. …[197]

S Peyer, 'Injunctive Relief and Private Antitrust Enforcement'[198]

The principles of effectiveness and equivalence order the national courts to award damages for the violation of the EU antitrust statutes. Provided that a national legal system arranges for injunctions for violations of national competition law, the same must apply when EU antitrust rules are breached. Whether the principle of effectiveness requires injunctive relief for the violation of EU competition law if the law of a Member State does not permit, or only in limited circumstances allows, the use of injunctive relief for breaches of national statutory provisions is a different matter. European law does not give an answer to this problem but the strong stance the CJ took in *Courage* and *Manfredi* may suggest that injunctions could be available with a similar rationale …

Applying this rationale, one could argue that the national courts should not reject an application for injunctive relief based on the infringement of Articles 101 or 102 if the denial would make it particularly difficult for the victim to enforce his rights. Instead, the injunction ought to be granted according to the principle of effectiveness to safeguard the directly applicable EU rights.

Although the CFI did not specify the available types of injunctions, the statement of the Advocate General Edward in *Automec* as for the character of injunctive relief implies that claimants can seek more than just a prohibitory injunction. He characterised *Automec's* request as a 'positive injunction' although only in the context of the EC's (non-existing) powers to grant such an injunction. Since *Automec* requested the EC to do something, this positive injunction was a claim for mandatory injunctive relief. In the absence of a final ruling (on a preliminary reference) but with regards to the stance the CJ took on injunctive relief in *Automec*, one could argue that EU law requires the existence and provision of prohibitory or mandatory permanent injunctions in the laws of the Member States.

---

[197] ibid 1238–39.
[198] S Peyer, 'Injunctive Relief and Private Antitrust Enforcement' (2011) *CCP Working Papers* 11-7, 10-11, footnotes omitted.

II.C.ii THE DIVISION OF POWERS BETWEEN THE EC AND THE NATIONAL COURTS

According to the EC, 'national courts are usually better placed than the EC to adopt interim measures'.[199] There appears to be a double reason why injunctive relief in competition cases, especially in the form of interim relief, is so popular at the national level (and therefore of importance in this casebook), even in cases of breach of EU competition law provisions.

First, private parties may choose to turn to national judges for interim relief as they have no right to claim interim relief from the EC. Second, national judges can grant *positive* injunctions, whereas in *Automec*,[200] the GC ruled that the EC does not have that power. We will briefly expand on both reasons.

II.C.ii.a Interim Relief in EU Competition Matters: Access to a National Judge But Not Necessarily to the EC

In *Camera Care*, the CJ established the power of the EC to order interim measures in relation to a suspected infringement of Articles 101 and 102 TFEU.[201] In order to do so, the EC has to prove a prima facie competition law infringement and urgency due to the risk of serious and irreparable harm to competition. In addition, the interim measures must be of a 'temporary and conservatory nature and restricted to what is required in the given situation' and must take into account 'the legitimate interests of the undertaking concerned'.[202]

In its judgment in *Camera Care*, the CJ made no distinction between different forms of injunctions, but it is interesting to note that the interim measure applied for was a positive injunction ('to make supplies').

Article 8(1) of Regulation 1/2003[203] codified this case law by explicitly empowering the EC to adopt interim measures. The decision to do so is now the sole right of the EC.[204] Regulation 1/2003 does not formally acknowledge the right of private parties to make requests for interim measures; private parties only have the possibility to *encourage* the

---

[199] Commission Notice on the handling of complaints by the EC under Articles 81 and 82 of the EC Treaty [2004] OJ C101/65, paras 16 and 80.

[200] GC *Automec* (n 12).

[201] CJ 17 January 1980 Case C-792/79 *Camera Care v Commission of the European Communities* [1980] I-00119 ECLI:EU:C:1980:18, paras 17–18. The power to adopt interim measures was not explicitly granted in the Treaty or in the EEC Council Regulation No 17 of 6 February 1962 (First Regulation implementing Articles 85 and 86 of the Treaty [1962] OJ 13/204). However, the CJ held that it stemmed from the tasks conferred upon the EC by the Treaty and Regulation No 17. The EC has since made full use of its powers; see, eg, Commission Decision 83/462/EEC of 29 July 1983 relating to a proceeding under Article 86 of the EEC Treaty (IV/30.698—*ECS/AKZO*: interim measures) [1983] OJ L252/13.

[202] CJ *Camera Care* (n 201) para 19. *cf*, eg, GC 24 January 1992 Case T-44/90 *La Cinq SA v Commission of the European Communities* [1992] II-00001 ECLI:EU:T:1992:5, paras 32–96.

[203] 'In cases of urgency due to the risk of serious and irreparable damage to competition, the Commission, acting on its own initiative may by decision, on the basis of a prima facie finding of infringement, order interim measures.' Council Regulation (EC) No 1/2003 of 16 December 2002 on the implementation of the rules on competition laid down in Articles 81 and 82 of the Treaty, OJ L 1/1, 4 January 2003.

[204] See Antitrust Manual of Procedures, *Internal DG Competition Working Documents on Procedures for the Application of Articles 101 and 102 TFEU*, March 2012. See also: http://ec.europa.eu/competition/antitrust/information_en.html.

EC to adopt such measures.[205] In this regard, one also observes an interesting evolution of the stated *ratio* for interim relief. In *Camera Care*, the CJ declared that interim measures are needed in certain circumstances, *inter alia* where a practice is 'causing damage to other undertakings'.[206] Regulation 1/2003 limits the ratio to the public interest, and no longer mentions the interest of individual undertakings.

II.C.ii.b Positive Injunctions Can Only Be Granted by National Judges

In its *Automec* judgment, the GC effectively denied the EC power to issue a positive injunction on the following grounds:

> [Now Article 101(1) TFEU] prohibits certain anticompetitive agreements or practices. Among the consequences which an infringement of that prohibition may have in civil law, only one is expressly provided for in [now Article 101(2) TFEU], namely the nullity of the agreement. The other consequences attaching to an infringement of [now Article 101 TFEU], such as the obligation to make good the damage caused to a third party or a possible obligation to enter into a contract … are to be determined under national law. Consequently, it is the national courts which, where appropriate, may, in accordance with the rules of national law, order one trader to enter into a contract with another.[207]

As a consequence, private parties that wish to obtain a positive injunction against an alleged infringer of competition law have to address a national judge. The case law that will be discussed in the following chapter will mostly illustrate the award of positive injunctions by national courts.

II.C.iii NATIONAL CASE LAW

Voorzitter Rechtbank van Koophandel Brussel (President Commercial Court Brussels), 12 February 2002[208]   **2.52 (BE)**

Sourcepower SA v Elia SA

INTERIM INJUNCTION

Dominant undertaking lacking in Christmas spirit

A positive injunction is granted against an electricity network operator which is found to abuse its dominant position

Facts: In the summer of 2001, a new entrant sought access to the Belgian electricity transmission network from 1 January 2002 onwards. The transmission system operator (Elia) sent the new entrant the contracts used in 2001 and stated that the 2002 contracts would be very similar. It did not, however, send the actual contract for 2002 until 18 December 2001 (after 6 pm) indicating that if access was required as of 1 January 2002, the contract needed to be signed by 20 December 2001. Moreover, a bank guarantee of €1,975,000 was to be provided by 15 January 2002. The new entrant sought an injunction from the President of the Commercial

---

[205] A. Nordsjo, 'Regulation 1/2003: Power of the Commission to Adopt Interim Measures' (2006) 27(6) *ECLR* 300.

[206] CJ *Camera Care* (n 201) para 14.

[207] GC *Automec* (n 12) para 50.

[208] President Commercial Court Brussels 12 February 2002 *JLMB* 2002, 1146 *Sourcepower SA v Elia SA*.

Court asking him to order the defendant to grant access to the network even though the bank guarantee was not provided within the time set, and to provide for a period of at least 12 weeks for the parties to negotiate a reasonable guarantee.

Held: The injunction was granted on the basis that the behaviour of the defendant constituted an abuse of dominant position.

Judgment: Consequently, the behaviour of the defendant constitutes an abuse of a dominant position on his part and on the part of *Electrabel*,[209] in so far as the defendant creates an unjustified obstacle to the network access by imposing contractual requirements that cannot, in such a short time, be fulfilled by the claimant, who intends to enter the Belgian market as a new competitor of *Electrabel*;
… Order the defendant to grant the claimant access to the electricity transport network, despite the absence of an established bank guarantee payable on first demand within the deadlines imposed by the defendant.

Notes:

(1) The judgment provides an example of a positive injunction granted by way of interim relief. According to the Court's President, excessive contractual demands to be fulfilled within very short time limits create barriers to entry. The President granted 16 weeks to negotiate a bank guarantee. In the meantime, the defendant was ordered to grant the claimant access to its electricity transport network. Under the EU *Automec* case law, the claimant might not have been able to obtain similar relief from the EC.

(2) This was not the first case where the Belgian courts granted positive injunctions to new entrants seeking protection from the anticompetitive practices of dominant operators. In *Lookdata v Belgacom*,[210] new entrant Lookdata claimed that telecoms incumbent Belgacom had unilaterally and abusively changed the terms of their contract by restricting Lookdata's access to specific telephone data in order to commercially exploit these data. The court held that Belgacom had abused its dominant position and granted an injunction, ordering Belgacom to provisionally give access to the detailed telephone data, as was the case under the original contract.

(3) Similarly, in the Austrian case *Westbahn v ÖBB*, an abuse of dominance by the incumbent railroad operator allegedly obstructed entry into the market by Westbahn, a new entrant in the market of passenger railway traffic. Westbahn filed a petition for interim measures against ÖBB, which had refused to include Westbahn's railway services in their printed railway guides, online journey planners and information hotline. In 2011, the Cartel Court of Vienna (*Kartellgericht Wien*) granted interim relief on the grounds that ÖBB had prima facie abused its dominant position on the market for journey planning media.[211] It ordered ÖBB to fully include the services offered by the new entrant.[212] *Rekurs* (cassation) against the first instance judgment was rejected.[213]

---

[209] *Electrabel* was the incumbent in the market for electricity supply.
[210] Interim proceedings before the Commercial Court Brussels 14 January 1997 *JT dr eur* 1997, 141 *Lookdata v Belgacom*.
[211] See: http://ec.europa.eu/competition/ecn/brief/01_2012/at_railway.pdf.
[212] Austrian Cartel Court of Vienna 28 November 2011 no GZ 26 Kt 70-72/11-21.
[213] Austrian Supreme Court 11 October 2012 no 16Ok1/12.

High Court of Justice Chancery Division,
21 December 2005[214]   **2.53 (UK)**

Attheraces Ltd v The British Horseracing Board Ltd

INTERIM INJUNCTION

Place your bets?

Under the 'balance of convenience' test, an interim injunction is granted to avoid potential losses which cannot be compensated in money

Facts: At the races (ATR) supplied websites, television channels and other audiovisual media with data on British horse racing, to be used by bookmakers and customers. The pre-race data ATR supplies were ultimately derived from British Horseracing Board's (BHB) database. ATR accused BHB of seeking to unilaterally impose its terms for the supply of the pre-race data. BHB indeed threatened to terminate the supply of pre-race date to ATR. This supply was handled by PA News (PA), to whom BHB contractually conferred the distribution of pre-race data to the end-users. Under the contractual agreement, PA was obliged to discontinue any supply after BHB reported that the end-user did not have the required licence. ATR claimed that BHB had abused its dominant position in the supply of UK pre-race data by an unreasonable refusal to supply, excessive and unfair pricing, and discriminatory pricing. ATR applied for an interim injunction.

Held: The High Court granted an interim injunction until judgment on the merits.

Judgment: 65 If no interim injunction is granted then the supply of pre-race data by PA to ATR will be stopped. It is essential to the conduct of its business because although similar data can be taken from the newspapers it is by no means necessarily up to date; up to date and accurate information is crucial to bookmakers and punters alike. I do not think that the loss of business so caused could be properly compensated in money.

66 Thus the balance of convenience as well as maintenance of the status quo both favour the grant of an injunction. There is no reason why such an injunction should encourage others to follow the example of ATR because ATR will be required to pay out that for which they are prospectively liable if they lose. But I remain concerned that BHB is not kept out of the money for any longer than may be necessary if, in the event, it is shown by the judgment at trial that it is entitled to it.

Notes:

(1) In this case, the High Court held that there was a serious issue to be tried and that it would be difficult to properly compensate ATR in money if ATR were not supplied with pre-race data. On the balance of convenience (see next note), the High Court granted the injunction, provided ATR continued to adequate payments pending judgment. On the merits of the case, the High Court subsequently determined that BHB had abused its dominant position. On appeal, this finding of an infringement was overturned in 2007.[215]

(2) The test applied in the UK in order to determine whether interim measures will be ordered is threefold. The court must be convinced of the following *facts:* a serious question is to be tried, damages are not an adequate remedy and the so-called 'balance

---

[214] *Attheraces Ltd v The British Horseracing Board Ltd* [2005] EWHC 1553, paras 65–66.
[215] *Attheraces Ltd v The British Horseracing Board Ltd* [2007] EWCA Civ 38; [2007] UKCLR 309; [2007] BusLR D77.

of convenience' lies in favour of granting interim measures.[216] In case of positive injunctions, the test will be stricter and require a significant, strong and clear case.[217]

(3) At the EU level, the EC needs to prove a prima facie competition law infringement to issue interim measures. This is different in the UK. In order to fulfil the first condition, no prima facie infringement needs to be established.[218] It will be sufficient to satisfy the court by demonstrating that a serious question is brought before it.

(4) Interim injunctions are not easily granted under English law. For another successful application, see *Dahabshiil v Barclays Bank* below. However, in *Intecare Direct Ltd v Pfizer*,[219] a healthcare provider's application for an interim injunction in order to compel a pharmaceutical company to provide it with a certain drug was rejected. The court held that the healthcare provider had failed to establish that it would succeed at trial in proving that the pharmaceutical company was abusing its dominant position in relation to the supply of that drug. An important factor in this case was the fact that the court was very unhappy with the late application of the claimants:

> It is extraordinary for the court to be faced with an application of this complexity in relation to proposals which have been well-known both publicly and to the claimants for several months. It is a strong thing for the court to interfere by interim injunction in the conduct of business, particularly on the scale proposed in this case. By depriving the defendants and the court of the proper opportunity of dealing with this application, *the delay greatly increases the risk of injustice if an injunction is granted*. The fact that the claimants chose to pursue their complaints with the OFT and to persist in doing so until the very last moment does not in my judgment provide a good ground for not bringing the matter before the court at a much earlier stage.

Also in *Chemistree Homecare v Abbvie*,[220] the English Court of Appeal rejected a claim for interim measures. *Chemistree* alleged that the reduction in supplies was an abuse of a dominant position. The High Court refused Chemistree's application for an interim measure, as it failed to establish that a serious question needed to be tried. This was later confirmed by the Court of Appeal, which, applying the 'SSNIP' test,[221] held that Chemistree had failed to identify any relevant product market on which Abbvie could conceivably be dominant.

(5) *Arriva The Shires Ltd v London Luton Airport Operations Ltd* concerned an exclusive coach concession at Luton Airport, for the service between the airport and Victoria Station. After Luton Airport had tendered out the bus service in early 2013, coach operator Arriva lost the concession which it had held for 30 years. Arriva then argued that the terms of the concession and the tendering process amounted to an abuse of dominance by Luton Airport, and sought an interim injunction which would allow it to continue to run the service pending a full trial. There was an interlocutory hearing on interim relief in 2013, but such relief was denied as the balance of convenience demonstrated no need for an interim

---

[216] *American Cyanamid v Ethicon* [1975] 2 WLR 316; [1975] AC 396; [1975] UKHL 1.
[217] *Leisure Data v Bell* [1987] Court of Appeal [1988] FSR 367.
[218] *American Cyanamid v Ethicon* (n 216).
[219] *Intecare Direct Ltd v Pfizer* [2010] EWHC 600 (Ch).
[220] *Chemistree Homecare v Abbvie* [2013] EWHC 264.
[221] SSNIP = small but significant non-transitory increase in price. Under this test, a hypothetical monopolist raises its prices by a small but significant amount (five per cent) on a permanent basis. If consumers switch to other products, these other products are substitutable and should be included in the relevant product market.

injunction.[222] Damages would suffice as a remedy if it became clear that the airport had actually abused its dominant position. However, the competent judge did rule that the full trial should be expedited and that the issues to be covered at the trial should be agreed between the parties. The parties agreed that Luton Airport effectively held a dominant position and in 2014 the High Court in London found that the exclusion of Arriva from accessing the bus station at the airport amounted to an abuse of this dominant position.

England and Wales High Court (Chancery Division),
5 November 2013[223]

2.54 (UK)

Dahabshiil v Barclays Bank

INTERIM INJUNCTION

Abuse by termination

A bank which terminates business relationships with a smaller business may be found to abuse its dominant position; the 'balance of convenience' favours an interim injunction against the bank

Facts: Dahabshiil was a money service business (MSB) enabling money transfers to and from people living in Somalia. An MSB was a very risky customer for a bank to have, since some of these types of businesses can be fronts for money laundering and terrorism financing.

In order to reduce its exposure to litigation risks, Barclays Bank ran an internal review in late 2012 and early 2013. After this review, it decided to terminate its contract with some MSBs, including Dahabshiil. Dahabshiil subsequently sued Barclays Bank to obtain an interim injunction in order to continue running its business.

Held: The interim injunction was granted.

Judgment: 73 I can deal with this part of the case much more briefly. It may at first sight seem counter-intuitive that a party in a dominant position in a market can abuse that dominant position by seeking to reduce its participation in it. This point is duly made by Mr Overd in his expert evidence on behalf of Barclays … On the other hand, there is at least some authority that a dominant undertaking may commit an abuse where, without justification, it cuts off supplies of goods or services to an existing customer: see *Jobserve* at paragraph [9], and the opinion of Advocate General Jacobs in *Case C-7/97, Oscar Bronner GmbH & Co. AG v Mediaprint Zeitungs-und Zeitschriftenverlag GmbH & Co. AG and others* [1999] 4 C.M.L.R. 112 at paragraph [43] of his Opinion. This is a question of law for determination at trial. I am satisfied that it is not suitable for summary determination.

76 Again, I can deal with this part of the case briefly. In the light of the evidence, it seems to me all but self-evident that damages would not be an adequate remedy for any of the claimants, and that the balance of convenience favours the grant rather than the refusal of interim relief. There is a far greater danger of irremediable prejudice to the claimants in refusing the grant of injunctions until trial than there would be in granting the injunctions. As matters now stand, the alternative banking arrangements that Dahabshiil has been able to make are far more limited than those previously provided by Barclays, and the arrangements made with Moneycorp may be precarious. As for Harada

---

[222] *Arriva The Shires Ltd v London Luton Airport Operations Ltd* [2014] EWHC 64 (Ch). The interlocutory hearing is discussed in para 6 of the judgment on the merits.
[223] *Dahabshiil v Barclays Bank* [2013] EWHC 3379 (Ch).

and BCG, they have been unable to find any bank willing to offer them standard banking facilities, and the refusal of an injunction would on the face of it either force them out of business or compel a merger with a competitor which still has banking facilities. Conversely, the grant of an injunction will require Barclays to do no more than continue providing banking services to established customers with impeccable records. I bear in mind Mr Reid's evidence that some concerns have been expressed within Barclays about Dahabshiil; but those concerns have never been raised with Dahabshiil, so Dahabshiil has not had an not opportunity to answer them. On the face of it, the continued provision of banking services to the claimants will be profitable to Barclays, albeit probably not at the level set by the review. In the unlikely event that Barclays suffers any loss as a result of the injunction, all three claimants are willing to offer the usual cross-undertaking in damages. In their skeleton argument, counsel for Barclays assert that there is 'a very real question mark' over the ability of the claimants to satisfy a cross-undertaking in damages. I heard no oral argument on this question. If it remains a live issue, it can be raised when this judgment is handed down.

Notes:

(1) *Dahabshiil v Barclays Bank* concerned a withdrawal of banking services to the claimants. The claimant alleged that Barclays' termination of banking services amounted to an abuse of a dominant position and that, in the absence of an alternative bank willing to offer it services, this would force Dahabshiil to cease its activity. The court ruled that Barclays' withdrawing from the market might constitute an abuse of dominance, but this should be determined during further trial. However, the court also found that the claimant had a serious question to be tried. As no other bank was found willing to provide banking services to the claimant, Dahabshiil faced the possibility of having to cease its activity if Barclays did not continue to provide banking services. The court found that the balance of convenience favoured interim measures, as damages would not be sufficient to compensate Dahabshiil if the injunction would not be granted. It issued an injunction requiring the continued supply of banking services pending trial.

(2) The judgment appears to be in line with what the EU courts define as 'irreparable' damage. According to the GC and the CJ, damage is 'irreparable' if it leads to market developments that will be very difficult to reverse.[224] This will also be the case if damage can no longer be remedied by a subsequent decision during the administrative procedure before the EC.[225]

Under EU law, financial loss is in general not regarded as irreparable unless the survival of the undertaking concerned is threatened. The fact that an undertaking is forced to request the opening of an insolvency procedure can constitute a serious and 'irreparable' harm.[226] However, the mere existence of an insolvency procedure will not suffice if it does not impede an undertaking to pursue its economic activity.[227]

---

[224] See, eg, GC T-184/01 R *IMS Health v Commission* [2001] II-3193 ECLI:EU:T:2001:259, paras 121–33.

[225] As a consequence, damage may be held to be 'irreparable' even if it can be repaired by a judgment of either a national or an EU court. See GC *La Cinq SA* (n 202) paras 79–80. See also Nordsjo (n 205) 302.

[226] Order of the President of the CJEU 14 December 1999 Case C-335/99P (R) *HFB Holding für Fern-wärmetechnik Beteiligungsgesellschaft mbH & Co KG et al v Commission of the European Communities* [1999] I-018705 ECLI:EU:C:1999:608, paras 56–58.

[227] GC 14 March 2008 Case T-440/07 R *Huta Buczek v Commission of the European Communities* [2008] II-00039 ECLI:EU:T:2008:77, paras 47–50 (summary).

(3) Common law resists attempts to conceptualize the 'balance of convenience' test, once again decisive in *Dahabshiil*. The 1975 statement of Lord Diplock in *American Cyanamid*[228] still fully applies:

> It is where there is doubt as to the adequacy of the respective remedies in damages available to either party or to both, that the question of balance of convenience arises. It would be unwise to attempt even to list all the various matters which may need to be taken into consideration in deciding where the balance lies, let alone to suggest the relative weight to be attached to them. These will vary from case to case.

In other words, the decision of where the balance lies is left to the discretion of the judge.

(4) In April 2014, the *Dahabshiil v Barclays* dispute was settled.

II.D DAMAGES

II.D.i OVERVIEW

Introductory Notes

1. No other aspect of private enforcement of competition law has attracted so much public attention recently as the actions for damages for infringements of competition law. For the past 15 years, since the seminal CJ judgment in *Courage v Crehan*, the EC has actively promoted the private enforcement of competition law through damages actions.

The different stages in the process are well known. The EC issued a Green Paper with rather radical ideas (double damages, common law-style discovery) in 2005[229] and a much more moderate White Paper in 2008.[230] In 2009 a Proposal for a Directive was widely circulated, although it was not officially made public. In 2010, a study on the quantification of antitrust damages was published with guidance to national courts,[231] followed in 2011 by a Draft Guidance Paper on the issue.[232] In 2011, the EC launched a public consultation on collective redress[233] leading to a Recommendation[234] and a Communication[235] in 2013.

---

[228] *American Cyanamid Co v Ethicon Ltd* (n 216).

[229] Commission Green Paper on Damages Actions for Breach of the EC Antitrust Rules (COM(2005) 672 final), accompanied by Commission Staff Working Paper, Annex to the Green Paper on Damages Actions for Breach of the EC Antitrust Rules (SEC(2005) 1732).

[230] Commission White Paper on Damages Actions for Breach of the EC Antitrust Rules, COM(2008) 165 final, accompanied by Staff Working Paper Accompanying the White Paper on Damages Actions for Breach of the EC Antitrust Rules (SEC(2008) 404).

[231] Oxera, Komninos et al, *Quantifying Antitrust Damages: Towards Non-binding Guidance for Courts*, Study prepared for the European Commission, December 2009. Available at: http://ec.europa.eu/competition/antitrust/actionsdamages/quantification_study.pdf.

[232] Draft Guidance Paper: Quantifying Harm in Actions for Damages Based on Breaches of Article 101 or 102 TFEU (Brussels, 2011).

[233] Commission Staff Working Document, Public Consultation: Towards a Coherent European Approach to Collective Redress (SEC(2011)173 final).

[234] Commission Recommendation 2013/396/EU of 11 June 2013 on common principles for injunctive and compensatory collective redress mechanisms in the Member States concerning violations of rights granted under Union Law [2013] OJ L201/60

[235] Communication from the EC to the European Parliament, the Council, the European Economic and Social Committee and the Committee of the Regions Towards a European Horizontal Framework for Collective Redress [2013] OJ C140/68.

This process culminated in the adoption on 26 November 2014 of Directive 2014/104/EU 'on certain rules governing actions for damages under national law for infringements of the competition law provisions of the Member States and of the European Union'[236] (hereinafter the Damages Directive).

Before starting the analysis of national case law, it seems appropriate to make the following general points about damages actions and the foreseeable impact of the Damages Directive thereupon.

2. As part of private enforcement of competition law, damages actions are fully complementary to public enforcement of competition law. Four differences appear between both enforcement techniques. Under public enforcement, EU or national (element 1) public authorities, usually administrative authorities (element 2), fine (or accept commitments, enter into settlements, ...) (element 3) and they do so in the public interest (element 4). Under private enforcement, national (element 1) judges (element 2), award damages (or declare null and void, or grant injunctive relief, etc) (element 3) to private parties acting in their private interest (element 4). The differences are substantial and exclude the application of *ne bis in idem*. They are not merely of an academic nature, but have practical consequences, as will be shown below. For example, when parties settle a conflict, they can agree to withdraw all private enforcement claims against each other, but they cannot withdraw their complaints with the EC or NCAs, as these are run in the public interest.

3. Although they are different, public and private enforcement impact upon each other. All actions taken under public enforcement should take private enforcement into account and vice versa. This appears already from the fact that most damages actions are nowadays not of the 'stand-alone' but of the 'follow-on' type, ie, damages are claimed after the EC or an NCA has already established (and fined) an infringement of competition law. Two other examples can illustrate the intricate link between public and private enforcement:

> The EC's Leniency Notice[237] and similar national leniency regimes grant conditional immunity to the first whistle-blower in a cartel, and a reduction of fines to cartelists who cooperate. Similarly, the EC's Settlement Notice and similar national settlement regimes grant a reduction of fines if parties to a cartel admit to an infringement. Leniency and settlement are part of public enforcement but have a direct impact on private enforcement. Leniency applicants and settling infringers are often the first to be exposed to private enforcement claims. As they admit to an infringement, a 'fault' under national tort law can more easily be established. There is a risk that the promotion of private enforcement effectively brings to a halt leniency and settlement programmes. Especially when harmed consumers or competitors obtain access to leniency statements or settlement notices, private enforcement risks to 'kill' leniency, which currently is the most successful tool for detection of cartelistic behaviour.

> The starting point of private enforcement litigation may depend on the arguments raised in public enforcement procedures. National judges may decide to suspend damages actions as long as the infringing undertakings challenge in court (typically before the GC or CJ in Luxembourg) the finding by the EC or by an NCA of a cartel infringement or an alleged abuse of dominance. If, on the other hand, alleged infringers only contest the *level of the fine* in a public enforcement

---

[236] [2014] OJ L349/1 (n 6).
[237] Commission Notice on immunity from fines and reduction of fines in cartel cases [2006] OJ C298/17.

case, national judges are seen to allow private enforcement damages claims to proceed in the national courts.

4. EU rules of international private law, which are not the focus of this chapter, allow for a certain degree of *forum shopping*.[238] As a consequence, damages actions are mostly concentrated in a limited number of jurisdictions (currently mainly in the UK, Germany and, to a lesser degree, the Netherlands, but this can quickly change). However, the close interaction between public and private enforcement, illustrated in note 2 above, makes the evolving European damages actions regime equally relevant for undertakings and enforcers in all European jurisdictions.

5. At least the following categories of legal questions typically arise in stand-alone and/ or follow-on damages actions:

— *Establishment of a fault*: does the mere infringement of the principled EU or national prohibition on restrictive practices and abuse of dominance qualify as a 'fault' under national tort law (to the extent that a fault is required under national tort law) or is a qualified infringement required? In a follow-on claim, is the finding of an infringement by the EC or an NCA binding on the national judge, to the extent that the national judge is obliged to recognise such finding as the establishment of a 'fault' under national tort law?
— *Extent of damages*: what types of damage can be compensated? Are judges limited to compensatory damages or can they also award restitutionary damages, or even exemplary, punitive or 'umbrella' damages? How should damages be calculated? Is the national judge allowed to estimate the damage? Are infringers allowed to raise a 'passing-on' defence and, if so, what is the position of indirect purchasers in this regard?
— *Causal link*: how is a sufficiently direct link between the 'fault' and the damage to be established? Is there a presumption that infringements of competition law cause damage?
— *Procedural issues*: who can start a damages action (*active standing*), against whom (*passive standing*) in which jurisdiction and before which national court (the latter may depend on *international private law*)? Is *collective action* possible and, if so, under what form (representative action, class action, opt-in or opt-out regime)? How is *access to evidence* organised? Is all access to evidence to be controlled by a judge or is some form of private party discovery allowed? Can claimants in a damage action obtain access to leniency statements or settlement notices? Which time limits apply?

6. These legal issues will be dealt with below, in the order of their listing above. It is important to note that these legal issues are, and will continue to be, settled mainly under national (private) law. The recent Damages Directive, which is due to be implemented by 27 December 2016, will impact upon some of these issues, but not on all of them (eg, not on collective redress or on international private law) and will not affect all of them

---

[238] See CJ 21 May 2015 Case C-352/13 *Cartel Damage Claims (CDC) Hydrogen Peroxide SA v Akzo Nobel NV and others* ECLI:EU:C:2015:335 on the interpretation of Council Regulation (EC) No 44/2001 of 22 December 2000 on jurisdiction and the recognition and enforcement of judgments in civil and commercial matters ([2001] OJ L 12, 1).

to the same degree (eg, it leaves considerable discretion for national law as regards the required causal link).

7. As indicated at the beginning of this chapter, our focus is on national case law. However, some of the existing national case law will have to change after the implementation of the Damages Directive. The first excerpted case below already illustrates this. Therefore, we will in the notes accompanying the excerpted cases also refer to the Damages Directive. At this point, the following general observations on the Damages Directive appear warranted.

As its title indicates, the Damages Directive will apply to 'actions for damages under national law'. Moreover, the competition law infringements which will lead to such actions for damages are *not* only infringements of EU law *but also* of purely national competition law.[239]

The stated aims of the Damages Directive include effective legal protection and consumer protection, but also the creation of a level playing field between undertakings. While certainly facilitating damages claims, the Damages Directive at the same time also limits both compensation and the initiative of private parties to obtain evidence. The following appear to be essential goals of the Damages Directive: the promotion of compensation of victims of infringements of Articles 101 and 102 TFEU, the prohibition of overcompensation, the promotion of leniency[240] (which is a remarkable achievement, since, as indicated, private enforcement normally obstructs leniency) and the promotion of alternative dispute settlement. The Damages Directive further applies to collective action, but does not organise it.

Rechtbank van Koophandel Brussel (Brussels Commercial Court),
24 November 2014[241]   **2.55 (BE)**

European Union v Otis, KONE, Schindler and ThyssenKrupp

DAMAGE AND CAUSAL LINK—STANDARD OF PROOF

Schindler's lift

As it predates the adoption of Directive 2014/104/EU on antitrust damages actions, the applicable national law knows no presumption of damage for cartelistic behaviour and imposes high standards of proof regarding damage and causal link

Facts: In February 2007, the EC fined four elevator companies more than €992 million for their participation in a market allocation cartel and bid-rigging scheme.[242] The EC, representing the EU, then started a follow-on

---

[239] The Damages Directive has a double legal basis: arts 103 (on competition law, with reference to 'national laws') and 114 (on the internal market).

[240] It is submitted that the Damages Directive promotes leniency by: (a) guaranteeing, much more effectively than the CJ had done previously, that courts will not grant damage claimants access to leniency statements and settlement submissions (art 6(6) of the Damages Directive); and (b) limiting joint and several liability of immunity recipients (art 11(4) and (6) of the Damages Directive).

[241] Brussels Commercial Court 24 November 2014 A.R/A08/06816 *European Union v Kone, Otis, Schindler and ThyssenKrupp*.

[242] Commission Decision of 21 February 2007 relating to a proceeding under Article 81 of the EC Treaty, Case COMP/E-1/38.823—PO/Elevators and Escalators. For the nature of the fined infringement, see art 1 of the Decision.

damages claim before the Commercial Court in Brussels, in order to be compensated for overcharges it had allegedly paid to the elevator companies for the maintenance and modernisation of elevators in the buildings of EU institutions.

Held: The Commercial Court dismisses the EC's claim for damages.

Judgment: Since the [EC] Proposal was adopted on 17 April 2014 as a Directive, legislation in EU Member States will have to comply with the Directive Proposal on damages actions for infringement of competition law within the implementation period of two years. Pursuant to Article 16 of the Directive it is presumed in case of a cartel infringement that the infringement caused damage. The infringing undertaking has the right to rebut this presumption. When establishing liability, a rebuttable presumption is therefore created that there is a *conditio sine qua non* connection between the damage and the cartel infringement. This is said to relate to research establishing that nine out of ten cartels indeed cause an illegitimate price increase.

However, the case at hand was initiated in 2008 and is hence to be assessed in accordance with the abovementioned rules of Belgian law, which are still applicable …

The court observes that, according to Belgian law, the claimant needs to make it plausible and hence not merely hypothetical that it suffered damage. A legal presumption (that every cartel infringement causes damage) as advocated by the Commission does not (yet) exist in the relevant provisions of Belgian law.

The court deems it generally plausible that a cartel leads to higher prices. Prices are nonetheless seldom determined by merely one cause …

A certain causal relation between, on the one hand, the infringement of the prohibition of cartels determined by the Commission and, on the other hand, the maintenance contracts containing the (according to the claimant) excessive prices cannot be merely assumed. Even if and in so far as the agreed prices were inexplicably high … a connection between the prohibited cartel agreements and those prices is not to be unreservedly established without further foundation, which is lacking. Parties in an agreement are in principle bound by that agreement, even in case the prices agreed or other elements of the agreement are disappointing upon closer inspection. The claimant has not presented any precise documents, facts or circumstances that lead to the conclusion that this principle is to be abandoned by the court.

The claimant has therefore failed, regarding each [EU] institution and each maintenance contract that relates to Belgium, to carefully demonstrate and quantify the extra costs to which the established infringement would actually have given rise.

…

In the case at hand, the claimant does not even provide prima facie evidence of having been deprived of a real chance of avoiding the so-called surcharges (she again bases her arguments on mere hypotheses), so that her claim is to be rejected.

Notes:

(1) The judgment is important as it marks the first attempt of the EC, representing the EU, to successfully claim damages before a national court after a breach of EU cartel regulations was established. The EC's attempt has so far been unsuccessful, but the first instance national court itself indicates that this may be due in large part to the non-implementation of the Damages Directive. The Damages Directive creates a rebuttable

presumption that cartels cause harm,[243] allows national judges to estimate the amount of harm,[244] allows them to seek assistance of NCAs when estimating the harm[245] and requires Member States to 'ensure that neither the burden nor the standard of proof required for the quantification of harm renders the exercise of the right to damages practically impossible or excessively difficult'.[246]

In the absence of all these provisions, currently applicable national law still requires the claimant in a damages claim to 'carefully demonstrate and quantify' the damage and the causal link between fault and damage, as in all other damages actions. According to the national court's extensively motivated judgment (only briefly excerpted here), the EC did not bring sufficient proof, or even the beginning of proof, of the components 'damage' and 'causal link', or even proof of the loss of a chance.

(2) Interestingly, the national court has no problem whatsoever with accepting that the EC's previous fining of the elevator companies constitutes sufficient proof of a 'fault' under national tort law. Given the supremacy of EU law, that finding appears to be correct—at least to the extent that, as the national court observes, 'parties do not dispute the facts established in the [fining] Decision'.[247] After the implementation of the Damages Directive, final decisions of *national* competition authorities or by *national* review courts will also be deemed to constitute irrefutable proof of an infringement of competition law (below).

(3) In this case, as in all others where the EC would start a *private enforcement* follow-on damages action after having fined the infringing undertakings involved in a *public enforcement* case, one could suspect a possible conflict of interest for the EC. This suspicion led the defending elevator companies to argue before the Brussels Commercial Court that the EC's claim for damages was inadmissible, and the national court referred a preliminary ruling on this question to the CJ. In its judgment of 6 November 2012,[248] the CJ ruled that 'in circumstances such as those at issue in the main proceedings' (ie, also where the EC has previously fined under public enforcement), the EC 'is not precluded from representing the European Union before a national court hearing a civil action for damages'. The CJ repeated that each person and individual, and therefore also the EC as a representative of the EU, should have the principled right to compensation for infringements of cartel law, in order to achieve full effectiveness of EU law. The CJ dispelled the defendant's fear that the EC would use confidential information gathered during the fining procedure for its damages claim afterwards. The EC declared that it had only used the non-confidential version of the fining decision to substantiate its damages claim. Moreover, Article 28(1) of Regulation No 1/2003[249] prohibits the use of information gathered

---

[243] The reference to art 16 in the excerpted judgment is to be read as a reference to art 17(2) of the final version of the Damages Directive: 'It shall be presumed that cartel infringements cause harm. The infringer shall have the right to rebut that presumption.'

[244] Damages Directive, art 17(1).

[245] ibid, art 17(3).

[246] ibid, art 17(1).

[247] If that were different, the national court might have had to await the outcome of the review of the EC's fining decision by the GC and possibly, on appeal, the CJ.

[248] CJ 6 November 2012 Case C-199/11 *European Union v Otis et al* nyr ECLI:EU:C:2012:684.

[249] Council Regulation (EC) No 1/2003 of 16 December 2002 on the implementation of the rules on competition laid down in Articles 81 and 82 of the Treaty, OJ L1/1, 4 January 2003.

in the course of the investigation for purposes other than those of the investigation. In these circumstances, the CJ saw no breach of the principle of equality of arms or of Article 47 of the Charter, which safeguards the right to an effective remedy and to a fair trial.

The CJ added that, whereas national courts are bound by the infringement decisions of the EC, national judges nevertheless remain free to decide whether damages should be awarded. On the basis of the answers received from the CJ, the Brussels Commercial Court decided to declare the EC's claim admissible. As we know now, the Commercial Court has also made full use of its 'freedom to decide whether damages should be awarded'.

(4) This case illustrates the problems in terms of the burden of proof which claimants in damages cases may encounter under national law, and how the Damages Directive may help them to overcome these problems. The EC, which was only able to rely on the non-confidential version of its fining decision (above), may also have suffered from a lack of access to evidence, in particular to 'direct evidence' (eg, internal documents of the cartelists about price-fixing agreements or their execution). The institution was only able to present to the national court a study of a 'sample' of maintenance contracts, the exact number of contracts was not even known. It was unable to prove with certainty that during the existence of the cartel, the prices were artificially raised. After the implementation of the Damages Directive, national judges may be better equipped to order the defendants to disclose any relevant (direct) evidence.[250]

(5) Early on in 2015, the EC lodged an appeal against the first instance judgment with the Brussels Court of Appeal. It has recently become public that in an interim judgment of 28 October 2015, the Court of Appeal, on application by the EC and by way of interim relief, has ordered the four Belgian elevator cartel members to disclose documents from the EC's cartel file.

(6) After the EC had launched a follow-on damages claim against the elevator companies, the Belgian state started a similar action, also before the Brussels Commercial Court.[251] This action was also dismissed, in part on the same grounds as the EC action. In addition, the judgment of 24 April 2015, among other things, focuses on the nature of the fined cartel as a market allocation cartel and bid-rigging scheme, but not, according to the court, a price-fixing cartel. As the EC did not fine the companies for price-fixing, the EC fining decision cannot serve to prove 'a fault, consisting in the imposition of overcharges in the agreements between claimant and defendants'.[252]

II.D.ii THE FAULT-BINDING CHARACTER OF EC AND NCA INFRINGEMENT DECISIONS ON NATIONAL COURTS

Introductory Notes

1. Multiple questions arise on the concept of fault in the context of actions for damages (eg, is there a separate fault requirement and, if so, what constitutes a 'fault'?). Given the rise of follow-on damages claims, the question whether infringement decisions of the EC or of NCAs are binding on national judges takes centre stage. On closer inspec-

---

[250] See arts 5 and 6 of the Damages Directive.
[251] Commercial Court Brussels 24 April 2015 *TBM* 2015-3, 212–27, *Belgische Staat v liftenproducenten.*
[252] ibid, point 3.5.2.2 sub b of the judgment.

tion, three different questions are to be distinguished, relating to the status, in damages actions before national courts, of: (a) final EC infringement decisions; (b) ongoing EC investigations or EC infringement decisions under review; and (c) NCA infringement decisions. We will deal with these questions, in this order, first in introductory notes and then through excerpts of cases and legislation.

2. The binding character of final EC infringement decisions for national courts dealing with follow-on damages claims is largely recognised. It originates from the principles of sincere cooperation and supremacy of EU law and from Article 16(1) of Regulation 1/2003, which prohibits a national court from taking a decision which would run counter to an EC decision. However, as will be made clear by the *Inntrepreneur Pub Company (CPC) v Crehan* judgment excerpted below, these principles still do not answer all queries that may arise in a follow-on damages claim. For example, the question arises whether sincere cooperation implies that national courts have to take into account EC decisions in cases that are *similar* to the case presented before them (and if so, how similar should the case be?), and whether national courts are required to stay proceedings when an EC investigation is still ongoing or when an EC infringement decision is still under review by the EU courts. These questions are to be answered by the national judiciary, if necessary with the help of the CJ through preliminary ruling questions.

3. As to the binding character of NCA infringement decisions in damages claims before national courts, the era before the Damages Directive was/is one of diversity in national legal systems: in a majority of Member States, the national judge currently remains free to appreciate the probative value of an infringement decision in a follow-on action, based on the perceived quality of the NCA's reasoning. The infringement decision may thus constitute persuasive authority, but not, in most Member States, binding authority.

4. The Damages Directive will to some extent unify the national laws in this area. Article 9(1) stipulates that in follow-on actions, 'an infringement of competition law found by a final decision of a [NCA] or by a review court is deemed to be irrefutably established for the purposes of an action for damages'. A final finding by an NCA or review court will thus be deemed to constitute irrefutable proof 'of an infringement of competition law' (not 'of a fault') before a national court of the same Member State in a damages action. It is left to national law to determine how a 'fault' is to be established in stand-alone actions.

Under Article 9(2), final decisions by the NCA or a review court in another Member State will not be binding, but constitute 'at least prima facie evidence' that an infringement has occurred. The Damages Directive is more restrictive on this point than the EC's Green Paper[253] and the 2008 EC White Paper, where the EC declared that it saw no reason why a final decision of an NCA in the European Competition Network (ECN) on Articles 101 and 102 TFEU should not be accepted in every Member State as irrefutable proof of the infringement.[254] It was only in the Damages Directive that a distinction was introduced between decisions rendered by the NCA of the same Member State and those rendered by an NCA of another Member State.

---

[253] Commission Green Paper on Damages Actions for Breach of the EC Antitrust Rules (n 229) 6.
[254] Commission White Paper on Damages Actions for Breach of the EC Antitrust Rules (n 230) 6.

It should be noted that Article 9 does not apply to so-called 'commitment decisions' which impose a change of behaviour on the defendant firm, but do not contain final findings on infringements of competition law.[255]

House of Lords, 19 July 2006 **2.56 (UK)**

Inntrepreneur Pub Company (CPC) v Crehan[256]

BINDING EFFECT OF EC FINDINGS IN A NATIONAL COURT

Last orders for Mr Crehan

An EC infringement decision in a case which is similar but involves different parties is only part of the evidence before the national court, it is not binding upon the national court

Facts: In 1991, the claimant, Mr Crehan, entered into agreements with the defendant, Inntrepreneur Pub Company, to take leases of two public houses belonging to the latter. The contracts were in standard form and contained ties which obliged Mr Crehan to buy his beer from Courage Limited at its list prices. Both businesses of Mr Crehan failed because, as the judge found, he could not compete with other public houses which were able to buy their beer at lower prices. As a consequence, he did not do enough trade to cover the rent he had agreed to pay. Mr Crehan surrendered his two leases in March and September 1993, having lost a substantial sum of money.

Held: The House of Lords overruled the Court of Appeal's decision to award damages to Mr Crehan and held that (now) Article 101 TFEU did not apply in this case.

Judgment: 69. There was a good deal of discussion, both before the Court of Appeal and in argument before the House, about the degree of 'deference' which a national court should show to a decision of the Commission. Mr Vaughan QC is recorded (in para 96 of the judgment of the Court of Appeal) as having constructed a scheme of three degrees of deference (absolute deference, very great deference and deference) which might have to be paid to a decision of the Commission. For my part, I do not find deference in this context a very helpful expression. It is commonly (if not altogether happily) used in administrative law when a court decides that the decision-making power on a particular question properly belongs to someone else and that the court should not substitute its own view. But the decision-making power on whether [now Article 101(1) TFEU] applies plainly belonged to the English court, exercising concurrent jurisdiction, and I find it difficult to see how the exercise of this power can be combined with 'deference' to the decision of someone else. The correct position is that, when there is no question of a conflict of decisions in the sense which I have discussed, the decision of the Commission is simply evidence properly admissible before the English court which, given the expertise of the Commission, may well be regarded by that court as highly persuasive. As a matter of law, however, it is only part of the evidence which the court will take into account. If, upon an assessment of all the evidence, the judge comes to the conclusion that the view of the Commission was wrong, I do not see how, consistently with his judicial oath, he can say that as a matter of deference he proposes nevertheless to follow the Commission. Only a

---

[255] See N Dunne, 'The Role of Private Enforcement within EU Competition Law' (2014) 16 *Cambridge Yearbook of European Legal Studies* 172–73.

[256] *Inntrepreneur Pub Company (CPC) v Crehan* [2006] 3 WLR 148; [2006] 30 EG 103; [2006] 30 EGCS 103; [2006] 4 All ER 465; [2006] ICR 1344; [2006] NPC 85; [2006] UKHL 38; [2007] 1 AC 333; [2007] AC 333.

rule of law, in the nature of an issue estoppel which obliges him to do so, could produce such a result and the Court of Appeal accepted that there was no such rule.

Notes:

(1) The excerpted judgment deals with the *status of EC infringement decisions* in follow-on damages claims before a national court. It illustrates the limits of the above-mentioned principle of supremacy and sincere cooperation, and of Article 16(1) of Regulation 1/2003. To repeat, the general rule is that an EC decision cannot be set aside by a national judge. When the dispute at the national level is a follow-on case, the relevant finding of the EC cannot be contradicted. *Inntrepreneur Pub* was indeed not the only owner of tied houses which had been found to breach competition law. In earlier cases, the EC already decided that *Bass*, *Whitbread* and several other brewers had infringed (now) Article 101 TFEU. Consequently, the claimant based a major part of his argumentation on the former EC findings, stating that the national judge was obliged to give deference to these decisions. Nevertheless, the reasoning of the earlier Court of Appeal's decision and the quoted decision of the House of Lords establish conflicting opinions on the extent of EC findings regarding similar cases. The reasoning of the Court of Appeal brought forward that a judge was obliged to give greater deference to the EC's earlier findings on the applicability of (now) Article 101 TFEU and was not free to come to a different conclusion. The House of Lords ruled that the English courts were not bound to follow factual findings of the EC which were reached in cases involving different parties, regarding different subject matter, even if they relate to the same market. The House of Lords thus qualified the earlier EC decisions as simple evidence.

(2) In its 2015 judgment in *Belgian State v Elevator Companies* (above), the Brussels Commercial Court ruled that the binding character of the EC fining decision only applies to the infringements referred to within that decision and only to the parties mentioned in that decision. The decision therefore cannot be extended towards other facts or to other parties, not even if these parties are subsidiaries of the addressees of the EC decision.[257]

(3) A connected but still different issue is that of the status of *ongoing EC investigations or of EC decisions under review* in follow-on damages claims before a national court. The decision of a national judge to stay proceedings until the EC has decided or until the EC fining decision has become final may imply that a damages claim is stayed for several years. In view of the principle of sincere cooperation and summarizing several CJ decisions, Bellamy & Child conclude as follows on the status of ongoing EC investigations:

> [I]f the Commission is investigating the relevant agreement or conduct, the national court should consider whether to stay its proceedings until the European Commission has taken its decision and, if necessary, grant interim relief. If a stay is required, the national proceedings may also need to await the outcome of any actions for annulment of the European Commission's decision before the General Court and the Court of Justice ... Where, however, it is clear how the Commission will deal with the matter or where it is possible to take a non-conflicting

---

[257] *Belgische Staat v liftenproducenten* (n 251) point 3.5.2.2, sub c.

decision, the national court may take its own decision without waiting for the conclusion of the European Commission's proceedings.[258]

(4) The Dutch *Equilib Netherlands v Koninklijke Luchtvaartmaatschappij (KLM)* case concerns the impact on a private enforcement damages action in a national court of a EC fining decision which is still under review before the EU courts in Luxembourg. In September 2010, Equilib launched a damages action against three air carriers for alleged participation in cartelistic behaviour. In November 2010, the EC fined these and other air carriers almost €800 million for their alleged participation in an air cargo cartel in Europe. Equilib then changed the basis of its damages claim, turning the claim into a follow-on claim based on the EC fining decision. As the air carriers launched actions for annulment against the EC decision before the GC, the Dutch first instance court decided to stay proceedings until the EC decision would become final.[259] Equilib appealed the decision. On appeal, the Court of Amsterdam reversed the judgment in first instance.[260] The appeal court inferred from Article 16(1) of Regulation 1/2003 (above) and from the CJ's *Masterfoods* judgment[261] that a national judge has a degree of discretion in deciding to stay or not to stay a damages action based on an EC fining decision which is still under review. Staying the national proceedings is only allowed when questions relating to the facts or the law in the national procedure depend on the validity of an EC decision and when there is a reasonable doubt as to whether the EC decision is in fact valid. Making good use of its discretion, the appeal court ruled that it is for the party who disputes the validity of the EC fining decision and who claims that national proceedings should be stayed to show that it: (a) launched an appeal against the EC decision in due time; (b) 'in reasonableness contests' the EC decision (ie, has reasonable arguments); and (c) sets out the defences in the national case, so that the national judge can check whether and to what extent the assessment of these defences depends on the validity of the EC decision. As the second and third conditions were not fulfilled *in casu*, the first instance judgment was reversed. The defendants were offered the opportunity to set out their arguments under (b) and (c) above.

The *Equilib* case shows how complex it is for national judges to strike a correct balance between, on the one hand, the interests of claimants in damages actions who should not fall victim to delaying tactics used by well-advised cartelists and, on the other hand, the interest of the defendants (and of procedural efficiency at large) in not having to spend unnecessary funds and time on fighting private enforcement actions based on EC decisions that may still be overturned in Luxembourg. In December 2015, and as if

---

[258] V Rose and D Baily (eds), *Bellamy & Child, European Union Law of Competition*, 7th edn (Oxford, Oxford University Press, 2013).

[259] District Court of Amsterdam 7 March 2012 ECLI:NL:RBAMS:2012:BV8444 para 4.10 *Equilib Netherlands v Koninklijke Luchtvaartmaatschappij (KLM)*.

[260] Dutch Court of Appeal of Amsterdam 24 September 2013 ECLI:NL:GHAMS:2013:3013 *Equilib Netherlands v Koninklijke Luchtvaart Maatschappij (KLM)*. In first instance, several air carriers had pleaded that the judgment in the Netherlands should also be stayed until judges in the UK and France had ruled. Their claims were rejected and that rejection was confirmed on appeal.

[261] CJ 14 December 2000 Case C-344/98 *Masterfoods Ltd v HB Ice Cream Ltd* [2002] I-11369ECLI:EU:C:2000:689.

to prove that last point, the GC annulled all the fines imposed by the EC in the air cargo cartel case.[262]

Article 152 of the Code on Civil Procedure   **2.57 (NL)**

1. Evidence can be submitted through any means, unless the law provides otherwise.
2. The value of the evidence is to be determined by the judge unless the law provides otherwise.

Proposed Article 161a Code on Civil Procedure

An irrevocable decision finding an infringement by the Consumers and Market Authority is irrefutable evidence of an identified infringement in a procedure in which damages are claimed for a breach of competition law within the meaning of Article 193k, part 1, Book 6 of the Civil Code.

Notes:

(1) This excerpt, and the following ones, concern the *status of an NCA's decisions* in follow-on damages claims before a national court.

(2) In the Dutch pre-proposal for an Act implementing the Damages Directive,[263] a new Article 161a is inserted into the Code of Civil Procedure. In line with Article 9(1) of the Damages Directive, it states that a final infringement decision of the Dutch NCA[264] is to be considered as irrefutable proof of an infringement of competition law in a follow-on proceeding. However, the proposal does not incorporate Article 9(2) of the Damages Directive, according to which final decisions by an NCA or a review court of another Member State will constitute 'at least prima facie evidence' that an infringement has occurred. The Explanatory Memorandum indicates that Dutch law is already in accordance with Article 9(2), because infringement decisions of NCAs in other Member States come under the scope of 'any means' in Article 152(1) of the Code on Civil Procedure. A Dutch court is therefore allowed (but not obliged) to accept an infringement as prima facie evidence.[265]

(3) The Polish Supreme Court[266] held in 2008 that a final decision of the President of the Polish NCA in a particular case is binding upon a national court dealing with the same issue. According to the Court: 'It shall not raise any doubts that it would be undesirable if the evaluation of the same practice by the court and the competition authority could be divergent ... the final decision of the competition authority on the abuse of a dominant position shall be binding upon the civil court. Such standpoint is consistent with the rule that civil courts are generally bound by final administrative decisions.'

---

[262] For the KLM fine, see GC 16 December 2015 Case T-62/11 *Air France-KLM v Commission* nyr ECLI:EU:T:2015:996. The judgment is under appeal in Case C-590/11 P (I).

[263] See *Kamerstukken II* 2015/16 34 490 no 3, 21: art II part B of the 'Voorontwerp Implementatiewet richtlijn privaatrechtelijke handhaving mededingingsrecht' (MvT). The consultation on this pre-proposal ended on 22 November 2015.

[264] 'Autoriteit Consument en Markt' or 'Consumers and Market Authority'.

[265] See *Kamerstukken II* 2015/16 34 490 no 3, 8 (MvT).

[266] Resolution of the Polish Supreme Court 23 July 2008 Case III CZP 52/08 *OSN* 2009 no 7–8 item 107.

(4) From a constitutional point of view, it is not at all self-evident that a national judge would be bound by the (final) decision of an NCA, to the extent that the NCA is an administrative authority (and not a court or administrative court as in so-called dualist systems of national cartel enforcement). Article 9 of the Damages Directive might be seen as encroaching upon the separation of powers. It is true that only *final* decisions of NCAs will bind national courts, so that these decisions may have been subject to judicial review. However, that will not always be the case. The Belgian situation may serve to illustrate this point. Article 159 of the Belgian Constitution provides as follows: 'Courts only apply general, provincial or local decisions and regulations provided that they are in accordance with the law.' On the basis of this provision, parties to any court procedure have the right to raise a so-called 'exception of illegality' before a national judge. Under this exception, ordinary courts may refuse to enforce an illegal administrative rule. If, after the proper implementation of Article 9 of the Damages Directive, a party would have doubts as to the legality of an NCA decision which has become final but has not been subjected (for whatever reason, eg, because the time limits for appeal have lapsed) to judicial review, that party might be barred from invoking the exception of illegality against the NCA decision. Belgian judges might feel bound by a possibly illegal NCA decision. Tension between the Damages Directive and the Belgian Constitution might surface. In the hierarchy of norms, the Constitution would prevail over the national implementation of Article 9, but most probably not over Article 9 itself. Moreover, in case of the perceived improper or only partial implementation of Article 9, the CJ would probably not hesitate to grant direct vertical effect to Article 9.

Corte di Cassazione (Italian Court of Cassation),
13 February 2009[267]   **2.58 (IT)**

ANCL v INAZ

BINDING EFFECT OF NCA DECISIONS IN NATIONAL COURTS

A trade association finds that the boot is on the other foot

Under Italian law, the NCA's finding of an infringement creates an authoritative presumption on which a court can base its decision

Facts: INAZ, the defendant, a software provider in the wages and welfare sector, was involved in a dispute with various professional consultant trade associations at the national and local level. After being reported to the NCA for misleading advertising, INAZ in its turn reported to the NCA that the professional associations were boycotting its activities. The NCA sanctioned the national association, but not the local associations. INAZ brought an action for declaration of nullity of the restrictive practice between the various professional associations, which it deemed to be in breach of antitrust law, as well as an action for injunctive relief and for damages. The Court of Appeal granted all the claims and condemned the national association to pay damages. The national association appealed the decision before the Italian Court of Cassation.

Held: The Court of Cassation upheld the judgment of the Court of Appeal, since the rules on the burden of proof were applied correctly. It ruled that an NCA decision which finds an infringement of competition law creates an authoritative presumption on which a court can base its decision. The NCA decision does not

---

[267] Cass it Section I 13 February 2009 no 3640.

constitute irrefutable proof (*in re ipsa*). Parties to the court case may present evidence either validating or invalidating the NCA decision.

Judgment: There is no doubt that the decision taken by the NCA or by the administrative judges which definitively confirms or reverses [that decision], plays a significant role in the finding of the agreement, of the concerted practice or of the abuse of a dominant position [and thus] constitutes privileged evidence of the existence of the behaviour ascertained or of the position retained in the market and of its possible abuse.

However, in the proceedings before civil courts it is possible to bring both evidence supporting such an assessment, regarding more directly the position of the single damaged party, as well as evidence against it. [The evidence] may be offered both by the party asserting the existence of the violation, where for instance there has been a rejection [of the complaint] by the NCA or a decision to close the file, as well as by the undertaking accused, which may bring evidence against the appraisals conducted and the conclusions drawn.

Notes:

(1) The annotated judgment grants the claimant the advantage of a presumption, since an administrative decision on the existence of an antitrust infringement already existed. Nevertheless, the court immediately offers the parties the opportunity to bring proof validating or invalidating the decision of the Italian NCA (the AGCM). The claimant can thus only count on a rebuttable presumption.

(2) This decision has repeatedly been confirmed by the Italian Court of Cassation. In the *Allianz spa v AE* case, a purely domestic case regarding the burden of proof, the court restated that the parties are allowed to challenge the NCAs decisions. The consumer (the defendant) had claimed and obtained before the Court of Appeal damages from the insurance company (the claimant) resulting from a restrictive practice, which caused an increase of the insurance premium and was ascertained by the national competition authority. The insurance company appealed claiming that the Court of Appeal did not take into consideration the proof that it had produced against the existence of a causal link. The Court of Cassation confirmed the earlier Court of Appeal decision, awarding damages to the defendant on the basis of a restrictive practice, since there existed no relevant proof against the infringement decision of the NCA.

(3) The possibility for parties to bring proof invalidating an infringement decision equally implies a certain degree of freedom assigned to judges, namely to set aside an NCA's findings. The 2011 judgment of the Court of Appeal of Rome in *Stream v Telepiù, Prima TV, Atena Servizi, Europa TV*[268] illustrates this. *Stream* brought its action before the Court of Appeal. At the time,[269] this court had jurisdiction over private enforcement in purely national competition cases, whereas other judges had jurisdiction if the violation affected the EU market. Telepiù (the defendant) claimed that the Court of Appeal had no competence since the matter fell within the scope of EU law. However, the Court of

---

[268] Jugment of 15 January 2011 published in (2002) II *Giurisprudenza Commerciale* 362.

[269] Law number 27 of 24 March 2012 ('Disposizioni urgenti per la concorrenza, lo sviluppo delle infrastrutture e la competitivitá') has abolished the jurisdiction of the Court of Appeal over claims concerning national cases. Nowadays, all private enforcement claims are brought before the court for undertakings (Tribunale delle Imprese).

Appeal rejected this argument. It held that the finding of the AGCM, which incidentally recognised the influence of the abuse of dominance on the EU internal market, was not binding in the civil proceeding before it.

(4) However, if Italy implements Article 9(1) of the Damages Directive correctly, the courts will have to apply a different approach with regard to decisions rendered by the Italian NCA. From then on, once the Italian NCA has ruled on the existence of a competition law infringement, an infringement is irrefutably established (see above). The national judge will thus no longer be able to take a divergent standpoint in the civil procedure pending before it.

(5) Concerning decisions rendered by an NCA of another Member State, the approach of the Court of Cassation remains valid. As set out above, Article 9(2) of the Damages Directive only requires that the findings of an NCA should at least be accepted as prima facie evidence of an infringement.

Corte di Cassazione (Italian Court of Cassation),
4 March 2013[270]   **2.59 (IT)**

Tommaselli v Axa Assicurazioni

BINDING EFFECT OF NCA DECISIONS IN NATIONAL COURT

A privileged presumption

The NCA's decision constitutes 'privileged evidence': the defendant cannot raise before a court the same arguments and evidence already rejected by the NCA

Facts: The claimant appealed to the Italian Court of Cassation in order to obtain the annulment of the judgment of the Court of Appeal. The latter had denied him compensation for sums paid to a motor insurance company (the defendant), which was part of a cartel sanctioned by the Italian competition authority in 2000.

Held: The Court of Cassation annulled the judgment of the Court of Appeal, considering its grounds as inadequate. It confirmed that the decision of the NCA has the value of 'privileged evidence' in follow-on actions. This implies that the defendant may provide evidence against the facts ascertained, but not on the basis of the same arguments and evidence rejected by the NCA.

The claimant could invoke the presumption that the sum paid was too high because of the defendant's anticompetitive conduct. The defendant could provide evidence against both the existence of the casual link and the damage suffered. Such evidence must nevertheless be accurate, detailed and adequate to prove that the final amount paid by the claimant had been determined by factors other than the anticompetitive behaviour. In bringing evidence against the existence of a causal link, the defendant could only rely on aspects not covered by the NCA's decision and on factors concerning the defendant himself, the claimant or the contract discussed, but not the market in general.

Judgment: 5. The case law of this court is now univocal in stating that, in the action brought by a consumer concerning a claim for compensation of the damage suffered as a consequence of an unlawful anticompetitive agreement set up by a business operator:

— the documents of the proceeding at the outcome of which the NCA has established the existence of a horizontal agreement between insurance companies and has imposed a fine on the undertaking constitute privileged proof[.] [This means] that the undertaking may provide evidence against the ascertained facts, without however

---

[270] Cass it Section VI 4 March 2013 no 5327.

being allowed in the civil action to call into question again the facts on the basis of which the existence of the infringement of competition rules has been affirmed, relying on the same evidence or arguments already dismissed on that previous occasion;[271]

— the insured party is entitled to avail himself of the presumption that the premium paid is higher than it was due as a consequence of the collusive conduct of the defendant insurance company, in proportion to the increase of premiums in comparison with the European average, with the result that the undertaking may provide evidence to the contrary concerning both the existence (or the interruption) of the causal link between the anticompetitive infringement and the damage, as also the extent of the damage itself[.] [H]owever, if the undertaking took part in the proceedings before the NCA, being condemned, it cannot provide only general arguments regarding the data influencing the setting of premiums in the market of insurance policies already considered by the NCA, but must provide detailed information on situations and specific conduct of the undertaking involved and of the single insured party which must be capable of demonstrating that the level of the premium has not been determined by the participation in the unlawful agreement but by other factors; ...

— the proof of the non-existence of the causal link cannot be drawn from general considerations concerning the data influencing the setting of premiums in the market of insurance policies, but must relate to circumstances and conduct that are specific to the undertaking involved: i.e. that relate to that particular insurance company, to that particular insured party or to that particular insurance policy, and which are apt to demonstrate that—in the case at hand—the level of the insurance premium has not been determined by the participation in the anticompetitive agreement; it should hence be demonstrated that (for instance) the defendant insurance company departed from the trend of premium increases which was ascertained by the NCA and which was common to the other insurance companies; or that the undertaking was in particular economic difficulties, which forced it to take certain price decisions; or that the contract covered particular risks, which are normally not included in the policy; or that it concerned insured parties whose behaviour was characterized by an abnormal accident rate; and so on: all these circumstances may not only be generically affirmed, but must be substantiated, indicating the criteria adopted in setting the insurance premiums, the cost components burdening the undertaking during the period in which the infringement took place.

Notes:

(1) In this judgment, the Italian Court of Cassation is moving towards the approach taken in the Damages Directive. In line with the previous cases, the decision of the AGCM is seen as establishing a rebuttable presumption. Nevertheless, the court is stricter in determining what evidence can be taken into account to rebut the presumption. It creates a 'privileged rebuttable presumption': the defendant is allowed to bring evidence against the facts ascertained, but not on the basis of the same arguments and evidence previously rejected by the NCA. Scholars have argued that in the Italian system, the defendant's right of defence in this type of actions has been gradually eroded.

(2) The judgment concerns an infringement decision of the home NCA. It will be interesting to observe which choice will be made after the implementation of the

---

[271] 'On that previous occasion' refers to the proceedings before the NCA.

Damages Directive. As explained, the findings of a Member State's own NCA will be upgraded to an irrefutable establishment of infringement. Decisions of NCAs from other Member States should at least constitute prima facie evidence. The unsolved question is whether the Court of Cassation will immediately apply its theory of privileged evidence to this second type of infringement decisions, or will stick to its former case law, under which the defendant was able to use all types of evidence and facts to invalidate the NCA's findings.

II.D.iii DAMAGE

II.D.iii.a Type of Damage

Introductory Notes

1. The type of damages awarded and the extent to which damages are awarded largely depend on national (case) law. However, the CJ has imposed certain minimum requirements, which are best summarised in its *Manfredi* judgment.[272]

The CJ repeats the well-known mantra on procedural autonomy. In the absence of EU rules governing the matter, it is for the domestic legal system of each Member State to set the criteria for determining the extent of the damages for harm caused by an agreement or practice prohibited under Article 101 TFEU provided that such rules are not less favourable than those governing similar domestic actions (principle of equivalence) and that they do not render practically impossible or excessively difficult the exercise of rights conferred by EU law (principle of effectiveness).[273] Applying these principles, the CJ sets out the following principles:

— Injured persons have a right to full compensation. They must be able to seek compensation not only for actual loss (*damnum emergens*) but also for loss of profit (*lucrum cessans*). A total exclusion of loss of profit would be such as to make reparation of damage practically impossible.[274]

— It must be possible to award particular damages, such as exemplary or punitive damages, pursuant to actions founded on EU competition rules, if such damages may be awarded pursuant to similar actions founded on domestic law.[275]

— An award of interest made in accordance with the applicable national rules constitutes an essential component of compensation[276]—as the CJ had already made clear in earlier case law.[277]

2. The principles set out by the CJ are now largely incorporated into the Damages Directive. The standard put forward in the Directive is that the victim of a competition

---

[272] CJ *Manfredi* (n 38).
[273] ibid, paras 62, 71–72, 77, 81, 92 and 98, and points 2–5 of the dictum.
[274] ibid, paras 95–96 and 100, and the dictum, *in fine*.
[275] ibid, paras 92–94, 99 and point 5, para 2 of the dictum.
[276] ibid, paras 95, 97 and 100, and the dictum, *in fine*.
[277] The CJ refers to CJ 2 August 1993 Case C-271/91 *Marshall v Southampton and South-West Hampshire Area Health Authority (Marshall II)* [1993] I-04367 ECLI:EU:C:1993:335, para 31.

infringement is entitled to full compensation, but not to overcompensation. The victim must be put back in the position which she or he would have been in had the infringement not been committed.[278]

The effects of the Damages Directive on national legal systems are limited and will differ. They are limited because the Directive's principles still cover a wide variety of legal realities. A recent study by the European University Institute, for example, compares 13 national legal systems on the issue of interest payments and finds them to be very divergent, to the extent that 'this is a field ripe for law reform at the EU level and … incremental adjustment by national courts would be insufficient'.[279] For example, in some national legal systems it is unclear whether interest may in effect run from the date of the loss instead of only from the date of the claim, in some systems a total ban to compound interest applies and in several national legal systems the case law is inconsistent.

The effects of the Damages Directive will differ in that in some legal systems, which claim to already apply these principles, no legislative amendments will be made. For example, in its proposal to implement the Damages Directive, the Dutch legislator abstained from incorporating a new Article within the Civil Code regarding the right of full compensation. The principles of the Directive are deemed to already form part of the Dutch law on liability claims.[280]

The German Civil Code (BGB) also explicitly states that damages should include loss of profit. According to §252 BGB, profit is considered to be lost where following the ordinary course of things, it could be expected as probable. On the basis of §252 BGB, the Higher Regional Court of Düsseldorf, for example, awarded more than €11.5 million in damages for breach of national and EU competition law in its 2014 *German State Lotteries* judgment.[281]

3. The following excerpts illustrate the important and complex choice between restitutionary, compensatory and/or exemplary awards. The last excerpt deals with the currently most controversial type of damages: damages awarded for the so-called 'umbrella pricing' effects of cartels.

[278] Damages Directive, art 3.
[279] G Monti (ed), *EU Law and Interest on Damages for Infringements of Competition Law: A Comparative Report* (Florence, EUI Working Paper Law 2016/11) 30.
[280] Article 6:96(1) of the Dutch Civil Code (BW) states that 'financial loss includes actual loss and loss of profit'. See *Kamerstukken II* 2015/16 34 490 no 3, 1-27 (MvT) (see nn 261 and 263).
[281] OLG Düsseldorf 9 April 2014 VI-U (Kart) 10/12. The claimant in the case was a company which generated lotto orders from private persons and transferred these to the state lottery companies in exchange for a provision. The lottery companies cooperated when the orders were generated over the internet, but when the claimant started a new business model, with physical generation of orders in fuel stations, supermarkets and the like, the state lotteries coordinated their behaviour in order to impede cooperation with the claimant. They refused to accept terrestrial mediated betting stakes from commercial gaming agents, in breach of national and EU competition law. In its 'Lottoblock' judgment of 14 August 2008 (KVR 54/07), the BGH ruled that there was an antitrust violation and prohibited the state lottery companies from continuing to implement the violation. The BGH's decision was binding for the OLG Düsseldorf, which held the defendant responsible for an antitrust violation which had (at least in part) caused the failure of the claimant's business model and awarded damages for lost profits.

Devenish Nutrition Ltd and others v Sanofi-Aventis SA (France) and others

RESTITUTIONARY AND EXEMPLARY DAMAGES

Keep taking the vitamins

Restitutionary damages cannot be awarded unless compensatory damages are inadequate

Facts: In 2001, the EC imposed fines of €855.22 million for participating in eight distinct secret market-sharing and price-fixing cartels affecting vitamin products.[283] In this follow-on damages case, the claimant claimed damages because it had purchased vitamins or products containing vitamins, during the cartel's existence, either for re-sale or for use in other products which were then re-sold. By way of a preliminary point of law, the question arose as to whether restitutionary damages could be claimed instead of only compensatory damages.

Held: In first instance, the High Court had ruled that restitutionary awards could not be made unless compensatory damages were inadequate to compensate the claimant for its loss, which the court held was not the case. The High Court also rejected exemplary damages. In the excerpted judgment, the Court of Appeal confirmed that no restitutionary damages are available (albeit on different grounds than the High Court), therefore dismissing the appeal. There was no appeal against the rejection of exemplary damages.

Judgment 2. This appeal involves a fundamental issue for the purposes of the law of tort, which may be summarised as follows. The aim of the law of tort is to compensate for loss suffered. The courts have exceptionally also awarded damages (commonly called 'user damages') by reference to the fair value of a right of which the defendant has wrongly deprived the claimant, and these awards have been made even if the claimant would not himself have sought to use that right and so incurred no loss. However, there is no question in this case of Devenish having been deprived of a proprietary right, that is, a right arising from property, to which such awards were formerly confined. Devenish relies on the recent case of *Attorney General v Blake* [2001] AC 268, in which a remedy of the type that it seeks in this case was awarded for a breach of contract not involving the deprivation of any property. It contends that compensatory damages will not be an adequate remedy.

134. The second question is whether the availability of a restitutionary award is necessary for the purposes of the effectiveness principle of Community law. [Counsel for the claimant] relies on Case 14/83 *Von Colson v Land Nordrhein-Westfalen* [1984] ECR 1891. This case concerned an application for damages pursuant to rights conferred by Directive 76/207/EEC for discrimination on the grounds of sex by a female applicant turned down for employment which was awarded to less qualified men. The Court of Justice held that, although the directive left Member States free to choose between the different solutions suitable for achieving its objective if compensation for this kind of breach was awarded it must be 'adequate in relation to the damage sustained'. This compensation, therefore, had to be more than purely nominal compensation such as, for example, the reimbursement only of the expenses incurred in connection with the application.

135. Van Colson was decided in a completely different context. Even so, it is clear that the remedy under national law need be no more than 'adequate in relation to the

---

[282] *Devenish Nutrition Ltd et al v Sanofi-Aventis SA (France) et al* [2009] EWCA Civ 1086; [2009] Ch 390; [2009] Bus LR 858; [2009] 3 WLR 198; [2009] 3 All ER 27; [2008] UKCLR 783.
[283] EC Decision 2003/2/EC of 21 November 2001 relating to a proceeding pursuant to Article 81 of the EC Treaty and Article 53 of the EEA Agreement (Case COMP/E-1/37.512—Vitamins) [2003] OJ L6/1.

damage sustained' ... It is also clear from cases such as *Manfredi* that purely compensatory damages are sufficient for the purposes of safeguarding the rights of private persons under [now Article 101 TFEU]. The doctrine of effectiveness is therefore directed to ensuring sufficient remedies rather than the fullest possible remedies. An action for compensatory damages fulfils the requirements of sufficiency. Accordingly I would dismiss the appeal on this ground.

Notes:

(1) As compensatory damages aim to put the victim of an infringement in the position which that victim would have been in if the infringement had not been committed, they are usually measured by the victim's loss. Restitutionary damages (in particular 'account of profits') are instead measured according to the tortfeasor's gain rather than the claimant's loss, and therefore tend to be higher. As set out above, in *Manfredi* the CJ did not oblige or prohibit Member States to award exemplary or restitutionary damages, but left the decision to award these damages to national law, subject to the principles of equivalence and effectiveness. The excerpted judgment is important as, together with the first instance judgment, it was the first to explore in such detail the types of remedy available against those participating in a cartel under UK law. It also exemplifies how difficult it is to strike the correct balance between public and private enforcement.

(2) Both the High Court and the Court of Appeal reject the award of restitutionary damages. The Appeal Court distinguished the case at hand from the situation in the seminal *Von Colson and Kamann* case—rightly so, it is submitted. The High Court had also made (and the Appeal Court partly reiterates) the following other arguments against the award of restitutionary and/or examplary damages in a private enforcement damages case:

- A restitutionary award would only be available for so-called 'proprietary torts' (eg trespass to land or interference with goods)[284] and not for 'non-proprietary torts' such as the one in issue, i.e. breach of a statutory duty.[285] The Appeal Court disagrees with the reasoning of the High Court on this point, but confirms the conclusion for this case.[286]
- It is difficult to assess the appropriate level of exemplary or restitutionary damages where there are multiple claimants and in light of the scale of the fines imposed.[287]
- Procedural problems may arise in a collective action, or if some victims opt for compensatory damages and others for restitutionary damages: 'some claimants with better evidence might choose an award of compensatory damages, while other claimants with worse evidence might choose an account of profits. I do not think that it would be fair for remedies to be mixed and matched'.[288]
- Similarly, it may be difficult to determine what the profits actually are: 'Finally, the scale of the inquiry that would be required in the case of these defendants all of which are or are parts of multi-national groups must be taken into account ... It is very likely that disclosure of documents would be both enormous and multi-lingual, would require consideration of

---

[284] In para 2 of the excerpted judgment, 'a proprietary tort' is defined as 'a tort for which a claimant entitled to property or a property right is entitled to sue for interference'.

[285] See High Court judgment, paras 106–10; Court of Appeal judgment, para 16.

[286] See Court of Appeal judgment, paras 42–86.

[287] See High Court judgment, para 107; Court of Appeal judgment, para 18.

[288] See High Court judgment, para 114; Court of Appeal judgment, para 19.

taxation and accounting methods in differing jurisdictions and a difficult exercise in allocating profits as between vitamins that formed part of the cartels and other products. In addition in the case of the Roche defendants, the relevant vitamin businesses have been sold to a third party with the result that the Roche defendants no longer have access to the relevant documents.'[289]

(3) The High Court had also raised the following arguments, mainly (but not only, as restitutionary damages may contain an element of deterrence as well) against the award of exemplary damages:

— The award of exemplary damages by a national court against a successful leniency applicant would undermine the public enforcement policy behind the leniency programme.
— Article 16 of Modernisation Regulation (EC) No 1/2003 precludes a national court from taking a decision that runs counter to a decision of the EC. In this case the EC had already determined the appropriate level of fines to punish and deter, so that another decision to do the same, this time before a national court and in a private enforcement case, threatens to conflict with the EC decision.
— The principle of *non bis in idem* would preclude an award of exemplary damages in circumstances where the defendants have already been fined (or have had fines imposed which were then reduced or commuted) by the EC in respect of the same unlawful conduct.[290]

These arguments relate to the difficult relationship between private and public enforcement, which has entered a new phase after the Damages Directive. In the framework of this chapter, two comments are warranted:

— As already indicated, the promotion of private enforcement damages claims may indeed negatively affect (or halt) leniency programmes. Undertakings may not want to step forward and confess to restrictive practices if subsequently they become the first victims of damages claims. It is all the more remarkable then that the Damages Directive has not only safeguarded leniency, but actually promotes it, in two ways: it provides very strong protection of leniency submissions against discovery in private enforcement cases[291] and it limits the joint and several liability of immunity recipients.[292]
— Under current EU competition law, application of the *ne bis in idem* principle[293] requires identity of the facts, unity of offender and unity of the legal interest protected.[294] This very strict interpretation by the CJ of the *ne bis in idem* principle is not in line with the interpretation of that same principle in other fields of EU law, where only identity of the facts and unity of the offender are required.[295] As long as it stands, however, the principle cannot be applied to a combination of public

---

[289] See High Court judgment, para 116; Court of Appeal judgment, para 20.

[290] *cf* Appeal Court judgment para 112.

[291] See art 6(6) of the Damages Directive.

[292] Article 11(4) and 11(5) of the Damages Directive, deviating from the general rule in art 11(1).

[293] See art 50 of the Charter of Fundamental Rights of the EU: 'No one shall be liable to be tried or punished again in criminal proceedings for an offence for which he or she has already been finally acquitted or convicted within the Union in accordance with the law.'

[294] CJ 14 February 2012 Case C-17/10 *Toshiba Corporation et al v Úřad pro ochranu hospodářské soutěže* ECLI:EU:C:2012:72, para 97.

[295] W Devroe, 'How General Should General Principles Be? *Ne Bis in Idem* in EU Competition Law' in Bernitz/Groussot/Shulyok et al (eds) 2013 401–42.

and private enforcement, which by nature serve different (general versus private) interests.

Competition Appeal Tribunal, 5 July 2012[296]   **2.61 (UK)**

2 Travel Group plc (in Liquidation) v Cardiff City Transport Services Ltd

EXEMPLARY DAMAGES

White bus

A follow-on damages claim leads to exemplary damages for the first time

Facts: The claim under section 47A of the Competition Act 1998 was based on a finding by the NCA (OFT) that Cardiff Bus had engaged in predatory conduct against 2 Travel and had thus abused its dominant position in the relevant markets. The abuse involved launching and operating its so-called 'white (bus) services' with exclusionary intent between 19 April 2004 and 18 February 2005. 2 Travel contended that it had sustained loss and damage as a result of the infringement under various different heads.

Held: The Competition Appeal Tribunal (CAT) awarded damages to 2 Travel in respect of its claim for lost profits in the amount of £33,818.79 plus interest. It rejected 2 Travel's claims for loss of a capital asset, loss of a commercial opportunity, wasted staff and management time and liquidation costs. The CAT awarded exemplary damages to 2 Travel to the sum of £60,000.

Judgment: 449. It has been held that exemplary damages should only be awarded if compensatory damages are insufficient alone to punish the defendant. Thus, Lord Devlin in *Rookes v Barnard* stated that exemplary damages should be awarded (at 1228):

> ... if, but only if, the sum [awarded as compensation] is inadequate to punish [the defendant] for his outrageous conduct' (Emphasis added) ...

... we consider that—unless we are compelled to by higher authority—to impose on undertakings an exposure to exemplary damages in all cases where a company proceeds with conduct despite there being a known risk of an infringement of the Chapter II prohibition would be wrong. It would have the effect of deterring actions that might well have a pro-competitive effect.

Obviously—as *Devenish* shows—exemplary damages can in theory be awarded where there is an intentional breach of the law i.e. the defendant acts knowing that what he does constitutes an infringement of competition law and intending that infringement. It is equally clear—from the case-law we have cited—that the jurisdiction to award exemplary damages extends beyond this core case, and that cases which may be termed cases of 'recklessness' can be sufficiently outrageous so as to fall within Lord Devlin's second category (see, in particular, paragraphs 466, 468, 470 and 471 above) ...

490. We consider that it will only be in those cases where an undertaking is aware that its proposed conduct is either probably unlawful or clearly unlawful that a risk can be classed as 'unacceptable'. Whether the risk is, in fact, 'unacceptable' will in addition depend upon all the facts of the case, including (for example): (1) Any expected pro-competitive effects of the conduct. (2) The degree and seriousness of any anticompetitive effects. (3) The motive of the undertaking for acting. (4) The practicability of achieving the

---

[296] *2 Travel Group plc (in Liquidation) v Cardiff City Transport Services Ltd* [2012] CAT 19. See also: www.catribunal.org.uk/238-7662/Judgment.html.

same commercial or pro-competitive aim by following a different course of action with less serious anti-competitive effects.

Notes:

(1) In normal circumstances, and for the reasons explained in *Devenish Nutrition* (see above), a claim for exemplary damages will not be available in a follow-on claim in the UK. The subjects of an EC infringement decision will either already have been fined or have been granted immunity or a reduction of fines under leniency. In the first hypothesis, the award of exemplary damages (which have a punitive character) may infringe *ne bis in idem,* while in the second hypothesis, the award of exemplary damages risks undermining leniency programmes.

However, the excerpted judgment concerns a situation which falls outside both hypotheses (no fine, no leniency) as *Cardiff Bus* enjoyed limited immunity from financial penalties for conduct of minor significance.[297] In this situation, comparable to de minimis under EU law,[298] the CAT awarded exemplary damages after finding that Cardiff Bus had deliberately sought to force 2 Travel out of the market in total disregard of the law.

(2) A 2013 judgment of the same CAT in *Albion Water*[299] illustrates just how high a threshold must be met for exemplary damages to be awarded under UK law. The CAT held that the price at which Dŵr Cymru was prepared to offer Albion a common carriage service to carry water through its pipes amounted to an abuse of dominant position. The CAT therefore ordered Dwr Cymru to pay £ 1.85 million in compensation to Albion Water for losses resulting from the abuse of dominance. However, the CAT also dismissed the claim for exemplary damages, ruling that the evidence provided by Albian Water was insufficient to substantiate such a claim.

(3) The 2013 EC Recommendation on collective redress[300] states the following under the heading 'Prohibition of punitive damages':

> The compensation awarded to natural or legal persons harmed in a mass harm situation should not exceed the compensation that would have been awarded, if the claim had been pursued by means of individual actions. In particular, punitive damages, leading to overcompensation in favour of the claimant party of the damage suffered, should be prohibited.

It is submitted that the words 'in particular' are surprising, as we now know that exemplary damages can be awarded under UK law. The recommended prohibition might even lead to inequality between individual claimants and participants in a collective action.

As punitive damages 'necessarily lead to overcompensation', the European Law Institute (ELI) qualifies the wording of the Recommendation as 'unfortunate' and a 'drafting deficiency' in its statement on collective redress of December 2014. The ELI refers

---

[297] Article 40 of the Competition Act 1998 (UK).

[298] Notice on agreements of minor importance which do not appreciably restrict competition under Article 101(1) of the Treaty on the Functioning of the European Union [2014] OJ C291/1. Under EU law, no similar de minimis regime is applicable to abuse of dominance.

[299] *Albion Water Ltd v Dŵr Cymru Cyfyngedig* [2013] CAT 16. See also: www.catribunal.org.uk/238-7977/ Judgment.html.

[300] Commission Recommendation 2013/396/EU of 11 June 2013 on common principles for injunctive and compensatory collective redress mechanisms in the Member States concerning violations of rights granted under Union Law [2013] OJ L201/60.

to 'a measure of ambivalence on the part of the EC towards punitive damages which prevented it from outlawing punitive damages altogether'.[301] The Institute rightly argues that punitive damages are not currently prohibited under EU law.

Cour d'appel de Paris (Court of Appeal of Paris),
14 December 2011[302]   **2.62 (FR)**

British Airways/Compagnie Emirates/SARL CHADEP ('Emirates')

COMPENSATORY DAMAGES FOR LOSS OF PROFIT

Airlines pricing to French travel agents

Discriminatory pricing in general sales conditions leads to compensatory damages, also for the loss of profits

Facts: Emirates' and British Airways' standard terms for travel agents provided that the agents are bound by the ticket prices available in their country and cannot benefit from lower ticket prices in other countries. A French travel agency found that the price of flights departing from London was substantially lower than the price of flights departing from Paris. The travel agency therefore purchased flights departing from London for its customers, but was asked by the airlines to pay a compensatory amount. The agency brought an action before the competent French courts, claiming a breach of competition law and seeking damages.

Held: The first instance court and the Paris Court of Appeal ruled that the terms and conditions of sales were in breach of EU competition law since they were abusive (unfair) and discriminatory. The Court of Appeal awarded damages in order to allow the travel agency to recover the compensatory payments made to the airlines and granted additional compensation for loss of sales.

Judgment: The practices in question could have discouraged certain customers, who were tempted to turn to English agencies to directly buy their ticket rather than use [the] services [of French travel agencies]. Considering the nature of the faults in question, namely anticompetitive agreements introducing discriminatory tariffs that, presumably, led to an important distortion of competition, and the specific nature of the harm caused, all the more important since the CHADEP agency is specialised in the sale of global flight tickets and consequently cannot recover its loss on classic airline tickets, this harm may, as a minimum, be established at 20,000 euros in respect of the year 2006.

Notes:

(1) In ordering compensation for the loss of profit, the judgment is in full conformity with the *Manfredi* case law of the CJ. The relative ease with which this compensation is calculated as 'as a minimum ... 20,000 euros in respect of the year 2006' will not surprise those familiar with French tort law. Moreover, this relative ease is also in line with EU law, as the Damages Directive now even imposes on Member States to allow their courts, under certain conditions, to estimate the amount of harm.[303]

---

[301] Statement of the European Law Institute on Collective Redress and Competition Damages Claims, 52. Available at: www.europeanlawinstitute.eu.

[302] French Court of Appeal of Paris 14 December 2011 *Compagnie Emirates/SARL CHADEP/British Airways*.

[303] See art 17(1), second sentence of the Damages Directive.

(2) In addition to the award of damages, the court pronounced the nullity of the contested clauses in the general sales conditions of the airlines, on the basis of Article L 420-3 of the French Commercial Code and of Article 101 TFEU.

CJ, 5 June 2014[304]   **2.63 (EU)**

Kone AG and others v ÖBB-Infrastruktur

DAMAGES FOR UMBRELLA PRICING

Elevator cartel may pay for the lifting of prices by non-cartelists

National tort law cannot a priori exclude compensation for losses resulting from umbrella pricing

Facts: In February 2007, the EC fined four elevator companies more than €992 million for their participation in a market allocation cartel and bid-rigging scheme.[305] The cartels involved the installation and maintenance of elevators in Belgium, Germany, Luxembourg and the Netherlands, but it led to higher prices throughout the sector, and not just by cartel members. ÖBB-Infrastruktur, the Austrian railways, claimed compensation for an alleged loss caused as a result of third parties (not cartelists) charging higher prices than they could have charged if the cartel had not existed.

The Austrian Court of First Instance rejected the claim, but the Appellate Court upheld it. The Austrian Supreme Court asked the CJ to clarify whether Article 101 TFEU also applies to this kind of 'umbrella pricing'.

Held: Article 101 TFEU precludes domestic legislation which categorically excludes civil liability of undertakings belonging to a cartel for the loss resulting from umbrella pricing.

Judgment: 29. ... It should be noted that market price is one of the main factors taken into consideration by an undertaking when it determines the price at which it will offer its goods or services. Where a cartel manages to maintain artificially high prices for particular goods and certain conditions are met, relating, in particular, to the nature of the goods or to the size of the market covered by that cartel, it cannot be ruled out that a competing undertaking, outside the cartel in question, might choose to set the price of its offer at an amount higher than it would have chosen under normal conditions of competition, that is, in the absence of that cartel. In such a situation, even if the determination of an offer price is regarded as a purely autonomous decision, taken by the undertaking not party to a cartel, it must none the less be stated that such a decision has been able to be taken by reference to a market price distorted by that cartel and, as a result, contrary to the competition rules.

30. It follows that, contrary to the assertions of Schindler Aufzüge und Fahrtrappen and Schindler Liegenschaftsverwaltung, a loss being suffered by the customer of an undertaking not party to a cartel, but benefiting from the economic conditions of umbrella pricing, because of an offer price higher than it would have been but for the existence of that cartel is one of the possible effects of the cartel, that the members thereof cannot disregard ...

33. The full effectiveness of Article 101 TFEU would be put at risk if the right of any individual to claim compensation for harm suffered were subjected by national law, categorically and regardless of the particular circumstances of the case, to the existence of a direct causal link while excluding that right because the individual concerned had no

---

[304] CJ 5 June 2014 Case C-557/12 *Kone AG et al v ÖBB-Infrastruktur AG* ECLI:EU:C:2014:1317.
[305] See n 40.

contractual links with a member of the cartel, but with an undertaking not party thereto, whose pricing policy, however, is a result of the cartel that contributed to the distortion of price formation mechanisms governing competitive markets.

34. Consequently, the victim of umbrella pricing may obtain compensation for the loss caused by the members of a cartel, even if it did not have contractual links with them, where it is established that the cartel at issue was, in the circumstances of the case and, in particular, the specific aspects of the relevant market, liable to have the effect of umbrella pricing being applied by third parties acting independently, and that those circumstances and specific aspects could not be ignored by the members of that cartel. It is for the referring court to determine whether those conditions are satisfied ...

37. In the light of all the foregoing considerations, the answer to the question referred is that Article 101 TFEU must be interpreted as meaning that it precludes the interpretation and application of domestic legislation enacted by a Member State which categorically excludes, for legal reasons, any civil liability of undertakings belonging to a cartel for loss resulting from the fact that an undertaking not party to the cartel, having regard to the practices of the cartel, set its prices higher than would otherwise have been expected under competitive conditions.

Notes:

(1) The annotated judgment is as much concerned with the causal link and the legal position of indirect purchasers (see below) as it is with the types of damage to be compensated. It does not *impose* liability in case of umbrella pricing, but merely prohibits Member States from categorically excluding such liability in case cartel members 'could not ignore' the potential effect of umbrella pricing. Once again, and in light of the principle of procedural autonomy, the CJ leaves it to the national judge to assess 'the circumstances of the case and, in particular, the specific aspects of the relevant market' that will determine whether compensation should be available.

(2) The Damages Directive does not explicitly refer to umbrella pricing, but its Recitals 12 and 13, read in combination with Article 1, certainly do not exclude the possibility of a damages claim in case of umbrella pricing.

(3) Legal practice is usually (far) ahead of textbooks and CJ judgments, which are typically pronounced years after a claim was started in a national court. We know of at least one pending case where a multinational company is faced with a very substantial claim brought by one of its customers, not because non-cartel members raised their prices 'under the umbrella' of the cartel, but because the cartelist itself raised prices for products which were not cartelised, but which were substitute products for the cartelised products. This new type of 'umbrella pricing' damages claim may rapidly gain ground.

II.D.iii.b Quantification of Harm

Introductory Notes

1. Quantification of harm in current competition damages cases is hardly an exact science. AP Komninos, leading scholar and practitioner in the field, aptly sketches the current situation as follows:

> The national courts and parties involved in damages claims have been consistently undecided as to what econometric model or formula to apply when trying to reach an accurate

calculation. Consequently, the most common argument used by the infringing party is that the model applied by the claimant is incorrect and fails to identify the correct market analysis if the infringement had not occurred. As a consequence, judges and the national courts will estimate the damage in between the estimates of the defendant and the claimant. It might also happen that a national court establishes the liability of the infringing undertaking, leaving the quantification of the damages for a later stage, hoping that the parties involved will reach a settlement in the meantime.[306]

2. From this perspective, quantification of harm has much in common with the establishment of a causal link. First, both legal issues tend to place great evidentiary burdens on claimants and in practice often lead to the unsuccessful outcome of private enforcement damages. Second, it is said that EU law does not devote much space and attention to these thorny issues—but that is only partly correct:

— In *Manfredi*,[307] the CJ expanded of the type of damage to be compensated, but remained silent on the quantification of the damage. In general, the CJ referred to the procedural autonomy principle and the twin conditions of equivalence and effectiveness, stressing the second of those conditions.
— The EC first raised the question on the quantification of damages in its Green Paper.[308] In the White Paper, the EC declared that it would draw up a framework as guidance in order to facilitate the calculation of damages[309] The EC certainly kept its promise, issuing a brief Communication, but also a very detailed non-binding 'Practical Guide' in 2013.[310]
— At first sight, the Damages Directive appears to do little better than the CJ. The Directive admits to being silent on causation ('aspects not dealt with in this Directive such as the notion of causal relationship between the infringement and the harm')[311] and devotes only one article to the quantification of harm.

3. However, the single Article 17 on 'Quantification of harm' in the Damages Directive could make a world of difference in practice. This is already apparent from the discussion of the EC's damages claim before the Brussels Commercial Court concerning the elevator cartel, excerpted above.[312] The EC lost its case, but, as the national court indicated, this may largely have been due to the non-implementation of the Damages Directive and, more particularly, its Article 17. Article 17 consists of four elements. The first one is not

---

[306] AP Komninos, 'Private Antitrust Enforcement in the National Courts—Second Generation Questions' [2012] *e-competition March*, 5.
[307] CJ *Manfredi* (n 38) paras 95–97.
[308] See the Commission Green Paper on Damages Actions for Breach of the EC Antitrust Rules (n 229) 7. See the annexed Commission Staff Working Paper (SEC(2005) 1732) 37–42.
[309] Commission White Paper on Damages Actions for Breach of the EC Antitrust Rules (n 230) 7.
[310] Communication from the Commission on quantifying harm in actions for damages based on breaches of Article 101 or 102 of the Treaty on the Functioning of the European Union (OJ C167/19, 13 June 2016). Commission Staff working document. Practical Guide. Quantifying harm in actions for damages based on breaches of Article 101 or 102 of the Treaty on the Functioning of the European Union. Accompanying the Communication from the Commission on quantifying harm in actions for damages based on breaches of Article 101 or 102 of the Treaty on the Functioning of the European Union. See also: http://ec.europa.eu/competition/antitrust/actionsdamages/quantification_guide_en.pdf.
[311] Recital 11 of the Damages Directive.
[312] Case 2.55 (BE).

new but still welcome: Member States have to make sure that neither the burden nor the standard of proof required for quantification of harm renders the exercise of the right to damages practically impossible or excessively difficult. Article 17 adds three elements that can very well make a difference in practice: (a) a rebuttable presumption is introduced that cartel infringements cause harm; (b) Member States must empower national courts to *estimate* the amount of that harm if it is established that a claimant suffered harm, but it is practically impossible or excessively difficult to precisely quantify the harm on the basis of the available evidence; and (c) Member States must allow national courts to ask NCAs to assist them with the quantification of harm 'where that [NCA] considers such assistance to be appropriate'.

4. The Italian judgment excerpted below provides a relatively rare instance (pre-Damages Directive) of a national court assisting the claimant, making it easy (too easy?) to quantify damages.

One should realise that there are many other cases where national courts find it impossible to award damages because the claimant does not quantify the damages with sufficient precision. Two Spanish judgments can illustrate this:

— In the Spanish *Antena 3* case, a TV channel claimed damages from the Spanish Football Association (LNFP) for abuse of dominance. The LNFP had excluded Antena 3 from long-term contracts offered to other TV channels. The Spanish NCA confirmed the abuse. However, in the follow-on damages case, the national courts dismissed the damages claim on the ground that the theoretical report supplied by Antena 3 did not suffice to quantify the damages. The courts found the criteria used in the report to be too subjective and unrealistic.[313]

— *Conduit Europe* concerned the opening of the Spanish market for directory enquiry services. The incumbent Telefónica was held to refuse to supply data, and later to supply only low-quality data to new market entrants. The national telecom regulator confirmed the abusive behaviour. Conduit filed a follow-on claim and submitted an expert report in order to estimate its additional costs and its loss of profits due to the competition infringements. For the loss of profits, Conduit's expert based its estimations on Conduit's position on the British market. The national court did not agree, holding that British market conditions were largely different from Spanish market conditions and that multiple elements other than the lack of qualitative data determined the claimant's market share. As a consequence, the court ruled that a causal link between the infringement and the damages was not sufficiently established and dismissed the claim for damages.[314]

5. One can safely assume that in the majority of cases, national judges play their normal role, ie, they allow reasonable claims and block unreasonable or unsubstantiated claims. This may lead to the partial or reduced award of claimed amounts. For example, the 2004

---

[313] Spanish Supreme Civil Court 14 April 2009 no ATS 4632/2009—858/2007 ECLI:ES:TS:2009:4632A. Firstly, the case was decided by the Madrid Court of First Instance no 4 on 7 June 2005. On appeal, the Madrid Provincial Court no 25bis ruled on 18 December 2006.

[314] Commercial Court of Madrid No 5 11 November 2005 no 85/05 *Conduit Europe SA v Telefónica de España* SAU. For a full analysis, see G Siotis and M Martínez-Granado, 'Sabotaging Entry: An Estimation of Damages in the Directory Enquiry Service Market'(2010) 6 *Review of Law & Economics* 1.

judgment of the Court of Appeal of Versailles in the *Vérimédia v Médiametrie* case.[315] Vérimédia was one of three 'media expertise' companies in France specialising in the audit of publicity agencies for their clients who order the publicity. Vérimédia needed the services of, among others, Médiamétrie, which had a monopoly on the electronic registration and analysis of the behaviour of panels of TV viewers. After a complaint by Vérimédia, the French NCA fined Médiamétrie in 1998 for the use of vague access conditions to its service and for deliberately delaying the communication of essential information to Vérimédia.[316] In a follow-on damages case, Vérimédia claimed €828,103 for loss of clientele, €2.027,572 being the difference between the projected business plan and the actual results and €15,000 for non-material damage ('préjudice moral'). In first instance, all claims were rejected and Vérimédia was ordered to pay damages for 'abusive use of procedure' ('procédure abusive'). The Court of Appeal reversed this ruling, recognising that the infringements established by the NCA qualified as a 'fault' in French tort law. The Court of Appeal reduced the damages to be awarded to a total of €100,000, explicitly qualifying this as an 'estimate' compensating 'the loss of a chance to penetrate more swiftly and more efficiently the market for TV audits'. The Court of Appeal took into account the fact that the damage was in part caused by Vérimédia's own behaviour (lack of precision of orders and lack of knowledge of sector specifics) and that the document which was claimed to set out the business plan was not based on 'any serious analysis' ('aucune analyse sérieuse').

6. In principle, damages awarded in private enforcement cases by national courts and fines imposed in public enforcement cases by competition authorities do not impact upon each other. Since compensation is the main aim of damages, fines can hardly be taken into account in a damages claim. The opposite would in theory be possible, ie, competition authorities might take paid damages into account, either as a mitigating circumstance or in order to safeguard the continued existence of the fined entity. However, there is little evidence in practice of such mutual influence.

Corte di Cassazione (Italian Court of Cassation),
18 December 2009[317]   **2.64 (IT)**

PV v Axa Assicurazioni spa

EASY PROOF FOR FOLLOW-ON ACTIONS

Italian insurance revisited

Facts: A consumer claimed damages from an insurance company which was involved in a restrictive practice that caused an increase of insurance premiums and that was sanctioned by the NCA. The Corte d'appello rejected the claim. Before the Corte di Cassazione, the claimant argued that the Corte d'appello wrongly imposed the burden of proof for establishing the causal link and the quantum of damages on the consumer.

Held: In order to prove damages in a follow-on claim, the insured party only needs to produce the fining decision of the NCA and the contract between the consumer and the insurance company. The damage can be

---

[315] French Court of Appeal of Versailles (12th Chamber) 24 June 2004 no 2002-07434 *SA Vérimédia v SA Médiamétrie et al*.

[316] French Competition Council 8 July 1998 no 98-D-53 (see: www.autoritedelaconcurrence.fr/pdf/avis/98d53.pdf)

[317] Cass it Section III 18 December 2009 no 26748 *PV v Axa Assicurazioni spa*.

calculated as the percentual difference between the premium paid by the insured party and the premium that he would have paid in absence of the restrictive practice.

Judgment: 2. The decision must be repealed and referred back to the Corte d'appello, in a different composition, so that it decides the dispute in conformity with the principles enunciated in the cited case law of the Corte di Cassazione, in particular with those according to which the judge may identify the causal link between the anticompetitive behaviour and the asserted damage also through criteria of high logical probability or through presumptions, and may come to an assessment in an equitable way, setting the amount for the compensation as a percentage of the premium paid, after tax and various burdens (Cass. civ. No. 2305/2007, cit.), it being understood that the civil judge has the duty to evaluate the possible opposing elements of proof provided by the insurer.

Notes:

(1) This judgment pre-dates similar judgments from the Italian Court of Cassation, which were excerpted above.[318] It again concerns a purely domestic case. In line with the judgments excerpted above, it raises three important issues concerning competition damages actions: the binding power of NCA infringement decisions for the national judge in a follow-on damages claim (this element was discussed above), the burden of proof regarding the causal link (see below) and the extent of damages. The excerpted judgments lower the burden of proof for the consumer as regards both the causal link and the quantification of damages. The Court of Cassation deemed it possible for the lower courts to calculate the harm as the percentual difference between the premium paid by the insured person and the premium that he would have paid in absence of the restrictive practice, without the claimant having to provide further information. This contrasts with judgments in other jurisdictions (some of them excerpted above), which, admittedly in more complex cases, subject even expert opinions to very high standards.

(2) The attitude of the Italian courts to claimants in competition law damages cases thus appears to be rather generous. This does not only become clear from this judgment and the judgments excerpted above, but also from the Italian follow-up judgment to the CJ's preliminary ruling in *Manfredi*. Referring to the principle of effectiveness and setting aside principles of the Italian Civil Code, the national court in that follow-up judgment apparently awarded double damages. The court intended to annul any economic advantage that the infringers could have obtained from their anticompetitive agreement. Allowing any further profit from the infringement would undermine the prohibition of restrictive practices.[319]

II.D.iii.c Passing-on Defence

Introductory Notes

1. '[A]n undertaking which purchases from a supplier engaged in anticompetitive behaviour could be in a position to mitigate its economic loss by passing the overcharge on to

---

[318] Cases 2.58 (IT) and 2.59 (IT).

[319] See P Nebbia, 'An Italian Court awards to a Consumer Damages Amounting to Twofold the Loss Suffered as a Result of a Cartel among Insurance companies after Obtaining an ECJ Preliminary Ruling (Manfredi)' (2007) *e-Competitions Bulletin May*, art no 41611.

its own customers. The damages caused by anticompetitive behaviour could therefore be passed down the supply chain or even suffered in entirety by the ultimate purchaser, the final consumer.'[320] If a tortfeasor in a private enforcement damages action (most often a cartelist) is allowed to invoke the 'passing-on defence', this implies that the tortfeasor will not have to compensate the victim for that part of the damages which were caused by the infringement, but which the victim has passed down the supply chain.

2. Under US law, the passing-on defence is prohibited.[321] In EU law, the EC introduced the idea of a passing-on defence in its Green and White Papers, arguing that a denial to allow the passing-on defence would result in the unjust enrichment of the purchaser who has passed on the overcharge. Introduction of the passing-on defence is now imposed by the Damages Directive.[322] As will be made clear in the excerpts below, increasing numbers of Member State courts also recognise the defence under national law, in what might be seen as an intriguing form of 'pre-emptive implementation' of the Damages Directive.

3. It is submitted that the reason for the growing divergence between US and EU law on this point is twofold:

i.   Whereas deterrence is an important function of private enforcement of competition law in the US, compensation is the main function of EU private enforcement. Deterrence is mostly left to public enforcement in the EU, as the ever higher fines make clear. The Damages Directive even prohibits overcompensation.[323]

ii.   The passing-on defence has since long been recognised in other areas of EU law, making it difficult to reject it in cases of private enforcement of competition law. The CJ first confirmed that the passing-on defence is not incompatible with EU law in the 1976 *Rewe* judgment.[324] Since then, the CJ has acknowledged the possibility of a passing-on defence in actions for extra-contractual liability of the EU under Article 340(2) TFEU[325] and in actions which undertakings launch against Member States for the recovery of duties levied in breach of EU law (ie, the EU law remedy of restitution).[326]

---

[320] Commission Green Paper on Damages Actions for Breach of the EC Antitrust Rules (n 229).

[321] See especially *Illinois Brick Co v Illinois* 431 US 720 (1977); *Hanover Shoe, Inc v United Shoe Machinery Corp* 392 US 481 (1986).

[322] Article 13 of the Damages Directive: 'Member States shall ensure that the defendant in an action for damages can invoke as a defence against a claim for damages the fact that the claimant passed on the whole or part of the overcharge resulting from the infringement of competition law. The burden of proving that the overcharge was passed on shall be on the defendant, who may reasonably require disclosure from the claimant or from third parties.' The CJ did not rule on the admissibility of the passing-on defence in the above-cited and seminal *Courage* and *Manfredi* judgments.

[323] Damages Directive, art 3(3).

[324] CJ 16 December 1976 Case 33/76 *Rewe-Zentralfinanz eG and Rewe-Zentral AG v Landwirtschaftskammer für das Saarland* [1976] I-01989 ECLI; EU:C:1976:188. See also Hartkamp 2016 no 122.

[325] CJ 29 October 1979 Case C- 238/78 *Ireks-Arkady GmbH v Council and Commission of the European Communities* [1979] I-02955 ECLI:EU:C:1979:226, para 14: 'it must be admitted that if the loss from the abolition of the refunds has actually been passed on, or could have been passed on, in the prices the damage may not be measured by reference to the refunds not paid. In that case the price increase would take the place of the refunds, thus compensating the producer'. See also CJ 4 October 1979 Joined Cases C-64 and 113/76, 167 and 239/78, 27-28 and 45/79 *P Dumortier frères SA et al v Council of the European Communities Dumortier Frères* [1979] I-03091 ECLI:EU:C:1979:223, para 15.

[326] CJ 27 February 1980 Case C-68/79 *Hans Just I/S v Danish Ministry for Fiscal Affairs* [1980] I-00501ECLI:EU:C:1980:57, para 26: 'that the protection of rights guaranteed ... does not require an order for the recovery of charges improperly made to be granted in conditions which would involve the unjust enrichment of those entitled. There is nothing therefore, from the point of view of Community law, to prevent

An additional reason for US courts to prohibit the passing-on defence is the complexity of the damages calculations which may follow from the defence. The Damages Directive may be seen to counter that objection by ensuring that national judges are allowed to estimate the share of any overcharge that was passed on, just as national judges are allowed to estimate the amount of harm in general.[327]

4. In EU competition law, there is a strong link between, on the one hand, the passing-on defence and, on the other, (a) causation and (b) the standing of indirect purchasers, whom the EC defined in its White Paper as 'purchasers who had no direct dealings with the infringement, but who nonetheless may have suffered considerable harm because an illegal overcharge was passed on to them along the distribution chain'.[328] When the EC first mentioned the passing-on defence in its Green Paper, it was because the EC noticed that indirect purchasers are confronted with evidentiary problems when proving the extent of their damages and the causal link with the infringing behaviour. This explains why the passing-on defence in EU law is coupled with a rebuttable presumption that illegal overcharges are passed on to the indirect purchasers. The rebuttable presumption is now incorporated into Article 14 of the Damages Directive. According to Article 14(1) the burden of proving the existence and scope of a passing-on rests in principle on the damages claimant.[329] However, the burden of proof is lowered for indirect purchasers and is made conditional upon prima facie evidence only:

[T]he indirect purchaser shall be deemed to have proven that a passing-on to that indirect purchaser occurred where that indirect purchaser has shown that:

(a) the defendant has committed an infringement of competition law;
(b) the infringement of competition law has resulted in an overcharge for the direct purchaser of the defendant; and
(c) the indirect purchaser has purchased the goods or services that were the object of the infringement of competition law, or has purchased goods or services derived from or containing them.

This paragraph shall not apply where the defendant can demonstrate credibly to the satisfaction of the court that the overcharge was not, or was not entirely, passed on to the indirect purchaser.[330]

5. More controversial than the introduction of the passing-on defence in the Damages Directive is the introduction of the rebuttable presumption in favour of indirect purchasers. In theory and according to the letter of the Directive, it is for the defendant (mostly an alleged or confirmed cartelist) to invoke and prove the defence, and/or to demonstrate that harm was not passed on to an indirect purchaser. In practice, there may be a clear

national courts from taking account in accordance with their national law of the fact that it has been possible for charges unduly levied to be incorporated in the prices of the undertaking liable for the charge and to be passed on to the purchasers'.
[327] See arts 12(5) and 17(1) of the Damages Directive, respectively. Article 16 stipulates that the EC shall issue guidelines for national courts on how to estimate the share of the overcharge that was passed on to the indirect purchaser.
[328] Commission White Paper on Damages Actions for Breach of the EC Antitrust Rules (n 230) 3–4.
[329] Damages Directive, art 4(1).
[330] ibid, art 14(2).

conflict of interests between the direct and the indirect purchaser now that the Damages Directive prohibits overcompensation and harm can therefore only be recovered once. It is to be feared that in practice, the direct and indirect purchasers, who are both victims and supposedly best friends (as they will often be in a supplier–client relationship), may be forced to directly or indirectly fight each other over whether harm was or was not passed on. If, for example, both a direct and an indirect purchaser claim damages from an infringer, Article 14 *in fine* leaves it to that infringer to 'demonstrate credibly to the satisfaction of the court that the overcharge was not, or was not entirely, passed on to the indirect purchaser'. But what is the incentive for the infringer to spend resources on such demonstration if he knows that he will only have to pay compensation once?[331]

6. For a long period, no harmonising legislation on passing-on existed at the EU level. In *Courage* and *Manfredi*, the CJ did not rule on whether a passing-on defence should or should not exist under national law. It merely confirmed the right for any private party to bring an action for damages against the infringer of EU competition law rules, leaving it to the national courts to decide, under their respective national laws, on the conditions, subject to the twin conditions of equivalence and effectiveness under procedural autonomy. The following excerpts serve to illustrate that the gradual recognition of the passing-on defence in Dutch, Spanish, German and French national law constitutes a recent and sometimes uncertain development.

Gerechtshof Arnhem-Leeuwarden (Court of Appeal of Arnhem-Leeuwarden), 2 September 2014[332]   **2.65 (NL)**

ABB Ltd v TenneT TSO BV

PASSING-ON DEFENCE

GIS *bis*

Dutch law recognises the passing-on defence, even though this may allow the cartellist to (temporarily) keep a part of the cartel's gains

Facts: In 2007, the EC fined a global cartel in the Gas Insulated Switchgear (GIS) sector for breach of (now) Article 101 TFEU.[333] ABB Ltd participated in this cartel, but received full immunity as it was the first leniency applicant. In a Dutch follow-on case, TenneT TSO BV then claimed damages from ABB, but ABB argued that TenneT had passed on any overcharges to its customers.

Held: The first instance court rejected the passing-on defence. It awarded the damages claim, but postponed calculation of the damages.[334] The appeal court accepted the passing-on defence, but denied that the overcharge was fully passed-on to indirect purchasers.

---

[331] See ibid, art 12(2).

[332] Dutch Court of Appeal of Arnhem-Leeuwarden 2 September 2014 ECLI:NL:GHARL:2014:6766 *ABB Ltd v Tennet TSO BV*.

[333] Commission Decision of 24 January 2007 relating to a proceeding under Article 81 of the Treaty establishing the European Community and Article 53 of the EEA Agreement (Case COMP/38.899—Gas Insulated Switchgear), OJ C5/7, 10 January 2008.

[334] Dutch District Court Oost-Nederland 16 January 2013 ECLI:NL:RBONE:2013:BZ0403 *Tennet TSO BV v ABB BV.*

Judgment: 3.32 According to the view of the court, the claim of TenneT c.s. will be reasonably established by the overcharge (the difference in price between what has been paid and what would have been paid without the cartel infringement), minus any part of that damage which has been passed-on by TenneT c.s. to its customers, all this insofar as these elements will be established in the damages assessment procedure, besides potential loss of profits and interest. The court also takes into account that in case of passing-on the harm, this results in fact in a deflection of this harm to those to whom the overcharge has been passed-on (the customers). As appears from what has been considered above, every person has the right to claim damages before the national judge for the harm suffered because of a competition infringement. Consequently, this also applies for the customers of TenneT c.s, provided that and as far as they have suffered any harm caused by the antitrust violation ...

Admittedly, the court realises that it cannot be excluded beforehand that ABB c.s. will not—immediately—be deprived of the surplus they have gained because of the cartel violation in 1993, but that is not the key priority when confronted with damages claims. The objective of damages claims is to compensate the harmed party—in this case TenneT c.s.—for the disadvantage they have suffered following the unlawful conduct of the party causing the harm—here ABB c.s. If and insofar as it is determined in the damage assessment procedure that TenneT c.s. has passed-on the overcharge, the harm of TenneT c.s. will no longer exist and they will already have been compensated by the increase of their prices, instead of by the award of damages.

Notes:

(1) On appeal, this court confirmed that it is possible to raise the passing-on defence under Dutch law, although it dismissed the defendant's position that the overcharge was *fully* passed-on to indirect purchasers. Just before this book was sent to print, we learned that the Dutch Supreme Court ('Hoge Raad') has confirmed the appeal judgment, leaving no doubt that the passing-on defence is now recognised in Dutch law.[335]

(2) The recognition of the defence is fully in line with EU law. The Gerechtshof refers to, among others, the *Courage* and *Manfredi* judgments, not only to establish the principled liability of infringers but also to underline the power of national judges to prevent unjust enrichment of the claimant; it also refers to the (at the time of the judgment still draft) Damages Directive.[336] The Damages Directive only has to be implemented by the end of 2016, but a proposal for implementation by the Dutch legislature is already available. The proposed implementing Act incorporates the possibility to raise the passing-defence, as well as the rebuttable and conditional presumption of passing-on to indirect purchasers.[337] No amendments are deemed necessary concerning the burden of proof and the disclosure of evidence related to the passing-on.[338]

---

[335] Hoge Raad, 8 July 2016, Case no 15/00167, ECLI:NL:HR:2016:1483.

[336] See the well-documented paras 3.26–3.27 of the excerpted judgment.

[337] Proposed arts 6:193q and 6:193r of the Dutch Civil Code.

[338] A sufficient legal basis is deemed to be present in the existing arts 150 and 843a of the Code on Civil Procedure. See Draft Implementing Act on Private enforcement of competition law ('Voorontwerp Implementatiewet richtlijn privaatrechtelijke handhaving mededingingsrecht'), 1–27, General Explanation ('Memorie van Toelichting), 17.

(3) The Gerechtshof admitted that a deduction of passed-on overcharges from the calculated harm could result in ABB being allowed to keep certain gains from its unlawful conduct. However, the judges rightly pointed at the specific, compensatory, aim of private enforcement damages claims. The word 'immediately' is also important in the excerpt: as soon as indirect purchasers launch their own claims, any remaining surplus of the unlawful conduct of infringer ABB can be expected to disappear.

Tribunal Supremo Madrid (Spanish Supreme Court),
7 November 2013[339]   **2.66 (ES)**

Sweets and Food Producer v Ebro Foods

PASSING-ON DEFENCE

The sweet taste of revenge

Spanish law recognizes the passing-on defence, but firmly imposes on the defendant, ie, on the alleged cartelist, the burden to prove the passing-on

Facts: Between 1995 and 1996, multiple sugar manufacturers organised a cartel covering the Spanish market. After the Spanish NCA adopted an infringement decision, several sweets and food producer filed follow-on damages claims for damages against sugar producer Ebro Foods. The defendant invoked a passing-on defence, raising the question whether such defence was valid under Spanish law.

Held: Subject to strict conditions, the passing-on defence was allowed. However, the burden of proof was on the defendant. As the defendant's arguments were rejected, full damages were awarded to the claimants.

Judgment: In the absence of specific EU regulation on compensation for damages in competition law, the issue must be resolved by applying the rules of national law. Under this [national law], it is permissible for the party from whom compensation for damages caused by a competition law infringement is sought (the defendant) to oppose to the claimant making the claim that the [claimant] has not suffered any damage since [it] has passed on the costs down the supply chain. Since compensation for damages resulting from a practice restrictive of competition is subject to criteria of compensation and since in this field of law, a principle of law applies that forbids unjust enrichment, it is not reasonable to compensate anyone who has not suffered damage.

It can be observed from the work performed in this regard in the European Union that the burden of proving the acts constituting the 'passing-on' should be on the offending company, and that the standard of proof for this defense should not be lower than that imposed on the claimant to prove the damage caused.

Notes:

(1) Like the Dutch judgment excerpted before, the judgment of the Spanish Supreme Court recognises that no harmonised EU law rules exist (as yet), but still relies on EU law, in particular on the CJ's mandate in *Courage* and *Manfredi* for national judges to prevent unjust enrichment of the claimant.

---

[339] Spanish Supreme Court Civil 7 November 2013 no 2472/2011 *Sweets and Food Producer v Ebro Foods.*

(2) The Spanish Court also refers to EU law for the burden of proof, which is on the defendant. The defendant should not only prove that the claimant has passed on the economic damage and loss to its customers, but also that the claimant's volume of sales has not decreased following the competition infringement. If harm was passed on but the claimant's sales went down, harm may still be caused and compensatory damages would still be justified. This reflects established CJ case law since *Comateb*:

> [E]ven where it is established that the burden of the charge has been passed on in whole or in part to the purchaser, repayment to the trader of the amount thus passed on does not necessarily entail his unjust enrichment ... the trader may have suffered damage as a result of the very fact that he has passed on the charge ... because the increase in the price of the product brought about by passing on the charge has led to a decrease in sales.

> In such circumstances, the trader may justly claim that, although the charge has been passed on to the purchaser, the inclusion of that charge in the cost price has, by increasing the price of the goods and reducing sales, caused him damage which excludes, in whole or in part, any unjust enrichment which would otherwise be caused by reimbursement.[340]

Bundesgerichtshof (Federal Court of Germany),
28 June 2011[341]   **2.67 (DE)**

ORWI

STANDING OF INDIRECT PURCHASERS AND PASSING-ON DEFENCE

Carbonless paper

Even before the coming into force of Directive 2014/104/EU on antitrust damages actions, German law recognises both the standing of indirect purchasers and the passing-on defence

Facts: In 2001, the EC fined 10 companies for taking part in price-fixing and market-sharing agreements in the carbonless paper industry.[342] A German manufacturer of pre-printed forms, ORWI, bought such paper from a wholesaler—a subsidiary of one of the cartel members. The printing company became insolvent and assigned its antitrust claims against the cartel members to a German bank. The bank brought an action in damages against the company's supplier. The German Federal Civil Court was asked to rule on the standing of indirect purchasers. It also addressed the issue of passing-on.

Held: Indirect purchasers have standing in a damages claim if their supplier passed on the price increase which followed from the anticompetitive behaviour to them. The passing-on defence is available to defendants.

Judgment: [22] To the extent that [legal scholars or courts] accept that also indirect purchasers may, in principle, claim damages, they either grant the passing-on defence on principle ... or they stress that ... a multiple (judicial) recourse against the cartel participant

---

[340] CJ 14 January 1997 Case C-192–218/95 *Société Comateb* [1997] ECR I-165, ECLI:EU:C:1997:12, paras 29–32.

[341] BGH 28 June 2011KZR 75/10 *ORWI*.

[342] Commission Decision 2004/337/EC of 20 December 2001 relating to a proceeding pursuant to Article 81 of the EC Treaty and Article 53 of the EEA Agreement (Case COMP/E-1/36.212—Carbonless paper), OJ L115/1, 21 April 2004.

[shall be avoided], through a settlement between the aggrieved parties or a deduction of damages already paid.

[23] b) Preferable is the opinion that also indirect purchases have a damage claim on the basis of Section 823 § 2 BGB in conjunction with Article 101 TFEU if they suffered damage from anticompetitive conduct.

[25] aa) To effectively achieve the objective pursued with recognising the cartel prohibition as protective legislation within the meaning of Section 823 para. 2 BGB it is necessary that indirect purchasers are entitled to claim damages based on competition law infringements.

In view of the importance of the cartel prohibition for the economic order it is necessary to grant law-abiding market participants the protection provided by tort law where an anticompetitive behaviour is being exercised to their detriment.

[26] The damaging effect of a cartel or any other conduct prohibited under Art. 101 TFEU often extends the directly involved countervailing market power.

Depending on the circumstances on the downstream markets also, or even primarily, purchasers on downstream levels and consumers may be economically affected and limited in their choices.

The restriction of supplies, partitioning of the market or price increase intended by the cartel regularly result in higher prices and less [choices/diversity of supply] for consumers.

This is provoked by direct purchasers who will attempt to pass on the increase in their purchase prices onto their customers.

Where they succeed—due to the conditions on the downstream markets being marked by the price level that the cartel causes—, the damage only occurs at the subsequent market level.

To generally exclude indirect purchasers from claiming damages would result in denying compensation to those primarily affected by cartels and other prohibited forms of behaviour.

[27] bb) … Furthermore, the larger the distance between the respective market levels of the claimant and the author of damage, the more the probability of a successful damages claim will decrease …

[34] dd) The EU principle of effectiveness also pleads in favour of entitling indirect purchasers to claim damages …

[37] It is correct that the [CJEU] considers that individual damage claims increase the effective enforcement of EU competition law rules and are suitable to deter business from anticompetitive conduct prohibited by law.

However, one cannot conclude from this that EU law allows or even demands that indirect purchasers who are actually suffering damage, be denied claims for compensation merely because a limitation to direct purchasers possibly would facilitate the private enforcement of competition law.

EU law rather requires that a workable coexistence is reached between [a] the individual rights of persons and [b] the public interest in effective enforcement of EU antitrust law …

[58] … Striking a fair balance between the conflicting interests involved in a case of damage requires, on the one hand, that the aggrieved party will not be made better off as compared to his/her situation without the damaging event. On the other hand, not all advantages resulting from the damaging event are to be deducted from the damages claim, but only those the consideration of which corresponds with the … function of the claim for compensation, i.e. as far as such deduction is reasonable for the injured party and does not unduly relieve the author of the damage.

Notes:

(1) The excerpted judgment is extremely rich and well motivated, and deserves to be read in its entirety. One could identify three parts in the reasoning. First, the BGH motivates why, in its view, indirect purchasers deserve to have standing in damages claims. Paragraphs 23–37 in the above excerpt relate to this part of the BGH's reasoning and decision, but many additional arguments pro and contra are discussed in the judgment. Paragraph 22 somehow links the standing of indirect purchasers and the passing-on defence: to the extent that indirect purchasers have standing, a passing-on defence appears to be necessary in order to avoid overcompensation. Paragraphs 58ff discuss the modalities of the passing-on defence in relation to the required causal link.

(2) On appeal before the case reached the BGH, the Oberlandesgericht Karlsruhe had struck a different 'fair balance between the conflicting interests involved in a case of damage'. It had rejected the passing-on defence, because the defence would give the infringing undertaking the opportunity to escape liability, thus hindering efficient enforcement, and it would be contrary to the general rule set out by the CJ that *any* victim of competition law infringements must have the right to claim damages.[343]

(3) According to Bellamy & Child, 'if account is taken of passing-on then indirect purchasers may encounter evidential difficulties when attempting to trace the effect of the anticompetitive charge through each stage of the supply chain'.[344] The BGH similarly states that when the distance between the claimant and the infringer increases, the chances of success of the damages claim decrease. To counter these concerns, the Damages Directive obliges Member States to write a rebuttable presumption in favour of indirect purchasers into their laws.[345] Indirect purchasers will merely have to prove that: (i) the defendant committed an antitrust infringement; (ii) this resulted in an overcharge for the direct purchaser; and (iii) the indirect purchaser bought the goods or services that were the object of the competition infringement. One could say that this presumption is supported by further presumptions. Regarding the first element, as discussed, final findings of infringements by the EC or by the national NCA will become binding for the court hearing the damages claim. Regarding the second element, the claimant may invoke the presumption that cartel infringements cause harm.[346]

---

[343] Oberlandesgericht Karlsruhe (6. Zivilsenat) 11 June 2010 *ORWI* 6 U 118/05 (Kart) (08).

[344] V Rose and D Baily (eds), *Bellamy & Child, European Union Law of Competition* (Oxford, Oxford University Press, 2013) 1255.

[345] Damages Directive, art 14. See n 4.

[346] ibid, art 17(2). See M Strand, 'Indirect Purchasers, Passing-on and the New Directive on Competition Law Damages' (2014) *European Competition Journal* 382.

Tribunal de Commerce de Paris (Tribunal de Commerce de Paris),
26 January 2007[347]   **2.68 (FR)**

Juva Santé et Juva Production SED v Société Hoffmann La Roche AG

PROOF OF DAMAGE AND OF QUANTUM OF DAMAGES

Vitamins

Commercial and financial harm are not presumed but have to be proven under French law

Facts: In 2001, the EC imposed fines of €855.22 million for participating in eight distinct secret market-sharing and price-fixing cartels affecting vitamin products.[348] Juva Santé and Juva Production brought a follow-on damages action against their suppliers Hoffmann La Roche and its subsidiaries. When a passing-on defence was raised, Juva argued that it could not have passed the overcharge for vitamins on to its customers since such an increase would have resulted in a loss of market share.

Held: The claims for compensation were dismissed.

Judgment: Even if the JUVA companies do not, in a credible manner, establish the *quantum* of harm resulting from the abnormal increase in the price of raw materials, it now needs to be examined whether they can claim a decrease of their sales margins …

As a matter of fact, it is recognised by all economists that for products considered by consumers as lacking substitution or as covering basic needs, which is often the case with health products, there is no price elasticity of demand, i.e. the volumes do not decrease in case of an increase in price.

Considering the reality of variations in price and margins throughout the period in question,

That the cost of the contentious raw materials constitutes a very small part of the sales price of products which use such raw materials,

As a consequence, a low increase in the sale price suffices to compensate for a major increase of the cost of raw materials.

… It hence sufficed, in order to compensate the alleged excess, to increase, at the beginning of the period and only once, the sales price of the package of 15 tablets with 1,3% and of the package of 30 tablets with 2,05% …

As such, it would be incorrect to state, as claimed by the JUVA companies, that 'the sales prices of finished products have only very slightly increased throughout the period of the agreement'; it is likewise incorrect to state that the price increases of raw materials resulted in 'a decrease of the sales margin realised by the JUVA Laboratories'.

The court, considering that the JUVA companies do not prove that the price increase of raw materials led to a decrease in their sales margin and that their claims for compensation for commercial harm are hence ill-founded, dismisses these claims, and likewise dismisses their claims regarding financial harm, considering that financial harm depends on commercial harm which, as stated, does not exist.

[347] RG03048044.
[348] EC Decision 2003/2/EC of 21 November 2001 relating to a proceeding pursuant to Article 81 of the EC Treaty and Article 53 of the EEA Agreement (Case COMP/E-1/37.512—Vitamins), OJ L 6/1, 10 January 2003.

*Cour de Cassation, chambre commerciale (Court of Cassation,
Commercial Division), 15 June 2010*[349]   **2.69 (FR)**

Doux aliments

PASSING-ON DEFENCE

Lysine

*The French Court of Cassation recognises the passing-on defence but does not place the
burden of proof on the alleged cartellist*

Facts: Ajinomoto Eurolyne (AE) supplied lysine to Ceva Santé Animale, which in turn supplied the poultry
farmer group Doux Aliments. In 2000, the EC imposed a fine of €110 million on five lysine producers, including AE.[350] Doux launched a follow-on damages claim against AE.

Held: The Court of Cassation struck down the appeal judgment because the appeal court had not checked
whether Doux had passed on the overcharge to its customers.

Judgment: Having regard to Article 1382 of the Civil Code;
    Considering that, in order to condemn company AE to pay damages to the *Doux* com-
panies, the judgment, after having observed that the existence of a fault committed by
company AE results from the decision of 7 June 2000 of the [EC] and after having pointed
out that this fault has caused, for the *Doux* companies, an extra cost in the purchases
of lysine, holds the fact that the *Doux* companies were able to pass on this extra cost
through price increases of the product to be without effect on their right to compensation
for damages; the judgment adds that the increased expenses incurred by those [*Doux*]
companies as a result of price increases, caused harm by a loss of competitiveness of their
products and form the cause of a loss of a chance ...
    Considering that, without analysing whether the *Doux* companies have, in full or in
part, passed on to their customers the extra costs resulting from the infringement by
company AE, so that the award of damages could have given rise to unjust enrichment,
the judgment by the Court of Appeal is without legal basis.

Notes:

    (1) The Paris Court of Appeal had rejected AE's argument that the claimant Doux
had passed on any overcharge to its consumers. It made use of the doctrine of loss of
a chance and concluded that Doux had to be compensated up to a level of 30 per cent
of the claimed amount of damages for the loss of a chance it had suffered as a result of
increased prices and decreased competitiveness.
    (2) The French Court of Cassation struck the appeal judgment down. Its ruling that the
Court of Appeal was required to consider a possible passing-on of overcharges amounts
to a formal recognition of that defence under French law. However, the Court of Cassation

---

[349] Court of Cassation, Commercial Division 15 June 2010 no 09-15816 *Ajinomoto Eurolysine c v Doux
aliments Bretagne et al.* See also C Lemaire and M Cousin, 'Passing-on Defence: The Court of Cassation
Cancels a Decision of the Court of Appeals Refusing the "Passing-on Defence" (Ajinomoto Eurolysine/Doux
Aliments Bretagne e.a.)' (2010) 4 *Concurrences Review November*, art no 33173, 205–07.
[350] EC Decision 2001/418/EC of 7 June 2000 relating to a proceeding pursuant to Article 81 of the EC
Treaty and Article 53 of the EEA Agreement (Case COMP/36.545/F3—Amino Acids), OJ L 152/24, 7 June
2001.

also appears to have allocated the burden of proof that no passing-on took place on the claimant, whereas Article 13, *in fine*, of the Damages Directive firmly places the burden of proof on the defendant.

(3) In its 2012 *Gouessant*[351] judgment, the Court of Cassation also confirmed that the parties in a follow-on damages claim can rely on the presumption that direct purchasers, victims of competition infringements, pass on any overcharge to their customers, ie, to indirect purchasers. It appears that the Court of Cassation leaves it to the direct purchaser to rebut the presumption by demonstrating that it suffered damage by the defendant's anticompetitive behaviour. Such division of the burden of proof would again have to change after the date for implementation of the Damages Directive, as Article 14(1) places the burden of proof on the defendant (see above, Introductory Notes).

II.D.iv CAUSAL LINK

Introductory Notes

1. We refer to the introductory notes (in particular notes 1 and 2) under 'Quantification of harm' and to the section on the passing-on defence. In practice, the establishment of a sufficiently direct causal link seriously hinders claimants from obtaining damages in private enforcement damages cases. The above-excerpted *EU v Otis* case in Belgium and the first of the two Dutch cases excerpted below may illustrate this.

2. EU tort law is not very well developed when it comes to causality. This is not specific to the competition law area, but is a general feature that is also present in the case law on Article 340 (liability of EU Institutions and civil servants) or on Member State liability. The very first casebook in this series of *Ius Commune* casebooks, the volume on *Tort Law* mostly written by the late Walter van Gerven in 2000, is very instructive in this regard: not much more could be derived from the EU courts' case law than that the causal link between infringement and damage has to be 'direct' or 'sufficiently direct'.[352] Little appears to have changed since. In its *Manfredi*[353] and other judgments, the CJ explicitly puts forth the requirement of a causal link between the damage suffered by the claimant and an infringement of antitrust rules, but leaves it to national legal systems to regulate the requirements in accordance with the principle of procedural autonomy.

This is not different in the CJ's *Kone* judgment on 'umbrella pricing'. However, as may appear from the excerpt above, the judgment nevertheless had a direct impact on the Austrian law on causation, at least in one particular setting. Austrian case law held that:

> [W]hen an undertaking not party to a cartel takes advantage of the effect of umbrella pricing, there is no adequate causal link between the cartel and the loss potentially suffered by a buyer, since it consists of an indirect loss: a side effect of an independent decision that a person not party to a cartel has taken on the basis of his own business considerations.

---

[351] Cour de cassation, Chambre Commerciale, 15 May 2012, arrêt no. 540, pourvoi no. 11-18.495.

[352] W van Gerven, J Lever and P Larouche, *Ius Commune Casebooks for the Common Law of Europe* (Oxford, Hart Publishing, 2000) 889–930.

[353] CJ *Manfredi* (n 38) para 61.

This case law would have to be reversed after *Kone*. Interestingly, the referring court also distinguished between: (a) consequences foreseeable 'in abstracto', including accidental consequences, for which the tortfeasor must provide compensation; and (b) atypical consequences, for which no compensation would have to be provided. The CJ did not expand on this, but the AG did.[354]

3. At first glance, causation appears to be an equally underprivileged topic in the Damages Directive. Recital 11 lists causation as an 'aspect not dealt with in this Directive'. However, this may amount to false modesty, since the introduction by the Damages Directive of certain presumptions does have a direct impact on at least the burden of proof when establishing a causal link. The (rebuttable) presumption that cartels cause harm[355] and the (rebuttable and conditional) presumption that overcharges were passed on to indirect purchasers[356] come to mind.

Rechtbank Midden-Nederland (District Court Midden-Nederland),
13 March 2013[357]   **2.70 (NL)**

Vereniging van eigenaars woningen 'Het Schip' v Otis BV

CAUSAL LINK

Elevators going Dutch

A causal link is not presumed; no damages will be awarded if the causal link is not sufficiently substantiated

Facts: In February 2007, the EC fined four elevator companies more than €992 million for their participation in a market allocation cartel and bid-rigging scheme.[358] Dutch homeowners' associations launched a follow-on damages claim against Otis. The claims concerned two maintenance contracts with Otis, for which the claimants allegedly paid an excessive price.

Held: The claims were dismissed due to a lack of causal link between the cartel infringement and the alleged damage.

Judgment: 4.2. It is apparent from the decision, as *Otis* uncontestably states, that the EC has only established that *Otis* and two other suppliers of elevators had made agreements in view of restricting competition in the light of a number of projects between 15 April 1988 and 5 May 2004. The EC has, on that basis, concluded that these agreements were prohibited agreements in the sense of (current) Article 101 TFEU.

VvE has not substantiated that those prohibited agreements also envisaged to close maintenance agreements for three elevators of VvE. Therefore one cannot establish a causal link between on the one hand the infringement of the cartel prohibition identified by the EC and on the other hand the maintenance contracts including (according to VvE)

---

[354] AG Kokott Opinion 30 January 2014 in Case C-557/12 *Kone et al v ÖBB-Infrastruktur AG* ECLI:EU:C:2014:45, paras 41–52.

[355] Damages Directive, art 17(2).

[356] ibid, art 14(2).

[357] Dutch District Court Midden-Nederland 13 March 2013 ECLI:NL:RBMNE:2013:CA1922 *Vereniging van eigenaars woningen 'Het schip' v Otis BV.*

[358] Commission Decision of 21 February 2007 relating to a proceeding under Article 81 of the Treaty establishing the European Community (Case COMP/E-1/38.823—Elevators and Escalators) [2008] OJ C75/19.

excessive prices and unreasonable conditions. For those reasons, the court does not agree with VvE's arguments. Even if, and to the extent that, the agreed prices were inexplicably high, as VvE has argued during its pleadings, the existence of a causal link between the prohibited agreements and the prices cannot be recognized without further substantiation, which is lacking.

Notes:

(1) The EC wrote in its fining decision that the possible effects of the elevator cartel could be felt for 20 to 50 years, since maintenance is often conducted by the same companies that installed the elevators and were parties to cartel agreements. However, the Dutch court ruled that the claimants did not prove a causal link between the anticompetitive conduct and the alleged excessive prices and unfair conditions. The claimants failed to prove that the fined restrictive agreements also covered the specific elevator maintenance contracts between them and Otis. The claimants bore the burden of proving that the cartel agreements also covered the specific contracts.

(2) This Dutch *Otis* judgment apparently contrasts with another Dutch judgment in a comparable follow-on damages claim. The *Tennet TSO BV v ABB BV* judgment pre-dates the *Otis* judgment and relates to Gas Insulated Switchgear (GIS), a sector where the EC also fined a global cartel. The Arnhem court in *Tennet* assumed that the global cartel members also entered into anticompetitive agreements with regard to the specific GIS projects. Although the earlier EC findings did not specifically identify these projects as falling under the cartel agreements, the national court based its decision on the EC's finding that the cartel had an impact on the Dutch market. The *Tennet* judgment, contrary to the *Otis* judgment, effectively assigned the burden of proof in relation to the causal link to the members of the cartel instead of to the claimants.

(3) It is equally interesting to now compare the Dutch case law with case law in other Member States:

— As discussed above, in *EU v Otis*,[359] the Brussels court of first instance rejected the EC's claim for damages in the elevator cartel case, in part for lack of sufficient proof of a causal link. An appeal is pending.

— In Germany, the Federal Supreme Court of Germany (BGH) held in its *ORWI* judgment,[360] also excerpted above, that indirect purchasers have standing to claim damages for competition infringements, but that they also bear the burden of proof when alleging that overcharges were passed on to them. A causal link between an overcharge and the relevant cartel agreement cannot be presumed according to the Federal Supreme Court. Taking into account the specific circumstances of the case, the claimant has to show that the price increase on his level is attributable to the cartel and not to other factors. The BHG's directives on how to establish this are rather precise.[361]

---

[359] Brussels Commercial Court 24 November 2014 A/08/06816 *Europese Commissie v Otis et al TBM* 2015 no 1–2, 37–46.

[360] BGH 28 June 2011 KZR 75/10 *ORWI*.

[361] For more details, see I Lianos, *Causal Uncertainty and Damages Claims for the Infringement of Competition Law in Europe* (London, CLES Research Paper 2/2015) 34–35.

— Several Italian judgments were excerpted above[362] that create rebuttable but authoritative presumptions, not only on (a) the binding power of NCA infringement decisions for national judges in follow-on damages claims and (b) the extent of damages, but also on (c) the burden of proof regarding the causal link.

— Like the judgment of the Versailles Court of Appeal in *Vérimédia v Médiametrie* discussed above, the Swedish judgment in *Europe Investor Direct*[363] illustrates that in some cases, a causal link can only be partially established. After a detailed assessment of the situation, the Stockholm City Court awarded only half of the amount claimed for breach of competition law. The Court ruled that part of the losses could have been avoided if the claimant had taken other business decisions, and it also took economic recession into account.

— French judgments on causality make use of the doctrine of loss of a chance 'which provides an escape valve to the strict requirements of certainty and directness of the causal link between the damage and the infringement, although this is not also without limits'[364] (compare the abovementioned judgment of the Versailles Court of Appeal in *Vérimédia v Médiametrie*). In its judgment in *Doux Aliments*—of which the passing-on aspects were discussed above—the French Court of Cassation held that the causal link between the damage and the infringement cannot be purely hypothetical. It held that the price fluctuations of lysine during the cartel period did not enable the establishment of a causal link. Following the judgment of the Court of Cassation, the Court of Appeal of Paris reconsidered the case in a different formation. Although this court held the expert report relied upon by the claimant to be partially based on imprecise methods, it came to the conclusion that damage was proven beyond doubt.[365]

— In the UK, the *Arkin*[366] judgment introduced a rule of 'dominant or effective cause of the loss'. In order to establish an effective causal link, English law applies a 'but for' test ('but for the action, the result would not have occurred'). This test guides the judges to find the dominant cause and to eliminate irrelevant elements. The approach was also applied in the *2 Travel Group*[367] judgment excerpted above. In certain cases of causal uncertainty, the 'but for' test was modified.[368]

---

[362] Cases 2.58 (IT), 2.59 (IT) and 2.64 (IT).

[363] Stockholm City Court 20 November 2008 Joined Cases T 32799-05 and T 34227-05 *Europe Investor Direct AB et al v VPC AB*.

[364] Lianos 2015 37 (see footnote 361).

[365] Paris Court of Appeal 27 February 2014 no 10/18258 *SNC Doux Aliments Bretagne etc v SAS Ajinamoto Eurolysine*. For more details on the case, see Lianos 2015 37–39 (see footnote 361).

[366] *Arkin v Borchard Lines Ltd and others* [2005] EWCA Civ 655.

[367] *2 Travel Group PLC (in Liquidation) v Cardiff City Transport Services Ltd* [2012] CAT 19.

[368] See *Fairchild v Glenhaven Funeral Services Ltd* [2002] UKHL 22.

II.D.v PROCEDURE

II.D.v.a Standing

Introductory Notes

1. Competition law infringements may have impact upon a large number of parties.

Bellamy & Child, European Union Law of Competition[369]   **2.71 (EU)**

Who can sue? A wide range of persons, including companies and individuals, may suffer loss or damage from a single infringement of Article 101 or 102. Claimants include actual purchasers from the infringing undertaking ('direct purchasers'), entities which might have, but did not, purchase from the infringing undertaking ('potential purchasers'), customers of the purchasers from the infringing undertaking ('indirect purchasers'), actual or potential suppliers to the infringing undertaking, competitors and the undertakings who are party to the unlawful agreements themselves.

EU law does not, or only marginally, determine under which conditions these categories of natural or legal persons have the right to start private enforcement action. Under reference to procedural autonomy, it is once more left to national law to determine who has the power to claim.

2. Applicable national regimes are divergent. For example, since the French Cour de cassation recognised the possibility of civil damages actions in competition law cases in its *Syndicat*[370] judgment, the case law has recognised rather generous conditions for standing. The German 'Schutznorm' concept, on the other hand, is considered to be more narrow. At first, only standing could only be guaranteed if the norm breached was intended to protect the claimant. Section 33(1) of the German Competition Act has broadened this to cover 'affected persons', including competitors and 'other market participants' (see also the excerpt from the *ORWI* judgment above). In Italy, a distinction was made between subjective rights (*diritti soggettivi*) and lawful interests (*interessi legitimi*). However, the *Ricciarelli/Unipol* judgment excerpted below changed this.

Corte di Cassazione (Court of Cassation), 4 February 2005[371]   **2.72 (IT)**

M Ricciarelli/Unipol Assicurrazioni SpA

STANDING OF FINAL CONSUMERS

Consumers can rest assured

Reversing its earlier case law, the Italian Court of Cassation grants standing to final consumers in antitrust damages actions, even though they are not party to the restrictive agreement concerned

Facts: A consumer brought a damages claim against an insurance company before a lower court (Giudice di pace), asking compensation for damages suffered as a consequence of a restrictive agreement between

---

[369] V Rose and D Baily (eds), *Bellamy & Child, European Union Law of Competition* (Oxford, Oxford University Press, 2013) 16.066, footnotes omitted.
[370] Cour de Cassation, Chambre commerciale, 1 March 1982, 80-15.834.
[371] Cass civ, 4 February 2005, no. 2207.

insurance companies which, according to the consumer, had increased insurance premiums. The Italian NCA had already fined the infringement.

Held: The Court of Cassation recognised standing for the consumer. It also ruled that only the Court of Appeal is competent to hear cases based on competition law, subject to appeal to the Court of Cassation.

Judgment: The difference between the protection from unfair competition provided for in the Code and the protection guaranteed by Antitrust Act L. 287/1990 as regards their scope and function rules out that the consumer, as a third party alien to agreement, might be denied standing before the civil judge … Contrary to what was held by the Court of Cassation in its judgment n. 17475/2002, Antitrust Act L. 287/1990 is not a law for undertakings only, but rather a law for all market actors, that is anyone who has an interest (relevant from a procedural point of view) in the preservation of the market's competitive nature, to the extent that he can allege a specific prejudice deriving from the rupture or the diminution of such competitive nature.

…

The consumer, which is the final buyer of the product offered on the market, closes the chain which starts with the production of the good. Thus the unlawful [character] of an agreement materializes by replacing the consumer's right to a real choice between competing goods with a choice that is merely apparent …

It should also be said, in light of the interpretative relevance of the principles of the Community legal order in this matter, that the judgment of the Court of Justice in *Courage* (C-453/1999) tends to expand the catalogue of subjects protected by competition law, in a perspective—so it appears to this court—that values damage actions as a means capable to ensure the effectiveness of the competitive structure of the market.

Notes:

(1) In this landmark judgment, the Court of Cassation overruled its previous case law[372] and gave full recognition to the standing of consumers who bring damages claims for infringement of antitrust rules. It emphasised that while the rules on unfair competition in the Civil Code primarily protect commercial enterprise against acts of competitors, the antitrust rules protect everyone on the market, including consumers who have been injured by anticompetitive behaviour of undertakings.

(2) The Court of Cassation referred to the role of competition in the EU legal system and to the CJ's statement in the *Courage* judgment that '*any* individual can rely on a breach of [now Article 101 TFEU] before a national court'.[373] After the excerpted judgment was handed down, the CJ repeated the statement in *Manfredi*,[374] which related to the same insurance cartel in Italy as the excerpted judgment. This time, the CJ more explicitly recognised standing for consumers who are not party to a restrictive agreement.

(3) The excerpted judgment is not only positive for consumers. Whereas many consumers had filed their claims before their Giudici di Pace (Justice of the Peace) and many of these lower courts had recognised jurisdiction, the Court of Cassation ruled that the Court of Appeal, subject to appeal to the Court of Cassation, has sole competence to rule

---

[372] Cass civ, sez. I., 9 December 2002, Axa, no 17475.
[373] CJ 20 September 2001 Case C-453/99 *Courage Ltd v Bernard Crehan and Bernard Crehan v Courage Ltd and others* [2001] ECR I-6297, ECLI:EU:C:2001:465, para 24.
[374] CJ *Manfredi* (n 38) para 59.

in competition matters. Consumer discontent may have led to one of the preliminary ruling questions in *Manfredi*: 'Is [now Article 101 TFEU] to be interpreted as meaning that it precludes the application of a national provision similar to that in Article 33 of Law [No 287/90] under which a claim for damages … must also be made by third parties before a court other than that which usually has jurisdiction for claims of similar value, thus involving a considerable increase in costs and time?' In its answer, the CJ simply refers to procedural autonomy.[375]

(4) The line of thinking set out in the excerpted judgment has been followed by the court which hears appeals against first instance *administrative* decisions. As a consequence, consumers can now also appeal decisions of the Italian Antitrust Authority.[376] This illustrates the close link between public and private enforcement procedures and rules.

II.D.v.b Collective Redress

Introductory Notes

1. Even if (end) consumers are provided standing under national law, other obstacles can still prevent them from bringing a claim for damages. 'Rational apathy' is one of the hurdles.

Van den Bergh, 'Private Enforcement of European Competition Law and the Persisting Collective Action Problem'[377] **2.73 (EU)**

The efficiency of collective actions and representative actions will be crucial for achieving an optimal degree of private enforcement in Europe. Both instruments can be seen as responses to a pervasive collective action problem. Victims of competition law infringements, such as consumers who paid excessively high cartel prices, may not bring an action in court because the costs of doing so are higher than the expected benefits. This is called rational apathy …

The casebook on *Consumer law* in this series[378] analyses collective action extensively, so the discussion here will be succinct.

2. The EC linked private enforcement of competition law and collective action already in its Green Paper.[379] In the White Paper, the EC proposed two complementary mechanisms of collective redress: representative action brought by qualified entities and collective opt-in action.[380] As indicated, the Damages Directive applies to collective action,

---

[375] See ibid, para 61.

[376] See T Salonico and A Barbiroli, 'The Italian Supreme Court Recognizes the Right of Consumers for Claim for Damages in Case of Violation of Antitrust ules (Mario Ricciarelli/Unipol Assicurrazioni)', *e-Competitions*, 4 February 2005, art no 23982.

[377] R van den Bergh, 'Private Enforcement of European Competition Law and the Persisting Collective Action Problem' (2013) 20(1) *Maastricht Journal of European and Comparative Law* 12, 14.

[378] *Cases, Materials and Text on Consumer Law* (Oxford, Hart Publishing, 2010).

[379] Commission Staff Working Paper, Annex to the Green Paper on Damages Actions for Breach of the EC Antitrust Rules, SEC(2005) 1732, 52–57.

[380] Commission White Paper on Damages Actions for Breach of the EC Antitrust Rules (n 230) 4.

but does not organise it.[381] The EC did adopt a Recommendation[382] and a Communication[383] on the topic in 2013.

The question arises as to the exact relationship between the Damages Directive and Recommendation 2013/396/EU, which recommends that Member States adopt mechanisms of collective redress for violations of rights conferred by the EU.[384] A comparative overview will be provided below on the implementation of this Recommendation in the national legal system of several Member States.

3. A lack of collective redress mechanisms in combination with the recognition of standing for indirect purchasers, a passing-on defence and a rebuttable presumption of passing-on (see above) can be problematic. The volume of purchased goods typically declines when descending the supply chain. Although the percentage of overcharge passed-on to purchasers may remain stable, in terms of absolute value per buyer, the overcharge becomes less important. The costs of private enforcement may surpass the possible gains from a successful damages claim. A system of collective redress might remedy.[385]

Whish and Bailey, Competition Law[386]   **2.74 (EU)**

Infringement of Articles 101 and 102 may cause economic harm to a large number of (natural and legal) persons, in particular where higher prices are passed on to many indirect purchasers. The harm to any one person may be small, and insufficient to merit the risk and cost of bringing an action for damages. In these circumstances the right to damages may be more theoretical than real in the absence of a possibility for collective redress, a procedural mechanism enabling many single claims to be bundled into a single court action.

4. The following judgments serve to illustrate potential and limits of collective redress.

---

[381] See Recital 13 of the Damages Directive.

[382] Commission Recommendation 2013/396/EU of 11 June 2013 on common principles for injunctive and compensatory collective redress mechanisms in the Member States concerning violations of rights granted under Union Law, OJ L201/60, 26 July 2013.

[383] Communication from the EC to the European Parliament, the Council, the European Economic and Social Committee and the Committee of the Regions, 'Towards a European Horizontal Framework for Collective Redress', doc COM(2013) 401 final of 11 June 2013.

[384] AM van den Bossche, 'Private Enforcement, Procedural Autonomy and Article 19(1) TEU Two's Company, Three's a Crowd' (2014) *Yearbook of European Law* 66–67.

[385] N Dunne, 'Courage and Compromise: The Directive on Antitrust Damages Actions' (2015) *European Law Review* 588.

[386] R Whish and D Bailey, *Competition Law*, 8th edn (Oxford, Oxford University Press, 2015) 319, footnotes omitted.

Consumers' Association v JJB Sports plc

COLLECTIVE ACTION BROUGHT BY A CONSUMERS' ASSOCIATION

Everyone wants the number 10 position

A damages action brought by an approved representative body was settled, as confirmed by court order

Facts: The UK Consumers' Association brought a damages claim against JJB Sports as a representative body approved under the Competition Act 1998 to bring actions on behalf of individual consumers who had suffered loss as a result of a breach of the competition rules. The claim was brought before the CAT on behalf of around 130 consumers who had purchased football kits which were the subject of a cartel.

Held: Upon settlement by the parties, the Competition Appeal Tribunal ordered (a) the claimant to withdraw its action, and (b) the defendant to pay the claimant reasonable costs.

Notes:

(1) On 9 January 2008, the Consumers' Association announced that it had reached a settlement with JJB. Under the terms of the settlement, JJB had agreed to pay back fans who were illegally overcharged. Consumers who had joined the Consumers' Association's class action were to receive £20 each. Consumers who had not participated in the class action could claim £5 or £10 each, provided that, before 5 February 2009, they could show proof of purchase of one of the products concerned at a JJB store. Given the small amounts of compensation, the settlement was generally not regarded as a major success for private enforcement or for collective action.

(2) Another UK case, *Emerald Supplies Ltd v British Airways*, proved even less successful from a collective action perspective. Emerald was a flower importer which, together with one other claimant, claimed damages from British Airways (BA), which had been convicted in the US for operating an air freight cartel with other airlines and was under investigation in the EU for similar practices. Emerald and its co-claimant sought certification under the UK Civil Practice Rules that they were representative of all other direct and indirect customers of BA. The Chancery Division of the High Court granted BA's application to strike the representative element of the 'opt out' claim[388] on the ground that applicable UK law required that the represented victims should have 'the same interest'. As part of the victims were not known, the High Court felt unable to evaluate the interests at stake. In addition, it decided that, even if all purchasers were known, the opposition between direct and indirect consumers prevented Emerald from representing both categories. Whereas direct purchasers would benefit from demonstrating that the overcharge was not passed-on, the opposite was true for BA's indirect customers (*cf* introductory note 5 under 'Passing-on defence'). If the damages claim would have been awarded, this would not have been equally beneficial for all consumers.

---

[387] Order of the Competition Appeal Tribunal, 14 January 2008, *The Consumers' Association v JJB Sports plc*, Case 1078/7/9/07.
[388] High Court, 23 July 2009, *Emerald Supplies Ltd v British Airways plc* [2009] EWHC 741 (Ch).

The representative element of the claim was therefore struck out. The Court of Appeal confirmed this.[389]

(3) In France, approved associations may bring collective damages claims if at least two of the consumers concerned give permission to do so. French law, however, indicates that this mandate cannot be sought by public appeal on radio, television or by letter.[390] In *UFC-Que Choisir v Bouygues*,[391] the Court of Cassation broadened the scope of that prohibition in view of the new ways of communication (internet). Consequently, the Court decided that the damages claims were in contradiction to the regulation on collective redress, and thus rejected the appeals before it.

Corte di Cassazione (Italian Court of Cassation),
18 August 2011[392]   **2.76 (IT)**

Codacons v Allianz Assicurazioni

STANDING OF CONSUMER ASSOCIATIONS IN FOLLOW ON ACTIONS

Consumer organisation to the rescue!

The Italian Court of Cassation grants conditional standing to a consumer organisation in a follow-on damages claim

Facts: The consumer association Codacons brought an action against motor insurance undertakings that were part of a price-fixing cartel which the Italian NCA had fined. Codacons hoped to recover overcharges paid by consumers. The Court of Appeal stated that this claim had to be considered as the sum of individual claims rather than as a claim of common interest for the category of consumers and denied standing to Codacons, which appealed.

Held: Codacons had standing if it acted within the limits of the collective interest of the category.

Judgment: Codacons also has the right, on the basis of those rules, to submit claims for restitution and damages following illegal competition practices, to the extent that it serves the common interest of the category of users of that type of assurance services to obtain a decision on aspects such as the existence of the infringement, the liability, the causal link between the infringement and the harm, the existence and possible extent of the damage (regardless of the particularities of each individual situation), and every other question suitable to facilitate the individual initiatives, relieving the individual from related costs and risks.

Notes:

(1) The Court of Cassation affirmed that acknowledging the standing of consumer associations in actions which concern many (damaged) consumers is consistent with EU law. It referred to the EC's Green and White Papers, which stress the need for consumer

---

[389] English Court of Appeal, 18 November 2010, *Emerald Supplies and another/British Airways* [2010] EWCA Civ 1284; [2011] CP Rep 14; [2011] Ch 345; [2011] 2 WLR 203; [2011] UKCLR 20.
[390] Consumer Code, art L 422-1.
[391] Cour de cassation (Première chambre civile), 26 May 2011, Case n°10-15.676, *UFC Que choisir.*
[392] Cass civ, sez III, 18 August 2011, No 17351.

protection against unfair commercial practices and anticompetitive conduct to counter the inertia of damaged parties in bringing an individual action.

(2) Regarding the representation requirements for collective redress procedures, the Belgian Constitutional Court recently annulled the relevant provision of the Economic Law Code because of its narrow scope. In its judgment, it ruled that certain elements of the relevant article discriminate against representative organisations of other Member States. Not only did the requirements of Belgian law violate provisions of the Constitutional Code, but they equally formed an obstacle hindering the principles expressed in the EU's Services Directive.[393] Consequently, the Court itself broadened the conditions under which a representative organisation from another Member State will be authorised to act as a group representative.[394]

Comparative overview

As indicated, the EC adopted Recommendation 2013/396/EU, which establishes common principles for national collective redress mechanisms.[395] This non-binding act applies to claims regarding EU law in areas such as consumer protection and competition, as well as data and environmental protection. It requires Member States to assess the legal standing of representative entities through clearly defined eligibility criteria. In each case: (i) the representative entity should have a non-profit character; (ii) there needs to be a direct relationship between the entity's objectives and the violated EU rights in question; and (iii) the entity should have sufficient resources and experience to represent multiple claimants acting in their best interest. The Recommendation prohibits contingency fees, which are said to risk inducing unnecessary litigation, and obliges parties who lose their case to reimburse the legal costs of the prevailing party (the 'loser pays principle'). In addition, the claimant should be formed on the basis of express consent of the natural or legal persons alleging to have been harmed (the 'opt-in' principle). Any exception to this principle, by law or by court order, should be duly justified by reasons of sound administration of justice.

Across the EU, collective redress regimes are still quite diverse.

— In *Belgium*, collective actions may be initiated by group representatives who fulfil pre-set conditions (eg, certain consumer organisations).[396] Contingency fees are not allowed. Deviating from the EC Recommendation, Belgian law allows courts to opt for either opt-in or opt-out approaches.[397]

— *France*, as opposed to Belgium, has regulated collective proceedings by sector[398] and has adopted a restrictive approach on legal standing. An opt-in system applies,

---

[393] [2006] OJ L376, 36–68.

[394] Belgian Constitutional Court, 17 March 2016, Judgment no 41/2016.

[395] Commission Recommendation 2013/396/EU of 11 June 2013 on common principles for injunctive and compensatory collective redress mechanisms in the Member States concerning violations of rights granted under Union Law, OJ L 201/60, 26 July 2013. This text paragraphs is in particular based on Recital 7 and paras 4, 7, 13, 21 and 30 of the Recommendation.

[396] See notably arts I.20 and XVII.35–69 of the Belgian Code of Economic Law (*Code de droit économique*).

[397] ibid, art XVII.43, §2, 3°.

[398] See arts L.423-1 to L.423-19 and R. 423-1–R.423-23 of the French Consumer Code (*Code de la consummation*).

contingency fees are prohibited and legal costs are usually borne by the party that loses the case.

— No general collective redress rules apply in *Germany*, but several sectoral regimes exist. Sectoral regimes can be opt-in (eg, 'Sammelklagen' under the *Rechtsdienstleistungsgesetz*)[399] or opt-out (eg, collective actions under the *Kapitalanleger-Musterverfahrensgesetz*)[400] and are based on a 'loser pays' principle. Exceptionally, contingency fees can apply.

— No general collective redress mechanism exists in *Italy*, where the 'azione di classe' is regulated on a sectoral basis.[401] Strict criteria regarding legal standing apply and collective action can be launched in case of both unfair or anticompetitive commercial practices. The opt-in and 'loser pays' principles apply.

— The general *Lithuanian* group action model[402] practises an opt-in approach and limits the representative entities, although not by means of the criteria established in the Recommendation. Competition-specific collective redress actions can only be brought by organisations representing the interests of undertakings or consumers.[403] The general model adheres to the 'loser pays' principle, but success fees are allowed.

— In *the Netherlands*, three general collective redress mechanisms apply,[404] each with its own requirements on legal standing. The mechanisms are both opt-in- and opt-out. Contingency fees are prohibited for members of the Dutch Bar.

— *Poland* has had class action laws since 2010.[405] Class actions are opt-in. Initiation is limited to class members and to regional consumer ombudsmen. The 'loser pays' principle applies and success fees are allowed but capped.

— The *Portuguese* general collective redress regime[406] contrasts with other Member States, as it grants legal standing to a considerably broader range of actors and is based on an opt-out mechanism. Contingency fees are not allowed.

— The *Spanish* legal system, although lacking a proper general collective redress mechanism, allows for collective litigation in, *inter alia*, consumer,[407] competition[408]

---

[399] ie, the 'Act on Legal Services' of 12 December 2007.

[400] ie, the 'Capital Markets Model Claims Act' of 19 October 2012.

[401] See art 140-bis of the Italian Consumer Code (*Decreto legislativo*), 6 September 2005, no 206.

[402] See art 49 of the Lithuanian Civil Procedure Code (*Lithuanian Civilinio proceso kodekso patvirtinimo, įsigaliojimo ir įgyvendinimo įstatymas*).

[403] See art 16 of the Lithuanian Law on Competition (*Lietuvos Respublikos konkurencijos įstatymas*).

[404] See arts 1013–18 of the Dutch Code of Civil Procedure (*Wetboek van Burgerlijke Rechtsvordering*) and arts 7:907-910 of the Dutch Civil Code (*Burgerlijk Wetboek*) for collective settlements, arts 3:305a–305d of the Dutch Civil Code for collective actions, and art 7:423 of the Dutch Civil Code for group mandates and transfer of claims.

[405] See Polish Class Actions Act (*Ustawa z dnia 17 grudnia 2009 r o dochodzeniu roszczeń w postępowaniu grupowym*).

[406] Portuguese Law of Popular Action (*Direito de participação procedimental e de acção popular, lei n.° 83/95, de 31 de Agosto*).

[407] Scattered over multiple laws, such as the Spanish Civil Procedure Act (*Ley de Enjuiciamiento civil*), the Spanish General Law for the Defence of Consumers and Users and Other Complementary Laws (*Real Decreto Legislativo 1/2007, de 16 de noviembre, por el que se aprueba el texto refundido de la Ley General para la Defensa de los Consumidores y Usuarios y otras leyes complementarias*) and the Spanish Act on General Contractual Conditions or Standard Form Contracts (*Ley 7/1998, de 13 de abril, sobre condiciones generales de la contratación*).

[408] See arts 32 and 33 of the Spanish Unfair Competition Act (*Ley 3/1991, de 10 de enero, de Competencia Desleal*).

and non-discrimination law.[409] Certain unfair competition actions can be brought by associations, professional corporations or representatives of economic interests in case the interests of their members are harmed. Depending on the case, both opt-in as well as opt-out mechanisms appear to be available. The 'loser pays' rule applies and it is allowed to agree on contingency fees.

— The *Swedish* general collective redress mechanism[410] allows for class actions by individual groups, organisations and governments (eg, the Swedish Competition Authority). The system, which is opt-in and in-court, is already largely in line with the EC Recommendation. The party losing the case pays the costs of litigation. Contingency fees are not allowed, but so-called 'risk agreements' are permitted (subject to certain fairness conditions), increasing or reducing the fees for attorneys if the case is won or lost. Apart from the general collective redress regime, group proceedings can also be initiated before the Swedish National Board for Consumer Disputes.

— The *UK* has both general collective redress mechanisms (ie, group litigation orders, representative actions and test cases—all on an opt-in basis) and sectoral mechanisms. In competition cases, actions for collective proceedings may be filed by any person who proposes to be the representative in those proceedings, as long as the UK Competition Appeal Tribunal (CAT) considers it just and reasonable for that person to act as a representative.[411] Deviating from the EC Recommendation's principles, the CAT may allow both opt-in and opt-out actions.

II.D.v.c Access to Evidence

Introductory Notes

1. The difficulty in obtaining evidence, often in the hands of infringing parties and public enforcers, constitutes one of the most important hurdles to successful private enforcement through damages claims. On the other hand, granting damages to claimants easy access to leniency submissions risks to effectively halt the leniency programmes which are so successful in public enforcement.

2. In its 2011 *Pfleiderer* judgment,[412] the CJ recognised the conflicting interests involved and ordered national courts to balance the interest of the injured party to the publication of the documents, with the interest of the protection of the information provided by the leniency applicant—without much further guidance. In the absence of mandatory EU law, national courts were nevertheless allowed to disclose leniency documents for use in liability actions 'on a case-by-case basis'.[413]

The CJ's 2013 *Donau Chemie* judgment[414] dealt with a request for access to documents by third parties that were not a party to national public enforcement proceedings.

---

[409] See art 19 of the Spanish Equal Opportunities Act (*Ley 51/2003, de 2 de diciembre, de igualdad de oportunidades, no discriminación y accesibilidad universal de las personas con discapacidad*).

[410] See the Swedish Group Proceedings Act (*Lag om grupprättegång*) of 30 May 2002.

[411] Consumer Rights Act, sch 8, s 47C, §8.

[412] CJ 14 June 2011 Case C-360/09, *Pfleiderer AG v Bundeskartellamt* [2011] ECR I-5161, ECLI:EU:C:2011:389.

[413] ibid, para 23.

[414] CJ 6 June 2013 Case C-536/11 *Donau Chemie* ECLI:EU:C:2013:366.

The request was clearly motivated by a possible action for damages against the undertakings subject to the public enforcement proceedings. The CJ ruled that, particularly in the light of the principle of effectiveness, EU law precludes a provision of national law which makes access to documents, including leniency documents, solely dependent on the consent of all the parties involved in the national proceedings, without any possibility for national courts to weigh the interests involved. National courts have to apply a balancing test: they do not have to grant full access to all documents in possession of the NCA, but the mere risk that the leniency programme would lose its effectiveness is insufficient to justify a refusal of access.[415]

3. The EC and the Council appear to choose more straightforwardly for the protection of leniency programmes. As from the White Paper, the EC opted for a minimum level of disclosure inter partes. Moreover, access to evidence should be based on fact pleading and strict judicial control. Disclosure of documents should only cover precise documents. Limiting the scope for disclosure even further, the EC stated that adequate protection against disclosure for corporate statement submitted in a leniency procedure has to be ensured.[416]

4. The Damages Directive is in line with these principles. Its Chapter II includes extensive regulation on the disclosure of evidence. Leniency statements and settlement submissions are 'blacklisted': no national court will be allowed to order a party or a third party to disclose them in a damages action.[417] For other types of documents (eg, settlement submissions that were later withdrawn), national courts can order disclosure only after public enforcement procedures are closed ('grey list').[418] The remainder of documents can in principle be disclosed subject to judicial control ('white list').[419] Member States also have to adopt sanctioning mechanisms.

High Court of Justice (Chancery Division),
4 April 2012[420]   **2.77 (UK)**

National Grid Electricity Transmission plc v ABB Ltd

DISCLOSURE OF LENIENCY DOCUMENTS

Not all gas is invisible

The High Court, aware of the CJ's Pfleiderer judgment and the German follow-up judgment, nevertheless orders disclosure of certain confidential procedural documents

Facts: In 2007, the EC fined a global cartel in the Gas Insulated Switchgear (GIS) sector for breach of (now) Article 101 TFEU (see above). In a follow-on action, the claimant claimed damages from cartel members.

---

[415] ibid, paras 30, 33 and 46. Only in the actual event that the disclosure of a particular piece affects the effectiveness will refusal be justified. See para 48.

[416] EC White Paper on Damages Actions for Breach of the EC Antitrust Rules (n 230) 5. *cf* EC Staff Working Paper, *Annex to the Green Paper on Damages Actions for Breach of the EC Antitrust Rules*, SEC(2005) 1732, 18–30.

[417] Damages Directive, art 6(6)–(8).

[418] ibid, art 6(5).

[419] ibid, art 6(9). See also art 5 with general conditions for disclosure of evidence.

[420] High Court of Justice (Chancery Division) 4 April 2012 *National Grid Electricity Transmission plc v ABB Ltd* [2012] EWHC 869 (Ch).

Held: The High Court ordered disclosure to the claimant of limited parts of the confidential version of the EC fining decision as well as certain replies to EC requests for information.

Judgment: 57. Some of the redactions from the non-confidential version of the Decision are made on the grounds of commercial confidentiality, or, as the Commission points out in its submissions, to reflect its policy of not publicly disclosing the source of evidence given through corporate statements. Those concerns are met by restricting any disclosure to the confidentiality ring. They do not affect a leniency applicant's defence to the damages claim.

58. The Decision comprises 552 recital paragraphs and two annexes. Having read the relevant parts of the Decision in unredacted form, I conclude that a number, but by no means all, of the redacted passages should be disclosed. I set out the list of paragraphs (or parts of paragraphs) to be disclosed in the Appendix to this judgment …

60 … I was supplied with a copy … of the judgment of the Amstgericht Bonn of 30 January 2012 in the *Pfleiderer* case, where the German court ruled against disclosure of leniency documents. However, I find that of little assistance since, as the ECJ made clear, the balancing exercise is to be conducted on a case-by-case basis; it is therefore very fact-sensitive to the particular proceedings, in the context of the relevant national procedural rules. Nor do I think that there is any ground for making a reference to the ECJ for a preliminary ruling … I regard the conclusion that *Pfleiderer* applies in this case and that EU law does not preclude the English court from ordering disclosure as *actes clairs*. And as for the particular application of the balancing exercise to the documents sought by NGET's application, that is, as I have just stated, a fact-sensitive exercise to be conducted on the basis prescribed by the ECJ in its ruling in *Pfleiderer* and does not therefore give rise to a question of EU law for reference.

Notes:

(1) The High Court referred in its judgment to the CJ's *Pfleiderer* judgment. Uncertain as to how to apply the balancing test, the High Court invited the EC to submit observations. The EC accepted and intervened as an *amicus curiae* before the national court, which rarely happens.[421]

(2) On the basis of self-imposed criteria ('Is the information available from other sources and what is the relevance of the information?'), the High Court concluded that certain limited parts of the confidential version of the EC Decision and of one answer to a request for information from the EC had to be disclosed. As regards all other documents, the High Court concluded that their relevance to the proceedings was not such that the interest of protecting information supplied under the leniency programme outweighed the interest of disclosure in an action for damages.

(3) In Germany, in yet another follow-on damages claim after the elevators cartel, a number of construction firms started legal action against the fined elevator constructors. The competent civil court (not the claimants directly) intended to review certain documents provided by the public prosecutor's office[422] and containing confidential information assembled during the public enforcement procedure. As a leniency statement and the

---

[421] See art 15(3) of Regulation 1/2003 (cited above). The EC submissions can be consulted online (http://ec.europa.eu/competition/court/antitrust_amicus_curiae.html).

[422] The NCA had handed over certain documents to the public prosecutor, with a view to the sanctioning of individuals who were involved in the cartel.

confidential version of the EC fining decision were among the documents, the elevator companies objected that this would violate their fundamental and constitutional rights.[423] However, their claims were rejected, first by the competent civil court and subsequently, after filing a *Verfassungsbeschwerde*, by the Federal Constitutional Court (*Bundesverfassungsgericht*), which did not accept to rule on the matter.[424]

II.D.v.d Time Limits, Limitation Periods and Prescription

Introductory Notes

1. Public enforcement procedures in competition law, often involving appeals before national and/or EU courts, may easily have a duration of 10 years or more. The longer these public enforcement procedures take, the more risk there is that follow-on private enforcement damages claims will be time barred under national procedural rules or will only permit partial recovery of damage (eg, damage which occurred up to 10 years before the damages claim was launched). Some of the cases excerpted below illustrate how limitation periods in national law may obstruct the success of damages claims.

2. The CJ recognised the problem in its 2006 *Manfredi* judgment:

> 78. A national rule under which the limitation period begins to run from the day on which the agreement or concerted practice was adopted could make it practically impossible to exercise the right to seek compensation for the harm caused by that prohibited agreement or practice, particularly if that national rule also imposes a short limitation period which is not capable of being suspended.

> 79. In such a situation, where there are continuous or repeated infringements, it is possible that the limitation period expires even before the infringement is brought to an end, in which case it would be impossible for any individual who has suffered harm after the expiry of the limitation period to bring an action.[425]

Then, the EC suggested in its White Paper to partially harmonise national law on limitation periods in this type of cases.[426] The Damages Directive now indeed obliges Member States to harmonise the limitation periods. The relevant provisions apply to all damages claims in case of a breach of national and/or EU competition law. They thus cover more than just follow-on claims and will also apply in purely internal cases, to be solved under national competition law alone.

3. Three aspects are harmonised: the starting point, the minimum duration and suspension during public enforcement investigations. As to the start of the limitation period, the Damages Directive states:

> Limitation periods shall not begin to run before the infringement of competition law has ceased and the claimant knows, or can reasonably be expected to know: (a) of the behaviour and the

---

[423] Article 12(1) of the German *Grundgesetz* protects business secrets.

[424] German Federal Constitutional Court 6 March 2014 *Aufzugskartell* n° 1 BvR 3541, 3543, 3600/13. The Bundesverfassungsgericht (BVerfG) decided that it would not accept the case for decision ('nicht zur Entscheidung annehmen'). However, it appears from the motivation of that decision that the BVerfG sees no serious risk of a breach of fundamental rights.

[425] CJ *Manfredi* (n 38) paras 78–79.

[426] Commission White Paper on Damages Actions for Breach of the EC Antitrust Rules (n 230) 8–9.

fact that it constitutes an infringement of competition law; (b) of the fact that the infringement of competition law caused harm to it; *and* (c) the identity of the infringer. (Emphasis added)

In particular the cumulative nature of these elements may halt the start of limitation periods.

As for duration, the Damages Directive imposes that limitation periods have a minimum duration of five years. Finally, limitation periods will have to be suspended for as long as the EC or an NCA 'takes action for the purpose of the investigation or its proceedings in respect of an infringement of competition law to which the action for damages relates'. 'The suspension shall end at the earliest one year after the infringement decision has become final or after the proceedings are otherwise terminated.'[427]

4. Whether the Damages Directive would allow a national limitation period to start running before the end of all court appeals against infringement decisions is not entirely clear.[428] Can a claimant be said to 'know, or reasonably be expected to know' that certain behaviour constitutes an infringement of competition law before all appeals against an infringement decisions are exhausted? And can one conclude that 'an infringement decision has become final' as long as it is still subject to judicial review?

5. The new regime on limitation periods in the Damages Directive will improve the position of claimants. Conversely, it will also lead to even longer competition procedures and to a further fragmentation of national tort and procedural laws, as rules for claims in competition matters will differ from rules for other claims.

Grondwettelijk Hof/Cour constitutionnelle (Belgian Constitutional Court), 10 March 2016[429] **2.78 (BE)**

Honda Motor Europe Logistics

NATIONAL LIMITATION PERIODS

Honda's race against time

The Belgian limitation period in the Civil Code is held to violate the constitutional principle of equality

Facts: In the early 1990s, the official importer of Honda motorbikes in Belgium obliged its dealers to obtain a 'certificate of conformity' from it for every Honda motorbike bought abroad from other suppliers than the official Belgian importer. In 1995, certain dealers filed a complaint with the Belgian NCA. In January 1999, the NCA fined the practice as an abuse of dominance. Its decision was confirmed by the Appeal Court in 2009 and by the Court of Cassation in 2011.

---

[427] See art 10 of the Damages Directive. Article 10(2) deals with the start of the limitation period, art 10(3) with the duration and art 10(4) with the suspension.

[428] The EC appears to answer in the negative in its 'Competition Policy Brief: The Damages Directive— Towards More Effective Enforcement of the EU Competition Rules', issue 2015-1, January 2015, 3: 'Once the investigation is over, victims have at least one year after the authority's final decision to bring their damages actions. These rules allow injured parties to wait for pulic enforcers, finally to establish the infringement, which helps them avoid unnecessary litigation costs.'

[429] Judgment No 38/2016 of 10 March 2016, answer to a preliminary ruling question in *Herman Verboven and others/Honda Motor Europe Logistics.*

When the dealers launched a damages claim against the Belgian Honda importer at the end of 2006, the defendant argued that the claim was time barred, as the Civil Code imposes a limitation period of five year after the claimant learned about the identity of the infringer and the damage. The claimants objected, referring to the quasi-criminal nature of competition law and to the fact that, under Belgian penal procedural law, civil damages claims connected to penal prosecutions are never time barred as long as the penal procedure runs.

The Ghent Commercial Court referred a request for a preliminary ruling to the Constitutional Court, asking whether the different treatment of civil claims in competition matters and in penal matters breached the constitutional principle of equality.

Held: The relevant provision of the Belgian Civil Code breached the constitutional principle of equality to the extent that the provision allows a damages claim in competition matters to be time barred before there is a final decision confirming the existence of a competition infringement.

Judgment: Following Directive 2014/104/EU of the European Parliament and of the Council of 26 November 2014 on certain rules governing actions for damages under national law for infringements of the competition law provisions of the Member States and of the European Union, the Union legislator is equally of the opinion that the victim of an infringement of the competition rules may not be hindered in his right on compensation for the reason that the limitation period for bringing claims for damages following that infringement can expire before the administrative enforcement of competition legislation has ended by way of a final decision ...

Article 2262*bis*, § 1, second paragraph of the Civil Code violates Articles 10 and 11 of the Constitution to the extent that the civil claim for damages following a competition infringement can expire before a final decision [*Editor's note:* not subject to further judicial review] establishes the competition violation.

Notes:

(1) This well-motivated judgment is remarkable for several reasons. First, the Constitutional Court rarely declared a provision of the Civil Code and/or its interpretation to be unconstitutional.

Second, the Constitutional Court made explicit reference to the upcoming Damages Directive and based its reasoning in large part on EU law. To some extent, one witnesses another instance of 'proactive implementation' of the Damages Directive, even though the Directive's provisions are more detailed, as indicated in the introductory notes.

Third, the original language version[430] of the judgment makes it very clear that according to the Constitutional Court, a civil claim in competition matters cannot be time barred. It cannot be time barred before the end of the administrative procedure, but also not before all possible judicial review of the administrative decision has ended (*cf* introductory note 4).

(2) The facts of the case make it painfully clear how long procedures in competition matters may take. Public enforcement and private enforcement procedures have a long duration in common, but when one adds public and private enforcement, the limits of the rule of law appear to be reached. In this case, the anticompetitive behaviour dated back to the early 1990s and the complaint to 1995. Public enforcement only ended in 2011, ie,

---

[430] The Constitutional Court refers to an administrative decision 'in kracht van gewijsde' (in French: 'force de chose jugée'). The notion is hard to translate in English, but indicates that no further judicial appeal against the decision is possible.

16 years after the complaint. Private enforcement started in 2006 and is, thanks to this judgment, still ongoing.

Supreme Court, 9 April 2014[431]   **2.79 (UK)**

Deutsche Bahn AG and others v Morgan Advanced Materials plc

NATIONAL LIMITATION PERIODS

Even German railways may arrive too late

Limitation periods are calculated for each fined cartel member separately, and may thus start to run much sooner for a successful immunity applicant than for other cartel members who appeal the EC fining decision

Facts: Morgan Advanced Materials plc and five other undertakings established an illegal cartel in the carbon and graphite industry. The EC imposed fines totalling €101.44 million, but Morgan disclosed the cartel to the EC and obtained immunity from fines.[432] Whereas the other undertakings contested the fining decision before the GC, Morgan did not appeal. The GC dismissed all appeals on 8 October 2008. Two infringing companies filed further appeals before the CJ, but these were declared inadmissible as they were brought after the expiration of the applicable time limit. On 15 December 2010, Deutsche Bahn and others filed follow-on damages claims against Morgan before the CAT. Morgan argued that the damages claims were time barred.

Held: The CAT ruled that the damages claim against Morgan was time barred. The Court of Appeal reversed. The Supreme Court unanimously allowed the appeal and held that the claim was time barred.

Judgment: 1. The issue on this appeal is whether claims against [Morgan] for loss allegedly suffered by reason of a cartel infringing [now Article 101(1) TFEU] are time-barred ...

4 ... The claims were 'follow-on' claims, that is claims made under section 47A of the Competition Act 1998 in reliance upon the [EC]'s finding (upheld in fact in all respects on the various appeals) that [now Article 101(1) TFEU] had been infringed ...

8. The issue thus arises whether the decision to which the above provisions refer is the Commission Decision viewed as a decision made against and not appealed by the appellant, or the Commission Decision viewed as a decision made against all the cartel members, appealed by most of them and finally upheld as to liability by the General Court. On the former approach the two-year limitation period began on 13 February 2004 when time expired for an appeal by the appellant to the General Court, and the present follow-on claims issued on 15 December 2010 were brought too late. On the latter approach it began only on 18 December 2008 when time expired for an appeal to the Court of Justice by those who had appealed to the General Court, and the follow-on claims were in time. The appellant therefore argue for the former approach, the respondents for the latter ...

21. The judgments in *Assi Domän* and *Galp Energia* establish that a Commission Decision regarding the existence of a cartel constitutes a series of decisions addressed to its individual addressees, which remain binding or not according to the lodging and

---

[431] *Deutsche Bahn AG and others v Morgan Advanced Materials plc (Formerly Morgan Crucible Co plc)* [2014] UKSC 24.
[432] EC Decision 2004/420/EC of 3 December 2003 relating to a proceeding under Article 81 of the EC Treaty and Article 53 of the EEA Agreement (Case No C.38.359—Electrical and mechanical carbon and graphite products) [2004] OJ L 125/45, 28 April.

outcome of any individual appeals. A successful appeal by one addressee, establishing that there was no cartel, has no effect on the validity and effects of the Decision determining that there was such a cartel and levying a fine as against another addressee who has not appealed …

22. It follows in the present case that, even if the appeals against infringement by alleged cartel members other than the appellant had succeeded, that would in European law have made no difference to the findings as to the existence and scope of the 'complex of agreements and concerted practices' in the relevant sector to which the Commission Decision found the appellant to have been party. The Commission Decision would have remained as against the appellant in full force and effect. That being the (only) Decision against the appellant in European law, it is also the only decision to which section 47A(5) and (9) apply.

Notes:

(1) Under the applicable UK law (section 47A(8) of the Competition Act 1998), no follow-on damages claim could be brought during the period up to the expiry of the time limit for pursuing any appeal against the administrative public enforcement (fining) decision, or the determination of any such appeal. As for the duration of the limitation period, a follow-on damages claim had to be launched within two years after the public enforcement *decision* had become *final*.

(2) There was no doubt about the notion 'final' in this case. Under the applicable law, 'final' meant that no further judicial review against the administrative decision was possible (*cf* introductory note 4). However, it was less clear what the 'decision' was in this case. If the relevant 'decision' was the EC's Decision in its entirety and against all the cartel members, then Deutsche Bahn had brought its follow-on claim in time. The EC decision in its entirety became indeed 'final' on 18 December 2008 (and Deutsche Bahn's claim was brought on 15 December 2010, ie, less than two years thereafter). However, if, as Morgan argued, one were to approach the EC decision as a bundle of individual decisions, each against one cartel member, then the Morgan decision had become 'final' on 13 February 2004 and Deutsche Bahn's claim was time barred.

(3) The Supreme Court sided with Morgan after a thorough exam of CJ case law, which results in part from an intervention in the case by the EC. This is indeed another of the few cases where the EC chose to intervene as an *amicus curiae* before a national court.[433] The conclusions of the Supreme Court are in line with the submissions of the intervening EC.

(4) We stated earlier that leniency applicants risk being the first victims of private enforcement claims. This risk has increased after the Supreme Court's ruling. In order not to miss the two-year deadline, potential damages claimants will now certainly want to launch their actions against the leniency applicant while the other infringers are still fighting fining decisions in Luxembourg or before national courts.

(5) The long duration of the procedure is again noticeable. The infringement dates back to 1 January 1994 and the EC fining decision was adopted in 2003. Private

[433] See art 15(3) of Regulation 1/2003 (cited above). The EC submissions can be consulted online (http://ec.europa.eu/competition/court/antitrust_amicus_curiae.html).

enforcement ended for Morgan in 2014 (and could have lasted much longer had the Supreme Court ruled differently and had the other undertakings launched the CJ appeals in time).

(6) In its 2012 judgment in *BCL Old Co Ltd and others v BASF plc and others*,[434] the Supreme Court already applied the EU law principles of effectiveness and legal certainty to the statutory limitation periods. It held the statutory limitation period applicable to a claim for damages for participation in an unlawful cartel, as it operated before the Competition Appeal Tribunal, to be compatible with EU law.

Cour d'appel de Paris (Court of Appeal of Paris),
26 June 2013[435]   **2.80 (FR)**

JCB v Central Parts

NATIONAL LIMITATION PERIODS

Compensation in part(s)

Although the finding of an infringement by the EC is binding on a national court, judicial review of that finding before EU courts does not suspend limitation periods under national tort law

Facts: Central Parts (CP) was a French undertaking importing and selling machinery and spare parts for public works. One of its suppliers was JCB Service Ltd. When it found that prices for JCB products were lower at JCB's French subsidiary than at the UK and Irish subsidiaries, it tried to order its products there. However, the UK and Irish subsidiaries were prohibited from engaging in 'passive sales' to clients outside their territory. After a complaint brought by CP in 1996, the EC fined the JCB group almost €40 million in 2000. The EC decision was confirmed by the GC in 2004 and by the CJ in 2006.

In 2004 and 2005, CP launched claims against JCB group members before the Commercial Court of Orléans in order to recover damages which it had allegedly suffered as from 1989. The Commercial Court awarded CP €600,000 in damages in 2008. The Orléans Court of Appeal largely confirmed the first instance ruling in 2010, but ordered an expert to calculate the damage. At the end of 2011, the Court of Cassation quashed the appeal judgment (but on a ground which is unrelated) and referred the case back to the Court of Appeal of Paris. This court also had to rule on the question whether judicial review before EU courts suspended the limitation period in France.

Held: Judicial review before EU courts did not suspend the national limitation period. The starting point of the limitation period is therefore the moment when the damage appeared. As a 10-year limitation period applies, damage which occurred more than 10 years before the claim was launched cannot be recovered.

Judgment: Considering that in application of Article 16 of Regulation EC No 1/2003 of the Council of 16 December 2002, on the implementation of the rules on competition laid down in Articles 81 and 82 of the Treaty, the finding of infringements is binding for the national courts; that therefore, the challenging [of these findings] by JCB, which claims that the refusals to supply are legal in light of the block exemption Regulations of 1999 and 2010 is not admissible,

Considering that the infringements of EU legislation amount to civil wrongs under French law ...

---

[434] *BCL Old Co Ltd and others v BASF plc and others* [2013] All ER 457; [2012] 1 WLR 2922; [2012] Bus LR 1801; [2013] UKCLR 23; [2012] WLR(D) 286; [2012] UKSC 45.

[435] *JCB v Central Parts*, Cour d'appel de Paris, Pôle 5—Chambre 4, 26 juin 2013, N° 12/04441.

Considering finally that it is for the Court to fix the period during which the infringements were committed in order to solve the dispute brought before the Court ...

Considering that the committed infringements will be taken into consideration as from the beginning of the year 1989 until 21 February 2001 ...

Considering that according to [CP], the prescription could not run when its damages claim depended on the condition of its recognition by the EU courts, [and] that the harm continued to exist after the [EC] injunction dated 20 December 2000,

Considering that under the former Article 2270-1 of the Civil Code which is applicable to the case, the limitation period starts to run as from the appearance of the harm; that Article 2233 Civil Code cannot be invoked usefully by [CP], since indeed its claim is not conditional and since nothing prohibited [CP] to refer the dispute to the national court, albeit in order for this court to stay proceedings when awaiting the final decision of the EU courts; that indeed, the passage before the EU courts, which aim to establish the infringements of EU legislation, to sanction them and not to compensate the harm which can be caused by these violations, cannot have suspended the prescription which has occurred here ...

Notes:

(1) The Paris Court of Appeal has no difficulty in recognising that under Modernisation Regulation 1/2003[436] (and under the doctrine of supremacy of EU law), the finding of an infringement of EU competition law by the EC (and later confirmed by the GC and the CJ in Luxembourg) is binding on the national judge. The Court added that this constitutes sufficient proof of a 'fault' for a tort claim under Article 1382 of the French Civil Code.

(2) Article 2270-1 of the French Civil Code, which the Court of Appeal refers to, states that 'the claims for tort liability are time barred after ten years from the appearance of the harm or of its aggravation'.[437] The damages claimant tries to intelligently extend this 10-year limitation period by referring to Article 2233 CC which states that 'the prescription does not run in relation to a claim that depends on a condition, until that condition occurs'.[438] The claimant presents the acceptance of its damages claim by the EC as a condition which has to be fulfilled before the limitation period can start to run. However, the Court of Appeal correctly countered that the EC does not recognise damages claims, but infringements of EU law. As a result, only the harm resulting from anticompetitive practices between 15 April 1995 and 21 February 2001 could be compensated, and not harm which occurred between 1989 and 15 April 1995. Consequently, CP could not enjoy its right on full compensation, as the harm caused by the practices implemented by the JCB Group between early 1989 and April 1995 could not be compensated.

(3) The Court of Appeal's pragmatic approach should also be noted. Even though, according to the Court, the damages claimant should have brought its actions while the

---

[436] Council Regulation (EC) No 1/2003 of 16 December 2002 on the implementation of the rules on competition laid down in Articles 81 and 82 of the Treaty [2003] OJ L1/1, 4 January. Article 16(1) prohibits a national court from taking a decision which would run counter to an EC decision.

[437] See the first sentence of the article (which was repealed in 2008): 'Les actions en responsabilité civile extracontractuelle se prescrivent par dix ans à compter de la manifestation du dommage ou de son aggravation.'

[438] 'La prescription ne court pas: 1° A l'égard d'une créance qui dépend d'une condition, jusqu'à ce que la condition arrive.'

EU courts were still examining the legality of the EC fining decision, this would not force the national courts to actively pursue the case. The courts could opt for immediate suspension awaiting a final ruling from Luxembourg. Such an approach could reconcile respect for the claimant's rights with procedural economy and respect for the supremacy of EU law and Regulation 1/2003. However, it would still entail a cost for the claimant. Depending on the correct interpretation of Article 10(4) of the Damages Directive (see introductory note 4), the position of the Court of Appeal may have to be revised.

(4) The infringements in this case date back to 1989 and the complaint to the EC dates from 1996. The 2013 judgment which is excerpted here does not mark the end of proceedings, as the court designated an expert to assess damages. Once again, the case illustrates how (further) extending the limitation periods will come at a price.

FURTHER READING

B Adkins and S Beighton, *Private antitrust litigation* (London, Sweet & Maxwell, 2013)

R Amaro, *Le contentieux privé des pratiques anticoncurrentielles—Etude des contentieux privés autonome et complémentaire devant les juridictions judiciaires* (Brussels, Bruylant, 2014).

D Ashton and D Henry, *Competition damages actions in the EU* (Cheltenham, Edward Elgar Publishing, 2013).

J Basedow, *Private enforcement of EC competition law* (Alphen aan den Rijn, Kluwer Law International, 2007).

M Bergström, MC Iacovides and M Strand, *Harmonising EU competition litigation: the new directive and beyond* (Oxford, Hart Publishing, 2016).

C Cauffman, 'Injunctions at the Request of Third Parties in EU Competition Law' (2010) *MJ* 58–86.

C Cauffman, 'The impact of voidness for infringements of Article 101 TFEU on related contracts' (2012) *European Competition Journal* 12 95–122.

G Cumming, B Spitz and R Janal, *Civil procedure used for enforcement of EC competition law by the English, French, and German civil courts* (Alphen aan den Rijn, Kluwer Law International, 2007).

N Dunne, 'The Role of Private Enforcement within EU Competition Law' (2014) *Cambridge Yearbook of European Legal Studies* Vol 16 143–187.

N Dunne, 'Umbrella effects and private antitrust enforcement' (2014) *Cambridge Law Journal* 73(3) 510–513.

N Dunne, 'Courage and Compromise: The Directive on Antitrust Damages Actions' (2015) *European Law Review* 40(4) 581–597.

T Eilmansberger, 'Zur Nichtigkeit kartellrechtswidriger Vereinbarungen und ihren Konsequenzen' (2009) (Teil. 1) *Juristische Blätter* 131(6) 337–350; (Teil. 2) *Juristische Blätter* 131(7) 427–436.

K Hüschelrath and H Schweitzer, *Public and private enforcement of competition law in Europe* (Berlin, Springer, 2012).

AP Komninos, *EC Private Antitrust Enforcement. Decentralised Application of EC Competition Law by National Courts* (Oxford, Hart Publishing, 2008).

AP Komninos, 'Effect of Commission Decisions on Private Antitrust Litigation Setting the Story Straight' (2007) *Common Market Law Review* 44(5) 1387–1428.

I Lianos, *Causal uncertainty and damages claims for the infringement of competition law in Europe* (London, CLES Research Paper, 2015).

V Milutinovićć, *The 'right to damages' under EU competition law: from Courage v. Crehan to the White Paper and beyond* (Alphen aan den Rijn, Kluwer Law International, 2010).

T Möllers and A Heinemann, *The enforcement of competition law in Europe* (Cambridge, Cambridge University Press, 2007).

K Paul, *Gesetzesverstoß und Vertrag im Wettbewerbs- und Regulierungsrecht. Eine Untersuchung der Schutz- und Verbotsgesetzeigenschaft wettbewerbsschützender Normen sowie deren Auswirkungen auf Folgeverträge* (Baden-Baden, Nomos, 2009).

B Rodger (ed.), *Competition law, comparative private enforcement and collective redress across the EU* (Alphen aan den Rijn, Kluwer Law International, 2014).

V Rose and D Baily (eds), *Bellamy & Child, European Union Law of Competition* (Oxford, Oxford University Press, 2013) Chapter 16.

K Schmidt *in* Immenga/Mestmäcker, *EU-Wettbewerbsrecht* (München, Beck, 2012) Chapter 3 and Chapter XI.

R Whish and D Bailey, *Competition law* (Oxford, Oxford University Press, 2015) Chapter 8.

F Wilman, *Private Enforcement of EU law before National Courts: The EU legislative Framework* (Cheltenham, Edward Elgar Publishing, 2015).

3

FUNDAMENTAL FREEDOMS:
TFEU PROVISIONS ON FREE MOVEMENT

Roel van Leuken, Blandine de Clavière, Jean-Sylvestre Bergé and Oliver Remien

I. INTRODUCTION

Since its creation in 1957, the primary objective of the EU—formerly the European (Economic) Community—has been the creation of an internal market, ie, 'an area without internal frontiers in which the free movement of goods, persons, services and capital is ensured'.[1] To achieve this goal, the TFEU (like its predecessor, the E(E)C Treaty) contains, inter alia, fundamental provisions that prohibit impediments to the free movement of goods (Articles 34 and 35 TFEU), the free movement of workers (Article 45 TFEU), the freedom of establishment (Article 49 TFEU), the freedom to provide and receive services (Article 56 TFEU), and the free movement of capital (Article 63 TFEU). Originally, it was assumed that these prohibitions were exclusively addressed to the Member States.[2] It follows from the CJ's case law, however, that (at least) some of the fundamental freedoms may also be applied directly to private law relationships ('horizontal'

---

[1] Art 26(2) TFEU.
[2] The broadly defined concept 'Member State' includes not only *public law* bodies (ie, all levels and branches of government), but also *private law* entities that are controlled and/or financed by the state. See, eg, CJ 24 November 1982 Case C-249/81 *Commission of the European Communities v Ireland (Buy Irish)* [1982] I-04005 ECLI:EU:C:1982:402; CJ 13 December 1983 Case C-222/82 *Apple and Pear Development Council v KJ Lewis Ltd et al* [1983] I-04083 ECLI:EU:C:1983:370.

relationships),[3] in the sense that they result in the creation, modification or extinction of rights and obligations between individuals (*direct horizontal effect*).[4]

The Treaty provisions on free movement—even those that do not produce *direct* horizontal effect—can affect private law relationships in an *indirect* manner too. They can do so via three legal mechanisms: (i) the realisation of the aim of a fundamental freedom through the interpretation of national (public or private) law;[5] (ii) a review of compatibility of national law with the fundamental freedoms in proceedings between individuals;[6] and (iii) the 'positive obligation' for the Member States to protect the rights deriving from the free movement provisions and to also safeguard these rights vis-s-vis their citizens in horizontal relationships.[7]

Sections II–V below discuss the abovementioned direct and indirect horizontal effects for each freedom, using the same arrangement: a brief sketch (without value judgment) of the relevant EU case law, followed by a more detailed study of how *national* courts deal with cases in which an individual raises an argument that is based on the direct horizontal effect of a fundamental freedom, and how they apply the different mechanisms of indirect horizontal effect.

In section VI, attention is paid to the system of justifications. The reason for this is that the accordance of direct horizontal effect to (some of) the fundamental freedoms raises the important question whether and to what extent individuals can successfully rely on an exception in order to justify an act that violates one of those Treaty prohibitions.

The chapter ends with section VII, which offers some conclusions.

II. FREE MOVEMENT OF GOODS (ARTICLES 34 AND 35 TFEU)

Free movement of goods presupposes the abolition of, in principle, all barriers to trade within the EU. Accordingly, Articles 30 and 110 TFEU prohibit all *tariff* obstacles to trade between Member States (customs duties and charges having equivalent effect, internal taxes etc), whereas Articles 34 and 35 TFEU ban all *non-tariff* impediments to intra-EU trade (quantitative restrictions and measures having equivalent effect).[8] Before the national courts, these Treaty provisions may be directly invoked by individuals against Member States (direct *vertical* effect), but—and this holds in particular for Articles 34 and 35 TFEU—they may also be invoked in legal proceedings between individuals (direct or indirect *horizontal* effect).

---

[3] The phrase 'individual' refers to all (legal) persons whose acts cannot be attributed to the state.
[4] See section II.A in Ch 1.
[5] See sections II.B.i and II.B.ii in Ch 1.
[6] See section II.B.iii in Ch 1.
[7] See section II.B.iv in Ch 1.
[8] See also art 37 TFEU, which requires Member States to organise any state monopolies of a commercial character so as to preclude any discrimination between nationals of Member States regarding the conditions under which goods are procured and marketed.

II.A SOURCES: THE TFEU, CJ CASE LAW, MATERIALS

Article 34 TFEU **3.1 (EU)**

Quantitative restrictions on imports and all measures having equivalent effect shall be prohibited between Member States.

Article 35 TFEU **3.2 (EU)**

Quantitative restrictions on exports, and all measures having equivalent effect, shall be prohibited between Member States.

K Lenaerts and P van Nuffel, European Union Law[9]

Quantitative restrictions. The Court of Justice has defined 'quantitative restrictions' as 'measures which amount to a total or partial restraint of, according to the circumstances, imports, exports or goods in transit'. These are measures which introduce a limitation depending upon the quantity or the value of the goods concerned. Since most trade 'quotas' had already been abolished before [now TFEU] entered into effect … the prohibition of quantitative restrictions raises per se only a few problems.

    Measures having equivalent effect. However, alongside quantitative restrictions, all measures having equivalent effect are also prohibited. This ancillary prohibition came to have great significance owing to its broad scope … Indeed, in the 1974 judgment in *Dassonville*, the Court of Justice held that, '[a]ll trading rules enacted by Member States which are capable of hindering, directly or indirectly, actually or potentially, intra-Community trade are to be considered as measures having an equivalent effect to quantitative restrictions' … That definition of 'measures having equivalent effect' takes in a complete range of legislative and administrative measures which are applicable without distinction to domestic and imported products, yet have a—sometimes minimal—effect on potential sales of imported products and hence on the free movement of goods … According to the Court, measures adopted by a Member State are to be regarded as measures having equivalent effect to quantitative restrictions where their object or effect is to treat products originating in other Member States less favourably or where they (otherwise) hinder the access of such products to the market of that Member State. The Court also clarified [in its *Keck* judgment] that the latter is normally not the case for selling arrangements that apply to all traders operating within the national territory and that affect in the same manner, in law and in fact, the marketing of domestic products and of products originating from other Member States.

    …

    Export restrictions. Traditionally, in contradistinction to the broad interpretation of the concept of measures having effect equivalent to quantitative restrictions on imports (Article 34 TFEU [ex Article 28 EC]), the Court of Justice regarded as measures having equivalent effect to quantitative restrictions on exports (Article 35 TFEU [ex Article 29 EC]): 'national measures which have as their specific object or effect the restriction of patterns

---

[9] Lenaerts and Van Nuffel 2011 214–18, footnotes omitted.

of exports and thereby the establishment of a difference in treatment between the domestic trade of a Member State and its export trade in such a way as to provide a particular advantage for national production or for the domestic market of the State in question at the expense of the production or the trade of other Member States' … In recent case law, however, the Court of Justice has shown itself prepared to adopt a broad interpretation of export restrictions, similar to the *Dassonville* interpretation of import restrictions.

II.A.i DIRECT HORIZONTAL EFFECT

A Hartkamp, European Law and National Private Law[10]

For a long time the case law of the Court of Justice suggested that a distinction must be made with regard to the freedoms between the free movement of goods on the one hand and the freedoms relating to the movement of persons and services (free movement of workers, freedom of services and freedom of establishment) on the other hand.

Various judgments seem to indicate that the ECJ denies direct horizontal effect to the provisions regarding the free movement of goods (art. 34 TFEU and art. 35 TFEU, relating to import restrictions and export restrictions, respectively).

Leaving aside the case law in the sphere of intellectual property rights,[11] the CJ for a long time rejected the direct horizontal effect of Articles 34 and 35 TFEU. In *Van de Haar*, for example, it stated that while '[now Article 101 TFEU] of the Treaty belongs to the rules on competition which are addressed to undertakings and associations of undertakings … [now Article 34], on the other hand belongs to the rules which seek to ensure the free movement of goods and, to that end, to eliminate measures taken by Member States which might in any way impede such free movement'.[12] This dichotomy was confirmed in *Vlaamse Reisbureaus*, where the Court held that '[now Articles 34 and 35 TFEU] of the Treaty concern only public measures and not the conduct of undertakings'.[13] And finally, in *Sapod Audic*, it noted (with reference to the famous *Dassonville* judgment) that a clause in an agreement between individuals 'cannot be regarded as

---

[10] Hartkamp 2016 no 57.

[11] Initially, the CJ held in some judgments that the exercise of intellectual property rights by their (private law) holders could amount to a quantitative restriction within the meaning of arts 34 and 35 TFEU, which were (thus) accorded direct horizontal effect. For a discussion of this early case law, see, eg, T Körber, *Grundfreiheiten und Privatrecht* (Tübingen, Mohr Siebeck, 2004) 695–97. Since the mid-1980s, however, the Court has made it unequivocally clear that it merely investigates whether arts 34 and 35 TFEU exclude the application of national legislation on intellectual property rights. See, inter alia, CJ 9 April 1987 Case C-402/85 *G. Basset v Société des auteurs, compositeurs et éditeurs de musique* [1987] I-01747 ECLI:EU:C:1987:197, para 17. As this case illustrates, the review of compatibility with arts 34 and 35 TFEU of national intellectual property law can also take place in proceedings between individuals (*indirect* horizontal effect).

[12] CJ 5 April 1984 Joined Cases C-177/82 and C-178/82 *Criminal Proceedings v Jan van de Haar and Kaveka de Meern BV* [1984] I-01797 ECLI:EU:C:1984:144, paras 11 and 12.

[13] CJ 1 October 1987 Case C-311/85 *ASBL Vereniging van Vlaamse Reisbureaus v ASBL Sociale Dienst van de Plaatselijke en Gewestelijke Overheidsdiensten* [1987] I-03801 ECLI:EU:C1987:418, para 30. See also CJ 27 September 1988 Case C-65/86 *Bayer AG and Maschinenfabrik Hennecke GmbH v Heinz Süllhöfer* [1988] I-05249 ECLI:EU:C:1988:488, para 11.

a barrier to trade for the purposes of [now Article 34] of the Treaty since it was not imposed by a Member State but agreed between individuals'.[14]

In *Fra.bo*,[15] however, the CJ cautiously appeared to change its position.[16] The facts of this case were as follows. Fra.bo, an Italian manufacturer and seller of copper fittings, initiated legal proceedings against the Deutsche Vereinigung des Gas- und Wasserfaches e.V. (DVGW), a certifying organization, arguing that the latter's cancellation of its product certificate was contrary to Article 34 TFEU and thus unlawful. Because the Higher Regional Court Düsseldorf established regarding this issue that it had indeed become virtually impossible for Fra.bo to distribute its copper fittings in Germany (due to, inter alia, the presumption of compliance conferred on products certified by the DVGW under national law), it asked the CJ whether the DVGW—a private law certification body that is neither controlled nor financed by the state—had to comply with Article 34 TFEU when certifying products for drinking water supply. The CJ's answer was affirmative: '[now Article 34 TFEU] must be interpreted as meaning that it applies to standardisation and certification activities of a private law body, where the national legislation considers the products certified by that body to be compliant with national law and that has the effect of restricting the marketing of products which are not certified by that body'.[17] Interestingly, the CJ did not—unlike AG Trstenjak—explicitly champion the analogous application of its own case law on the direct horizontal effect of Articles 45, 49 and 56 TFEU.[18] Therefore, and due to the very specific facts of this case, *Fra.bo* should not be interpreted too broadly: the CJ has not (yet) ruled that the Treaty provisions on the free movement of goods (Articles 34 *and* 35 TFEU) apply directly to all acts of individuals.

The national follow-up to *Fra.bo* is discussed in sections II.B.i and VI.B below.

II.A.ii INDIRECT HORIZONTAL EFFECT

It follows from the case law of the CJ that the Treaty provisions on the free movement of goods can also have an *indirect* effect on legal relationships between individuals. Three mechanisms will now be briefly illustrated: the realisation of the purport of Article 34 and 35 TFEU through the interpretation of a national rule of (private) law, the review of compatibility of national law with Articles 34 and 35 TFEU in legal proceedings between individuals, and the so-called 'positive obligation' that Articles 34 and 35 TFEU impose on Member States.

---

[14] CJ 6 June 2002 Case C-159/00 *Sapod Audic v Eco-Emballages SA* [2002] I-05031 ECLI:EU:C:2002:343, para 74.

[15] CJ 12 July 2012 Case C-171/11 *Fra.bo v Deutsche Vereinigung des Gas- und Wasserfaches* [2012] ECLI:EU:C:2012:453.

[16] See N Nic Shuibhne, 'The Treaty is Coming to Get You' (2012) *EL Rev* 367–68; H van Harten and T Nauta, 'Towards Horizontal Direct Effect for the Free Movement of Goods. Comment on *Fra.bo*' (2013) 5 *EL Rev* 677; W-H Roth, 'Die "horizontale" Anwendbarkeit der Warenverkehrsfreiheit (Art. 34 AEUV)' (2013) *EWS* 16. For a different opinion, see P Oliver, 'L'article 34 TFEU peut-it avoir un effet direct horizontal? Réflexions sur l'arret *Fra.bo*' (2014) 50(1) *CDE* 77.

[17] CJ *Fra.bo* (n 15) para 32.

[18] A short summary of (the argumentation in) that case law can be found in section III.A.i (art 45 TFEU) and section IV.A.ii (arts 49 and 56 TFEU).

II.A.ii.a Interpretation of National (Private) Law in the Light of Articles 34 and 35 TFEU

Indirect horizontal effect of Articles 34 and 35 TFEU through interpretation by the national courts will mainly take the form of influence exerted by these Treaty provisions through open-ended principles of private law (eg, reasonable and fairness, generally accepted conduct and public order).[19] The national case that led to the CJ's judgment in *Dansk Supermarked*[20] illustrates this.

A Danish company (Imerco) ordered a British manufacturer (Broadhurst) to produce commemorative dinner services for its fiftieth anniversary, with the intention of selling them in Denmark exclusively through its shareholders (hardware merchants). Imerco allowed Broadhurst to market approximately 1,000 substandard pieces it had rejected, under the express condition that these items would not be exported to Danish territory. The manufacturer accordingly sold the rejected pieces to British wholesalers subject to a prohibition on their resale to Denmark. A Danish company (Dansk Supermarked) nonetheless obtained some of the substandard services and offered them for sale in Denmark at a price below the price charged by Imerco for the original pieces. Imerco sought an injunction to prohibit the sale of the services in question, arguing that Dansk Supermarked had infringed the Danish law on unfair competition. Because Dansk Supermarked invoked the principle of mutual recognition[21] enshrined in Article 34 TFEU as a defence, the Danish court referred the case for a preliminary ruling to the CJ, which first remarked that EU law does not, in principle, 'have the effect of preventing the application in a Member State to goods imported from other Member States of the provisions on marketing in force in the state of importation'.[22] As a result, 'the marketing of imported goods may be prohibited if the conditions on which they are sold constitute an infringement on the marketing usages considered proper and fair in the Member State of importation'.[23] However, the CJ then emphasised that the actual fact of the importation of goods which have been lawfully marketed in another Member State *cannot* be considered as an improper or unfair act 'since that description may be attached only to offer or exposure for sale on the basis of circumstances distinct from the importation itself'.

Dansk Supermarked provides a clear example of *indirect* horizontal effect of Article 34 TFEU: the behaviour of an individual (Dansk Supermarked) as against another individual (Imerco) is tested against an open-ended rule of national law (the Danish rule on unfair competition) that, on this occasion, is interpreted in the light of Article 34 TFEU.[24]

---

[19] See section II.B.ii in Ch 1.

[20] CJ 22 January 1981 Case C-581/80 *Dansk Supermarked A/S v A/S Imerco* [1981] I-00181 ECLI:EU:C:1981:17.

[21] Mutual recognition is the principle that a product lawfully marketed in one Member State, and not subject to EU harmonisation, should be allowed to be marketed in any other Member State, even when the product does not fully comply with the technical rules of the Member State of destination. See CJ 20 February 1979 Case C-120/78 *Rewe Zentrale AG v Bundesmonopolverwaltung für Branntwein (Cassis de Dijon)* [1979] I-00649 ECLI:EU:C:1979:42.

[22] CJ *Dansk Supermarked* (n 20) para 15.

[23] ibid.

[24] In, para 17 of the *Dansk Supermarked* judgment (n 20), the CJ also held 'that it is impossible in any circumstances for agreements between individuals to derogate from the mandatory provisions of the Treaty

II.A.ii.b Review of Compatibility of National Law with Articles 34 and 35 TFEU in Proceedings between Individuals

If there is a dispute about whether a national rule of (private) law is compatible with Article 34 or 35 TFEU, individuals may submit the conflict to the national courts for assessment. This may happen in conflicts between an individual and the state ('vertical proceedings'), but also in conflicts between individuals ('horizontal proceedings').[25] In *Delhaize*,[26] for example, Article 35 TFEU was successfully invoked by a Belgian super-market (Delhaize) to contest: (i) the legality of a Spanish law that prohibited the export of Rioja wine; and consequently also ii) the defence of force majeure of its contractual counterparty (Promalvin).[27] Although in this case the non-applicability of the national law ultimately did have consequences for the legal relationship between two individuals (Delhaize won and Promalvin lost because of Article 35 TFEU), this should not be called *direct* horizontal effect, because it was not the Treaty provision *itself* but, in the absence of force majeure, the agreement between the parties that created rights and obligations in this relationship between individuals.

II.A.ii.c Positive Obligation for the Member States to Safeguard the Free Movement of Goods on their Territory

Articles 34 and 35 TFEU can be construed to imply an obligation for the Member States to protect the rights deriving from these prohibitions and to safeguard these rights vis-a-vis their citizens, also in horizontal relationships. This follows from the *Spanish Strawberries* case.[28]

For many years, French farmers had been impeding the import and sale of agricultural products from (in particular) Spain. Despite the violent nature of these acts, the national authorities did not intervene. The EU therefore initiated infringement proceedings under Article 258 TFEU. In the judgment that followed, the CJ established that the fact that a Member State *abstains* from adopting adequate measures to prevent obstacles to the free movement of goods that are created by actions by private individuals on its territory is just as likely to obstruct intra-EU trade as are Member State *actions*. Consequently, it ruled that Article 34 TFEU requires the Member States not only to abstain from adopting or engaging in conduct liable to constitute an obstacle to trade (*negative* obligation), but

---

on the free movement of goods'. When isolated from its context, this sentence may be construed as a recogni-tion of the *direct* horizontal effect of art 34 TFEU. See, eg, P Pescatore, 'The Doctrine of "Direct Effect": An Infant Disease of Community Law' (1983) *EL Rev* 163. However, as the judgment primarily concerned the lawfulness of the acts of Dansk Supermarked, this reading is not imperative. See Hartkamp 2016 no 59, who adds that: 'It is, however, clear that nullity of the stipulation would support the view that the conduct of Dansk Supermarked was not unlawful.'

[25] Substantively, there is no difference whatsoever between these two situations. See P Oliver and W-H Roth, 'The internal market and the four freedoms' (2004) *CMLR* vol 41 no 2 p 421; Hartkamp 2016 no 21.

[26] CJ 9 June 1992 Case C-47/90 *Delhaize v Promalvin SA and AGE Bodegas Unidas SA* [1992] I-03669 ECLI:EU:C:1992:250.

[27] See for another example CJ 10 November 1982 Case C-261/81 *Walter Rau Lebensmittelwerke v De Smedt PVBA* [1982] I-03961 ECLI:EU:C:1982:382.

[28] CJ 9 December 2009 Case C-265/95 *Commission v France* [1997] I-06959 ECLI:EU:C:1997:595.

also, when read in conjunction with Article 4(3) TEU, to take all necessary and appropriate measures to ensure that individuals respect this fundamental freedom on their territory (*positive* obligation).[29]

At the time of this judgment, Article 34 TFEU had not yet been accorded direct horizontal effect, meaning that producers or importers of Spanish agricultural products could not invoke it *directly* against those responsible for the violent protest actions to claim damages. If the producers/importers had initiated proceedings against the French farmers, Article 34 TFEU could have produced an *indirect* horizontal effect, though, as the national judge might have interpreted the relevant provisions of national (tort) law in the light of this Treaty provision.

II.B NATIONAL CASE LAW

II.B.i DIRECT HORIZONTAL EFFECT

As it was not until 2012 (in the *Fra.bo* case; see section II.A.i above) that the CJ cautiously accepted some direct horizontal effect of Article 34 TFEU, it may not come as a surprise that there is hardly any national case law yet in which Article 34 (or 35) TFEU is applied directly to a legal relationship between individuals. In fact, the only national case we are aware of is the German proceedings in *Fra.bo* following the CJ preliminary ruling.

Oberlandesgericht Düsseldorf (Higher Regional Court Düsseldorf), 14 August 2013[30]   **3.3 (GERM)**

Fra.bo SpA v Deutsche Vereinigung des Gas- und Wasserfaches eV—'Technisch-Wissenschaftlicher Verein

DIRECT HORIZONTAL EFFECT OF ARTICLE 34 TFEU: PRIVATE LAW CONSEQUENCES

Fra.bo (national follow-up)

A private law association is held liable for breach of duty (§ 280 BGB) because it has acted contrary to Article 34 TFEU

Facts: See section II.A.i above. In short, the CJ answered the Higher Regional Court Düsseldorf that Article 34 TFEU must be interpreted as meaning that it applies to standardisation and certification activities of

---

[29] See ibid, paras 30–32. If a Member State (in this case, the French Republic) has 'manifestly and persistently abstained from adopting appropriate and adequate measures' to end the actions of individuals that hinder the free movement of goods and thus breaches this positive obligation, it may be liable in damages against the individuals whose rights were not adequately protected. See also CJ 12 June 2003 Case C-112/00 *Schmidberger, Internationale Transporte und Planzüge v Republik Österreich* [2003] I-06569 ECLI:EU:C:2003:33, in which the CJ held that the fact that the Austrian authorities did not ban a demonstration as those of the case at hand (which differed considerably from the circumstances in *Spanish Strawberries*) was not incompatible with arts 34 and 35 TFEU, read together with art 4(3) TEU.

[30] OLG Düsseldorf 14 August 2013 VI-2 U (Kart) 15/08 *Fra.bo SpA v Deutsche Vereinigung des Gas- und Wasserfaches eV—Technisch-Wissenschaftlicher Verein*.

a private law body (the DVGW), where the national legislation considered the products certified by that body to be compliant with national law and that had the effect of restricting the marketing of products not certified by that body. Consequently, the national court had to establish whether the cancellation of Fra.bo's product certificate for copper fittings constituted a restriction on the free movement of goods.

Held: The cancellation of Fra.bo's product certificate constituted an unjustified restriction on the free movement of goods. As a result, the DVGW was liable for breach of duty (§ 280 BGB). Fra.bo was awarded damages and, in addition, it had to be granted a (renewed) product certificate.

Judgment: [53] The corresponding prohibition applies also to the standardisation and certification activities of the respondents as private law bodies (CJ EU, 12 July 2012—'C-171/11, grounds 24–32). The respondents—the respondent under 2 having, on 1 August 2007, become the legal successor to the relevant legal rights and obligations of the respondent under 1—are the only bodies authorised to grant access to the German market for products such as the copper fittings in this case. The requirement for an ozone test and a 3000-hour test (DVGW technical standard W 534) makes it significantly more difficult for the applicant to market its fittings in Germany, where virtually the only such fittings purchased and installed are those certified by the respondents. The—theoretical— possibility of obtaining individual certification in the form of a report from an expert other than DVGW is not practical and cannot be expected to be obtained by those seeking to offer such products in the market.

…

[55] The restriction on the free movement of goods as practised by the respondents cannot be regarded as justified.

…

[72] The cancellation of the certificate for the water sector (registration number GW-8511BL0457), which is not in compliance with the Treaty, must consequently be reversed and payment of compensation made (§ 280 para. 1, German Civil Code). The certificate must be re-issued by the respondent under 2, who, through divestment of the certification activities, is the legal successor of the respondent under 1 with regard to certain legal rights and obligations, with effect from 1 August 2007.

[73] The defendants failed to demonstrate that the unlawful cancellation of the certificate was not attributable to them (§ 280 para. 1, German Civil Code). On the contrary, the defendant under 1, whose activities are attributable to the defendant under 2, was found in any event to have been negligent in cancelling the certificate. The defendant under 1 must have been aware that as a private law body had, in these circumstances, to take the EU provisions on free movement of goods into account in its standardisation and certification activities. It was the responsibility of the defendant under 1 to carefully examine its legal status and the decisions of the highest courts and, where necessary, to obtain legal advice. The Court of Justice's judgment of 12 July 2012 in this case was not at all surprising; indeed, as the Advocate-General stated in her opinion (points 27 *et seq.* and 30 *et seq.*), it was in line with a whole series of earlier decisions in the years to 2005, which gave expression not only to a broad interpretation of the term infringement of fundamental freedoms but also to the tendency of the Court to extend the scope of applicability of fundamental freedoms to include acts by private law bodies. Either, therefore, the defendant under 1 did not form its legal opinion on the scope of the fundamental freedom of the free movement of goods with sufficient care (including the requirement for an ozone test on its terms and conditions) or it chose to disregard the matter and to accept that its standardisation and certification activities were not compliant with EU law. The same applies to the justification sought for the measure. In the circumstances, the respondent under 1 must have been aware that the 3000-hours test could not be justified

under [now Article 36 TFEU] and that any justification based on unwritten grounds would be open to question. To that extent, therefore, it acted at its own, identifiable risk.

Notes:

(1) In this case, Article 34 TFEU influenced the substance of a horizontal legal relationship *directly*: because an individual (the DVGW) disproportionately[31] restricted the right to free movement of goods of the other individual (Fra.bo), it was held liable in damages for breach of duty (§ 280(1) of the German Civil Code (BGB)). Moreover, it was ordered to remove the restriction by granting a renewed product certificate.

(2) It follows from § 280(1), sentence 2 BGB that an obligee (Fra.bo) cannot claim damages from the obligor (the DVGW) if the latter is not responsible for the breach of duty. However, in para 73 of its judgment, the German court made it unequivocally clear that the DVGW *was* responsible for the breach, as it should have known that, in the current circumstances, it had to respect Article 34 TFEU. This rather EU-friendly approach of the Higher Regional Court Düsseldorf contrasts with the general reticence of German scholars[32] and courts[33] to apply the fundamental freedoms directly to legal relationships between individuals.

II.B.ii. INDIRECT HORIZONTAL EFFECT

In this section, attention will be paid to national cases in which Article 34 or 35 TFEU had an *indirect* effect on private law relationships. While, in this respect, the case law of the CJ illustrates that at least three types of legal mechanisms can be distinguished (see section II.A.ii above), all reported national cases concern proceedings between individuals in which Article 34 TFEU was invoked to contest the legality of a national rule.

Voorzitter Koophandel Antwerpen (President of the Commercial Court Antwerp), 19 June 2003[34]   **3.4 (BE)**

Firma de Meurichy NV v Tango België Pilot BVBA

BOUNDARIES OF ARTICLE 34 TFEU: PURELY INTERNAL SITUATIONS, SELLING ARRANGEMENTS

Unmanned fuel stations

Article 34 TFEU does not apply to purely internal situations, nor is it applicable to national legislation that imposes a general prohibition on resale at a loss

Facts: The claimant, a Belgian reseller of fuels, brought a cease and desist action against a Belgian proprietor of unmanned fuel stations, arguing that the latter had infringed the Belgian Act on Commercial Practices and

---

[31] See section VI.B below.

[32] A concise summary of opinions is found in, eg, S Perner, *Grundfreiheiten, Grundrechte-Charta und Privatrecht* (Tübingen, Mohr Siebeck, 2013) 152–55.

[33] See, eg, OLG Hamm 31 March 2008 Az. 8 U 222/07. This case will be discussed below in section V.B.

[34] President Commercial Court Antwerp 19 June 2003 *Jaarboek Handelspraktijken & Mededinging* 2003, 380 *Firma de Meurichy NV v Tango België Pilot BVBA*.

Consumer Protection by selling at a loss (*vente à perte*). The defendant asked the Belgian court to make a preliminary referral to the CJ in order to find out whether the Belgian prohibition to sell at a loss was compatible with Article 34 TFEU.

Held: The Belgian court rejected the defendant's request.

Judgment: The defendant raises a preliminary question for the CJEU because of the alleged conflict of Article 40(2) and (3) with the free movement of goods.

The defendant refers, however, to (possible) future law ('Proposal') that is not effective yet.

Moreover, the present case concerns purely Belgian law on the one hand, and Belgian parties and/or selling arrangements on the other hand (it does not concern the import of products from other Member States).

In addition, it has already been established that national rules concerning selling arrangements, such as a prohibition of sale at a loss, are not contrary to the free movement of goods if they apply to all affected traders operating within the national territory and provided that they affect in the same manner, in law and fact, the marketing of domestic products and those from other Member States (CJ 24 November 1993, Jaarboek Handelspraktijken 1993, 130).

Notes:

(1) It is settled case law of the CJ that the Treaty provisions on free movement do not apply to 'purely internal situations'. However, as Article 34 TFEU applies to all national measures which are capable of hindering, *directly or indirectly*, *actually or potentially*, trade between the Member States,[35] the existence of a cross-border element is quickly assumed.[36]

(2) By suggesting that Article 34 TFEU does not apply to the present case because all facts are situated in one Member State, the national court ignores that, according to the CJ, '[now Article 34 TFEU] cannot be considered inapplicable simply because all the facts of the specific case before the national court are confined to a single Member State'.[37]

(3) The national court is correct, though, in stating that the Belgian prohibition on resale at a loss falls outside the scope of Article 34 TFEU because it constitutes a non-discriminatory selling arrangement.[38] Consequently, the defendant can invoke the national rule of law to underpin its action against the claimant.

---

[35] CJ 11 July 1974 Case C-8/74 *Procureur du Roi v Benoît and Gustave Dassonville* [1974] I-00837 ECLI:EU:C1974:82, para 5.

[36] C Barnard, *The Substantive Law of the EU: The Four Freedoms* (Oxford, Oxford University Press, 2016) 88–9.

[37] CJ 7 May 1997 Joined Cases C-321/94–C-324/94 *Criminal Proceedings v Jacques Pistre, Michèle Barthes, Yves Milhau and Didier Oberti* [1997] I-02343 ECLI:EU:C:1997:229, para 44.

[38] CJ 24 November 1993 Joined Cases C-267/91 and 268/91 *Criminal Proceedings v Bernard Keck and Daniel Mithouard* [1993] I-06097 ECLI:EU:C:1993:905, para 16 (see section II.A above).

Voorzitter Koophandel Antwerpen (President Commercial
Court Antwerp), 8 May 2008[39]   **3.5 (BE)**

Maisons du Monde BVBA v Casa International NV

INCOMPATIBILITY OF A NATIONAL LANGUAGE REQUIREMENT WITH ARTICLE 34 TFEU

Product labelling

The incompatibility of a national language requirement with Article 34 TFEU does not affect the applicability of another provision from the same national law to the private law relationship

Facts: Maisons du Monde was sued by a competitor for infringement of Article 13 of the Act on Commercial Practices and Consumer Protection (ACPCP), which requires that user instructions need to be available in the language of the linguistic region where the goods are marketed.[40]

Held: In first instance, Maisons du Monde was sentenced by default and prohibited from offering and/or selling in the Flemish region products whose labelling, mandatory information, user instructions and warranty documents are not set in the Dutch language. Maisons du Monde opposed this judgment, claiming inter alia that Article 13 ACPCP was contrary to the free movement of goods. The appeal judge agreed that the national rule was contrary to Article 34 TFEU, but ruled that Maisons du Monde still had to comply with Article 30 ACPCP, which requires the seller to provide the consumer with appropriate and useful information about the characteristics and conditions of sale of the product, taking into account its reasonably foreseeable use.

Judgment: It is true that the Court of Justice repeatedly held that Article 13 ACPCP is incompatible with [now Article 34 TFEU], which prohibits quantitative import restrictions and measures of equivalent effect, because … it excludes the possibility of ensuring that the consumer is informed by other means such as designs, symbols or pictograms. However, this does not affect the applicability of Article 30 ACPCP, which requires the seller to provide the consumer with appropriate and useful information concerning the characteristics and conditions of sale of the product, taking into account its reasonably foreseeable use.

Article 30 ACPCP therefore imposes no specific language but lays down an obligation to use an intelligible language, which—depending on the circumstances—can be done either via pictograms, designs, symbols … or by written text and then for distribution in the Flemish part of the country—in the Dutch language.

Article 30 ACPCP does not contain an exhaustive list of the information to be provided but this can be generally defined as the mandatory information, user and safety instruction and guarantee certificates.

It is therefore clear that the mandatory information, user and safety instruction and guarantee certificates must be drawn up in the Dutch language or be indicated by means of pictograms, designs or symbols.

---

[39] President Commercial Court Antwerp 8 May 2008 *Jaarboek Handelspraktijken & Mededinging* 2008,182 *Maisons du Monde BVBA v Casa International NV.*

[40] Art 13 ACPCP required user instructions. This Act has now been replaced by the Code of Economic Law.

Note:

The Belgian court correctly stated that the CJ has repeatedly concluded that the language requirement imposed by Article 13 ACPCP is contrary to Article 34 TFEU.[41] As a consequence, this national provision cannot be applied in the present case.

Sąd Najwyższy (Supreme Court of Poland),
23 October 2013[42]   **3.6 (PL)**

AP Inc v SFP SA

COMPATIBILITY WITH ARTICLE 34 TFEU OF A STATUTORY EXCEPTION
(STRICTLY INTERPRETED) TO A PATENT MONOPOLY

Solifenacin succinate

Claimant seeks to enforce his patent rights against the defendant who argues that its actions did not constitute unlawful infringement of patent rights since they fell within the scope of fair use as provided for in Article 69(1)(4) of the Polish Industrial Property Act

Facts: The claimant (AP Inc, a company with its registered office in Japan) obtained in Poland a patent for producing a substance named 'solifenacin succinate'. In spite of this, the defendant (SFP SA, a company with its registered office in Poland) produced this substance in its Polish factory and sold it to its customers in, inter alia, Germany without the authorisation of the patent holder. The claimant sought an injunction ordering the defendant to cease and desist from infringing its patent rights. The defendant asserted that its actions did not constitute unlawful infringement of patent rights since they fell within the scope of fair use as provided for in Article 69(1)(4) of the Industrial Property Act of 30 June 2003 … Moreover, the defendant argued that this exemption, in conjunction with Article 34 TFEU, conferred the right to manufacture and to offer the product covered by the patent to entities from other EU Member States that would use it within the scope of fair use for the purposes specified in the aforementioned provision.

Held: The restrictive interpretation of Article 69(1)(4) of the Polish Industrial Property Act was not contrary to Article 34 TFEU.

Judgment: The dispute between the parties concentrated on the issue whether certain actions of the defendant fell within the scope of the fair use exemption provided for in Article 69((1)(4) of the Industrial Property Act (the so-called Bolar exemption). Pursuant to this provision a patent is not infringed by exploiting an invention to the extent necessary with a view to perform acts required by law to obtain registration or a permit as a precondition for the admission of certain products to the market for their stated purpose, in particular medicinal products. The content and meaning of this provision will be construed in the light of EU law.

…

The scope of the exemption should be construed strictly with a view to the purpose of its introduction. The restriction on the patent right previously in force, which authorized

---

[41] See, eg, CJ 18 June 1991 Case C-369/89 *Piageme et al v BVBA Peeters* [1991] I-02971 ECLI:EU:C:1991:256; CJ 12 October 1995 Case C-85/94 *Groupement des Producteurs, Importateurs et Agents Généraux d'Eaux Minérales Etrangères, VZW (Piageme) et al v Peeters NV* [1995] I-02955 ECLI:EU:C:1995:312; CJ 3 June 1999 Case C-33/97 *Colim NV v Bigg's Continent Noord NV* [1999] I-03175 ECLI:EU:C:1999:274.

[42] Polish Supreme Court 23 October 2014 nos 7–8 item 80 *AP Inc v SFP SA.*

the use of the invention for the purposes of research and experiments (currently Article 69(1)(3) of the Industrial Property Act), interpreted in conformity with EU law, did not apply to research conducted for commercial purposes. Consequently, it did not suffice to solve the problem concerning the market introduction of a so-called generic drug, i.e. a product comparable to a listed reference medicinal product (the original product) (Article 2(35)(9)(b)) and Article 15 of the Act of September 6, 2001—the Pharmaceutical Law, consolidated text: J.L. 2008, No. 45, item 271). The essential characteristic of a generic drug is that its active substance has the same qualitative and quantitative composition as the reference medicinal product, provided that its bioequivalence to the original has been confirmed by appropriate tests. The admission of a generic drug to the market is subject to a specific legal regime and long-term, multi-step proceedings. The exclusion of the possibility of conducting the tests needed to collect the documentation necessary for obtaining admission of the drug to the market (after expiry of the patent) prolongs the actual operation of the patent monopoly. The restriction ('Bolar exemption') under consideration makes it possible, even while the patent is still in force, to carry out the experiments necessary to demonstrate bioequivalence of products for the purpose of obtaining their admission to the market, thus enabling manufacturers of generic drugs to have these products available in a relatively short time after the expiration of the patent on the original drug.

...

For these reasons, it should be held that the patent holder may only be deprived of its prohibitive rights under Article 66(1) of the Industrial Property Act by the person who performs the steps required by law to obtain the registration or permit required for admission of the generic drug on the market.

This privilege does not extend to the use of an invention by an entity that does not intend applying for registration and does not run the necessary tests for such registration, but which instead is producing the product using someone else's invention in order to subsequently offer it for resale to sell it to others. This is not an activity falling within the scope of actions required to obtain the permit or the registration that is a condition for admission of the generic drug on the market, thus there is no reason why the patent holder should be deprived of its prohibitive rights vis-a-vis such entity.

...

The defendant used the claimants invention to produce the substance protected by the patent without the patent holder's permission. It did not intend to apply for admission to the market of a generic drug based on the active substance of the reference drug and did not take the steps for obtaining such admission; moreover, the sole purpose of producing the active substance was to sell it to third parties, so as to generate income from the profitable exploitation of someone else's invention during the patent protection period. Such an action, which—as explained—is not covered by the Bolar exemption, constituted infringement of the claimant exclusive rights under the patent.

The defendant's allegation that the Court of Appeal's reading of Article 69(1)(4) of the Industrial Property Act implies an erroneous interpretation of Article 34 TFEU namely that it provides that quantitative restrictions on imports and all measures having equivalent effect shall be prohibited between Member States, and thus lays down the principle of the free movement of goods, must likewise be dismissed. This provision is meant to eliminate unjustified obstacles to trade between Member States and to avoid a breaking down into national markets and it relates primarily to protectionist and discriminatory measures. Furthermore, Article 36 of the Treaty, i.e. in a provision which derogates from the prohibition provided for in Article 34, permits introducing restrictions on imports, exports or goods in transit if they are justified on grounds of the protection of other important rights, including the right to industrial property, hence respecting the national laws on industrial property. Derogation from the principle of free movement of goods is deemed justified only in relation to the rights making up the core of industrial property law, yet there is no reason for assigning to the category of rights beyond this core the right to the exclusive use of one's invention and the right to oppose encroachments on one's sphere of exclusivity. The restrictive interpretation of the exceptional restriction of these rights, which in the Polish legal system is laid down in Article 69(1)(4) of the Industrial Property Act, cannot be regarded as an erroneous reading of the legal norm of Article 34 TFEU and does not lead to arbitrary discrimination nor to concealed restraint of trade between Member States.

Note:

In this case, the claimant claimed an injunction based on infringement of a patent. The defendant invoked an exception based on a national statute (Article 69(1)(4) of the Industrial Property Act), but the lower courts dismissed that argument because the exception had to be interpreted strictly. As a result, the injunction was granted. The defendant appealed to the Polish Supreme Court, where it argued unsuccessfully that the (too) restrictive interpretation of the statutory exception was contrary to Article 34 TFEU. In the end, Article 34 TFEU therefore did not have an (indirect) impact on the legal relationship between the two individuals.

III. FREE MOVEMENT OF WORKERS (ARTICLE 45 TFEU)

III.A SOURCES: THE TFEU, CJ CASE LAW, MATERIALS

Article 45 TFEU   3.7 **(EU)**

1. Freedom of movement for workers shall be secured within the Union.

2. Such freedom of movement shall entail the abolition of any discrimination based on nationality between workers of the Member States as regards employment, remuneration and other conditions of work and employment.

3. It shall entail the right, subject to limitations justified on grounds of public policy, public security or public health:

(a) to accept offers of employment actually made;

(b) to move freely within the territory of Member States for this purpose;

(c) to stay in a Member State for the purpose of employment in accordance with the provisions governing the employment of nationals of that State laid down by law, regulation or administrative action;

(d) to remain in the territory of a Member State after having been employed in that State, subject to conditions which shall be embodied in regulations to be drawn up by the Commission.

4. The provisions of this Article shall not apply to employment in the public service.

Article 45(2) TFEU prohibits all *direct* and *indirect* discrimination between nationals (workers) of a given Member State and nationals (workers) of other Member States.

K Lenaerts and P van Nuffel, European Union Law[43]

Discrimination is direct where a measure employs a prohibited distinguishing criterion (e.g. nationality) or subjects different cases to formally similar rules. Indirect discrimination arises where, although not making use of an unlawful distinguishing criterion, a provision has effects coinciding with or approaching those of such a distinguishing criterion (nationality) as a result of its use of other distinguishing criteria which are not as such prohibited.

Initially, Article 45 TFEU was only applied to *discriminatory* measures that restrict the free movement of workers (see on the conjunction between the provisions on the fundamental freedoms and the caselaw of the CJ on Article 18 TFEU: sections III.A.i and V.C in Chapter 4). However, since *Bosman*,[44] it is established case law that Article 45 TFEU also catches *non-discriminatory* rules that impede the access of workers to the employment market of another Member State.

III.A.i DIRECT HORIZONTAL EFFECT

As set out in section II in Chapter 1, a provision of EU law has direct horizontal effect when it creates, modifies or extinguishes rights and obligations between individuals.

In the landmark case of *Walrave and Koch*, the CJ held for the first time that the non-discrimination rule of Article 45 TFEU not only applies to the acts of public authorities (direct vertical effect), but also to acts of any other nature aimed at regulating gainful employment in a *collective* manner (such as the rules and regulations of private law sporting organisations and collective labour agreements).[45] In *Angonese*, the direct horizontal effect of the prohibition of discrimination enshrined in Article 45 TFEU was even expanded to *non-collective* agreements between individuals.[46]

As a prohibition of restrictions, Article 45 TFEU is capable of producing direct horizontal effect too. It follows from cases like *Bosman*,[47] *Lehtonen*,[48] *Olympique*

---

[43] Lenaerts and Van Nuffel 2011 172.

[44] CJ 15 December 1995 Case C-415/93 *Union royale belge des sociétés de football association ASBL v Jean-Marc Bosman, Royal club liégeois SA v Jean-Marc Bosman et al and Union des associations européennes de football (UEFA) v Jean-Marc Bosman* [1995] I-04921 ECLI:EU:C:1995:463.

[45] CJ 12 December 1974 Case C-36/74 *BNO Walrave and LJN Koch v Association Union cycliste internationale, Koninklijke Nederlandsche Wielren Unie and Federación Española Ciclismo* [1974] I-01495 ECLI:EU:C:1974:140. See also CJ 14 July 1976 Case C-13/76 *Gaetano Donà v Mario Mantero* [1976] I-01333 ECLI:EU:C:1976:115. See on the conjunction between the provisions on the fundamental freedoms and the caselaw of the CJ on art 18 TFEU: section III.A.i and section V.C Ch 4.

[46] CJ 6 June 2000 Case C-281/98 *Angonese vCassa di Risparmio di Bolzano SpA* [2000] I-04139 ECLI:EU:C:2000:296. See also CJ 17 July 2008 Case C-94/07 *Andrea Raccanelli v Max-Planck-Gesellschaft zur Förderung der Wissenschaften eV* [2008] I-05939 ECLI:EU:C:2008:425; CJ 28 June 2012 Case C-172/11 *Georges Erny v Daimler AG—Werk Wörth* nyr ECLI:EU:C:2012:399.

[47] CJ *Bosman* (n 44).

[48] CJ 13 April 2000 Case C-176/96 *Jyri Lehtonen and Castors Canada Dry Namur-Braine ASBL v Fédération royale belge des sociétés de basket-ball ASBL (FRBSB)* [2000] I-02681 ECLI:EU:C:2000:201.

Lyonnais[49] and *Casteels*[50] that non-discriminatory collective measures of individuals can also be tested against this fundamental Treaty provision. To date, the CJ has not yet decided whether the same holds for the non-discriminatory, non-collective acts of individuals.

The CJ's main argument in favour of direct horizontal effect of Article 45 TFEU is based on the principle of effectiveness: the Treaty prohibition would lose its useful effect if it were merely binding upon the Member States, because restrictions on the free movement of workers can also come about as a result of the acts of individuals. Another argument is that certain subject matters (eg, terms of employment) are sometimes governed by provisions laid down by law or regulation and sometimes by agreements and other acts concluded or adopted by private persons. Limiting Article 45 TFEU to acts of a public authority would result in the dissimilar application of this provision, thereby undermining its effectiveness. For this reason, according to the CJ, it is not the public or private origin of an act that is decisive, but rather its effect on the functioning of the internal market.

III.A.ii INDIRECT HORIZONTAL EFFECT

Section II.A.ii illustrated three mechanisms of indirect horizontal effect of Articles 34 and 35 TFEU (free movement of goods): interpretation of a rule of national (private) law in the light of a provision of EU law; the positive obligation for the Member States; and a review of compatibility with EU law of a rule of national (private) law in proceedings between individuals. Article 45 TFEU, one must assume, is capable of producing the same indirect horizontal effects. The case law of the CJ, however, only provides some examples of legal situations in which this Treaty prohibition is invoked in a horizontal dispute to contest the legality of a national rule of law. One of them is *Las v PSA Antwerp*.[51]

On the basis of an employment contract of 10 July 2004, drafted in English, a Dutch resident, Anton Las, was employed as Chief Financial Officer for an unlimited period by PSA Antwerp NV, a company established in Antwerp (Belgium), but belonging to a multinational group whose registered office is in Singapore. By letter dated 7 September 2009, drafted in English, Las was dismissed with immediate effect. Pursuant to Article 8 of the aforementioned employment contract, PSA Antwerp made him a payment in lieu of notice equal to three months' salary and an additional payment equal to six months' salary. Las, however, brought an action before the Antwerp Labour Tribunal seeking an order for PSA Antwerp to pay him amounts which were considerably higher than those received. In support of his claims, he relied in particular on the fact that Article 8 of his employment contract, which was drafted in English, was vitiated by absolute nullity

---

[49] CJ 16 March 2010 Case C-325/08 *Olympique Lyonnais SASP v Olivier Bernard and Newcastle UFC* [2010] I-02177 ECLI:EU:C:2010:143.

[50] CJ 10 March 2011 Case C-379/09 *Maurits Casteels v British Airways plc* [2011] I-01379 ECLI:EU:C:2011:131.

[51] CJ 16 April 2013 Case C-202/11 *Anton Las v PSA Antwerp NV* nyr ECLI:EU:C:2013:239.

because it infringed the provisions of the Flemish Decree on Use of Languages, which provides for Dutch to be used in undertakings whose place of business is established in the Dutch-language region of Belgium. The defence of PSA Antwerp was that the decree could not be applied to situations in which a person exercises his right of freedom of movement as a worker, as the decree would then constitute an unwarranted obstacle to that fundamental freedom.[52] In answer to preliminary questions of the national court, the CJ ruled that the Flemish Decree on Use of Languages indeed caused a disproportionate restriction on the free movement of workers and thus could not be applied.

In this case, the horizontal relationship *itself* (the employment contract) was not tested against Article 45 TFEU (no *direct* horizontal effect). *Indirectly*, though, as an instrument for reviewing national legislation, the Treaty prohibition did affect the legal relationship between the employer and its employee. Because Article 45 TFEU precluded the application of the decree (and the nullity sanction it contained), the labour contract turned out to be valid and PSA Antwerp won (and Las lost) the proceedings.

III.B NATIONAL CASE LAW

III.B.i DIRECT HORIZONTAL EFFECT

This section discusses national cases in which Article 45 TFEU was applied (or should have been applied) *directly* to legal relationships between individuals. Coincidentally, all of them are cases decided after the CJ had given preliminary rulings: the Italian *Angonese* case, the German *Raccanelli* case and the French *Olympique Lyonnais* case.

Corte di Cassazione (Italian Court of Cassation),
11 October 2004[53]   **3.8 (IT)**

Cassa di Risparmio di Bolzano SpA v Roman Angonese

DIRECT HORIZONTAL EFFECT OF THE NON-DISCRIMINATION RULE OF ARTICLE 45 TFEU

Angonese (national follow-up)

The requirement of a particular language certificate imposed by a private employer upon job applicants is contrary to Article 45 TFEU

Facts: Angonese, an Italian national of German mother tongue from Bolzano, had been studying in Austria between 1993 and 1997. In August 1997, in response to a notice published in the local Italian daily *Dolomiten* on 9 July 1997, he applied to take part in a competition for a post with a private banking undertaking in Bolzano, the Cassa di Risparmio. One of the conditions for entry was possession of a type-B certificate of bilingualism in Italian and German delivered by the public authorities of the province of Bolzano after an

---

[52] In addition, PSA Antwerp NV argued that the employment contract must be respected since the document in question was in accordance with the will of the parties, which was expressed in a language that each party could understand, namely English, it being established that the director of that company who signed it was a Singapore national who was unfamiliar with Dutch.

[53] Cass it Labour Division 11 October 2004 no 20116 *Roman Angonese v Cassa di Risparmio di Bolzona SpA.*

examination held only in that province. Angonese (who was perfectly bilingual) did not own such a certificate. With a view to gaining admission to the competition, he had submitted a certificate showing completion of his studies as a draughtsman and certificates attesting to his studies of languages (English, Slovene and Polish) at the Faculty of Philosophy at Vienna University, and had stated that his professional experience included practising as a draughtsman and translating from Polish into Italian. Nevertheless, the Cassa de Risparmio did not allow him to enter the competition. The District Magistrates' Court Bolzano drew attention to the fact that non-residents of Bolzano may have difficulty obtaining the certificate in good time. The requirement of the certificate imposed by the Cassa de Risparmio was founded on Article 19 of the National Collective Agreement for Savings Banks of 19 December 1994, which provides: 'The institution has the right to decide whether the recruitment of staff referred to in paragraphs 1 and 2, subject in any event to Article 21 below, is to be by way of an internal competition on the basis of either qualifications and/or tests or in accordance with selection criteria specified by the institution. The institution must lay down as and when necessary the conditions and rules for internal competitions, must appoint selection panels and must lay down the selection criteria mentioned in the first paragraph.'

In the legal proceedings that followed, Angonese acknowledged the Cassa di Risparmio's right to select its future staff from persons who are perfectly bilingual, but he complained that the requirement to have and produce the certificate was unlawful and contrary to the principle of the freedom of movement for workers laid down in Article 45 TFEU. Angonese claimed that the requirement be declared void and that the Cassa di Risparmio be ordered to compensate him for his loss of opportunity and to reimburse him the costs he had incurred in the proceedings.

Held: After consulting the CJ, the District Magistrates' Court Bolzano declared the requirement null and void, and condemned the Cassa di Risparmio to compensate Angonese for loss of opportunity (approximately €43,000). The Court of Appeal confirmed this judgment, but lowered the compensation payment. The appeal judgment was upheld by the Italian Court of Cassation.

Judgment: The Court of Appeal interpreted the CJ ruling to mean that in addition to non-citizen workers, the same situation of serious difficulty may also occur, for citizens who, like the defendant, have enrolled as students at a foreign university and exercise the rights conferred by Directive 93/96 on the right of residence for students.

This interpretation is not a forced application of the principles affirmed by the CJ and must be fully shared. The appeal court took the ground that the fact that the defendant was enjoying the rights conferred by Directive 93/96 constitutes a sufficient link to allow him to invoke the advantages offered by the provisions on free movement of workers even if he had not yet acquired a title at the time of the facts, as he was abroad for the purpose of acquiring a professional title which could have been recognized in Italy, too.

The scope of [now Article 45 TFEU] may be lawfully extended to cover situations of students living outside the Member State of which they are citizens, who are looking for a job in the same Member State when they have almost finished their studies abroad. The CJ itself has stated (judgment 7.2.1979 *Knoors*, judgment 31.3.1993, *Kraus*) that there is a sufficient link with EU law when a citizen of a Member State has been regularly resident in another Member State and has acquired a professional qualification recognized by EU law and this citizen is in the same situation in relation to the Member state of citizenship as all those who enjoy the rights and freedoms recognized by the Treaty. Undoubtedly in this case of Angonese, who was finishing his studies and was looking for a job in Italy, the clause requiring the certificate of bilinguism was an objective obstacle to his right of free movement.

…

The CJ … has ruled that the clause of the competition regulation by which the employer required applicants to give evidence of their linguistic knowledge solely through a particular diploma issued only in a province of the Member State by a local public administration is contrary to [now Article 45 TFEU], as it makes it difficult or even impossible to acquire the certification for those applicants who are not resident in this province, the majority of whom having the Italian citizenship, with the further consequence that such a requirement puts nationals of other Member States at a disadvantage by comparison with Italian citizens.

As, for the reasons stated above … the situation of workers who are not citizens must be considered equivalent to the situation of citizens who—like Angonese—are living in another Member State for the purpose of acquiring a professional title which is also recognized in Italy, it must be concluded that the clause under consideration is vitiated by absolute nullity and cannot produce any effect, as it is contrary to an EU rule which cannot be derogated from.

As a consequence, according to the principles of the national legal system, the nullity can be invoked by anyone having an interest, since relative nullity operates only if specifically provided for and since no such provision exists in this case. The Court of Appeal correctly found the clause to be null because it was contrary to a mandatory rule and also recognized that the party concerned had an interest in invoking its nullity.

Notes:

(1) This national decision given after the CJ's *Angonese* judgment had been obtained is interesting for several reasons, one of which is that Article 45 TFEU was applied directly to a legal relationship between two individuals from the same Member State. In addition, it clearly illustrates the private law consequences of the direct horizontal effect of Article 45 TFEU. *Angonese* is also dealt with in Chapter 4, Case 4.14 (IT).

(2) In the proceedings before the CJ, the Cassa di Risparmio argued that the case presented a purely internal situation to which Article 45 TFEU did not apply. The CJ, however, considered it 'far from clear' that the requested interpretation of Article 45 TFEU had no relation to the actual facts of the case or to the subject matter of the main action and left it to the national court to address the matter.[54]

(3) According to the national courts (the District Magistrates' Court Bolzano, the Court of Appeal and the Italian Court of Cassation), there was a sufficient connecting factor with EU law: as Angonese had exercised his right to free movement as a student for the purpose of acquiring an Austrian professional title that could be recognised in Italy, his situation was considered similar to that of nationals of other Member States who could benefit from the rights guaranteed by Article 45 TFEU.[55]

(4) Given the 'European' nature of the case, the national courts applied Article 45 TFEU directly to the (horizontal) legal relationship between Angonese and the Cassa di Risparmio, and ruled, in conformity with the CJ's judgment, that the requirement to produce the particular certificate of bilingualism had the effect of making it difficult, or even impossible, for job applicants who are not resident in the province of Bolzano to acquire the certificate. Consequently, the requirement was considered a discriminatory restriction of the free movement of workers.

---

[54] CJ *Angonese* (n 46) para 19.
[55] For a contrasting view, see AG Fennelly Opinion 25 November 1999 in Case C-281/98 *Angonese v Cassa di Risparmio di Bolzano SpA* [2000] I-04139 ECLI:EU:C:1999:583, paras 14–37.

(5) Because the requirement was held to be contrary to Article 45 TFEU, it was declared null and void on the basis of national law. According to the relevant provisions of the Italian Civil Code, this nullity was found to be absolute (Article 1418) and might be relied upon by anyone having an interest (Article 1421).

(6) The District Magistrates' Court Bolzano also awarded Angonese damages for loss of opportunity. Although the amount was reduced on appeal, the ground for awarding damages (probably the unlawful act resulting from the infringement of Article 45 TFEU) was upheld on appeal and in cassation.

Arbeitsgericht Bonn (Employment Tribunal Bonn),
27 November 2008[56]   **3.9 (GERM)**

Andrea Raccanelli v Max-Planck-Gesellschaft zur Förderung
der Wissenschaften eV

DIRECT HORIZONTAL EFFECT OF THE PROHIBITION OF DISCRIMINATION
ON GROUNDS OF NATIONALITY ENSHRINED IN ARTICLE 45 TFEU

Raccanelli (national follow-up)

A private law organisation is not bound to observe the principle of non-discrimination enshrined in Article 45 TFEU vis-a-vis a PhD student who cannot be classified as a worker

Facts: From 7 February 2000 to 31 July 2003, Andrea Raccanelli—an Italian PhD student—stayed at the Max-Planck-Institut für Radioastronomie in Bonn. During this period, the Max-Planck-Gesellschaft (the MPG—a private law association incorporated under German law) paid him a grant that did not oblige him to undertake any work as an employee of the Max-Planck-Gesellschaft, but merely served as a contribution to the cost of living. Therefore, the grant was exempt from income tax (and consequently also exempt from social security contributions). Unlike German PhD students, Raccanelli was not given the opportunity to opt for an employment contract (a so-called BAT IIa contract, which is a more favourable option financially). Being of the opinion that the MPG thus violated the non-discrimination rule of Article 45 TFEU, he initiated legal proceedings before the Employment Tribunal Bonn to claim damages for loss of income. Because the national court doubted whether a private law organisation like the MPG was bound by Article 45 TFEU, it referred the case to the CJ for a preliminary ruling. In its judgment, the CJ held that a private law organisation, such as the MPG, must observe the principle of non-discrimination enshrined in Article 45 TFEU. However, the CJ left it to the national court to decide whether Raccanelli must be regarded as a worker within the meaning of that Treaty provision and, if the answer to that question was in the affirmative, whether there had been unequal treatment of domestic and foreign doctoral students.

Held: The claimant could not rely on Article 45(2) TFEU because he could not be classified as a worker.

Judgment: 53 1. A worker is defined as a person required to perform work for and under the direction of another party under a private law contract in a relationship based on personal dependency. The employment relationship is a continuing obligation, based on an exchange of work and remuneration. The contractually required work is performed

---

[56] ArbG Bonn 27 November 2008—1 Ca 4192 *Andrea Raccanelli v Max-Planck-Gesellschaft zur Förderung der Wissenschaften eV.*

within a labour structure organised by another party. Inclusion in the other party's labour structure is specifically demonstrated by directions given to the worker (employee) by his contractual partner (employer). These directions may cover the contents, implementation, time, duration and place of the activities. A worker is a person who is not essentially free to structure his activities and determine his hours of work. All circumstances of the individual case have to be taken into account and assessed in their entirety. The nature of the contract is determined by the actual nature of the activities. In the event of a discrepancy between the agreement and its actual implementation, the latter prevails (Federal Labour Court, 25 May 2005, 5 AZR 347/04, Juris).

...

66. It follows from the overall assessment of the circumstances in this case that the relationship existing between the parties did not constitute an employment contract. The applicant has no entitlement, therefore, to the usual remuneration payable in the sum of half of a BAT IIa contract.

67 II. Similarly, no entitlement to claim such amount arises under [now Article 45(2) TFEU] in conjunction with Article 7 of EEC Directive 1612/68. For such entitlement, this Directive, too, would require the applicant to have the status of an employee.

Notes:

(1) Article 45(2) TFEU, which has direct horizontal effect, can only be invoked by Member State nationals who are considered 'workers'. In *Raccanelli*, the CJ confirmed that this concept has a specific EU law meaning and must not be interpreted narrowly: 'Any person who pursues activities which are real and genuine, to the exclusion of activities on such a small scale as to be regarded as purely marginal and ancillary, must be regarded as a "worker". The essential feature of an employment relationship is, according to that case-law, that for a certain period of time a person performs services for and under the direction of another person in return for which he receives remuneration.'[57]

(2) Whereas the CJ left it to the German court to apply this *EU law* definition to the present case, it appears from paragraph 53 of the national judgment that the Employment Tribunal incorrectly chose to use the *national* definition of employee to assess the status of Raccanelli.

(3) The national court concluded that Raccanelli could not be considered as a worker (and could therefore not rely on Article 45(2) TFEU) because, in particular, the acceptance of the grant did not oblige him to perform tasks of an employee for the MPG and because the grant was thus exempted from income tax and social insurance contributions.

(4) Application of the (correct) EU law definition of 'worker' would probably not have resulted in a different outcome, as the facts of the case suggest that there was no relationship of subordination between the parties and that the grant did merely serve as a contribution to the cost of living (and not as a remuneration for work performed).

---

[57] CJ *Raccanelli* (n 46) para 33.

Cour de cassation (Ch Soc) (Court of Cassation,
Social Chamber), 6 October 2010[58] **3.10 (FR)**

Olympique Lyonnais SASP v Olivier Bernard, Newcastle UFC

DIRECT HORIZONTAL EFFECT OF ARTICLE 45 TFEU

Olympique Lyonnais (national follow-up)

Article 45 TFEU precludes a non-discriminatory provision in the Charter of a national football association, according to which a youth player has to sign his first contract as a professional football player with the club that trained him

Facts: Olivier Bernard, a young football player, signed a 'joueur espoir' contract with the French football club Olympique Lyonnais for three years. Before that contract was due to expire, Olympique Lyonnais offered him a professional contract. Bernard declined, but accepted another offer to play professionally for the English club Newcastle United. At the time, the rules governing professional football in France—more specifically, Article 23 of the Football Charter—rendered him liable in damages to the French club. Olympique Lyonnais sued both Bernard and Newcastle United before the Conseil de prud'hommes (Employment Tribunal) in Lyon, seeking an award of damages. The amount claimed was around € 53,000—equivalent to the remuneration which Bernard would have received over one year if he had signed the contract offered by Olympique Lyonnais. The Conseil de prud'hommes considered that Bernard had terminated his contract unilaterally, and ordered him and Newcastle United jointly to pay Olympique Lyonnais damages of approximately €23,000. The defendants appealed to the Court of Appeal of Lyon, which quashed the first judgment. Olympique Lyonnais then appealed to the French Court of Cassation. The Court of Cassation decided to stay the proceedings and to ask the CJ whether Article 23 of the Football Charter constituted an unjustified restriction on the free movement of workers. After the CJ's affirmative answer, the Court of Cassation substantively assessed the claim for damages.

Held: Olympique Lyonnais' claim for damages was rejected.

Judgment: Considering that by judgment of 16 March 2010 (C-325/08), the CJ decided several questions referred by the Cour de cassation for a preliminary ruling; that it stated that Article 45 TFEU does not preclude a scheme which, in order to attain the objective of encouraging the recruitment and training of young players, guarantees compensation to the club which provided the training if, at the end of his training period, a young player signs a professional contract with a club in another Member State, provided that the scheme is suitable to ensure the attainment of that objective and does not go beyond what is necessary to attain it; that a scheme such as the one at issue in the main proceedings, under which a 'joueur espoir' who signs a professional contract with a club in another Member State at the end of his training period is liable to pay damages calculated in a way which is unrelated to the actual costs of the training, is not necessary to ensure the attainment of that objective;

Considering that the scheme resulting from Article 23 of the Football Charter is characterised by the payment to the club which provided the training, not of compensation for training, but of damages, to which the player concerned would be liable for breach of his contractual obligations and the amount of which is unrelated to the real training costs incurred by the club;

---

[58] French Court of Cassation Chamber Social 6 October 2010 no 07-42023 *Olympique Lyonnais SASP v Olivier Bernard, Newcastle UFC.*

Considering that such a rule, according to which a 'joueur espoir', at the end of his training period, is required, under pain of being sued for damages, to sign a professional contract with the club which trained him, is likely to discourage that player from exercising his right of free movement and constitutes a restriction on freedom of movement for workers guaranteed within the European Union by Article 45 TFEU.

Notes:

(1) With explicit reference to the CJ's preliminary ruling,[59] the French Court of Cassation rejected the claim for damages that Olympique Lyonnais had brought against Oliver Bernard and Newcastle United.

(2) After establishing that Article 45 TFEU applied to the French Football Charter (a collective agreement), the CJ held that a rule 'according to which a 'joueur espoir', at the end of his training period, is required, under pain of being sued for damages, to sign a professional contract with the club which trained him [is] likely to discourage that player from exercising his right of free movement'.[60] Consequently, it established that Article 23 of the Football Charter constituted a restriction on the free movement of workers.

(3) The CJ then ruled that 'a scheme providing for the payment of compensation for training where a young player, at the end of his training, signs a professional contract with a club other than the one which trained him can, in principle, be justified by the objective of encouraging the recruitment and training of young players. However, such a scheme must be actually capable of attaining that objective and be proportionate to it, taking due account of the costs borne by the clubs in training both future professional players and those who will never play professionally'.[61] In the present case, the CJ concluded that Article 23 of the Football Charter did not satisfy this test, because a breach of this provision would result in an obligation to pay damages, the amount of which was unrelated to the real training costs incurred by the club.[62]

(4) After having recapitulated the above parts of the CJ judgment, the French Court of Cassation concluded (on the basis of national law) that Article 23 of the Football Charter was null and void. Accordingly, it rejected the claim for damages that was based on the breach of this (invalid) provision.

III.B.ii INDIRECT HORIZONTAL EFFECT

As was illustrated in section III.A.ii by reference to *Las v PSA Antwerp NV*, Article 45 TFEU can be invoked in legal proceedings between individuals to argue that a national rule of law is contrary to the free movement of workers and can on this ground be disapplied. However, since Article 45 TFEU only applies to cases with a cross-border element, this opportunity will in principle not arise when a situation is purely internal to a Member State. As the following two national cases demonstrate, this may lead to the result that a

---

[59] CJ *Olympique Lyonnais* (n 49).
[60] ibid, para 35.
[61] ibid, para 45.
[62] ibid, para 46.

national case is decided in a way that is less favourable to an individual than if his case would have been covered by EU law. As set out in section IV.D in Chapter 1, such reverse discrimination by a Member State of its own citizens can only be countered by the law of that Member State declaring in a general fashion that the resulting discrimination against its own citizens is forbidden by national law.

Arbeidshof Antwerpen (Labour Court Antwerp),
17 December 2013[63]   **3.11 (BE)**

X (Employee) v Y (Employer)

PURELY INTERNAL SITUATION: NO INDIRECT HORIZONTAL
EFFECT OF ARTICLE 45 TFEU

No bonus

Article 45 TFEU does not apply to purely internal situations. Consequently, it cannot be invoked by an individual in legal proceedings against another individual to contest the legality of a national rule of law

Facts: Employee X claimed a bonus fee from employer Y for the year in which he had been fired. Although Y admitted to the existence of a company bonus scheme, it pointed to an English-drafted policy clause according to which the right to a bonus is not available for employees who have been fired. X initiated legal proceedings against Y, claiming that this clause was contrary to Article 5 of the Flemish Language Decree, which requires employers that have their place of business in the Flemish part of Belgium to use the Dutch language in relations with its employees. The fact is that Article 10 of the Decree states that: 'Documents or acts that are contrary to the provisions of this Decree shall be null and void.'

Held: Because Y's policy clause was drafted in English, it infringed Article 5 of the Flemish Language Decree and was therefore declared null and void.

Judgment: For the sake of completeness, the Labour Court Antwerp remarked that a recent ruling of the CJ (CJ 16 April 2013, Las/PSA Antwerpen NV, Case C-202/11) does not alter this conclusion.

In said judgment, the CJ concluded that Article 45 TFEU must be interpreted as precluding legislation of a federated entity of a Member State, such as that at issue in the main proceedings, which requires all employers whose established place of business is located in that entity's territory to draft cross-border employment contracts exclusively in the official language of that federated entity, failing which the contracts are to be declared null and void by the national courts of their own motion.

According to its own wording, this CJ judgment only concerns labour agreements (and related social relations) having a cross-border nature, which is the case when one of the parties originates from another Member State and does not speak the official language of the relevant region.

---

[63] Labour Court Antwerp 17 December 2013 *Limburgs Rechtsleven* 2014 vol 2 143 *X (Employee) v Y (Employer)*.

Nothing indicates that this condition formulated by the CJ is fulfilled in the present case: there are no elements or indications on which the existence of such a cross-border labour agreement can be based.

As a result, the CJ's judgment cannot be applied by analogy.

Note:

Unlike *Las v PSA Antwerp NV* (see section III.A.ii above), the national court found no cross-border elements. Consequently, it ruled that Article 45 TFEU was not applicable, so that the Belgian employee (X) could successfully claim that the English-drafted clause in the bonus scheme was null and void because it infringed the Flemish Language Decree.

Legfelsőbb Bíróság (Hungarian Supreme Court),
21 December 2009[64]   **3.12 (HU)**

Dunaferr SE v A Limited Company

IRRELEVANCE OF THE *BOSMAN* DECISION FOR PURELY NATIONAL CASES

Transfer of ice-hockey players

The Bosman decision is only relevant for transfers having a cross-border nature, so the practice of national clubs of asking fees for the training of players is legal

Facts: This case concerned a dispute between an ice-hockey club and a company that held certain players' licences. In October 2002, the parties agreed that three players would continue their career in the applicant club (Dunaferr SE). After some discussion, the parties further agreed that the applicant would also pay half of the so-called 'solidarity fee' to the respondent by way of compensation for the costs of training of these ice-hockey players. However, the applicant contested the legality of this amount, since, according to the applicant, it was clearly contrary to the relevant provisions of the 'Sport Act' regulating the conditions of licence transfers in general.

Held: The court of first instance (the local court) decided in favour of the applicant and it required the respondent to pay back the solidarity fee, based on the rules on unjust enrichment. However, the appeal court reversed the decision, finding that the legal reasoning of the local court was incorrect because the 'Sport Act' did not explicitly prohibit these fees. Furthermore, the appeal court pointed out that the licence contract was not contrary to any other legal provisions and that it was in conformity with the rules of the Hungarian Ice Hockey Federation. The Hungarian Supreme Court upheld the decision of the appeal court.

Judgment: According to the Hungarian Supreme Court, the contested decision stated correctly that the licence contract between the parties breached neither the provisions of the Sport Act that were in effect when the contract was concluded, nor any other legal provision. As members of the Hungarian Ice Hockey Federation they had accepted the rules of the Federation, therefore their contract, being in conformity with these rules, is valid.

Even though Hungary was not a Member State of the EU at the moment when the contract was made, the Hungarian Supreme Court has examined—at the request of the

---

[64] Hungarian Supreme Court 21 December 2009 Pfv X.21.266/2009/5 *Dunaferr SE v A Limited Company.*

parties—how the CJ decided an earlier case. In *Bosman*, the CJ discussed intra-Union transfers and club-changes. According to a correct interpretation of this decision it can be said that this decision of the CJ does not affect fees relating to training, transfer etc. which only exist in a given Member State. The CJ did not touch upon the various solutions of the Member States when declaring that the free movement of players was in accordance with [now Article 45 TFEU], but only prohibited claiming training or other fees if a player moved from a given Member State to another one.

Notes:

(1) In *Bosman*,[65] the CJ applied Article 45 TFEU to the transfer rules of a private law organisation (*direct* horizontal effect).

(2) The application of Article 45 TFEU to transfer rules that are regulated by law *cannot* be qualified as direct horizontal effect. However, if such transfer rules are reviewed for compatibility with the free movement of workers in legal proceedings between individuals, Article 45 TFEU may produce an *indirect* horizontal effect.

(3) In the present case, the Hungarian Supreme Court jumped to the conclusion that Article 45 TFEU did not apply to domestic transfer rules. However, while the CJ did indeed rule that the fundamental freedoms are not applicable to internal situations in one Member State, sometimes a potential link to EU law may be sufficient to trigger their application.[66] As the Hungarian Supreme Court's reasoning is rather brief, it is unclear whether it searched for such a (potential) connection with EU law.

IV. FREEDOM OF ESTABLISHMENT AND FREEDOM TO PROVIDE AND RECEIVE SERVICES (ARTICLES 49 AND 56 TFEU)

IV.A SOURCES: THE TFEU, CJ CASE LAW, MATERIALS

Article 49 TFEU   **3.13 (EU)**

Within the framework of the provisions set out below, restrictions on the freedom of establishment of nationals of a Member State in the territory of another Member State shall be prohibited. Such prohibition shall also apply to restrictions on the setting-up of agencies, branches or subsidiaries by nationals of any Member State established in the territory of any Member State.

Freedom of establishment shall include the right to take up and pursue activities as self-employed persons and to set up and manage undertakings, in particular companies or firms within the meaning of the second paragraph of Article 54, under the conditions laid down for its own nationals by the law of the country where such establishment is effected, subject to the provisions of the Chapter relating to capital.

---

[65] CJ *Bosman* (n 44).
[66] For art 45 TFEU, see CJ *Angonese* (n 46).

Article 56 TFEU   **3.14 (EU)**

Within the framework of the provisions set out below, restrictions on freedom to provide services within the Union shall be prohibited in respect of nationals of Member States who are established in a Member State other than that of the person for whom the services are intended.

Like Article 45 TFEU, the Treaty provisions on the freedom of establishment and the freedom to provide and receive services initially applied to *(in)directly discriminatory* measures only.[67]

As from the 1990s, though, the CJ recognised that Articles 49 and 56 TFEU also apply to *non-discriminatory* obstacles to the freedom of establishment and the freedom to provide and receive services.[68]

IV.A.i DIRECT HORIZONTAL EFFECT

P Craig and G de Búrca, EU Law: Text, Cases and Materials[69]

We saw … how the ECJ ruled that … the provisions of Article 45 are binding on the state but also on private bodies. In the field of services, the ECJ ruled in the early case of *Walrave and Koch* that the Treaty rules applied not only 'to the action of public authorities but extends likewise to rules of any other nature aimed at regulating in a collective manner gainful employment and the provision of services'. It remained unclear however, even after the case of *Angonese* in the field of free movement of workers which explicitly deemed Article 45 TFEU to be applicable to private persons, whether the Treaty provisions on establishment and services were equally fully horizontally applicable, in the sense of imposing legal obligations on all individuals and not just on powerful, self-regulating collective actors such as sporting organizations, which possess powers akin to public law.

Originally, it was thought that the Treaty provisions on the freedom of establishment and the freedom to provide and receive services only applied to measures of the Member States (direct vertical effect). Since the mid-1970s, we know that this assumption is not correct: Articles 49 and 56 TFEU also apply to discriminatory[70] and non-discriminatory[71] *collective* acts of individuals, and are thus capable of creating,

---

[67] See, eg, CJ 21 June 1974 Case C-2/74 *Jean Reyners v Belgian State* [1974] I-00631 ECLI:EU:C:1974:68 (art 49 TFEU); CJ 3 December 1974 Case C-33/74 *Johannes Henricus Maria van Binsbergen v Bestuur van de Bedrijfsvereniging voor de Metaalnijverheid* [1974] I-01299 ECLI:EU:C:1974:131 (art 56 TFEU). A definition of the concepts of direct and indirect discrimination can be found in Lenaerts and Van Nuffel 2011 172 (cited in section III.A above).

[68] A brief description of this development (with references to relevant case law) can be found in Barnard 2016 (n 36) 271-74, 395-99 (art 49 TFEU) and 303–309 (art 56 TFEU).

[69] Craig and De Búrca 2015 797-98.

[70] See CJ *Walrave and Koch* (n 45) (art 56 TFEU); CJ *Donà* (n 45) (art 56 TFEU); CJ 9 June 1977 Case C-90/76 *Srl Ufficio Henry van Ameyde v Srl Ufficio centrale italiano di assistenza assicurativa automobilisti in circolazione internazionale (UCI)* [1977] I-01091 ECLI:EU:C1977:101 (art 49 TFEU); CJ 13 December 1984 Case C-251/83 *Eberhard Haug-Adrion v Frankfurter Versicherungs-AG* [1984] I-04277 ECLI:EU:C:1984:397 (art 56 TFEU). See on the conjunction between the provisions on the fundamental freedoms and the caselaw of the CJ on art 18 TFEU: section III.A.i and section V.C Ch 4

[71] See CJ 11 April 2000 Joined Cases C-51/96 and C-191/97 *Christelle Deliège tegen Ligue francophone de judo et disciplines associées ASBL, Ligue belge de judo ASBL, Union européenne de judo and François Pacquée* [2000] I-02549 ECLI:EU:C:2000:199 (art 6 TFEU); CJ 19 February 2002 Case C-309/99 *JCJ Wouters, JW Savelbergh and Price Waterhouse Belastingadviseurs BV v Algemene Raad van de Nederlandse Orde*

modifying and extinguishing rights and obligations between individuals (direct horizontal effect). The CJ has yet to decide whether the Treaty provisions on freedom of establishment and freedom to provide and receive services can be invoked to challenge *non-collective* acts of individuals as well.

The arguments on which the CJ has based the direct horizontal effect of Articles 49 and 56 TFEU are identical to those underpinning the direct horizontal effect of Article 45 TFEU. First, the Treaty provisions on freedom of establishment and freedom to provide and receive services would lose their useful effect if they were merely binding upon the Member States, because restrictions of these freedoms can also come about from acts of individuals. Second, limiting the scope of Articles 49 and 56 TFEU to acts of the Member States would entail the risk of dissimilar application of these provisions throughout the EU, as certain subject matter may be governed by provisions laid down by law or regulation in one Member State, and by agreements and other acts concluded or adopted by private persons in the other. Therefore—and also because both Articles are mandatory in nature—it is not the public or private origin of an act that is decisive for the CJ, but rather its effect on the functioning of the internal market.

IV.A.ii INDIRECT HORIZONTAL EFFECT

In addition to *direct* horizontal effect, the Treaty provisions on the freedom of establishment and the freedom to provide and receive services can have several *indirect* horizontal effects. Three mechanisms have been distinguished (see section II.A.ii above) in this respect: the interpretation of a rule of national (private) law in the light of a provision of EU law; the positive obligation for the Member States; and the review of compatibility with EU law of a rule of national (private) law in proceedings between individuals. Although Articles 49 and 56 TFEU are capable of producing indirect effect via each of these three mechanisms, CJ case law only provides some examples of these provisions being invoked in horizontal proceedings to contest the legality of a national rule of law, one of them being the *Parodi* case.[72]

Back in 1984, de Bary—a bank incorporated and established in the Netherlands—granted a mortgage loan in the amount of DM 930,000 to Parodi, a French real estate company. Six years later, in 1990, Parodi brought an action against de Bary seeking that the loan be declared null and void on the grounds that the bank had not, when it granted the loan, been authorised as required by French law (No 84–46 of 24 January 1984 on the activity and supervision of credit institutions). In addition, Parodi sought reimbursement of approximately FF 1,250,000, representing the amount of the charges and interest it had paid to de Bary. In first instance and on appeal, Parodi's claim was dismissed, inter alia on the grounds that the French law was contrary to Articles 49 and

---

van Advocaten [2002] I-01577 ECLI:EU:C2002:98 (arts 49 and 56 TFEU); CJ 11 December 2007 Case C-438/05 *ITWF v Viking* [2007] I-10779 ECLI:EU:C:2007:772 (art 49 TFEU); and CJ 18 December 2007 Case C-341/05 *Laval v Unions* [2007] I-11767 ECLI:EU:C:2007:809 (art 56 TFEU).

[72] CJ 9 July 1997 Case C-222/95 *Société civile immobilière Parodi v Banque H. Albert de Bary et Cie* [1997] I-03899 ECLI:EU:C:1997:345.

56 TFEU. Answering a preliminary question of the French Court of Cassation, the CJ indeed held that:

> With regard to the period preceding the entry into force of Second Council Directive 89/646/ EEC of 15 December 1989[73] ... [now Article 56 TFEU] must be construed as precluding a Member State from requiring a credit institution already authorized in another Member State to obtain an authorization in order to be able to grant a mortgage loan to a person resident within its territory, unless that authorization (1) is required of every person or company pursuing such an activity within the territory of the Member State of destination, (2) is justified on grounds of public interest, such as consumer protection, and (3) is objectively necessary to ensure compliance with the rules applicable in the sector under consideration and to protect the interests which those rules are intended to safeguard, and the same result cannot be achieved by less restrictive rules.[74]

See section IV.B.ii below for a French case in which the CJ's judgment in *Parodi* was applied.

IV.B NATIONAL CASE LAW

IV.B.i DIRECT HORIZONTAL EFFECT

This section discusses the national cases in which the Treaty provisions on the freedom of establishment and/or the freedom to provide and receive services were or should have been applied directly to a legal relationship between individuals. Starting with the exemplary Swedish follow-up on the important judgment of the CJ in *Laval*, it will be demonstrated that some national courts are reluctant to apply Articles 49 and/or 56 TFEU directly to a horizontal relationship.

Arbetsdomstolen (Swedish Labour Court),
2 December 2009[75]   **3.15 (SE)**

Laval un Partneri Ltd v Svenska Byggnadsarbetareförbundet, Svenska Byggnadsarbetareförbundets avdelning 1, Byggettan, Svenska Elektrikerförbundet

DIRECT HORIZONTAL EFFECT OF ARTICLE 56 TFEU

Laval (national follow-up)

A trade union can be liable in damages vis-a-vis another individual for breach of Article 56 TFEU

Facts: The case essentially concerned collective actions taken by the main Swedish trade union in the building sector (Byggnads) against a Latvian company based in Riga (Laval) that had posted workers in Sweden

---

[73] Second Council Directive 89/646/EEC of 15 December 1989 on the coordination of laws, regulations and administrative provisions relating to the taking up and pursuit of the business of credit institutions and amending Directive 77/780/EEC [1989] OJ L386/1.

[74] CJ *Parodi* (n 72) para 32.

[75] Swedish Labour Court 2 December 2009 judgment no 89/09 case no A 268/04 *Laval un Partneri Ltd v Unions*.

to work on building sites but had refused to enter into a collective agreement with Byggnads. The action, which included sympathy actions by other trade unions, took the form of a blockade of a building site in the municipality of Vaxholm where Laval's Latvian workers were engaged in rebuilding a school. Because of the action, Laval was ultimately forced to stop working on the site. Somewhat later, Vaxholm requested termination of the contract.

Laval brought proceedings before the Swedish Labour Court against Byggnads et al, seeking a declaration that the blockading and the sympathy actions were illegal and an order that such action should cease. It also sought an order that the unions pay compensation for the damage suffered. After consulting the CJ—which held that the collective actions of the trade unions amounted to an unjustified restriction on the freedom to provide services—the Swedish Labour Court decided on Laval's claims.

Held: The Swedish Labour Court rejected Laval's claim for economic damages (because of lack of proof), but granted the claim for exemplary damages on the ground that Byggnads' actions violated Article 56 TFEU.

Judgment: In its request for a preliminary ruling the Swedish Labour Court did not submit any questions to the [CJ] concerning the potential liability for damage of the Labour Unions. The issue is therefore whether the general principles for damage liability which the [CJEU] has developed in its case law can give sufficient guidance. In the opinion of the Labour Court and in accordance with the points upon which the parties appear to be in agreement, the first requirement for damage liability to exist is that the [EU] legal provisions breached by the Labour Unions have horizontal direct effect in the relationship between the Company and the Labour Unions. The Swedish Labour Court will therefore examine this question first.

In its preliminary ruling the [CJ] established that [now Article 56 TFEU] is directly applicable to the situation under consideration, and that it confers rights on the Company which it can invoke before the courts and which the national courts are to protect, in other words, this provision has direct effect in this case. In addition, the [CJ] held that compliance with [now Article 56 TFEU] is also required in the case of rules which are not public in nature but which are designed to regulate, collectively, the provision of services, since associations and organizations not regulated by public law—such as the Labour Unions—could also, by exercising their legal autonomy, raise obstacles to the free movement of services.

…

As demonstrated above, the [CJ] includes non-public associations such as the Labour Unions, attorney bar associations and sport associations, in the ambit of [now Article 56 TFEU], which is natural against the background of the fact that these types of associations serve important societal interests, have authority and influence and also play an active role in setting standards. With regard to violations of [EU] law regulations that apply to both the state and individuals, it can therefore be seen as odd to make a distinction between damage claims using the criterion whether the violator is a state body or happens to be independent of the state.

The Swedish labour unions enjoy a large degree of self-regulation and considerable authority when it comes to taking collective action to compel employers to sign collective agreements. They can be seen as having exercised what the [CJ] termed 'their legal autonomy', contrary to [now Article 56 TFEU], when they took the industrial actions and sympathy actions at issue to force the signing of a collective agreement. Against this background it therefore appears to be possible to find that the Labour Unions are liable for damage, assuming that the remaining criteria for such liability are fulfilled.

As mentioned above, it is settled case law that state liability for damage can arise under [EU] law provided that that three conditions are fulfilled, namely that the rule that was violated is intended to create rights for individuals, that the violation is sufficiently clear, and that there is a causal connection between the violation and the harm. If these criteria are applied to the situation under consideration, the Labour Court holds, having regard to the above grounds, that the first condition can be found to be fulfilled, and that it may be deemed evident that the required causal connection exists. What remains to be examined is the condition that the violation is sufficiently clear. In its judgments in *Brasserie du pêcheur* and *Factortame* the [CJ] stated with respect to Member States liability for acts that are in violation of [EU] law, that a violation of [EU] law is sufficiently clear when a Member State has obviously and seriously misjudged the bounds of its margin of appreciation. Further circumstances to be taken into consideration include the intentional or unintentional nature of the Treaty violation or the harm caused, the excusable or inexcusable nature of a potential error of law, or the fact that a stance taken by a[n EU] institution could have contributed to the individual's acting in violation of [EU] law'.

Without expressing an opinion the question whether it is possible to give full application to the above in the present situation, the Labour Court finds that according to the preliminary ruling of the [CJ] the actions of the Labour Unions at issue, i.e. the industrial actions, constitute a serious violation of the Treaty, as they were contrary to a fundamental principle of the Treaty, namely the freedom to provide services. Even though the right to take industrial action has been recognized by the European [Union] as a fundamental right, too, the concrete industrial actions were ruled to be unacceptable because they were not proportionate, despite their objective of protecting workers. The Labour Court finds that the position taken by the [CJ] on these issues means in the present case that there has been a sufficiently clear violation of [EU] law. Consequently, the conditions for finding liability for damage are fulfilled. Whether the [CJ] may consider the possibility of finding the Swedish State liable for damage is a question that ought not affect the Labour Court's judgment. It can, however, be added here that the [CJ] has stated that [EU] law does not preclude a legal subject other than a Member State from incurring liability for damage in addition to the Member State's own liability for damage caused by an individual through measures taken by this legal subject that were contrary to [EU] law ...

In summary and against the background of the above grounds, the Labour Court rules that the full effectiveness of [EU] law would be impaired if the Labour Unions could not be ordered to pay compensation to the Company for the harm the Company can prove it has suffered as a result of the fact that the Labour Unions took the concrete industrial actions contrary to with [EU] law.[76]

Notes:

(1) Two years after the (much-discussed) preliminary rulings of the CJ in *Viking*[77] and *Laval*,[78] the Swedish Labour Court delivered its judgment in the latter case.[79] As the CJ had established that the collective actions of Byggnads et al were contrary to Article 56 TFEU, it primarily focused on the follow-up question: can the trade unions be held liable in damages for the breach of Article 56 TFEU? The Labour Court started by mentioning, in particular, the principles of sincere cooperation (Article 4(3) TEU), the

---

[76] Excerpt based on an unofficial translation (by L Carlson) that was published in M Rönnmar (ed), *Labour Law, Fundamental Rights and Social Europe* (Oxford, Hart Publishing, 2011) 227–76.

[77] CJ *Viking* (n 71).

[78] CJ *Laval* (n 71).

[79] The *Viking* case, which concerned collective actions of trade unions that restricted the freedom of establishment, was settled outside the (national) court.

Francovich principle of state liability and the principle of effectiveness. It then went on to establish 'that liability for damages on an [EU] law basis has been extended in the case law of the European Court of Justice to exist in situations in which an individual claims rights under [EU] law as against another individual'. With reference to CJ judgments like *Courage v Crehan*, *Manfredi* and *Raccanelli*, the Labour Court reached the conclusion that 'in order for damage liability for violations of [EU] law to exist between individuals, the [EU] legal regulations that are violated must have direct [horizontal] effect at the national level'.[80]

(2) In its preliminary reference, the Labour Court had not asked questions about the conditions governing the trade unions' liability for breach of Article 56 TFEU. From the CJ's case law on state liability, it nevertheless inferred that an individual's liability for breach of EU law arises if: (1) a rule of EU law has been breached; (2) the breached rule is intended to create rights for an individual; and (3) there is a direct causal link between the damage suffered and the breach. It is unlikely that the breach of EU law is required to be 'sufficiently and serious' for the individual liability to exist; this assumption is based on the automatic application of the conditions for EU and Member State liability to individual liability without giving attention to the need to adjust the conditions to the capacity of the party that breaches EU law.[81]

High Court of Justice (Queen's Bench Division
Commercial Court), 20 June 2013[82]   **3.16 (UK)**

British Airways plc and International Consolidated Airlines Group SA v Sindicato
Espanol de Pilotos de Lineas Aereas (SEPLA) and the International Federation of
Airline Pilots Association (IFALPA)

DIRECT HORIZONTAL EFFECT OF ARTICLE 49 AND 56 TFEU REJECTED

Air pilot strike

Articles 49 and 56 TFEU cannot be invoked against a trade union, since these Treaty prohibitions only impose obligations on the Member States

Facts: British Airways proposed launching a new low-cost airline in Spain. SEPLA, which represented Spanish airline pilots, was hostile to the proposal and took strike action. The second defendant (IFALPA), a federation of airline pilots of which SEPLA was a member, asked its members to take supporting action. British Airways brought English proceedings for damages and declaratory and injunctive relief alleging that the strikes of Spanish airline pilots organised by SEPLA were unlawful under Spanish law, in that they were in breach of its right to freedom of establishment, and to provide cross-border services under Articles 49 and 56 TFEU. British Airways contended that the English court had jurisdiction over its claims against SEPLA under Article 6 of Regulation 44/2001 on the basis that IFALPA was domiciled in England at the time that the claim

---

[80] See U Bernitz and N Reich, 'Case No. A 268/04, The Labour Court, Sweden (Arbetsdomstolen) Judgment No. 89/09 of 2 December 2009, *Laval un Partneri Ltd. v. Svenska Byggnadsarbetareforbundet et al.*' (2011) 48(2) *CMLR* 608–10.

[81] CH Sieburgh, 'EU Law and Non-contractual Liability of the Union, Member States and Individuals' in Hartkamp/Sieburgh/Keus/Kortmann/Wissink (eds) 2014 529.

[82] *British Airways plc and International Consolidated Airlines Group SA v Sindicato Espanol de Pilotos de Lineas Aereas and The International Federation of Airline Pilots Association* [2013] EWHC 1657 (Comm).

form was issued, and the claims against SEPLA and IFALPA were so closely connected that it was expedient to hear and determine them together to avoid the risk of irreconcilable judgments resulting from separate proceedings. British Airways also contended that the court had jurisdiction under Article 5(3) of the Regulation on the ground that harm caused by the strikes was suffered by British Airways within the jurisdiction. SEPLA submitted that the claims against it based on Articles 49 and 56 were public law claims and not 'civil and commercial matters' within the meaning of Article 1 of the Regulation.

Held: The claim by British Airways was not considered a 'civil and commercial matter' for the purposes of Article 1 of Regulation 44/2001, with the result that the English court did not have jurisdiction under the Regulation to determine the claim.

Judgment: [35] In my judgment, [the] contention that the Claimants' claims are not 'civil and commercial' matters is well founded. The prohibitions on restrictions on the freedoms of establishment and the provision of services within the EU expressed in Articles 49 and 56 TFEU import treaty obligations laid upon the Member States, with the result in my view that the enforcement of those obligations is not a civil or commercial matter but one involving the application of public law. True it is that trade unions have been held to be subject to the obligation to maintain the fundamental freedoms enshrined in the [EU] predecessors to Articles 49 and 56, but this in my opinion is because for this purpose they are to be deemed to be emanations of the state.

[36] I would observe that it remains the case that the source of the fundamental freedoms are treaty provisions imposing obligations on states. Moreover, it is extremely difficult to conceive of circumstances where a private individual's acts could constitute a breach of the rights of establishment and free movement of goods and I accept Mr Flynn's submission that SEPLA's obligations to respect the Article 49 and Article 56 freedoms are exorbitant to those obligations to which it is subject as a matter of ordinary private law.

Notes:

(1) The claimant in this case followed the same strategy as the Finnish ferry operator in the national *Viking* case.[83] In order to justify the jurisdiction of the English court, British Airways (Viking) alleged that IFALPA (ITWF), which was domiciled in England at the time the claim was issued, had passed on a letter from SEPLA (FSU) asking for support in their industrial actions. Nevertheless, whereas jurisdiction was granted in *Viking*, the English court in the present case held that the claim (which was exclusively based on the breach of the right to the freedom of establishment and to provide cross-border services under Articles 49 and 56 TFEU) was not a 'civil and commercial matter' within the meaning of Article 6 of Regulation 44/2001.[84] It consequently did not fall within the scope of application of the Regulation, allowing the judge to refuse jurisdiction on grounds of *forum non conveniens*. To justify this exclusion, the judge first referred to the CJ's judgment in *Viking* and observed, in particular, that 'the source of the fundamental freedoms are Treaty provisions imposing obligations on States'. He considered that the basis on which trade unions were held liable in *Viking* relied on the fact that trade unions are for the purposes of 'the EC predecessors to Articles 49 and 56 ... deemed to be

---

[83] See J Prassl, 'Three Dimensions of Heterogeneity: An Overview of Member State Experiences' in M Freedland and J Prassl (eds), *EU Law in the Member States: Viking, Laval and Beyond* (Londen, Bloomburry Publishing, 2014) 273–75.

[84] Council Regulation (EC) No 44/2001 of 22 December 2000 on jurisdiction and the recognition and enforcement of judgments in civil and commercial matters [2000] OJ L012/1.

emanations of the State'. Second, the judge noted that 'a court having to decide whether SEPLA was in breach of Articles 49 and 56 TFEU will have to conduct a sensitive balancing exercise in which it weighs SEPLA's constitutional right to strike and the fundamental right to strike which forms part of the general principles of [EU] Law against the fundamental freedoms enshrined in Articles 49 and 56'. The judge considered that the resolution of this conflict of fundamental rights 'involve[s] a resort to notions of public law rather than to private law'.

(2) This exclusion of the litigation from the material scope of Regulation 44/2001 is surprising, as it is established case law of the CJ that Articles 49 and 56 TFEU have direct horizontal effect and are thus binding upon individuals as well. In *Viking*, the CJ even observed that trade unions are organisations that are *not* public law entities, but exercise the legal autonomy conferred on them by national law.[85] The English court's assertion that the trade unions in *Viking* and *Laval* were bound by Articles 49 and 56 TFEU because they were 'deemed to be emanations of the State' is therefore incorrect.

Gerechtshof 's-Gravenhage (Court of Appeal of The Hague),
11 January 2011[86]   **3.17 (NL)**

Stichting Euro-Sportring (ERS) v Stichting Garantiefonds Reisgelden (SGR)

DIRECT HORIZONTAL EFFECT OF ARTICLE 56 TFEU REJECTED

Guarantee fund

Entrepreneurial behaviour of a private law organisation should be assessed on the basis of the rules laid down in the Articles 101 and 102 TFEU, and not on the basis of Article 56 TFEU

Facts: ERS was a private law corporation (non-profit foundation) that organised sports tournaments (including travel and accommodation) for amateur athletes in, inter alia, EU Member States. SGR was a private law corporation (which did not perform a statutory task and had no regulatory powers) whose main goal was to make payments to or for consumers with regard to travel contracts offered and concluded on the Dutch market, in the event that they suffered damage as a result of the travel agent's financial inability to perform under the contract. The dispute between ERS and SGR was about the question whether SGR was required to insure travel and accommodation offered by ERS to the extent ERS offered it to teams and tournament participants from Member States other than the Netherlands. SGR took the view that its scope was limited to trips offered and concluded on the Dutch market and that the foreign activities of ERS were not covered. ERS believed that SGR was also obliged to provide cover for its overseas operations. Not covering these activities would, in the opinion of ERS, constitute a breach of Article 56 TFEU.

Held: Article 56 TFEU did not apply to the entrepreneurial activities of a private law association such as ESR.

Judgment: 5.2 The court ruled as follows. Article 56 TFEU is in principle applicable only to public bodies. It is only in a few cases that the CJ has made an exception to this rule with regard to collective actions having an effect that is comparable to government regulation and not typical market behaviour. The court observes that these situations are

---

[85] CJ *Viking* (n 71) para 60.
[86] Court of Appeal of The Hague 11 January 2011 *LJN* BP6112 ECLI:NL:GHSGR:2011:BP6112 *Stichting Euro-Sporting v Stichting Garantiefonds Reisgelden.*

not comparable to the present case, where it is typical entrepeneurial behaviour of SGR (which is a private legal person without any task or regulatory authority having its basis in the law) to determine on which market(s) it wants to offer its product. Such entrepreneurial behaviour should be assessed on the basis of the rules laid down in the Articles 101 and 102 TFEU and not on the basis of the free movement rules.

Notes:

(1) As set out under section IV.A above, the Treaty provisions on the free movement of workers, the freedom of establishment and the freedom to provide and receive services not only apply to acts of public authorities, but also to collective acts of individuals. As a result, the distinction between the addressees of, on the one hand, Articles 45, 49 and 56 TFEU and, on the other hand, Articles 101 and 102 TFEU has blurred to some extent.

(2) The CJ has accepted that the aforementioned free movement provisions and the competition rules can both apply to the same horizontal situation,[87] but at the same time it curiously refused to accept such a concurrence between the Treaty provisions on the free movement of goods (Articles 34 and 35 TFEU) and the Treaty rules on competition (Articles 101 and 102 TFEU).[88] The judgment in *Fra.bo*, however, might indicate that this unconvincing distinction will eventually disappear.[89]

(3) The CJ has not yet had the occasion to decide whether Articles 49 and 56 TFEU apply directly to non-collective acts of individuals. To conclude nevertheless that these Treaty prohibitions (in this case Article 56 TFEU) cannot be applied to the private law act under consideration in this case is premature, as one cannot rule out that the direct horizontal effect of both provisions will eventually be extended to non-collective acts of individuals (as a matter of fact, the non-discrimination rule of Article 45 TFEU already applies to acts of a non-collective nature).

Hoge Raad der Nederlanden (Supreme Court of the Netherlands),
1 February 2013[90]   **3.18 (NL)**

X v Stichting Volkshuisvesting Arnhem

DOES ARTICLE 56 TFEU APPLY TO THE LEASE REGULATIONS
OF A PRIVATE LAW HOUSING CORPORATION?

Satellite dish

National case that illustrates the potential scope of Article 56 TFEU

Facts: X had attached a satellite dish to the balcony of his rental apartment without permission of the housing corporation (a private law organisation). With reference to its lease regulations, the latter demanded the

---

[87] CJ *Bosman* (n 44); CJ *Wouters* (n 71); CJ 18 July 2006 Case C-519/04 P *David Meca-Medina and Igor Majcen v Commission of the European Communities* [2006] I-06991 ECLI:EU:C:2006:492.
[88] See, eg, CJ *Van de Haar* (n 12). Additional case law is mentioned in section II.A.i above.
[89] CJ *Fra.bo* (n 15), discussed in section II.A.i above.
[90] HR 1 February 2013 *RvdW* 2013/229 ECLI:NL:2013:BX9761 *X v Stichting Volkshuisvestiging Arnhem*.

removal of the dish. X argued, inter alia, that these rules restricted access to broadcasting services from other Member States and therefore infringed Article 56 TFEU. After both the District Court and the Court of Appeal had ignored this argument, X appealed to the Supreme Court.

Held: The Supreme Court of the Netherlands quashed the Court of Appeal's judgment because it was inadequately reasoned.

Judgment: The complaints succeed. The claimant explicitly relied on Article 56 TFEU, with proper substantiation. The defendant disputed this allegation, and the court of appeal established in para. 4.6 that the claimant's claims were based in part on Article 56 TFEU. Because the court then did not proceed to consider this essential allegation of the claimant it failed to state adequate grounds for its judgment. The challenged judgment must therefore be quashed.

Notes:

(1) Dutch civil procedural law allows a court to disregard the arguments of a party if it considers those arguments to be of no importance for its final decision. Essential allegations ('essentiële stellingen'), however, may not remain undiscussed.

(2) By considering the claimant's reliance on Article 56 TFEU an essential allegation, the Supreme Court of the Netherlands indicated that it might be crucial to the outcome of the case. Implicitly, therefore, the Supreme Court thus deemed it possible that Article 56 TFEU could be applicable to the lease regulations of a private law housing corporation.

(3) In this case, Article 56 TFEU was invoked against a *collective* act (a clause in the lease regulations) of a housing corporation. But what if the contested clause had been incorporated into an *individual* lease agreement between the parties? Despite the identical impact on the tenant's possibilities to receive broadcasting services from other Member States, it is unclear whether Article 56 TFEU would be applicable in that case; the CJ has yet to decide if Article 56 TFEU applies to non-collective acts of individuals as well.

IV.B.ii INDIRECT HORIZONTAL EFFECT

Articles 49 and 56 TFEU can produce several mechanisms of indirect horizontal effect (see section IV.A.ii above). Unfortunately, illustrations from national case law are just as scarce as examples in the case law of the CJ. The only national case that was brought to our attention is connected with the *Parodi* case,[91] already discussed above, and concerned review of compatibility of a national (French) rule of law with Article 56 TFEU in legal proceedings between individuals.

---

[91] CJ *Parodi* (n 72). See section IV.A.ii above.

Cour de Cassation Assemblée plénière (Court of Cassation),
4 March 2005[92]   **3.19 (FR)**

Société Lauga v Caisse hypothécaire anversoise

REVIEW OF COMPATIBILITY WITH ARTICLE 56 TFEU IN LEGAL
PROCEEDINGS BETWEEN INDIVIDUALS

Mortgage loans

Claimants cannot rely on a national rule that is contrary to Article 56 TFEU to argue that a loan agreement is null and void because the loan was granted by a bank that was not authorised in accordance with that national rule

Facts: The dispute was between Caisse hypothécaire anversoise (Caisse), established in Belgium, and M, X, Y, Z, and a company named Lauga, all of them French parties (hereinafter Lauga et al) concerning mortgage loans granted to the latter by Caisse. Lauga et al brought an action against Caisse, seeking that the loans would be declared null and void on the grounds that the bank, when it granted the loan, had not been authorised as required by French law.

Held: The French Court of Cassation rejected the claim; the loans were not declared null and void.

Judgment: Considering that the [CJ] has held (CJ, 9 July 1997, *Société civile immobilière Parodi v Banque H. Albert de Bary et Cie*, C-222/95) that with regard to the period preceding the entry into force of Second Council Directive 89/646/EEC … [now Article 56 TFEU] must be construed as precluding a Member State from requiring a credit institution already authorized in another Member State to obtain an authorization in order to be able to grant a mortgage loan to a person resident within its territory, unless that authorization is required of every person or company pursuing such an activity within the territory of the Member State of destination, is justified on grounds of public interest such as consumer protection, and is objectively necessary to ensure compliance with the rules applicable in the sector under consideration and to protect the interests which those rules are intended to safeguard, and the same result cannot be achieved by less restrictive rules;

…

Considering that the Court of Appeal decided that French legislation in force at that time was going beyond what is necessary to attain the objective pursued, namely to protect the interests at stake, and was therefore not compatible with the provisions of [Union] law applicable at the time the bank loans were granted;

…

Considering, however, that the mere fact that the credit institution was ignoring the pre-condition of the approval requirement imposed by article 15 of Act n° 84-46 of 24 January 1984, which became articles L. 511-10, L. 511-14 and L. 612-2 of the Monetary and Financial Code, in order to carry out its business, is not such as to entail the invalidity of the contracts it has concluded.

Notes:

In its *Parodi* judgment (see section IV.A.ii above), the CJ held that Article 56 TFEU in principle precludes a national rule that requires a credit institution already authorised in

---

[92] French Court of Cassation 4 March 2005 no 03-11725 *Société Lauga v Caisse hypothécaire anversoise.*

another Member State to obtain an authorisation in order to be able to grant a mortgage loan to a person who resides within its territory. As the French Court of Cassation established in the present case that the French law went beyond what was necessary to attain its objective (the protection of creditors), it concluded that the claimants could not rely on it against the bank. Consequently, the loan agreements that were concluded between the parties remained valid.

V. FREE MOVEMENT OF CAPITAL (ARTICLE 63 TFEU)

V.A SOURCES: THE TFEU, CJ CASE LAW, MATERIALS

Article 63 TFEU　　　　　　　　　　　　　　　　　　**3.20 (EU)**

1. Within the framework of the provisions set out in this Chapter, all restrictions on the movement of capital between Member States and between Member States and third countries shall be prohibited.

K Lenaerts and P van Nuffel, European Union Law[93]

Free movement of capital constitutes a necessary support for the [other] freedoms …: a transaction in goods or services or establishment in another member State will often require investment necessitating a capital movement to another Member State.

…

The prohibition of restrictions on movements of capital aims at more than eliminating discrimination based on nationality on the financial market and precludes all rules which make free movement of capital illusory by preventing market participants from investing in other Member States or by rendering it difficult for undertakings to raise capital in another Member State. Accordingly, national measures dissuading nationals of the Member State in question from taking out loans or making investments in other Member States or making direct foreign investment dependent on authorisation are incompatible with the free movement of capital. Even if such measures apply without distinction to both residents and non-residents, they are prohibited if they are liable to deter investors from making investments in another Member State and, consequently, affect access to the market.

　　Although the Treaties do not define the term 'movement of capital', it is settled case law that, inasmuch as Article 63 TFEU substantially reproduces the content of Article 1 of Directive 88/361, the nomenclature of capital movements annexed thereto retains an indicative value for the purposes of defining the term 'movement of capital', subject to the qualification, contained in the introduction to the nomenclature, that the list set out therein does not only cover investments and loans, but also inheritances and deduction for tax purposes of gifts in money or in kind.

---

[93] Lenaerts and Van Nuffel 2011 285–87, footnotes omitted.

V.A.i DIRECT HORIZONTAL EFFECT

While nowadays it is well established that Article 63(1) TFEU can be invoked by individuals against the Member State (direct *vertical* effect),[94] the CJ has not yet decided if the prohibition may also be directly applied to legal relationships between individuals, in the sense that it results in the creation, modification or extinction of rights and obligations between individuals (direct *horizontal* effect). However, the issue has already been raised by the defending Member State in a number of cases relating to Article 258 TFEU cases.[95] In *Commission v Germany (Volkswagen)*,[96] for example, the German Republic argued that Article 63(1) TFEU did not apply to its Volkswagen Law[97] because this national measure originated from a private agreement concluded in 1959 between individuals and groups who had disputed the ownership of the Volkswagen company. The CJ rejected the argument without addressing the issue of direct horizontal effect of Article 63(1) TFEU: 'Even if, as the Federal Republic of Germany submits, the VW Law does no more than reproduce an agreement which should be classified as a private law contract, it must be stated that the fact that this agreement has become the subject of a Law suffices for it to be considered as a national measure for the purposes of the free movement of capital. The exercise of legislative power by the national authorities duly authorised to that end is a manifestation *par excellence* of State power.'[98]

As restrictions on the free movement of capital (eg, shareholders' rights) can also emerge from acts of a truly private law nature (eg, agreements between shareholders, the articles of association of a company),[99] the CJ will eventually have to answer the question whether Article 63(1) TFEU has direct horizontal effect.

V.A.ii INDIRECT HORIZONTAL EFFECT

Even though Article 63(1) TFEU may, in theory, have an indirect effect on private law relationships through (i) the interpretation of a rule of national (private) law, (ii) a 'positive obligation' it imposes on the Member States, or (iii) the review of compatibility of

---

[94] See, eg, CJ 14 December 1995 Joined Cases C-163/94, C-165/94 and C-250/94 *Criminal Proceedings v Lucas Emilio Sanz de Lera, Raimundo Díaz Jiménez and Figen Kapanoglu* [1995] I-04821 ECLI:EU:C:1995:541, paras 41 and 47; CJ 18 December 2007 Case C-101/05 *Skatteverket v A* [2007] I-11531 ECLI:EU:C:2007:804, para 21. The case law of the CJ on art 63(1) TFEU, which has direct vertical effect, has already touched upon a number of private law questions. See O Remien, 'Kapitalverkehrsfreiheit und Privatrecht in der Rechtsprechung des Europäischen Gerichtshofes' in J Dammann, W Grunsky, Th Pfeiffer and M Wolf (eds), *Gedächtnisschrift für Manfred Wolf* (Munich, Verlag CH Beck, 2011) 717–23.

[95] CJ 26 September 2000 Case C-478/98 *Commission of the European Communities v Kingdom of Belgium* [2000] I-07587 ECLI:EU:C2000:497; CJ 13 May 2003 Case C-98/01 *Commission of the European Communities v United Kingdom of Great Britain and Northern Ireland* [2003] I-04641 ECLI:EU:C:2003:273.

[96] CJ 23 October 2007 Case C-112/05 *Commission of the European Communities v Federal Republic of Germany (Volkswagen)* [2007] I-08995 ECLI:EU:C:2007:623.

[97] Derogating from general company law, the Volkswagen Law capped the voting rights of every shareholder at 20 per cent and fixed a blocking minority at 20 per cent. Moreover, it gave both the Federal State and the Land of Lower Saxony the right to appoint two representatives to the supervisory board of Volkswagen AG.

[98] CJ *Commission v Federal Republic of Germany (Volkswagen)* (n 96) paras 26 and 27.

[99] See section V.B below.

national law in disputes between individuals, the case law of the CJ only offers some examples of the third category. One of them is *Burtscher v Stauderer*.[100]

In 1975, the Austrian parents of Burtscher wanted to sell a holiday home to Stauderer, a German national. At the time, the relevant national legislation (paragraph 7 of the *Vorarlberger Grundverkehrsgeset*) provided that: 'Acquisitions of built-on land ... are not subject to authorisation by the competent land transfer authority if the purchaser provides a written declaration ... that (a) the land is built-on, (b) he is an Austrian *citizen* ... and (c) the acquisition is or is not for holiday purposes.'[101] To exclude the application of this statutory restriction, the parties signed a lease for a term of 99 years without the possibility of termination. In 2000, however, Burtscher applied for an order against Stauderer to vacate the land concerned, claiming that the agreement concluded in 1975 was fraudulent and void ab initio. With regard to this issue, the national courts took the view that transactions designed to circumvent the law had to be subject to the rules applicable to the transaction actually intended. By then, the provisions governing the acquisition of built-on land no longer required prior authorisation from the competent land transfer authority; purchasers needed merely to make a declaration to that authority within a period of two years in accordance with paragraph 7 of the Vorarlberger Grund-verkehrsgeset, failing which the transaction would be retroactively invalid. The courts inferred from the foregoing that in the absence of a timely declaration provided by Stau-derer, the agreement of 1975 must, in principle, be regarded as void and that the lessee therefore had to vacate the premises. However, in a special appeal, the Austrian Supreme Court (Oberster Gerichtshof) asked the CJ whether Article 63(1) TFEU: 'Should ... be interpreted as precluding national legislation [the Vorarlberger Grundverkehrsgeset] by which ... failure by the acquirer to declare by the due date that the land is built on, that the acquisition is not for holiday purposes, and that he is, or should be treated as, an Austrian national, results in the retrospective invalidity of the transaction.'[102] The CJ's affirmative answer resulted in Article 63(1) TFEU having an indirect (but decisive) impact on the horizontal relationship between Burtscher and Stauderer: by precluding the statutory ground for nullity, the Treaty prohibition saved the lease agreement from voidness and thereby prevented Staudeler from having to vacate the holiday home.

V.B NATIONAL CASE LAW

The material provided by the national reporters in preparation of this chapter suggests that there is not much national case law on the direct or indirect horizontal effect(s) of Article 63(1) TFEU. Having stated this, this section will focus on a single but highly interesting case from Germany.

---

[100] CJ 1 December 2005 Case C-213/04 *Edwald Burtscher v Josef Stauderer* [2005] I-10309 ECLI:EU:C:2005:731.

[101] ibid, para 6.

[102] ibid, para 25.

Oberlandesgericht Hamm (Higher Regional Court Hamm),
31 March 2008[103]   **3.21 (GERM)**

Shareholders v ThyssenKrupp

NATIONAL COURT REJECTS DIRECT HORIZONTAL EFFECT OF ARTICLE 63(1) TFEU

Appointment right of a private shareholder

A decision of the general meeting of a private law company cannot be tested against Article 63(1) TFEU

Facts: On 19 January 2007, the general meeting of ThyssenKrupp AG (a German company limited by shares) decided by a majority of 78.91 per cent to amend the articles of association of the company so as to grant the Alfried Krupp von Bohlen und Halbach-Stiftung—which at the time held 25.1 per cent of the share capital—the right to appoint at least one member of the Supervisory Board (when holding a minimum of 10 per cent of the shares), but not more than three members (when holding 25 per cent or more of the shares). Three shareholders who had voted against the amendment initiated legal proceedings in which they contested the resolution, alleging that it was contrary to, inter alia, Article 63 TFEU

Held: The claim of the shareholders was rejected.

Judgment: (77) The creation of an appointment right for the Alfried Krupp von Bohlen und Halbach-Stiftung does not infringe [EU] Law, notably the free movement of capital (Article 63 TFEU).

...

(81) It is true that the CJ repeatedly ruled that the creation of an appointment right may also result in an act that restricts the free movement of capital, if it is likely to prevent or limit the acquisition of shares by other shareholders in the undertakings concerned ... A significant restriction in this respect is not only possible in the form of direct state intervention (e.g. legislative act), (cf. CJ 23 October 2007, C-112/05), but also by amendment of the articles of association by the company itself (CJ 6 December 2007, C-463/04 and C-464/04).

(82) In the present case, however, one cannot speak of an action restricting the capital market freedom, since the articles of association in question are based on a general rule of German company law (§ 102 Abs. 2 AktG) and since they create an appointment right for a *private* shareholder only. In the above-mentioned judgments of the CJ, the appointment rights were based either directly on legal provisions (§4 Volkswagen Act) or on a rule applying only to the *State* or *public* bodies for the benefit of public actors (Article 2449 of the Italian Codice Civile). In these two cases the CJ mainly focused on these special rights for public bodies and thus found decisive grounds to find restriction on the free movement of capital. There are no objections then to regulations made by the shareholders themselves for the benefit of private shareholders ...

(83) The claimants nonetheless take the position that violation of the fundamental freedoms can also be relevant in legal relationships between individuals, at any rate where the state has failed to take adequate measures ('Untermaßverbot'). In a dispute between individuals, therefore, national law should also be applied in conformity with the fundamental freedoms or, under certain circumstances, be disapplied. In the present case, this is not necessary.

---

[103] OLG Hamm 31 March 2008 Az 8 U 222/07 *Shareholders v ThyssenKrupp.*

(84) It is true that European fundamental freedoms can also play a role in legal relationships between individuals and are capable of conferring rights on e.g. private undertakings (cf. CJ 11 December 2007, C-438/05, paras. 55, 66, 74 concerning the freedom of establishment, Article 49 TFEU). However, the Member States have a margin of appreciation in preventing obstacles to the movement freedoms being raised by actions of individuals. Even in cases falling within their scope, the free movement provisions do not replace the national law that constitutes the relevant normative framework for assessing disputes between individuals. Rather, Member States remain free to regulate the conduct of individuals as long as they respect the boundaries set by [EU] law (cf. Opinion of Advocate General Maduro delivered on 23 May 2007 on CJ Case C-438/05, para. 51).

(85) The circumstances to be assessed in the present case do not exceed the limits of [EU] Law, in particular not those of the free movement of capital (Article 63 TFEU) between individuals. Particularly the CJ-decision 'Viking Line' (CJ Case C-438/05), on which the claimants rely to substantiate their position that the fundamental freedoms apply in the present case, too, was based on a provision which directly and specifically affected freedoms of third persons (in that case: the freedom of establishment of the company in question). The appointment rights at issue in the present case have no such infringing nature at all.

(86) Furthermore, the creation of an appointment right for the foundation did not grant this shareholder influence in excess of its shareholding. The ECJ held that the restrictive effect of an appointment right granted to a public body infringed the free movement of capital among other things because the beneficiaries were granted influence in excess of their shareholdings since the appointment rights were not linked to a corresponding participation in the share capital of the companies (CJ Case C-112/05, paras. 63, 64, 69; CJ Case C-463, 464/04, para. 24). In the present case the situation is different.

Notes:

(1) By holding that the resolution of the general meeting of ThyssenKrupp AG could not be reviewed against the free movement of capital provisions, the Higher Regional Court Hamm clearly rejected direct horizontal effect of Article 63(1) TFEU. For a number of reasons, this judgment can be subject to criticism.

(2) First, given the fact that (i) it is the exclusive competence of the CJ to interpret EU law, and (ii) the CJ has not yet decided on the direct horizontal effect of Article 63(1) TFEU, it is not for a national court to rule, on the basis of an *a contrario* reading of *Commission v Germany (Volkswagen)*, that this prohibition cannot be applied directly to legal relationships between individuals.

(3) Second, the national court's interpretation of *Viking* seems at odds with the CJ's rather clear and unconditional statement (in paragraph 33 of its judgment) that the Treaty provisions on the free movement of persons and services 'do not apply only to the actions of public authorities but extend also to rules of any other nature aimed at regulating in a collective manner gainful employment, self-employment and the provision of services'. What is more, the reasoning of the CJ in *Viking* provides no evidence that the CJ adopted AG Maduro's[104] line of reasoning (which is cited by the national court).

---

[104] AG Maduro Opinion 23 May 2007 in Case C-438/05 *Viking* [2007] I-10779 ECLI:EU:C:2007:292.

(4) Arguably, the claimants relied on *Viking* to demonstrate that the grounds on which the CJ based the direct horizontal effect of Articles 45, 49 and 56 TFEU can and should be applied analogously to Article 63(1) TFEU. Since this is still unknown territory, it is curious that neither the Higher Regional Court nor the Federal Supreme Court of Germany (Bundesgerichtshof)[105] made a preliminary reference to the CJ. The shareholders' constitutional complaint that their right of access to the courts enshrined in the German Constitution had been infringed was nevertheless rejected by the Federal Constitutional Court of Germany (Bundesverfassungsgericht).[106]

(5) The question which the CJ's judgment in *Commission v Germany (Volkswagen)* should have induced the national court to ask itself (and refer to the CJ for a preliminary ruling) was whether the contested resolution of the general meeting of ThyssenKrupp AG was liable to make it less attractive for foreign investors to invest in the share capital of the company and, if so, whether this private law act—like the appointment rights created by the Volkswagen Law—constituted a restriction on the free movement of capital, which is in principle prohibited.

VI. EXCEPTIONS (OR JUSTIFICATIONS): INVOCABILITY BY INDIVIDUALS

The accordance of direct horizontal effect to (some of) the fundamental freedoms raises the important question whether the (un)written exceptions based on the general interest, which may constitute grounds for justifying *Member State* measures that violate the prohibitions, can also be invoked successfully by *individuals*. To answer it, the current system of (un)written exceptions is briefly introduced (section VI.A) and relevant national 'horizontal' cases are explored (section VI.B).

VI.A SOURCES: THE TFEU, CJ CASE LAW, MATERIALS

A Hartkamp, European Law and National Private Law[107]

(a) A first group of exceptions is stated in the Treaty, each time together with the freedom concerned. The exceptions to the free movement of goods are listed in article 36 TFEU:

> The provisions of Articles 34 and 35 shall not preclude prohibitions or restrictions on imports, exports or goods in transit justified on grounds of public morality, public policy or public security; the protection of health and life of humans, animals or plants; the protection of national treasures possessing artistic, historic or archaeological value; or the protection of industrial and commercial property. Such prohibitions

---

[105] BGH 8 June 2009 II ZR 111/08 *ZIP* 2010,36. The Higher Regional Court did not admit a further appeal (*Revision*) to the BGH. This non-admission was challenged before the BGH, but the latter replied: 'The creation of an appointment right in the articles of association of the defendant is not a measure of equivalent effect prohibited by [now Article 63 TFEU], infringing the free movement of capital.'

[106] Constitutional Court of Germany 30 October 2009 Az 1 BvR 1892/09.

[107] Hartkamp 2016 no 64.

or restrictions shall not, however, constitute a means of arbitrary discrimination or a disguised restriction on trade between Member States.

Article 45(3) TFEU (freedom of movement for workers) declares restrictions justified 'on grounds of public policy, public security or public health'. Article 52 TFEU states the same restrictions on the freedom of establishment, which pursuant to Article 62 TFEU apply to the freedom of services as well. The free movement of capital and the free movement of payments are subject to the exceptions of public policy and public security, and also some other grounds, all of them subject to the condition that they do not constitute a means of arbitrary discrimination or a disguised restriction on the free movement of capital and payments (art. 65 TFEU).

(b) A second group of exceptions has been created by the Court of Justice, starting in the judgment in *Cassis de Dijon* ... with respect to the movement of goods and subsequently also with respect to the other freedoms. This is connected with the fact that the ECJ extended the scope of the prohibitions, which initially were only directed against discrimination (in the sense of distinction based on nationality or distinction between national and imported goods, services, etc.), to include national legislative and administrative measures which did not make any such distinction but which entailed restrictions on the freedoms 'without distinction'. Unlike discriminatory measures, which usually serve a protectionist objective, 'without distinction measures' are often taken to serve a respectable public interest. In order to take account of this fact, the ECJ, as a counterpart to the extension of scope, introduced a new category of grounds of justification based on so-called 'mandatory requirements' or 'rule of reason exceptions'. These exceptions include general interests of a non-economic nature such as the protection of consumers, environmental protection, protection of language and culture, protection of media plurality, tax system coherence and spatial planning ... The mandatory requirements may in principle only be invoked to justify 'without distinction measures', not to justify discriminatory measures. In principle the ECJ applies the exceptions listed in the treaty strictly with regard to the latter (but see also sub (e) below). The mandatory requirements, on the other hand, are not listed exhaustively.

...

(e) A spectacular extension of 'the exceptions' resulted from the ground of justification introduced in *Schmidberger* (C-112/00), namely the protection of the fundamental rights (in this case the freedom of expression), in which connection the ECJ expressly referred to the ECHR, as it usually did when applying human rights before the entry into force of the Charter. See also no. 204 below. The judgment is consistent with earlier case law in the sense that the Court had already ruled before (for example in *Defrenne v. Sabena II*, C-149/77, mentioned in no. 53) that human rights, too, form part of the general principles of Community law which the Court has a duty to protect. In view of the wordings of the ECJ, in which the fundamental freedoms and the fundamental rights rank equal, I think it likely that justification based on fundamental rights ranks equal with the exceptions mentioned under (a) above, so that they may not only be invoked in connection with a 'without distinction measure', but also in connection with a discriminatory measure.

Exceptions to free movement provisions can be classified into three groups: Treaty exceptions which can be invoked to justify both discriminatory and non-discriminatory measures (distinctly and indistinctly applicable measures); *rule of reason* exceptions (which, in principle, can only be invoked to justify non-discriminatory measures/'without distinction'measures); and the exception based on the protection of fundamental rights (which is likely to be invoked to justify discriminatory and non-discriminatory measures).

It appears from the case law of the CJ that, at least in theory, individuals can rely on these grounds for justification too. With regard to the exceptions formulated in Article 45(3) TFEU, this follows explicitly from the *Bosman* case.[108] In response to the plea of UEFA that the accordance of direct horizontal effect to Article 45 TFEU makes this prohibition more restrictive for individuals than for Member States, the CJ stated in paragraph 86 of its judgment: 'That argument is based on a false premise. There is nothing to preclude individuals from relying on justifications on grounds of public policy, public security or public health. Neither the scope nor the content of those grounds of justification is in any way affected by the public or private nature of the rules in question.'[109] While in theory the Court's proposition is correct, private law practice learns that individuals will usually not be able to satisfy the requirement that the justification invoked is related to the protection of a public interest mentioned in Article 45(3) TFEU. Since the same holds for Articles 36, 52 and 65 TFEU, the Treaty exceptions provide only little or no room for manoeuvre for individuals.

Looking at the CJ case law, it becomes clear that individuals can also rely on the unwritten *rule of reason* exceptions to justify an infringement of a fundamental freedom having direct effect. In *Bosman*, for example, the CJ ruled that the UEFA transfer rules could, in principle, be justified by the need to encourage the recruitment and training of young football players, which is a legitimate aim, while in *Wouters*,[110] the CJ held that a regulation of the Dutch Bar Association was justified by the need to ensure the proper practice of the legal profession. Although these judgments show that the CJ is willing to add some public interests raised by individuals to its catalogue of unwritten exceptions, this second group of exceptions does not (yet) cover truly private interests.

As regards the third group of exceptions, CJ case law suggests that individuals can invoke the protection of fundamental rights as a justification ground. In *Viking*,[111] for example, the CJ ruled that the fundamental right to take collective action, including the right to strike, 'is a legitimate interest which, in principle, justifies a restriction of one of the fundamental freedoms guaranteed by the Treaty'. Though it must be admitted that, in this case, the fundamental right (to strike) was absorbed by a *rule of reason* exception (protection of workers), there is every reason to believe that—given the equal status of fundamental freedoms and fundamental rights—the protection of fundamental rights can also function as an autonomous justification ground for individuals. In that capacity, the private law potential of fundamental rights is significant: arguments relating to party autonomy can be extracted from the arsenal of fundamental rights (laid down, for example, in the EU Charter) which an individual can use to construe or modify the obligations ensuing for him from a free movement provision having direct horizontal effect, in a way that does justice to the specific nature of the private legal relationship.[112]

For a restrictive measure (of a Member State) or act (of an individual) to be justified by a legitimate aim, it is necessary that it passes the proportionality test.

---

[108] CJ *Bosman* (n 44).
[109] See also CJ 7 May 1998 Case C-350/96 *Clean Car Autoservice GesmbH v Landeshauptmann von Wien* [1998] I-02521 ECLI:EU:C:1998:205, para 24; CJ *Erny* (n 46) para 48.
[110] CJ *Wouters* (n 71).
[111] CJ *Viking* (n 71).
[112] See CH Sieburgh, 'A Method to Substantively Guide the Involvement of EU Law in Private Law Matters' (2013) 21(5) *ERPL* 1182–84.

P Craig and G de Búrca, EU Law: Text, Cases and Materials[113]

In any proportionality inquiry the relevant interests must be identified, and there will be some ascription of weight or value to those interests, since this is a necessary condition precedent to any balancing operation. There will normally be three stages in a proportionality inquiry: whether the measure was suitable to achieve the desired end; whether it was necessary to achieve the desired end; and whether the measure imposed a burden on the individual that was excessive in relation to the objective sought to be achieved (proportionality stricto sensu).

There has been some doubt whether stage three is part of the ECJ's proportionality inquiry. The reality is that the ECJ will consider part three when an applicant addresses an argument concerning this stage of the inquiry. It may not do so where no such specific argument has been raised, more especially where the case can be resolved at one of the earlier stages. Moreover, in some cases the ECJ may distinguish stages two and three on the inquiry; in others it may in effect 'fold' stage three of the inquiry back into stage one or two.

VI.B NATIONAL CASE LAW

Oberlandesgericht Düsseldorf (Higher Regional Court Düsseldorf), 14 August 2013[114]   **3.22 (GERM)**

Fra.bo SpA v Deutsche Vereinigung des Gas- und Wasserfaches eV—'Technisch-Wissenschaftlicher Verein

JUSTIFICATION FOR BREACH OF ARTICLE 34 TFEU: PROPORTIONALITY TEST

Fra.bo (national follow-up)

The invocation of a Treaty exception by an individual is unsuccessful because the restriction on the free movement of goods is not proportionate to the aim pursued. Furthermore, the individual cannot successfully rely on Articles 15 and 16 of the Charter (freedom of association and freedom to conduct a business) to justify the de facto restriction on free movement

Facts: See case 3.3 (GERM) above. After consulting the CJ, the Higher Regional Court Düsseldorf established that the cancellation by the DVGW of Fra.bo's product certificate constituted a restriction on the free movement of goods. It then went on to investigate whether the breach of Article 34 TFEU could be justified.

Held: DVGW could not successfully rely on the protection of public health (Article 36 TFEU) and/or Articles 12 and 16 of the Charter (freedom of association and freedom to conduct a business) to justify the restriction on the free movement of goods. As a result, the DVGW was liable for breach of duty (§ 280 BGB). Fra.bo was awarded damages and, in addition, it had to be granted a (renewed) product certificate.

---

[113] Craig and De Búrca 2015 551.
[114] OLG Düsseldorf 14 August 2013 VI-2 U (Kart) 15/08 (n 30). See also section II.B.i above.

Judgment: [58] No general grounds for justification given.

[59] Pursuant to [now Article 36 TFEU], [now Article 34 TFEU] does not preclude import restrictions if these are justified on the grounds *inter alia* of protecting human health and life. Such restrictions are not permitted, however, to constitute a means of discrimination or a disguised restriction on trade between Member States.

...

[62] Protecting public health by preventing the pollution of drinking water is without doubt essential. The national legislator is permitted in principle to take appropriate measures to counter such threats, and these measures may go beyond the minimum standards set by the European Union. The respondents, too, are allowed to do this.

[63] A pre-requisite for such measures, however, is a verifiable and acceptable analysis of the relevant risks and threats by the Member State (i.e. the respondents), which analysis also reflects the probability of the drinking water supply becoming contaminated and the implications that this would have for public health. The respondents in this case have not submitted an assessment that includes an appropriate and satisfactory evaluation of these risks and threats ...

...

[68] Similarly, no unwritten grounds are given to justify the 3000-hours test. Such justification would require an overriding requirement recognised in the case law of the Court of Justice, while the measure must also be suited for achieving the desired aim and not go beyond what is necessary to achieve this aim (cf. CJ EU judgment, 10 November 2005—'C-432/03, Commission/Portugal, ground 42 with citations). Based on the opinion of the Advocate-General and the references to Court of Justice case law, the respondents have invoked special grounds in the private interest, objective reasons (protection of public health, consumer protection, security of supply) and fundamental rights set out in the Charter of Fundamental Rights of the European Union (Article 12—Freedom of association; Article 15—Freedom to choose an occupation and engage in work; Article 16—Freedom to conduct a business). The primary focus of the defence is on invoking the freedom to conduct a business and the freedom of association, depending on whether certification and the setting of standards are seen as an economic activity. As the applicant correctly pointed out, the freedom to choose an occupation and engage in work is subsumed in the fundamental right to conduct a business. Objective considerations such as the protection of public health, consumer protection and security of supply have previously been assessed with reference to general grounds for justification. No re-assessment is required. No special grounds in the private interest have been established. Consequently, the assessment can be limited to an examination of the fundamental rights of the freedom of association and the freedom to conduct a business (Articles 12 and 16 TFEU).

[69] Contrary, however, to the opinion of the respondents, fundamental rights do not automatically reduce the level of justification required to be provided by private individuals, a registered association such as the respondents under 1 or a legal person under private law, such that they should no longer have to meet the need for overriding requirements, as recognised in Court of Justice case law. Under Court of Justice case law, these requirements prevail over the free movement of goods or may prevail in the event of proper consideration being given in a concrete case. The contrary opinion held by the respondents overlooks the fact that, in their general interpretation, the fundamental freedom guaranteed in [now Article 34 TFEU] and essential for giving effect to the fundamental EU freedom of the free movement of goods can be circumvented and invalidated, which contradicts the principle of uniform and effective implementation of EU law by the Member

States (and their courts) (see also the opinion, ground 49). Their opinion also overlooks the fact that, in §12 para. 4 of the Ordinance on General Conditions for the Supply of Water [*AVBWasserV*], the German legislator established that products complying with the standards set by the respondent under 1 and certified by the respondent under 2 would be compliant with national legislation (CJ EU judgment, 12 July 2012—C-171/11, ground 27). It also overlooks the fact that the respondent under 2—in the absence of legislation in the Federal Republic of Germany, or in fact any reference to a DVGW certificate—is the only body authorised to certify products such as the copper fittings at issue in these proceedings and thus allow such products access to the German market (CJ EU judgment, 12 July 2012—C-171/11, grounds 28 and 31).

[70] In the present case, invoking the fundamental rights of the freedom to conduct a business and the freedom of association as set out in the Charter of Fundamental Rights of the European Union does not suffice to override the free movement of goods. Under the competences conferred on them by the doctrine of *effet utile*, the respondents are bound in law by the free movement of goods in the same way as the Member State the Federal Republic of Germany and should be treated in exactly the same way. This significantly weakens the ranking and importance of the fundamental rights claimed by the respondents under the Charter, especially since the sole interests pursued by the respondents are economic interests or the interests of their own association. For this reason the respondents' fundamental rights cannot prevail over the fundamental freedom of the free movement of goods under [now Article 34 TFEU] … Irrespective of this, the respondents' intended restriction on the free movement of goods does not respect the principle of proportionality (see above).

Notes:

(1) In this part of the judgment, the national court (the Higher Regional Court Düsseldorf) investigated whether the DVGW could successfully rely on a ground for justification.

(2) First, it explored whether the restriction on the free movement of goods that is caused by the introduction of the so-called 3,000-hour test is justified on the ground of public health (Article 36 TFEU). Regarding this issue, the national court acknowledged (at paragraph 82) that Member States and, as in this case, private bodies may take measures to protect public health against drinking water pollution. However, those measures have to satisfy the proportionality test. It becomes clear from paragraphs 62 and 65 that, in the opinion of the German court, the DVGW did not succeed in proving that the introduction of the 3,000-hour test is suitable and necessary to achieve this goal. For this reason, the DVGW could not successfully rely on protection of public health as a ground for justification.

(3) Further on, in paragraphs 68–70, the national court then investigated whether the DVGW could successfully invoke Articles 12, 15 and/or 16 of the Charter (freedom of association, freedom of occupation and freedom to conduct a business) as a justification ground. According to the Higher Regional Court Düsseldorf, the answer must be negative, in particular because the DVGW did not rely on any interests other than private, economic interests. This reasoning is not convincing, since the fundamental rights at stake protect public as well as private interests.

VII. CONCLUDING REMARKS

1. Although the Treaty provisions on free movement were originally assumed to be binding only on the Member States and capable of being relied on by individuals against the state (direct *vertical* effect), it follows from the case law of the CJ that at least some of these fundamental freedoms can also be applied to certain acts of individuals (direct *horizontal* effect). The 'horizontal' scope of Article 45 TFEU (free movement of workers) is the most sizeable, as it not only applies to discriminatory and non-discriminatory collective behaviour of individuals, but also to non-collective acts that are (in)directly discriminatory. Until now, the CJ has not been given the opportunity to extend the direct horizontal effect of Article 49 TFEU (freedom of establishment) and Article 56 TFEU (freedom to provide and receive services) in the same manner. It is, however, established case law that (non-)discriminatory collective acts of individuals can be tested against both provisions. The greatest uncertainty exists about the (extent of the) direct horizontal effect of the Treaty provisions on the free movement of goods (the judgment in *Fra.bo* appears to be multi-interpretable) and Article 63 TFEU (there has been no CJ decision on the matter yet).

2. National case law in which the fundamental freedoms are directly applied to legal relationships between individuals are scarce (or, as regards Article 63 TFEU, non-existent) and can mostly be linked to preliminary rulings of the CJ (*Angonese, Raccanelli, Laval, Olympique Lyonnais* and *Fra.bo*). Whether acting on their own initiative or at the instigation of one of the parties to the legal proceedings, the fact that the national courts referred questions to the CJEU in these cases implies that they were aware of the possibility that these Treaty provisions might have a direct impact on the private law relationship at issue. Unfortunately, the stand-alone cases (ie, national cases in which the CJ was not asked for guidance) illustrate that this awareness is not always present: in some cases, the national court clearly misinterpreted (or ignored) the CJ's case law on the direct horizontal effect of Articles 45, 49 and 56 TFEU, thereby depriving an individual of an argument that could potentially have won the case for it. To increase the awareness and/ or knowledge of the actors in national proceedings, academic research should, in our opinion, not only provide a critical assessment of the current state of the law regarding direct horizontal effect of the fundamental freedoms, but should also focus on how far this effect could or might come to reach in the future. Such a proactive research should necessarily include the question of how the current system of (un)written justifications can be accommodated to the needs of private law.

3. Although all fundamental freedoms can, in theory, produce several types of *indirect* horizontal effect, national cases typically concerned situations in which a fundamental freedom was invoked in legal proceedings between individuals to contest the legality of a provision of national law.

FURTHER READING

J Baquero Cruz, 'Free Movement and Private Autonomy' (1999) 24 *EL Rev* 603.

C Barnard, *The Substantive Law of the EU: The Four Freedoms* (Oxford, Oxford University Press, 2016).

U Bernitz and N Reich, 'Case No. A 268/04, The Labour Court, Sweden (Arbetsdomstolen) Judgment No. 89/09 of 2 December 2009, Laval un Partneri Ltd. v. Svenska Byggnadsarbetareforbundet et al' (2011) 48(2) *CMLR* 603.

P Craig, *EU Administrative Law*, 2nd edn (Oxford, Oxford University Press, 2012).

P Craig and G de Búrca, *EU Law. Text, Cases, and Materials* (Oxford, Oxford University Press, 2015) 2015

G Davies, 'Freedom of Contract and the Horizontal Effect of Free Movement Law' in D Leczykiewicz and S Weatherill (eds), *The Involvement of EU Law in Private Law Relationships* (Oxford, Hart Publishing, 2013).

S de Vries and R van Mastrigt, 'The Horizontal Direct Effect of the Four Freedoms: From a Hodgepodge of Cases to a Seamless Web of Judicial Protection in the EU Single Market?' in Bernitz/Groussot/Schulyok et al (eds) 2013.

T Ganten, *Die Drittwirkung der Grundfreiheiten* (Berlin, Duncker & Humblot, 2000).

AS Hartkamp, 'EU Law and General Contract Law' in Hartkamp/Sieburgh/Keus/Kortmann/ Wissink (eds) 2014.

AS Hartkamp, *European Law and National Private Law* (Antwerp, Intersentia, 2016)

MT Karayigit, 'The Horizontal Effect of the Free Movement Provisions' (2011) 3 *MJ* 303.

T Körber, *Grundfreiheiten und Privatrecht* (Tübingen, Mohr Siebeck, 2004).

C Krenn, 'A Missing Piece in the Horizontal Effect "Jigsaw": Horizontal Direct Effect and the Free Movement of Goods' (2012) 49(1) *CMLR* 177.

K Lenaerts and P van Nuffel, *European Union Law*, 3rd ed (London, Sweet & Maxwell, 2011).

S Löwisch, *Die horizontale Direktwirkung der Europäischen Grundfreiheiten. Zur Frage der unmittelbaren Verplichtung Privater durch die Grundfreiheiten des EG-Vertrages* (Baden-Baden, Nomos, 2009).

PJ Oliver, S Enchelmaier, M Jarvis, A Johnston, S Norberg, C Stothers and S Weatherill (eds), *Oliver on Free Movement of Goods in the European Union*, 5th edn (Oxford, Hart Publishing, 2010).

S Perner, *Grundfreiheiten, Grundrechte-Charta und Privatrecht* (Tübingen, Mohr Siebeck, 2013).

M Quinn and N MacGowan, 'Could Article 30 Impose Obligations on Individuals?' (1987) 12 *EL Rev* 163.

W-H Roth, 'Drittwirkung der Grundfreiheiten?' in O Due, M Lutter and J Schwarze (eds), *Festschrift für Ulrich Everling* (Baden-Baden, Nomos, 1995).

CH Sieburgh, 'General Principles and the Charter in Private Law Relationships: Constructive and Critical Input from Private Law' in Bernitz/Groussot/Schulyok et el (eds) 2013.

CH Sieburgh, 'A Method to Substantively Guide the Involvement of EU Law in Private Law Matters' (2013) 21(5–6) *European Review of Private Law* 1165.

CH Sieburgh, 'EU Law and Non-contractual Liability of the Union, Member States and Individuals' in Hartkamp/Sieburgh/Keus/Kortmann/Wissink (eds) 2014.

S van den Bogaert, 'Horizontality: The Court Attacks?' in C Barnard and J Scott (eds), *The Legal Foundations of the Single Market: Unpacking the Premises* (Oxford, Hart Publishing, 2002).

H van Harten and T Nauta, 'Towards Horizontal Direct Effect for the Free Movement of Goods? Comment on *Fra.bo*' (2013) 5 *EL Rev* 677.

RWE van Leuken, Private Law and the Internal Market. Direct Horizontal Effect of the Treaty Provisions on Free Movement (forthcoming, Intersentia, 2017).

4
NON-DISCRIMINATION PROVISIONS IN THE TFEU

Carla Sieburgh

I. GENERAL APPROACH

It was already mentioned in Chapter 2 that chapters in this casebook aim to be different from, and bring added value to existing textbooks and casebooks on topics of substantive EU law, which in this chapter is non-discrimination. It will be different in that it focuses as much as possible on national case law. A casebook on non-discrimination in general already exists. This chapter aims to study national case law from a range of Member States, and will search not only for both differences and common features in the national legal systems, but also for characteristics of the interaction between national law and primary EU non-discrimination law.

The non-discrimination principle flows from a variety of sources of EU law and it is therefore a subject discussed in several chapters in this book:

— This chapter deals only with primary EU law.
— Non-discrimination law following from directives and producing horizontal effects is discussed in Chapter 6.
— The prohibitions of discrimination as part of the provisions on fundamental freedoms are discussed in Chapter 3.
— The general principle of non-discrimination and its expression in Article 21 of the Charter are discussed in section II in Chapter 5.

Most importantly, the present chapter is part of a casebook that aims to describe the exchange and interaction between national law and EU law when these laws are applied to horizontal relationships. The following techniques of exchange and interaction are distinguished.

I.A CATEGORIES OF PRIVATE LAW CASES INFLUENCED BY TREATY PROVISIONS ON NON-DISCRIMINATION

The principle of equality plays a special role in EU law and it manifests itself in several ways. This chapter will focus on how the principle of equality as enshrined in Articles 18, 19 and 157 TFEU influences private law without the support of any other applicable rule of EU law.

There are different ways in which EU law can exert influence on private law, as has already been demonstrated by Hartkamp.[1] In the adjudication of private law disputes between individuals, the primary question is whether a provision of EU law has direct horizontal effect. For the purposes of this casebook, the concept of direct horizontal effect means that a provision of EU law directly influences the (legal) relationship between individuals in the sense that it creates, modifies or extinguishes rights or obligations between them.[2]

If no rule of EU law with direct horizontal effect is applicable to the legal relationship, this does not mean an end to the role of EU law. Rules of EU law can indirectly affect horizontal relationships in various ways. The term 'indirect horizontal effect' refers, inter alia, to the process of interpreting a rule of national private law in conformity with a rule of EU law (harmonious interpretation).[3]

It should be mentioned that the harmonious interpretation of national law may replace the direct application of EU law in horizontal relationships, provided that the same substantive result is reached.

Moreover, a rule of EU law can also exert influence regardless of the nature of the legal relationship. This happens when the applicable provision of national origin is subject to review against a rule of EU law and must be disapplied if it conflicts with it. If the provision of national origin is disapplied in a private law dispute, the disapplication does not (or at any rate not *immediately*) change the private law relationship, but rather the rule on the basis of which the relationship must be assessed. Via this mechanism, however, the EU law rule may generate changes in the private law relationship.[4]

---

[1] AS Hartkamp, 'Horizontal Effects (or "Effects in Relationships between Individuals") of EU Law' in Hartkamp/Sieburgh/Keus/Kortmann/Wissink (eds) 2014 57–71; Hartkamp 2011 nos 6, 7 and 11–13 and for an extensive discussion of the forms of influence exerted by the TFEU: Hartkamp 2016 nos 31 ff (review of national private law legislation against the TFEU), nos 42 ff (direct horizontal effect of the TFEU), nos 92 ff (indirect horizontal effect of the TFEU), nos 96 ff (interpretation of national law in light of the TFEU), nos 143 ff (review of national legislation and direct horizontal effect of the general principles of EU law), nos 154 (the operation of directives in private law) and nos 181 ff (harmonious interpretation).

[2] See section II.A in Ch 1 of this casebook. See also the literature mentioned in footnote 1.

[3] See section II.B.ii in Ch 1.

[4] See section II.B.iv in Ch 1. It should be pointed out that according to settled case law of the CJEU, the plea that a rule of national origin must be disapplied because it conflicts with a directive provision cannot be raised in disputes between individuals; see section II.B.i. in Ch 6.

So far, the CJ has not applied the general EU law principle of non-discrimination by according it direct horizontal effect in the sense described above. This means that the principle does not directly influence legal relationships between individuals: it does not create, modify or extinguish rights or obligations between them. The principle does not by itself create rights and obligations for individuals on which they can rely against another individual in the national courts.[5]

However, the principle has been used as a criterion for reviewing national legislation. In a private law relationship, disapplication of national provisions on account of conflict with the general EU law principle can have the result that the private law relationship comes into conflict with the law that revives after such disapplication. It is precisely in this step that surprises are lurking in the private law context. Cases in which this mechanism finds expression are discussed in section II in Chapter 5.

Since EU law may exert its influence on a horizontal relationship via different mechanisms, this chapter classifies case law into categories on the basis of the mechanism used. These mechanisms are: (i) direct effect of the EU rule; (ii) indirect effect of the EU law rationale via a national rule that is in conformity with a rule of EU law, by harmonious interpretation of a national rule that is not in conformity with EU law or by review of an incompatible rule of national law against EU law; (iii) positive obligation of Member States. Category (iv), 'miscellaneous', comprises cases in which national private law is influenced in yet other ways.

The reader should be aware of the following. In my discussion of category (ii), I will include the use of an open norm of national law to ensure conformity of national law with EU law, whether or not this is imposed by EU law (see sections II.B.i and II.B.ii in Chapter 1). It is possible, for example, to interpret an open norm such as a national standard of due care by reference to Article 108(3) TFEU (obligation to inform the EC of intentions to grant aid)[6] or to a directive which has not or not yet been implemented or which has been implemented incorrectly.[7] Moreover, under (iv) 'miscellaneous', I will discuss cases in which a national law that is *not* in conformity with EU law is nevertheless applied. These cases are examples of judgments in breach of EU law. If delivered by the highest national court, they can be a basis for Member State liability under the *Francovich* doctrine.

I.B STRUCTURE OF THIS CHAPTER

This chapter opens with an introduction to the principle of non-discrimination as part of EU law (section II). Section III describes the sources: the Treaty provisions on non-discrimination, the relevant case law of the CJ, and the integration of the prohibition into the laws of the Member States and into soft law. The description of cases of national courts in section IV is followed by a comparison in section V, which aims at making clear the different approaches taken by the courts of the Member States when they apply EU law and national law in horizontal relationships. Further Reading contains references to legal doctrine.

---

[5] Possibly, the CJ hints at the direct horizontal effect of the prohibition of discrimination in CJ 15 January 2014 Case C-176/12 *Association de médiation sociale v Union locale des syndicats CGT et al* nyr ECLI:EU:C:2014:2, para 47. See, with references, Hartkamp 2016 nos 231a ff.

[6] Hartkamp 2011 no 13; Hartkamp 2016 no 94.

[7] See sections II.B and V in Ch 6.

II. INTRODUCTION TO THE PRINCIPLE OF NON-DISCRIMINATION

EU law contains a number of concrete provisions specifying the principle of equality.[8] In primary EU law, these include Articles 2 and 3(3), second para TEU; Articles 8, 10, 18, 19, 21, 40(2), 45, 49, 56, 63, 106(1), 110, 111, 157 TFEU; and Articles 20, 21(1) and 23(1) of the Charter read in conjunction with Article 6 TEU.[9] Other principles which likewise have the nature of primary EU law are the principles of equal treatment and non-discrimination recognised by the CJEU[10] and the principles of non-discrimination on grounds of sex,[11] age,[12] sexual orientation[13] and nationality[14] that the CJEU has developed as general principles of EU law. The CJ has construed the last-mentioned principle (nationality) to be 'a specific expression of the general principle of equality, which is itself one of the fundamental principles of [EU] law'.[15] In secondary EU law, the principle of equality is enshrined in numerous directives, for example, in the anti-discrimination directives.[16]

General principles of EU law fill gaps, and their own specific meaning is determined on the basis of the Charter.

In its judgment in *ČEZ*, the CJ inferred the principle of non-discrimination from the Treaty text, namely from [now Article 18 TFEU] which prohibits any discrimination on grounds of nationality. In *Test-Achats*,[17] the CJ refers to Articles 21 and 23 of the Charter and to Articles 157 and 19 TFEU. The reasoning by which the CJ has arrived at formulating general principles of EU law makes it likely that it will use Article 21(1) of the Charter as a basis for also recognising as general principles of EU law the prohibitions

---

[8] For an interesting and detailed discussion of cases in which grounds of discrimination concur, see D Schiek, 'Age Discrimination before the ECJ: Conceptual and Theoretical Issues' (2011) 48(3) *CMLR* 777 ff. Schiek points out that (seemingly justified) discrimination on grounds of age often conceals discrimination on grounds of sex or race, for which there is usually no justification.

[9] An exhaustive overview is presented in K Lenaerts, 'L'Égalité de Traitement en Droit Communautaire, un principe unique aux apparences multiples' (1991) 27 *CDE* 3 ff.

[10] CJ 13 October 2005 Case C-458/03 *Parking Brixen GmbH v Gemeinde Brixen and Stadtwerke Brixen AG* [2005] I-8585 ECLI:EU:C:2005:605, para 52 (see Hartkamp 2011 no 12).

[11] CJ 15 June 1978 Case C-149/77 *Defrenne v Sabena (Defrenne III)* [1978] I-01365 ECLI:EU:C:1978:130, para 27.

[12] CJ 19 January 2010 Case C-555/07 *Kücükdeveci v Swedex* [2010] I-00365 ECLI:EU:C:2010:21.

[13] CJ 10 May 2011 Case C-147/08 *Römer v Freie und Hansestadt Hamburg* [2011] I-03591 ECLI:EU:C:2011:286, paras 59 and 60.

[14] CJ 27 October 2009 Case C-115/08 *Land Oberösterreich v ČEZ as* [2009] I-10265 ECLI:EU:C:2009:660.

[15] ibid, para 89.

[16] Council Directive 2004/113/EC of 13 December 2004 implementing the principle of equal treatment between men and women in the access to and supply of goods and services [2004] OJ L373/37; Council Directive 2000/43/EC of 29 June 2000 implementing the principle of equal treatment between persons irrespective of racial or ethnic origin [2000] OJ L180/226; Council Directive 2000/78/EC of 27 November 2000 establishing a general framework for equal treatment in employment and occupation [2000] OJ L303/16; Directive 2006/54/EC of the European Parliament and of the Council of 5 July 2006 on the implementation of the principle of equal opportunities and equal treatment of men and women in matters of employment and occupation [2006] OJ L204/23.

[17] CJ 1 March 2011 Case C-236/09 *Test-Achats ASBL et al v Conseil des ministres* [2011] I-00773 ECLI:EU:C:2011:100.

of discrimination on grounds of race, colour, ethnic or social origin, genetic features, language, religion or belief, political or any other opinion, membership of a national minority, property, birth or disability.[18]

All handbooks on substantive EU law stress the importance of equality as a legal concept in EU law.

T Tridimas, The General Principles of EU Law[19]

In [EU] law, equality as a legal concept is omnipresent. It operates at a number of different levels and it may be said that, in contemporary [EU] law, equality is understood primarily as participation, integration, opportunity and empowerment. Although these functions are inter-related and overlapping, they underlie different strands in the case law.

T Tridimas, The General Principles of EU Law[20]

The principle of equality binds the [EU] institutions and also the Member States, where they implement, or act within the scope of, [EU] law. In certain circumstances, it may bind natural and legal persons. This occurs in particular in three areas: prohibition of discrimination on grounds of nationality, prohibition of sex discrimination, and prohibition of anti-competitive conduct.

According to the case law of the CJEU, many provisions on non-discrimination in primary EU law produce direct horizontal effect. The advantages seem to override the drawbacks. Nevertheless, it remains essential to assess the specificity of private law and horizontal relationships. It should be accepted that justifications reflecting private law interests may be available to individuals.

T Tridimas, The General Principles of EU Law[21]

The case law accepts that certain provisions of the EC Treaty [now the TFEU] may produce horizontal effect. In *Defrenne v. Sabena* it was held that [now Article 157 TFEU], which provides for the principle of equal pay between men and women for equal work, establishes a right to equal pay which can be relied on in national courts against both public and private employees. In *Walrave and Koch v. Association Union Cycliste Internationale* it was held that the prohibition of discrimination on grounds of nationality, as incorporated in [now Articles 18, 40 and 56 TFEU], does not apply only to the actions of public authorities but extends also to rules of private organisations which aim at regulating in a collective manner gainful employment and the provision of services.

Subsequently, in *Bosman* the Court reiterated that [now Article 45 TFEU], which provides for the free movement of workers, applied to the football transfer rules of the international football federations FIFA and UEFA. Both in *Walrave* and *Bosman*, however, the provisions of the Treaty on free movement were applied against private associations

---

[18] See with respect to religion or belief, disablement and sexual orientation and, by analogy, race or ethnic origin CJ 22 November 2005 Case C-144/04 *Mangold v Helm* [2005] I-09981 ECLI:EU:C:2005:709, para 74.
[19] Tridimas 2006, 60.
[20] ibid 74–75. See also Hartkamp 2016 no 53; Craig and De Búrca 2015 564 ff, 892 ff; K Lenaerts and P van Nuffel, *Constitutional Law of The European Union*, 3rd edn (London, Sweet & Maxwell, 2011) 500–06.
[21] Tridimas 2006, 49–50.

which exercised some type of regulatory action and had therefore a quasi-public character. More recently, in *Angonese v. Cassa die Risparmio di Bolzano SpA*, the court unequivocally held that [now Article 45] has horizontal direct effect and binds private employers also. It pointed out that the principle of non-discrimination in [now Article 45] is drafted in general terms and is not specifically addressed to the Member States. It then referred to its reasoning in *Defrenne* and held that it applied a fortiori in the case of [now Article 45] which lays down a fundamental freedom. The extension of [now Article 45] to cover fully-fledged horizontal situations has been criticised mainly on two grounds. First, on the ground that the Court intervenes in the sphere of private autonomy and creates legal uncertainty, and second, on the ground that it upsets the balance of competence between the community and the Member States by intervening in the sphere of private law which falls within the remit of the latter. This however does not appear a persuasive criticism. The judicial arguments underlying the progressive extension of horizontality are the need to ensure the effectiveness of fundamental freedoms and, as the Court put it in *Angonese*, to avoid discrimination in the labour market. Within the European polity, the prohibition of discrimination can best be viewed as norms of constitutional status whose value and effects are not exhausted in vertical situations. Also, the competence of the [EU] to harmonize key areas of national private law, such as contract law, is well settled. Against this background, it would be the denial of horizontal effect of [now Article 45] against a private employer that could be viewed as an aberration rather than its acceptance. This is not to say that horizontality is without problems. Once it is accepted that [now Article 45] binds private employers, it should also be accepted that the latter have available to them the derogations from the free movement of workers recognized in the Treaty and the case law. These however have been designed as defences for public and not for private action. Inevitably, those derogations will need to be tailored to the defence of private parties and, in some contexts, interpreted more broadly.

The Court has not unequivocally pronounced on the horizontality of the other fundamental freedoms, but the reasoning of *Angonese* may apply also, at least in some respects, to the freedom to provide services and the right of establishment. Notably, in a recent case, the Queen's Bench Division held that a maritime company could rely on the right of establishment, as guaranteed by [now Article 49 TFEU], to obtain an injunction against trade unions threatening strike action. Such uncompromising application of [now Article 49 TFEU] raises fundamental issues pertaining to the scope and objectives of free movement.

The consequences for private law (eg, sanctions for violation of a prohibition), private law relationships and reasoning in private law (eg, justification) can and should be assessed, given the importance of the prohibition of discrimination and given the interpretation by the CJEU of provisions on non-discrimination in EU primary law.

A Hartkamp, European Law and National Private Law[22]

Outside the competition regulations, the question whether provisions of the TFEU have direct horizontal effect plays a role in connection with the provisions relating to discrimination and the free movement provisions. The main provisions relating to discrimination—apart from the prohibitions implied in the free movement provisions—are

---

[22] Hartkamp 2016 nos 53, 55, 64 and 66. See also Tridimas 2006 49–50.

article 18(1) TFEU (discrimination based on nationality) and article 157(1)TFEU (equality of pay for male and female workers). The case law of the Court of Justice shows that these provisions have direct horizontal effect …

The judgments do not say anything about sanctions for violation of a prohibition on discrimination. In principle, these are governed by national law and depend on the circumstances of the case. Naturally, nullity of a legal act will be one of the possible sanctions … The fact that a nullity sanction is consistent with the system of European discrimination law is also apparent from article 7(4) of Directive 1612/68 on the free movement for workers, which declares that any clause of a collective or individual agreement or of any other collective regulation concerning eligibility for employment, remuneration and other conditions of work or dismissal shall be null and void in so far as it lays down or authorises discriminatory conditions in respect of workers who are nationals of other member states.

A problem with according direct horizontal effect to treaty provisions on discrimination and on the free movement of persons and services is that their wording or context shows that within the system of the treaty they were intended as regulations addressed to the member states. This raises the question whether the exceptions based on the general interest, which may constitute grounds for justifying national measures that violate the prohibitions, may also be relied on by individuals and—more importantly—whether individuals can also invoke other grounds to restrict the scope of the prohibition. A move in this direction is necessary. It is likely that such a move will take place on the basis of the general principles of EU law and the Charter …

In my opinion it is not acceptable to accord direct horizontal effect to treaty provisions on the one hand, while leaving the system of exceptions unchanged on the other hand, so that the requirement would apply that the justification invoked by a defendant must relate to the protection of a public interest. Though it is not excluded that individuals may rely on public interest exceptions, as is rightly stated in *Bosman* (see sub (c) above) … individuals will usually not be able to satisfy this requirement. Such a system, which does not allow for the balancing of party interests that is typical of private law, would too severely restrict the freedom of individuals to act in general and their freedom to contract in particular, also in view of the weight given to the freedom to contract as being of equal value as a fundamental right …

III. SOURCES

III.A EU RULES PRODUCING DIRECT HORIZONTAL EFFECT

III.A.i ARTICLE 18 TFEU

Article 18 TFEU **4.1 (EU)**

1. Within the scope of application of the Treaties, and without prejudice to any special provisions contained therein, any discrimination on grounds of nationality shall be prohibited.

2. The European Parliament and the Council, acting in accordance with the ordinary legislative procedure, may adopt rules designed to prohibit such discrimination.

The right to equal treatment irrespective of nationality is one of the cornerstones of EU law.

In *Walrave*,[23] the CJ interpreted Article 18 TFEU in conjunction with Article 45 TFEU (free movement of workers) and Article 56 TFEU (freedom of services) to mean that any discrimination on grounds of nationality is prohibited and that this prohibition does not only apply to actions of public authorities, but likewise extends to rules of any other nature aimed at regulating in a collective manner gainful employment and the provision of services. The CJ ruled that:

> [T]he abolition as between Member States of obstacles to freedom of movement for persons and to freedom to provide services, which are fundamental objectives of the [EU] contained in Article 3(c) of the [EEC] Treaty, would be compromised if the abolition of barriers of national origin could be neutralized by obstacles resulting from the exercise of their legal autonomy by associations or organizations which do not come under public law … Since, moreover, working conditions in the various Member States are governed sometimes by means of provisions laid down by law or regulation and sometimes by agreements and other acts concluded or adopted by private persons, to limit the prohibitions in question to acts of a public authority would risk creating inequality in their application.

Accordingly, it held that a provision in the rules of the International Cycling Union relating to medium-distance world cycling championships behind motorcycles, according to which the pacemaker must have the same nationality as the stayer, was incompatible with the free movement of persons. According to some authors, this judgment must be understood as restricting the horizontal effect of Article 18 TFEU to collective agreements only. However, subsequent case law has shown that this is not the case.

In *Haug-Adrion*,[24] the CJ held that Article 18 TFEU, in combination with Articles 45 (free movement of workers), 56 and 61 (freedom of services) TFEU, was applicable to a stipulation in the general conditions of an insurance agreement. However, there was nothing to suggest that the clause in question, which refused a no-claims bonus to insured persons resident in another Member State who owned a vehicle registered under custom plates, gave any advantage whatever to national products or to the domestic market. Consequently, the CJ held that the refusal was not contrary to any provision of EU law insofar as it was based solely on objective actuarial criteria applied in a non-discriminatory manner. In *Ferlini*,[25] the CJ ruled that in the absence of an objective justification, the application by a group of healthcare providers, on a unilateral basis, of higher fee scales for medical and hospital maternity care to EC officials than to residents affiliated to the national social security scheme constituted discrimination on grounds of nationality prohibited under Article 18 TFEU. Moreover, it underlined the applicability of Article 18 TFEU in cases where a group or organisation exercises a certain power over individuals and is in a position to impose on them conditions which adversely affect the exercise of the fundamental freedoms guaranteed under the Treaty.

---

[23] CJ 12 December 1974 Case C-37/74 *Walrave and Koch v Association Union cycliste internationale, Koninklijke Nederlandsche Wielren Unie and Federación Española Ciclismo* [1974] I-01495 ECLI:EU:C:1974:140.

[24] CJ 13 December 1984 Case C-251/83 *Haug-Adrion v Frankfurter Versicherungs-AG* [1984] I-04277 ECLI:EU:C:1984:397.

[25] CJ 3 October 2000 Case C-411/98 *Ferlini v Centre hospitalier de Luxembourg* [2000] I-08081 ECLI:EU:C:2000:530.

Just as in *Ferlini*, the CJ reiterated in *Angonese*[26] that Article 45 TFEU (free movement of workers) constitutes a specific application of the general prohibition of discrimination contained in Article 18 TFEU and is thus designed to ensure that there is no discrimination on the labour market. Consequently, it held that the prohibition of discrimination on grounds of nationality laid down in Article 45 TFEU applied to individuals as well. As a result, this Article precluded an employer from requiring applicants who applied to take part in a recruitment competition to provide evidence of their linguistic knowledge exclusively by means of one particular diploma issued only in one particular province of a Member State. The same legal grounds were again stated in *Raccanelli*[27] regarding the inequality in opportunities to conclude an employment contract with the research centre between domestic and foreign doctoral students. As neither Article 45 TFEU nor Regulation No 1612/68[28] prescribed a specific measure to be taken by the Member States or associations like the research centre in question in the event of a breach of the prohibition of discrimination, so the CJ held, the Member States are free to choose between the different solutions suitable for achieving the objective of the respective provisions, depending on the different situations which may arise. As a result, the national court must assess the nature of the compensation which the applicant would be entitled to claim in the light of the national legislation applicable in relation to non-contractual liability.

It will be seen that in national case law, the general prohibition to discriminate on the basis of nationality is replaced, in conformity with standing case law of the CJEU, by more specific Treaty provisions, such as those on fundamental freedoms.[29]

T Tridimas, The General Principles of EU Law[30]

Viewed in historical perspective, the right to equal treatment irrespective of nationality is the most important right conferred by substantive [EU] law … [now Article 18 TFEU] has direct effect. According to the case law it produces both vertical and, at least in some cases, horizontal direct effect so that national courts must enforce rights deriving from that provision not only against public authorities but also against individuals. The prohibition of discrimination on grounds of nationality is implemented in specific spheres of [EU] law by a number of Treaty provisions, e.g. [now Article 45 TFEU] (free movement of workers), [now Article 49 TFEU] (right of establishment), [now Article 56 TFEU] (free movement of services) and [now Article 55] (participation of non-nationals in the capital companies). [now Article 18 TFEU] has a residual character. It is of autonomous application only in situations governed by [EU] law in relation to which the Treaty does not lay down a specific prohibition of discrimination. It performs therefore a 'gap-filling' function … As we shall see, the case law has understood [now Article 18 TFEU] as being an autonomous source of rights and obligations outside the sphere of free movement.

---

[26] CJ 6 June 2000 Case C-281/98 *Angonese v Cassa di Risparmio di Bolzano SpA* [2000] I-04139 ECLI:EU:C:2000:296.

[27] CJ 17 July 2008 Case C-94/07 *Raccanelli v Max-Planck-Gesellschaft zur Förderung der Wissenschaften eV* [2008] I-05939 ECLI:EU:CL2008:425.

[28] Regulation (EEC) No 1612/68 of the Council of 15 October 1968 on freedom of movement for workers within the Community [1968] OJ L257/2.

[29] See also J Temple Lang, 'Emerging European General Principles in Private Law' in Bernitz/Groussot/Schulyok et al (eds) 2013 75–77.

[30] Tridimas 2006 118–20.

X Groussot, General Principles of Community Law[31]

It ought to be noted that two general provisions are based on discrimination on grounds of nationality ([now Article 18 TFEU] …) and of gender ([now Article 157 TFEU] …). These provisions are general in the sense that they may spill over into different fields of [EU] law without touching a specific area of policy. Concerning [now Article 18 TFEU], the case-law has often linked it conscientiously to the free movement provisions. However, the recent jurisprudential development makes it a self-standing provision.

The interpretation given by the CJEU to Article 18 TFEU includes its capability of producing direct horizontal effect. A comprehensive and coherent reading of the CJEU's case law shows that this direct horizontal effect is not limited to collective agreements. The consequences of direct horizontal effect for private law (eg, sanctions for violation of a prohibition) and private law relationships are left to national law.

A Hartkamp, European Law and National Private Law[32]

Direct horizontal effect: prohibitions on discrimination. Outside the competition regulations, the question whether provisions of the FEU Treaty have direct horizontal effect plays a role in connection with the provisions relating to discrimination and the free movement provisions. The main provisions relating to discrimination—apart from the prohibitions implied in the free movement provisions—are article 18(1) TFEU (discrimination based on nationality) and article 157(1) TFEU (equality of pay for male and female workers). The case law of the Court of Justice shows that these provisions have direct horizontal effect.

With regard to the predecessor of article 157 TFEU (article 141(1) EC), the Court of Justice ruled in *Defrenne v Sabena I* (43/75) that the principle of equal pay is one of the foundations of the [EU], and that the provision is mandatory in nature so that 'the prohibition on discrimination between men and women applies not only to the action of public authorities, but also extends to all agreements which are intended to regulate paid labour collectively, as well as to contracts between individuals'. It should be noted that the fact that the provision is addressed to the member states did not prevent the conclusion at which the Court arrived. In *Defrenne v Sabena II* (149/77) the ECJ added that there is no doubt that the elimination of discrimination based on sex forms part of the fundamental rights, the respect for which is one of the general principles of [EU] law and the observance of which it has a duty to ensure.

…

The fact that the same holds true for article 18 TFEU appears from the judgment in *Walrave* (36/74), in which that provision was interpreted, in conjunction with Article 45 TFEU, free movement for workers and Article 56 TFEU, freedom of services, to mean that all discrimination on grounds of nationality is prohibited and that this prohibition does not only apply to the action of public authorities but extends likewise to rules of any other nature aimed at regulating in a collective manner gainful employment and the provision of services:

The abolition as between Member States of obstacles to freedom of movement for persons and to freedom to provide services, which are fundamental objectives of the

---

[31] X Groussot, *General Principles of Community Law* (Groningen, Europa Law Publishing, 2006) 162.
[32] Hartkamp 2016 nos 53, 54 and 61.

[EU] contained in article 3(c) of the (EEC) Treaty, would be compromised if the abolition of barriers of national origin could be neutralized by obstacles resulting from the
exercise of their legal autonomy by associations or organizations which do not come
under public law.

The judgment further states that Article 45 TFEU also extends to agreements and rules
which do not emanate from public authorities, including non-collective agreements
between individuals as well. This extension is not repeated in the operative part of the
judgment, from which some authors inferred that the horizontal effect of article 18 TFEU
is restricted to 'collective arrangements'. Subsequent case law has shown that this is not
correct. In *Haug-Adrion* (251/83) the provision was found applicable to stipulations in an
insurance agreement. This line is continued in subsequent judgments (*Ferlini*, C-411/98,
and *Angonese*, C-281/98): in *Ferlini* the ECJ observes that Article 45 TFEU implements
the prohibition of Article 18 TFEU with regard to the freedom of movement for workers (paragraph 40), while it ruled in *Angonese* (with reference inter alia to *Walrave* and
Defrenne v Sabena I) that the prohibition of discrimination on grounds of nationality laid
down in Article 45 TFEU applies to individuals as well (paragraph 36). This is repeated in
Raccanelli (C-94/07) …

   … The ECJ does not make any specific mention of the consequences of horizontal
effect. It usually confines itself to establishing that the aforementioned treaty provisions
are also applicable to the challenged provision of the collective rules or the agreement.
The consequences are manifestly left to national law, albeit subject to review by the ECJ,
which extends to cover both proportionality (*Olympique Lyonnais*, C-325/08) and effectiveness. It is clear that nullity is one of those consequences and this is confirmed by the
considerations in *Walrave* and in *Dona* (13/76), where the ECJ states that the provisions
of [now Article 18 TFEU], [now Article 45 TFEU] and [now Article 56 TFEU] may (or must,
respectively) be taken into account by the national court in judging the 'validity or the
effects' of a provision inserted in the rules of a sporting organization …

III.A.ii ARTICLE 157 TFEU

Article 157 TFEU   **4.2 (EU)**

1. Each Member State shall ensure that the principle of equal pay for male and female
workers for equal work or work of equal value is applied.
   2. For the purpose of this Article, 'pay' means the ordinary basic or minimum wage or
salary and any other consideration, whether in cash or in kind, which the worker receives
directly or indirectly, in respect of his employment, from his employer.
   Equal pay without discrimination based on sex means:

(a) that pay for the same work at piece rates shall be calculated on the basis of the
same unit of measurement;
(b) that pay for work at time rates shall be the same for the same job.

3. The European Parliament and the Council, acting in accordance with the ordinary
legislative procedure, and after consulting the Economic and Social Committee, shall
adopt measures to ensure the application of the principle of equal opportunities and
equal treatment of men and women in matters of employment and occupation, including
the principle of equal pay for equal work or work of equal value.
   4. With a view to ensuring full equality in practice between men and women in
working life, the principle of equal treatment shall not prevent any Member State from

maintaining or adopting measures providing for specific advantages in order to make it easier for the underrepresented sex to pursue a vocational activity or to prevent or compensate for disadvantages in professional careers.

In *Defrenne I*,[33] concerning compensation claimed by an air hostess from her employer on the ground that as a female worker she was discriminated against in terms of pay as compared with male colleagues doing the same work as cabin stewards, the CJ ruled that Article 157 TFEU is mandatory in nature so that 'the prohibition on discrimination between men and women applies not only to the action of public authorities, but also extends to all agreements which are intended to regulate paid labour collectively, as well as to contracts between individuals'. As a consequence, Article 157 may be relied upon before the national courts and these courts have a duty to ensure the protection of the rights conferred on individuals by this provision. In *Defrenne II*,[34] the CJ added that there is no doubt that the elimination of discrimination based on sex forms part of the fundamental rights, the respect for which is one of the general principles of EU law and the observance of which it has a duty to ensure. However, Article 157 TFEU cannot be interpreted to mean that, in addition to equal pay, it prescribes general equality of the other working conditions applicable to men and women.

Even in its early case law, the CJEU interpreted Article 157 TFEU as being capable of producing direct horizontal effect. The CJEU has placed greater emphasis on the Article's social aim than on its economic aim.

See additionally section III.A.i with an excerpt from A Hartkamp, *European Law and National Private Law* and the following text:

P Craig and G de Búrca, EU Law: Text, Cases and Materials[35]

While the equal pay rule was undoubtedly intended to 'level the playing field' by ensuring that employers in no one Member State would have this competitive advantage over those in another Member State, the CJ declared, even in its early case law, that Article 157 had a social and not just an economic aim. In the first *Defrenne* case, Belgium argued that the aim of this provision was economic only, namely 'to avoid discrepancies in cost prices due to the employment of female labour less well paid for the same work than male labour. The court rejected this view in *Defrenne II* ...

Thus the social aim of Article 157 TFEU, read in the light of the CJ's case law on fundamental human rights, had come to take precedence over its economic rationale. Moreover, while *Schröder* is an equal pay case, the Court's ruling seemed to refer to Article 157 TFEU and the equal treatment principle more generally.

The emphasis on human rights rather than on economic competitiveness as the primary rationale for EU equal treatment law is evident now in the preambles to recent legislation, including the consolidating Directive 2006/54 as well as in the Article 19 anti-discrimination Directives adopted in 2000.

---

[33] CJ 25 May 1971 Case C–80/70 *Gabrielle Defrenne v Belgian State (Defrenne I)* [1971] I-00445 ECLI:EU:C:1971:55.

[34] CJ 8 April 1976 Case C-43/75 *Gabrielle Defrenne v Société anonyme belge de navigation aérienne Sabena (Defrenne II)* [1976] I-00455 ECLI:EY:C:1987:56.

[35] Craig and De Búrca 2015 896–860. See also Tridimas 2006, excerpt in this chapter, section II.

III.B EU RULES NOT PRODUCING DIRECT HORIZONTAL EFFECT

III.B.i ARTICLE 19 TFEU

Article 19 TFEU   **4.3 (EU)**

1. Without prejudice to the other provisions of the Treaties and within the limits of the powers conferred by them upon the Union, the Council, acting unanimously in accordance with a special legislative procedure and after obtaining the consent of the European Parliament, may take appropriate action to combat discrimination based on sex, racial or ethnic origin, religion or belief, disability, age or sexual orientation.

2. By way of derogation from paragraph 1, the European Parliament and the Council, acting in accordance with the ordinary legislative procedure, may adopt the basic principles of Union incentive measures, excluding any harmonisation of the laws and regulations of the Member States, to support action taken by the Member States in order to contribute to the achievement of the objectives referred to in paragraph 1.

Even though Article 19 TFEU does not itself impose any specific legal obligations on Member States, let alone on individuals, it has an important symbolic and legal value for EU law. In view of its wording, it serves as a basis for secondary legislation, such as Directive 2000/78/EC[36] establishing a general framework for equal treatment in employment and occupation. This Directive played a role in *Mangold* and *Kücükdeveci*.[37] It also served as the basis for Directive 2004/113[38] on equal treatment between men and women in the access to and the supply of goods and services, which played a role in *Test-Achats*.[39] For these cases, see sections II.B and II.C.iv and cases 5.2 (GERM), 5.6 (GERM), 5.10 (BE) and 5.11 (BE) in Chapter 5. See also section V.B in Chapter 6.

To date, Article 19 TFEU has had limited importance in private law. In the future, this Article may exert influence on private law relationships through the techniques distinguished in sections II.C.v and II.C.vi in Chapter 1, section I.A in Chapter 4 and section II.A.ii in Chapter 5.

T Tridimas, The General Principles of EU Law[40]

[Now Article 19 TFEU], inserted by the Treaty of Amsterdam, provides an all-embracing legal basis for the adoption of measures to combat discrimination 'based on sex, racial or ethnic origin, religion or belief, disability, age or sexual orientation'. This is an important provision which has a symbolic and legal value … [now Article 19 TFEU] provides the basis for taking action to combat discrimination but does not itself impose any specific legal obligations on Member States. It does not therefore have direct effect.

---

[36] [2000] OJ L303/12 (n 16).
[37] CJ *Mangold* (n 18); and CJ *Kücükdeveci* (n 12).
[38] [2004] OJ L373/37 (n 16).
[39] CJ *Test-Achats* (n 17).
[40] Tridimas 2006 64.

III.C INTEGRATION OF NON-DISCRIMINATION INTO THE LAWS OF THE MEMBER STATES

For national legislation and for the way in which non-discrimination has in general been adopted in civil law systems and common law systems, see the *Ius Commune Casebook on Non-discrimination Law*.[41] Where this is important for the discussion in this chapter, I will give separate consideration to how the EU rules on non-discrimination have been adopted (eg, how Articles 18 and 157 TFEU have been implemented in the national legislation of the UK: see section IV.B.ii.a below).

For an elaboration of the directives dealing with non-discrimination, see the *Ius Commune Casebook on Non-discrimination Law*.[42]

III.D SOFT LAW

DCFR Book II Chapter 2: Non-discrimination   **4.4 (EU)**

Article II.-2:101: Right not to be discriminated against
   A person has a right not to be discriminated against on the grounds of sex or ethnic or racial origin in relation to a contract or other juridical act the object of which is to provide access to, or supply, goods, other assets or services which are available to the public.

Article II.-2:102: Meaning of discrimination
   (1) 'Discrimination' means any conduct whereby, or situation where, on grounds such as those mentioned in the preceding Article:
   (a) one person is treated less favourably than another person is, has been or would be treated in a comparable situation; or
   (b) an apparently neutral provision, criterion or practice would place one group of persons at a particular disadvantage when compared to a different group of persons.

   (2) Discrimination also includes harassment on grounds such as those mentioned in the preceding Article. 'Harassment' means unwanted conduct (including conduct of a sexual nature) which violates a person's dignity, particularly when such conduct creates an intimidating, hostile, degrading, humiliating or offensive environment, or which aims to do so.
   (3) Any instruction to discriminate also amounts to discrimination.

Article II.-2:103: Exception
Unequal treatment which is justified by a legitimate aim does not amount to discrimination if the means used to achieve that aim are appropriate and necessary.

Article II.-2:104: Remedies
   (1) If a person is discriminated against contrary to II.-2:101 (Right not to be discriminated against) then, without prejudice to any remedy which may be available under Book VI (Non-contractual liability for damage caused to another), the remedies for

---

[41] D Schiek, L Waddington and M Bell (eds), *Ius Commune Casebooks for the Common Law of Europe, Cases, Materials and Text on National, Supranational and International Non-discrimination Law* (Oxford, Hart Publishing, 2007).
[42] ibid.

non-performance of an obligation under Book III, Chapter 3 (including damages for economic and noneconomic loss) are available.

(2) Any remedy granted should be proportionate to the injury or anticipated injury; the dissuasive effect of remedies may be taken into account.

Article II.-2:105: Burden of proof

(1) If a person who considers himself or herself discriminated against on one of the grounds mentioned in II.-2:101 (Right not to be discriminated against) establishes, before a court or another competent authority, facts from which it may be presumed that there has been such discrimination, it falls on the other party to prove that there has been no such discrimination.

(2) Paragraph (1) does not apply to proceedings in which it is for the court or another competent authority to investigate the facts of the case.

DCFR Book III Chapter 1: General   **4.5 (EU)**

Article III.-1:105: Non-discrimination

Chapter 2 (Non-discrimination) of Book II applies with appropriate adaptations to:

(a) the performance of any obligation to provide access to, or supply, goods, other assets or services which are available to members of the public:

(b) the exercise of a right to performance of any such obligation or the pursuing or defending of any remedy for non-performance of any such obligation: and

(c) the exercise of a right to terminate any such obligation.

These provisions are not part of current law. Nevertheless, I will discuss them here because they can serve as a source of inspiration for EU private law when one has to deal with issues of non-discrimination.

As Articles II-2:101 and III-1:105 show, the provisions only cover (the performance of) contracts and other juridical acts aimed at creating obligations to provide access to, or supply, goods, other assets or services which are available to the public.

For the subject of this casebook—the influence of primary EU law on horizontal relationships—it is important to note that these provisions, which are aimed at horizontal relationships, expressly provide for a general exception: Article II-2:103. If the exception is applicable, unequal treatment is justified.

The provisions do not define any specific grounds for exceptions. Most probably the legitimacy of the appropriate and necessary aim must be assessed in the context of the horizontal relationship under scrutiny. This approach implies that aims relating to private law interests can be a ground for justifying discrimination.

Possible remedies are those available for non-contractual liability for damage caused to another and for non-performance of an obligation, including damages for economic and non-economic loss.

IV. NATIONAL CASE LAW

This section presents cases decided by national courts in horizontal relationships in which Articles 18 and 157 TFEU were applied (or should have been applied). No national case law has been reported with respect to Article 19 TFEU.

The users of this casebook are kindly invited to report developments in national case law involving Articles 18, 157 and 19 TFEU in horizontal relationships which might be interesting for a second edition of this book.

Relevant cases were selected on the basis of the following criteria: does the case involve a situation between individuals and, if not, are there horizontal relationships behind the litigating Member State and individual (eg, third parties that have a horizontal relationship with the individual or whose legal relationship changes due to a CJ ruling against the Member State) on which EU law exerts influence? What are the facts and what are the rules of national origin which are primarily applicable?

Subsequently, each case was subjected to the following sequence of questions: (i) did the case involve unequal treatment?; if so, (ii) did it fall within the scope of EU law?; if so, (iii) was the unequal treatment prohibited under EU law?; if so, (iv) did the national court use a mechanism (eg, direct application of EU law, harmonious interpretation or positive Member State obligation) to uphold the TFEU provision?; if so, (v) what were the consequences for the private law relationship?

IV.A NATIONAL CASE LAW WITHIN THE SCOPE OF ARTICLE 18 TFEU

IV.A.i DIRECT EFFECT OF THE EU RULE

This subsection presents cases from national jurisdictions in which the national courts applied Article 18 TFEU directly to the horizontal relationship.[43]

Individuals can only rely on the rights provided for by EU law if their case is covered by EU law (case 4.9 (FR)). The first step to determine the effect (if any) of EU law on a horizontal relationship is to assess whether or not it is covered by EU law.

In some of the cases presented below, the direct effect of provisions of primary EU law was or could have been responsible for remarkable substantive changes of the horizontal relationship, both regarding the effectuation of the right provided for by EU law and the enforcement of a right by, eg, the award of damages in case of infringement. See, for example, the Labour Division of the Court of First Instance of Bolzano 20 July 2011, in which the Italian court explicitly stated that Article 18 TFEU may also apply in horizontal relationships, even though the case in question concerned a vertical relationship between a female citizen of Czech nationality living in the town of Bolzano, and the Autonomous Province of Bolzano/South Tyrol, which refused to grant her a subsidy for rent on the ground of nationality.[44]

In other cases the effect of EU law did not change the substance of the horizontal relationship. Nevertheless, these cases are important because they demonstrate that national courts explicitly applied EU law and, by doing so, showed that they were aware of the fact that EU law is part of the framework regulating and thus shaping the horizontal relationship (case 4.8 (FR)).

---

[43] For the method of selecting cases and the structure of the presentation of the cases, see section IV below.

[44] Court of First Instance of Bolzano Labour Division 20 July 2011 no 342/2011 L.

One case shows that the national court was willing to consider an objective and reasonable justification for discrimination based on nationality (case 4.8 (FR)).

EU law does not protect against unfavourable treatment by a Member State of its own individuals as compared to nationals of other Member States (case 4.9 (FR)). This so-called reverse discrimination should be dealt with by mechanisms of national law.

Courts tend to derive diverse arguments from the situation that a citizen of their own Member State is treated less favourably. They sometimes even argue, erroneously, that a claim of a citizen from another Member State has to be refused for the reason that if the claim would be granted, he would be treated better than citizens who are nationals of the court's own Member State (case 4.13 (FR)).

Reverse discrimination is also discussed in sections IV.A.ii and IV.A.iv below.

Rechtbank van eerste aanleg Brussel (Court of First Instance of Brussels), 14 September 1992[45]   **4.6 (BE)**

C Markakis v Fédération Royale des Sociétés de Basketball

DISCRIMINATION BASED ON NATIONALITY

Shooting hoops

Pursuant to (now) Article 18 TFEU the provision in the regulations of a sporting league allowing only Belgians to participate in certain competitions may not be applied to professional sportsmen

Facts: Markakis, a Greek citizen and professional basketball player, had entered into a contract with a basketball club, under which he competed for remuneration in different competitions of the 1992–93 season. This contract was subject to the regulations of the Belgian basketball federation, which allowed only Belgians to participate in national and provincial basketball divisions. Therefore, Markakis was banned from these matches.

Held: Markakis invoked (now) Article 18 TFEU in interlocutory proceedings and sought a declaratory judgment that the regulations of the Belgian basketball federation were incompatible with this Article, which prohibits discrimination on grounds of nationality.

Judgment: Pursuant to [now Article 18 TFEU], which prohibits any discrimination on grounds of nationality, the provisions in the regulations of a sport federation which allow only Belgian nationals to participate in certain competitions, are not applicable to a foreigner engaging in a sports activity for remuneration. Given the urgency of the situation, the court in interlocutory proceedings may authorize the foreigner to engage in his sports activity for remuneration in the agreed competitions and may order the federation to refrain from preventing him from doing so until the court deciding on the merits has pronounced judgment.

... it is sufficiently likely that these principles apply to the facts of this case; the legal form of the defendant does not affect the problem before us; the fact that the regulations of the defendant were drawn up with the consent of the representative of inter alia the

---

[45] Court of First Instance of Brussels 14 September 1992 *Pas* 1992 III 103 *C Markakis v Fédération Royale des Sociétés de Basketball.*

club ... does not prevent Markakis from asserting the rights he derives in particular from [now the TFEU] and the Regulation adopted in implementation of it, and on which he may rely before the national courts; the difficulties do not lie at club membership level ... which the defendant does not as such criticize, but in the exercise of his profession as a basketball player, which is his livelihood, which implies that he must be able to participate in the championships, which article 245 of the defendant's regulations specifically prohibit.

Notes:

(1) A Greek citizen and professional basketball player entered into a contract with a basketball club under which the player was obliged to play basketball. One of the provisions of the regulations of the Belgian basketball federation which formed part of the contract excluded non-Belgian basketball players from participation in national and provincial basketball divisions.

(2) Applying Article 18 TFEU directly to the horizontal relationship, the Belgian national court hearing interlocutory proceedings set aside the contractual clause. Consequently, the professional basketball player was allowed to participate in the competitions. The Belgian basketball federation was ordered to allow the professional basketball player to perform his obligations under the contract concluded with the basketball club.

(3) The application of Article 18 TFEU reshaped two horizontal relationships. Transposed into private law reasoning, the national court intervened in both the contractual relationship between the player and the club, and the extra-contractual relationship between the player and the federation. After the court had set aside the contract clause that prevented the basketball player from playing, he was able to perform his obligations under the remaining provisions of the contract. By adding the injunction against the Belgian basketball federation, the national court ensured the effectiveness of the basketball player's right to perform his contractual obligations. The intervention in the extra-contractual relationship implied that the federation was acting unlawfully by maintaining the provision in its regulations concerning non-Belgium citizens in cases covered by EU law.

Cour de Cassation (Court of Cassation), 10 December 2002[46]   **4.7 (FR)**

Goethe Institut Association for the Promotion of the German Language Abroad and Cultural Exchanges v Bataille Zamolo

UNEQUAL COMPENSATION BASED ON NATIONALITY

Poetry employer

A dual system of remuneration on the basis of nationality is regarded as prohibited discrimination

Facts: Zamolo had worked since February 1985 as executive secretary at the Goethe Institute in Lille. Until 31 March 1991, the collective agreements of the Institute offered a compensation system benefiting only the

---

[46] French Court of Cassation 10 December 2002 *Bulletin* 2002 V no 373, 368 *Goethe Institut Association for the Promotion of the German Language Abroad and Cultural Exchanges v Bataille Zamolo.*

staff of German nationality hired before that date. Zamolo, a French citizen, was thus paid a different salary compared to a German employee performing the same function and scoring similarly on the criteria of seniority, marital status and education.

Held: On 18 February 2000, the Douai Court of Appeal granted Zamolo's request for payment of outstanding wages on the basis of prohibited discrimination on grounds of nationality. The Court of Cassation found the practice at issue to be discriminatory. It ruled that [now Article 18 TFEU], [now Article 45 TFEU] and Article 7 of Regulation (EEC) No 1612/68 of the Council of 15 October 1968 on freedom of movement for workers within the [EU] were directly applicable in domestic law. They were held to confer individual rights which the national courts must safeguard and to have supremacy over the national legislation. This meant that the Goethe Institute could not maintain the advantages in favour of the German employees employed before 31 March 1991, while denying these advantages to the French employees also employed before 31 March 1991. This practice sustained a discrimination prohibited by [EU] law.

Judgment: [Now Article 18 TFEU] prohibits discrimination on grounds of nationality; [now Article 45 TFEU] lays down the principle of non-discrimination and its paragraph 2 provides that freedom of movement for workers implies the abolition of any discrimination based on nationality between workers of the Member States as regards employment, remuneration and other conditions of work and employment; Article 7 of Regulation (EEC) No 1612/68 on freedom of movement for workers within the [EU] provides that any clause of a collective or individual agreement or of any other collective regulation concerning, in particular, remuneration, shall be null and void in so far as it lays down or authorises discriminatory conditions in respect of workers who are nationals of the other Member States; those texts are directly applicable in the Member States and create rights for individuals which the national courts must protect; they take precedence over all contrary national measures ...

The Court of Appeal, which had jurisdiction, found that pursuant to the above texts the Institute was precluded from adopting a different system of remuneration in France based on the nationality of its staff. The Court could therefore decide, stating sound reasons and without giving rise to the grounds for cassation, that maintaining a salary system for the benefit of the German workers employed before 31 March 1991 that was more favourable than the salary system provided for the French workers employed before this date, constituted prohibited discrimination against the latter. On the basis of this reason alone the Court of Appeal has legally justified its decision. The ground for cassation is unfounded ...

Notes:

(1) It is not easy to establish how EU law influenced this case. It seems as if the French Court of Cassation held the predecessors of Article 18 TFEU (in combination with the provisions regarding free movement of workers) directly applicable to the horizontal relationship between Zamolo and the Goethe Institute. It can equally be argued, however, that in this case, the Court of Cassation found Article 132-8 of the French Labour Code (Code du travail), and thus the collective agreement based upon it, in breach of EU law and on that ground precluded application of these rules. In this view, the European influence was realised by way of a legality review against the non-discrimination provision.

(2) Contrary to the above judgment by the Belgian national court (case 4.6 (BE)), the French national court elaborated upon the issue of direct applicability of the relevant EU law provisions in the law of the Member States.

(3) The application of Article 18 TFEU reshaped the horizontal relationship. After the contractual clause that was in conflict with the prohibition of discrimination had been set aside, Zamolo's employer was obliged to pay outstanding wages to Zamolo to ensure the equal treatment of its French and its German employees.

Cour de Cassation (Court of Cassation), 17 June 2003[47]   **4.8 (FR)**

MY v Groupe Alitalia

UNEQUAL COMPENSATION BASED ON NATIONALITY

Italian restrictions

A difference in treatment of employees is permitted under EU law when based upon an objective and reasonable justification, independent of the nationality of the workers concerned and proportionate to the legitimate aim pursued

Facts: As part of restructuring the Alitalia Group, Alitalia SpA and the Italian unions involved agreed upon workforce reductions in Italy in exchange for employee participation in the company's capital in the form of options on newly created shares. This benefit was conferred on all employees of Alitalia whose permanent contracts were governed by Italian law. Other employees with contracts under French law were not given the same benefit.

Held: On 16 January 2001, the Paris Court of Appeal dismissed the request of MY to benefit from the agreement made between Alitalia SpA and the Italian unions, since it found that the benefit conferred on employees whose contracts were governed by Italian law was based upon an objective reason unrelated to any discrimination on grounds of nationality. The Court of Cassation took the ground that the benefit conferred by the collective agreement was the counterpart of the sacrifices to which only the Italian employees had agreed. Indeed, these sacrifices did not concern the French employees. The benefits granted to the Italian employees were based on objective reasons unrelated to any discrimination on grounds of nationality. Consequently, there was no discrimination prohibited under [now Article 45 TFEU] and Article 14 of the European Convention on Human Rights, supplemented by Article 1 of its Additional Protocol.

Judgment: [A] difference in treatment between workers can be justified when it is based on objective reasons unrelated to any prohibited discrimination ... the grant of options on the newly created shares only to employees whose contracts were governed by Italian law was the counterpart of the sacrifices these employees had accepted as part of the company's 1996 restructuring plan and it has not been found that the plan concerned the workers employed in France since no provision had been made for restructuring accompanied by workforce reductions in France ... the benefit to workers whose contracts were governed by Italian law was based on an objective justification, unrelated to any discrimination on grounds of nationality.

Notes:

(1) The party relied on a restriction of the right to free movement of workers (Article 45 TFEU) caused by discrimination based on nationality. The national court found an objective reason for the difference in treatment, so it implicitly dismissed the

---

[47] French Court of Cassation 17 June 2003 *Bulletin* 2003 V no 195, 193 *MY v Groupe Alitalia*.

alleged violation of Article 45 TFEU. It is not clear how EU law influenced this case. It may be that the French Court of Cassation assessed the horizontal relationship between Alitalia and MY directly against Article 45 TFEU. However, it can equally be argued that in this case the Court of Cassation assessed the employment contract between Alitalia and MY against a provision of national law that was in conformity with Article 45 TFEU.

(2) The Court of Cassation held that the difference made between employees with an employment contract under Italian law and those with an employment contract under French law did not constitute prohibited discrimination on grounds of nationality. It did so because the difference in treatment of employees with an employment contract under Italian law and those with an employment contract under French law was not based on nationality and was, moreover, justified by the fact that the employees with a contract under Italian law had accepted sacrifices in the context of company restructuring in exchange for being granted options on newly created shares. This case shows that the Court of Cassation was willing to consider an objective and reasonable justification for discrimination based on nationality.

(3) Even though it is technically true that the difference in treatment was not directly discriminatory since the employment contract under Italian law could apply to employees of other nationalities as well, there might have been a risk of indirect discrimination. It was likely that the contracts under Italian law would in actual fact apply to Italian employees only. The Court of Cassation did not deal with this aspect of discrimination.

(4) Taking into regard the reason why the Court of Cassation held the difference in treatment to be justified, the possibility of indirect discrimination was irrelevant in this case.

(5) In this case, the application of either Article 45 TFEU or a provision of national law that was in conformity with Article 45 TFEU did not reshape the horizontal relationship, because in this case, the horizontal relationship was not at variance with EU law. Nevertheless, the EU law provision was part of the framework regulating and thus shaping the horizontal relationship. In other words, employment contracts have to be moulded to fit the boundaries set by EU law. The Court of Cassation was clearly aware of that fact.

Cour de Cassation (Court of Cassation), 17 April 2008[48]   **4.9 (FR)**

Wattecamps v Sté European Synchrotron

INTERPRETATION OF THE SCOPE OF EU LAW

Scientific excellence

Article 18 TFEU can only be applied in situations governed by EU law

Facts: Wattecamps, a French citizen living in Grenoble, was an employee of the company European Synchrotron. Among other national and international regulations, the company's collective agreements granted an expatriation premium to employees of foreign nationality for the sole purpose of attracting them for a job by way of compensating their possible disadvantages.

---

[48] French Court of Cassation 17 April 2008 *Bulletin* 2008 V no 95 *Wattecamps v Sté European Synchrotron*.

Held: On 13 September 2006, the Grenoble Court of Appeal dismissed the request of Wattecamps for payment of the expatriation allowance reserved for employees of foreign nationality. It accepted the premium for foreign employees on the grounds that the goal of creating an international centre of scientific excellence to be achieved thereby justified the discrimination and that the premium was granted to all foreign employees. The Court of Cassation stated that the principle of non-discrimination on grounds of nationality as set out in [now Article 18 TFEU] applied only to situations covered by [EU] law. Under [now Article 45 TFEU], this principle of non-discrimination aims to ensure the free movement of workers. [Now Article 18 TFEU] and consequently [now Article 45 TFEU] can only be invoked by workers who have exercised their freedom of movement.

Judgment: [T]he principle of non-discrimination on grounds of nationality enshrined in [now Article 18 TFEU] applies only to situations governed by [EU] law; in the context of employment law its sole aim under [now Article 45 TFEU] is to ensure the free movement of workers; therefore, these articles cannot be relied on by an employee who has not exercised this freedom of movement to go and work in another Member State;

... It then follows from the preamble of the Paris Convention of 16 December 1988 ... and art. 50 of the aforementioned collective agreement ... that the expatriation premium ... is intended to compensate the employee and his family for the disadvantages arising from their expatriation ...; withholding this advantage from the French employees is therefore based on an objective and adequate reason, unrelated to any prohibited discrimination and proportionate to the legitimate objective pursued by the Contracting States.

Notes:

(1) The French Court of Cassation was the first to correctly hold that the EU principle of non-discrimination can only apply if the factual situation falls within the scope of EU law. This was not the case here because the freedom of movement was not at issue.

(2) By way of obiter dictum, the Court of Cassation hypothetically presupposed that EU law was applicable. If in that case Article 18 TFEU would have been applied to the company's regulations granting an expatriation bonus to employees of foreign nationality only, there would have been room for justification. The Court of Cassation stated that this regulation was based on an objective reason so that the alleged prohibited discrimination was proportionate to the legitimate aim pursued by the Member States.

(3) Both the *Vredestein* case (case 4.11 (NL)) and this case show that EU law does not protect against unfavourable treatment by a Member State of its own nationals as compared to nationals of other Member States.

IV.A.ii INDIRECT EFFECTS OF THE EU RULE

This section is intended to present cases from national jurisdictions in which the national courts applied the rationale of a relevant EU law via a national rule that was in conformity with the rule of EU law, or by harmonious interpretation of a national rule that was not in conformity with EU law, or by reviewing an incompatible rule of national law against EU law.

The application of national law that is already in conformity with Article 18 TFEU is interesting for this casebook because such a national rule may result from the implementation of an EU law provision into national law. Moreover, it is also important because the national courts must comply with new or evolving interpretations of the rule of

EU law on which the national rule is based. With regard to Article 157 TFEU, some interesting examples from UK case law that illustrate this dynamic will be examined in section IV.B.ii.a below.

As mentioned before (section IV.A.i), EU law does not protect against unfavourable treatment by a Member State of its own individuals as compared to nationals of other Member States (case 4.11 (NL)). This so-called reverse discrimination should be solved by techniques of national law. See also section IV.A.iv below.

IV.A.ii.a Application of the EU Law Rationale via a National Rule that is in Conformity with the Rule of EU Law

EU law can exert an indirect effect on the substance of a horizontal relationship via national rules that are in conformity with EU law. The legislator of a Member State may, for example, regard an existing national rule as an anticipatory enactment of the substance and, for that reason, as an implementation of a directive that was established and entered into force afterwards. Such a national rule is in the first place part of the framework regulating horizontal relationships. In the second place, legal actors have to be aware of the fact that the rule of national law is required to be constantly in conformity with EU law (and with its interpretation by the CJEU).

Since cases in this category generally do not trigger any questions relating to EU law in the national courts deciding them, they are not recognised as being influenced by EU law. Moreover, they normally do not create problematic situations. An exception is the situation where the national court is aware of a possible incompatibility between the national legislation and the interpretation given by the CJEU to the rule of EU law. In this case, the national court will either refer a preliminary question to the CJ or interpret the national rule in conformity with the EU rule. Those situations are dealt with separately in sections IV.A.ii.b and IV.B.ii.b.

A situation that must be distinguished from the above is where an open norm of national law is interpreted in conformity with EU law (see section I.A above). Case 4.12 (GERM)) resembles this situation.

IV.A.ii.b Application of the EU Law Rationale by Harmonious Interpretation of a National Rule that is Not in Conformity with EU Law

EU law can exert an indirect effect on the substance of a horizontal relationship via harmonious interpretation of a national rule that is not in conformity with EU law. This way of interpreting national law may substantively change the framework regulating horizontal relationships.

The reader should be aware of the fact that under this type of cases is also included the situation in which a national court applies national law that is *not* in conformity with EU law. Such a situation may occur when the national court is unable to harmoniously interpret the national provision and also cannot apply an alternative technique (eg, positive obligation–see sections IV.A.iii and IV.B.iii). Since no such cases have been reported, I discuss this situation in the context of case 4.10 (BE), note 5.

Hof van Beroep Antwerpen (Court of Appeal of Antwerp),
5 March 2007[49]   **4.10 (BE)**

Scarade NV v Bonyad Shipping Line Europe Ltd and BVBA
Van Doosselaere & Achten

CLAIM FOR PROVISION OF SURETY PURSUANT TO BELGIAN NATIONAL LAW

Iranian tools

Article 18 TFEU precludes application of Article 851 of the Belgian Judicial Code against subjects of other Member States

Facts: Scarade contacted Van Doosselaere & Achten for the shipment of certain tools from Antwerp to Bandar Abbas (Iran) in the period between 23 and 26 November 2003. Van Doosselaere & Achten offered Scarade the shipping services of Bonyad, a shipping company under the laws of Malta, which Scarade accepted. However, Bonyad failed to ship the objects in the agreed period of time.

Held: Scarade unsuccessfully invoked Article 851 of the Belgium Judicial Code to have the proceedings suspended pending provision of surety by Bonyad for an amount equal to the sum of the counterclaim.

Judgment: The 'cautio judicatum solvi' (exception of surety for legal costs by a foreign claimant) raised by the appellant against Scarade should be rejected as unfounded.

Article 851 of the Judicial Code provides for a procedural suspensive exception aimed at protecting Belgian defendants from pecuniary loss resulting from unfounded actions brought by foreigners who offer no guaranty in Belgium ensuring payment of any costs and damages that may be awarded against them.

The term 'foreigners who are required to provide surety, subject to treaty-based exemption' means all foreigners acting as lead claimant or as intervening party.

It is generally assumed that treaties which contain an MFN clause or a clause that equates foreigners with a country's own national, implicitly confer exemption from the 'cautio judicatum solvi'.

One of the main multilateral treaties leading to exemption from the obligation to provide surety is the [now TFEU]. [Now Article 18 TFEU] must be interpreted to mean that it precludes a Member State from requiring surety for legal costs from a national of another Member State who has brought an action before one of the civil courts of the former Member State against one of its subjects, if nationals of this State cannot be required to do so.

In other words, Belgian defendants cannot raise the 'cautio judicatum solvi' exception in disputes in which the claimant is an EU national.

It is irrelevant in the present case that on the date on which the summons was issued, being 09/04/2004, Malta – the country in which Bonyad has its registered place of business – was not yet an EU Member State, since at the time of assessing whether the exception is well-founded Scarade is a national of a Member State of the European Union, so that it cannot be ordered to provide surety.

The 'cautio judicatum solvi' exception (exception of surety by a foreign claimant for legal costs) raised by the appellant against Scarade must therefore be rejected as unfounded.

[49] Court of Appeal of Antwerp 5 March 2007 *Eur Vervoerr* 2007 vol 6, 739 *Scarade NV v Bonyad Shipping Line Europe Ltd and BVBA Van Doosselaere & Achten.*

Notes:

(1) This case is an example of how national courts can use the method of harmonious interpretation to ensure EU rights in a horizontal relationship. The problem was a national procedural rule which provided Belgian citizens with the possibility of invoking the *cautio judicatum solvi* against foreigners.[50] The court's interpretation of [now Article 18 TFEU] made clear that the term foreigner in Article 851 of the Belgian Judicial Code may be interpreted as to include a subject of another Member State because Belgium does not impose the obligation of the Article on its own inhabitants.

(2) Another technique which the national courts could have used was that of setting aside the national rule after reviewing its legality and subsequently filling the resulting gap in conformity with EU law.

(3) Indirectly, the harmonious interpretation of the rule of national law that was not in conformity with EU law reshaped the horizontal relationship. After the court's harmonious interpretation of the national rule, Scarade could no longer rely on Article 851 of the Belgian Judicial Code. Consequently, Scarade could not, on the ground of the insolvency risk, suspend payment of the amount due to the Maltese company Bonyad. The other side of the coin was that the Maltese company was treated in the same way as Belgian companies.

(4) However, the general acceptation that certain treaties provide an escape from the obligation of *cautio judicatum solvi* imposed on non-Belgium residents together with this harmonious interpretation make the Belgium provision consistent with EU law. Such harmonious interpretation might imply a *contra legem* interpretation of national law. As repeatedly set out by the CJ,[51] the EU obligation to harmoniously interpret national law cannot serve as the basis for an interpretation *contra legem* of national law (see also section I.C.iii in Chapter 5). The question arises as to whether the interpretation of Article 851 of the Belgian Judicial Code should be considered *contra legem* since the term foreigner does not leave much margin for construing it other than as meaning 'non-Belgian'.

(5) If the Belgian court should not have managed to find a technique to harmoniously interpret the national provision (and should not have relied on positive obligation either – see sections IV.A.iii and IV.B.iii), the rule it would have applied would have been the national provision that runs counter to the requirements set by EU law. In that case, the individual could not have relied on the right conferred on it by EU law. This gap may be covered by the doctrine of Member State (*Francovich*) liability.[52]

---

[50] For comparable cases decided by the CJEU, see CJ 26 September 1996 Case C-43/95 *Data Delecta Aktiebolag and Forsberg v MSL Dynamics Ltd* [1996] I-04661 ECLI:EU:C:1996:357, paras 17 and 22; CJ 20 March 1997 Case C-323/95 *Hayes v Kronenberger GmbH* [1997] I-01711 ECLI:EU:C:1997169, para 19.

[51] See, eg, CJ 10 March 2011 Case C-109/09 *Deutsche Lufthansa AG v Gertraud Kumpan* [2011] I-01309 ECLI:EU:C:2011:129, para 54.

[52] CJ 30 September 2003 Case C-224/01 *Köbler v Republik Österreich* [2003] I-10239 ECLI:EU:C:2003:513; CJ 13 June 2006 Case C-173/03 *Traghetti del Mediterraneo SpA v Repubblica italiana* [2006] I-05177 ECLI:EU:C:2006:391.

IV.A.ii.c Application of the EU Law Rationale by Reviewing an Incompatible
Rule of National Law against EU Law

To avoid a result in a horizontal relationship that is at variance with the requirements of
EU law, a national court can review a rule of national law against Article 18 TFEU. If the
national provision is found to be incompatible, it has to be set aside. Subsequently, the
remaining provisions of national law or the applicable provisions of EU law will have to
lead to a solution that is not discriminatory. Possible legal doctrines that can be used to
achieve this result include nullity, damages and undue payment.

*Hoge Raad der Nederlanden (Supreme Court of the
Netherlands), 11 May 2001*[53]   **4.11 (NL)**

Vredestein Fietsbanden BV v Stichting Ring 65

REVERSE DISCRIMINATION

Deep profile

*Applying the Berne Convention in international situations only does not entail impermis-
sible discrimination under EU law against the Member State's own nationals since EU law
does not prohibit reverse discrimination*

Facts: In 1988, the Dutch company Vredestein Fietsbanden BV marketed Perfect bicycle tyres, named Perfect-
Old. In 1995, Vredestein BV slightly modified the profile of the Perfect-Old tyres. It deposited this new profile
model, named Perfect-New, with the International Bureau of the World Intellectual Property Organization so
as to be protected in the Benelux countries as well. In April 1997, Vredestein BV cancelled the Perfect-New
registration without making a conservation statement as required under Article 21(3) Benelux Tekeningen en
Modellen Wet (BTMW). Ring 65, a Dutch cooperation, distributed a number of bicycle tyres of the Anello
brand among its members to bring this tyre on the Dutch market on a larger scale. The profile of the Anello tyre
showed a remarkable similarity to the profiles of both the Perfect-Old and the Perfect-New models. In 1996,
Ring 65 registered the tyre profile with the International Bureau of the World Intellectual Property Organization.

Held: The court of first instance granted the claim of Ring 65 for a declaratory judgment that the profile of the
Perfect-tyres was not protected by the Dutch Copyright Act 1912 and that Ring 65's marketing of bicycle tyres
with a profile similar to that of the Perfect-tyres did not constitute unfair competition vis-a-vis Vredestein BV,
and it also granted its claim for annulment of the Benelux shape trademark application by Vredestein BV. On
the basis of the counterclaim of Vredestein BV, it further declared void the 1996 design application by Ring 65.
The Court of Appeal confirmed the judgment of the court of first instance and ruled that Vredestein BV did
not enjoy any form of copyright protection due to the cancellation without the conservation statement required
pursuant to Article 21(3) BTMW.

Judgment: The Supreme Court of the Netherlands upholds the judgment of the Court of
Appeal.
    3.3.3 The Court of Appeal furthermore rejected Vredestein's allegation that
articles 2(7), 5(2) and 7(4) of the Berne Convention for the protection of literary and artis-
tic works prevented the lapse of the copyright pursuant to article 21(3) BTMW. It based

---

[53] HR 11 May 2001 *NJ* 2002, 55 ECLI:NL:HR:2001:AB1558 *Vredestein Fietsbanden BV v Stichting
Ring 65*. In HR 13 December 2013 *NJ* 2015, 307 ECLI:NL:HR:2013:1881 *Montis Design BV v. Goossens
Meubelen BV* para 6.4.1 and 6.4.2 the Supreme Court of the Netherlands reiterated the reasoning relevant for
the analysis of the Vredestein case.

this decision in the first place on its finding that the Berne Convention only applies in international situations and that a Dutch author cannot rely on the Berne Convention in the Netherlands with regard to a work having its origin in the Netherlands. This decision is correct, as is also clear from article 5(1) and (3) first sentence, of the Berne Convention. Contrary to what is argued in part 1.3.1 of the ground for cassation, this does not entail a discrimination of Dutch copyright holders as compared with foreign copyright holders that is inadmissible in the light of [now Article 18 TFEU], since a more unfavourable treatment by a Member State of its own individuals as compared to individuals of other Member States does not constitute discrimination prohibited by [now Article 18 TFEU].

Notes:

(1) This case is an example of a situation in which a national court reviewed a decision of the lower court against what is now Article 18 TFEU. According to the Supreme Court of the Netherlands, the decision of the Court of Appeal was not in breach of Article 18 TFEU.

(2) In the situation under consideration, the Dutch claimant argued that it was treated less favourably than an individual of another Member State. The national court assessed whether the ensuing legal situation was at variance with Article 18 TFEU. In line with the case law of the CJEU, the national court affirmed that EU law does not protect citizens of a Member State from being treated less favourably by that Member State than citizens from other Member States.[54]

(3) This is a regular finding in case law. Courts tend to derive diverse arguments from the situation where a citizen is treated less favourably by his own Member State. They sometimes even reason, erroneously, that a claim of a citizen from another Member State has to be refused on the ground that granting the claim would lead to his being treated more favourably than the Member State's own citizens. See also case 4.13 (FR).

(4) The situation is different in jurisdictions where the national principle of equality requires the courts to treat domestic situations in the same way as cross-border situations. On the basis of such a doctrine (enshrined in the national constitution or in case law of a constitutional court), nationals of that country are protected against being treated less favourably than citizens from other countries (based, eg, on EU law).[55]

(5) In the *Vredestein* case, the legal situation of Vredestein did not change. Nevertheless, it is clear that the national court was prepared to review a provision and a judgment against EU law.

IV.A.iii POSITIVE OBLIGATION OF MEMBER STATES THAT IMPACT ON HORIZONTAL RELATIONS BETWEEN INDIVIDUALS

This section presents a case from a national jurisdiction which indirectly involved a horizontal relationship and in which the national court based a positive obligation of the Member State on Article 18 TFEU, which had consequences for the horizontal

---

[54] See case law cited by AG Sharpston Opinion 30 September 2010 in Case C-34/09 *Zambrano v Office national de l'emploi* [2011] I-01177 ECLI:EU:C:2010:560, fn 103.
[55] Hartkamp 2016 no 100. See also section IV.D in Ch 1.

relationship.[56] To avoid a result in a horizontal relationship that is at variance with the requirements of EU law, a national court may rely on this technique.

A positive obligation can cause remarkable substantive changes in horizontal relationships, as in the following case, in which the group of persons who could exercise the right provided for by EU law was widened.

Bundesverfassungsgericht (Federal Constitutional Court of Germany), 19 July 2011[57] **4.12 (GERM)**

SrL v MX

FOREIGN LEGAL PERSONS WHO ARE DOMICILED IN THE EU CAN BE CARRIERS OF MATERIAL FUNDAMENTAL RIGHTS OF THE GERMAN CONSTITUTION

Stylish furniture

Extension of the scope of application of Article 19(3) of the German Constitution to include legal persons domiciled elsewhere in the EU to ensure the protective effect of the basic rights as an interpretative reaction to the development of EU law

Facts: The applicant, a company with limited liability incorporated under Italian law and having its registered office in Italy, was a producer of furniture designed by the deceased architect and furniture designer Le Corbusier. The applicant sublicensed the copyright on these pieces of Le Corbusier furniture. However, some Le Corbusier replicas were found in a cigar lounge in Germany owned by the defendant. The defendant had purchased these replicas from a Bologna company, also an intervening party to in the proceedings, to whom no copyright rights had been granted.

Held: Pursuant to Articles 17(1) and 96 of the German Copyright Act, the applicant had brought an action before the German court claiming that the defendant be ordered to refrain from the exploitation of unauthorised reproductions of copyrighted Le Corbusier furniture models in Germany. The applicant's claim was dismissed on appeal by the Federal Court of Justice of Germany on 22 January 2009. The applicant lodged a constitutional complaint alleging violation of its right of ownership under Article 14 of the German Constitution.

Judgment: The Federal Constitutional Court of Germany allowed the constitutional complaint. It applied the rule of national law (Article 19 German Constitution) that was not in conformity with EU law in a way adjusted to the requirements set by EU law.

[56] 1. a) Article 19(3) of the German Constitution does not preclude a claim for breach of Article 14(1) of the German Constitution.

[57] It is true that, until now, the German Constitutional Court has in its previous case law rejected extending the general applicability of material fundamental rights to foreign legal persons, with reference to the wording of Article 19(3) of the German Constitution. More recently, however, decisions by a Constitutional Court chamber left open the question of whether this case law could also apply to legal persons domiciled in other Member States of the [EU]. In view of the prohibition of discrimination in EU law, as interpreted by the European Court of Justice, it would in any event seem possible that the fundamental constitutional right of ownership applies to the applicant in this case, who is domiciled in Italy ...

---

[56] For the method of selecting cases and the structure of the presentation of the cases, see above, first paragraph of this section.

[57] Federal Constitutional Court of Germany 19 July 2011 *NZG* 2011, 1262 *SL v MX*.

[68] 1. The applicant, a legal person domiciled in Italy, has fundamental rights under the German Constitution. Based on the primacy of application of the fundamental freedoms in the internal market (Article 26(2) TFEU) and the general prohibition of discrimination on grounds of nationality (Article 18 TFEU), the extension of the scope of application to legal persons from other Member States of the European Union constitutes a treaty-based extension of the protection provided under the German Constitution.

[69] 1. Pursuant to Article 19(3) of the German Constitution, the fundamental rights apply also to domestic legal persons insofar as they are by their very nature applicable to them. The fundamental rights alleged to have been breached in this case are evidently applicable by their very nature.

[70] a) The Senate, on the other hand, has until now decided that foreign legal persons cannot invoke material fundamental rights … It justified these decisions by referring to the wording and meaning of Article 19(3) of the German Constitution, which it held to prohibit such an extended interpretation. In other decisions, the two Senates of the German Constitutional Court expressly left open the question of whether foreign legal persons were entitled to the protection provided by fundamental rights.

[71] The German Constitutional Court has not yet considered in any further detail the specific question of whether legal persons domiciled elsewhere in the [EU] can invoke the material fundamental rights guaranteed by the German Constitution. However, and without giving any further reasons, a ruling in 1968 declared the constitutional appeal by an association established under French law and domiciled in France to be inadmissible, while a ruling in 1973 expressly left open the question of a French trading company's basic legal capacity in such circumstances. In professional literature the issue remains controversial.

[72] b) According to the wording of Article 19(3) of the German Constitution, the fundamental rights apply to 'domestic legal persons'. Given the restriction to domestic legal persons, extension of the scope of applicability cannot be justified by referring to the wording of Article 19(3). Interpretation in conformity with EU law and with the term 'domestic' being construed to mean 'German and including European' legal persons would go beyond the limits of this wording. Even though, in the light of the area of 'freedom, security and justice without internal frontiers in which the free movement of persons is ensured' (Article 3(2) TEU), the territories of the Member States of the European Union are no longer regarded as abroad in the classic sense of the word, this does not make them 'domestic' within the meaning of territorial jurisdiction.

[73] The legislative provision was not, however, based on any intention of the legislator to permanently exclude legal persons from Member States of the European Union from the opportunity to invoke fundamental constitutional rights. The Parliamentary Council's general drafting committee concluded in a draft of Article 20(a) of the German Constitution, which corresponds to the current Article 19(3), that there 'should be no reason for the protection afforded by the Constitution also to be granted to foreign legal persons.' Von Mangoldt, the chairman of the Policy Dialogue Committee, consequently proposed adding the word 'domestic', and this proposal was accepted by the committee.

[74] In 1948–49 the development of a [internal] market in Europe was still in its infancy. The European Union has since increasingly taken shape and now forms a highly integrated 'union of states', in which the Federal Republic of Germany participates under Article 23(I) of the German Constitution. The extension of the scope of application of Article 19(3) of the German Constitution reflects this development.

[75] 2. Extending the scope of application of the protection of fundamental rights to legal persons from elsewhere in the European Union accords with the obligations

assumed as a result of the European treaties, as reflected in particular in the European fundamental freedoms and, at a secondary legislative level, in the general prohibition of discrimination set out in Article 18 TFEU. The fundamental freedoms and the general prohibition of discrimination constitute a barrier to unequal treatment between domestic and foreign enterprises in cases falling within the scope of application of EU law and, to that extent, are contrary to the restriction to domestic legal persons of the constitutional protection provided for by Article 19(3) of the German Constitution.

[76] a) … In an earlier preliminary ruling procedure requested by the German Federal Court of Justice, the European Court of Justice ruled that the freedom of establishment provided for in European law, requires a non-discriminatory assessment of a person's legal capacity and, consequently, of that person's capacity to be a party to legal proceedings in German civil courts.

[77] b) Extending the scope of application cannot be considered unnecessary by arguing that the applicant is assured of equivalent protection elsewhere. It is true that, in non-constitutional proceedings, legal persons domiciled in another EU Member State can in any event rely on the direct effect of primary EU law and that their inability to rely on the German fundamental rights will therefore not leave them without legal protection. However, for enjoying protection of at least equivalent value under the EU prohibition of discrimination, it is not sufficient for foreign legal persons to be able to claim substantive equality with domestic legal persons in non-constitutional proceedings, while being unable to enforce their rights under Article 93(I) No. 4(a) of the German Constitution before the Federal Constitutional Court because the German fundamental rights do not apply to them.

[78] c) Infringement of the EU-law prohibition of discrimination arising from the fundamental freedoms and Article 18 TFEU presupposes that the activities of the legal persons in question domiciled in the [EU] fall within the scope of application of EU law. The Treaties' scope of application is governed by the current state of primary and secondary legislation of the [EU] and thus by the sovereign powers transferred to Union law under the European Treaties. This manifests itself in particular with regard to the realisation of the fundamental Treaty freedoms and the enforcement of EU law. In this sense, the activities of the applicant, who relies *inter alia* on its copyrights under the harmonised (or at least partially harmonised) EU copyright law which it alleges to have been infringed by economic activities in Germany, fall within the scope of application of the Treaties.

[80] e) The Federal Constitutional Court is not required to refer the question to the European Court of Justice as the national courts themselves are competent to interpret national law in conformity with EU law. The correct interpretation of the EU-law prohibition of discrimination is so evident in this case as to leave no scope for reasonable doubt.

[81] 3. The extension of the scope of application of Article 19(3) of the German Constitution to include legal persons from other EU Member States reflects developments of the EU treaties and EU law and avoids a collision with European Union law. The Federal Republic of Germany is bound by Article 18 TFEU and the prohibition of discrimination arising under the fundamental freedoms, including their primacy over national law. Extended application respects the principle that the supranational law of the European Union does not have the effect of setting aside or nullifying the law of Member States, but instead merely reduces its scope insofar as required by the Treaties and permitted by the ratification granted by the Act of Consent. The law of a Member State thus merely becomes inapplicable. The EU-law provisions do not supersede Article 19(3) of the German Constitution, but simply cause the protection of the fundamental rights to extend

to include other entities within the internal market. Subject to the conditions stated in Article 79(2) and (3) of the German Constitution, Article 23(I), (2) and (3) of the German Constitution allow sovereign powers to be transferred to the [EU] to the extent that this will amend or supplement the scope of the safeguards provided by the Constitution, without invoking the citation requirement of Article 79(I) of the Constitution. The same holds true with respect to the scope of application of the fundamental rights insofar as the protection of a fundamental right needs to be extended to legal persons domiciled elsewhere in the European Union in order to avoid unequal treatment with regard to fundamental rights in cases falling under the EU-law prohibitions of discrimination. The individual fundamental rights enshrined in the Constitution are not changed, however, by the extension of the scope of application of Article 19(3).

[82] 4. What obviously remains intact is the authority of the Federal Constitutional Court to review EU law for preservation of the identity of the national constitution, observance of the limits of the competences conferred on the EU and maintenance of a level of protection essentially equivalent to that of the German constitution. The extension of the scope of application of Article 19(3) clearly does not affect the identity of the constitution.

Notes:

(1) The Federal Constitutional Court of Germany stated very systematically and clearly which steps had to be taken to arrive at the correct decision. The Court elaborated upon the different ways in which EU law can and must have an influence on this case. First, it focused on the harmonious interpretation of Article 19 of the German Constitution (Grundgesetz) to make its application consistent with EU law. In the Court's opinion, however, the wording of this Article ('The basic rights shall also apply to domestic legal persons to the extent permitted by the nature of such rights') could not justify extending the protection of fundamental rights to legal persons domiciled in other Member States. Consequently, the method of harmonious interpretation could not be used, in contrast to the judgment of the Antwerp Court of Appeal of 5 March 2007 (case 4.10 (BE)). Such an interpretation of the Article in conformity with EU law would be *contra legem*. The Constitutional Court could (and did) manage to extend the scope of application of the constitutional provision by taking account of the development of the EU and the main objectives of EU law, including the prohibition of discrimination laid down in Article 18 TFEU. Taking the position that Germany was bound by the EU provisions and was thus obliged to avoid collision with EU law, it extended the scope of application of Article 19 of the German Constitution (*Anwendungserweiterung*) to include legal persons from other Member States. Whereas the wording of Article 19(3) of the German Constitution explicitly states that it applies to domestic legal entities, the German Constitutional Court took the ground that it had not been the legislator's intention to exclude legal entities domiciled in other Member States from relying on the fundamental rights. The basis of the reasoning of the Constitutional Court of Germany was its commitment to sincere cooperation towards fulfilling the obligations under the Treaty. By doing so, it bridged doctrinal issues recognised under German Constitutional law.

(2) The Constitutional Court did not explicitly say that it had used any method other than harmonious interpretation or interpretation. This case rather appears to be an example of the mechanism that the Member States have a positive obligation to ensure the

effectiveness of EU law. Even though the reasoning is clearly aimed at avoiding the technique of harmonious interpretation, using the technique of 'extended application' instead will lead to a similar result. Extending the scope of application resembles the mechanism of using an open norm of national law to ensure the conformity of national law with EU law (see sections II.B.i and II.B.ii in Chapter 1).

(3) It is striking how well the Constitutional Court has elaborated its considerations regarding EU law. For example, it stressed the importance of fundamental rights being enforceable (not only before the CJ but) also before the Constitutional Court. Moreover, it explained in its judgment (paragraph 80) why it was not necessary to refer questions to the CJ.[58]

(4) The application (rather than interpretation) of the rule of national law (Article 19 of the German Constitution) that lacked conformity with EU law in a way that was adjusted to the requirements set by EU law indirectly reshaped the horizontal relationship. After the national rule had been applied in conformity with EU law, the Italian company (and holder of the licence to (re)produce copyrighted Le Corbusier designer furniture) could rely on the right of ownership granted under Article 14 of the German Constitution. Consequently, it could bring an action against the German defendant and claim an injunction ordering the defendant to refrain from the exploitation of unauthorised reproductions.

(5) Translated into private law reasoning, this judgment enables individuals from other Member States to equally rely on the right of ownership in extra-contractual relationships. No matter whether the defendant violates a right of ownership of a German citizen or of an individual of another Member State, his conduct is equally unlawful.

IV.A.iv MISCELLANEOUS

This subsection describes and explains some other ways, different from those dealt with above in sections IV.A.i–IV.A.iii, in which Article 18 TFEU can influence national private law.

As mentioned above (sections IV.A.i and IV.A.ii), courts tend to derive diverse arguments from the situation that a citizen of their own Member State is treated less favourably. They sometimes even reason, erroneously, that a claim of a citizen from another Member State has to be refused for the reason that if the claim would be granted, he would be treated better than the Member State's own nationals (case 4.13 (FR)).

---

[58] Stating reasons for such a decision is required by ECHR 8 April 2014 no 17120/09 *Dhahbi v Italy*.

Cour de Cassation (Court of Cassation), 11 March 2009[59]   **4.13 (FR)**

Denis X v Société nationale des chemins de fer français (SNCF)

STAFF REGULATIONS CONTAINING DISCRIMINATION
BASED ON AGE AND NATIONALITY

Belgian French

If an age limit and staff regulations that do not take previous work experience into account apply without distinction to nationals of the Member State concerned and nationals of the other Member States, they cannot be considered discriminatory or otherwise in breach of rules of EU law

Facts: Since 1992, Mr Denis X, a Belgian citizen, had been in the employ of the national Society of Belgian Railways (SNCB), in which he served as a skipper and later as deputy chief of station. After he moved to France in 2000, he applied for similar positions at the national Society of French Railways (SNCF). He was hired by the French station by contract of 7 January 2002 as 'agent Annex 25 CPS technician circulation' and was assigned to Nîmes on a three-month trial period. When Mr X requested that his employer grant him permanent appointment as a technician, he was confronted with an age limit depriving him of the opportunity to hold the position.

Held: On 21 November 2007, the Court of Appeal of Montpellier ruled that the staff regulations of SNCF violated [now Article 45 TFEU] and Council Regulation EEC 1612/ 68 of 15 October 1968. Contrary to the court of first instance, the Court of Appeal awarded Mr X's claim for damages. The Court of Cassation declared the challenged contractual provision void because it infringed [now Article 45 TFEU] and Article 7(1) of Regulation (EEC) No 1612/68 of the Council of 15 October 1968 on freedom of movement for workers within the [EU].

Judgment: Having regard to [now Article 45 TFEU] and Art. 7(1) of Council Regulation (EEC) No 1612/68 of the Council of 15 October 1968 on freedom of movement for workers within the [EU], further referred to as 'Regulation 1612/68'.

It follows from these texts that freedom of movement for workers, which is ensured within the [EU], implies that a worker who is a national of a Member State may not, in the territory of another Member State, be treated differently by reason of his nationality than workers having that other Member State's nationality in respect of any condition of employment and work, in particular as regards remuneration, dismissal, occupational reintegration or re-employment after being unemployed;

... no provision of the collective staff regulations agreed between SNCF and its employees obliges SNCF, when deciding to deny the claimant's claim for a salary adjustment on the basis of seniority, to take account of seniority attained at another company when determining a salary; this rule applies without distinction to nationals of the Member State concerned and to other [EU] citizens; that consequently the complaint of wage discrimination on grounds of nationality is unfounded;

... Having regard to the fact that a migrant worker, when a provision of national staff regulations applicable within a public undertaking provides for a seniority-based promotion system ... for the employees of this undertaking, must be able to rely on periods of employment in a comparable field of activity completed previously in the employment of

[59] French Court of Cassation 11 March 2009 Bulletin *2009 V* no 71 *Denis X v Société nationale des chemins de fer français (SNCF)*.

a public undertaking in another Member State, the Court of Appeal has, in so deciding, breached the aforementioned texts ...

Having regard to [now Article 45 TFEU] and Article 7(1) of Council Regulation (EEC) No 1612/68;

...

Having regard to the fact that a public undertaking in a Member State may not, when recruiting staff, refuse to take account of the seniority, experience and qualifications previously acquired by the candidates in a comparable field of activity in a public undertaking of another Member State, the Court of Appeal breached the aforementioned texts.

... The Court of Appeal breached the aforementioned texts ...

Notes:

(1) A Belgian citizen who was employed by the Belgian railway company moved to France and changed employers. He was employed by the French railway company and asked a salary that corresponded with his experience and seniority. However, the staff regulations of the French railway company allowed it to not take account of seniority attained at another employer. The Court of Appeal took the position that relevant experience acquired by migrant workers whilst being employed by a public company in another Member State should be taken into account. However, the employee in this case could not rely on his claim based on seniority because he exceeded the age limit laid down in the same staff regulations. This age limit applied to all employees. Finally, the Court reasoned that French employees, too, did not get credits for seniority built up at another company.

(2) The relevant Treaty provision in this case was not Article 18 TFEU, but Article 45 TFEU, which regulates the free movement of workers. As already mentioned, it follows from the case law of the CJ that cases that are covered by fundamental freedoms provisions are not dealt with on the basis of the general non-discrimination provision of Article 18 TFEU. The Court of Cassation based its entire ruling on the free movement of workers. Consequently, it also applied Article 45 TFEU to the claim of adjusted salary for seniority. Within the context of the free movement of workers, the courts applied the rationale behind the prohibition of age discrimination instead of directly applying Article 18 TFEU to the supposedly discriminatory provision of the staff regulations. Decisions in such cases therefore shed light on the method used when a case is merely covered by Article 18 TFEU.

(3) A remarkable part of the reasoning of the Court of Appeal implies that an interpretation of the company's staff regulations that differed from the interpretation given to them by the Court of Appeal and that would result in higher payment for seniority would positively discriminate non-French citizens. Under EU law, however, this is not a valid ground for denying a claim. As we have seen in earlier cases, EU law does not prevent citizens who exercise rights conferred on them by EU law from being treated more favourably than citizens who do not exercise these rights.

(4) The Court of Cassation quashed the entire reasoning of the Court of Appeal, resulting in a substantive change in the horizontal relationship between SNCF and the Belgian employee. The employee was entitled to rely on his experience acquired whilst being employed at the Belgian company. Possible remedies available to him were damages and an open-ended employment contract.

(5) This case shows that EU law is part of the framework that sets the boundaries for private autonomy. Since courts are obliged to apply that framework, individuals should be aware of the requirements set by the different rules in order to proactively ensure the validity of their agreements.

Corte di Cassazione (Court of Cassation),
11 October 2004[60]   **4.14 (IT)**

Cassa di Risparmio di Bolzano SpA v Roman Angonese

DISCRIMINATION ON THE BASIS OF NATIONALITY

Italian

The scope of Article 45 TFEU includes situations relating to students who are citizens of a certain Member State, studying abroad to acquire a qualification and looking for a job when they have almost finished their studies abroad. The requirement in the regulation is therefore null and void

Facts: Angonese, an Italian national of German mother tongue from Bolzano, had been studying in Austria between 1993 and 1997. In August 1997, in response to a notice published in the local Italian daily *Dolomiten* on 9 July 1997, he applied to take part in a competition for a post with a private banking undertaking in Bolzano, the Cassa di Risparmio. One of the conditions for entry was possession of a type-B certificate of bilingualism (in Italian and German) delivered by the public authorities of the province of Bolzano after an examination held only in that province. Angonese (who was perfectly bilingual) did not own such a certificate. With a view to gaining admission to the competition, he had submitted a certificate showing completion of his studies as a draughtsman and certificates attesting to his studies of languages (English, Slovene and Polish) at the Faculty of Philosophy at Vienna University and had stated that his professional experience included practising as a draughtsman and translating from Polish into Italian. Nevertheless, the Cassa di Risparmio did not allow him to enter the competition. The District Magistrates' Court Bolzano drew attention to the fact that non-residents of Bolzano may have difficulty obtaining the certificate in good time. The requirement of the certificate imposed by the Cassa de Risparmio was founded on Article 19 of the National Collective Agreement for Savings Banks of 19 December 1994, which provides: 'The institution has the right to decide whether the recruitment of staff referred to in paragraphs 1 and 2, subject in any event to Article 21 below, is to be by way of an internal competition on the basis of either qualifications and/or tests or in accordance with selection criteria specified by the institution. The institution must lay down as and when necessary the conditions and rules for internal competitions, must appoint selection panels and must lay down the selection criteria mentioned in the first paragraph.'

In the legal proceedings that followed, Angonese acknowledged the Cassa di Risparmio's right to select its future staff from persons who are perfectly bilingual, but he complained that the requirement to have and produce the certificate was unlawful and contrary to the principle of the freedom of movement for workers laid down in Article 45 TFEU. Angonese claimed that the requirement be declared void and that the Cassa di Risparmio be ordered to compensate him for his loss of opportunity and to reimburse him the costs he had incurred in the proceedings. According to the national court, the requirement to hold the certificate in order to provide evidence of linguistic knowledge may, contrary to [EU] law, penalise job candidates not resident in Bolzano and, in the present case, could have been prejudicial to Angonese, who had taken up residence in another Member State for the purpose of studying there. Moreover, the national court took the view that if the requirement at issue were held to be inherently contrary to [EU] law, it would be void under Italian law.

---

[60] Cass it 11 October 2004 no 20116 *Roman Angonese v Cassa di Risparmio di Bolzona SpA.*

Held: Following a preliminary reference procedure, the CJ ruled that [now Article 45 TFEU] precluded an employer from requiring persons applying to take part in a recruitment competition to provide evidence of their linguistic knowledge exclusively by means of one particular diploma issued only in one particular province of a Member State. Following the CJ's decision, the referring judge (District Magistrates' Court Bolzano) declared null the requirement of the recruitment competition regulation issued by the bank. This requirement for admission to the competition constituted discrimination on grounds of nationality contrary to [now Article 45 TFEU], as ruled by the CJ. The District Magistrates' Court Bolzano ordered the defendant to compensate Mr Angonese for loss of opportunity (the equivalent of about €43,000). The Court of Appeal confirmed this decision and reduced damages by half. The judgment was appealed by the bank. The Italian Court of Cassation confirmed the decision given by the Court of Appeal. The requirement in the regulation issued by the bank was declared null and void, and the nullity was held to be absolute in nature as [now Article 45 TFEU] is a mandatory provision protecting a general interest (Article 1418 of the Italian Civil Code) and may be relied upon by anyone having an interest (Article 1421 of the Italian Civil Code).

Judgment: The Court of Appeal interpreted the CJ ruling to mean that in addition to non-citizen workers, the same situation of serious difficulty may also occur for citizens who, like the defendant, have enrolled as students at a foreign University and exercise the rights conferred by Directive 93/96 on the right of residence for students.

This interpretation is not a forced application of the principles affirmed by the CJ and must be fully shared. The appellate court took the ground that the fact that the defendant enjoyed the rights conferred by Directive 93/96 constituted a sufficient link to allow him to invoke the advantages offered by the provisions on free movement of workers even if he had not yet acquired a title at the time of the facts, as he was abroad for the purpose of acquiring a professional title which could have been recognized in Italy, too.

The scope of Article 39 of the Treaty [now Article 45 TFEU] may be lawfully extended to cover situations of students living outside the Member State of which they are citizens, who are looking for a job in the same Member State when they have almost finished their studies abroad. The CJ itself has ruled (judgment 7.2.1979 *Knoors*, judgment 31.3.1993, *Kraus*) that there is a sufficient link with EU law when a citizen of a Member State has been regularly resident in another Member State and has acquired a professional qualification which is recognized by EU law and this citizen is in the same situation in relation to the Member State of citizenship as all those who enjoy the rights and freedoms recognized by the Treaty. Undoubtedly in this case of Angonese, who was finishing his studies and was looking for a job in Italy, the clause requiring the certificate of bilingualism was an objective obstacle to his right of free movement.

The third ground of the complaint must be rejected as well.

In the above decision the CJ confirmed that the recruitment competition rule by which the employer required applicants to provide evidence of their linguistic knowledge solely through a particular diploma issued only in a province of the Member State by a local public administration is contrary to Article 39 of the EC Treaty [now Article 45 TFEU], as it makes it difficult or even impossible to acquire the certification for those applicants who are not resident in this province, the majority of whom are Italian citizens, with the further consequence that such a requirement puts nationals of other Member States at a disadvantage by comparison with Italian citizens.

Since, for the reasons established above with respect to the second ground for cassation, the situation of workers who are not citizens must be considered equivalent to the situation of citizens who – like Angonese – are living in another Member State for the purpose of acquiring a professional title which is also recognized in Italy, it must be concluded that the clause under consideration is vitiated by absolute nullity and cannot produce any effect, as it is contrary to an EU rule which cannot be derogated from.

This has the consequence that according to the principles of the national legal system, the nullity can be invoked by anyone having an interest, since it is relative nullity that only operates when specifically provided for and since no such provision exists in this case. The Court of Appeal correctly found the clause to be null because it was contrary to a mandatory rule and also recognized that the party concerned had an interest in invoking its nullity.

Notes:

(1) This follow-up decision taken after the CJ had given its judgment in the *Angonese* case is interesting for several reasons. The relevant Treaty provision in this case is not Article 18 TFEU, but Article 45 TFEU on the free movement of workers (*Angonese* is also dealt with in case 3.8 (IT) in Chapter 3). Moreover, the national court applied CJ case law on Article 45 TFEU to Italian nationals. Two remedies can be distinguished. The national court declared the clause to be null and it awarded damages.

(2) The Italian Court of Cassation first established the existence of a connecting factor with EU law in order to justify the application of the provisions of Article 45 TFEU to the situation of Angonese. It demonstrated that his situation was not internal to a Member State by observing that since Angonese was born in Italy and could be regarded an Italian citizen, he had exercised his right of free movement which Directive 93/96[61] conferred on him as a student by sojourning in Austria for his studies, with the purpose of acquiring a professional title which could also be recognised in Italy. Thus, in relation to his Member State of citizenship, Angonese's situation was considered similar to that of nationals of other Member States who could benefit from the freedoms guaranteed by Article 45 TFEU. Accordingly, Angonese could rely on the Treaty provision. Most probably, an additional reason was the Italian Constitution, which protects against reverse discrimination.[62]

(3) The statement by the CJ in *Angonese* that the principle of non-discrimination on grounds of nationality laid down in Article 45 TFEU applies to individuals too may also apply in connection with the right of establishment and the freedom to provide services. National case law may therefore evolve, applying the prohibition to discriminate on grounds of nationality to a variety of cases in the realm of the fundamental freedoms.

(4) The Court of Cassation held the clause to be contrary to Article 45 TFEU. This had the result that the clause was null and incapable of producing effects. Under Italian law, the nullity was absolute, meaning that pursuant to the general rule on nullity, it could be relied upon by anyone having an interest, as opposed to relative nullity, which only operates in cases provided for by law.

(5) In addition to its finding of nullity, the court of first instance had awarded damages for loss of opportunity (€43,000). While the appeal court mitigated the amount of the damages awarded, it upheld the substantive decision of recognising damages as a remedy for the nullity.

---

[61] Council Directive 93/96/EEC of 29 October 1993 on the right of residence for students [1993] OJ L317/59.
[62] See section V.E below for more details.

(6) This case makes very clear that the prohibition of discrimination confers rights on individuals in their relationship with other individuals. Angonese could rely on his right not to be discriminated against by a future employer. The clause set by the future employer was declared null. This clause was drafted by an employer who was a private entity not exercising public powers.

(7) By awarding damages to Angonese, the national court provided an effective remedy for the future employer's infringement. In this case, the ground for liability in damages is most likely an unlawful act resulting from on infringement of a statutory provision.

IV.B NATIONAL CASE LAW WITHIN THE SCOPE OF ARTICLE 157 TFEU (EQUAL TREATMENT OF MEN AND WOMEN)

IV.B.i DIRECT EFFECT OF THE EU RULE

This subsection presents cases from national jurisdictions in which the national courts applied Article 157 TFEU directly to a horizontal relationship.[63]

It should be noted that individuals can only rely on rights provided for by EU law if their case falls within the scope of EU law (see case 4.9 (FR) in section IV.A.i above). The first step in determining the effect of EU law on a horizontal legal relationship is to assess whether or not EU law covers the legal relationship.

In some of the cases presented below, the direct effect of provisions of primary EU law is responsible for remarkable substantive changes in the horizontal relationship, both as regards realising the right provided for by EU law and the enforcement of rights by, eg, obtaining damages in case of infringement.

The case law presented below shows that national courts in Belgium and the French Court of Cassation applied Article 157 TFEU directly to horizontal relationships, with the result that a clause in a contract was null and void. The Dutch national court, by way of obiter dictum, explicitly considered this very possibility.

In the first French case (case 4.17 (FR)), the national court explicitly used the primacy of EU law as a rationale for its direct application in a horizontal relationship. The Belgian courts (cases 4.15 (BE) and 4.16 (BE)) used the doctrine of direct effect to insist on the need to assess the contractual clause or the treatment at issue. The Dutch court (case 4.19 (NL)) did not elaborate upon any EU law doctrines. One of the reasons for this may be that the Netherlands has a monistic system in which EU law automatically becomes part of national law. With regards to the second French case (case 4.18 (FR)), it remains unclear whether the national court would have decided in the same vein if no national rule addressing non-discrimination had existed.

In one case (case 4.20 (NL)), the application of EU law did not change the substance of the horizontal relationship. It is nevertheless an interesting case because it demonstrates that national courts explicitly apply EU law and thus shows they are aware of

---

[63] For the method of selecting cases and the structure of the presentation of the cases, see above, first paragraph of this section.

the fact that EU law is part of the framework regulating and thus shaping horizontal relationships.

Arbeidsrechtbank Nijvel (Labour Tribunal of Nijvel),
24 May 1989[64]   **4.15 (BE)**

Plapied and Gallez v UCL

UNEQUAL PAY FOR MEN AND WOMEN BY WAY OF SUPPLEMENTARY FAMILY ALLOWANCES
GRANTED VIA A COLLECTIVE AGREEMENT

Counterpartial inequality

The mere fact that female workers must take administrative action to obtain payment of supplementary family allowances while male workers need not do so can be construed as a prohibited discrimination under Article 157 TFEU

Facts: Both Plapied and Gallez were female employees of the Catholic University of Leuven (UCL). On the basis of its collective agreement of 28 July 1969, UCL granted supplementary family allowances to members of the administrative and technical staff. Under the collective agreement, married female workers living with their spouse and children only rarely received supplementary family allowances, while UCL systematically paid these allowances to their male counterparts in the same situation. The collective agreement had been concluded for an indefinite period and was replaced by a new collective agreement on 13 June 1973, which included broader provisions on supplementary allowances.

Held: Plapied and Gallez sought a judgment ordering the UCL, pursuant to [now Article 157 TFEU], to pay them supplementary family allowances as provided for in the collective agreement of the administrative and technical staff of the UCL of 28 July 1969 with respect to the years 1976–85.

Judgment: The Belgian Court rightly applied [now Article 157 TFEU] directly to the contract clauses and set them aside.

14. [Now Article 157 TFEU] applies not only to the actions of the public authorities but also extends to all agreements for regulating paid work in collective ways and to contracts between individuals' (CJ, 8 April 1976, *Defrenne II v. Sabena*, 43/75, para 39).

15. Accordingly, [now Article 157 TFEU] applies to contractual relationships, both individual or collective, between the U.C.L. and its employees.

16. The principle of equal pay has applied in full in Belgium since 1 January 1962 …

19. Therefore, to the extent that the elimination of unequal pay between male and female workers does not require any amendments to the legislation and regulations in force in Belgium but only a change in the provision(s) based on agreements or established unilaterally by the employer, [now Article 157 TFEU] is directly applicable.

20. Accordingly, in so far as Ms. Plapied and Ms. Gallez establish that the difference in the amount of pay to which they object is based on gender discrimination, [now Article 157 TFEU] applies directly in the sense that the workers concerned may rely on it in law to obtain equal pay and that national courts must take [now Article 157] into consideration as an element of [EU] law …

…

---

[64] Labour Tribunal of Nijvel 24 May 1989 *JTT* 1990, 203 *Plapied and Gallez v UCL*.

47. Indeed, to change the order of priority and become recipients of statutory family allowances, workers living with the father of their child(ren) must complete administrative procedures of which the outcome is uncertain since it depends on either 'the agreement of the holder of the priority', in other words the father of the child or children … or, if he refuses such agreement, on the decision of the Minister of Social Affairs …

48. The mere fact of having to engage in administrative procedures to obtain the payment of supplementary family allowances, while male workers in the same situation need not do so, should be considered as resulting in discrimination as prohibited by [now Article 157 TFEU] …

50. In addition and as a subsidiary consideration, the court reminds the U.C.L. that the system for the granting of family allowances as organised by the consolidated legislation on family allowances does not involve any discrimination against women since all the children of male or female paid workers ultimately receive family allowances, whereas, by contrast, in the system of supplementary family allowances as devised by the U.C.L., the children of married female workers whose spouses do not work for the U.C.L. are excluded.

Notes:

(1) This judgment illustrates one of the techniques that national courts can use when applying EU law. EU law can, moreover, influence a case in various ways, even via the application of one and the same technique. In this case, the Belgian court opted for direct application of [now Article 157 TFEU] to the horizontal relationship between the female workers and UCL. The Court explicitly held that [now Article 157 TFEU] applied to both the individual and the collective contractual relationships between UCL and its staff.

(2) However, as the discrimination in question was made by reference to a fixed priority allocation system established by the legislator (paragraph 50), the Belgian Court could also have reviewed this Belgian legislation against EU law. If the national rule is found to be contrary to EU law, it must be set aside, which indirectly affects the horizontal relationship by depriving the provisions of the collective agreement of their legal basis. The lacuna in the collective agreement can then be filled with EU law or a national rule interpreted in the light of EU law. It remains unclear, given the full effect of Article 157 TFEU and given its direct horizontal effect as formulated by the court, why the court deemed it to be relevant that Article 157 TFEU was only directly applicable to the extent that the elimination of unequal pay between male and female workers did not require the laws and regulations in force in Belgium to be amended, but merely that the provision(s) based on agreements or established unilaterally by the employer be changed. In its reasoning, the court seems to have avoided the direct vertical effect of Article 157 TFEU and to have regarded direct horizontal effect as less far-reaching. Moreover, it is a misconception that a rule of EU law can produce direct horizontal effect without producing direct vertical effect. However, the Belgian Court rightly applied [now Article 157 TFEU] directly to the contract clauses and set them aside.

(3) The application of Article 157 TFEU reshaped the horizontal relationships. Female employees were granted the same family benefits under the same conditions as male employees.

Rechtbank van Koophandel Brussel (Brussels Commercial Court), 5 April 1994[65]

4.16 (BE)

Heyrman v SA Sabena

UNEQUAL PAY FOR AND WOMEN

Flying pension schemes

Article 157 TFEU precludes an insurance policy containing discrimination based exclusively on gender and not justified by any objective factor

Facts: On 31 May 1978, Sabena agreed in consultation with the social partners on a disability insurance for its staff. The policy concluded with Royale Belge provided for payment of a pension to members as compensation for the financial consequences in case of temporary or permanent inability to fly. However, the period of guaranteed coverage differed between men and women; under the policy the guaranteed coverage for male staff would end not earlier than on the fifty-fifth birthday and not later than on the sixtieth birthday; for female personnel, the guaranteed coverage ended at the end of the month in which the insured turned 50. As a result, Heyrman, a former air hostess in the service of Sabena who was declared unfit to fly in March 1984, received less payment than she would have received had she been a man.

Held: Heyrman alleged that Sabena had taken out an insurance policy with Royale Belge that was discriminatory for women. She claimed payment by Sabena of a sum equal to the difference between what she had already received and what she would have received under the policy had she been a man.

Judgment: The Court grants Heyrman payment of a sum equal to the difference between what she had already received and what she would have received under the policy had she been a man.

Whereas [now Article 157 TFEU] guarantees equal pay for male and female workers ...;
This article is directly applicable, as agreed by the parties ...;
Whereas there is no difficulty of interpretation; the insurance taken out by the Sabena company constitutes pay in the sense of [now Article 157]; it does not therefore seem useful to seek a ruling from the European Court of justice ... Whereas Article 10 of the insurance policy discriminates solely on the basis of gender and which is not justified by any objective and extraneous factor ...;
Discrimination of this kind is contrary to [now Article 157 TFEU]; Stéphanie Heyrman rightly claims restoration of equal pay in the sense of [now Article 157 TFEU].

Notes:

(1) In this judgment, the Belgian Court applied [now Article 157 TFEU] directly to the contractual relationship between the employer Sabena and the employee Heyrman.

(2) Since the contract concluded between Sabena and Heyrman referred to an insurance policy that differentiated between men and women with regard to the guaranteed period of coverage, that part of the contract infringed [now Article 157 TFEU].

(3) It is not clear from the judgment whether the national court disapplied or annulled the contractual clause.

(4) However, it is very clear from the judgment that the individual could directly invoke her right to equal pay under [now Article 157 TFEU].

---

[65] Brussels Commercial Court 5 April 1994 *TBH* 1996, 242 *Heyrman v SA Sabena.*

(5) The application of [now Article 157 TFEU] reshaped horizontal relationships. Female employees were granted the same remuneration scheme as male employees.

(6) Regarding the remedies that are available for infringement of the prohibition of discrimination in a horizontal relationship, there is an interesting related case by the highest Belgian national court: Court of Cassation, Third Chamber 23 December 1991 Chr. D.S. 1992, 7 p 287 ff. The Court of Appeal had rendered null the part of a contractual clause that excluded female employees from a payment for termination of the employment contract, although the employer had alleged that [now Article 157 TFEU] did not allow for such partial nullity and that, for that reason, the entire clause should have been rendered null. The Supreme Court quashed the decision because the Court of Appeal had not discussed the employer's allegation. The Supreme Court did not decide on the facts, but referred the case to another court. The subsequent Court of Appeal confirmed the approach of the first Court of Appeal: it was possible to render the clause partially null.[66]

Cour de Cassation (Court of Cassation),
18 December 2007[67]   **4.17 (FR)**

Société Régie autonome des transports parisiens (RATP) v M Somazzi

DISCRIMINATION ON GROUNDS OF AGE AND, IN THIS CONNECTION, OF GENDER

Parisian permanent staff

A provision in staff regulations reserving to certain women the benefit of an exemption from the age limit and excluding men who are in the same situation is contrary to Article 157 TFEU

Facts: The Independent Paris Transport Authority (RATP) was a public industrial and commercial establishment in France. Its staff regulations included a provision that the age limit of 35 years of Article 9 of the RATP Staff Regulations may not be applied to widows, divorced women who have not remarried, mothers of three or more children, and single women obliged to work with at least one dependent child. This provision gives priority access to permanent staff status at RATP. Somazzi, a divorced male employee of RATP, alleged that he was discriminated against, since he had been denied permanent agent status and the benefit attached thereto.

Held: On 4 July 2006, the Paris Court of Appeal rejected the application of Article 9 of the Staff Regulations and granted Somazzi the benefit of permanent staff status, ruling that the provision was contrary to the [EU] law principle of equal treatment. The RATP appealed to the Court of Cassation. The Court of Cassation reiterated that a contractual provision which gives absolute and unconditional priority to some groups of women without according the same benefit to men in the same situation infringed the [EU] principle of equal treatment between women and men.

---

[66] Several decisions by the Employment Tribunal Mons 10 October 1994; see, eg, Employment Tribunal Mons, Second Chamber 10 October 1999 *RG* 11290, *Luc Tillie v SA Sabena*; Employment Tribunal Mons, Second Chamber 10 October 1994 *RG* 11291 *Léopold Dethier v SA Sabena*. See also: http://jure.juridat.just. fgov.be/view_decision.html?justel=F-19941010-4&idxc_id=18085&lang=FR.

[67] French Court of Cassation 18 December 2007no 06-45132 *Bulletin* 2007 V no 215 *Société Régie autonome des transports parisiens (RATP) v M Somazzi*.

Judgment: Whereas, according to the contested confirmatory judgment (Paris, 4 July 2006), Mr. Somazzi, relying on the provisions of Article 9(2) of the staff regulations of the RATP (the 'staff regulations') which provide that the age limit of 35 years is not applicable to widows and women who are divorced or not remarried, to mothers of three children and more and to unmarried women with at least one dependent child who are obliged to work, has instigated proceeding with the Labour Court, arguing that he was discriminated against since he had been deprived of the benefit of the status of permanent officer and the associated benefits even though he satisfied the conditions;

...

Whereas, subsequently, in referring to the primacy of [EU] law without assessing the legality of Article 9 of the staff regulations, the appeal court rightly decided that this text could not prevent the application of the principle of equal treatment for male and female workers in matters of employment and occupation resulting from Article 141(4) of the EC Treaty [now Article 157 TFEU] and Article 2(4) of Directive 76/207/EEC of 9 February 1976;

...

But whereas having found that the regulations at issue granted absolute and unconditional priority to the candidacies of certain categories of women, which include women who have divorced and not re-married and who are obliged to work, and reserved to these women the benefit of the non-applicability of the age limits for access to the status of permanent officer with the RATP, to the exclusion of men who have divorced and not re-married and who are in the same situation, the appeal court, which was not required to respond to the invalid conclusions allegedly omitted according to the second part, rightly decided that such regulations were contrary to the [EU] principle of equal treatment for men and women in matters of employment and occupation as it follows from Article 141(4) of the EC Treaty [now Article 157 TFEU] and Article 3(1) and Article 2(4) of Directive 76/207/EEC ...

Notes:

(1) In this case, the French Court of Cassation referred to the primacy of EU law. It held that the text of the provision of the Staff Regulations of the company and employer RATP could not prevent the application of the principle of equal treatment of men and women.

(2) The national court referred to both [now Article 157 TFEU] and the directive, and upheld the ruling of the Court of Appeal that the provision of the Staff Regulations was not applicable.

(3) EU law was applied directly in this relationship. Since RATP was mentioned to be a public industrial and commercial establishment, it is not clear whether the relationship was vertical or horizontal. However, under French law, private law applies equally to both public and private companies. Therefore, the court's decision would have been the same if the company had been a private company.

(4) This case is therefore an example of direct horizontal effect: the contractual relationship was directly influenced.

(5) The consequence for the horizontal relationship between the male worker and the employer was that the provision of the Staff Regulations no longer impeded the possibility of permanent employment for the male employee.

(6) This case does not provide information about (effective) remedies. If, for example, an employer has no vacancies which the male worker can fill, damages could be an alternative remedy.[68]

Cour de Cassation (Court of Cassation),
27 February 1991[69]   **4.18 (FR)**

CPAM de la Mayenne v Ferandin et al

A PROVISION IN THE COLLECTIVE AGREEMENT GRANTING A NURSERY
ALLOWANCE TO SINGLE MOTHERS IS CONSIDERED AS UNEQUAL PAYMENT

Singularity

Any provision in a collective labour agreement that grants one or more workers of the one sex less than workers of the opposite sex for equal work is null and void

Facts: Ferandin and others were employed by Mayenne. The collective agreement applying to the workers of this company granted a nursery allowance only to single mothers employed by social security bodies, but denied this benefit to men in a similar situation.

Held: On 30 November 1989, the Angers Court of Appeal granted the claim of Ferandin and others for payment of the allowance, since any benefit paid by an employer to a female worker in connection with her employment constitutes pay and must therefore also be paid to men who satisfy the required conditions. The Court of Cassation also held the challenged contractual provision to be void because it violated [now Article 157 TFEU] and Article L 140-2 of the French Labour Code by breaching the principle of equal pay for women and men. Mayenne was ordered to pay the nursery allowance at issue to the men who satisfied the conditions set out in the collective agreement.

Judgment: [P]ursuant to [now Article 157 TFEU] and Article L. 140-2 of the Labour Code, any benefit paid by an employer to its employees under their employment contract constitutes pay; pursuant to article L. 140-4 of the Labour Code, any provision laid down in a collective agreement … which includes, for one or several workers of the one sex, lower pay than that accorded to the workers of the other sex, for the same job or a job of equal value, is null and void …

After establishing that for the period in question the agreement of 2 July 1968 provided for a nursery allowance to certain women employed by the social security institutions, but denied this benefit to men in a similar situation, the Court of Appeal then rightly ordered [Mayenne] to pay this allowance to fathers who satisfied the conditions laid down in the agreement.

Notes:

(1) It is not clear whether the French Court of Cassation found nullity in this case on the basis of EU law or of national law (or both). EU law and national law seem to have mutually supported the outcome of the case.

---

[68] CJ Case C-14/83 *Sabine von Colson and Elisabeth Kamann v Land Nordrhein-Westfalen* [1984] I-01891 ECLI:EU:C:1984:153, paras 22 ff.
[69] French Court of Cassation 27 February 1991 *Bulletin* 1991 V no 101, 63 *CPAM de la Mayenne v Ferandin et al.*

(2) The French Court of Cassation explicitly mentioned [now Article 157 TFEU] in its judgment to underline the fact that not only the national Labour Code, but EU law too requires equal payment of men and women. Since, however, EU law says nothing whatsoever about the legal consequences of a violation of this provision, the Court of Cassation rightly used its national law as the basis for declaring the provision of the collective agreement granting the allowance null and void.

(3) Just as in case 4.17 (FR), it was a male employee who was discriminated against. The question arising after the declaration of nullity was how the unequal treatment was to be remedied. The national court ruled that the invalid remuneration must be substituted by operation of law so that in similar situations, male employees are paid the same higher pay as enjoyed by female employees. The employer was obliged to grant the higher pay to male employees as well.

(4) The nullity pronounced in this case was a remedy provided for by national law.

(5) The impact of EU law (directly via [now Article 157 TFEU] and indirectly via the Article in the national Labour Code) is evident. A provision in a contract was declared null and was substituted to ensure that the horizontal relationship was consistent with the requirements set by EU law.

Hoge Raad der Nederlanden (Supreme Court of the Netherlands), 5 January 2007[70]   **4.19 (NL)**

Bijenkorf cs v Boersma-Leenmeijer cs

INDIRECT DISCRIMINATION OF PART-TIME EMPLOYEES
AND TEMPORARY WORKERS

Freedom of choice

Part-timers will only find themselves in a more unfavourable position than full-time workers with regard to the possibility of participating in the pension plan if the conditions under which they can use their right to opt for participation constitute such a barrier as to render their participation in the pension scheme practically impossible

Facts: Boersma-Leenmeijer and other defendants had been employed as assistants or part-time workers by several Dutch companies, including Bijenkorf. Their main activities involved selling goods. Until 1 January 1987, the collective pension scheme offered by the companies excluded assistants and part-time workers. The scheme was amended with effect from 1 December 1986 to the extent that, as far as is relevant here, the applicable waiting period for part-timers for compulsory participation in the pension scheme was reduced to one year. As of 1992, the waiting period was abolished altogether so that all workers could participate in the scheme from the commencement of their employment.

Held: The Court of Appeal of Amsterdam allowed the claims of Boersma-Leenmeijer and others for compensation for damages with respect to the years for which they were not included in the pension scheme, holding that pursuant to [now Article 157 TFEU] the scheme for part-timers was not equal to and was disadvantageous compared with the scheme for full-time workers.

---

[70] HR 5 January 2007 *NJ* 2007, 320 ECLI:NL:HR:AY8771 *Bijenkorf cs v Boersma-Leenmeijer cs.*

Judgment: The Supreme Court of the Netherlands quashed the judgment of the Court of Appeal. It did not see any discrimination in the facts as presented in the judgment of the Court of Appeal. Like the Court of Appeal, the Supreme Court applied Article 157 TFEU.

3.3.2 Part 2.1.1 of the ground of cassation claims – in brief – that in para. 4.9 the Court of Appeal failed to appreciate that the mere fact of the freedom of choice whether or not to participate in the pension scheme offered at the time to part-timers did not constitute such a barrier as to make participation impossible. The risks attached to this freedom of choice which the Court of Appeal held to be disadvantageous do not as such constitute an exclusion from participation that is prohibited by [now Article 157 TFEU] nor do they make the pension scheme more unfavourable for part-timers than for full-timers ...

The Part raises the question of whether the optional participation included in the pension scheme constituted discrimination against part-timers as prohibited under [now Article 157 TFEU] regarding their participation in the pension scheme. As can be assumed with a sufficient degree of certainty on the basis of the case law of the Court of Justice of the European Union, the decisive criterion regarding this question in this case ... is whether the circumstances in which the part-timers could use their right to opt for participation in the pension scheme during the waiting period constituted such a barrier to free choice on the part of the part-timers as to make it practically impossible for them to participate, with the result that the part-timers were de facto excluded from participating in the scheme. Only then it could be said that the part-timers were in a less favourable position as regards the possibility to participate in the pension scheme than the full-timers.

None of the risks mentioned by the Court of Appeal – which it apparently derived from general experience – were of such a nature, however, that generally speaking and considered objectively they constituted such a real obstacle for the part-timers to their joining the pension scheme during the waiting period as to entail their de facto exclusion from participation.

Notes:

(1) In this case, the Supreme Court of the Netherlands quashed the judgment of the Court of Appeal. The Supreme Court did not find any discrimination in the facts as presented in the judgment of the Court of Appeal. Like the Court of Appeal, the Supreme Court applied Article 157 TFEU.

(2) After cassation by the Supreme Court, another Court of Appeal would have to decide upon the facts of the case. In such further adjudication of a case, the Court of Appeal can decide either to declare the pension scheme discriminatory for other reasons than those mentioned by the first Court of Appeal or to declare the pension scheme non-discriminatory.

(3) Another issue which the Court of Appeal would have to consider was the influence of EU law on horizontal relationships by reviewing the law of prescription against the principle of effectiveness. The Supreme Court observed that the right to equal participation in a pension scheme based on Article 157 TFEU could be affected if, due to limitation, the pension entitlement built up over different working periods is reduced in the event that not all periods of work are counted when calculating the retirement pay.

(4) This reasoning implies that Article 157 TFEU can be a ground for setting aside the national law of limitation. Consequently, an individual relying on the national

limitation rules can be confronted with the obligation to perform. Until now, the CJ has not been inclined to rule that national time limits are incompatible with the principle of effectiveness.[71]

Gerechtshof' s-Gravenhage (Court of Appeal of The Hague),
17 March 2009[72]   **4.20 (NL)**

X cs v Cooperation Centraal Bureau Rijvaardigheidsbewijzen (CBR)

INDIRECT DISCRIMINATION OF PART-TIME EMPLOYEES
AND TEMPORARY WORKERS

Excluded examiners

Offering an option for employment contracts with different rights to participation in the pension scheme and insisting on making a choice for one of the contracts does not have the effect of eliminating the exclusion of part-time workers from the pension plan during this period

Facts: The appellants worked at CBR during the years 1977–79 as secondary examiners on the basis of a contract for the provision of certain services. Until 1990, the employment regulations of CBR provided for a pension plan that excluded married women and part-time employees from participation. As of 1 January 1990, CBR applied a pension scheme which no longer contained exclusions. From 1986, due to a reorganisation of the functions of the secondary examiners, CBR had worked with a system that only recognised three types of employment contracts, each with a different right to participation in the pension scheme.

Held: The court of first instance dismissed the appellants' claims for payment of damages with respect to the years they were not included in the pension scheme, as it held that those claims were time barred.

Judgment: The Court of Appeal upheld the decision of the lower court.

10. It has neither been alleged nor become apparent that the issue of 'pension repair' by CBR was already 'on the agenda' in a way known to the appellants – at the time when CE contracts were concluded between CBR and [appellants] – or that CBR had presented the waiver of all and any claims to pension repair – with respect to past periods – to be a consequence of concluding a CE contract. For this reason alone – having regard to the Haviltex criterion – the Court of Appeal holds that it cannot be inferred from the mere fact that [the appellants] opted to conclude a CE contract (without a pension scheme), that by doing so they waived all and any claims to pension repair with respect to past periods. Especially not given the fact that their choice was based on the fact that they could not meet the requirements set by CBR for concluding a contract *with* a pension scheme – as was known to CBR.

11. In the opinion of the Court of Appeal the foregoing also applies mutatis mutandis to claims to pension repair with respect to the (brief) period between the conclusion of the CE contracts and 1 January 1990 (effective date of the new pension rules). This is so because choosing a contract without a pension scheme in a situation in which CBR insisted on choosing one of the three types of contract it had established does not

---

[71] Hartkamp 2016 no 113.
[72] Court of Appeal of The Hague 17 March *PJ* 2009,76 ECLI:NL:GHSGR:2009:BH9352 *X cs v Cooperation Centraal Bureau Rijvaardigheidsbewijzen.*

mean – in the circumstances referred to under 10. above – that in this period there was no longer a situation in which part-timers were excluded under the 'old' pension scheme. [The appellants] can therefore not be considered to have waived all and any claims in connection with said exclusion: this requires more than merely signing a CE contract knowing that it does not provide for a pension scheme.

Notes:

(1) The Court of Appeal of The Hague ruled explicitly that this case concerned 'equal payment claims for men and women on the basis of [now the TFEU]'. This explicit reference to the TFEU makes the case exceptional and worth noticing.

(2) In this case, limitation periods were also relevant for the eventual claims the applicants might have. In the same way as the Supreme Court of the Netherlands did in the case of 5 January 2007 (case 4.19 (NL)) that was discussed above, the Court of Appeal reviewed the limitation provisions, being procedural rules, against the EU principle of effectiveness when it considered the alleged waiver of rights (paragraphs 13 and 16).

(3) The Court of Appeal gave extensive consideration to the question whether the applicants had been effectively able to file their claims and whether they had been treated less favourably than in cases governed by national law. The remarkable conclusion was that the relevant national rule of limitation applied to all claims for damages and for that reason was not at variance with the principle of effectiveness.

(4) It can be questioned whether CBR is an individual or is to be regarded as an individual performing public functions. If the latter is the case, then according to EU law, it must be dealt with as a public institution. Since under Dutch law the same private law rules apply to individuals and public parties (see case 4.17 (FR)), the case is relevant to the subject of this casebook.

(5) In this case, the legal situation of the parties did not change. Nevertheless, it is clear that the national court is prepared to apply Article 157 TFEU directly to a horizontal relationship and to review a national provision that is applicable to that relationship against the EU law principle of effectiveness.

IV.B.ii INDIRECT APPLICATIONS OF THE EU RULE

This section presents cases from national jurisdictions in which the national courts applied the rationale of a relevant EU rule via a national rule that was in conformity with the rule of EU law, by harmonious interpretation of a national rule that was not in conformity with EU law or by reviewing an incompatible rule of national law against EU law.

The application of national law that is already in conformity with Article 157 TFEU is interesting for this casebook because such a national rule may be the result of the implementation of the provision of EU law by the national legislator. Furthermore, it is important because the national courts must also comply with new or evolving interpretations of the rule of EU law on which the national rule is based. With regard to Article 157 TFEU, some interesting examples of this dynamic from UK case law are discussed in section IV.B.ii.a below.

As will become clear, UK cases generally fall in this category. This can be explained by the fact that the UK generally has a good transposition record (transposition is done by the enactment of domestic secondary legislation, pursuant to the European Communities Act 1972). Sometimes substantive problems may arise.

IV.B.ii.a Application of the Rationale of the Rule of EU law via a National Rule that is in Conformity with the EU Rule

EU law can exert an indirect effect on the substance of a horizontal relationship via national rules that are in conformity with EU law. For example, the legislator of the Member State concerned may regard an existing national rule as an anticipatory enactment of the substance, and for that reason as an implementation, of a directive that was established and entered into force afterwards. Such a national rule is in the first place part of the framework regulating horizontal relationships. In the second place, legal actors have to be aware of the fact that the rule of national law is required to be in conformity with EU law (and with its interpretation by the CJEU).

Since cases in this category decided by national courts generally do not trigger any questions relating to EU law, they are not recognised as being influenced by EU law. Moreover, usually, they do not create problematic situations. An exception is the situation where the national court is aware of a possible incompatibility between the national legislation and the interpretation by the CJ of the rule of EU law. In such cases, the national court either refers a preliminary question to the CJ or interprets the national rule in conformity with the EU rule. Those situations are discussed separately in sections IV.A.ii.b and IV.B.ii.b.

A distinction must be made between these cases and the situation that an open norm of national law is interpreted in conformity with EU law (see section I.A above).

Court of Appeal, 27 April 1978[73]   **4.21 (UK)**

Shields v E Coomes Holdings Ltd

UNEQUAL PAY OF WOMEN AND MEN

Betting shop

A difference in work is not of practical importance if it does not arise during the actual performance of the work

Facts: Ms Shields worked as a counterhand in a betting shop in south-east London, one of 90 such establishments owned by E Coomes Holdings Ltd. Compared to a male counterhand working at the same shop, she was paid less. As the employer considered the shop to be situated in a highly criminal neighbourhood, they paid the male counterhand more than a woman similarly employed, because the male counterhand was also to act as a deterrent, to render immediate physical assistance if required, to be available in case of trouble when opening the shop and to carry cash between the betting shops. However, there had been no trouble of the kind feared in the betting shop.

---

[73] *Shields v E Coomes Holdings Ltd* [1978] 1 WLR 1408.

269

Held: The Industrial Tribunal dismissed the employee's complaint for equality of pay with the male counterhand on the ground that although they were employed in work of a broadly similar nature, there were differences of practical importance within the meaning of section 1(4) of the Equal Pay Act 1970. Therefore, the employee was not employed on like work within the meaning of section 1(2). The Employment Appeal Tribunal, however, allowed the employee's appeal holding that since male counterhands were paid more than the women whether or not they were fulfilling the protective role, the differences between the work of the employee and the male counterhand were not of practical importance in relation to the terms and conditions of employment and that, in any event, section 1(3) of the Act could not apply because the extra payment was made because the counterhand was a man and not because he was trained for security work; therefore, if there was a material difference, it was one of sex. The Court of Appeal upheld the result.

Judgment: [D]ismissing the appeal, (1) that, although the appeal tribunal's decision was based on the erroneous belief that male counterhands were employed in all the 90 betting shops the employee was doing work of a broadly similar nature to the man and, therefore, under section 1(4) of the Act consideration had to be given to whether the differences between her duties and those undertaken by the man were of practical importance; that the man's contractual obligations were irrelevant unless those obligations resulted in actual and not infrequent differences in practice; and that, since the man's responsibility to deal with trouble if it ever occurred could not represent a difference between the things done by him and the employee as counterhands, it had not been shown that there were differences of practical importance between their work and the employee was entitled to succeed on her claim under section 1(2)(a) of the Act.

(2) That, even if the employers could succeed under section 1(4) of the Act, the counterhand was employed because he was a man and not because he was trained in security duties and, therefore, the employees could not bring themselves within the provisions of section 1(3) that the variation in the terms of his contract was genuinely due to a material difference other than sex.

Lord Denning M.R. The difficulty posed by the industrial tribunal's finding that the differences between the employee's work and that of the man were 'real and existing and of practical importance' has been resolved by giving supremacy to [EU] law. Under that law it is imperative that pay for work at time rates should be the same for the same job and all discrimination on the ground of sex should be eliminated with regard to all aspects and conditions of remuneration. The differences found by the majority of the tribunal are all based on sex. They are because he is a man.

Notes:

(1) The English court seemingly enforced the national Equal Pay Act 1970 in combination with the Sex Discrimination Act 1975. Both statutes are considered to be 'plainly designed to implement the [now TFEU] and the Directives issued by the Council'. However, the approach taken by Lord Denning MR sheds light on the possibility of giving straightforward supremacy to EU law. By taking this approach, the court applied Article 157 TFEU rather than the national Acts. This circumvented the drawbacks of harmonious interpretation of a national rule of which it was not entirely clear whether it was already in conformity with EU law and which apparently left scope for an interpretation not in conformity with EU law. See *Pickstone v Freemans plc*[74] for a comparable consideration of interpreting the national Acts in conformity with EU law.

---

[74] *Pickstone v Freemans plc* [1989] 3 WLR 265.

(2) This case shows that the English court was sympathetic to accepting an EU law interpretation of national rules in appeal proceedings, even though the lower court did not give consideration to EU law. See also *Lawson and others v Britfish Ltd.*[75] Since the UK generally uses the system of transposing EU law into national law, which is, moreover, amended if new developments via either the EU legislator or the CJ so require, it can be regarded as a judicial technique when the courts, where necessary, reinterpret the national implementing law in the light of further developments in EU law and apply it accordingly.

(3) The impact of EU law (directly via [now Article 157 TFEU] and indirectly via the intermediary article in the national Equal Pay Act 1970) is evident. A provision in a contract was deemed null. The nullity was remedied to ensure that the horizontal relationship corresponded with the requirements laid down in EU law. The employer had to pay equal wages to the female employee. The employee had realised her EU right to be paid the same as her male colleague.

Employment Appeal Tribunal, 1 November 2005[76]   **4.22 (UK)**

Sharp v Caledonia Group Services Ltd

CRITERION FOR JUSTIFICATION OF DIFFERENCE IN PAY

Personal nature

In an equal pay claim, the defence of genuine material difference under section 1(3) of the Equal Pay Act 1970 requires justification by objective criteria

Facts: The claimant, a woman named Sharp employed as a financial accountant, was paid less than a male office manager, who had also acted as private secretary to the chairman of the employers until the chairman's death, and whose salary had been initially set by the chairman to reflect the personal nature of that relationship and had been allowed by the employers to rise with inflation after his death.

Held: The claimant brought an equal pay claim against her employers, and an independent expert rated her work as of equal value to that of the comparator. The employers relied on the defence in section 1(3) of the Equal Pay Act 1970 that the variation was due to a material factor that was not the difference of sex. The employment tribunal dismissed the claim on the ground that the employers had established a genuine reason that caused the difference in pay, which was unrelated to any discrimination based on sex.

Judgment: The Employment Appeal Tribunal quashed the decision of the employment tribunal.

... allowing the appeal, that, on a claim for equal pay, once like work or work rated as equivalent or work of equal value had been established, a prima facie case of discrimination existed, which equated to the primary facts found in a case of sex discrimination whereby the burden of proof shifted onto the employer to show that there was no discrimination whatsoever; that in all such cases there was a need for objective justification unrelated to any discrimination linked to the difference in sex; and that, accordingly, the

[75] *Lawson and others v Britfish Ltd* [1987] ICR 726.
[76] *Sharp v Caledonia Group Services Ltd.* [2006] ICR 218.

tribunal had been wrong in approaching the genuine material defence factor from a subjective rather than an objective view, and the matter would be remitted for rehearing.

... We can see no reason whatsoever for not following the Brunnhofer decision which provides clear guidelines in equal pay cases as to the need for objective justification in all cases; in so far as there is a conflict between that decision and earlier United Kingdom decisions then we must now follow the European decision.

Notes:

(1) In establishing the criterion for assessing whether a variation in payment is justified by material difference, as laid down in national law, the Employment Appeal Tribunal was clearly guided by EU law, more specifically EU case law. It followed *Brunnhofer v Bank der osterreichischen Postsparkasse AG*,[77] which provides clear guidelines in equal pay cases as to the need for objective justification in all cases.

(2) In the context of the system adopted in the UK for complying with EU law, it is important that the Tribunal stated explicitly that insofar as a conflict occurs between the *Brunnhofer* decision and earlier UK decisions, the EU decision must be followed.

(3) Whether this explicit statement will result in a substantive change of the horizontal relationship depends on the decision of the national court after its re-examination of the case. The Employment Appeal Tribunal immediately granted both parties leave to appeal (paragraph 53 of the decision), yet neither professional literature nor the case law database yields any discussion of a decision of the Court of Appeal on the case. It can therefore be assumed that the case has been settled.

IV.B.ii.b Application of the Rationale of the EU Rule by Harmonious Interpretation of a National Rule that is Not in Conformity with EU Law

EU law can exert an indirect effect on the substance of a horizontal relationship by harmonious interpretation of a national rule that is not in conformity with EU law. This way of interpreting national law may substantively change the framework regulating horizontal relationships.

To avoid a result in a horizontal relationship that is at variance with the requirements of EU law, the national courts can interpret a rule of national law in conformity with Article 157 TFEU. Subsequently, the application of the reinterpreted rule of national law will have to lead to a solution that is not discriminatory. The possible legal doctrines to achieve this result are, eg, nullity, damages and undue payment.

The reader should be aware that in my consideration of this type of case, I include the situation in which the national court applies national law that is *not* in conformity with EU law. Such a situation may occur when the national court can neither harmoniously interpret the national provision nor apply an alternative technique (like positive obligation – see sections IV.A.iii and IV.B.iii).

---

[77] CJ 26 June 2001 Case C-381/99 *Susanna Brunnhofer v Bank der österreichischen Postsparkasse AG* [2001] I-04961 ECLI:EU:C:2001:358.

IV.B.ii.c Application of the Rationale of the EU Rule by Reviewing
an Incompatible Rule of National Law against EU Law

To avoid a result in a horizontal relationship that is at variance with the requirements of
EU law, a national court can review a rule of national law against Article 157 TFEU. If
the national provision is found to be incompatible, it has to be set aside. Subsequently,
the remaining national law provisions or the applicable EU law provisions will have to
lead to a solution that is not discriminatory. The possible legal doctrines to achieve this
result are, eg, nullity, damages and undue payment.

IV.B.iii POSITIVE OBLIGATION OF MEMBER STATES THAT IMPACT ON HORIZONTAL RELATIONS BETWEEN INDIVIDUALS

This section is intended to present cases from national jurisdictions involving a horizontal relationship, in which the national court finds on the basis of Article 157 TFEU
that the Member State has a positive obligation that indirectly affects that horizontal
relationship.[78] A national court may use this technique to avoid a result in a horizontal
relationship that is at variance with the requirements of EU law.

 As became clear from case law of the CJ and the ECHR and in section IV.A.iii
(Article 18 TFEU), a positive obligation can be responsible for remarkable substantive
changes in a horizontal relationship.

IV.B.iv MISCELLANEOUS

Under this heading, I set out and explain ways in which Article 157 TFEU can influence
national private law that are different from those dealt with in sections IV.B.i–IV.B.iii
above.

 A mechanism known from the case of *Test-Achats* (which will be discussed in cases
5.10 (BE) and 5.11 (BE) in section II.C.iv in Chapter 5) goes as follows. A provision
of secondary EU law is established to be applicable to the horizontal relationship via a
national provision implementing it. Subsequently, the provision of secondary EU law is
reviewed against a provision of primary EU law prohibiting discrimination and found to
be incompatible. After it has been set aside, the prohibition of discrimination governs
the horizontal relationship (eg, via a national provision that is in conformity with EU
primary law or via the provision of primary EU law itself). This has the consequence that
the horizontal relationship breaches the (remaining) applicable provisions and has to be
reshaped.

IV.C NATIONAL CASE LAW WITHIN THE SCOPE OF ARTICLE 19 TFEU

As explained in section III.B.i above, Article 19 TFEU has had limited importance in
private law so far. Since Article 19 TFEU has important symbolic and legal value within

---

[78] For the method of selecting cases and the structure of the presentation of the cases, see section IV.

EU law, it may well come to exert influence in private law relationships in future cases via the techniques distinguished in sections II.C.v and II.C.vi in Chapter 1, in section I.A in Chapter 4 and in section II.A.ii in Chapter 5.

V. FINAL OBSERVATIONS

This chapter has dealt with a variety of cases from most of the jurisdictions included in this casebook. It is interesting to note that the number of cases in which courts relied on Article 18 TFEU is significant. Apparently, Article 18 TFEU has practical relevance, separate from the free movement provisions.

After the above detailed discussion of reported case law in terms of facts, the legal relationships concerned, the techniques and mechanisms of EU law and national law, the substance of rules of EU law and national law, and the substantive implications of the prohibition of discrimination on grounds of nationality and gender, including available remedies, it is now possible to make some general observations that shed light on the differences and commonalities between the various judgments as regards the substantive and formal interaction between EU law and national (private) law. These are relevant to actors (scholars, judges, legal practitioners and parties) dealing with non-discrimination and private law in particular, and more generally also to actors dealing with the interaction between EU law and private law.

These observations give an insight into the substantive changes of a private law relationship after a confrontation with EU law (section V.A). They also throw light on the constitutional structures and techniques that frame the reasoning of national courts when they are dealing with the application of EU law in private law relationships (section V.B). They draw attention to the phenomenon that the fundamental freedoms are becoming an instrument to apply the rationale of non-discrimination (section V.C). Furthermore, they relate to the remedies used to achieve a result that is in conformity with EU law (section V.D). A striking phenomenon in the field of non-discrimination is that national courts run into problems and are surprised when they discover that the application of EU non-discrimination rules to citizens of other EU countries may result in a more favourable treatment of those citizens compared to the treatment of the Member State's own nationals under its domestic law. Since the appropriate attitude towards this phenomenon is partially covered by EU law, this issue will be considered too (section V.E).

V.A ARTICLES 18 AND 157 TFEU MAY SUBSTANTIVELY CHANGE HORIZONTAL RELATIONSHIPS

As explained before, EU law has developed several mechanisms via which it affects national (private) law. Article 18 or 157 TFEU may thus lead to substantive changes in horizontal relationships, regardless of whether they are applied directly or indirectly. An individual who infringes the prohibition of discrimination may be confronted with both contractual and non-contractual obligations. Where EU law imposes obligations upon individuals, it may be expected that it will also provide for appropriate grounds for justification on which individuals can rely.

Infringement of the prohibition of discrimination can, eg, constitute an unlawful act (cases 4.6 (BE) and 4.14 (IT)), a ground for rendering a contractual relationship null and void (cases 4.16 (BE), 4.18 (FR) and 4.21 (UK)), and for (subsequently) filling a contractual gap (cases 4.18 (FR) and 4.21 (UK)), for setting aside (cases 4.6 (BE), 4.7 (FR), 4.15 (BE) and 4.16 (BE)) or disapplying (case 4.17 (FR) a contractual clause, for granting a party a right under EU law (cases 4.17 (FR) and 4.14 (IT)), for granting a party a right under national law, eg, the right of ownership (case 4.12 (GERM) or for precluding a party from relying on rights derived from national law, eg, the right to suspend or to invoke national prescription rules (cases 4.10 (BE), 4.19 (NL) and 4.20 (NL)).

As a matter of fact, the direct or indirect confrontation of a horizontal relationship with EU law may also lead to the conclusion that the relationship is not in breach of any obligation under EU law. In such cases, EU law still has an effect on the horizontal relationship (cases 4.8 (FR), 4.11 (NL), 4.13 (FR) and 4.20 (NL)).

The accordance of direct horizontal effect to Articles 18 and 157 TFEU implies that individuals should be able to rely on appropriate grounds of justification (for the fundamental freedoms, see section VI in Chapter 3).

V.B NATIONAL COURTS DO EXPLICITLY CONSIDER THE CONSTITUTIONAL FRAMEWORK OR MECHANISM(S) OF INTERACTION BETWEEN EU LAW AND PRIVATE LAW

National systems vary in terms of the way they adapt to supranational and international legal rules. Particularly in dualistic systems, the courts tend to elaborate on how a rule of EU law takes effect in the national jurisdiction (case 4.7 (FR)), taking into consideration the development of EU law and its relationship to national law (4.12 (GERM)). Such considerations are seen less frequently in, eg, Dutch case law. The Netherlands has a monistic system in which EU law automatically becomes part of national law. Supremacy does not raise problems. Some courts explicitly take account of the principle of supremacy (cases 4.17 (FR), 4.21 (UK) and 4.22 (UK)) and direct horizontal effect (cases 4.15 (BE), 4.16 (BE) and 4.20 (NL)).

The possibility of complying with EU law may reach its limit when compliance would call for *contra legem* interpretation (case 4.10 (BE)).

EU law can only have an impact on national law in cases that come under its scope of application (case 4.9 (FR)).

Furthermore, national courts give consideration to the mechanism(s) to be used to ensure that EU law takes effect in private law (relationships) (cases 4.10 (BE), 4.11 (NL) and 4.21 (UK)). Even so, it does not always become clear which mechanism the court has used (cases 4.7 (FR) and 4.8 (FR)).

In some cases, the national court tried to find a justification for the infringement of EU law in its national law (cases 4.8 (FR) and 4.9 (FR)).

There is only one case that included an explicit consideration regarding the need to refer a preliminary question to the CJ (case 4.12 (GERM)).

V.C FUNDAMENTAL FREEDOMS AS AN INSTRUMENT TO APPLY THE RATIONALE OF NON-DISCRIMINATION

In line with the approach of the CJ, cases covered by fundamental freedom provisions are not dealt with under the general non-discrimination provision of Article 18 TFEU. Please take due note of the fact that this doctrine means that discrimination on grounds of age, for example, is found in case law on the fundamental freedom provisions. Decisions in these cases therefore shed light on the method used in cases decided exclusively on the basis of Article 18 TFEU (cases 4.8 (FR), 4.13 (FR) and 4.14 (IT)). In addition, courts apparently do not always require cases to be cross-Member State in nature. It may be sufficient if a case has cross-regional elements for the courts to hold that the fundamental freedoms, and consequently the general prohibition of discrimination, apply. Moreover, the statement by the CJ in *Angonese*[79] that the prohibition of discrimination on grounds of nationality laid down in Article 45 TFEU applies to individuals too may also apply in connection with the right of establishment and the freedom to provide services. National case law may therefore evolve so as to apply the prohibition to discriminate on grounds of nationality to a variety of cases in the realm of the fundamental freedoms.

V.D NATIONAL COURTS USUALLY FIND SUITABLE REMEDIES IN CASE OF INFRINGEMENT OF EU LAW

National courts usually find suitable remedies in their national systems, eg, injunctions (cases 4.6 (BE) and 4.12 (GERM)), order to pay equal wages, remuneration or benefits (cases 4.7 (FR), 4.15 (BE), 4.16 (BE), 4.18 (FR) and 4.21 (UK)), damages for loss of opportunity (case 4.14 (IT)) and enforcement of the existing obligation to perform (cases 4.19 (NL) and 4.20 (NL)). Moreover, courts review limitation provisions governing the enforceability of a right to establish whether they are compatible with the EU principle of effectiveness (cases 4.19 (NL) and 4.20 (NL)).

In one case, a problem that could not be solved within the private law relationship was solved by an explicit reference to Member State liability (case 4.10 (BE)).

V.E REVERSE DISCRIMINATION

EU law does not protect against unfavourable treatment by a Member State of its own nationals as compared to nationals of other Member States (cases 4.9 (FR) and 4.11 (NL)). In two cases, the court elaborated extensively on the method to achieve that individuals of other Member States were covered by national provisions addressed to domestic legal persons (case 4.12 (GERM)) or, conversely, to exclude nationals of other Member States from the definition of 'foreigner' (case 4.10 (BE)).

However, in a judgment of a lower court that was quashed by the highest national court, one of the reasons for not granting the claim was that the positive discrimination of individuals from other Member States is to be avoided (case 4.13 (FR)).

---

[79] CJ *Angonese* (n 26).

An approach that will avoid this situation is found in some Member States, eg, Italy, Belgium and Austria. In these jurisdictions, the (national) principle of equality requires the courts to treat domestic situations in the same way as cross-border situations (case 4.14 (IT)). On the basis of such a doctrine (enshrined in the national constitution or in the case law of a constitutional court),[80] citizens having the nationality of that country are protected against being treated (on the basis of, eg, EU law) less favourably than citizens from other countries.

FURTHER READING

Aristotle, *Ethica Nicomachea*, Book V, Chapter 3 nos 1–7, translated by H Rackman (Loeb Classical Libary).

J Basedow, 'Der Grundsatz der Nichtdiskriminierung im europäischen Privatrecht' (2008) *ZEuP* 230–51.

CD Classen, 'Freiheit und Gleichheit im öffentlichen und im privaten Recht – Unterschiede zwischen europäischem und deutschem Grundrechtsschutz' (2008) *EuR* 627–53.

JH Gerards, *Judicial Review in Equal Treatment Cases* (Leiden, Martinus Nijhoff Publishers, 2005).

X Groussot, *General Principles of Community Law* (Groningen, Europa Law Publishing, 2006).

S Huster, 'Gleichheit im Mehrebenensystem: Die Gleichheitsrechte der Europäischen Union in systematischer und kompetenzrechtlicher Hinsicht' (2010) *EuR* 325–37 ff.

K Koch and A Nguyen, 'Schutz vor mittelbarer Diskriminierung – Gleiches Recht für alle? Das Verbot der mittelbaren Diskriminierung in der höchstrichterlichen Rechtssprechung' (2010) *EuR* 364–77.

K Lenaerts, 'L'Égalité de Traitement en Droit Communautaire, un principe unique aux apparences multiples' (1991) 27 *CDE* 3–41.

A Metzger, 'Allgemeine Rechtsgrundsätze in Europa – dargestellt am Beispiel des Gleichbehandlungsgrundsatzes' (2011) 75(4) *RabelsZ* 845–81.

M de Mol, 'Horizontal Direct Effect of Union Prohibitions of Discrimination' in Hartkamp/Sieburgh/Keus/Kortmann/Wissink (eds) 2014 219–49.

M de Mol, *De directe werking van de grondrechten van de Europese Unie* (Oisterwijk, Wolf Legal Publishers, 2014).

E Muir, 'Of Ages in – and Edges of EU Law' (2011) 48(1) *CMLR* 39–62.

N Reich, 'The Impact of the Non-discrimination Principle on Private Autonomy' in D Leczykiewicz and S Weatherill (eds), *The Involvement of EU Law in Private Law Relationships* (Oxford, Hart Publishing, 2013) 253–78.

---

[80] Italian law has now introduced a specific provision that applies to such situations. The Italian general law on the participation of Italy in the formation and implementation of EU legislation and policy (Legge 24 December 2012 no 234 *Norme generali sulla partecipazione dell'Italia alla formazione e all'attuazione della normativa e delle politiche dell'Unione europea*) provides that the equality of treatment between Italian citizens and citizens of other EU Member States must be guaranteed when implementing EU legislation; Italian citizens may in any event not be treated less favourably (Article 32, co 1, lett i; Article 52). Before being transposed into legislation, the principle had already been recognised by the Italian Constitutional Court (Corte Costituzionale) (in particular, see Constitutional Court 30 December 1997 no 443) on the basis of Article 3 of the Italian Constitution and by the administrative tribunals. See for Belgium Constitutional Court of Belgium 30 June 2014 ECLI:NL:XX:2014:901*Schaarbeek v Belgium*.

N Reich, *General Principles of EU Civil Law* (Antwerp, Intersentia, 2014).

D Schiek, 'Age Discrimination before the ECJ: Conceptual and Theoretical Issues' (2011) 48(3) *CMLR* 777–99.

CH Sieburgh, 'The Union-Law Principle of Equality and its Effect on Private Law' in Hartkamp/Sieburgh/Keus/Kortmann/Wissink (eds) 2014 271–95.

J Temple Lang, 'Emerging European General Principles in Private Law' in Bernitz/Groussot/Schulyok et al (eds) 2013.

5

GENERAL PRINCIPLES OF EU LAW

I. GENERAL PRINCIPLES OF A PUBLIC LAW NATURE

Roel van Leuken and José Caramelo Gomes

I.A INTRODUCTION

This section concisely demonstrates the private law significance of three general principles that originate from public law: the principle of effectiveness (section I.B), the principle of legal certainty (section I.C) and the principle of proportionality (section I.D). In the absence of much reported national case law, the effects of these EU law principles on horizontal situations are primarily illustrated by examples from the case law of the CJ.

I.B THE PRINCIPLE OF EFFECTIVENESS

In *Van Gend & Loos*,[1] the CJ famously held that EU law 'not only imposes obligations on individuals, but is also intended to confer on them rights ... that arise not only where they are expressly granted by the Treaty, but also by reason of obligations which the Treaty imposes upon the Member States and upon the institutions of the [EU]'. In the absence of EU rules governing the substance and enforcements of these rights, it is for the national courts (acting in their supplementary capacity as EU courts) to uphold them according to

---

[1] CJ 5 February 1963 Case C-26/62 *Van Gend & Loos v Netherlands Inland Revenue Administration* [1963] I-00001 ECLI:EU:C:1963:1.

the substantive and procedural rules of their national law. As a result, there is a division of functions between the EU and national legal systems, with the former providing the *rights*, and the latter the *procedures* and *remedies*.[2] If national law lacks suitable rules for this purpose, the CJ may fill the gap through the application of the principle of effective judicial protection (section I.B.i). As we shall see, the primary considerations behind this principle are closely linked to fundamental rights and, ultimately, to the idea of the rule of law.[3] Another important aspect of the principle of effectiveness, sometimes referred to as procedural autonomy, is that it subjects the national rules governing actions brought to enforce rights derived from EU law to a certain measure of review by the CJ. Such rules must satisfy the requirements of equivalence and effectiveness (section I.B.ii).

I.B.i THE PRINCIPLE OF EFFECTIVE JUDICIAL PROTECTION

A Hartkamp, European Law and National Private Law[4]

[T]he principle of effective judicial protection. It imposes a duty on the member states to ensure that possibilities are available to their citizens to enforce their right in court proceedings.

In *Johnston* (222/84) this right was based on a provision of Directive 76/207/EEC (equal treatment in employment), which in general terms granted the right to pursue claims by judicial process, in combination with articles 6 and 13 ECHR. Subsequently, the same decision was reached in situations where a specific provision of EU law could not be invoked. The ECJ has often stated article 10 EC (currently art. 4(3) TEU) as the basis for the obligation of the member states to ensure judicial protection. A well-known case is *Factortame I* (C-213/89), in which the ECJ ruled that the national court must set aside a national rule that precludes it from granting interim relief (in this case against the English Crown) in favour of an individual invoking EU law, because such a restriction of its powers would prevent EU law from having full force and effect, even though only temporarily. See also the judgment given in *Unibet* (C-432/05).

Eventually, this aspect of the principle of effectiveness was codified in the Charter of Fundamental Rights. Article 47(1) of the Charter provides that everyone whose rights and freedoms guaranteed by the law of the Union are violated has the right to an effective remedy before a tribunal in compliance with the conditions laid down in this article ...

S Prechal and R Widdershoven, 'Redefining the Relationship between "Rewe-Effectiveness" and Effective Judicial Protection'[5]

[T]he cases decided by the ECJ ... illustrate which aspects of procedures and remedies can be affected by the principle [of effectiveness] and what the possible implications are of the requirement that the protection should be *effective*. Thus, for instance, the principle

---

[2] *cf* W van Gerven, 'Of Rights, Remedies and Procedures' (2000) 37(3) *CMLR* 501.
[3] S Prechal and R Widdershoven, 'Redefining the Relationship between "Rewe-Effectiveness" and Effective Judicial Protection' (2011) 4(2) *Review of European Administrative Law* 46.
[4] Hartkamp 2016 no 110.
[5] Prechal and Widdershoven (n 3) 36, footnotes omitted.

requires that there must be actual access to the courts, which must be independent and impartial and be competent to rule on both facts and the law. The possibility of applying to a court for a remedy may not be restricted, and certainly not denied altogether. This may of course have consequences for 'standing' requirements or pre-trial obligations, such as mandatory mediation or other out-of-court settlements. Furthermore, the principle may entail a shift in the burden of proof and it may imply that a preparatory act which would not normally be open to an appeal according to national law may nevertheless be regarded as a decision against which an appeal is possible. The ECJ has also implied from the principle an obligation on the part of the national authorities to give reasons for the decisions they take, so that the person concerned is able to defend his rights under the best possible circumstances. As a standard for national systems of judicial protection, the principle has also had significant consequences for the remedies that must be made available for breaches of EU law. Above we have already pointed out that in the case of *Unibet*, the *Factortame* rule, requiring interim measures to be available, was also explicitly based on the principle of effective judicial protection. A second, even more clearly articulated case was *Francovich*. According to the Court, the principle of state liability for loss caused to individuals whose rights are infringed follows from the requirement that Member States must ensure EU rules take full effect and must protect the rights they confer on individuals.

I.B.ii THE *REWE* DOCTRINE: THE REQUIREMENTS OF EQUIVALENCE AND EFFECTIVENESS

The second, highly important aspect of the principle of full effectiveness of EU law is that it subjects the procedural and substantive national rules governing actions brought to enforce rights derived from EU law to a certain measure of review by the CJ. Such rules must be no less favourable than those governing similar domestic actions (requirement of equivalence) and must not render practically impossible or excessively difficult the exercise of rights conferred by EU law (requirement of effectiveness). This so-called *Rewe* doctrine[6] has been applied by the CJ to several kinds of national rules of private (procedural) law.

A Hartkamp, European Law and National Private Law[7]

Many judgments are about time limits, both about time limits for filing complaints and objections whose non-observance results in loss of the possibility of commencing a legal action; and about limitation and prescription periods set for commencing the legal action itself. This was the issue of the *Rewe* judgment … in which the requirements of equivalence and effectiveness were formulated for the first time in a case concerning an administrative appeal period for recovering an import charge levied in violation of [now Article 38 TFEU]. In principle, the ECJ will respect the time limits set for such actions.

---

[6] CJ 16 December 1976 Case C-33/76 *Rewe Centralfinanz eG and Rewe Central AG v Landwirtschaftskammer für das Saarland* [1976] I-1989 ECLI:EU:C:1976:188.
[7] Hartkamp 2016 no 113.

However, as is observed by Craig and De Búrca, even reasonable time limits may be rendered incompatible with EU law 'where the effective protection of EU rights is negatively affected by other factors, for example: where the date on which the period begins to run is unclear; or commences before the applicant knew or should have known of the violation', or 'where the limitation period applies retroactively', or 'the national court has too much discretion in determining whether proceedings were brought 'promptly".[8]

The requirements of equivalence and effectiveness have been applied to other areas of private (procedural) law too. Examples concern, inter alia, abuse of rights (see section III), the *ex officio* application of legal grounds (see Chapter 7) and—as *Courage v Crehan*[9] illustrates—*nemo auditur*, the passing-on defence, and rules of evidence. In this landmark judgment, the CJ held that an *absolute* bar to a damages action brought by a party to a contract in breach of Article 101 TFEU is at variance with the principle of effectiveness, but explicitly added that EU law does *not* preclude national law from denying a party who is found to bear significant responsibility for the distortion of competition the right to obtain damages from the other contracting party.[10] *En passant*, the CJ also ruled that the passing-on defence does not in itself impair the effectiveness of Article 101 TFEU.[11] However, from cases concerning the undue payment of taxes/charges levied contrary to EU law, it appears that the principle of effectiveness opposes national presumptions or rules of evidence intended to place upon the claimant (who paid the tax/charge) the burden of establishing that the tax/charge unduly paid has not been passed on to other persons.[12] In the same vein, the principle can oppose national rules that oblige a claimant to prove that he has not passed on his damages resulting from an anti-competitive agreement.[13]

I.C THE PRINCIPLE OF LEGAL CERTAINTY

The principle of legal certainty expresses the fundamental premise that those subject to the law must know what the law is so as to be able to plan their actions accordingly.[14] In the interaction between EU law and national law, the principle mainly sets limits on the application of EU law.[15] The following examples may illustrate this.

---

[8] Craig and De Búrca 2015 242–43 (including references to relevant CJ case law).

[9] CJ 20 September 2001 Case C-453/99 *Courage v Crehan* [2001] I-06297 ECLI:EU:C:2001:465.

[10] CJ *Courage v Crehan* (n 9) paras 28 and 31–33.

[11] ibid, para 30. See section II.D.iii.c in Ch 2 and section IV.C in Ch 5.

[12] See, eg, CJ 9 November 1983 Case C-199/82 *Amministrazione delle Finanze dello Stato* v *SpA San Giorgio* [1983] I-03595 ECLI:EU:C:1983:318.

[13] See art 13 of Directive 2014/104/EU on antitrust damages actions: 'The burden of proving that the overcharge was passed on shall be on the defendant, who may reasonably require disclosure from the claimant or from third parties.'

[14] Tridimas 2006 242. See also X Groussot, *General Principles of Community Law* (Groningen, Europa Law Publishing, 2006) 189.

[15] Sometimes, though, the principle of legal certainty *permits* EU law to prevail. See LAD Keus, 'The Principle of Legal Certainty' in Hartkamp/Sieburgh/Keus/Kortmann/ Wissink (eds) 2014 299–300.

I.C.i SIGNIFICANT LEGAL UNCERTAINTY MAY INVOLVE A BREACH OF THE PRINCIPLE OF EFFECTIVENESS

UK Supreme Court, 24 October 2012[16]   **5.1 (UK)**

BCL Old Co Ltd et al v BASF plc et al

COMMENCEMENT OF A NATIONAL LIMITATION PERIOD
IS SUFFICIENTLY FORESEEABLE

Vitamins unlimited

As the operation of the statutory time limit is sufficiently clear, precise and foreseeable, the statute did not render it excessively difficult for the appellants to exercise their EU law rights

Facts: In November 2001, the Commission adopted a decision finding that a number of undertakings, including BASF, had participated in a cartel with respect to the sale of vitamins, in breach of Article 101 TFEU. In March 2006, BASF appealed against the fine that had been imposed, but not against its liability for the infringement. Two years later, in March 2008, BCL filed a claim for damages against BASF under section 47A of the Competition Act. According to rule 31 of the Competition Appeal Tribunal Rules 2003, any such claim for damages required to be made within two years from: (i) the date on which the cause of action accrued; (ii) the date on which a right to bring an appeal expires; or (iii) the date of the final judgment in an appeal. The Competition Appeal Tribunal considered BCL's action as within time. Subsequently, however, the Court of Appeal found that an appeal solely against a fine did not extend the deadline for a claim for damages. BCL appealed to the Supreme Court, arguing that the operation of the two-year limitation period was a legally uncertain matter, which rendered it 'excessively difficult' to pursue its claim against BASF in time.

Held: Unanimously dismissing the appeal, the Supreme Court ruled that there was no failure to comply with the EU law principles of effectiveness and legal certainty.

Judgment: Lord Mance: The principles of effectiveness and legal certainty on which … BCL relies are well-recognised … in … Case C-453/99 *Courage Ltd v Crehan* [2002] QB 507, [2001] ECR I-6297, Case C-445/06 *Danske Slagterier v Germany* [2009] ECR I-2119 and Case C-456/08 *Commission v Ireland* [2010] ECR I-859 …

Resuming the effect of these cases: in *Courage Ltd v Crehan* the Court of Justice was concerned with an English law rule which rendered recourse impossible, but pointed out that it was also impermissible for a rule of law to render the exercise of European legal rights 'excessively difficult'. In *Danske Slagterier* the Court was concerned with the latter situation, and held it to apply where it was not ascertainable 'with a reasonable degree of certainty' or not 'sufficiently foreseeable' whether a limitation period applied. The same test, whether a national rule renders it 'impossible or excessively difficult' to exercise European rights is stated and restated in [paragraphs] 53 and 62 in *Commission v Ireland*. In paragraphs 61, 65 and 66 the Court joins this with references to the need for Member States to create a legal situation which is 'sufficiently, precise, clear and foreseeable' or 'sufficiently clear and precise' to enable individuals to ascertain and avail themselves of their rights, and (in that case) to exclude the risk of their being deprived of the right to challenge a public procurement decision by a decision 'handed down by a national court

---

[16] *BCL Old Co Ltd et al v BASF plc et al* [2012] UKSC 45.

on the basis of its own interpretation' of its Rules. In [paragraph] 58 the Court summarised its conclusion in *Commission v* Ireland as being that it was not compatible with the Directive if the scope of the period laid down in Order 84A(4) was 'extended to cover the review of interim decisions … without that being clearly expressed in the wording thereof'.

…

Taking the statutory provisions by themselves, I have no doubt about the answer to the question whether the commencement of the two-year limitation period was sufficiently foreseeable. The Court of Appeal's analysis was impeccable and it was in my opinion well-justified in speaking of 'the plain and ordinary meaning of the statutory language' and of the legal position as 'clear'.

…

The domestic legal position resulting from the course of events outlined in paragraphs 32 to 36 is now unchallenged and unchallengeable. But it took time and a process of appeals to reach this position. Does that mean that English law lacked the requisite legal certainty, that its requirements or effect were not 'sufficiently foreseeable' or that it was 'excessively difficult' for BCL to take advantage of the possibility of making a claim for damages against BASF?

…

The Tribunal decisions considered in paragraphs 32 to 38 above were irrelevant to BCL's actual conduct. But do they demonstrate objectively the existence of such uncertainty in English law as to infringe the relevant European legal principles? Clearly, it is unfortunate if Competition Appeal Tribunals arrive at conclusions on the commencement of a limitation period and on the power to grant an extension of time which are held erroneous on appeal to the Court of Appeal. But an appellate system is there to remedy error and to establish the correct legal position. I do not accept that its ordinary operation is the hallmark of a lack of legal certainty or effectiveness.

Notes:

In this case, the UK Supreme Court had to rule whether the operation of a two-year national limitation period for bringing a damages claim for breach of Article 101 TFEU was contrary to the EU law principles of effectiveness and legal certainty. To that end, paragraphs 10–28 contained a detailed review of the relevant EU and ECHR case law. First, the Supreme Court recalled that the principle of effectiveness as established in *Courage v Crehan*[17] requires national courts to avoid the application of national procedural rules that 'render practically impossible or excessively difficult the exercise of rights conferred by [EU] law' (paragraph 10). Second, it referred to the judgment in *Danske Slagterier*,[18] in which it was held that a 'situation marked by significant legal uncertainty may involve a breach of the principle of effectiveness, because reparation of the loss or damage caused to individuals by breaches of [EU] law … could be rendered excessively difficult in practice if the individuals were unable to determine the applicable limitation period with a reasonable degree of certainty' (paragraph 12). From this, the Supreme Court concluded that EU law does not require that the effect of a statutory

---

[17] CJ *Courage v Crehan* (n 9).
[18] CJ 24 March 2009 Case C-445/06 *Danske Slagterier v Bundesrepublik Deutschland* [2009] I-02119 ECLI:EU:C:2009:178.

limitation period be clear beyond doubt (paragraphs 20–22). What is required is that national law is sufficiently clear, precise and foreseeable to enable individuals to ascertain their rights and obligations and exercise those rights without excessive difficulty (paragraphs 23–24). That was the case here according to the Supreme Court.

I.C.ii LEGAL CERTAINTY AS A LIMIT TO THE RETROACTIVE EFFECT OF PRELIMINARY RULINGS

K Lenaerts and P van Nuffel, European Union Law[19]

In the Union legal order, the case law of the Court of Justice, the General Court and the specialised courts constitutes an important source of law. Although they play a crucial role in developing the law, their task is formally limited to interpreting and applying each of the other sources of [EU] law …

The interpretation which the Union Courts give to a rule of Union law defines the meaning and scope of that rule as it must be or ought to have been understood and applied from the time of its coming into force. It follows that a rule of Union law interpreted in this way must be applied to legal relationships which arose or were formed before the Court gave its ruling on the question on interpretation. In practice, however, such an interpretation may have unexpected effects. A judicial ruling holding that a provision has direct effect may, for instance, impose considerable burdens where authorities or individuals are faced with unforeseen claims from individuals. Accordingly, in exceptional cases, the Court of Justice will impose restrictions on grounds of legal certainty on the *ex tunc* effect of its preliminary rulings on Union law.

The first time the CJ reserved the right to limit the temporal effect of its preliminary rulings was in *Defrenne II*.[20] Since then, it has only imposed such a restriction in a few cases.[21] Limitation of the temporal effect is subject to two conditions. First, such a limitation may only be considered when there is a risk of serious economic repercussions owing in particular to the large number of legal relationships entered into in good faith on the basis of national rules considered to be valid and in force. Second, it must be apparent that the individuals and the national authorities have been led into adopting practices which do not comply with EU legislation by reason of objective, significant uncertainty regarding the implications of EU provisions to which the conduct of other Member States or the EC may even have contributed.[22]

---

[19] Lenaerts and Van Nuffel 2011 para 22-113, footnotes omitted.

[20] CJ 8 April 1976 Case C-43/75 *Gabrielle Defrenne v Société anonyme belge de navigation aérienne Sabena (Defrenne II)* [1976] I-00455 ECLI:EU:C:1976:56.

[21] See, eg, CJ 27 March 1980 Case C-61/79 *Amministrazione delle finanze dello Stato v Denkavit italiana Srl* [1980] I-01205 ECLI:EU:C:1980:100; CJ 2 February 1988 Case C-24/86 *Blaizot v University of Liège et al* [1988] I-00379 ECLI:EU:C:1988:43; CJ 17 May 1990 Case C-262/88 *Barber v Guardian Royal Exchange Assurance Group* [1990] I-1889 ECLI:EU:C:1980:209; CJ 16 July 1992 Case C-163/90 *Administration des Douanes et Droits Indirects v Legros et al* [1992] I-04625 ECLI:EU:C:1992:326; CJ 15 December 1995 Case C-415/93 *Union royale belge des sociétés de football association ASBL v Jean-Marc Bosman, Royal club liégeois SA v Jean-Marc Bosman et al and Union des associations européennes de football (UEFA) v Jean-Marc Bosman* [1995] I-04921 ECLI:EU:C:1995:463; CJ 1 March 2011 Case C-236/09 *Test-Achats ASBL et al v Conseil des ministres* [2011] I-00773 ECLI:EU:C:2011:100 (discussed in section II.C.iv below).

[22] AG Sixt-Hackl Opinion in Case C-292/04 5 October 2006 *Meilicke, Weyde and Stöffler v Finanzamt Bonn-Innenstadt* [2007] I-01835 ECLI:EU:C:2006:642, paras 37–38.

I.C.iii LEGAL CERTAINTY AS A LIMIT TO THE OBLIGATION OF NATIONAL COURTS TO INTERPRET AND APPLY THEIR NATIONAL LAWS IN CONFORMITY WITH DIRECTIVES

According to settled case law, individuals cannot invoke a directive against each other to argue that one individual can derive a right or a defence against another individual from the directive or to argue that a national rule is incompatible with the directive and must therefore be disapplied.[23] The absence of these two types of horizontal effect does not, however, exclude a directive from having an impact on private law relationships through the obligation of national courts to interpret and apply their national laws in conformity with EU directives.[24]

L Keus, 'The Principle of Legal Certainty'[25]

From a legal point of view, the obligation to interpret national law in conformity with directives is open to debate. National courts must interpret national law in conformity with directives, but only if the dispute falls within the scope of EU law. That implies that differing interpretations may be given to the same national rule, depending on whether or not EU law is applicable. This ... might suggest that the national court is forced to deprive the national rule of its true and proper meaning, just to bring it into line with EU law. From that perspective it is appropriate that the Court of Justice has also paid attention to the limits of the obligation to interpret national law in conformity with EU law, especially those resulting from the principle of legal certainty.

Summarizing its case law, the Court of Justice held in the *Adeneler* Case 'that the obligation on a national court to refer to the content of a directive when interpreting and applying the relevant rules of domestic law is limited by general principles of law, particularly those of legal certainty and non-retro-activity, and that obligation cannot serve as the basis for an interpretation of national law *contra legem*'.

I.D THE PRINCIPLE OF PROPORTIONALITY

A Hartkamp, European Law and National Private Law[26]

By far the most important principle when reviewing legislation is the proportionality principle. This principle plays a role when a national measure is incompatible with a prohibition, in particular with a provision that safeguards any of the freedoms enshrined in the TFEU and therefore prohibits its violation, while the measure is argued to be justified because it falls under a ground of justification or 'exception' (see no. 64) approved in the treaty (or in case law), which authorises the member states to realise a specific policy

---

[23] See section III.A in Ch 6.

[24] See section III.C.ii in Ch 6 (and, in particular, case 6.16 (FR), which exemplifies a rather bold harmonious interpretation of national law by the French Court of Cassation).

[25] LAD Keus, 'The Principle of Legal Certainty' in Hartkamp/Sieburgh/Keus/Kortmann/Wissink (eds) 2014 303–04.

[26] Hartkamp 2016 no 131.

objective. The principle means that for the plea of a ground of justification to be success-ful, the member state must prove that the measure is suitable for achieving the objective and does not go beyond what is necessary to achieve it. The principle is so highly impor-tant because it allows the courts on the one hand to respect the member state's margin of appreciation as to the desirability of the measure and thus refrain from giving a political decision, and on the other hand to give a decision of a more juristic nature on the ques-tion whether the measure is suitable for achieving the objective pursued and—in particu-lar—whether a less far-reaching measure would have sufficed to achieve the objective ...

The principle of proportionality can (in)directly affect private law relationships. To the extent that an individual relies on a *Member State* measure that does not comply with a provision of EU law and invokes a ground of justification for that measure, another individual is entitled to invoke the principle of proportionality to test the justification ground.[27] The proportionality test may also be directly applied to (legal) acts of *individu-als*. This is clearly illustrated by the case law in which a free movement provision that has direct horizontal effect is invoked against a private party who, as a defence, relies on a written or unwritten exception. In *Viking*, for example, the principle of proportional-ity was employed to reconcile the right of establishment of a Finnish undertaking with the right to strike of (inter)national trade unions.[28] The principle can play a similar role outside the field of free movement law. In a private competition law dispute, for instance, 'where a market operator questions if an undertaking could not have developed a less restrictive alternative to its potentially anticompetitive distribution system'.[29]

In section III below, attention will be paid to a particular application of the principle of proportionality: the prohibition to abuse rights granted by EU law.

FURTHER READING

W Devroe and P van Cleynenbreugel, 'The Impact of General Principles of EU Law on Private Law Relationships' in Hartkamp/Sieburgh/Keus/Kortmann/Wissink (eds) 2014 187–218.

X Groussot, *General Principles of Community Law* (Groningen, Europa Law Publishing, 2006).

AS Hartkamp, *European Law and National Private Law. Effect of EU Law and European Human Rights Law on Legal Relationships between Individuals*, 2nd ed (Cambridge, Intersentia, 2016).

LAD Keus, 'The Principle of Legal Certainty' in Hartkamp/Sieburgh/Keus/Kortmann/Wissink (eds) 2014 297–314.

S Prechal and R Widdershoven, 'Redefining the Relationship between "Rewe-Effectiveness" and Effective Judicial Protection' (2011) 4(2) *Review of European Administrative Law* 31–50.

T Tridimas, *The General Principles of EU Law*, 2nd ed (Oxford, Oxford University Press, 2006).

W van Gerven, 'Of Rights, Remedies and Procedures' (2000) 37(3) *CMLR* 501–36.

---

[27] See section VI.A in Ch 3.

[28] CJ 11 December 2007 Case C-438/05 *ITWF v Viking* [2007] I-10779 ECLI:EU:C:2007:772, paras 75–90. The CJ provided rather strict guidance as to how the proportionality test should be applied: if the national court were to conclude that 'the jobs or conditions of employment of the union's members liable to be adversely affected by the reflagging of the *Rosella* are in fact jeopardised or under serious threat, it would then have to ascertain whether the collective action initiated by FSU is suitable for ensuring the achievement of the objective pursued and does not go beyond what is necessary to attain that objective'.

[29] W Devroe and P van Cleynenbreugel, 'The Impact of General Principles of EU Law on Private Law Relationships' in Hartkamp/Sieburgh/Keus/Kortmann/Wissink (eds) 2014 205.

II. THE PRINCIPLE OF NON-DISCRIMINATION

Carla Sieburgh

II.A INTRODUCTION

This section deals with the principle of non-discrimination as part of EU law. For the elaboration of this principle in Articles 18 and 157 TFEU, see sections I, II and III in Chapter 4. This section will focus on how the principle of non-discrimination influences private law, either as a general principle of EU law or as a Charter provision.

As will be seen, there is not much national case law yet on the autonomous application of the general principle of non-discrimination in horizontal relationships. Nevertheless, this section will elucidate the various ways in which the general principle can influence private law relationships. These descriptions may assist students, scholars, judges and lawyers in structuring their arguments in future cases.

II.A.i DESCRIPTION OF THE GENERAL PRINCIPLES AS DEVELOPED BY THE CJEU AND THEIR RELATION TO THE TREATY PROVISIONS AND TO THE CHARTER

Equal treatment of equal cases (and unequal treatment of unequal cases in proportion to the extent of their differences) is a general commandment of justice forming the very foundation of law. The commandment is enshrined in national law,[30] in international law (see, eg, Article 14 ECHR, Article 1 Protocol 12 ECHR and Article 26 ICCPR) and in supranational law. There are a number of forms of (un)equal treatment for which more detailed rules have been laid down.[31]

There are several reasons why the principle of equality is important to EU law.[32] In the first place, standards of substantive law ensue from the principle, for instance, the prohibitions of discrimination enshrined in the freedoms of movement.[33] Enforcement of these equality rights is a necessary prerequisite for realising and maintaining the internal market. Second, a structural aspect of the EU law equality rights ensues from the principle of equality. In the multi-layered legal order in Europe, they serve as an instrument to achieve unity and thus reinforce the actual weight of EU law relative to legislation

---

[30] See, eg, arts 10–11bis of the Belgian Constitution, the Preamble of the French Constitution, art 3 of the German Basic Law, Germany's General Act on Equal Treatment, art 3 of the Italian Constitution, art 1 of the Dutch Constitution, arts 5–7a of the Dutch Equal Treatment Act and the UK Equality Act. For more national regulations, see the Table of Legislative Instruments in D Schiek, L Waddington and M Bell (eds), *Ius Commune Casebooks for the Common Law of Europe*, Cases, Materials and Text on National, Supranational and International Non-Discrimination Law (Oxford, Hart Publishing, 2007).

[31] See, for extensive sources, Schiek, Waddington and Bell (n 30).

[32] Tridimas 2006 59 ff; Hartkamp 2016 no 57 ff, both containing further references; S Huster, 'Gleichheit im Mehrebenensystem: Die Gleichheitsrechte der Europäischen Union in systematischer und kompetenzrechtlicher Hinsicht' (2010) *EuR* 330 ff.

[33] Articles 34, 45(2), 49, 56 and 63 TFEU.

of national origin. And, finally, the equality rights legitimate the power of the CJEU to review rules of EU law and of legislation of national origin.

Because the powers of the EU are limited and because the EU seeks to achieve uniformity in limited areas only, the EU law prohibitions of discrimination are not merely derivatives of the general principle of equality. The substance of the prohibitions is partly determined by the specific nature of the EU. This specific nature manifests itself in the limitation of the kind of areas covered by EU law (it hardly concerns equality in electoral laws, for example) and in the interpretation given to the concept of equality. In EU law matters, the concept of equality is interpreted against the background of EU law, including its political and economic objectives. This interpretation may therefore differ from interpretations given to national and international concepts of equality.

Section II in Chapter 4 lists a number of concrete EU law provisions specifying the principle of equality. The relevant provisions for the present section are Articles 20, 21(1) and 23(1) of the Charter read in conjunction with Article 6 TEU. Other principles which likewise have the nature of primary EU law are the principles of equal treatment and non-discrimination recognised by the CJ,[34] and the principles of non-discrimination on grounds of sex,[35] age,[36] sexual orientation[37] and nationality[38] that the CJ has developed as general principles of EU law. The CJ has construed the last-mentioned principle concerning nationality to be 'a specific expression of the general principle of equality, which is itself one of the fundamental principles of [EU] law'.[39] In secondary EU law, the principle of equality is enshrined in numerous directives, for example, the anti-discrimination directives.[40]

The general principles of EU law fill in gaps, and their own specific meaning is determined on the basis of the Charter.

In *ČEZ*, the CJ derived the principle prohibiting any discrimination on grounds of nationality from what is now Article 18 TFEU. In *Test-Achats*, the CJ referred to Articles 21 and 23 of the Charter and to Articles 157 and 19 TFEU.[41] The way in which the CJ has arrived at formulating general principles of EU law makes it likely that it will use Article 21(1) of the Charter as a basis for recognising as general principles of EU

---

[34] CJ 13 October 2005 Case C-458/03 *Parking Brixen GmbH v Gemeinde Brixen and Stadtwerke Brixen AG* [2005] I-8585 EU:C:2005:605, para 52 (see Hartkamp 2011 no 12).

[35] CJ 15 June 1978 Case C-149/77 *Defrenne v Sabena* (Defrenne III) [1978] I-01365 ECLI:EU:C:1978:130, para 27.

[36] CJ 19 January 2010 Case C-555/07 *Kücukdeveci v Swedex* [2010] I-00365 ECLI:EU:C:2010:21.

[37] CJ 10 May 2011 Case C-147/08 *Römer v Freie und Hansestadt Hamburg* [2011] I-03591 ECLI:EU:C:2011:286, paras 59 and 60.

[38] CJ 27 October 2009 Case C-115/08 *Land Oberösterreich v ČEZ as* [2009] I-10265 ECLI:EU:C:2009:660.

[39] ibid, para 89.

[40] Council Directive 2004/113/EC of 13 December 2004 implementing the principle of equal treatment between men and women in the access to and supply of goods and services [2004] OJ L373/37; Council Directive 2000/43/EC of 29 June 2000 implementing the principle of equal treatment between persons irrespective of racial or ethnic origin [2000] OJ L180/22; Council Directive 2000/78/EC of 27 November 2000 establishing a general framework for equal treatment in employment and occupation [2000] OJ L303/16; Directive 2006/54/EC of the European Parliament and of the Council of 5 July 2006 on the implementation of the principle of equal opportunities and equal treatment of men and women in matters of employment and occupation [2006] OJ L204/23.

[41] CJ *Test-Achats* (n 21) paras 18 and 19.

law the prohibitions of discrimination on grounds of race, colour, ethnic or social origin, genetic characteristics, language, religion or belief, political or other opinions, association with a national minority, property, birth or disability.[42]

II.A.ii CATEGORIES OF PRIVATE LAW CASES INFLUENCED BY THE GENERAL PRINCIPLE OF NON-DISCRIMINATION AND BY THE CHARTER

The principle of equality, or non-discrimination, plays a special role in EU law and it manifests itself in several ways. This section will focus on how the principle of non-discrimination, as a general principle of EU law and/or as a Charter provision, influences private law.

So far, the CJ has not applied the general EU law principle of non-discrimination by according it direct horizontal effect as described in section II.A in Chapter 1 and section I.A in Chapter 4. This means that the principle does not interfere directly with the legal relationship between individuals: it does not create, modify or extinguish rights or obligations between them. So the principle as such does not create rights and obligations for individuals which they can invoke against another individual in the national courts.[43]

However, the principle has been used as a criterion for reviewing national legislation. In a private law relationship, disapplication of one or more national provisions because they conflict with this general EU law principle can result in the private law relationship coming into conflict with legal provisions which then become applicable (eg, subsequent or reviving provisions). It is precisely in this step that the impact of EU law may take actors in private law by surprise. Cases in which this mechanism operates will be discussed in this section.

In *Mangold, Kücükdeveci, ČEZ and Dansk Industri*, the CJ ruled, through the autonomous application of the general EU law principle of equality, that legislation of national origin which conflicts with the principle must be disapplied.[44]

Section II.C.iv below analyses a case, *Test-Achats*, in which the CJ's ruling that an act of the EU, namely a directive, was invalid because it conflicted with the principle of equality enshrined in the Charter indirectly caused effects in horizontal relationships.

EU law may exert influence on a horizontal relationship via different mechanisms (see section II in Chapter 1 and section I.A in Chapter 4). This section classifies case law into

---

[42] See with respect to religion or belief, disability and sexual orientation and, by analogy, race or ethnic origin CJ 22 November 2005 Case C-144/04 *Werner Mangold v Rüdiger Helm* [2005] I-09981 ECLI:EU:C:2005:709, para 74. See additionally CJ 19 April 2016 Case C-441/14 *Dansk Industri v Estate of Karsten Eigil Rasmussen* ECLI:EU:C:2016:278.

[43] Possibly, the CJ hints at direct horizontal effect of the prohibition of discrimination in CJ 15 January 2014 Case C-176/12 *Association de médiation sociale v Union locale des syndicats CGT et al* nyr ECLI:EU:C:2014:2, para 47. See, with references, Hartkamp 2016 no 231a ff.

[44] By autonomous application, I mean the use of the general EU law principle of equality as an independent review ground. In those cases, the operation of the principle (separately from a Charter provision) is not unlocked by a written provision of EU law in which the principle is embodied or by the interpretation of a written provision of EU law or of national law.

categories on the basis of the mechanism used. These mechanisms are: (i) direct effect of an EU rule; (ii) indirect effect of the EU law rationale via a national rule that is in conformity with a rule of EU law, by harmonious interpretation of a national rule that is not in conformity with EU law or by review of an incompatible rule of national law against EU law; and (iii) positive obligation of Member States. Category (iv), 'miscellaneous', comprises cases in which national private law is influenced in yet other ways.

The reader should be aware of the following. In my discussion of category (ii), I will include the use of an open norm of national law to ensure conformity of national law with EU law, whether or not this is imposed by EU law (see sections II.B.i and II.B.ii in Chapter 1). It is possible, for example, to interpret an open norm of national private law (reasonableness and fairness, generally acceptable conduct, public order/public policy, public morals etc) while taking into account the requirements arising from the principle of non-discrimination (see the *ČEZ* case, discussed in section II.B below, for an example from CJ case law on non-discrimination). Moreover, category (iv), 'miscellaneous', could include cases in which a national law that is *not* in conformity with EU law is nevertheless applied. Such cases are examples of judgments in breach of EU law. If delivered by the highest national court, they can be a basis for Member State liability under the *Francovich* doctrine.

II.B SOURCES

For materials in books I refer to Chapter 4. In this section, I will consider case law in which the CJ developed the general EU law principle of non-discrimination and ruled that national law applicable to a horizontal relationship must be reviewed against this principle. See also section V.B in Chapter 6.

In both *Mangold* and *Kücükdeveci*, which are about legal relations between employees and employers, provisions of German employment contract law were reviewed against the general principle of EU law that prohibits (age) discrimination (as expressed in Directive 2000/78/EC).[45] After the CJ decisions in *Mangold* and *Kücükdeveci*, the Federal Labour Court of Germany referred another preliminary question to the CJ. National case law formulating a preliminary question gives insight into how national courts reason when carving out the question. In this section, one preliminary question is presented as a source, since no follow-up decision by the national court is available in this case. See for a comparable case 5.5 (GERM). Two other preliminary questions (cases 5.7 (GERM) and 5.10 (BE)) will be discussed together with the follow-up decisions by the national court in sections II.C.ii.c and II.C.iv.

---

[45] [2000] OJ L303/16 (n 40).

Arbeitsgericht München (Employment Tribunal Munich),
29 October 2003[46]   **5.2 (GERM)**

Mangold v Helm

DISCRIMINATION ON GROUNDS OF AGE BY PROVIDING FOR THE POSSIBILITY
OF FIXED-TERM EMPLOYMENT CONTRACTS FOR OLDER EMPLOYEES ONLY,
WITHOUT REQUIRING OBJECTIVE JUSTIFICATION

Younger old

The national court stayed the proceedings in order to obtain a preliminary ruling
from the CJ

Facts: The claimant, Mr Mangold, who was 56 years old, was in the employment of the defendant, Mr Helm.
The employment contract between the parties had been concluded for eight months. Whereas normally no
fixed-term employment contracts could be concluded without objective justification, according to a provision
of national law (§14(3) of the German Act on Part-Time Work and Fixed-Term Employment Contracts), no
objective justification was required for employees older than 52.

Held: Mangold sought a declaratory judgment that the employment relationship between the parties did
not expire after eight months, but had instead been concluded for an indefinite period. He alleged that the
fixed-term clause of the employment contract was ineffective and that the contract represented a permanent
employment relationship. He therefore claimed that Helm was obliged to continue employing him on the same
conditions of employment as other employees. He took the position that the limitation of the employment
relationship based on age laid down in the employment contract, although based on a provision of national law,
was contrary to higher-ranking EU law (Directives 1999/70/EC and 2000/78/EC).

Judgment: The Employment Tribunal has stayed the proceedings on the following grounds:

According to the written employment contract, the fixed term of the contested employment relationship is based on the fixed-term option provided in §14(3) of the German Act
on Part-Time Work and Fixed-Term Employment Contracts (TzBfG). If this provision were to
be compatible with higher-ranking European law, the time limitation would be effective
and the claim would have to be rejected. If the standard were not to be applied on the
grounds of infringement of higher-ranking law, the time limitation would be ineffective
and the claim would have to be allowed.

As far as can be seen, the CJ has not yet expressed views on the question of the compatibility of §14(3) of the above Act or the question of the admissibility and, as the case may
be, justification of the exclusion of entire age cohorts from the protection afforded by the
said directives.

For reasons of legal certainty it would also seem appropriate to await a decision by the
CJ. The provisions in §14(3) of the aforementioned Act are intended to facilitate the integration of older workers into the labour market. Irrespective of whether such provisions
are suitable for achieving the stated purpose, they fail on the grounds that the greater
part of literature on the subject considers them to be incompatible with European law.
This includes, for example, the Confederation of German Employers' Associations (BDA),

---

[46] ArbG Munich 29 October 2005 *NZA-RR* 2005, 43 *Mangold v Helm.*

which advises against entering into fixed-term employment relationships based on this provision …

The national court concludes from this that §14(3) of the above Act is wholly inapplicable and that the standard of §14(1) of the above Act, whereby an objective ground of justification is required, should apply.

The following questions will be referred to the CJ for a preliminary ruling:

1(a) Is Clause 8(3) of the Framework Agreement to be interpreted, when transposed into domestic law, as prohibiting a reduction of protection following from the lowering of the age limit from 60 to 58?

1(b) Is Clause 5(1) of the Framework Agreement to be interpreted as precluding a provision of national law which—like the provision at issue in this case—does not contain any of the three restrictions set out in paragraph 1 of that clause?

2. Is Article 6 of Directive 2000/78 to be interpreted as precluding a provision of national law which, like the provision at issue in this case, authorises the conclusion of fixed-term employment contracts, without any objective reason, with workers aged 52 and over, contrary to the principle requiring justification on objective grounds?

3. If one of those three questions is answered in the affirmative: must the national court refuse to apply the provision of domestic law which is contrary to [EU] law and apply the general principle of internal law, under which fixed terms of employment are permissible only if they are justified on objective grounds?

Notes:

(1) This is an interesting judgment in more than one respect. In the first place, the preliminary questions formulated in it, followed by others in the same vein, formed the basis of a new line of rulings by the CJ regarding the possibility for general principles of EU law to have effect in a private law relationship. As such, it has opened an entirely new method of reasoning within the field of national private law and its relationship towards EU law.

(2) Second, the national court anticipated that the national provision would be held at variance with EU law and that it should be set aside.

(3) Third, the national court referred to the fact that in by far the greater part of the literature, the provision of national law was considered to be incompatible with the requirements set by EU law. As will be seen, this observation is important when national courts consider the question whether the consequences of the influence of the general EU law principle of non-discrimination are running counter to the legitimate expectations of the employer(s).

(4) A follow-up decision of a national court is not available. The parties settled the case. See case 5.5 (GERM) below for a decision of a German national court on comparable facts.

(5) Even though a follow-up decision is not available, it is clear that after the provision of national law had been set aside, the contract clause infringed the general rule (laid down in Article 14(1) German Act on Part-Time Work and Fixed-Term Employment Contracts). Under German law, the clause would for that reason be regarded ineffective

(*unwirksam*). The employee's claim that he be permitted to continue working under the same employment conditions would be allowable.

In *Mangold*, the German provision permitting employers, without restriction, to conclude fixed-term contracts of employment with workers over the age of 52 served as the basis on which Mr Mangold, then 56 years old, entered into a contract with Mr Helm for the duration of eight months. The German provision fell within the scope of EU law, being a measure implementing Directive 1999/70. The period prescribed for the transposition into domestic law of Directive 2000/78/EC had not yet expired. Nevertheless, the CJ held that EU law, more particularly Article 6(1) of Directive 2000/78/EC laying down the principle prohibiting discrimination on grounds of age, must be interpreted as precluding the provision of domestic law under scrutiny. The CJ stated that 'in those circumstances it is the responsibility of the national court, hearing a dispute involving the principle of non-discrimination in respect of age, to provide, in a case within its jurisdiction, the legal protection which individuals derive from the rules of [EU] law and to ensure that those rules are fully effective, setting aside any provision of national law which may conflict with that law'.[47]

In *Kücükdeveci*, the CJ confirmed the *Mangold* judgment.[48] In *Kücükdeveci*, national legislation made it possible not to take into account periods of employment completed by the employee before reaching the age of 25 in calculating the notice period for dismissal. As a result, Ms Kücükdeveci was dismissed by her employer with a notice period calculated on the basis of three years of employment, although she had been employed for 10 years. Again, the CJ established that the national rule was incompatible with the principle prohibiting discrimination. Thus, it ruled that 'the need to ensure the full effectiveness of the principle of non-discrimination on grounds of age, as given expression in Directive 2000/78/EC,[49] means that the national court, faced with a national provision falling within the scope of EU law which it considers to be incompatible with that principle and which cannot be interpreted in conformity with that principle, must decline to apply that provision'. See case 5.6 (GERM) below for the follow-up decision by the national court.

The CJ's decision in *Mangold* led to another preliminary question by the German court regarding another aspect of the provision of national law. The German court wanted to know whether in this case too, the *Mangold* doctrine applied. See for doubts amongst national courts caused by the CJ's *Mangold* decision the cases presented in section V.B in Chapter 6.

The CJ judgment of 10 March 2011 in *Lufthansa v Kumpan*[50] does not elaborate upon the general principle of EU law prohibiting discrimination on the ground of age. Its reasoning relies on the Framework Agreement on fixed-term work and the obligation of national courts to interpret national law in conformity with EU law. In paragraph 56, the CJ elaborates on the measures to be taken by national courts to meet the requirement of

---

[47] CJ *Mangold* (n 42) para 77.
[48] See case 5.6 (GERM) for the follow-up decision.
[49] [2000] OJ L303/16 (n 40).
[50] CJ 10 March 2011 Case C-109/09 *Deutsche Lufthansa AG v Gertraud Kumpan* [2011] I-01309 ECLI:EU:C:2011:129.

consistent interpretation: 'It is therefore for the national court, to the fullest extent possible, and where there has been misuse of successive fixed-term employment contracts, to interpret and apply the relevant provisions of national law in such a way that it is possible duly to penalise the abuse and to nullify the consequences of the breach of EU law.'

The follow-up decision of the Federal Labour Court makes clear that the national court held the opinion that its questions had not been adequately answered (paragraph 16). Nevertheless, it followed the suggestion of the CJ. After having reinterpreted the national provisions, it decided that the labour contract must be regarded to have been concluded for unlimited duration and consequently had not terminated. For details on the rather unclear reasoning, see the follow-up decision of the national court (case 5.8 (GERM)).

In the *ČEZ* judgment, a provision of the Austrian Civil Code pertaining to nuisance was reviewed against the prohibition of discrimination on grounds of nationality. ČEZ was the operator of a nuclear power plant in Temelín in the Czech Republic. Temelín lies near the Austrian border. ČEZ possessed the Czech licences required for operating the plant. Moreover, the nuclear power plant had been inspected in accordance with the European Atomic Energy Community (EAEC) Treaty. Land Oberösterreich was the owner of agricultural land located in Austria, at a distance of approximately 60 km from the Temelín nuclear power plant. Land Oberösterreich and other (private) owners[51] suffered nuisance from the ionising radiation which the operation by ČEZ entailed because the radiation interfered with the normal use of the land. Land Oberösterreich and the other private owners brought actions before the Austrian Court (*Landesgericht Linz*) seeking an order that ČEZ put an end to the actual or potential nuisance or, if that was impossible, to cease operating the nuclear power plant. §364a of the Austrian Civil Code (ABGB) provides that a landowner cannot bring an action for cessation of nuisance if it is caused by an officially authorised installation. In such cases, a landowner is entitled only to bring court proceedings for compensation for the damage caused by the nuisance. According to the Austrian case law dating from before 4 April 2006, the latter rule was also applicable with respect to installations authorised by foreign authorities where it appeared that the nuisance in question was authorised by international law and the conditions of authorisation applicable in the state of origin were, in essence, equivalent to those prevailing in Austria. However, according to the interpretation which the Austrian Supreme Court (Oberste Gerichtshof) has given to §364a ABGB since 4 April 2006, a prohibition is allowable if the nuisance emanates from installations granted official authorisation by a foreign authority. It is only when the nuisance emanates from installations granted official authorisation by the Austrian authorities that it is impossible to bring an action for cessation of nuisance.

The interpretation which the Austrian Supreme Court chose to give to §364a ABGB discriminated between authorisation granted by Austrian authorities and authorisation not granted by Austrian authorities. The CJ came to the conclusion that the situation was governed by EU law.[52] It took a firm step: it ruled that [now Article 18 TFEU], which

---

[51] CJ *ČEZ* (n 38) para 41.
[52] ibid, paras 87–91.

prohibits any discrimination on grounds of nationality, is a specific expression of the general principle of equality, which itself is one of the fundamental principles of EU law.[53] The prohibition of any discrimination on grounds of nationality is a general principle of EU law,[54] which is also applicable under the EAEC Treaty. Subsequently, the CJ found that the way in which §364a ABGB had been applied led to discrimination on grounds of nationality. No justification existed for this discrimination, inter alia because of the existence of an EU framework offering protection against the risks of nuclear power plants.[55]

According to the CJ, the discrimination on grounds of nationality contrary to EU law had the consequence that the national courts must as far as was possible interpret the national provisions they had to apply in a way which accorded with the requirements of EU law. When such interpretation in conformity with EU law was impossible, the national courts must fully apply EU law and protect the rights conferred thereby on individuals, if necessary by disapplying domestic provisions if their application would, in the circumstances of the case, lead to a result contrary to EU law. This had the consequence that the interpretation which the Austrian court must give to §364a ABGB would not result in prohibited discrimination. This could only be achieved if the court did not follow the interpretation given to the provision by the Austrian Supreme Court in its judgment of 4 April 2006 and disapplied that interpretation. The legal consequence was that the owner of the land, Land Oberösterreich, could not seek prohibition of the nuisance, but only compensation for the damage caused by the nuisance.

Another case in which the CJ ruled on the general principle of non-discrimination is *Test-Achats*. An action was brought by the Belgian Verbruikersunie Test-Achats and two individuals before the Belgian Constitutional Court about the constitutionality of a Belgian law implementing Directive 2004/113.[56] When examining the constitutionality of the Belgian implementing law, the Belgian Constitutional Court raised the question whether Article 5(2) of the Directive was contrary to Article 6(2) TEU and, more specifically, contrary to the principle of equality and non-discrimination safeguarded by that provision. The CJ reviewed the provision of the Directive against Articles 21 and 23 of the Charter. It ruled that the possibility of discriminating without temporal limitation as permitted by the Directive was incompatible with the intended purpose of Article 19(1) TFEU, namely to combat social exclusion and discrimination and to promote social justice and protection, equality of men and women, solidarity between generations and the protection of the rights of children. The possibility was also ruled to be inconsistent with the aim of the EU in all its activities to eliminate inequalities and to promote equality between men and women, as provided in Article 8 TFEU. The Directive provision permitting the Member States to maintain exceptions to the rule of gender-neutral premiums and benefits without temporal limitation was ruled to be contrary to the realisation of the Directive's objective of equal treatment between men and women and incompatible

---

[53] ibid, para 89.

[54] ibid, para 91.

[55] CJ *ČEZ* (n 38) paras 108–36. This obviously does not imply that any foreign authorisation must be equated with a domestic authorisation.

[56] [2004] OJ L373/37 (n 40); art 10 of the Act of 10 May 2007 to prevent discrimination between men and women.

with Articles 21 and 23 of the Charter. The CJ declared the relevant Article of the Directive invalid effective from 21 December 2012. Notwithstanding the transitional period, the declaration of invalidity of the Directive provision had a major impact on contracts concluded under national law designed in conformity with the provision in the Directive that was now deemed to be at variance with the prohibition of discrimination on grounds of sex. To avoid uncertainty, the Commission communicated guidelines.[57] For a detailed elaboration, see cases 5.10 (BE) and 5.11 (BE).

More recently, the CJ[58] was confronted with a case between two individuals, namely AMS, an association participating in the implementation of social mediation measures and measures for the prevention of crime, and Mr Laboubi, who had been appointed representative of the trade union section created within AMS and other organisations. AMS challenged that appointment and took the view that its staff numbers were lower than 11 and, a fortiori, lower than 50 employees and that, as a result, it was not required, under national legislation, to take measures for the representation of employees. When counting its employees, AMS, in accordance with French law, excluded from its relevant staff numbers apprentices, employees with an employment-initiative contract or accompanied-employment contract and employees with a professional training contract. The issue at hand focused on the validity of this French provision under EU law, more specifically Article 27 of the Charter. The CJ considered it necessary 'to ascertain … whether the situation in the case in the main proceedings is similar to that in the case which gave rise to *Kücükdeveci*, so that Article 27 of the Charter, by itself or in conjunction with the provisions of Directive 2002/14, can be invoked in a dispute between individuals in order to preclude, as the case may be, the application of the national provision which is not in conformity with that directive'. What is striking is that the CJ reconstructed *Kücükdeveci*, where it raised the possibility that Charter provisions can be invoked not only 'in conjunction with the provision of the Directive', but also 'by itself'.[59] The CJ has elevated the Charter, with the result that a Charter provision may operate by itself.

However, it concluded that it was not possible to infer from the wording of Article 27 of the Charter a prohibition on excluding from the calculation of the staff numbers in an undertaking a specific category of employees initially included in the group of persons to be taken into account. In that way, the facts of this case may be distinguished from those giving rise to *Kücükdeveci*, insofar as the principle of non-discrimination on grounds of age at issue in that case and laid down in Article 21(1) of the Charter was sufficient by itself to confer on individuals an individual right which they may invoke as such. Consequently, the CJ held that: 'Article 27 of the Charter cannot, as such, be invoked in a dispute, such as that in the main proceedings, in order to conclude that the national provision which is not in conformity with Directive 2002/14 should not

[57] Communication from the Commission, Guidelines on the application of Council Directive 2004/113/EC to insurance, in the light of the judgment of the Court of Justice of the European Union in Case C-236/09 (Test-Achats), Brussels 22 December 2011 C(2011) 9497 final. See also: http://ec.europa.eu/justice/gender-equality/files/com_2011_9497_en.pdf.
[58] CJ *AMS* (n 43).
[59] ibid, para 23.

be applied. That finding cannot be called into question by considering Article 27 of the Charter in conjunction with the provisions of Directive 2002/14, given that, since that article by itself does not suffice to confer on individuals a right which they may invoke as such, it could not be otherwise if it is considered in conjunction with that directive.'[60]

However, the individual injured as a result of domestic law not being in conformity with EU law can rely on the doctrine of Member State (*Francovich*) liability for a breach of EU law.

In general, *AMS* makes clear that a Charter provision may constitute a basis for reviewing a provision of national law applicable to the horizontal relationship provided that this Charter provision is by itself sufficient to confer on individuals an individual right which they may invoke as such. In other words, the reasoning developed by the CJ regarding the general principle of EU law prohibiting discrimination is applicable to Charter provisions prohibiting discrimination.

It is plausible that the technique developed by the CJ in *Mangold* for the general principle of EU law of non-discrimination, and equally applied in *AMS* and *Dansk Industri* to Charter provisions dealing with the prohibition of discrimination, will become applicable as soon as the CJ interprets a Charter provision as being by itself sufficient to confer on individuals an individual right which they may invoke as such.

II.C NATIONAL CASE LAW

This section presents cases decided by national courts in which a horizontal relationship was at issue and in which the court dealt with (or should have dealt with) a principle of non-discrimination.

The users of this casebook are kindly invited to report developments in national case law involving the principle of non-discrimination in horizontal relationships, which might be interesting for a second edition of this book.

Relevant cases were selected on the basis of the following criteria: does the case involve a situation between individuals and, if not, are there horizontal relationships behind the litigating Member State and the individual (eg, third parties that have a horizontal relationship with the individual or whose legal relationship changes due to a CJ ruling against the Member State) on which EU law exerts influence? What are the facts and what are the rules of national origin which are primarily applicable?

Subsequently, each case was subjected to the following sequence of questions: (i) did the case involve unequal treatment?; if so, (ii) did it fall within the scope of EU law?; if so, (iii) was the unequal treatment prohibited under EU law?; if so, (iv) did the national court use a technique (direct application of EU law, construction in conformity, positive Member State obligation etc) to uphold the principle of non-discrimination?; if so, v) what were the consequences for the private law relationship?

---

[60] CJ *AMS* (n 43) paras 48 and 49.

II.C.i DIRECT EFFECT OF THE EU RULE

This section is intended to present cases from national jurisdictions in which the national court applied the principle of non-discrimination directly to the horizontal relationship.[61]

However, as stated in section II.A.ii above, the CJEU has not applied the general EU law principle of non-discrimination or Charter provisions on non-discrimination by according either of them direct horizontal effect.

II.C.ii INDIRECT EFFECTS OF THE EU RULE

This section presents cases from national jurisdictions in which the national court applied the rationale of the general EU law principle of non-discrimination or Charter provisions on non-discrimination by harmonious interpretation of a national rule that was not in conformity with EU law or by reviewing an incompatible rule of national law against EU law.[62]

The application of national law that is already in conformity with the principle of non-discrimination is interesting for this casebook because such a national rule may well be the result of the implementation of the principle by the national legislator. Moreover, it is important because the national courts have to comply with new or evolving interpretations of this principle of EU law on which the national rule is based.[63]

II.C.ii.a Application of the Rationale of EU Law via a National Rule that is in Conformity with the EU Rule

EU law can exert an indirect effect on the substance of a horizontal relationship via national rules that are in conformity with EU law. For example, the legislator of the Member State concerned may regard an existing national rule as an anticipatory enactment of the substance, and for that reason as an implementation, of a directive that was established and entered into force afterwards. In the first place, such a national rule is part of the framework regulating horizontal relationships. Second, legal actors have to be aware of the fact that the rule of national law is required to be in conformity with EU law (and with its interpretation by the CJEU).

Since cases in this category decided by national courts generally do not trigger any questions related to EU law, they are not recognised as being influenced by EU law. Moreover, usually, they do not create problematic situations. An exception is the situation in which the national court is aware of a possible incompatibility between the national legislation and the interpretation by the CJ of the rule of EU law. In such cases, the national court either refers a preliminary question to the CJ or interprets the national rule in conformity with EU law (see section II.C.ii.b).

---

[61] For the method of selecting cases and the structure of the presentation of the cases, see section II.C.

[62] See previous note.

[63] With regard to art 157 TFEU, we saw some interesting examples in UK case law of this dynamic: see section IV.B.ii in Ch 4.

Tribunale di Roma (Rome Court of First Instance),
12 June 2012[64]   **5.3 (IT)**

FIOM and CGIL Nazionale v Fabbrica Italiana Pomigliano SpA

DISCRIMINATION AGAINST WORKERS ON GROUNDS OF ASSOCIATION
WITH A TRADE UNION

Previous share

A national court must set aside any discriminatory provision of national law and apply to members of the disadvantaged category the same arrangements as those enjoyed by members of the other category

Facts: Two trade unions, FIOM and CGIL Nazionale, brought an action before the Rome Court of First Instance based on discriminatory conduct of the employer, Fabbrica Italiana Pomigliano SpA, with regard to their members. Fabbrica Italiana Pomigliano SpA had fired a number of its employees exclusively selected from those associated with the aforementioned trade unions.

Held: The Italian court found that the employer's conduct towards the employees associated with a specific trade union was discriminatory and remedied this discrimination by disapplying its national law which was not in conformity with EU law.

Judgment: According to the EU case law on non-discrimination—which is particularly relevant to this case, since the Decreto Legislativo no. 216 of 2003 is the national measure implementing Directive 2000/78—once the infringement of the right to equal treatment has been established, the remedy can be no other than to acknowledge the 'good' that has been denied without justification (*cf Commission v Italy*).

In particular, the CJ stated that:

> [I]t is for the authorities of the Member State concerned to adopt the general or specific measures necessary to ensure that [EU] law is complied with in their territory, those authorities retaining the choice of measures to be taken to ensure that national law is changed so as to comply with [EU] law and that the rights which individuals derive from [EU] law are given full effect. Where the national court finds discrimination contrary to [EU] law, it must set aside any discriminatory provision of national law for as long as measures reinstating equal treatment have not been adopted, without having to request or await its prior cancellation by the legislature, and apply to members of the disadvantaged category the same arrangements as those enjoyed by the persons in the other category.[65]

Notes:

(1) It is not clear whether this case falls within the scope of EU law. Nor is it clear which specific provision of EU law would apply to this horizontal relationship. There is no cross-border element. Nevertheless, the court argued that in such cases, the national courts are obliged under EU law to remedy the discrimination, eg, by interpreting in

---

[64] Court of First Instance of Rome 12 June 2012 Foro it 2013 I 1674 *FIOM and CGIL Nazionale v Fabbrica Italiana Pomigliano SpA.*

[65] The quotation by the Italian Court is taken from CJ 16 January 2008 Joined Cases C-128/07–C-131/07 *Molinari et al v Agenzia delle Entrate—Ufficio di Latina* [2008] I-00004 ECLI:EU:C:2008:15, para 23.

conformity or setting aside any national provision that is discriminatory. If a party should have successfully alleged that the case did not fall within the scope of EU law, the national court must have applied national law, even though it referred to EU law. If a party should have successfully alleged that the case did fall within the scope of EU law, the national court apparently did not require a cross-border element in non-discrimination cases.

(2) The case is original because of the atypical remedy granted by the court within the margin of discretion it was allowed by its domestic law to eliminate the discrimination and to restore equality. The court reasoned that, given the unequal treatment, the remedy could be no other than acknowledging the 'good' that had been denied without justification. It ordered the employer to hire such number of members of the particular trade union as would re-establish the previous proportion of such members relative to the overall number of employees in the establishment.

(3) The court referred to CJ case law because both national and EU law give the courts broad discretion as to which remedy to apply in actual cases in order to restore equality. The reference to the CJ decision serves the purpose of justifying and reinforcing the choice of a measure—even if atypical—which is appropriate in the actual case.

(4) The Court of Appeal upheld the main reasoning of the first instance judgment (Court of Appeal Rome, order 10 November 2012 *Foro it.* 2013 I 1674). The award of compensation for non-pecuniary damage was reversed. The first instance decision had ordered FIOM to pay compensation for non-pecuniary damage to each worker who had been fired and the Court of Appeal set aside this decision on the ground that there was no evidence of damage suffered by the workers.

(5) With regard to the remedy awarded by the Court of First Instance, namely an order to hire employees who were members of the disadvantaged category, the Court of Appeal specified that this remedy could be justified on the basis of internal law which in this respect was in conformity with EU law.

(6) It is clear that the Italian courts were concerned about giving full effect to the right which individuals derive from the principle of non-discrimination. The remedy considerably changed the relationship between the employer and the category of employees who were members of the particular trade union. Whereas before the proceedings, the employees who were members of that trade union had been fired, after the court decision, the employer had to hire such number of employees in this category as would re-establish the previous proportion of this category relative to the overall number of employees in the establishment.

II.C.ii.b Application of the Rationale of EU Law by Harmonious Interpretation of a National Rule that is Not in Conformity with EU Law

EU law can also exert an indirect effect on the substance of a horizontal relationship by harmonious interpretation of a national rule that is not in conformity with EU law. This way of interpreting national law may substantively change the framework regulating horizontal relationships.

The reader should be aware of the fact that I understand this type of cases to include the situation in which the national court applies national law that is *not* in conformity with EU law. Such a situation may occur when the national court is unable to harmoniously interpret the national provision and also cannot apply an alternative technique (like positive obligation of a Member State; see section II.C.iii below).

II.C.ii.c Application of the Rationale of EU Law by Reviewing an Incompatible Rule of National Law against EU Law

The cases presented in this section are of German origin. They all relate to employment contracts and age discrimination. Nevertheless, they differ significantly. The cases are divided into categories in order to keep the materials accessible. The first category contains cases that are similar to the *Mangold* judgment: an older employee is offered a fixed-term employment contract for no other reason than his age. The legal basis for this exception to the general rule of §14(1) of the German Act on Part-Time Work and Fixed-Term Employment Contracts lay in the fourth sentence of §14(3) of the German Act on Part-Time Work and Fixed-Term Employment Contracts,[66] which the CJ ruled in

---

[66] To understand the differences between category (i) and category (iii), it is important to read §14 of the TzBfG and to know that para (3) has been amended (which was relevant for the *Mangold* decision):
'(1) A fixed-term employment contract may be concluded if there are objective grounds for doing so. Objective grounds exist in particular where:
— the operational manpower requirements are only temporary,
— the fixed term follows a period of training or study in order to facilitate the employee's entry into subsequent employment,
— one employee replaces another,
— the particular nature of the work justifies the fixed term,
— the fixed term is a probationary period,
— reasons relating to the employee personally justify the fixed term,
— the employee is paid out of budgetary funds provided for fixed-term employment and is employed on that basis, or
— the term is fixed by common agreement before a court.

(2) The term of an employment contract may be limited in the absence of objective reasons for a maximum period of two years. Within that maximum period a fixed-term contract may be renewed three times at most. The conclusion of a fixed-term employment contract within the meaning of the first sentence shall not be authorised if that contract is immediately preceded by an employment relationship of fixed or indefinite duration with the same employer. A collective agreement may fix the number of renewals or the maximum duration of the fixed term in derogation from the first sentence. Employers and workers in a sector in which such a collective agreement has been made but who are not bound thereby may agree to the agreement.

(3) The conclusion of a fixed-term employment contract shall not require objective justification if the worker has reached the age of 58 by the time the fixed-term employment relationship begins. A fixed term shall not be permitted where there is a close objective connection with a previous employment contract of indefinite duration concluded with the same employer. Such a connection shall be presumed to exist inter alia where the interval between the two employment contracts is less than six months.

(4) The limitation of the duration of an employment contract must be fixed in writing in order to be enforceable.'

Paragraph 14(3) of the TzBfG was amended by the First Law on the Modern Supply of Services on the Labour Market (*Erstes Gesetz für moderne Dienstleistungen am Arbeitsmarkt*) of 23 December 2002 (BGBl 2002 I 4607). The new version of that provision, which took effect on 1 January 2003, provided:

'The conclusion of a fixed-term employment contract shall not require objective justification if the worker has reached the age of 58 by the time the fixed-term employment relationship begins. A fixed term shall not be permitted where there is a close objective connection with a previous employment contract of indefinite duration concluded with the same employer. Such a connection shall be presumed to exist inter alia where the interval between the two employment contracts is less than six months. Until 31 December 2006, the first sentence shall be applied as if it read "the age of 52" instead of "the age of 58".'

Mangold to be at variance with the general principle of EU law prohibiting discrimination on grounds of age and which the national courts must disapply. In the second category, I discuss the follow-up decision in *Kücükdeveci*: the periods of employment completed by the employee before reaching the age of 25 were not taken into account in calculating the notice period for dismissal. The legal basis for this exception to the general rule lay in §622(2)2 of the German Civil Code (BGB), which the CJ ruled in *Kücükdeveci* to be at variance with the general principle of EU law that prohibits discrimination on grounds of age and which the national courts must disapply. In the third category, I consider two cases in which the applicable collective labour agreement provided that the employment contract would terminate without notice being required at the end of the month in which the employee reached the age of 60. This age limit differed from the default age limit.

Age Discrimination: Fixed-Term Contracts for Older Employees without Objective Justification

Bundesverfassungsgericht (Federal Constitutional Court
of Germany), 6 July 2010[67]   **5.4 (GERM)**

Honeywell v X

DISCRIMINATION ON GROUNDS OF AGE

Car trouble

The legislative exception for concluding fixed-term contracts has to be disregarded to the detriment of the applicant if it is contrary to EU law

Facts: Honeywell, a company in car components, employed several workers under contracts for a fixed term based on a provision of national law (§14(3) of the German Act on Part-Time Work and Fixed-Term Employment Contracts) to cover production peaks. Some of these employees had already reached the age of 52, including the claimant, so the fixed-term contracts could be concluded without objective justification.

Held: The employee challenged the validity of the limited duration of the contract based on the provision of national law (§14(3) of the German Act on Part-Time Work and Fixed-Term Employment Contracts) because of its incompatibility with EU law (two directives). He sought a judgment ordering that the employment relation be continued. The Court of first instance dismissed the action on the ground that individuals cannot rely on the direct effect of directives. The Labour Court of Appeal upheld the judgment of the Court of first instance. The employee challenged this decision by bringing an action before the Federal Labour Court of Germany. The Federal Labour Court ruled that the employment relation between the parties had not ended upon the expiry of the agreed fixed term. It arrived at this decision by holding the provision of national law (§14(3) of the German Act on Part-Time Work and Fixed-Term Employment Contracts), the legal basis of the fixed-term clause, to be incompatible with EU law and therefore inapplicable by the national courts. Honeywell filed a constitutional complaint, alleging that the judgment of the Federal Labour Court based on the case law of the CJ violated his right of freedom of contract, enshrined in the Basic Law of Germany. The Constitutional Court upheld the judgment by the Federal Labour Court.

Judgment: 49I. The complainant's (employer's) freedom of contract under Article 12.1 and Article 2.1 of the Basic Law has not been violated for the reason that the challenged judgment of the Federal Labour Court is based on a non-permissible further development of the law by the European Court of Justice.

---

[67] Federal Constitutional Court of Germany 6 July 2010 *NJW* 2010, 3422 *Honeywell v X*.

...

The challenged judgment does not violate Article 101.1 sentence 2 of the Basic Law, given that the Federal Labour Court, by deciding not to make a submission to the European Court of Justice, did not deny the complainant (employer) his right to a hearing before the judicial body provided for by law.

In the event of full confirmation of the Mangold ruling, the Federal Labour Court furthermore could and should have examined whether and to what extent there were possible solutions in conformity with European law which would at least in terms of outcome have respected the will of the legislature expressed in §14(3) 4 TzBfG, for instance deciding the present legal dispute, under disapplication of the aforementioned provisions, on the basis that the legal basis of the contract had ceased to exist. It is only when this approach, too, should have proved impossible, that the Federal Labour Court could and should have taken the path of judicial review pursuant to Article 100(1) of the Basic Law to have the Constitutional Court formally establish the exceeding of competence [by the CJ]. This shows, moreover, that *ultra vires* review can largely take place in an EU law-friendly and cooperative way. Consequently, the actual establishment by the Constitutional Court that the Court of Justice has exceeded its competence and that its ruling is therefore inapplicable remains an ultimate measure.

Notes:

(1) This case is interesting since the employer challenged a decision of a national court that was in conformity with the *Mangold* judgment of the CJ. The Federal Labour Court found that the fixed-term employment contract which had been concluded with an employee older than 52 had not ended on the agreed end date. It arrived at this decision by holding that the provision of national law (§14(3) of the German Act on Part-Time Work and Fixed-Term Employment Contracts), which was the legal basis of the fixed-term contract, was incompatible with EU law and must therefore be disapplied by national courts. Under German law, the clause would then be regarded as ineffective (*unwirksam*). As in *Mangold*, the legal relationship between the employer and the employee changed. The employee's claim that he be allowed to continue working under the same employment conditions was granted.

(2) The employer filed a constitutional complaint. He argued that the application of the *Mangold* decision to the case resulted in a violation of his right of freedom of contract as laid down in Articles 12 I and 2 I of the Basic Law of Germany. The Federal Constitutional Court decided that the reasoning of the Federal Labour Court was in conformity with EU law and that it was not required to refer a preliminary question to the CJ. Moreover, it decided that the decision did not violate the claimant's constitutional right of freedom of contract.

(3) This decision has been of major importance for the relationship between EU law and the German Constitution. The Federal Constitutional Court of Germany decided that the 'ultra vires test' (whether or not the CJ acted within the limits of the competences conferred upon it) can be performed in an EU law-friendly and cooperative way.

(4) The effects for the horizontal relationship take place via the legality review of national law against the principle of non-discrimination. Even though this technique does not directly affect the horizontal relationship, it has far-reaching consequences for the actual legal relationship. Because the provision of national law (§14(3) of the German

Act on Part-Time Work and Fixed-Term Employment Contracts) was disapplied, the fixed-term clause in the employment agreement had to be reviewed against the rule of national origin that restricts the possibility of concluding fixed-term employment agreements. The clause was ineffective. Consequently, the employment relation between parties had not ended at the end of the fixed term.

Bundesarbeitsgericht (German Federal Labour Court), 26 April 2006[68]   **5.5 (GERM)**

X v Y

DISCRIMINATION ON GROUNDS OF AGE

Unlimited limit

Following the decision of the CJ of 22 November 2005 (Mangold), the provision of national law violates EU law and shall not be applied by the national courts

Facts: The employee, who was born on 13 February 1950, had been in the employment of the defendant as a production and machinist assistant. Since 12 July 1999, several fixed-term contracts had been concluded between the parties. On the basis of a provision of national law (§14(3) of the German Act on Part-Time Work and Fixed-Term Employment Contracts), the last contract that was concluded provided for a fixed-term employment relationship for the period from 19 February 2003 to 31 March 2004.

Held: The employee brought an action before a German Labour Tribunal claiming that the tribunal should declare that the employment relation between the parties did not end on 31 March 2004 as provided by the fixed-term clause and should order the employer to continue the employment relationship in unmodified form after the fixed end date. The employee based the ineffectiveness of the stipulated fixed term in the employment contract on the incompatibility of the relevant German employment provisions with EU law (a directive). The German Labour Tribunal did not grant the action. At appeal, the employee's claim was again dismissed. The employee then lodged an appeal with the German Federal Labour Court. The Federal Labour Court granted the claim of the employee.

Judgment: The claimant's action, duly filed (§17(1) TzBfG), for a fixed-term complaint is founded. The temporal limitation agreed in the last employment contract is ineffective. It cannot be justified by reference to the provisions of the Act on Part-Time Work and Fixed-Term Employment Contracts (TzBfG). The contested temporal limitation is not justified by an objective reason within the meaning of §14(1) TzBfG The conditions for temporal limitation without objective justification laid down in §14(2) TzBfG are not fulfilled. The defendant cannot rely on the possibility of temporal limitation pursuant to §14(3)1 and 4 TzBfG. The provision is contrary to [EU] law and is therefore not applicable, and it is also not applicable on grounds of legitimate expectations on the part of the defendant. The Senate was not called upon to decide on the claim under 2 aimed at provisionally continuing the employment for the duration of the proceedings.

...

C. The defendant cannot rely on §14(3) 1 and 4 TzBfG to justify the temporal limitation ... §14(3)4 TzBfG, which until 31 December 2006 lowered the age limit of §14(3)1 TzBfG to 52, is incompatible with [EU] law. The national courts may not apply this provision. This follows from the ruling of the CJ (*Mangold*) that is binding on the Senate.

---

[68] German Federal Labour Court 26 April 2006 NZA 2006, 1162 *X v Y*.

This also applies to fixed-term agreements made prior to the ruling of the CJ. The Senate is not bound to refer the question to the CJ pursuant to [now Article 267(3) TFEU], because the incompatibility of §14(3)4 TzBfG with Union law has been clarified by the CJ. The pronouncement of inapplicability does not violate national constitutional law, so that submission to the Federal Constitutional Court under Article 100 of the Basic Law does not come into consideration.

...

aa ... The Federal Constitutional Court has approved the fundamental rights proofing of the CJ oriented towards the general principle of equality and the prohibition of discrimination and has regarded it as a reason for withdrawing its judicial competence when applying secondary Union law to this extent.

...

This does not conflict with the fact that pursuant to art. 100 Basic Law the unconstitutionality of a law can only be established by the Federal Constitutional Court. The issue in the present case is the compatibility of a national provision with directly applicable Union law. Unlike unconstitutionality, incompatibility of a national provision with Union law does not result in nullity. Rather, the national provision continues to exist and may be applied as soon as the incompatibility with Union law ceases to exist ...

It is true, though, that due to these EU law considerations concerning the merely indirect effect of directives a private employer should not assume, a priori, that a fixed-term contract agreed under §14(3)4 TzBfG is invalid. Because the discussion about the consequences of incompatible national law had not been settled yet at the time when §14(3)4 TzBfG came into force, the situation was that until the CJ would have finally clarified the issue, private employers (also) could not unreservedly rely on the validity of fixed-term employment contracts without objective justification with employees, who had reached the age of 52 at the time of concluding the contract. The literature on employment law also advised private employers to make no or only sparing use of the possibility of fixed term contracts without objective justification under §14(3) TzBfG because of the „anything but clear legal situation'. The defendant has indeed not alleged that he must be regarded as worthy of protection in view of the early assertion of the ineffectiveness of the agreed fixed term and the possibilities available to him to otherwise terminate the contract.

Notes:

(1) The facts in this case are comparable to the facts in *Mangold* and in the case decided in 2010 by the Federal Constitutional Court of Germany discussed above (case 5.4 (GERM)). The decision of the Federal Labour Court of Germany has several aspects that are relevant for this casebook. Even though the decision was delivered before the decision by the Federal Constitutional Court of Germany (case 5.4 (GERM)), it more or less follows the same type of reasoning. It starts by pointing out the characteristics of EU law, it then deals with the interaction between EU law and German law, it discusses the implication of the *Mangold* decision and evaluates its consequences for the provision of national law at issue, and finally it decides upon the specific question whether the employment relationship between the parties had ended.

(2) The court reviewed the national provision against the general principle of EU law that prohibits discrimination.

(3) Moreover, it dealt with three related problems that are relevant for individuals: the retroactive effect of the case law of the CJ (paragraphs 40, 42–46), the protection of

legitimate expectations of individuals and the possibility that directives may influence national law before the expiration of the implementation deadline. Since the latter aspect goes beyond the scope of this casebook, these notes do not deal with it.

(4) Even though CJ case law may change relationships between individuals, in *Mangold*, the CJ did not impose any time restriction on the effects of its judgment. The Federal Labour Court of Germany made explicit that only the CJ has competence to restrict the effects of its judgments in time.

(5) As a logical corollary, the protection of legitimate expectations of (one of the) individuals is irrelevant in EU law. According to the Federal Labour Court of Germany, however, the national court has the discretion to protect legitimate interests by applying a national concept of protection of legitimate expectations. But in this case, the Federal Labour Court of Germany held that there were no facts available to make a plausible case for protecting the employer's expectations. The Court reasoned that the employer might have used alternative legal possibilities to terminate an employment contract. For details on facts that may justify the protection of legitimate expectations, see case 5.6 (GERM). Moreover, similar to case 5.2 (GERM), the Court referred to the approach taken by the majority of German legal authors before the CJ delivered its *Mangold* judgment (see note 3). They advised employers not to rely or to rely only cautiously on the relevant provision of national law (§14(3) of the German Act on Part-Time Work and Fixed-Term Employment Contracts).

(6) The possibility of reviewing an applicable national rule against the general EU law principle of non-discrimination is liable to have consequences that lead to major changes in horizontal relationships. Instead of no longer being employed, the employee was employed for an indefinite period, and instead of no longer employing the employee, the employer was employing him for an indefinite period.

Age Discrimination: Limiting Notice Periods for Young(er) Employees by Excluding Period of Employment Completed before a Specified Age

Landesarbeitsgericht Düsseldorf (Labour Court of Appeal of Düsseldorf), 17 February 2010[69]   **5.6 (GERM)**

Küçükdeveci v Swedex GmbH & Co KG

DISAPPLICATION OF A NATIONAL PROVISION REGULATING NOTICE PERIODS
CONTRARY TO THE PROHIBITION OF DISCRIMINATION UNDER EU LAW

Too short a notice period

The prohibition of age discrimination under EU law requires disapplication of §622(2)2 BGB, with the result that the minimum notice period for termination of contracts with young(er) employees is ineffective and replaced by the correct notice period applicable to older employees

Facts: The claimant, Ms Küçükdeveci, who was born in 1978, had been in the employment of the defendant Swedex GmbH as a transit worker since the age of 18. The minimum notice period, laid down in the terms and conditions applicable to the employment relationship between the parties, was based on §622(2)2 BGB and

---

[69] Labour Court of Appeal Düsseldorf *NZA-RR* 2010, 240 *Küçükdeveci v Swedex GmbH & Co KG*.

did not take into account the working years completed before the employee had reached the age of 25. This resulted in termination of the claimant's contract in 2006 with a notice period of one month instead of the four months that would have applied after 10 years of service.

Held: Kücükdeveci alleged that the statutory minimum notice period based on §622(2) BGB, which disregarded length of employment completed before the age of 25 in calculating the notice period, was discriminatory against younger people. The provision of the BGB should be disregarded as it was contrary to the prohibition of age discrimination in EU law. The Mönchengladbach court of first instance dismissed the claim insofar as it sought a declaration that the termination was ineffective and that the employment relationship was continuing. It referred a question to the CJ for a preliminary ruling, which led to the requested disapplication of the German national provision. The parties settled their dispute at a closed session on 3 February 2010 and requested a court decision on the litigation costs.

Judgment: I. The notice of termination dated 19 December 2006 could not dissolve the employment relationship between the parties, which at the time of the notice had existed for more than ten years, before 30 April 2007 with due observance of the notice period of §622(2) 1 No. 4 BGB. It is true that according to §622(2)2 BGB periods worked before the employee had reached the age of 25 must not be taken into account when calculating the decisive length of service pursuant to para. 1. In the present case, however, the exception rule must be disapplied on the basis of the harmonious development of the law that is permitted and required …

III. The incompatibility of §622(2)2 BGB with the prohibition of discrimination on grounds of age has the result that the courts may no longer apply the provision to notices of termination given after 2 December 2006 …

3. After the preliminary ruling of the CJ (para 51) the commitment to protection of EU law can make it necessary for the national courts to disapply a national legal provision that is contrary to the prohibition of discrimination on grounds of age.
   a) Disapplication of §622(2)2 BGB eliminates the inherent discrimination on grounds of age.
   The provision on notice periods is not inapplicable in its entirety. What no longer applies is in fact the restriction of its scope of application, which discriminates against employees who entered the employment of the business before reaching the age of 25. For notices of termination given after 2 December 2006 the discrimination on grounds of age can therefore be remedied only by 'upward adjustment'.
   Suspension until the law will have been adjusted is not necessary. Suspension would only come under consideration when as a result of disapplication of the discriminating provision existing unequal treatment would not be eliminated or would even be increased. That is not the case here. Disapplication of §622(2)2 BGB results in proper equal treatment of the employees, while the extension of the notice period depends only on the duration of the employment relationship.

IV. Legal consequences are attached to the primacy of EU law which can only have effect with respect to the parties involved within the framework of the constitutional fundamental principle of the rule of law.
   …
   However, the fundamental principles of protection of legitimate expectations and of legal certainty are not the only essential elements of the rule of law. Achieving material justice is just as much (such) an essential element. With regard to §622(2)2 BGB, there is on the one hand the confidence of employers, strengthened by articles 20(3) and 97(1) Basic Law, that a statutory age threshold which was not subject to constitutional objections would be applied by the courts, and on the other hand the right of

the disadvantaged employee to be treated without discrimination compared with the employees who entered the company's employment after they had reached the age of 25. In view of the duty of the court to give full effect to the EU principle of equal treatment, the enforcement of prohibition of discrimination (Art. 21 CFREU) carries particular weight in balancing the interests of concerned.

2. …

d. The starting point for the assessment process must be that as of 2 December 2006 the expiry of the period for transposition of Directive 2000/78/EC led to a change in the law, namely that §622(2)2 BGB became inapplicable. From this point of view a 'spurious retroactive effect' exists, because the CJ judgment of 19 January 2010 merely clarified the legal situation. Nevertheless, the change in the law brought about by EU law has not entirely done away with the obligation to protect legitimate expectations based on current legislation, because the parties concerned have frequently relied on the continuation of the legal situation shaped by published laws and have in the past adapted their conduct to it. The rule of law therefore calls for balancing the interest of adjusting the law to the further development of EU law on the one hand and the interest of protecting legitimate expectations on the other hand. In the opinion of the Chamber, the protection of legitimate expectations should not outweigh the other aspect if the dispute between the parties involved concerning the notice period is still pending, and the extension of the notice period with 'retroactive' effect is not unreasonably onerous for the employer and does not endanger the latter's existence …

…

V.2. The termination at too short notice must be regularly construed as having been made with the 'correct' notice period …

The legal consequence that the proper termination takes effect at the end of the extended notice period is in conformity with the EU law requirement that the provision of §622(2)2 BGB be disapplied when calculating the notice period in order to ensure the full effectiveness of the prohibition of discrimination on grounds of age. The contrary view that the notice of termination cannot be construed differently pursuant to §140 BGB and is therefore ineffective, gives too broad an interpretation to the prohibition of partial retention (geltungserhaltende Reduktion) and will, in violation of the prohibition of discrimination, lead to a more favourable treatment of 'younger' employees whose contracts were terminated with too short a notice period and whose termination was therefore ineffective, compared to 'older' employees whose contracts were terminated with a proper notice period from the start. Where – as in this case – the employer merely adjusts his acts to the statutory time frames and otherwise does not show any conduct of his own aimed at discrimination on grounds of age, the punitive nature of anti-discrimination law cannot serve as an argument for nullity of the notice of termination.

Notes:

(1) A provision of national law (§622(2)2 BGB) permitted not taking into account periods of employment completed by an employee before reaching the age of 25 when calculating the notice period for dismissal. As a result, Ms Kücükdeveci, who was younger than 25 when her employment contract was concluded, was dismissed by her employer with a notice period calculated as if she had three years' length of service, although she had been employed for 10 years. There were more such cases.[70]

---

[70] Labour Court of Appeal Berlin-Brandenburg 24 July 2007 *NZA-RR* 2008, 17.

(2) This judgment was a follow-up decision in the case of *Kücükdeveci*. After the CJ had delivered its ruling, the parties settled their dispute. They requested the national court to give a decision on the litigation costs. In its decision, however, the national court elaborated upon the systematic steps it would have to take in adjudicating on this case.

(3) In the first place, the Labour Court of Appeal made it clear that it was not necessary to set aside the entire provision of national law relating to the notice period to be observed when terminating an employment contract. It sufficed to limit the provision's applicability so that it did not apply to employees who had entered into an employment contract before reaching the age of 25 (see judgment III sub 3.a). As a result, the provision still applied to employees who had entered into a contract after the age of 25.

(4) Moreover, the Labour Court of Appeal made it very clear that the termination of the employment contract with a notice period of one month was not entirely ineffective. If the termination were ineffective, the employment contract would not have ended. This situation would result in unequal treatment of employees older than 25, whose contracts could be terminated within the regular notice period, and employees younger than 25, whose contracts would not be terminated at all (see judgment sub V.2). Rather than regarding the termination ineffective, the termination should be construed as having taken place under the conditions required by the applicable provision of national law. This meant that the termination with one month's notice was construed as termination with four months' notice.

(5) The Labour Court of Appeal elaborated upon the restrictions to be taken into account under national law and held that the prohibition of 'geltungserhaltende Reduktion' did not preclude construing the termination as lawful termination.

(6) The result of thus construing the termination was that the employer had to pay wages for three additional months. The legality review of the provision of national law had consequences for the private law relationship. The employer was obliged to pay the employee wages for three additional months and the employee was entitled to be paid wages for three additional months.

(7) In this decision, the national court also elaborated upon the problem of legitimate expectations of individuals who design their acts in conformity with national law (see also case 5.5 (GERM)). Protection of legitimate expectations entered the picture because a legality review against a general principle of EU law in a case in which the national rule might not be reviewed against the directive resulted in unexpected obligations and rights in the relationship between individuals. The national court reasoned that in the judgments of the CJ, the prohibition of discrimination clearly outweighs the protection of legitimate expectations. However, this approach is not decisive for the national courts. From the perspective of the rule of law, German national courts balance the need to shape the rule of national law in conformity with EU law and protection of legitimate expectations. The Labour Court of Appeal argued that the protection of legitimate expectations did not outweigh the former aspect if the dispute concerning the notice period was still pending and the extension of the notice period was not unreasonably onerous and did not endanger the employer's continued existence.

(8) Individuals are therefore confronted with unexpected obligations. This has been recognised by the CJ, which in this connection refers explicitly to the liability of the Member State under the *Francovich* doctrine.

Age Discrimination: Automatic Termination When the Employee Reaches a Specified Age

This section presents a preliminary question and the follow-up decision by the Federal Labour Court.

Bundesarbeitsgericht (Federal Labour Court of Germany),
16 October 2008[71]   **5.7 (GERM)**

Lufthansa v Kumpan

DISCRIMINATION ON GROUNDS OF AGE

High (age) in the sky I

The national court suspended the proceedings in order to obtain a preliminary ruling from the CJ

Facts: Kumpan, who was born on 12 April 1945, worked for Lufthansa as a flight attendant. Since 15 March 1971, several fixed-term contracts had been concluded between the parties. The contract concluded on 15 March 1991 provided for an employment relationship that would terminate, under the applicable collective agreement, at the end of the month in which the employee reached the age of 55. The employment relationship of Kumpan was thus to end on 12 April 2000. However, the collective agreement contained an optional clause, which was used by the parties, to extend the employment relationship by successive fixed-term contracts for part-time employment, each time for a period of one year, with the employment relationship finally terminating at the end of the month in which the employee reached the age of 60. In the case of Kumpan, the employment relationship would thus terminate without notice on 30 April 2005.

Held: The Employment Tribunal dismissed the claim of Kumpan (the employee), who asked the court to declare that the employment contract between the parties had not ended on 30 April 2005 and to order the continuation of the employment relationship between the parties for the position of flight attendant. At appeal, the Labour Court of Appeal (Landesarbeitsgericht) upheld the complaint and ruled in favour of the claimant. The defendant (the employer) challenged this decision by bringing an action before the Federal Labour Court of Germany alleging that the age limitation for cabin crew was in accordance with a provision of national law (§14(3) TzBfG). The Federal Labour Court of Germany suspended the proceedings in order to acquire a preliminary ruling from the CJ.

Judgment: The decision in this case depends on the compatibility with Union law of §14(3)1 TzBfG in the version applicable in the period 01.01.2001—30.04.2007. The fixed-term clause in the employment contract is not justified by an objective reason within the meaning of §14(3)1 TzBfG old version. The action must, however, be dismissed if the agreed fixed term can be justified by the option laid down in §14(3)1 TzBfG old version to allow a temporal limitation, without objective justification, in an employment contract with an employee who had reached the age of 58 at the start of the employment relationship. Furthermore, the compatibility of the provision with Union law has significant relevance to the decision in this case. This issue can be decided only by the CJ. According to its considerations in the Mangold judgment relating to the inapplicability of §14(3)4 TzBfG old version, §14(3)1 TzBfG old version may likewise be contrary both to the principle of equality in employment and occupation enshrined in primary law and to art. 6I of Directive 2000/78/EC. The Senate additionally holds that §14(3) TzBfG old version does not conform to the requirements of Clause 5(1) of the Framework Agreement. Finally, it remains unclear whether a breach of art. 6I of Directive 2000/78/EC or Clause

---

[71] Federal Labour Court of Germany *NZA* 2009, 378–385 *Lufthansa v Kumpan*.

5(1) of the Framework Agreement leads to inapplicability of §14(3)1 TzBfG old version. The questions in the operative part of the order for reference have not yet been the subject of interpretation by the CJ and they cannot be answered unambiguously and unequivocally either …

[23]II. Thus, the fixed-term clause in the employment contract of 23.01.2004 can be justified only under §14(3)1 TzBfG old version, the conditions of which are met in this case. It is doubted, however, whether this provision is compatible with Union law. Incompatibility could result in the national courts being unable to apply the norm …

[31] The Senate cannot, therefore, give a final judgment on the claimant's complaint concerning the decision on the fixed term clause which under national law is ready for judgment in the claimant's favour …

[33] For this reason, §14(3)1 TzBfG old version is not included in the pronouncement of inapplicability in the CJ's ruling in the Mangold case. Under national law, therefore, temporal limitation without justification in contracts with employees who had reached the age of 58 at the start of the employment relationship was permitted until 30.04.2007, subject to the additional conditions of §14(3)2 and 3 TzBfG old version …

[43] In principle, the inapplicability of §14(3)1 TzBfG old version arises only if the provision is contrary to primary Union law. If this is not the case, the Senate, when interpreting §14(3)1 TzBfG old version, would only be authorized to take account of Directive 2000/78/EC, which by way of its advance effect already applied when the employment relationship commenced on 1 May 2004. §14(3)1 TzBfG old version cannot be interpreted in conformity with Union law, though. The provision is admittedly aimed at preserving and creating employment … However, the wording of the provision, which in this respect is unambiguous, does not permit consideration of the labour market objectives pursued by this provision as a condition for a fixed-term contract without objective justification.

[44]dd) Another reason why it is necessary to start a preliminary ruling procedure under [now Article 267 TFEU] is that the Senate is unable to determine clearly and unambiguously the principles that apply, according to CJ case law, to the proportionality assessment of unequal treatment on grounds of age …

[51]b) The Senate cannot assess with the required degree of clarity whether the decision of the CJ in the Mangold case must be understood to mean that a national court is not permitted to apply a provision of national law enacted during the period allowed for transposing a directive if that provision contravenes the objectives pursued by the directive.

Bundesarbeitsgericht (Federal Labour Court of Germany),
19 October 2011[72]   **5.8 (GERM)**

Lufthansa v Kumpan

DISCRIMINATION ON GROUNDS OF AGE

High (age) in the sky II

Under Article §14(3) TzBfG, the employment relationship must be considered to be for an indefinite duration in spite of the reference in the current contract to the provision in the collective agreement for an age limit

Facts: See case 5.7 (GERM).

[72] Federal Labour Court of Germany *BeckRS* 2012, 68565 *Lufthansa v Kumpan*.

Held: See case 5.7 (GERM). In its judgment, the Federal Labour Court followed the suggestion by the CJ of relying on a different provision of national law and ruled in favour of the claimant.

Judgment: [16] 1. The question whether §14(3)1 TzBfG old version is compatible with [EU] law has not been conclusively settled … Instead, the CJ has ruled that Clause 5(1) of the Framework Agreement should be interpreted to mean that the concept of 'close objective connection with a previous contract of employment of indefinite duration with the same employer', as referred to in §14(3)2 TzBfG old version, should be applied to certain circumstances that are specified in detail.

[17] 2. After reassessing the case in the light of the order for reference, the Senate concludes that in the present case the conformity of §14(3)1 TzBfG old version with EU law is ultimately irrelevant because application of the disputed provision is contrary to §14(3)2 TzBfG old version. The 'close objective connection' required by this provision exists also if there were several successive fixed-term contracts, without interruption, between the earlier employment contract of indefinite duration and the last fixed-term contract. If any conclusion to the contrary can be drawn from the order for reference of 16 October 2008, the Senate will not adhere to it. The assumption of a previous employment contract of indefinite duration within the meaning of §14(3)2 TzBfG old version is not precluded by the applicability of a collectively agreed, higher age limit to the earlier employment contract concluded for an indefinite duration …

[26](2) In the present case, harmonious interpretation of §14(3)2 TzBfG old version is both necessary and possible. To this extent the Senate follows the reasoning of the CJ (C-109/09, *Deutsche Lufthansa*).

[27](a) The CJ did not exceed its competence in its judgment C-109/09 (*Deutsche Lufthansa*). By ruling that EU law required a specific interpretation of §14(3)2 TzBfG old version, it did not interpret national law, but rather provided an interpretation of EU law. The fact that this did not answer the question asked by the Senate in its request for a preliminary ruling does not mean that the CJ evidently exceeded its competence.

[28](b) According to the CJ, §14(3)1 TzBfG old version leads to a lower level of social protection for all older employees as they are deprived of all the protective measures specified in Clause 5(1) of the Framework Agreement and aimed at preventing abusive recourse to consecutive fixed-term employment contracts. §14(3)2 TzBfG old version is the sole restriction on the possibility allowed by §14(3)1 TzBfG old version to conclude an unlimited number of consecutive fixed-term contracts without objective justification with people who have reached the age of 58. In order to avoid limiting the scope of application of this sole restriction, EU law requires the assumption of a 'close objective connection', as referred to in §14(3)2 TzBfG old version, also in cases in which there is an interval of several years between the last fixed-term contract and the earlier contract of indefinite duration, provided that the original employment relationship, involving the same work and the same employer, continued under an uninterrupted series of fixed-term contracts throughout this period.

[29](c) The Senate shares this view. b) The assumption of a previous employment contract of indefinite duration, as referred to in §14(3)2 TzBfG old version, does not preclude a collectively agreed, higher age limit from applying to the earlier employment contract concluded for an indefinite duration. The nature of such contracts is that of consolidated 'normal working relationships'. They are often regarded as contracts concluded 'for an indefinite period', without this resulting in a waiver of any age limit. For the purposes of §14(3)2 TzBfG old version, they are taken to be 'of indefinite duration' …

[31] 3. Consequently, the employment relationship between the parties has not ended on 30 April 2005.

Notes:

(1) The judgment of the Federal Labour Court (case 5.7 (GERM)) clearly illustrates how a national court analysed a preliminary ruling of the CJ and the reasoning it used to decide how to apply the CJ ruling to the case under scrutiny. The facts and the point of law differed from those in the *Mangold* case. The provision under scrutiny made it possible to conclude fixed-term employment contracts without objective justification with workers who had reached the age of 58 at the commencement of the fixed-term employment relationship.

(2) The Federal Labour Court took *Mangold* as a starting point. It confirmed (in paragraph 32) that the CJ ruled within the limits of its competence. Subsequently, the court tried to discover whether the general principle of EU law that prohibits discrimination on grounds of age as developed in *Mangold* also applied to the provision of national law that was applicable in this case. In its preliminary question, the Federal Labour Court held the opinion that §14(3)1 of the German Act on Part-Time Work and Fixed-Term Employment Contracts applied. Its question was whether under the circumstances of the case, this provision was at variance with Directive 2000/78,[73] with the general principle of non-discrimination on grounds of age and with clause 5(1) of the Framework Agreement on fixed-term employment, and must therefore be disapplied.

(3) The court was therefore looking for clarification of the scope of the general principle. A national court is not allowed to review a provision of national law applicable to a horizontal relationship against a provision in a directive. Therefore, if the general principle did not cover this case, the national court would not be allowed to review the national provision.

(4) Furthermore, the national court wanted the CJ to determine whether the provision of national law in this case survived the legality review against the general principle of non-discrimination, as the provision might be considered to be proportionate in view of its intended aim (the employment of older people). In this case, the national court could not use the CJ's reasoning in *Mangold* on whether the provision of national law was appropriate and necessary to achieve a legitimate objective. Tailoring this reasoning to the provision in the case under consideration had to be done by the CJ.

(5) As we learn from case 5.8 (GERM), the CJ suggested a different approach to assessing the national rules applicable to the horizontal relationship. The provision of national law (§14(3) of the German Act on Part-Time Work and Fixed-Term Employment Contracts) may be construed in conformity with EU law. The suggested technique was to use an option already available under national law, namely to restrict the opportunities for concluding fixed-term employment contracts (§14(3)2 of the German Act on Part-Time Work and Fixed-Term Employment Contract). The German court presupposed that this restriction (a fixed-term contract is not permitted if there is a close objective connection between that contract and a previous employment contract of indefinite duration concluded with the same employer) did not apply to the case. The CJ held, however, that where there has been abuse of successive fixed-term employment contracts, the relevant provisions of national law can be interpreted and applied in such a way as to make it

---

[73] [2000] OJ L303/16 (n 40).

possible to duly penalise the abuse and nullify the consequences of the breach of EU law. Moreover, the CJ argued that a close objective connection with a previous employment contract of indefinite duration concluded with the same employer is assumed to exist even when a fixed-term contract was not immediately preceded by a contract of indefinite duration and an interval of several years separates those contracts, provided that the initial employment relationship continued for the same work and with the same employer throughout the entire period by means of an uninterrupted series of successive fixed-term contracts.

(6) The Federal Labour Court adjusted its legal reasoning and followed the reasoning of the CJ. The effect of this on the horizontal relationship was that the employment relationship was taken to be for an unlimited duration and therefore the contract did not end when the employee turned 60.

Bundesarbeitsgericht (Federal Labour Court of Germany),
15 February 2012[74]					**5.9 (GERM)**

Z v X

DISCRIMINATION ON GROUNDS OF AGE

Piloting

An age limitation for cockpit personnel constitutes violation of the EU law principle of non-discrimination on grounds of age. Even if there are safety reasons for such an age limit, they were applied in a disproportionate way

Facts: The claimant, a UK citizen, worked for the defendant as a pilot. The contract he had concluded provided for an employment relationship that would end, in accordance with the applicable collective agreement, at the end of the month in which the employee reached the age of 60. The employment relationship thus ended without notice being required.

Held: The parties had a dispute as to whether the employment relationship had ended when the claimant turned 60. The collective agreement (*Manteltarifvertrag*) provided that the employment ended when the employee turned 60. The claimant alleged that such an arrangement infringed the principle prohibiting age discrimination. The Federal Labour Court held that the arrangement between the parties violated the EU law prohibition of discrimination. As far as there were safety reasons for such an age limit, they were applied in a disproportionate way. The employment relationship had not ended.

Judgment: [17]1 ... The question whether EU law precludes an age limit laid down in national law must therefore be examined on the basis of the general principle of EU law which prohibits any discrimination on grounds of age and which has been specified in the Framework Directive on Equal Treatment (see CJ 19 January 2010 – C-555/07 – [*Kücükdeveci*] paragraph 27).

[34](3) Guaranteeing the safety of air traffic is a legitimate purpose of the collectively agreed age limit.

[34](4) The collective bargaining parties have imposed on the airline pilots a disproportionate requirement within the meaning of the general legal principle expressed in

---

[74] Federal Labour Court of Appeal of Germany *NZA* 2012, 866 *Z v X*.

Article 4(1) of the Framework Directive on Equal Treatment, by setting the age limit after which the pilots are considered to be no longer physically able to carry out their professional activities at the end of the month in which they reach the age of 60. The national and international licence regimes allow pilots to carry out this activity until they have reached the age of 65 where there are two (co-)pilots in the cockpit, provided that one of them has not yet reached the age of 60. There are no sufficiently reliable findings that the public law restrictions guaranteeing the safety of air traffic in force at the time are not adequate and that further collective restrictions are necessary.

[37]3. The collective age limit of §19(1) MTV No. 1, which occurs before the statutory retirement age is reached, is therefore contrary to the primary-law prohibition of discrimination on grounds of age, which must be regarded as a general principle of EU law and which has been further specified in the Framework Directive on equal treatment in employment and occupation.

Notes:

(1) According to the collective labour agreement applicable to the employment contract, this contract ended without notice at the end of the month in which the employee turned 60. This age limit differed from the default age limit, which was 65. According to the national court, there was no objective justification for the age limit of 60 set in the collective agreement. The Federal Labour Court of Germany relied on the general principle of non-discrimination and held that the provision in the collective employment agreement should have been disapplied by the German courts.

(2) Technically, the German Court applied the principle of non-discrimination directly to the collective labour agreement and consequently to the horizontal relationship. But the reasoning of the national court seems to have had its basis in the technique of legality review (paragraphs 28 and 37 of the decision). Most probably, the German Court took the same approach to a collective labour agreement as to a provision of national law.

(3) The effect on the contract between employee and employer was that the employment contract did not end at the age of 60; the employee would be employed until the default age: 65.

(4) See sections III and V.B in Chapter 6 for a Belgian case on termination of an employment contract on the basis of age.

II.C.iii POSITIVE OBLIGATION OF MEMBER STATES WITH IMPACT ON HORIZONTAL RELATIONS BETWEEN INDIVIDUALS

This section presents cases from national jurisdictions which indirectly involve a horizontal relationship and in which a national court finds on the basis of the principle of non-discrimination that a positive obligation of the Member State exists, which has consequences for the horizontal relationship.[75] A national court may rely on this mechanism to avoid a result in a horizontal relationship that is at variance with the requirements of EU law.

---

[75] For the method of selecting cases and the structure of the presentation of the cases, see section II.C.

II.C.iv MISCELLANEOUS

This category comprises cases in which national private law is influenced by the EU principle of non-discrimination in yet other ways than those dealt with in sections II.C.i–II.C.iii.

A case in which the CJ ruled that an act of the EU, namely a directive, was invalid because it conflicted with the principle of equality enshrined in the Charter is *Test-Achats* (see case 5.10 (BE) and 5.11 (BE)). This case does not involve the autonomous operation of a general principle of EU law,[76] yet it is interesting and relevant. It is interesting because it shows the links between the Charter and the general principles of EU law. Gaps existing in EU law can be filled by reference to general principles of EU law. These principles may in turn be derived from the Charter.[77]

Grondwettelijk Hof België (Constitutional Court
of Belgium), 18 June 2009[78]   **5.10 (BE)**

Association Belge des Consommateurs Test-Achats ASBL, Yann
van Vugt & Charles Basselier v Conseil des ministres

DISCRIMINATION ON GROUNDS OF SEX

Policing policies I

The national court suspended the proceedings in order to obtain a preliminary ruling from
the CJ

Facts: The Belgian legislator had implemented Directive 2004/113/EC. The Directive orders Member States to ensure equal treatment between men and women by prohibiting all sex-related differences in contracts concluded after 21 December 2007. However, pursuant to Article 5(2) of the Directive Member States may decide before this date to permit proportionate differences in individuals' premiums and benefits where the use of sex is a determining factor in the assessment of risk based on relevant and accurate actuarial and statistical data. Belgium made use of this option of Article 5(2) of the Directive with regard to life assurance contracts.

Held: The claimants claimed annulment of the Belgian provisions transposing the Directive and more specifically of Article 5(2) of the Directive, alleging that the Belgian legislation was in conflict with the principle of equality between men and women, as it allowed gender-based discrimination by permitting unequal premiums and benefits under (life) insurance agreements. The Belgian court suspended the proceedings to refer a question for a preliminary ruling and asked the CJ to determine whether the Belgian legislation, which contained an exception for insurance companies allowing them to deviate from the prohibition of discrimination based on sex, operated against achieving the objective of equal treatment between men and women, and whether it was compatible with (the purpose of) Directive 2004/113 and with Articles 21 and 23 of the Charter.

---

[76] Review against the Charter will not always replace review against a general principle of EU law. Now that the Charter has come into effect, the case law on the autonomous operation of general principles of EU law will not be replaced in its entirety by adjudication based on review against the Charter. As will be demonstrated below, the former can moreover be important even if the court does (primarily) review against the Charter.

[77] CJ 27 June 2006 Case C-540/03 *European Parliament v EU Council* [2006] I-05769 ECLI:EU:C:2006:429, para 38. See on this issue K Lenaerts and JA Gutiérrez-Fons, 'The Constitutional Allocation of Powers and General Principles of EU Law' (2010) 47 *CMLR* 1654–60. These authors hold that it cannot be excluded that the CJEU would have referred to the Charter if CJ *Mangold* (n 42) had been pronounced later than CJ *European Parliament v EU Council*.

[78] Constitutional Court of Belgium 18 June 2009 Belgisch Staatsblad 31 July 2009 arrest no 103/2009 (2nd edn) 2691 *Association Belge des Consommateurs Test-Achats ASBL, Yann van Vugt & Charles Basselier v Conseil des ministres*.

Judgment: B.3 The first plea, like the two other pleas, is derived from violation 'of articles 10, 11 and 11bis of the Constitution, read in conjunction with [now Article 19 TFEU], Council Directive 2004/113/EC of 13 December 2004 implementing the principle of equal treatment between men and women in the access to and supply of goods and services, articles 20, 21 and 23 of the EU Charter of Fundamental Rights, article 14 of the European Convention on Human Rights, article 26 of the International Convention on Civil and Political Rights and the International Convention on the elimination of all forms of discrimination against women'.

...

B.5.1 Since the challenged statute makes use of the option of article 5(2) of the Directive of 13 December 2004, and since the criticism formulated by the applicants in their first plea with regard to the statute applies equally to this article 5(2), the issue of the validity of that provision of this directive will first have to be resolved before the Court can give a decision on the appeal.

B.5.2 The Court is not competent to rule on the question whether or not that directive provision is compatible with the prohibition of discrimination on grounds of sex, enshrined inter alia in the aforementioned article 6(2) of the Treaty on European Union ...

B.7 The parliamentary documents of the challenged provision show that initially the legislator considered extending its scope to various insurance classes, such as health insurance, vehicle damage insurance, insurance against civil liability with respect to motor vehicles, and insurance activities falling in the area of 'life' insurance ... but that eventually it was restricted to life insurance contracts ...

If the answer to the first preliminary question is negative, the CJ must be asked whether a derogation that is restricted to life insurance contracts is also incompatible with the principle of equality and non-discrimination ...

The following questions are referred to the Court for a preliminary ruling:

1. Is Article 5(2) of Directive 2004/113 compatible with Article 6(2) [EU] and, more specifically, with the principle of equality and non-discrimination guaranteed by that provision?

2. If the answer to the first question is negative, is Article 5(2) of the Directive also incompatible with Article 6(2) [TEU] if its application is restricted to life assurance contracts?

Grondwettelijk Hof België (Constitutional Court
of Belgium), 30 June 2011[79]   **5.11 (BE)**

Association Belge des Consommateurs Test-Achats ASBL,
Yann van Vugt & Charles Basselier v Conseil des ministres

DISCRIMINATION ON GROUNDS OF SEX

Policing policies II

The Belgian legislation implementing Article 5(2) of Directive 2004/113/EC is invalid and a transitional period in relation to the effects of its invalidity is applied from 21 December 2012

Facts: See case 5.10 (BE).

---

[79] Constitutional Court of Belgium 30 June 2011 Belgisch Staatsblad 11 August 2011 p 45813 arrest no 116/2011 *Association Belge des Consommateurs Test-Achats ASBL, Yann van Vugt & Charles Basselier v Conseil des ministres.*

Held: See case 5.10 (BE). The Constitutional Court of Belgium annulled the national provision.

Judgment: B.7 As observed before, the first plea in the main proceedings alleges that the use made in the challenged statute of the option of derogation laid down in article 5(2) of Directive 2004/113/EC is contrary to the provisions on which the plea relies, since said article 5(2) is itself contrary to the principle of sex equality enshrined in Union law …

B.11 When the criterion under consideration is based on the gender of the persons involved, articles 10, 11 and 11bis(1) of the Constitution must be taken into account, as well as the international provisions that are binding on Belgium and that have a scope that is analogous to said provisions of the Constitution; the safeguards contained in those international provisions form an indissociable whole with the safeguards included in the aforementioned provisions of the Constitution. These provisions, read in conjunction with one another, compel legislators to observe particular prudence when they introduce a difference of treatment on grounds of sex. Such a criterion is acceptable only if it is justi-fied by a legitimate objective and relevant with regard to that objective. Review is more stringent when the fundamental principle of sex equality is at issue.

B.12 For the reasons stated by the Court of Justice in its abovementioned judgment of 1 March 2011, in particular in paragraphs 30–32—in which it draws specific attention to undermining the principle of equal treatment of women and men enshrined in articles 21 and 23 of the EU Charter of Fundamental Rights—there is no reasonable justification for the different treatment at issue. This finding applies equally to article 3 of the challenged statute and its article 4, which provides for a transitional arrangement; it also applies to the other provisions of the statute of 21 December 2007, because they are connected with these articles 3 and 4.

B.13 The first plea in law is well-founded. Consequently, the challenged statute should be annulled in its entirety.

Notes:

(1) Case 5.10 (BE) related to an action brought by Belgian Verbruikersunie Test-Achats and two individuals before the Belgian Constitutional Court about the constitu-tionality of a provision of a Belgian law.[80] This law implemented Directive 2004/113.[81] Article 10(1) provided, in derogation of Article 8 (which prohibited discrimination), that a proportional direct difference might be made on grounds of sex where the use of sex was a determining factor in the assessment of risk based on relevant and accurate actu-arial and statistical data. This derogation applied exclusively to life insurance contracts.

(2) Article 10(1) of the Belgian law was based on Article 5(2) of the Directive, which permits Member States to make sex-related differences in individuals' premiums and benefits where the use of sex is a determining factor.

(3) The issue of the constitutionality of the Belgian implementing law raised the ques-tion in the Belgian Constitutional Court whether Article 5(2) of the Directive was con-trary to Article 6(2) TEU and, more specifically, contrary to the principle of equality and non-discrimination safeguarded by that provision.

(4) The CJ reviewed the provision of the Directive against Articles 21 and 23 of the Charter. It ruled that the option of discriminating without temporal limitation as

---

[80] The Law of 21 December 2007 transposing Directive 2004/113 into Belgian law.
[81] [2004] OJ L373/37 (n 40).

permitted by the Directive was incompatible with the intended purpose of Article 19(1) TFEU. It was also ruled to be inconsistent with the aim of the EU to eliminate inequalities and to promote equality between men and women in all its activities, as provided in Article 8 TFEU. See also section II.B above.

(5) The CJ repeated that the principle of equality required that comparable situations must not be treated differently and that different situations must not be treated similarly unless such treatment is objectively justified. The question whether the situations in which men and women find themselves with regard to determining insurance premiums are comparable must be assessed in the light of the subject matter and the purpose of the EU measure which introduced the distinction in question: Directive 2004/113. The purpose of this Directive in the insurance services sector is the application of unisex rules on premiums and benefits. It is therefore based on the assumption that the situations in which men and women find themselves with regard to the premiums and benefits of the insurance agreements they have concluded are comparable. The provision giving the Member States the option of maintaining exceptions to the rule of unisex premiums and benefits without temporal limitation was ruled to be contrary to the realisation of the Directive's objective of equal treatment between men and women and incompatible with Articles 21 and 23 of the Charter. The CJ declared the relevant article of the Directive invalid effective from 21 December 2012 and ruled that the national implementing law had to be set aside.

(6) The CJ did not specify what the precise implications of the transitional period are. It may happen that before the expiry of the transitional period, an individual relies on the general principle of EU law prohibiting discrimination on grounds of sex to obtain a judgment that the national law must be disapplied because it conflicts with the EU law principle. In that case, the individual would be relying on the approach taken in *Mangold*, *Kücükdeveci* and *ČEZ*, according to which conflict with EU law has immediate consequences. This would de facto make ineffective the transitional period recognised in the case of *Test-Achats*, just as the remaining implementation period became ineffective in the *Mangold* case. If one disregards this possibility (which has not yet been tested in practice) of relying on the general principle of EU law, this means that the legislature is allowed time to adjust its national legislation and individuals are thus allowed time to revise their legal relationships. Notwithstanding the transitional period, the declaration of invalidity of the directive provision had a major impact on contracts concluded under a national law that had been designed in conformity with the invalidated provision of the Directive. To avoid uncertainty, the Commission communicated guidelines.[82]

(7) The question submitted to the CJ in *Test-Achats* and the CJ's ruling on the matter did not concern the autonomous operation of a general principle of EU law or a legal relationship between individuals. The case was about the validity of an act of the EU (issuing a directive provision) and it did not concern the autonomous application of a principle of EU law because the CJ reviewed the provision against the Charter.

---

[82] Communication from the Commission, Guidelines on the application of Council Directive 2004/113/EC to insurance, in the light of the judgment of the Court of Justice of the European Union in Case C-236/09 (Test-Achats), Brussels 22 December 2011 C(2011) 9497 final.

The primary mechanism that in this situation set in motion an effect on the legal relationships between individuals was the declaration by the Belgian court that the Belgian (implementing) act was unconstitutional. But these specific aspects of the case do not change the fact that the invalidation of the Directive will also cause effects in other Member States. Where Member States have likewise enacted implementing provisions that correspond with the invalidated Directive provision, they will have to amend their legislation. This has the legal consequence that a clause in an insurance agreement which differentiates, in accordance with the possibility of discriminating on grounds of sex, in the determination of insurance premiums and benefits will come to be contrary to the law of national origin.

(8) In her opinion for the judgment, AG Kokott[83] included a thorough discussion of the question whether discrimination on grounds of gender is a consequence of the fact that a difference between men and women can be established. In this context, she dealt with the pitfall that in actual practice the distinction is easy to make and is therefore used, for the sake of convenience, as a substitute criterion for other distinguishing factors. In the context of life insurance, these are factors like stressful professional activities, the use of stimulants and practising sports. In present-day social circumstances, the extent to which these factors are present or absent is not or is no longer gender-linked. Consequently, it is not possible to establish an objective justification for discrimination on grounds of sex in the rules for determining insurance premiums and benefits.

(9) It was only after having obtained the CJ's answer that the Constitutional Court of Belgium was able to review the provision of national law (case 5.11 (BE)). The invalidation of the provision of the Directive obliged the Belgian Constitutional Court to invalidate the provision of the implementing law that was based on the provision of the Directive.

(10) It is clear that agreements concluded after the national provision (which formed part of the implementing law) had been declared unconstitutional or ceased to apply may not conflict with the resulting (eg, subsequent or reviving) law (of national, supranational or international origin). The policy conditions will have to be adjusted in such a way that there is no discrimination on grounds of sex with regard to premiums and benefits. For the time being, it is still uncertain what the fate will be of clauses in agreements concluded before the provision of the national implementing law was declared unconstitutional or ceased to apply. In this respect, the implications of this ruling differ from the implications of the CJ's case law concerning provisions of national law that infringed a general principle of EU law or a Charter provision.

(11) With regard to the consequences for private law, the rules of national transitional law are important. However, it is doubtful whether these rules will lead to this issue being definitely settled in the end. Where national transitional law leaves intact clauses that were legally valid at the time of making the agreement even if subsequently they conflict with resulting (eg, subsequent or reviving) legislation, then individuals would have no protection against a conflict between national legislation and EU law. It is indeed

---

[83] AG Kokott Opinion in Case C-236/09 *Test-Achats ASBL et al v Conseil des ministres* [2011] I-00773 ECLI:EU:C:2010:564.

conceivable that in this situation, also in light of effectiveness, the CJ will allow the plea that either the result generated by the rule of national transitional law or the insurance agreement concluded in the past conflicts with the general principle of EU law prohibiting discrimination on grounds of sex. If this should happen, the fact that the implementing law conflicts with EU law would have the result that the contractual clauses pertaining to the calculation of premiums come into conflict with the resulting (eg, subsequent or reviving) law (whether of national or international origin) and are null and void because they conflict with either the general principle of EU law or the law of national origin. The consequences (eg, conversion or supplementing a different clause by operation of the principle of reasonableness and fairness) must be decided in accordance with national law. At any rate, a clause that is void must be replaced by a clause that calculates the same premium for men and women. Based on logical reasoning, one would have expected that premiums for women would fall and those for men would rise. However, in reality, this ruling resulted in premiums rising for both women and men.

II.D FINAL OBSERVATIONS

This section has dealt in detail with reported case law in terms of facts, the legal relationship concerned, the techniques and mechanisms of EU law and national law, the substance of rules of EU law and national law, and the substantive implications of the prohibition of discrimination, including available remedies. The analyses resulted in general observations that shed light on the differences and commonalities regarding the substantive and formal interaction between EU law and national (private) law. These are relevant to actors (scholars, judges, legal practitioners and parties) dealing with non-discrimination and private law in particular, and more generally also to actors dealing with the interaction between EU law and private law.

These observations give insight into the substantive changes of a private law relationship after a confrontation with EU law (section II.D.i). They also shed light on the constitutional structures and techniques that frame the reasoning of national courts when they are dealing with the application of EU law in private law relationships (section II.D.ii). They relate to the remedies used to achieve a result that is in conformity with EU law (section II.D.iii). A striking finding that can be signalled in relation to the application of the general EU law principle of non-discrimination is that a balance must be struck between the enforcement of the right to be not discriminated against and the protection of legitimate expectation (section II.D.iv). Interestingly, these expectations may have their basis in provisions of national law envisioned to implement EU law.

II.D.i THE GENERAL PRINCIPLE OF NON-DISCRIMINATION MAY SUBSTANTIVELY CHANGE HORIZONTAL RELATIONSHIPS

As explained before, EU law has developed several mechanisms via which it affects national (private) law. The general EU law principle of non-discrimination may thus lead to substantive changes in the horizontal relationship. An individual who infringes the prohibition of discrimination, for example, by observing national provisions that are at variance with the principle, may be confronted with both contractual and non-contractual obligations. Where EU law imposes obligations upon individuals, it may be expected that it will also provide for appropriate grounds for justification on which individuals can rely.

Infringement of the prohibition to discriminate can, for example, be the reason to render a contractual relationship null and void (case 5.11 (BE)), to consider a juridical act as ineffective (case 5.5 (GERM)), to construe a juridical act (termination or an entire contract) in such a way that it becomes lawful (cases 5.6 (GERM) and 5.8 (GERM)), to fill gaps in a contract (case 5.8 (GERM)), to set aside or disapply a contractual clause (case 5.9 (GERM)), to grant a party a right (eg, payment of wages) under EU law or national law (cases 5.3 (IT) and 5.6 (GERM)) or to bar a party from relying on rights derived from national law (eg, the ending of an employment contract) (cases 5.5 (GERM), 5.6 (GERM), 5.8 (GERM) and 5.9 (GERM)).

Courts give consideration to the objective justifications for infringement of EU law caused by national law (cases 5.5 (GERM), 5.6 (GERM), 5.7 (GERM) and 5.9 (GERM)). On the general principle of proportionality in EU law, see section I.C in Chapter 5.

II.D.ii NATIONAL COURTS DO EXPLICITLY CONSIDER THE CONSTITUTIONAL FRAMEWORK OR MECHANISM(S) OF INTERACTION BETWEEN EU LAW AND PRIVATE LAW

National systems vary in terms of the way they adapt to supranational and international legal rules. The CJ's judgments in *Mangold* and *Kücükdeveci* raised the fundamental question whether the CJ acted within the limits of the competences conferred upon it and whether national actors feel bound to adapt to the requirements set by these judgments (cases 5.4 (GERM), 5.5 (GERM), 5.6 (GERM), 5.7 (GERM) and 5.8 (GERM)).

In their considerations, national courts deal with the supremacy of EU law (cases 5.3 (IT), 5.4 (GERM) and 5.7 (GERM)), the relationship between primary and secondary EU law (case 5.7 (GERM)), the fact that directives do not have direct effect in horizontal relationships (cases 5.5 (GERM) and 5.7 (GERM)), the duty to interpret national law in conformity with EU law (case 5.8 (GERM)), the duty to disapply national law that is not in conformity with EU law (case 5.3 (IT)), the duty to refer a preliminary question to the CJ (cases 5.4 (GERM) and 5.7 (GERM)) and the fact that the CJ has not answered the preliminary question (case 5.8 (GERM)).

EU law can only have an impact on a case if it falls within the scope of application of EU law (case 5.7 (GERM)).

Besides, national courts give consideration to the mechanism(s) to be used in order to achieve the result that EU law has effect in private law and in private law relationships (cases 5.3 (IT), 5.6 (GERM) and 5.8 (GERM)).

II.D.iii NATIONAL COURTS USUALLY FIND SUITABLE REMEDIES IN CASE OF INFRINGEMENT OF EU LAW

National courts usually find and adjust suitable remedies in their national systems, for instance, injunctions (case 5.3 (IT)) and modifying a contract in order to avoid its ending upon the expiry of a fixed term (case 5.8 (GERM)). In case 5.3 (IT), the national court created an inventive remedy. It ordered the employer to hire a sufficient number of members of the particular trade union to re-establish the previous proportion of such members relative to the overall number of employees in the establishment.

When moulding the remedy, the courts try to prevent the remedy from resulting in a subsequent discrimination (case 5.6 (GERM)).

II.D.iv NATIONAL COURTS GIVE CONSIDERATION TO THE PROTECTION OF LEGAL CERTAINTY AND LEGITIMATE EXPECTATIONS

The consequences for horizontal relationships of the CJ judgments in *Mangold*, *Kücük-deveci* and *ČEZ* were perceived as startling. Current national law had to be disapplied because it conflicted with the EU law principle of equal treatment. Individuals who were subsequently confronted with consequences they could not have foreseen (an unexpected obligation to continue employing the employee, to pay wages or to make a higher sever-ance payment) tried to rely on legal certainty and the protection of legitimate expecta-tions. The courts did take legal certainty and legitimate expectations into consideration (cases 5.4 (GERM), 5.5 (GERM), 5.6 (GERM) and 5.11 (BE)). In case 5.6 (GERM), the court took the ground that both justice (*Gerechtigkeit*) and the rule of law required that the change in the rules applicable to the horizontal relationship imposed by EU law do not necessarily entail setting aside the protection of expectations based on the law that was applicable prior to the change. According to the courts, the following factors are important when assessing the weight to be given to expectations: is the case still pending in court or has it been closed, and are the obligations arising under the unexpected legal situation unreasonably onerous for the individual or do they endanger his existence? However, in none of the reported cases were the expectations considered to be decisive and to outweigh the unlawful discrimination. In cases 5.2 (GERM) and 5.5 (GERM), the court also referred to the approach taken in the greater part of German professional literature before the CJ delivered its *Mangold* judgment. In the literature, employers were advised to not or only cautiously rely on the relevant provision of national law (§14(3) of the German Act on Part-Time Work and Fixed-Term Employment Contracts). In case 5.6 (GERM), the court made clear that though the rule of law includes the elements of legal certainty and legitimate expectations, it calls primarily for substantive justice. In that regard, the protection against discrimination seems to prevail.

Analysed against the background of the interaction between EU law and national law, the reason why the principle of legal certainty cannot outweigh the EU principle of non-discrimination may be twofold: the way in which the principle of non-discrimination works (the 'operational mechanism') and the level at which legal uncertainty occurs. The technique applied by the CJ has shown that the operational mechanism of the principle of non-discrimination is the doctrine of primacy: EU law has primacy over national law that is contrary to it. The disapplication of the rule of national law clears the way for the expression of other rules that are not contrary to EU law. These can be rules of EU law origin, but also (as in *Mangold*, *Kücükdeveci* and *ČEZ*) of national origin. The issue of legal certainty does not play a role in the doctrine of primacy. Primacy has the objective of ensuring the full force and effect of EU law, and it will practically by definition entail legal uncertainty, since primacy finds expression only where the applicable law leads to a result that conflicts with EU law. Primacy is only effectuated by achieving a result that is not contrary to EU law. If legal certainty were to play a relevant role in this mechanism, primacy would eventually die a quiet death.

The following can be said about the level at which legal uncertainty occurs. As will be explained in section II.D.v below, the case law regarding the autonomous application of general principles of EU law which the CJ has developed so far has not resulted in a structural collapse of the law of national origin. Legal uncertainty primarily affects an individual who, for example, suddenly turns out to have employed a person under an employment agreement for an indefinite period, or who must suddenly make a higher severance payment, or who suddenly cannot seek a prohibitory injunction to protect his property. It is important to overcome these uncertainties, but it is doubtful whether the uncertainty on the part of a particular individual carries sufficient weight to put a halt to EU law. On legal certainty as a general principle of EU law, see section I.C in Chapter 5.

II.D.v ADDITIONAL REMARKS

To paraphrase the words of Van Gerven:[84] 'the principle of equality is a principle with a great history and a great future'. It has generative power.[85] Its relevance to private law provisions and horizontal relationships is therefore not limited to ex post review by the courts. The principle of equality is part of the framework regulating private law and horizontal relationships. For that reason, actors (attorneys at law, individuals, judges, governments) must anticipate its applicability and consequences at an early stage, ie, in the legislative process and in the process of creating horizontal relationships.

While it is not surprising that the principle is applicable even if applied autonomously as a general principle of EU law, the consequences at a micro level (private law relationships) can be instantaneous and far-reaching. Current national law has had to be disapplied because it conflicted with the EU law principle of equal treatment. It has frequently been pointed out that giving such effect to a general principle of EU law will lead to an unlimited operation of the principle that will cause incoherences in national legislations. Generally speaking, this speculation cannot be said to be nonsense. The CJ has given effect to the EU law principle of non-discrimination in a way that has had enormous force. This force can be both constructive and destructive. However, in the cases on which the CJ has ruled, it seems that no threat of any structural incoherence has arisen. In *Mangold*, the disapplication concerned a special provision of law which constituted an exception to the national rule prohibiting the conclusion of fixed-term employment agreements. The

---

[84] W van Gerven, 'Het evenredigheidsbeginsel: een beginsel met een groot verleden en een grote toekomst' in *In het nu, wat worden zal*, Opstellen aangeboden aan HCF Schoordijk (Deventer, Kluwer, 1991) 75 ff.

[85] In his Opinion 16 March 2006 in Case C-13/05 *Chacón Navas v Eurest Colectividades SA* I-06467 ECLI:EU:C:2006:184, paras 48–56, AG Geelhoed argued (unsuccessfully, as became clear after the judgment in *Kücükdeveci* was issued) in favour of a more sparing application of the general principle of equality than the CJ has chosen to use in the *Mangold* case. In para 54, he describes the possible consequences of an extensive interpretation of the principle, as applied by the CJ in *Mangold*. 'So broad an interpretation ... results, as it were, in the creation of an Archimedean position, from which the prohibitions of discrimination defined in Article 13 EC (currently 19 TFEU) can be used as a lever to correct, without the intervention of the authors of the Treaty or the [EU] legislature, the decisions made by the Member States in the exercise of the powers which they—still—retain.'

structure of the law of national origin was deprived of an exception. This is not a reason to argue that the entire private law system will collapse. *Kücükdeveci* likewise concerned an exception to the main rule for calculating severance payments. The judgment did not put the structure of the law at risk. And in *ČEZ*, the restrictive interpretation which the Austrian Supreme Court did not start giving to a provision until 4 April 2006 was inconsistent with EU law. The interpretation which the Austrian Supreme Court had given to the provision in its judgments pre-dating April 2006 shows that it is quite possible to interpret and apply the provision in conformity with EU law. Viewed from this perspective, it would not even be necessary to disapply the rule.

Moreover, the EU law 'mean' achieved in these three cases is entirely compatible with the private law mean (see, eg, case 5.6 GERM)). Is that coincidence? Is it self-evident that the disapplication of a rule of national origin on account of conflict with the principle of non-discrimination would lead to serious infringement of the private law frame of thought? This could only happen in the case of provisions that constitute a pillar of the private law system and which directly or indirectly confirm the discrimination. Until now, no such private law provisions have been reported (with the possible exception of family law).

FURTHER READING

See Further Reading of Chapter 4: Non-discrimination provisions in the TFEU.

III. ABUSE OF RIGHTS AS A GENERAL PRINCIPLE OF EU LAW

Jeremias Prassl

III.A INTRODUCTION

This section focuses on the prohibition of abuse of law as a general principle of EU law, with a view to explore how this principle, couched in the language of a general principle of EU law and now set out in this section, has influenced or might come to influence legal relationships between individuals.

The material provided by the national reporters in the preparation of this section suggests that there is not much national case law which relies on the autonomous application of the general principle of prohibition of abuse of rights in horizontal relationships. Moreover, cases where the principle is discussed tend to base their reasoning on national concepts, such as that of good faith, thus reducing their potential direct applicability in other jurisdictions. That said, the solutions reached and approaches observed might still serve as guidance in similar cases. It is in the hope of showing up these *possibilities* in which the general principle *could* influence private law relationships that the principle will be explained, and the case law set out and discussed.

III.B SOURCES

The material in the first part of this section aims to provide a brief overview of the development and role played by abuse of law as a general principle of EU law.[86] It is organised first to set out the origins of the principle and some of the most important cases in which it was developed (section III.B.i). Discussion then turns to competing analyses of the principle's role in the EU legal order (section III.B.ii)—a discussion with significant practical impacts for the purposes of section III.B.iii, which explores the potential horizontal impact of the abuse principle in general and its implications for national private law in particular.

III.B.i THE DEVELOPMENT AND ROLE PLAYED BY ABUSE OF LAW AS A GENERAL PRINCIPLE OF EU LAW: OVERVIEW

The European Treaties do not contain an explicit provision setting out a notion of abuse of law. This, of course, is not an obstacle to their recognition as a general principle in the EU legal order, given the two main sources usually cited by the CJEU in the development of general principles: international legal obligations set out in Treaties and the common constitutional traditions of the Member States.[87] It has been demonstrated that Member States with civilian legal origins have long known of principles which prohibit the abuse of rights, even though both its sources and criteria are fundamentally diverse even across that legal family,[88] and suggested furthermore that in other systems, such as the common law, 'pragmatic solutions are found through the use of concepts that, in concrete situations, will lead to a similar result as the prohibition of abuse of rights would do'.[89]

The earliest recognition of the principle before the CJEU is usually said to have been the decision of *Van Binsbergen*,[90] when the CJ suggested that 'a Member State cannot be denied the right to take measures to prevent the exercise ... of the Freedom guaranteed by Article 59 [now Article 56 TFEU] for the purposes of avoiding the professional rules of conduct which would be applicable to him if he were established within that State'.[91] Even though the language of abuse was not explicitly deployed as such there, the principle soon began to take hold in the EU legal order. A leading author suggests that two key factors played a role in the development of a general principle out of these humble roots: 'First, as litigants sought to stretch to the maximum the scope of Treaty

---

[86] For an in-depth analysis, see the contributions in De la Feria and Vogenauer (eds) 2011. The discussion in this section III draws on various chapters of that volume.

[87] CJ 14 May 1974 Case C-4/73 *Nold, Kohlen- und Baustoffgroßhandlung v Commission of the European Communities* [1974] I-00491 ECLI:EU:C:1974:51, para 13.

[88] A Lenaerts, 'The General Principle of the Prohibition of Abuse of Rights: A Critical Position on its Role in a Codified European Contract Law' (2010) 18(6) *ERPL* 1122, 1125–28. See also J Gordley, 'The Abuse of Rights in the Civil Law Tradition' in De la Feria and Vogenauer (eds) 2011 33–48.

[89] Lenaerts (n 88) 1125.

[90] CJ 3 December 1974 Case C- 33/74 *Johannes Henricus Maria van Binsbergen v Bestuur van de Bedrijfsvereniging voor de Metaalnijverheid* [1974] I-01299 ECLI:EU:C:1974:131.

[91] See ibid, para 13.

freedoms, defendant governments resorted to the doctrine of abuse as a countervailing force. Secondly, the proliferation of [EU] legislation in areas such as indirect tax and subsidies inevitably increased opportunities for improper use of [EU] benefits.'[92]

The principle can therefore not be said to be limited to any one particular area of EU law, or even the CJEU's case law—it has been recognised in a wide range of secondary legislation, not least in the area of tax law.[93] Article 54 of the Charter furthermore specifically recognises the principle's importance within the EU legal order, as it stipulates that: 'Nothing in this Charter shall be interpreted as implying any right to engage in any activity or to perform any act aimed at the destruction of any of the rights and freedoms recognised in this Charter or at their limitation to a greater extent than is provided for herein.'[94]

A key area from which the origins of the principle are often traced is the fundamental freedoms, even though it has been argued that 'in the area of free movement of goods and services there is no need to develop an independent "abuse" doctrine', as alternative mechanisms have come to take account of the underlying problems.[95] This high threshold approach can be illustrated by reference to the much-discussed decision in *Centros*,[96] where the CJ found that the incorporation of a subsidiary in order to avoid the application of domestic Danish company law could, in itself, not constitute an abuse of the freedom of establishment,[97] as well as the subsequent decision in *Cadbury Schweppes*.[98]

In *Emsland-Stärke*,[99] the CJ was faced with traders who had exported potato starch products to Switzerland for the sole purpose of receiving export refunds, before re-importing the selfsame to Germany. Having noted that 'the scope of [EU] regulations

---

[92] T Tridimas, 'Abuse of Rights in EU Law with a Focus on Financial Law' in De la Feria and Vogenauer (eds) 2011 169, 170. However, note that the precise relationship between legislative expressions of the principle, and its operation in the guise of a general principle, is rather unclear: see especially K Engsig Sørensen's reading of *Kofoed* in De la Feria and Vogenauer (eds) 2011 30 ff.

[93] See notably CJ 21 February 2006 Case C-255/02 *Halifax plc et al v Commissioners of Customs & Excise Halifax* [2006] I-01609 ECLI:EU:C:2006:121 and CJ 5 July 2007 Case C-321/05 *Hans Markus Kofoed v Skatteministeriet* [2007] I-05795 ECLI:EU:C:2007:408. See also, eg, art 35 of Directive 2004/38/EC of the European Parliament and of the Council of 29 April 2004 on the right of citizens of the Union and their family members to move and reside freely within the territory of the Member States ... [2004] OJ L158/35. However, note that this provision was *not* relied upon by the Grand Chamber in its recent decision in CJ 11 November 2014 Case C-333/13 *Elisabeta Dano and Florin Dano v Jobcenter Leipzig* nyr ECLI:EU:2014:2358.

[94] Article 54 of the Charter. *cf* art 17 of the ECHR, whence this text is taken. In his book, *General Principles of EU Civil Law*, Reich addresses art 54 the Charter in the context of the (potentially) emerging principle of good faith and of a prohibition of abuse of rights, stressing the importance of the principle of good faith for the current debate. See N Reich, *General Principles of EU Civil Law* (Cambridge, Intersentia, 2014) 208–12.

[95] See, eg, S Weatherill, 'Fitting "Abuse of Rights" into the Free Movement of Goods and Services' in De la Feria and Vogenauer (eds) 2011 49.

[96] CJ 9 March 1999 Case C-212/97 *Centros Ltd v Erhvervs- og Selskabsstyrelsen* [1999] I-01459 ECLI:EU:C:1999:126. For commentary, see, eg, M Adenas, 'Free Movement of Companies' (2003) 119 *LQR* 221.

[97] CJ *Centros Ltd* (n 96) para 27.

[98] CJ 12 September 2006 Case C-196/04 *Cadbury Schweppes plc and Cadbury Schweppes Overseas Ltd v Commissioners of Inland Revenue* [2006] I-07995 ECLI:EU:C:2006:544. See, eg, para 51: 'a national measure restricting freedom of establishment may be justified where it "specifically relates to wholly artificial arrangements" aimed at circumventing the application of the legislation of the Member State concerned'.

[99] CJ 14 December 2000 Case C-110/99 *Emsland-Stärke GmbH v Hauptzollamt Hamburg-Jonas* [2000] I-11569 ECLI:EU:C:2000:695, para 51.

must in no case be extended to cover abuses on the part of a trader', it went on to formulate a two-pronged test, including 'first, a combination of objective circumstances in which, despite formal observance of the conditions laid down by the [EU] rules, the purpose of those rules has not been achieved'[100] and 'second, a subjective element consisting in the intention to obtain an advantage from the [EU] rules by creating artificially the conditions laid down for obtaining it'.[101] At the same time, the CJ made it clear that it was 'for the national court to establish the existence of [the key elements of the abuse of law test], evidence of which must be adduced in accordance with the rules of national law, provided that the effectiveness of [EU] law is not thereby undermined'.[102]

A second crucial area for the development of the general principle of abuse of law has been EU tax law. In *Halifax*,[103] the Grand Chamber of the CJEU relied, inter alia, on the just-cited paragraphs of *Emsland-Stärke* to find that the 'principle of prohibiting abusive practices [viz "[EU] law cannot be relied on for abusive or fraudulent ends"][104] also applies to the sphere of VAT'.[105] It was in a subsequent tax case, *Kofoed*, that the CJ deployed the explicit terminology of general principles of EU law when it held that the directive in question 'reflects the general [EU] law principle that abuse of rights is prohibited. Individuals must not improperly or fraudulently take advantage of provisions of [EU] law. The application of [EU] legislation cannot be extended to cover abusive practices, that is to say, transactions carried out not in the context of normal commercial operations, but solely for the purpose of wrongfully obtaining advantages provided for by [EU] law'.[106]

III.B.ii DISCUSSION SURROUNDING THE PRECISE NATURE OF THE PRINCIPLE

The CJ's decision in *Kofoed* seems to provide clear evidence for the recognition of the general principle in EU law. Upon closer inspection, however, the position might not be as straightforward as that case might suggest. Extensive debate continues to rage in the literature. One author, for example, has argued that whilst the CJ did indeed recognise a general law principle in the above-cited paragraph in *Kofoed*, it 'seems improbable that [the first chamber] was intending to give birth to a new general principle', especially when that case is juxtaposed with the Grand Chamber's more careful formulation in *Halifax*.[107]

This debate as to the precise nature of the principle can even be traced through the leading volume on abuse of law. One contributor's conclusion that 'the prohibition of abuse is too uncertain in its application and potentially damaging to the proper functioning of the Union to be accorded the constitutional status of a general principle of Union

---

[100] ibid, para 52.
[101] ibid, para 53.
[102] ibid, para 54.
[103] CJ *Halifax* (n 93).
[104] ibid, para 68.
[105] ibid, para 70.
[106] CJ *Kofoed* (n 93) para 38.
[107] A Arnull, 'What is a General Principle of EU Law?' in De la Feria and Vogenauer (eds) 2011 20.

law [and that it] should instead be considered a maxim of interpretation',[108] for example, stands in stark contrast with the opinion of one of the collection's editors, who concludes his extended survey of the principle by finding that: 'According to the judge-made pro-hibition of abuse of EU law, a given rule of law will not be applied where (1) a particular set of facts is clearly and unambiguously covered by the wording of the rule but (2) the result of applying the rule would be contrary to the purpose of that rule and (3) the person's reliance on the rule is abusive.'[109]

Even those who are in agreement that the principle exists in principle, so to speak, differ as to its precise nature and/or scope of operation. The second editor, for example, notes that whilst it is 'appropriate to accept the application of the principle of prohibition of abuse of law to all areas of EU law, without exception', this cannot be done without 'acknowledging that in some [areas of EU law] abuse of law will be harder to find'.[110] Yet another contributor, on the other hand, suggests that whilst abuse of law 'can certainly be described as a general principle of interpretation [it] does not have all the facets of other recognised general principles'.[111]

The debate as to precisely what sort of principle the prohibition of abuse of law is within the EU legal order is of deep significance for any discussion surrounding the potential horizontal impact of the putative general principle, insofar as 'if the principle is a principle of construction, the issue of horizontal effect does not arise, but if it is a general principle, it could'.[112]

III.B.iii CATEGORIES OF PRIVATE LAW CASES INFLUENCED BY THE GENERAL PRINCIPLE OF ABUSE OF RIGHTS

The impact of abuse of law on EU private law has been the subject of a small-scale survey by a leading German author, focusing on EU intellectual property law, civil procedure and EU contract law, before suggesting that it is only in the former two areas that abuse of law can be said to play a significant role.[113] Whilst 'one could well imagine cases in which the use of contractual remedies such as the consumer's right to withdraw from the contract could be seen as abusive ... the principle ... has only rarely been invoked in European and national courts with regard to contractual rights and remedies rooted in the *acquis communautaire*'.[114] He strongly disagrees with suggestions that the Unfair

---

[108] See ibid 23.

[109] S Vogenauer, 'The Prohibition of Abuse of Law: An Emerging General Principle of EU Law' in De la Feria and Vogenauer (eds) 2011 571.

[110] R de la Feria, 'Introducing the Principle of Prohibition of Abuse of Law' in De la Feria and Vogenauer (eds) 2011 xix.

[111] P Farmer, 'Prohibition of Abuse of (European) Law: A Response' in De la Feria and Vogenauer (eds) 2011 4.

[112] K Engsig Sørensen, 'What is a General Principle of EU Law? A Response' in De la Feria and Vogenauer (eds) 2011 28. See also her earlier piece: K Engsig Sørensen, 'Abuse of Right in Community Law: A Principle of Substance or Merely Rhetoric?' (2006) 43(2) *CMLR* 423.

[113] A Metzger, 'Abuse of Law in EU Private Law: A (Re-)Construction from Fragments' in De la Feria and Vogenauer (eds) 2011 237, 247.

[114] See ibid, 246.

Contract Terms Directive's provisions are a legislative expression of the principle[115] and concludes that as regards EU contract law, 'abuse of law is neither supported by EU legislation nor is it recognised by the CJ's case law ... [existing] fragments do not amount to the recognition of a general principle of law'.[116] This argument is supported by a leading commentator's warning of the questionable 'constitutional appropriateness of recognition of a "general principle" of "abuse of law" in the context of the "European private law" or EU contractual *acquis* given the nature of the legislation in this area'.[117] The study's conclusion that 'the rare examples [of invocation before national courts] do, for most part, fail to match the concept of abuse of law as it has emerged in the Court's case law in other areas of law'[118] is therefore clearly in line with the meagre findings of the present section.

It is beyond doubt today that EU law can have an impact on private law at the national level.[119] However, the material developed in this section raises difficult questions at the very edges of the impact that EU law might have on Member State systems, as it deals with the potential horizontal impact of a still-developing general principle. Following the CJ's decision in *Mangold*,[120] such impact cannot be excluded completely.[121] That said, the CJ's line of reasoning in this area has come under sustained criticism[122] and now looks likely to be confined to the specific context of non-discrimination,[123] which subject has been further discussed in section II above.

Indeed, it has been argued that in *Kofoed*, 'the ECJ stopped short of recognising that the principle was self-executing. This contrasts with its judgment in *Mangold* ... This difference in approach may be explained by a number of reasons. In *Mangold* the dispute was between individuals whilst in *Kofoed* it was conversely vertical, i.e. involved a state authority relying on a directive against an individual. More importantly, *Mangold* involved equal treatment, which is a fundamental constitutional principle receptive to a dynamic interpretation'.[124] For the present purposes, these different explanations of the CJ's approach in *Kofoed* and *Mangold* are of critical importance—if the limitation to the equal treatment context turns out to be the CJ's key motivation in future cases, it is unlikely that the general principle of abuse of law per se would be able to exert a strong horizontal influence in national private law.

---

[115] Council Directive 93/12/EEC of the European Communities of 5 April 1993 on unfair terms in consumer contracts [1993] OJ L095/29. *cf*, for example, Tridimas (n 92) 171.

[116] Metzger (n 113) 251.

[117] S Whittaker, 'Comments on "Abuse of Law" in European Private Law' in De la Feria and Vogenauer (eds) 2011 253, 259.

[118] Metzger (n 113) 246–47.

[119] See Ch 1. See also Hartkamp 2011 nos 6, 7 and 11–13; and for an extensive discussion of the forms of influence exerted by the TFEU, see Hartkamp 2016.

[120] CJ *Mangold* (n 42).

[121] See, in a similar light, the CJ's subsequent decision in CJ *Kücukdeveci* (n 36).

[122] See, eg, the essays in M Adams, H de Waele, J Meeusen, and G Straetmans (eds), *Judging Europe's Judges: The Legitimacy of the Case Law of the European Court of Justice* (Oxford, Hart Publishing, 2013).

[123] CJ *AMS* (n 43) para 47: 'the facts of the case may be distinguished from those which gave rise to *Kücukdeveci* in so far as the principle of non-discrimination on grounds of age at issue in that case, laid down in Article 21(1) of the Charter, is sufficient in itself to confer on individuals an individual right which they may invoke as such'.

[124] Tridimas (n 92) 175–76.

III.C NATIONAL CASE LAW

Bundesgerichtshof (Federal Supreme Court of Germany),
22 December 2004[125]   **5.12 (GERM)**

C v B

VENIRE CONTRA FACTUM PROPRIUM: *MISREPRESENTATION OF*
A BUSINESSPERSON AS A CONSUMER

Cheapy Barchetta

The buyer pretended to be a business man and cannot in good faith rely on being a consumer

Facts: In the course of purchasing a used car in October 2002, the claimant—in spite of his intentions to act as a private purchaser—agreed to a 'special agreement' as part of the purchase contract, which stipulated that the sale was 'without guarantee' as it was a 'deal between business persons'. This stipulation had been inserted on the seller's behalf precisely in order to exclude any warranties, which would not have been possible in dealing with consumers. Technical problems soon appeared, and the claimant demanded a rescission of the agreement, which had also included misleading statements as regards the car's original registration.

Held: The claimant's demands were dismissed both at first instance and upon appeal, including on 22 December 2004 by the Federal Supreme Court of Germany. As the claimant had pretended to be a trader in order to take advantage of the reduced price offered, he could not now rely on their consumer protection rights pursuant to §474ff BGB. The Court rejected any suggestion that consumer protective provisions should apply regardless of the purchaser's misrepresentation.

Judgment: II.2.a) A person who wants to buy a product from a businessman who is not prepared to enter into a consumer purchase transaction because he does not want to give a warranty for the product purchased, may not deviously obtain the protection of consumer purchases provisions in his favour by untruthfully pretending to be a dealer in order to induce the trader to make the sale. If he does so, then subsequently he cannot in good faith invoke the fact that he is in reality a consumer ('venire contra factum proprium') ....

...

To counter the argument of revision, the businessman who has been misled by the other contracting party is not, in such a case, limited to contesting the contract on the ground of fraudulent misrepresentation concerning his consumer capacity. It would be contrary to good faith if the misleading party to the contract would be able to achieve the goal of withdrawing from the contract with the subsequent disclosure of the misrepresentation by invoking the legislation on consumer protection. The businessman may therefore keep his contractual partner to the latter's own false statements and thus to the contract that is not covered by consumer protection.

...

The principle of good faith (§242 BGB) must prevail over the interest of the dishonest party to the contract

...

II.2.b) On the one hand the principle of good faith is also recognised in [EU] law (...). This is an argument supporting the view that under [EU] law, too, a person who pretends

---

[125] BGH 22 December 2004 VIII ZR 91/04 *NJW* 2005, 1045. A detailed summary by C Rodorff and J Mertens can be found at: www.eu-consumer-law.org/caseabstracts_en.cfm?JudgmentID=1.

to be acting for a commercial business purpose cannot subsequently rely on strictly private use, in contradiction with his own statement when he concluded the contract. ....
For this result it is irrelevant – both under [EU] law and under German law (see II.2.a above) – whether the misleading contractor is denied consumer capacity on the basis of his pretending to be acting for business purposes, or whether, even though in theory he is considered a consumer, he is barred from relying on his consumer capacity in good faith.

Notes:

(1) The Federal Supreme Court of Germany held that a claimant who had intentionally presented themselves as a businessman could not later invoke his role as a consumer and rely on the protection of consumers and the BGB provisions implementing the Consumer Sales Directive.[126] The decision refers to the principle of *Treu und Glauben* (good faith) under §242 BGB, before turning to synonymous discussions in EU law. It does not, however, rely directly on abuse of law, deploying instead the notion of good faith. The crucial point to note for the present purposes can be found in paragraph II.2.b of the judgment: the CJ does *not* rely on the autonomous notion as found in EU law, but merely contents itself with pointing out the *parallel* recognition of the principle at stake in the EU legal order.

(2) Axel Metzger, in commenting on this decision, has noted that: 'Although the Federal Supreme Court of Germany explicitly emphasised the abusive character of the consumer's behaviour, the case is not squarely covered by the concept of abuse presented by *Emsland-Stärke* and *Halifax*. One might consider the consumer's conduct as against the purpose of consumer protection law ... In this respect, the case has more resemblance to ECJ abuse of law cases like *Van Binsbergen*.'[127]

Arbeidsrechtbank Brussel (Labour Tribunal Brussels),
22 December 2005[128]   **5.13 (BE)**

VP v Royal Football Association

INDIRECT EFFECT OF NON-DISCRIMINATION DIRECTIVE THROUGH
THE PROHIBITION OF ABUSE OF RIGHTS

Finished whistling I

Application of a directive using the concept of abuse of right

Note:

This case is discussed in sections IV and V.B in Chapter 6; see cases 6.21 (BE) and 6.22 (BE).

---

[126] Directive 1999/44/EC of the European Parliament and of the Council of 25 May 1999 on certain aspects of the sale of consumer goods and associated guarantees [1999] OJ L171/12.
[127] Metzger (n 113) 248. See discussion of CJ *Van Binsbergen* [1974] (see footnote 91), supra: the CJ evoked the broad idea underpinning the notion, without however naming it explicitly.
[128] Labour Tribunal Brussels 22 December 2005 *Sociaalrechtelijke Kronieken* 2008 vol 1 p 48–51 *V.P. v Royal Belgian Football Association.*

FURTHER READING

M Adams, H de Waele, J Meeusen and G Straetmans (eds), *Judging Europe's Judges: The Legitimacy of the Case Law of the European Court of Justice* (Oxford, Hart Publishing, 2013).

M Adenas, 'Free Movement of Companies' (2003) 119 *LQR* 221.

A Arnull, 'What is a General Principle of EU Law?' in De la Feria and Vogenauer (eds) 2011 7–24.

K Engsig Sørensen, 'Abuse of Right in Community Law: A Principle of Substance or Merely Rhetoric?' (2006) 23(2) *CMLR* 423–59.

K Engsig Sørensen, 'What is a General Principle of EU Law? A Response' in De la Feria and Vogenauer (eds) 2011 25–32.

P Farmer, 'Prohibition of Abuse of (European) Law: The Creation of a New General Principle of EC Law through Tax: A Response' in De la Feria and Vogenauer (eds) 2011 3–6.

J Gordley, 'The Abuse of Rights in the Civil Law Tradition' in De la Feria and Vogenauer (eds) 2011 33–48.

R de la Feria, 'Introducing the Principle of Prohibition of Abuse of Law' in De la Feria and Vogenauer (eds) 2011.

R de la Feria and S Vogenauer, *Prohibition of Abuse of Law: A New General Principle of EU Law?*, (Oxford, Hart Publishing, 2011).

A Lenaerts, 'The General Principle of the Prohibition of Abuse of Rights: A Critical Position on its Role in a Codified European Contract Law' (2010) 18(6) *ERPL* 1121–54.

A Metzger, 'Abuse of Law in EU Private Law: A (Re-)Construction from Fragments' in De la Feria and Vogenauer (eds) 2011 235–52.

N Reich, *General Principles of EU Civil Law* (Cambridge, Intersentia, 2014).

T Tridimas, 'Abuse of Rights in EU Law: Some Reflections with Particular Reference to Financial Law' in De la Feria and Vogenauer (eds) 2011 169–92.

S Vogenauer, 'The Prohibition of Abuse of Law: An Emerging General Principle of EU Law' in De la Feria and Vogenauer (eds) 2011 521–72.

S Weatherill, 'Fitting "Abuse of Rights" into the Free Movement of Goods and Services' in De la Feria and Vogenauer (eds) 2011 49–62.

S Whittaker, 'Comments on "Abuse of Law" in European Private Law' in De la Feria and Vogenauer (eds) 2011 253–60.

IV. THE PRINCIPLE OF UNJUST ENRICHMENT

Marloes van de Moosdijk

IV.A INTRODUCTION

Section IV.A analyses the principle of unjust enrichment as part of EU law. The principle or concept of unjust enrichment is not mentioned in the EU Treaties and is seldom used in secondary legislation.[129] It has been recognised in the case law of the CJ. The CJ has

---

[129] Council Regulation (EC) No 6/2002 of 12 December 2001 on Community Designs [2001] OJ L3 5/1/2002, 1–24 and Council Regulation (EC) No 207/2009 of 26 February 2009 on the Community Trade

employed the principle in different ways,[130] as will be further discussed in sections IV.B. and IV.C below. The CJ has given the following description of the EU concept of unjust enrichment and its consequences: 'a person who has suffered a loss which increases the wealth of another person without there being any legal basis for that enrichment has the right, as a general rule, to restitution from the person enriched, up to the amount of the loss'.[131]

This casebook focuses on the various ways in which EU law can exert influence on relationships between individuals. The concept of unjust enrichment, as a (general) principle of EU law, could potentially affect horizontal relationships without the support of another applicable rule of EU law in the same manner as was described in Chapter 1.[132] Until now, the CJ has not had many opportunities to apply the principle of unjust enrichment as a general principle of EU law in horizontal relationships. When the occasion presented itself in the case of *Bostock*, the CJ left it to national law to decide whether on the termination of the lease, an obligation arising from unjust enrichment could exist between a lessee and a lessor in connection with the transfer of the value of a milk quota.[133] In *Messner*, the CJ referred to unjust enrichment as a principle of civil law to interpret Directive 97/7/EC[134] on the protection of consumers in respect of distance contracts in a horizontal relationship.[135] It is uncertain whether the designation of unjust enrichment as a principle of civil law instead of EU law has implications. In any case, the principle of unjust enrichment is part of EU law and, as such, could be employed in

---

Mark [2009] OJ L78/1. In the old version of the Consumer Credit Directive 87/102/EEC of 22 December 1986 OJ L42/48, the concept was used to 'ensure that where the creditor recovers possession of the goods the account between the parties shall be made up so as to ensure that the repossession does not entail any unjust enrichment'.

[130] For example, CJ 10 April 2008 Case C-309/06 *Marks & Spencer plc v Commissioners of Customs & Excise* [2008] I-02283 ECLI:EU:C:2008:211 and CJ 14 January 1997 Case C-192/95 *Société Comateb et al v Directeur General des Douanes et Droits Indirects* [1997] I-00165 ECLI:EU:C:1997:12.

[131] CJ 16 December 2008 Case C-47/07 P *Masdar (UK) Ltd v Commission of the European Communities* [2008] I-9761 ECLI:EU:C:2008:726, para 44.

[132] See also AS Hartkamp, 'The General Principles of EU Law and Private Law' (2011) 6–7 *RabelsZ* 11–13 and, more specifically, Hartkamp 2014 (I) 567–88.

[133] C Semmelmann, 'The General Principles of EU Law in the Light of the Public-Private Distinction' in S Besson and P Pichonnaz (eds), *Les principes en droit européen/Principles in European Law*, vol 2 (Zürich, Schulthess Verlag, 2011) 233, 240. An illustration of a case in which the principle of unjust enrichment is regarded in a horizontal relationship is CJ 24 March 1994 Case C-2/92 *The Queen v Ministry of Agriculture, Fisheries and Food ex parte Dennis Clifford Bostock* [1994] ECLI:EU:C:1994:116. See section IV.B.

[134] Directive 97/7/EC of the European Parliament and of the Council of 20 May 1997 on the protection of consumers in respect of distance contracts [1997] OJ L144/19.

[135] CJ 3 September 2009 Case C-489/07 *Pia Messner v Firma Stefan Krüger* [2009] I-07315 ECLI:EU:C:2009:502, paras 26 and 29. Ms Messner exercised her right of withdrawal from the contract concluded with Firma Stefan Krüger to buy a second-hand laptop via the internet. She also sought reimbursement of the price, but was confronted with a counter-claim for compensation for the use made of the laptop. The claim for compensation could be successful under German law, but the national court questioned the compatibility with the Directive and started a preliminary ruling procedure. The CJ held that the Directive must be interpreted so as to preclude a provision of national law that provides in general that, in the case of withdrawal by a consumer within the withdrawal period, a seller may claim compensation for the value of the use of the consumer goods acquired under a distance contract. Those provisions do not prevent the consumer from being required to pay compensation for the use of the goods if he has made use of those goods in a manner that is incompatible with the principles of civil law, such as those of good faith or unjust enrichment.

horizontal relationships as well. Until now, however, there has been little EU case law on the subject. It is not surprising that national case law on the autonomous application of the EU law principle of unjust enrichment in horizontal relationships is not yet available.

The principle has been applied in relationships between public bodies and individuals. It has functioned as a criterion for judicial review of legislative, administrative and factual acts of EU institutions. The principle of unjust enrichment has also been used to interpret EU legislation and to construe the obligation to pay interest on a sum of money unlawfully withheld. In addition, it can serve as cause of action for a remedy, meaning that the principle can take the form of a legal action for compensation. The action for compensation can be based on unjust enrichment or on undue payment ('condictio indebiti'), though the CJ prefers to base the latter on the system of EU law in combination with the principle of effectiveness.[136] The action arising from unjust enrichment is presented in section IV.B. The principle can also be condensed into an exception, which is dealt with in section IV.C. Though national case law on the principle in horizontal relations is currently absent, it will be elucidated in this section how exactly the CJ has used the concept of unjust enrichment under EU law. The judgments that reveal the substantive meaning of the concept vary according to the influence exerted on the relationships involved. The differences are due to the variation in the actual claims pleaded, as well as the specificities of their factual contexts. In the following, I will first set out and distinguish between the most relevant decisions of the CJ according to the legal consequences which the principle had for the parties involved: being either ensuring judicial protection, ultimately by way of an action resulting in compensation, or its use as a defence against a claim. Subsequently, I will construe the possible influence that the principle could have in the future on private law relationships. Knowledge of the possible influence can be of assistance to students, scholars, judges and lawyers in structuring their arguments in future cases.

IV.B THE ACTION ARISING FROM UNJUST ENRICHMENT

Most of the following decisions of the CJ concern a relationship between an EU institution and an individual. The principle of unjust enrichment is used to ensure judicial protection. Its reviewing standard can result in the nullity of a legal act and in the award of damages after unlawful acts. In *Masdar v Commission*, the CJ eventually allowed the principle to condense in a legal action arising from unjust enrichment against the EU institutions.[137]

In *Hellenic Republic v Commission*, the CJ held for the first time that the EC cannot act in a way that would 'unjustly [enrich] the [EU] contrary to the general principles of [EU] law'.[138] In this case, the CJ annulled an EC decision on the clearance of

---

[136] Hartkamp 2014 (I) 568.

[137] GC 16 November 2006 Case T-333/03 *Masdar (UK) Ltd v Commission of the European Communities* [2006] II-04377 ECLI:EU:T:2006:348; and CJ *Masdar v Commission* (n 131).

[138] CJ 10 July 1990 Case C-259/87 *Hellenic Republic v Commission of the European Communities* [1990] I-02845 ECLI:EU:C:1990:287 (summary).

the Member States' expenditure accounts for the European Agricultural Guidance and Guarantee Fund at the request of Greece. The EC had refused to take into account the sums received on an irregular sale of agricultural products by the European Agricultural Guidance and Guarantee Fund. As the refusal led to the EC's enrichment at the expense of the Member States, the decision was held to be void. The judgment is a first example of the possibility of reviewing legislative or administrative acts of EU bodies against the principle prohibiting unjust enrichment. The review can result in the nullity of these acts if they are found to be incompatible with the principle.[139]

Subsequently, in *Corus v Commission*, the GC explicitly recognised the prevention of unjust enrichment as a general principle of EU law to underline that the restitution of a fine also includes payment of interest.[140] Corus UK Ltd, an individual, had paid a fine of nearly €32 million imposed by the EC for infringing EU competition provisions. In proceedings before the GC, this amount was reduced, and the EC repaid the €12 million difference to Corus. However, it refused to pay the interest accrued over the five years during which it had retained the sum. Corus started proceedings before the GC and argued that the EC, by not paying the interest accrued, was liable in damages for violation of its obligations. The GC dismissed the claim for damages because there had been no unlawful act of the EC, but it did order the EC to pay interest. It qualified the payment of interest as an essential component of the EC's obligation to restore the applicant to its original position.[141] The GC added that 'a failure to reimburse interest could result … in the unjust enrichment of the [EU], which would be contrary to the general principles of [EU] law'.[142] With reference to *Hellenic Republic v Commission*, it ordered the EC to reimburse not only the principal amount of the fine unduly paid, but also the amount of any enrichment or benefit it had obtained as a result of the payment. The reasoning of the GC was thus partly based on unjust enrichment. The GC pointed out that the right to receive interest was not subject to proof of damage and discussed the calculation of the amount of interest based on 'the lower of the two amounts corresponding to the enrichment and the loss'.[143] *Corus v Commission* signals that the prohibition of unjust enrichment is one of the general principles of EU law.[144] It serves as an example of how the principle of unjust enrichment can lead to liability of the EU on a legal basis other than Article 340(2) TFEU.

---

[139] Another example of the reviewing function of the general principle of unjust enrichment is GC 29 June 2000 Case T-7/99 *Medici Grimm KG v Council of the European Union* [2000] II-2671 ECLI:EU:T:2000:175, which annulled a provision in an anti-dumping regulation denying retroactive effect to the amended regulation because that would result in unjust enrichment of the EU at the expense of the applicant, an undertaking.

[140] GC 10 October 2001 Case T-171/99 *Corus UK Ltd v Commission of the European Communities* [2001] II-02967 ECLI:EU:T:2001:249, para 54.

[141] ibid.

[142] ibid, para 55.

[143] ibid, paras 56 and 60.

[144] Though see GC 21 April 2005 Case T-28/03 *Holcim (Deutschland) AG (Formerly Alsen AG) v Commission of the European Communities* [2005] II-01357 ECLI:EU:T:2005:139 on the limited applicability of the *Corus* approach. If an undertaking, instead of paying the fine, prefers to furnish a bank guarantee, it cannot recover the costs involved on the basis of unjust enrichment of the EU.

In *Dolianova v Commission*,[145] the CJ did not yet recognise the principle's capability to condense in a legal claim arising from unjust enrichment against EU institutions. Instead, the GC held that the EU can be liable in damages under Article 340(2) TFEU for a sufficiently serious breach of the principle of unjust enrichment. The case revolved around a loss suffered by wine producers. The producers supplied wine to a distillery, which went bankrupt before it had paid the purchase price. In accordance with the requirements of Regulation 337/79,[146] the price included an amount of EU aid to be paid by the distillery to the producers. The distillery had received the aid as an advance payment from the Italian intervention agency. In return, it provided a guarantee to secure the transaction in the form of a bond issued by an insurance company for the benefit of the Italian agency. As a result of financial difficulties, the distillery failed to pay the wine producers for the wine received and was later declared bankrupt. The Italian agency had in the meantime collected the guarantees. The wine producers asked the EC to call on Italy to pay the purchase price of the wine delivered to the distillery. After the EC rejected the request, the producers started legal proceedings. They claimed the annulment of the EC's rejection and called for a declaration that they were entitled, on the grounds of unjust enrichment or unlawful act, to receive the EU aid which had not been paid by the distillery and which had been recovered by the Italian agency under the guarantee and refunded to the relevant EU body. The GC dismissed the claim of the wine producers insofar as it was based on unjust enrichment, holding it inadmissible on the ground that the Treaty lacked a provision for bringing such an action arising from unjust enrichment.[147] The GC did, however, allow the claim for compensation insofar as it was based on an unlawful act of the EC. The GC reasoned that the Regulation did not include a provision guaranteeing payment of aid to producers in the event of insolvency of the distillery. The Regulation was therefore held to be vitiated by a sufficiently serious breach of the principle prohibiting unjust enrichment.[148] Although the GC did not accept the action based on unjust enrichment at the EU level, it re-affirmed the prohibition of unjust enrichment as a general principle of EU law while citing *Hellenic Republic v Commission* and *Corus v Commission*.[149] A sufficiently serious breach of the principle can thus lead to the EU being liable in damages under Article 340(2) TFEU.[150]

---

[145] GC 23 November 2004 Case T-166/98 *Cantina sociale di Dolianova Soc. coop arl et al v Commission of the European Communities* [2004] II-03991 ECLI:EU:T:2004:337.

[146] Council Regulation (EEC) No 337/79 of 5 February 1979 on the common organization of the market in wine [1979] OJ L54/1.

[147] GC *Cantina sociale di Dolianova et al v Commission* (n 145) para 84.

[148] ibid, para 162.

[149] ibid, para 160. The GC also referred to the following case: GC 3 April 2003 Joined Cases T-44/01, T-119/01 and T-126/01 *Eduardo Vieira, SA et al v Commission of the European Communities* [2003] II-01209 ECLI:EU:T:2003:98. In this case, the principle of unjust enrichment was used to interpret a fisheries agreement between the EU and Argentina to grant the EC the right to suspend the payment of financial aid under certain circumstances. At appeal, the CJ construed the instrument without referring to the principle.

[150] When the case was brought before the CJ, the only question raised was the date from which time began to run against the applicants. Since they were out of time, it annulled the decision of the GC without considering any of the issues relating to the unjust enrichment of the EU; see CJ 17 July 2008 Case C-51/05 P *Commission of the European Communities v Cantina sociale di Dolianova Soc coop arl et al* [2008] I-05341 ECLI:EU:C:2008:409.

In *Masdar v Commission*, on the other hand, the GC ruled that Article 340(2) TFEU imposed an obligation on the EU to make good any damage caused by its institutions in accordance with the general principles common to the laws of the Member States, also in the absence of unlawful conduct. A claim arising from unjust enrichment could therefore be brought against the EU under Article 340(2) TFEU.[151] However, the GC did not award compensation based on unjust enrichment due to the factual circumstances of the case. The case involved a three-party situation, consisting of a contractual relationship between the EC and Helmico on the one hand, and an agreement between Helmico and Masdar on the other hand. Both contracts regulated the execution of technical services in underdeveloped agricultural areas in Moldavia and Russia under an EU aid programme. Though the EC paid Helmico, and Masdar performed the services as agreed, Helmico was late in paying Masdar. When Masdar contacted the EC, it discovered that Helmico had in fact received full payment. The EC eventually wrote to Helmico requiring payment of over €2 million because it had discovered Helmico's fraudulent behaviour. Masdar then sued Helmico before the UK courts for the sum of money owing under the contract and brought an action against the EC for reimbursement based on unjust enrichment at the EU level. The GC held that 'any enrichment of the EC or impoverishment of the applicant, as it arose from the contractual framework in place, cannot be described as being without a cause'.[152]

On appeal, the CJ upheld the judgment of the GC. The CJ confirmed that the principles common to the laws of the Member States include an obligation arising from unjust enrichment. It based responsibility of the EU on Article 340(2) TFEU. If such liability were denied, the result would be contrary to the principle of effective judicial protection as safeguarded in the case law of the CJ and confirmed in the Charter.[153] The CJ did not comment on the action arising from unjust enrichment being an alternative or subsidiary action. As Craig notes, 'the CJ affirmed in *Masdar* that although unjust enrichment did not fit in perfectly with the criteria for recovery in cases of non-contractual liability, it would be contrary to the principle of effective judicial protection if Articles 274 and 340(2) were construed to preclude such recovery'.[154] Like the GC, the CJ recognised the obligation from unjust enrichment, but did not find for the claimant on its basis. According to both the GC and the CJ, the enrichment of the EU, which consisted of Masdar's fulfilment of the EU aid projects in Russia and Moldavia without the EU being obliged to make a counter-performance, was not unjust, but was based on continued contractual relations. The CJ also repeated the GC's conclusion that the loss suffered by Masdar was a common commercial risk inherent to all contractual relationships, namely the risk that a party will not perform the contract satisfactorily or that it will become insolvent.[155]

---

[151] GC *Masdar v Commission* (n 137); GC *Corus v Commission* (n 141).
[152] GC *Masdar v Commission* (n 137) para 99.
[153] CJ *Masdar v Commission* (n 131) para 50.
[154] P Craig, *EU Administrative Law* (Oxford, University Press, 2012) 698.
[155] CJ *Masdar v Commission* (n 131) para 59.

The recognition of the action for unjust enrichment against EU institutions raises the question whether the action is also available to the EU bodies themselves or to parties in other legal relationships, viz between individuals and Member States and between individuals.

In *Penycoed*, the CJ was confronted with the issue of whether the EU could avail itself of the principle of unjust enrichment to bring an action for unjust enrichment against an individual.[156] The case concerned the additional levy on milk established by Regulation 3950/92,[157] which was owed by milk producers but collected by the Intervention Board from the purchasers of the milk, who in their turn recovered the levy from the producers by deducting it from the purchase price payable to the latter. Penycoed circumvented the Regulation by means of an arrangement to the effect that Penycoed rented part of its land and cattle to Elm Farms and TDM, and was paid by the latter companies to maintain and milk the herd on their behalf. This had the result that, technically speaking, Penycoed was not a producer and Elm Farms and TDM were not purchasers within the meaning of the Regulation, though milk was supplied between them without payment of the levy. Under the Regulation, the Intervention Board could only claim the levy from the purchasers and in this case, it had no recourse against them. The question arose whether the Intervention Board could collect the levy from Penycoed as a milk producer even though the Regulation did not provide a legal basis for doing so. The CJ held that the Member States' positive obligation under Article 4(3) TEU to ensure the collection of the levy in the event of frustration of the mechanism provided for in the Regulation includes the power to take direct action against the producer.[158] AG Geelhoed, however, had on the one hand based his opinion on the issue on the principle of effectiveness like the CJ did, but on the other hand also observed that the action was permitted because the producers would be unjustly enriched if they would not have to pay the additional levy.[159] Though the CJ refrained from doing so, the AG had thus invoked the principle of unjust enrichment to ensure the claim and, consequently, the effectiveness of EU law.

The CJ has also had opportunities to shed light on the principle of unjust enrichment in a horizontal relationship, but it neither confirmed nor opposed the prohibition of unjust enrichment of individuals as a general principle of EU law.[160] The CJ has recognised unjust enrichment as a general principle of civil law derived from the legal systems of the Member States.[161] This reasoning suggests that the principle will be extended beyond EU institutions to public bodies of Member States and to individuals.

---

[156] CJ 15 January 2004 Case C-230/01 *Intervention Board for Agricultural Produce v Penycoed Farming Partnership* [2004] I-00937 ECLI:EU:C:2004:20.

[157] Council Regulation (EEC) No 3950/92 of 28 December 1992 establishing an additional levy in the milk and milk products sector [1992] OJ L405/1.

[158] CJ *Intervention Board v Penycoed* (n 156) paras 36–39.

[159] AG Geelhoed Opinion 13 February 2003 in Case C-230/1 *Intervention Board of Agricultural Produce v Penycoed Farming Partnership* [2004] I-00937 ECLI:EU:C:2003:97.

[160] See, eg, CJ *Bostock* (n 133); CJ *Courage v Crehan* (n 9); CJ 21 September 2000 Joined Cases C-441/98 and C-442/98 *Kapniki Michaïlidis AE v Idryma Koinonikon Asfaliseon (IKA)* [2000] I-07145 ECLI:EU:C:2000:479; CJ 13 July 2006 Joined Cases C-295/04 to C-298/04 *Vincenzo Manfredi et al v Lloyd Adriatico Assicurazioni SpA et al* [2006] I-06619 ECLI:EU:C:2006:461; and CJ *Messner* (n 136).

[161] CJ *Messner* (n 136).

A significant judgment in this regard is *Bostock*. In those preliminary ruling proceedings, the CJ was directly confronted with an issue of unjust enrichment between individuals. It concerned a dispute about an alleged obligation to pay compensation between a lessee and a lessor regarding the transfer of the value of a milk quota on termination of the lease. English legislation did not provide for payment of compensation to the tenant upon the surrender of his milk quota to the lessor. The claimant argued that under EU law, the principles of non-discrimination and respect for property are binding on the Member States and require a Member State to introduce a scheme for payment of compensation by a lessor to an outgoing lessee or indeed directly confer on the lessee a right to compensation from the lessor. The CJ held that Member States have a duty to respect fundamental rights when they implement EU law, but it did not follow the appellant's argument.[162] In this case, the lessee sought compensation from the lessor on the ground that the fruits of his labour and his investments had contributed to the acquisition or the increase in the reference quantity.[163] It may be argued that the CJ was not willing to accept that a general principle of EU law can impose obligations upon individuals in their relationship with other individuals,[164] since it emphasised that the law of the relevant Member State governed legal relations between the lessor and the lessee. The consequences of unjust enrichment in that relation were not a matter of EU law.[165]

IV.C THE DEFENCE OF UNJUST ENRICHMENT

EU law cannot avoid having to deal with the issue of undue payments to and by public bodies of the EU or Member States. Where money has been paid by or to a public authority in breach of EU rules, the CJ requires repayment of the sums ('condictio indebiti').[166] The CJ has not yet been explicitly confronted with the *condictio indebiti* in a horizontal relationship. The general wording concerning the obtaining of compensation via all the legal remedies available and the rationale behind the judgment *Courage v Crehan* make it plausible that its reasoning will also apply to actions for recovery of any performance between individuals under a contract that is void due to a breach of Article 101 TFEU.[167] The obligation to refund amounts unduly paid in vertical relationships has been primarily based on the need to ensure the effective protection of EU rights and to preserve the effectiveness of EU law. However, the obligation could also be independently justified as an instrument to reverse the unjust enrichment of the payee. Where a right to restitution

---

[162] CJ *Bostock* (n 133) para 20.

[163] ibid.

[164] However, the EU concept of non-contractual liability arising from unlawful act shows that the CJ has also accepted liability on account of breach of EU law between individuals; see CH Sieburgh, 'EU Law and Non-contractual Liability of the Union, Member States and Individuals' in Hartkamp/Sieburgh/Keus/Kortmann/Wissink (eds) 2014 518 ff.

[165] CJ *Bostock* (n 133) para 26.

[166] CJ 9 November 1983 Case C-199/82 *Amministrazione delle Finanze dello Stato* v *SpA San Giorgio* [1983] I-03595 ECLI:EU:C:1983:318. See A Jones, *Restitution and European Community Law* (London, Mansfield Press, 2000).

[167] CJ *Courage v Crehan* (n 9).

exists under EU law, the national courts and tribunals are obliged to protect this right. It is for the domestic system of each Member State to determine the measures that must be taken to ensure such protection. The national conditions set out by the Member States must not make it virtually impossible or excessively difficult to exercise the right under EU law, and these national rules governing recovery in EU cases must not be less favourable than those relating to similar claims of a domestic nature.

Where repayment of a tax that was wrongly paid would entail unjust enrichment of the persons concerned, it can be refused.[168] In certain circumstances, granting a *condictio indebiti* under EU law is barred by the application of the principle of unjust enrichment.[169] In *Just v Danish Ministry for Fiscal Affairs*, the CJ held that EU law 'does not require an order for the recovery of charges improperly made to be granted in conditions which involve the unjust enrichment of those entitled'.[170] It 'does not prevent the fact that the burden of the charges may have been passed on to other traders or to consumers from being taken into consideration'.[171] In this case, the claimant had paid taxes, which were ruled to be discriminatory in contravention of [now Article 110 TFEU]. The CJ confirmed that the national court could, in recovery proceedings, take account of the fact that it had been possible for the undertaking liable for the unduly levied charges to incorporate those charges into prices and to pass them on to consumers. It was recognised that a defence of passing-on could be applied to prevent the claimant's recovery of charges which had been levied by a Member State in breach of EU law. To do otherwise might unjustly enrich economic operators as they would be allowed recovery of the undue payment though they had not suffered any loss as a result, since the costs were passed on to the purchasers, whereas no effective remedy could be offered to the purchasers as they would not often be able to recover their losses from the trader or the national authorities that levied the charge.[172] As such, the passing-on defence has become a firm part of EU law. Moreover, the CJ judgments in cases of payment to and by public bodies have had some influence on the remedy of claiming restitution that is available in some national systems, even in cases not involving EU law. An example is the UK decision in *Woolwich Equitable*

---

[168] More recently, the CJ has so ruled in CJ 6 September 2011 Case C-398/09 *Lady & Kid A/S et al v Skatteministeriet* [2011] I-07375 ECLI:EU:C:2011:540 and CJ 16 May 2013 Case C-191/12 *Alakor Gabonatermelő és Forgalmazó Kft v Nemzeti Adó- és Vámhivatal Észak-alföldi Regionális Adó Főigazgatósága nyr* ECLI:EU:C:2013:315. The CJ has similarly also referred to the passing-on defence in the context of a claim arising from unlawful act. In CJ 13 March 1991 Case C-377/89 *Cotter and McDermott v Minister for Social Welfare and Attorney General* [1991] I-01155 ECLI:EU:C:1991:116 concerning social security entitlement and the issue of unequal treatment of men and women, the CJ rejected the defence of unjust enrichment on the ground that withholding the benefit from married women constituted unlawful discrimination. It seems as though the principle of unjust enrichment may operate more strongly in economic relations than in a social security environment. However, the unjust enrichment of the claimant, a married woman, remains uncertain because the fact that the benefit was granted to both spouses does not entail unjust enrichment of the claimant. See Hartkamp 2014 (I) 583–86 nos 15–16.

[169] It can be questioned whether such a bar to acceptance of the *condictio indebiti* by way of the principle of unjust enrichment is correct from a private law perspective, as the suffering of any loss by the claimant generally does not affect the decision to allow recovery of an undue payment.

[170] CJ 16 February 1980 Case C-68/79 *Hans Just I/S v Danish Ministry for Fiscal Affairs* [1980] I-00501 ECLI:EU:C:1980:57.

[171] ibid, paras 26 and 27.

[172] CJ *Lady & Kid A/S et al* (n 168) para 19.

Building Society v Inland Revenue Commissioners.[173] Furthermore, concepts discussed at the EU level, such as the passing-on defence (see section II.D.iii.c in Chapter 2), have been discussed in national debates and have influenced national legislation.

There are other cases not involving any passing on of the sums unduly levied in which the full recovery of the undue payment would similarly result in unjust enrichment of the claimant.[174] In *Lady & Kid* and, more recently, *Alakor*, the rationale behind the passing-on defence was deployed. Both cases concerned the restitution of an unlawful tax. In *Lady & Kid*, the introduction of a tax, which was in breach of an EU directive, had been accompanied by the abolishment of social security contributions. Both the tax and the social contributions were levied on the same undertakings. The claim of recovery of the tax unduly paid was contested with the (rationale of the) passing-on defence. The CJ refused to accept the defence on the ground that it was to be considered a limitation of the EU right to restitution. The defence was to be interpreted narrowly, meaning that the sole exception to this right was where the sum unduly paid had been directly passed on to purchasers.[175] In *Alakor*, the defence put forward by the State was accepted, although there had been no passing on of the unduly paid tax to purchasers.[176] In this case, a project of Alakor was subsidised by a Hungarian state institution. According to the applicable national provision, the subsidised project was subject to a tax that was partly non-deductible. The national provision violated EU law. Alakor therefore claimed back the non-deductible amount of the taxes. The question arose as to whether the state could refuse repayment because it had provided compensation in the form of a subsidy. The CJ allowed the state's defence on the condition that the compensation covered the whole economic burden imposed by the tax unduly paid, being the entire amount of the tax declared non-deductible in breach of EU law. The reason for the distinction made between *Lady & Kid* and *Alakor* might be the fact that there must be a connection between the loss created by the undue payment and the gain enjoyed by the claimant.[177] In *Alakor*, this connection was apparently more direct than in *Lady & Kid*. In conclusion, the CJ has accepted that in certain circumstances, the defence of unjust enrichment can also be a valid defence for tax authorities, even if the party that paid the unlawful tax has not fully passed on the tax to purchasers, but has been compensated in another way. However, national law is not obliged under EU law to allow such a defence.

IV.D FUTURE EFFECTS OF THE PRINCIPLE OF UNJUST ENRICHMENT

This section elaborates on the effects which the principle of unjust enrichment as currently recognised as part of EU law could have on horizontal relations in the future. The recognition of the principle at EU level implicitly introduced its interpretative function,[178]

---

[173] *Woolwich Equitable Building Society v Inland Revenue Commissioners* [1993] AC 70.
[174] Hartkamp 2014 (I) 583.
[175] CJ *Lady & Kid A/S et al* (n 168).
[176] CJ *Alakor* (n 168).
[177] Hartkamp 2014 (I) 586.
[178] See GC *Eduardo Vieira, SA et al v Commission of the European Communities* (n 149) para 86.

and also its controlling function and its gap-filling or generative function into EU law.[179] Case law of the CJ has already confirmed that the principle of unjust enrichment, being a general principle of EU law, can affect the relationship between an individual and an institution of the EU. The legislative and administrative acts binding the parties in this vertical relationship can be reviewed against the principle. If such an act is incompatible with the principle, it is considered void. A factual act of an EU institution can also be contrary to the principle, which results in a right to compensation. The principle of unjust enrichment is applied to interpret the vertical relationship or to fill in any gaps. The relationship can be supplemented or modified. In this vertical relationship, the principle has taken the form of an independent cause of action arising from unjust enrichment. This has the result that an individual has the right, under Article 340(2) TFEU, to claim reimbursement of an unjust enrichment obtained at his expense by an EU institution. Other Treaty provisions or EU rules, for example, a provision in a directive, can also result in the right of an individual to bring a claim for unjust enrichment against an EU body.

In vertical relationships between an individual and a Member State institution, the CJ has accepted the obligation of the latter to refund undue payments. This obligation is subject to the defence of unjust enrichment of the individual. The CJ has not yet generally confirmed that the principle of unjust enrichment, as a general principle of EU law or as a cause of action, can create rights and obligations for individuals in such relationships. However, it has acknowledged the non-contractual liability arising from an unlawful act (the infringement of a rule of EU law) in both vertical relationships. Article 340(2) TFEU regulates the EU's non-contractual liability for damage. A similar liability as regulated in Article 340(2) TFEU for EU institutions rests on the Member States and their bodies, although it lacks a basis in the EU Treaties. This liability has been created by the CJ. It derives from the objectives and the nature of EU law, including Article 340(2) TFEU. Moreover, it ensures that the EU rules have full effect and that the EU law rights conferred on individuals are protected if they are infringed as a result of a breach of EU law by a Member State.[180] It is likely that in a case covered by EU law which concerns a vertical relationship between an individual and a Member State body, the CJ will follow a similar reasoning and will recognise the same rights and obligations arising from unjust enrichment as it has in the legal relationship between an individual and an EU institution.

In horizontal relationships, the CJ seems hesitant to apply the principle of unjust enrichment as a general principle of EU law. It may be inferred that the CJ leaves it to national law to decide whether an obligation arising from unjust enrichment exists between individuals. This would be in line with the fact that the CJ has allowed Member States to apply national provisions on unjust enrichment to rights derived from the application of EU law. In *Bostock*, however, parties requested legal arrangements concerning unjust enrichment for an issue falling outside the scope of EU law. Consequently, the CJ could not grant such a claim for EU law did not govern the case. In *Messner*, moreover,

---

[179] For the different functions of general principles of EU law, see Tridimas 2006; and CH Sieburgh, 'Principles in Private Law: From Luxury to Necessity – Multi-layered Legal Systems and the Generative Force of Principles' (2012) 20(2) *ERPL* 295.

[180] CJ 19 November 1991 Joined Cases C-6/90–C-9/90 *Andrea Francovich and Danila Bonifaci et al v Italian Republic* [1991] I-05357 ECLI:EU:C:1991:428, paras 32 ff.

the principle of unjust enrichment was applied to limit the compensation rights and obligations in a horizontal relationship. EU law is therefore not blind to issues of unjust enrichment between private parties. It is plausible that the CJ's reasoning with regard to unjust enrichment as a separate source of rights and obligations in relationships between an individual and an EU institution would also apply in horizontal relationships. Again, the case law on unlawful act may serve as a frame of reference. After acknowledging the obligation resting on the bodies of the EU and Member States to make good damages caused by an unlawful act, the CJ, in *Courage v Crehan*, recognised the liability of individuals for violation of EU law in order to ensure the full effectiveness of EU law and to protect the rights it confers on individuals.[181] The principle of effectiveness has served as the driving force behind the acknowledgement of the liability of individuals for breaches of EU law. The principle has been instrumental in the establishment of new (private law) remedies of EU origin in various legal relationships.[182] The CJ could in a similar way develop the existence of rights and obligations arising from unjust enrichment under EU law in horizontal relationships, using a connecting factor found in the Treaties or the general principles of EU law.[183] In *Masdar v Commission*, the CJ already recognised the right of an individual to hold the EU liable for unjust enrichment under Article 340(2) TFEU, referring to the principle of effective judicial protection. The most plausible ground for recognising the cause of action arising from unjust enrichment in the other legal relationships will be a combination of the principle of unjust enrichment and the principle of effectiveness. The CJ's case law, including those cases that involve issues of unjust enrichment, shows that the principle of effectiveness is used to safeguard judicial protection. It justifies the availability of remedies in situations that call for reimbursement to protect the EU law rights of individuals. In those situations, the absence of a remedy could be at variance with both the principle of effectiveness (or effective judicial protection) and the principle of unjust enrichment.

If the CJ were to acknowledge the direct horizontal effect of the principle of unjust enrichment, horizontal relationships could thereby be supplemented or modified, resulting in compensation rights and obligations. A contract might then be reviewed against[184] or interpreted in the light of that principle, and factual conduct of an individual might be considered to constitute a ground for liability towards another individual because the contract or act conflicts with the principle of unjust enrichment. The principle could also affect a relationship between individuals indirectly. Indirect effect could occur in various ways. EU law could, for example, impose a duty on national courts to interpret national law in such a way that it conforms with the principle in the situation where a directive has not been implemented or has been implemented incorrectly in the national legal system. Or the review of a national rule against the principle could lead to its disapplication,

---

[181] CJ *Courage v Crehan* (n 9).
[182] Hartkamp 2016 no 109.
[183] Hartkamp 2014 (I) 575.
[184] If the contract is at variance with the principle, it may be wholly or partially void. With regard to unjust enrichment, it will not often happen that a contract is declared void in its entirety since in most cases only a part of the agreement will be at variance with the principle of unjust enrichment.

which may have consequences for the validity of contracts concluded while the national rule was in force. It can be difficult to establish in national case law how exactly the EU law principle of unjust enrichment has influenced national law. It may be hard to distinguish its application from the application of the national principle of unjust enrichment as long as the material differences between them are insignificant.[185]

In addition, the principle could be condensed into a right of reimbursement based on unjust enrichment under EU law in horizontal relationships. An EU law remedy of claims for unjust enrichment between individuals could then exist under Treaty provisions or other EU rules that have been recognised to have direct horizontal effect, such as Article 101 TFEU. This would have the result that an individual could hold another individual accountable for unjust enrichment under EU law.[186] If the CJ should already have pronounced its judgments in *Masdar v Commission* and *Courage v Crehan* at the time it had to deal with *Bostock*, the latter case might well have been decided differently and a right of compensation based on unjust enrichment might have been recognised. At any rate, such a right may probably be assumed to be acceptable now. Two different reasonings can be followed to establish the right, both aimed at safeguarding judicial protection. Which reasoning will be followed depends on whether the CJ will proceed on the basis of the principle of effectiveness in its gap-filling function and whether the CJ wishes to leave the national legislatures free to determine the substantive and procedural rules through which the EU law right to reimbursement for unjust enrichment is to be realised.[187]

In the first reasoning, the right is based on the principle of effectiveness in its gap-filling function in combination with the principle of unjust enrichment. The CJ could ultimately rule that the EU principle of unjust enrichments confers an explicit and general cause of action on individuals in horizontal relationships, which is to be given effect through national law. This means that the national rules effectuating the EU law cause of action are subject to EU law, following the example of *Courage v Crehan*.[188] According to this scenario, the lessee in *Bostock* could have availed himself of that cause of action.

In the second reasoning, the CJ would interpret the EU principle of unjust enrichment to mean that it does not confer a cause of action in horizontal relationships, but merely sets a standard for reviewing the rules of national law on compensation in cases involving an enrichment issue that falls within the scope of EU law, which requires application of the principles of equivalence and effectiveness.[189] The national rules could be reviewed

---

[185] Unlike a national principle of unjust enrichment, the principle can only exert influence as an EU principle when the case falls within the scope of EU law. A case involving unjust enrichment will most likely fall within the scope of EU law if the enrichment of the defendant has occurred on the basis of (a violation of) an EU rule. The criterion of coverage by EU law is used to select the relevant national cases presented throughout the casebook.

[186] See Hartkamp 2014 (I) 575–76.

[187] Hartkamp 2016 nos 109 ff.

[188] CJ *Courage v Crehan* (n 9).

[189] CJ 16 December 1976 Case C-33/76 *Rewe Centralfinanz eG and Rewe Central AG v Landwirtschaftskammer für das Saarland* [1976] I-1989 ECLI:EU:C:1976:188. The review function of the principles of effectiveness and equivalence would also exist in the first design of the right of reimbursement arising from unjust enrichment, insofar as the national rules giving effect to the EU law cause of action will also be reviewed by the CJ against these principles.

against both principles and set aside if they are held to be incompatible with the principles because they preclude individuals in such cases from being awarded compensation or because the compensation offered is not awarded on the same conditions that would have applied to domestic cases.[190] In this way, the CJ would be able, without recognising an EU law cause of action arising from unjust enrichment, to give more or less detailed rules on the circumstances under which the EU right of reimbursement arising from unjust enrichment must be available and whether the national remedies must include the possibility of compensation. Consequently, review of the national rules governing compensation with respect to enrichment issues could result in reimbursement being awarded if EU law so requires, but the national rules do not provide for this remedy. Such review would thus make it possible for an individual to rely on a national cause of action in situations governed by EU law via an adjusted interpretation of the requirements which the national claim must satisfy and the establishment of the minimum scope of the obligation to provide compensation. An example could be the situation where under national law, a certain loss suffered as a result of illicit competition is not recoverable via the cause of action arising from unjust enrichment though EU law requires this remedy to be available. Pursuant to EU law, this restriction could then be set aside after it has been reviewed against the principle of effectiveness. With such judgments, the CJ would lay down a standard of protection by review that goes beyond merely requiring the national rules to be reviewed against the principles of effectiveness and equivalence, since it also gives directions regarding the interpretation of the required scope of the obligation to provide compensation. Without determining the precise definition and operation of the remedy in national law, the CJ would give an interpretation of the conditions and scope of the obligation based on unjust enrichment. According to this second reasoning, a national remedy would be available to the lessee in *Bostock* against the lessor in *Bostock* that would result in compensation of the unjust enrichment occurring. The relevant national substantive and procedural rules of this remedy would be subject to review against the EU law principles of effectiveness and equivalence and, if available, the CJ's interpretation of its conditions and scope.

The CJ could thus apply the principle of unjust enrichment to develop a right of reimbursement for unjust enrichment under EU law by recognising an EU law cause of action or by requiring a minimum level of protection in national law. In both alternatives, the EU law principle of effectiveness will be instrumental in creating an EU law counterpart to the national concepts of unjust enrichment and will affect their application in cases falling within the scope of EU law.

---

[190] See, eg, CJ 10 April 1984 Case C-14/83 *Sabine von Colson and Elisabeth Kamann v Land Nordrhein-Westfalen* [1984] I-01891 ECLI:EU:C:1984:153; CJ 2 August 1993 Case C-271/91 *Marshall v Southampton and South-West Hampshire Area Health Authority (Marshall II)* [1993] I-04367 ECLI:EU:C:1993:335; CJ 12 May 1998 Case C-367/96 *Kefalas et al v Elliniko Dimosio (Greek State) and Organismos Oikonomikis Anasygkrotisis Epicheiriseon AE (OAE)* [1998] I-02843 ECLI:EU:C:1998:222; CJ 23 December 2000 Case C-373/97 *Diamantis v Elliniko Dimosio (Greek State) and Organismos Ikonomikis Anasygkrotisis Epicheiriseon AE (OAE)* [2000] I-01705 ECLI:EU:C:2000:105.

FURTHER READING

AS Hartkamp, 'Unjust enrichment and *condictio indebiti* in European Union law' in Hartkamp/
Sieburgh/Keus/Kortmann/Wissink (eds) 2014 p 567–588.

MMC van de Moosdijk, 'Het verrijkingsbeginsel en de niet-contractuele aansprakelijkheid van de
Europese Unie' (2013) 6977 *WPNR* 420–27.

R Williams, *Unjust Enrichment and Public Law, A Comparative Study of England, France and the
EU*, (Oxford, Hart Publishing, 2010).

6

DIRECTIVES

Sander Van Loock, Ilse Samoy and Jerzy Pisuliński

I. INTRODUCTION

This chapter deals with the private law effects of directives. Its purpose is not to describe the (correct) transposition of directives into the different national systems or to discuss the details of specific directives in the field of private law. Instead, the chapter starts with an analysis of the obligation of the Member States to implement directives (see section II below). It then focuses on the legal techniques available to the national courts to ensure the effectiveness of directives, even if they have not been implemented or have not been implemented correctly or on time. In such cases, the absence of direct horizontal effect of the provisions of a directive does not preclude these provisions from having certain effects on the legal position of the authorities or individuals concerned.[1] Where these

---

[1] See Hartley 2010 234 ff; Lenaerts and Van Nuffel 2011, para 22-086.

effects on the relationship between individuals are indirect or incidental, they can be called 'indirect horizontal effects'.[2]

The terminology used in legal doctrine and jurisprudence to refer to the indirect horizontal effect of directives is often confusing and misleading. In line with Chapter 1, we distinguish the following techniques:

i. Harmonious interpretation imposed by EU law, meaning that the national courts are obliged to use the methods of interpretation available to them under national law in order to interpret national law as far as possible in conformity with a directive. See section III below.

ii. Harmonious interpretation not imposed by EU law, ie, interpretation of open-ended principles of national private law, such as good faith, reasonableness and fairness, in conformity with EU law instruments, *in casu* directives. See section IV below.

iii. Review of national law in the light of provisions of EU law (including general principles of EU law) and, exceptionally, the disapplication of national law which conflicts with EU law. See section V below.

iv. Positive obligations, ie, obligations for Member States to safeguard the rights deriving from EU law vis-a-vis their citizens, also in horizontal relationships. As no national cases have been reported in which this fourth technique was used in connection with directives, we will not deal with it further in this chapter.

As Member State liability also influences private law relationships in the Member States (albeit in vertical relationships, viz between individuals and Member States), this chapter will also deal briefly with cases in which a Member State had failed to transpose a directive into national law or had failed to do so correctly and on time, and had caused damage to an individual. See section VI below.

Finally, we will discuss so-called 'spillover' effects of directives. The concept refers to the situation where a directive is voluntarily (or mandatorily—eg, by applying the national principle of equality) implemented in a way that reaches further than EU law requires. See section VII below.

II. OBLIGATION OF THE MEMBER STATES TO IMPLEMENT A DIRECTIVE

Article 288(3) TFEU **6.1 (EU)**

A directive shall be binding, as to the result to be achieved, upon each Member State to which it is addressed, but shall leave to the national authorities the choice of form and methods.

Directives are not directly applicable in the domestic legal systems of the Member States. They are only binding as to the result to be achieved. In other words, a directive lays down an objective, but leaves Member States free to determine the way in which the objective is to be achieved. Directives only acquire their full legislative effect after they

---

[2] See Hartkamp 2016 no 17.

have been transposed into the national legal order through the adoption of the neces-sary implementing measures.[3] The provisions of directives must be implemented with unquestionable binding force and with the specificity, precision and clarity necessary to satisfy the requirements of legal certainty. This means that Member States will not have fulfilled their obligations under Article 288, third paragraph TFEU by maintain-ing existing administrative practices, even though they are consonant with the directive, because administrative practices can be changed without sufficient publicity as and when it pleases the authorities.[4] Directives usually specify a time limit within which Member States must adopt the necessary measures and put them into effect in order to achieve the result envisaged by the directive. For Member States, the obligation to implement a directive is an 'obligation to achieve a fixed result' (*obligation de résultat*). Member States cannot justify their failure to comply with the deadline for implementation by referring to problems at the national level.[5]

II.A PROHIBITION TO ADOPT OR MAINTAIN NATIONAL PROVISIONS NOT IN CONFORMITY WITH THE PROVISIONS OF A DIRECTIVE

Although Member States are under no obligation to adopt transposition measures before the period prescribed for implementing a directive has expired, this does not mean that they are entirely free. Pursuant to Article 4(3) TEU, Member States must refrain from taking any measures which might seriously compromise achievement of the result pre-scribed by the directive. It is up to the national courts to assess whether that is the case by considering, in particular, the effects in practice of applying the incompatible provi-sions and their duration in time.[6] A provision of national law adopted after the directive entered into force may compromise this result, regardless of whether it is connected with the transposition of the directive or not.[7]

II.B ABSENCE OF THE DIRECT HORIZONTAL EFFECT OF PROVISIONS OF AN UNIMPLEMENTED OR INCORRECTLY IMPLEMENTED DIRECTIVE

II.B.i SOURCES: CJ CASE LAW

In vertical relationships, ie, between the authorities and individuals, the CJ has held that a provision of a directive can have direct effect if that provision is unconditional

---

[3] See Hartley 2010 218; Lenaerts and Van Nuffel 2011 para 22-075/76; Dashwood/Dougan/Rodger/Spaventa/Wyatt 2011 258.

[4] CJ 6 May 1980 Case C-102/79 *Commission of the European Communities v Kingdom of Belgium* [1980] I-01473 ECLI:EU:C1980:120, para 11. See Lenaerts and Van Nuffel 2011 para 22-077; Dashwood/Dougan/Rodger/Spaventa/Wyatt 2011 258.

[5] See Lenaerts and Van Nuffel 2011 para 22-078.

[6] CJ 18 December 1997 Case C-129/96 *Inter-Environnement Wallonie ASBL v Région wallonne* [1997] I-07411 ECLI:EU:C:1997:628, paras 45–47.

[7] CJ 22 November 2005 Case C-144/04 *Werner Mangold v Rüdiger Helm* [2005] I-09981 ECLI:EU:C:2005:709, para 68.

and sufficiently precise, and the period prescribed for implementing the directive has expired.[8] In *Van Duyn*, the seminal case on this issue, the CJ gave two reasons for according direct vertical effect.[9] The first reason is functional and is that the effectiveness (*'effet utile'*) of a directive would be weakened if individuals could not rely on it before a national court. The nature of the second reason is textual. The fact that national courts can refer questions concerning any EU measure to the CJ implies that such measures can be invoked by individuals before the national courts.[10] In *Ratti*, the CJ added a third rationale for according direct effect to directive provisions. It held that 'a Member State which has not adopted the implementing measures required by the directive in the prescribed periods may not rely, as against individuals, on its own failure to perform the obligations which the directive entails'.[11] This argument, which prevents a Member State from taking advantage of its own failure to implement a directive properly, reflects the civil law principle of *nemo auditur* and the common law principle of estoppel.[12]

The situation is completely different in horizontal relationships, ie, between individuals. As was discussed in Chapter 1, provisions (and principles) of EU law may have a variety of horizontal effects, so it is necessary to distinguish between them. Directives cannot be invoked in horizontal relations, ie, between individuals. A directive cannot of itself impose obligations on individuals, nor can a provision of a directive as such be relied on against an individual, eg, to review whether a provision of national law is compatible with a directive.[13] A directive cannot directly create, modify or extinguish rights and obligations between parties. In *Marshall I*, the CJ clarified that 'a directive may not of itself impose obligations on an individual and that a provision of a directive may not be relied upon as such against such a person'.[14] In *Faccini Dori*, this meant that in the

---

[8] See Craig and De Búrca 2015 200–204; Kapteyn 2008 525; Lenaerts and Van Nuffel 2011 para 22-080; Dashwood/Dougan/Rodger/Spaventa/Wyatt 2011 259–60.

[9] CJ 4 December 1974 Case C-41/74 *Yvonne van Duyn v Home Office* [1974] I-01337 ECLI:EU:C:1974:133, para 12.

[10] Craig and De Búrca 2015 201; Kapteyn 2008 526; Hartley 2010 219–20, who distinguishes three reasons. Note that the CJ, too, has used this argument in CJ 7 March 1985 *Van Gend & Loos v Inspecteur der Invoerrechten en Accijnzen, Enschede* [1985] I-00779 ECLI:EU:C:1985:104 to support the direct effect of Treaty provisions.

[11] CJ 5 April 1979 Case C-148/78 *Criminal Proceedings v Ratti* [1979] I-01629 ECLI:EU:C:1979:110, para 23.

[12] AG Van Gerven Opinion 30 January 1990 in Case C-262/88 *Douglas Harvey Barber v Guardian Royal Exchange Assurance Group* [1990] I-01889 ECLI:EU:C:1990:34, para 49; Craig and De Búrca 2015 203; Hartley 2010 220; Dashwood/Dougan/Rodger/Spaventa/Wyatt 2011 261. The estoppel argument was first put forward in AG Warner Opinion 25 October 1977 in Case C-38/77 *Enka BV v Inspecteur der Invoerrechten en Accijnzen Arnhem* [1977] I-02203 ECLI:EU:C:1977:168 2226. According to Van Gerven, the principle of estoppel is better suited to justify the vertical direct effect of directives, considering the broad interpretation of 'Member State': W van Gerven, 'The Horizontal Effect of Directive Provisions Revisited: The Reality of Catchwords' in D Curtin and T Heukels (eds), *Institutional Dynamics of European Integration: Essays in Honour of Henry G. Schermers, Volume II* (Dordrecht, Martinus Nijhoff, 1994) 335, 343–45. According to other authors, the 'estoppel-like notion' is a consequence of, rather than a basis for, the direct effect of directives: Prechal 2005 220–26; and Kapteyn 2008 526 fn 76.

[13] See Hartkamp 2016 no 156; and section II.C in Ch 1.

[14] CJ 26 February 1986 Case C-152/84 *MH Marshall v Southampton and South-West Hampshire Area Health Authority (Teaching) (Marshall I)* [1986] I-00723 ECLI:EU:C:1986:84, para 48.

absence of measures transposing Directive 85/577/EEC[15] on consumer contracts negotiated away from business premises within the prescribed time limit, consumers could not derive from the directive itself a right of cancellation against traders with whom they had concluded a contract nor enforce such a right in a national court.[16] Moreover, an individual may not rely on a directly effective provision of a directive against a public authority where this would directly lead to obligations being imposed on another individual by the directive.[17] In *Wells*, the CJ ruled in a similar vein that 'an individual may not rely on a directive against a Member State where it is a matter of a State obligation directly linked to the performance of another obligation falling, pursuant to that directive, on a third party'.[18] So where a Member State would be obliged by the individual's reliance on the directive to make another individual comply with an obligation arising under the directive, direct effect is not possible.[19] However, in *Wells*, the CJ qualified this by ruling that an individual may rely on the direct effect of provisions of a directive against a Member State, even though this might have adverse repercussions on another individual.[20] The mere adverse repercussions on the rights of third parties, even if these are certain, do not justify preventing an individual from invoking the provisions of a directive against the Member State concerned.[21]

The case law of the CJ in which it refuses to allow individuals to invoke provisions of directives, but allows several forms of indirect horizontal effect (see below), is criticised in legal doctrine.[22] Sacha Prechal summarised the arguments pro and contra allowing direct horizontal effect as follows.[23]

---

[15] Council Directive 85/577/EEC of 20 December 1985 to protect the consumer in respects of contracts negotiated away from business premises [1985] OJ L372/31.

[16] CJ 14 July 1994 Case C-91/92 *Faccini Dori v Recreb Srl* [1994] I-03325 ECLI:EU:C:1994:292, para 25.

[17] CJ 4 December 1997 Case C-97/96 *Verband deutscher Daihatsu-Händler eV v Daihatsu Deutschland GmbH* [1997] I-068843 ECLI:EU:C:1997:581, paras 24 and 26. See Lenaerts and Van Nuffel 2011 para 22-083.

[18] CJ 7 January 2004 Case C-201/02 *Delena Wells v Secretary of State for Transport* [2004] I-00723 ECLI:EU:C:2004:12, para 56.

[19] Prechal 2005 265, with reference to CJ *Verband deutscher Daihatsu-Händler eV v Daihatsu Deutschland GmbH* [1997] (see footnote 17).

[20] Craig and De Búrca 2015 208; Hartley 2010 227–28; Lenaerts and Van Nuffel 2011 para 22-085.

[21] CJ *Wells* (n 18) paras 56–57; CJ 17 July 2008 Joint Cases C-152/07–C-154/07 *Arcor AG & Co KG, Communication Services TELE2 GmbH and Firma 01051 Telekom GmbH v Bundesrepublik Deutschland* [2008] I-05959 ECLI:EU:C:2008:426, paras 34–43.

[22] P Craig, 'Directives: Direct Effect, Indirect Effect and the Construction of National Legislation' (1997) 22(6) *EL Rev* 519; P Craig, 'The Legal Effects of Directives: Policy, Rules and Exceptions' (2009) 34(3) *EL Rev* 349; Craig and De Búrca 2015 200–209; D Kinley, 'Direct Effect of Directives: Stuck on Vertical Hold' (1995) 1(1) *EPL* 79; T Tridimas, 'Horizontal Effect of Directives: A Missed Opportunity' (1994) 19 *EL Rev* 621. See also the attempts of three AGs in the early 1990s to alter this case law: AG Van Gerven Opinion 26 January 1993 in Case C-271/91 *MH Marshall v Southampton and South-West Hampshire Area Health Authority (Marshall II)* [1993] I-04367 ECLI:EU:C:1993:30, para 12; AG Jacobs Opinion 27 January 1994 in Case C-316/93 *Nicole Vaneetveld v Le Foyer SA and Le Foyer SA v Fédération des Mutualités Socialistes et Syndicales de la Province de Liège* [1994] I-00763 ECLI:EU:C:1994:32, paras 18 ff; AG Lenz Opinion 9 February 1994 in Case C-91/92 *Paola Faccini Dori v Recreb Srl* [1994] I-03325 ECLI:EU:C1994:45, paras 43 ff

[23] Note that she uses the term 'horizontal direct effect' referring to the *Marshall* judgment which, in the terminology of this casebook, encompasses both 'direct horizontal effect' (see section II.A in Ch 1) and indirect horizontal effect as described in section II.B in Ch 1. See, for further clarification, sections II.C and III in Ch 1.

The *first argument* against horizontal direct effect of directives draws upon the definition of directives in [now Article 288(3) TFEU]. According to this definition directives are
binding upon the Member States and therefore not upon private individuals. For this
reason they cannot impose obligations on individuals but only on Member States. In its
judgment in *Marshall I* the Court found in favour of this textual argument keeping close
to the terms of [now Article 288(3) TFEU]. This approach is, however, difficult to reconcile
with the Court's case law on direct effect of, notably, Treaty provisions. From this case law
it appears, firstly, that direct effect is not conditional upon the addressee of the relevant
provision and that the nature of the legal relationship involved plays no part in the matter at all. Further, the case law on direct effect of Treaty provisions has made clear that in
determining the legal effects, it is the content of the measure rather than its form which is
decisive. There has been no indication that direct effect is dependent on the legal character of the act in which the relevant provision has been laid down. According to some, the
mere fact that Member States are obliged, under [now Article 288(3) TFEU], to implement
the directive does not as such decide the question as to the potential legal effects of the
substantive provisions.

The *second argument* against horizontal direct effect of directives refers to the difference between regulations and directives. Only the former are, according to [now Article
288 TFEU], directly applicable and may, for that reason, impose obligations on private
individuals. Accepting horizontal direct effect of directives would amount to assimilating
directives to regulations. This argument was embraced by the Court in *Faccini Dori* when
it held that the acceptance of horizontal direct effect would mean 'to recognize a power
in the [EU] to enact obligations for individuals with immediate effect, whereas it has competence to do so only where it is empowered to adopt regulations'. This argument of—no
doubt—constitutional character is often also considered an expression of the rule of law
or, more precisely, the 'principle of legality'. Yet, with respect to the distinction between
regulations and directives, it has been observed that such an argument is the same as
that put forward against direct effect of directives in general, which has, however, been
dismissed by the Court. Moreover, allowing horizontal effect of directives would change
nothing with respect to the obligation to implement them, nor would it alter the choice of
form and methods left to the Member States. To this one may add that 'the directive', as
an instrument of [EU] law, has undergone an important development to which, however,
[now Article 288 TFEU] has not been adapted.

The *third argument* relates to legal certainty. It comprises two distinct elements. Firstly,
there was no legal requirement to publish directives in the Official Journal. This rather
formalistic argument according to some is considered by certain other scholars to be an
important one. Advocate General Lenz made a distinction in this respect between publication with 'constitutive' effect and a merely declaratory publication. In his opinion, '[t]he
basic condition for a burden imposed on the citizen by legislative measures is their *constitutive publication* in an official organ'. The entry into force of directives is, under the 'old'
EEC Treaty, made dependent upon their notification and not their publication. This is now
different under [now Article 297 TFEU].

Secondly, it was maintained that to allow directives to be pleaded against individuals
would create a situation of considerable legal insecurity. In principle, certainly as far as

---

[24] Prechal 2005 255–58.

obligations are concerned, individuals must be able to rely on national law. If horizontal direct effect were accepted, individuals would be required to scrutinize both national law and the relevant [EU] directives, which would impose a heavy burden on them. This argument has been countered that neither the situation under national law nor the situation with respect to regulations is much different. However this might be, the Court seems to attribute quite some weight to this argument. In a recent case it held that 'the principle of legal certainty prevents directives from creating obligations for individuals'.

However, even with the issue of legal certainty which lies at the heart of the entire discussion, there are at least two scenarios. On the one hand, there is the legal certainty of those who are entitled to expect that their position as safeguarded by the directive will be protected. On the other hand, there is the legal certainty of those who would be confronted with an obligation which is not laid down in national law. The ultimate question is: whose legal certainty deserves protection? In my view this question cannot be answered once and for all, and in general terms. Depending on the context of the case the outcome may differ. As a rule, for the reasons already presented above, an individual should be able to rely on and enforce a provision of a directive against another individual. The latter may raise in his defence that he was not and in all reasonableness could not have been acquainted with the obligations resulting from the directive at issue. Whether this defence will succeed depends on several factors, such as the publication of the directive, the experience and vigilance of the defendant etc.

The *fourth argument* against horizontal direct effect of directives appeared in *Ratti* where the Court held that a Member State which has not adopted the implementing measures required by the directive at issue may not rely, *vis-à-vis* individuals, on its own failure to perform the obligation which the directive entails. It has been reiterated in other cases, such as *Faccini Dori*, where the Court maintained that its case law on direct effect of directives seeks to prevent the State from taking advantage of its own failure to comply with [EU] law and thus depriving the individuals of the benefit of the rights which directives may confer on them. This so-called 'principle of estoppel' has already been discussed at length in Subsection 9.2.2. The most obvious counter-argument is indeed that the Court of Justice has never attached much importance to the principle of estoppel as a conceptual basis. It was rather doctrine which declared this principle to be the ultimate rationale of direct effect of directives.

An important argument in favour of horizontal direct effect draws upon the need for uniform application and the '*effect utile*' of [EU] law. To allow horizontal direct effect of directives would increase their effectiveness, and would constitute a further incentive for the Member State to implement directives in time and safeguard as far as possible uniform application of [EU] law and the protection for rights which individuals derive from it. The latter would be compromised not only by a denial of horizontal direct effect as such but also by fresh discrimination to which such a denial would lead. The anomalies to which the denial of horizontal direct effect of directives would lead, was particularly conspicuous after the *Marshall I* judgment, where the Court introduced an unfair distinction between private employees and State employees: the latter may rely on a directive while the former may not. Such a distinction may vary over time, as in the case of privatization of nationally run businesses, and from Member State to Member State, with as a consequence discriminations and inequalities in conditions of competition, which can hardly be considered compatible with [EU] law as such. In other—general—terms, both from the perspective of the functioning of the internal market as from the perspective of equality as a fundamental right, the Court's approach is deemed highly unfortunate.

*Corte di Cassazione, sezione lavoro (Italian Court of Cassation,
Labour Division), 5 April 1995*[25]   **6.3 (IT)**

Mosca v Fabbian

NO DIRECT HORIZONTAL EFFECT OF DIRECTIVE PROVISIONS

Time is money

Article 3(1) of Directive 77/187/EEC has no direct effect in a horizontal relationship

Facts: In assessing the conditions governing an employee's employment contract, the current employer did not take into account all the rights deriving from the relationship between that employee and his previous employers.

Held: According to the Italian Court of Cassation, Article 3(1) of Directive 77/187/EEC cannot be applied between private parties, even if the relevant provisions of the Directive are sufficiently clear and unconditional. The employee can, however, claim compensation from the state.

Judgment: Italy's failure to comply with the obligations under the Treaty regarding the implementation of the directive was established by the decision of the Court of Justice of the European Communities of 10 July 1986 in Case 235/84.

The problem that arises in this case is whether, despite the failure to implement the Directive on time ... that directive can exert some influence in the decision of this case ...

And yet, although a direct application of the Directive in respect of Member States' citizens should be excluded, it has been accorded some effectiveness under certain conditions.

According to the development of the case law of the CJ, and endorsed by the Constitutional Court ...: 'wherever the provisions of a directive appear, as far as their subject matter is concerned, to be unconditional and sufficiently precise, those provisions may be relied upon by an individual against the State where that State fails to implement the directive in national law by the end of the period prescribed or where it fails to implement the directive correctly' ...

However, this direct effect of an unimplemented directive only recognizes individual rights against the (defaulting) State and in relation to other public authorities (so-called vertical effects), but is not capable of creating legal situations unfavourable towards individuals, decreasing the rights or increasing duties or otherwise imposing obligations (inadmissibility of horizontal effects) ...

Therefore with regard to this case, where the relations between individuals are at issue, the failure to implement the Directive at the time of termination of the employment relationship does not allow the recognition of an immediate and direct effect of the Directive's provisions, even if unconditional and precise, but for the State's liability to pay damages for the failure to implement the Directive ...

---

[25] Italian Court of Cassation, Labour Division 5 April 1995 no 3974, *Rivista giuridica lavoro* 1995, II 706. *Foro italiano* 1997, I, 3663.

Notes:

(1) Pursuant to Article 3(1) of Council Directive 77/187/EEC[26] on the approximation of the laws of the Member States relating to the safeguarding of employees' rights in the event of transfers of undertakings, the transferor's rights and obligations arising from a contract of employment or from an employment relationship existing on the date of a transfer shall, by reason of such transfer, be transferred to the transferee. Member States may provide that the transferor shall continue to be liable, in addition to the transferee, in respect of the obligations arising from the employment contract. Italy did not implement the Directive in time.

(2) As that provision of the Directive is not directly effective in a horizontal relationship, the employee could not rely on its protection and the Italian courts had to apply the old Article 2112 of the Italian Code Code (*Codice Civile*). Pursuant to that Article, when an undertaking is transferred, the employment contract with the transferee continues if the transferor does not terminate the contract in a timely fashion. The employee retains all rights acquired for the period preceding the transfer. Pursuant to that version, there is no joint liability between the transferor and the transferee towards the employee. Article 2112 currently adds that the transferor and the transferee are jointly liable for all rights which the employee had at the time of the transfer of the undertaking.

(3) Unable to rely on the unimplemented provision of the Directive, the employee's only possibility is to claim damages from the Italian state for not implementing the Directive in time.

II.C BROAD INTERPRETATION OF THE CONCEPT OF 'STATE'

II.C.i SOURCES: CJ CASE LAW

This strict approach of the CJ in denying directive provisions direct horizontal effect is somewhat nuanced by a broad interpretation of the term 'Member State'. In *Marshall I*, the CJ ruled that the capacity in which the state is acting is irrelevant. It held that 'where a person involved in legal proceedings is able to rely on a directive as against the State he may do so regardless of the capacity in which the latter is acting, whether as employer or public authority'.[27] The argument on which the CJ based this decision is that 'a Member State which has not adopted the implementing measures required by the directive within the prescribed period may not plead, as against individuals, its own failure to perform the obligations which the directive entails'. The case also demonstrates that the concept of public authorities is not limited to central authorities, but inter alia embraces an Area Health Authority as well. In *Foster*, the CJ clarified its broad interpretation of 'Member State'. According to the CJ, 'a body, whatever its legal form, which has been made

---

[26] Council Directive 77/187/EEC of 14 February 1977 on the approximation of the laws of the Member States relating to the safeguarding of employees' rights in the event of transfers of undertakings, businesses or parts of businesses [1977] OJ L61/26.

[27] CJ *Marshall I* (n 14) para 49.

responsible, pursuant to a measure adopted by the State, for providing a public service under the control of the State and has for that purpose special powers beyond those which result from the normal rules applicable in relations between individuals is included in any event among the bodies against which the provisions of a directive capable of having direct effect may be relied upon'.[28] This line of cases confirms that an individual may rely against a government body on rights derived from a directive regardless of: (a) the capacity of the body concerned; or (b) whether that body was entrusted with the implementation of the directive in national law.[29] The broad interpretation of 'Member State' has been criticised in legal doctrine because a body that might be connected with the state is held responsible for a failing of the state itself, even where it had no control over the relevant event. This seems to undermine the very rationale for allowing only the vertical (and not the horizontal) effect of provisions of directives.[30]

II.C.ii NATIONAL CASE LAW

Corte di Cassazione (Italian Court of Cassation),
23 January 2002[31]   **6.4 (IT)**

Assitalia v Bartoloni

NATIONAL JUDGE MUST ASSESS WHETHER *FOSTER* CRITERIA
ARE MET BEFORE DIRECTLY APPLYING DIRECTIVE PROVISIONS

Accidents may happen

A national judge may only directly apply the provisions of a directive after assessing whether the criteria established by the CJ in Foster are met

Facts: A victim brought an action against an insurance company claiming compensation for damage suffered after having been hit by an unidentified vehicle. The victim invoked Directive 84/5/EEC, which obliges Member States to set up or authorise a body which provides compensation for damage caused by unidentified vehicles. The first instance judge and the Court of Appeal awarded damages. The insurance company brought the case before the Court of Cassation.

Held: The decision of the Court of Appeal was quashed because Directive 84/5/EEC was applied without ascertaining whether the necessary requirements were met and, in particular, whether the relationship under consideration could be considered as vertical according to the criteria laid down by the Court of Justice in *Foster*. The case was referred to another division of the Court of Appeal that had to carry out the verification.

Judgment: Moreover, the Court of Justice stated that 'Unconditional and sufficiently precise provisions of a directive can be relied on against organizations or bodies which are

---

[28] CJ 12 July 1990 Case C-188/89 *A. Foster et al v British Gas plc* [1990] I-03313 ECLI:EU:C:1990:313, para 20.
[29] See Craig and De Búrca 2015 206–209; Hartley 2010 231; Dashwood/Dougan/Rodger/Spaventa/Wyatt 2011 262–63; Lenaerts and Van Nuffel 2011 para 22-083.
[30] Craig and De Búrca 2015 208; Dashwood/Dougan/Rodger/Spaventa/Wyatt 2011 263.
[31] Cass it 23 January 2002 no 752 *Responsabilità civile e previdenza* 2002 738 note Caranta.

subject to the authority or control of the State or have special powers beyond those which result from the normal rules applicable to relations between individuals. In any case, those provisions may be relied upon against a body, whatever its legal form, which has been made responsible, pursuant to a measure adopted by the State, for providing a public service under the control of the State and has for that purpose special powers beyond those which result from the normal rules applicable in relations between individuals' ... The FGVS, a body without legal personality, established to meet the social interest of not leaving victims of road accidents without compensation, should be held to fall within the above mentioned categories.

The indices that are relevant in this regard are that, under Article. 20 L. 990-1969 in its current formulation, the fund is managed under the control of the Ministry of Industry, Commerce and Handicrafts and Consap, and that under Article 31 of the same law it is financed by contributions authoritatively imposed on the companies authorized to provide insurance for civil liability for damage caused by auto vehicles.

Therefore, the national court is bound to apply the Directive 84/5/EEC, which set the maximum insurance, in relations between the FGVS and individuals, and to disapply conflicting national provisions, once it has verified the existence of the conditions required for this purpose.

In the present case the contested judgment 'purely and simply' applied the Directive without ascertaining whether those conditions were met. Therefore, the judgment should be repealed and the case should be referred to a court in another division of the Court of Appeal of Rome.

The national court must carry out the omitted verification, and—if the outcome is positive—apply the directive to the relationship between the designated company and the victim of the accident, and rule on the costs of the Cassation proceedings.

Notes:

(1) This case relates to the implementation of Directive 84/5/EEC[32] on the approximation of the laws of the Member States relating to insurance against civil liability in respect of the use of motor vehicles. Pursuant to Article 1(4) of this Directive, Member States must set up or authorise a body with the task of providing compensation, at least up to the limits of the insurance obligation for damage to property or personal injuries caused by an unidentified vehicle. A victim of an accident sought to directly invoke that provision.

(2) The question arose whether the *Fondo di Garanzia per le Vittime della Strada* (FGVS), set up, inter alia, to provide compensation for victims where the damage has been caused by an unidentified vehicle, could be considered to be a government body as referred to in the *Foster* decision. The Court of Cassation quashed the decision of the Court of Appeal because it had implemented the provisions of the directive directly without assessing whether the criteria laid down in the *Foster* decision were met.

---

[32] Second Council Directive 84/5/EEC of 30 December 1983 on the approximation of the laws of the Member States relating to insurance against civil liability in respect of the use of motor vehicles [1984] OJ L008/17.

Sąd Najwyższy (Polish Supreme Court),
of 13 March 2008[33]   **6.5 (PL)**

Wojciech v Samodzielny Publiczny Zaklad Opieki Zdrowotnej Wojewódzkiego

BROAD INTERPRETATION OF 'MEMBER STATE'

Calculation of working time

An employee can directly invoke provisions of a directive which are unconditional and sufficiently precise against his employer which is a private limited liability company and whose sole shareholder is an inter-municipal public law association dedicated to social welfare issues

Facts: An employee brought an action against his employer, the Independent Public Health Care Unit, in order to obtain back payments for overtime work and an allowance for on-call duty time, during which he had to be present at the hospital. He argued that his on-call duty time should be considered as overtime work.

Held: National legislation according to which the time of medical on-call duty is not included in working time is not in conformity with the interpretation of the concept of working time as established in the case law of the CJ. The employee could directly invoke Directive 93/104/EC[34] against the employer whose sole shareholder was an inter-municipal public law association.

Judgment: Article 32j(2) of the Act on Health Care Units, according to which the time of medical on-call duty is not included in working time, is clearly inconsistent with the interpretation of the concept of 'working time' established in the case law of the Court relating to Directive 93/104 which was mentioned above. The inclusion in working time of the whole time spent on medical on-call duty at the working place is a consequence of the direct effect of a directive in relations between an individual and the State, applying the broad interpretation of the concept of 'State' established in the case law of the Court with respect to the direct effect of a directive. There is no doubt that the provisions of the directive concerning minimum rest periods are unconditional and sufficiently precise, therefore they may be applied directly. With regard to the concept of 'State', the case law of the Court considers this term to include organizational entities subordinated to or controlled by public authorities, even if they have a separate legal personality ...

The failure of an employer to grant time off as specified by law undoubtedly constitutes a breach of its duties in the employment relationship. If the other conditions are met, especially if the employee has suffered damage, the employee may claim compensation pursuant to [national law on contractual liability]. At the same time, however, such unlawful behaviour of the employer ... constitutes a tort ... As a result there will be a concurrence of tortuous and contractual liability ...

Provisions of the Employment Code that introduce minimum rest periods are aimed at protecting the health of employees.

Since health is an interest enjoying general protection, causing damage to health constitutes a tort. Liability of the State for breach of [EU] law will also need to be

---

[33] Polish Supreme Court 13 March 2008 *OSNAPiUS* 2008 no 17–18 247.
[34] Council Directive 93/104/EC of 23 November 1993 concerning certain aspects of the organization of working time [1993] OJ L307/18.

considered … The mere failure to grant time off in itself does not constitute a cause of damage. Nevertheless, the claim for damages will be admissible if an employee demonstrates damage consisting in loss of pecuniary profit caused by failure to grant time off, or if the failure has caused health complaints.

Notes:

(1) This case demonstrates how the broad interpretation of the concept of 'state' can come to the aid of an individual who seeks to rely on provisions of a directive.

(2) According to Article 32j(2) of the Act on Health Care Units, the time of medical on-call duty is not included in working time. This was held to be inconsistent with the concept of working time as developed in the case law of the CJ on Directive 93/104/EC. The Polish Supreme Court ruled that the entire time of medical on-call duty should be included in the calculation of working time on the basis of the Directive having direct effect in relations between an individual and a state entity, as interpreted broadly by the CJ.

(3) The Polish Supreme Court ruled that the failure of an employer to grant time off work as specified by law constituted a breach of his duties in the employment relationship as well as a tort within the meaning of the Polish Civil Code. It allowed the application of the provisions on protection of personal interests such as health, as well as the application of Article 448 of the Civil Code, which empowers the courts to award an appropriate amount as monetary compensation for non-pecuniary damage in case of infringement of one's personal interests.

(4) An Act of 17 June 2004[35] changed the provisions on state liability in Poland. A new article of the Civil Code now regulates liability for damage caused by an act or omission of an organ of the state, a local government body or any other legal person exercising public authority.[36]

III. HARMONIOUS INTERPRETATION (INTERPRETATION IN CONFORMITY WITH A DIRECTIVE) IMPOSED BY EU LAW

III.A SOURCES

III.A.i CJ CASE LAW

The most important way to ensure the effectiveness of directives in spite of the refusal to accord them horizontal direct effect as explained in the previous section, has been the development by the CJ of the principle of harmonious interpretation. According to this

---

[35] DzU no 162 item 1692.

[36] See more on this provision in the judgment of the Court of Appeal Warsaw of 9 November 2011 cited below in section VI.B.ii.

principle, national courts are under an obligation to use the methods of interpretation available to them under national law to interpret national law as much as possible in conformity with a directive.[37]

The principle of harmonious interpretation was established in *Von Colson and Kamann*, where the CJ held that 'in applying the national law … national courts are required to interpret their national law in the light of the wording and the purpose of the directive'.[38] This is necessary in order to achieve the result referred to in Article 288(3) TFEU.[39] In *Pfeiffer*, the CJ added that this requirement 'is inherent in the system of the Treaty'.[40]

The requirement to interpret national law in conformity with a directive is not dependent on whether its provisions have direct effect. Harmonious interpretation has thus 'been imposed in particular where a provision of a directive lacks direct effect, be it that the relevant provision is not sufficiently clear, precise and unconditional to produce direct effect or that the dispute is exclusively between individuals'.[41] The requirement of harmonious interpretation is not dependent on the identity or capacity of the parties to the relevant proceedings.[42] It can be invoked in a vertical relationship where individuals are seeking to enforce their EU law rights against the public authorities of a Member State (*Von Colson and Kamann*). Conversely, the requirement equally applies where a Member State tries to enforce EU law obligations against an individual (*Kofoed*).[43] Moreover, the CJ has confirmed that the duty of harmonious interpretation exists in horizontal situations as well (*Marleasing*). As a result, such interpretation may result in an individual being ordered by the court to comply with certain obligations under national law or in the individual being precluded from effectuating claims against another individual.[44] In such cases, the issue of a non-implemented directive imposing obligations on individuals does not arise, since any obligation falling on individuals would be based on the relevant provision of national law.[45]

The obligation of a national court to interpret its domestic law harmoniously is, however, subject to important limitations. This doctrine is limited by general principles of law, such as those of legal certainty and non-retroactivity. Moreover, national courts are not required to resort to a *contra legem* interpretation of their domestic law. These limitations are discussed in depth in section III.C. below.

---

[37] Craig and De Búrca 2015 209; Prechal 2005 180–81; Dashwood/Dougan/Rodger/Spaventa/Wyatt 2011 239.

[38] CJ 10 April 1984 Case C-14/83 *Sabine von Colson and Elisabeth Kamann v Land Nordrhein-Westfalen* [1984] I-01891 ECLI:EU:C:1984:153, para 26.

[39] See ibid, para 27.

[40] CJ 5 October 2004 Joined Cases C-397/01–C-403/01 *Pfeiffer et al v Deutsches Rotes Kreuz* [2004] I-08835 ECLI:EU:C:2004:584, para 114.

[41] CJ 4 July 2006 Case C-212/04 *Konstantinos Adeneler et al v Ellinikos Organismos Galaktos (ELOG)* [2006] I-06057 ECLI:EU:C:2006:443, para 113.

[42] Dashwood/Dougan/Rodger/Spaventa/Wyatt 2011 240.

[43] CJ 5 July 2007 Case C-321/05 *Hans Markus Kofoed v Skatteministeriet* [2007] I-05795 ECLI:EU:C:2007:408, para 45.

[44] CJ 13 November 1990 Case C-106/89 *Marleasing SA v La Comercial Internacional de Alimentacion SA* [1990] I-04135 ECLI:EU:C:1990:395, paras 6–9. See Craig and De Búrca 2015 211–12; Lenaerts and Van Nuffel 2011, para 22-089.

[45] CJ *Kofoed* (n 43) para 45.

III.A.ii NATIONAL CASE LAW

Arbeitsgericht Hamm (Employment Tribunal Hamm),
6 September 1984[46]   **6.6 (GERM)**

Von Colson and Kamann v Land Nordrhein-Westfalen

HARMONIOUS INTERPRETATION

Von Colson and Kamann

The interpretation in conformity with EU law trumps the principles of systematic and historical interpretation

Facts: Two women applied for a job at a prison. Their applications were rejected and two male candidates were appointed. The two women sought a declaration that they had not been appointed solely because of their sex. They claimed that they should be offered an employment contract or should be paid damages amounting to six months' salary. In such cases, however, German law only provided for compensation for 'Vertrauensschaden', expenses incurred by the would-be employee as a result of his or her reliance on the fact he or she would not be refused a post due to a breach of the prohibition of discrimination. German law expressly did not allow compensation of the positive interest.

Held: In a preliminary ruling requested by the Employment Tribunal Hamm, the CJ held that although Directive No 76/207/EEC, with regard to imposing a sanction for a breach of the prohibition of discrimination, leaves the Member States free to choose between the different solutions suitable for achieving its objective, it nevertheless requires that if a Member State chooses to penalise breaches of that prohibition by the award of compensation, then in order to ensure that it is effective and that it has a deterrent effect, that compensation must in any event be adequate in relation to the damage sustained. It must therefore amount to more than purely nominal compensation, for example, the reimbursement of only the expenses incurred in connection with the application. It is for the national court to interpret and apply the legislation adopted for the implementation of the directive in conformity with the requirements of EU law, insofar as it is given discretion to do so under national law. The Employment Tribunal Hamm accordingly awarded damages for the positive interest.

Judgment: This decision [CJ C-14/83 *Von Colson and Kamann*] has made it possible to award the claimants compensation that is adequate in relation to the damage sustained and which at the same time has a deterrent effect to avoid further discriminations, as required by the CJ, if a State has chosen compensation as the sanction for a breach of Directive 76/207, as is the case in §611a BGB. The CJ has created this possibility by deciding—apparently for the first time—that 'it is for the national court to interpret and apply the legislation adopted for the implementation of the directive in conformity with the requirements of [EU] law, in so far as it is given discretion to do so under national law' (No. 3 of the operative part of the judgment). The CJ thereby evidently followed the opinion of the German Government, that §611a BGB does not exclude the application of §823 BGB …

The German Constitutional Court has always recognized the duty and the authority of the courts to further develop the law ('*Rechtsfortbildung*'). This authority is however exceeded when the creative judicial construction is contrary to the wording, the sense and the legislative aim … The court would have exceeded this framework in the present case

---

[46] Employment Tribunal Hamm 6 September 1984 *ZIP* 1984,1525 *Von Colson and Kamann v Land Nordrhein-Westfalen.*

if it had adopted the position defended by the German Government before the CJ. This is so because in cases of discrimination the second paragraph of §611a BGB only provides for compensation for *Vertrauensschaden*, and because according to the intention of the legislature and the general rules of systematic interpretation, these provisions exclude the application of §823 BGB. Harmonious interpretation, which is required by the CJ, trumps the principles of systematic and historical interpretation and finds its limits only in the wording of the legal provision ... This has the result that the second paragraph of §611a BGB, interpreted in the light of the decision of the CJ, regulates only one specific case of compensation, without excluding the application of the more far-reaching provisions of §823 BGB.

Notes:

(1) This national case gave rise to the *Von Colson and Kamann* decision of the CJ in which the principle of harmonious interpretation was established. The CJ held that 'the Member States' obligation arising from a directive to achieve the result envisaged by the directive and their duty under [now Article 4(3) TEU] to take all appropriate measures, whether general or particular, to ensure the fulfilment of that obligation, is binding on all the authorities of Member States including, for matters within their jurisdiction, the courts'. As a result, 'in applying the national law and in particular the provisions of a national law specifically introduced in order to implement [the directive], national courts are required to interpret their national law in the light of the wording and the purpose of the directive in order to achieve the result referred to in the third paragraph of [now Article 288 TFEU]'.[47] The Employment Tribunal of Hamm interpreted §611a(2) BGB in conformity with Directive 76/207/EEC.[48] It was held not to exclude recourse to the more general provisions for damages such as §823 BGB. The CJ had stressed in its decision that 'in order to ensure that it is effective and that is has a deterrent effect, that compensation must in any event be adequate in relation to the damage sustained and must therefore amount to more than purely nominal compensation'.[49]

(2) The judgment illustrates the reaction of a national court which is confronted with a novel principle of EU law. The court underlines that the judicial development (interpretation of §611a(2) BGB) goes further than what would be allowed in a purely national situation. The interpretation of that paragraph by the court would be a judicial development which runs contrary to the principles of German constitutional law, if this were a purely internal case. However, the requirement of an interpretation which is in conformity with EU law and the directive trumps the ordinary principles of systematic and historical interpretation.[50] According to the court, judicial development in conformity with a directive is only limited by the wording of the law.

---

[47] CJ *Von Colson and Kamann* (n 38) para 27.
[48] Council Directive 76/207/EEC of 9 February 1976 on the implementation of the principle of equal treatment for men and women as regards access to employment, vocational training and promotion and working conditions [1976] OJ L39/40.
[49] CJ *Von Colson and Kamann* (n 38) para 28.
[50] Prechal 2005 195.

III.B DUTY OF INTERPRETATION AND SCOPE

III.B.i SOURCES: CJ CASE LAW

After a period of uncertainty, the CJ established that the general obligation of harmonious interpretation of a directive only arises once the period for its transposition has expired. Before that date, however, national courts are nonetheless under an obligation to refrain as far as possible from interpreting national law in a manner which might seriously compromise the attainment of the objective pursued by the directive after the period for transposition has expired.[51]

It is now well established that once the time limit for implementation has expired, it is obligatory for the national courts to interpret the whole corpus of national law as far as possible in conformity with the directive.[52] This includes judge-made law, private law agreements which implement a directive and collective agreements.[53] In *Von Colson and Kamann*, the CJ had held that this duty of harmonious interpretation related to the interpretation of legislation adopted for the implementation of the directive.[54] Subsequently, the CJ in *Marleasing* further expanded the scope of the duty of harmonious interpretation to include national legislation irrespective of 'whether the provisions in question were adopted before or after the directive'.[55] In *Pfeiffer*, the CJ clarified that while it is true that this duty chiefly concerns provisions which are enacted to implement a directive, it furthermore requires a national court to consider national law as a whole. Therefore, a national court must 'consider national law as a whole in order to assess to what extent it may be applied so as not to produce a result contrary to that sought by the directive'.[56]

There has been discussion on how far national courts have to go in interpreting the otherwise clear provisions of national law in order to comply with a directive. The Treaty obligation on national courts to take all measures possible to comply with EU law limits the interpretative discretion that national courts would otherwise have under national law.[57] In *Pfeiffer*, the CJ stressed the strength of this obligation and ruled that 'the principle of interpretation in conformity with Union law thus requires the referring court to do whatever lies within its jurisdiction, having regard to the whole body of rules of national law'.[58] In *Marleasing*, the CJ already held very firmly that a national court must interpret national law 'as far as possible' in conformity with a directive.[59] The limits on this duty will be discussed in section III.C below.

---

[51] CJ *Adeneler* (n 41) para 123. For more details, see C Hofmann, '§16 Die Vorwirkung von Richtlinien' in M Gebauer and T Wiedmann (eds), *Zivilrecht under europäischem Einfluss* (Stuttgart, Richard Boorberg, 2010) 366–87; M Klamert, 'Judicial Implementation of Directives and Anticipatory Indirect Effect: Connecting the Dots' (2006) 43(5) *CMLR* 1251.

[52] Craig and De Búrca 2015 212–13; Gebauer 2010 122–23; Lenaerts and Van Nuffel 2011 para 22-087; Prechal 2005 184–87; Roth 2010 315.

[53] S Prechal, 'Joined Cases C-397/01–C-403/01, *Bernhard Pfeiffer et al*' (2005) 42(5) *CMLR* 1445, 1460.

[54] CJ *Von Colson and Kamann* (n 38) para 28.

[55] CJ *Marleasing* (n 44) para 8.

[56] CJ *Pfeiffer* (n 40) para 115.

[57] Craig and De Búrca 2015 213.

[58] CJ *Pfeiffer* (n 40) para 118.

[59] CJ *Marleasing* (n 44) para 8.

III.B.ii NATIONAL CASE LAW

Cour d'Appel Mons (Court of Appeal Mons),
30 May 2005[60]   **6.7 (BE)**

P v SPRL Garage B

INTERPRETATION OF BELGIAN SALES LAW IN CONFORMITY WITH
THE CONSUMER SALES DIRECTIVE: ACTION TO BE BROUGHT
WITHIN SHORT PERIOD OF TIME

You can't drive my car

*As the Belgian legislature belatedly implemented Directive 1999/44/EC, national courts
must interpret national sales law in conformity with that Directive, so that the short period
referred to in the Belgian Civil Code cannot be shorter than two years, the period referred
to in the Directive*

Facts: On 26 March 2002, a consumer bought a second-hand van from a professional seller. A few months
later, the consumer sought to rescind the contract and argued that the price was much higher than the real value
of the van and that the car presented many (hidden) defects. The question arose as to whether the consumer had
brought his action against the seller within a short period of time as required by Article 1648 of the Belgian
Civil Code.

Held: The consumer had brought his action in a timely manner, as the 'short period' was to be interpreted in
conformity with Article 5(2) of Directive 1999/44/EC.

Judgment: He has asked the court to find that his action was brought within a short
period and that this period cannot be inferior to two years from the time of delivery, in
conformity with Article 5 of the Directive 1999/44/EC of the European Parliament and of
the Council of 25 May 1999 on certain aspects of the sale of consumer goods and associated guarantees.

He has argued with pertinence that it should have been implemented into national law
not later than 1 January 2002 and that, notwithstanding that it was only implemented by
an Act of 1 September 2004, all authorities of the Member States, including the courts,
must interpret national law in the light of the wording and the purpose of the directive
in order to achieve the result pursued by the latter and thereby comply with the third
paragraph of [now Article 288(3) TFEU] …

In effect, the court must apply national law, Article 1648 of the Civil Code in particular, in the light of the wording and the purpose of the directive, which should have been
implemented in Belgian law at the moment the contract was concluded …

Even when its starting point and its duration are not determined by law, the starting
point and the duration of this period are discretionarily assessed by the court, taking into

---

[60] Court of Appeal Mons 30 May 2005 *JLMB* 2005, 1473 *v SPRL Garage B.*

account all the circumstances of the case, the short period imposed by Article 1648 of the Civil Code for the buyer to introduce his action on the merits must be considered to be a limitation period.

Pursuant to Article 5(1) second section and recital 17 of the preamble to the Directive, this period cannot be shorter than two years from the time of delivery.

Under these circumstances, the action must be considered to have been brought within a short period.

Cour d'Appel Liège (Court of Appeal Liège),
10 October 2007[61]   **6.8 (BE)**

Brun et al v Bose automobiles sa

INTERPRETATION OF BELGIAN SALES LAW IN CONFORMITY
WITH THE CONSUMER SALES DIRECTIVE: PRESENCE OF HIDDEN
DEFECT AT THE TIME OF TRANSFER OF OWNERSHIP AND RISKS

Pouring oil on troubled waters

As the Belgian legislature belatedly implemented Directive 1999/44/EC, national courts must interpret national sales law in conformity with that Directive, so that consumers can rely on the presumption established in Article 5(3) of Directive 1999/44/EC to prove, as required by Belgian law, that the hidden defect was present at the time of the transfer of ownership and risks

Facts: On 6 August 2003, a consumer bought a car that apparently had a hidden defect: it used an excessive amount of oil. Therefore, the consumer sought to rescind the contract. In order for his claim to be successful, he had to prove that the hidden defect was already present at the moment of the transfer of ownership and risks (requirement of anteriority).

Held: The requirement of anteriority was satisfied, as it was interpreted in the light of the presumption established in Article 5(3) of Directive 1999/44/EC, according to which any lack of conformity which becomes apparent within six months of delivery shall be presumed to have existed at the time of delivery.

Judgment: For a successful claim under the guarantee for hidden defects, the buyer is required pursuant to the general sales law to prove that the defect existed at the moment of transfer of ownership and risks.

In determining whether the condition of anteriority is satisfied, the court seized of a case relating to a contract concluded on 6 August 2003, must, in line with the principle of harmonious interpretation, apply Article 5(3) of the directive.

Consequently, whenever, as in the present case, it is not contested that the buyer informed the seller of the defects in the vehicle within the period of six months, the hidden defects ... must, without proof to the contrary, be presumed to have existed at the time of delivery of the vehicle.

---

[61] Court of Appeal Liège 10 October 2007 *JT* 2008 177 annotated by Glansdorff *Brun et al v Bose automobiles sa.*

Hof van Beroep Antwerpen (Court of Appeal Antwerp),
1 March 2010[62]   **6.9 (BE)**

NV J v RR and GB

INTERPRETATION OF BELGIAN SALES LAW IN CONFORMITY WITH THE CONSUMER SALES
DIRECTIVE: ACTION BROUGHT WITHIN A SHORT PERIOD OF TIME AND THE PRESENCE OF
HIDDEN DEFECT AT THE TIME OF TRANSFER OF OWNERSHIP AND RISKS

Faulty reparation

*As the Belgian legislature belatedly implemented Directive 1999/44/EC, national courts
must interpret national sales law in conformity with that Directive, so that the short period
referred to in Article 1648 of the Belgian Civil Code cannot be shorter than two years, the
period referred to in Article 5(1) of Directive 1999/44/EC, and the consumer can rely on
the presumption established in Article 5(3) of the Directive to prove, as required by Belgian
law, that the hidden defect was present at the time of the transfer of ownership and risks*

Facts: On 6 September 2004, a consumer bought a second-hand car from a professional seller. Directly after
the sale, the car showed deficiencies which were not satisfactorily repaired by the seller. Therefore, the consumer sought to obtain €6,000 in damages. Two questions arose: (a) whether the consumer had brought his
action against the seller within a short period of time as required by Article 1648 of the Belgian Civil Code;
and (b) whether the hidden defect was already present at the time of the transfer of ownership and risks
(requirement of anteriority).

Held: The consumer brought his action in a timely manner since the 'short period' was interpreted in conformity with Article 5(2) of Directive 1999/44/EC, and the requirement of anteriority was satisfied since it was
interpreted in the light of the presumption established in Article 5(3) of Directive 1999/44/EC, which provides
that any lack of conformity that becomes apparent within six months of delivery shall be presumed to have
existed at the time of delivery.

Judgment: The appellant alleges that the short period was exceeded in this case, so that
the action of the respondents must be declared inadmissible on those grounds ...

When a Member State fails to implement a directive into national law, an individual
cannot directly invoke the provisions of the directive against another individual. However,
once the implementation period has expired, the national courts must interpret national
law in conformity with the directive and must as far as possible interpret the national law
to be applied by the court in the light of the substance of the directive and the purpose
pursued by it.

Since the implementation period for the Consumer Sales Directive into Belgian law had
indeed expired when the sales contract was concluded, the court must take the provisions
of the directive into account when assessing the short period of Article 1648 of the Civil
Code, and must assess the issue in its light. With respect to the limitation period, the Consumer Sales Directive provides that if national legislation provides for a limitation period
regarding the relevant rights of consumers, this period cannot expire within a period
of two years from the time of delivery (art. 5(1) second sentence). The 'short period' of
Article 1648 of the Civil Code must be considered as a limitation period, since the buyer is
obliged to bring his claim before the expiration of that period. Harmonious interpretation

---

[62] Court of Appeal Antwerp 1 March 2010 *Limburgs Rechtsleven* 2010, 202 annotated by Ponet *NV J
v RR and GB.*

of Article 1648 of the Civil Code leads to the conclusion that the short period of Article 1648 of the Civil Code may in any case not be shorter than two years from the delivery of the goods …

From the foregoing, the court can with certainty establish that the grave defects, including the defect of the gearbox, became apparent within six months of delivery of the vehicle … Based on this fact the court establishes the presumption that the defects to the vehicle existed at the time of delivery.

In this connection the court refers to Article 1649*quater*, §4 of the Civil Code, which introduces a legal presumption of anteriority when the lack of conformity becomes apparent within six months of delivery.

The appellant rightly argues that this provision, which was introduced by the implementation of the Consumer Sales Directive into Belgian law, is only applicable to sales contracts concluded after 1 January 2005. The late implementation of said directive into Belgian law once again compels the court to use harmonious interpretation with respect to this issue and justifies the presumption of anteriority with regard to defects becoming apparent within six months of delivery of the vehicle.

Notes:

(1) Article 11 of Directive 1999/44/EC provides that Member States must implement the Directive into national law not later than 1 January 2002. The Belgian legislature implemented the Directive with effect from 1 January 2005.[63]

(2) Amongst other things, the Directive sets several time limits. Article 5(1) provides that the seller is liable where the lack of conformity becomes apparent within two years as from delivery of the goods and that a national limitation period may not expire within a period of two years from the time of delivery. Moreover, Article 5(3) establishes a rebuttable presumption that any lack of conformity which becomes apparent within six months of delivery of the goods shall be presumed to have existed at the time of delivery unless this presumption is incompatible with the nature of the goods or the nature of the lack of conformity. This protection was not afforded under national general sales law.

(3) The three cases above show how the Belgian courts awarded protection to consumers by resorting to the technique of harmonious interpretation. The three Courts of Appeal interpreted national general sales law in the light of the Directive.

(4) The first issue, discussed by the Courts of Appeal of Mons and Antwerp, is whether the consumer/buyer brought his action against the professional seller in time. Article 1648 of the Belgian Civil Code provides that actions for hidden defects by a buyer against a seller must be brought within a short period (*bref délai/korte termijn*). It is for the court to determine the starting point and the duration of this period, taking into account all the circumstances of the case, such as the nature of the good sold, the nature of the defects, customary practice and the capacity of the parties. In both cases, the seller argued that the action of the consumer was not brought within this short period. However, the Courts of Appeal ruled that the short period referred to in Article 1648 of the Belgian Civil Code is a limitation period that cannot expire within a period of two years from the time of delivery. Both courts came to this conclusion by interpreting the open norm of

---

[63] Belgian Official Gazette 21 September 2004 no 138 6834-68388.

'short period' in the light of Article 5(1) of the Directive. It is doubtful whether a purely domestic interpretation would have led to the same result.

(5) The second issue, discussed by the Courts of Appeal of Liège and Antwerp, was whether the requirement of anteriority was satisfied. Under Belgian law, the buyer who brings an action against the seller must provide evidence that the hidden defect was present at the moment of the transfer of ownership and risks. This proof may be provided by all legal means. The Court of Appeal of Liège ruled that it had to interpret Belgian general sales law in conformity with Article 5(3) of the Directive to determine whether the requirement of anteriority was fulfilled. It held that the defects became apparent within the six-month period and that the consumer could rely on the presumption established by Article 5(3). It seems that the Court of Appeal went further than mere harmonious interpretation and actually stretched the national law too far. It seems to have given direct effect to the Directive by reversing the burden of proof to the detriment of the professional seller. The same can be said of the judgment of the Court of Appeal of Antwerp. It even referred first to the provision which implements Article 5(3) of the Directive (Article 1649*quater*, §4 of the Belgian Civil Code) and only then to the Directive in general without mentioning its Article 5(3). This could lead one to conclude that both judgments directly applied Article 5(3) of the Directive (or its implementation) rather than interpreting Belgian law in conformity with that provision.

(6) One could even argue that the interpretation of the Courts of Appeal of Liège and Antwerp amounts to interpretation *contra legem* of Article 870 of the Belgian Judicial Code which states that every party must produce proof of the facts it alleges. However, the decisions might be justified as a harmonious interpretation of the Article of the Belgian Civil Code which states that a court can accept presumptive evidence. It becomes clear that the duty of harmonious interpretation obliges national courts to interpret their national law as whole in conformity with a directive.

(7) In France, an Ordinance of 17 February 2005 changed the flexible 'short period' in Article 1648 of the French Civil Code into a fixed period of two years.

Hoge Raad der Nederlanden (Supreme Court of the Netherlands),
29 December 1995[64]   **6.10 (NL)**

Buyck v Van den Ameele BV

HARMONIOUS INTERPRETATION OF GROUNDS OF ANNULLABILITY

Late Christmas present

An employee is not required to invoke the annullability of the termination in time since, pursuant to harmonious interpretation, she remains employed

Facts: An employee was dismissed without the required dismissal permit just before the company that employed her was transferred to another company. More than six months later, she claimed a salary from that

---

[64] Supreme Court of the Netherlands 29 December 1995 *NJ* 1996, 418 annotated by PA Stein ECLI:NL:HR1995ZC1943 *Buyck v Van den Ameele BV.*

other company, as she considered herself employed by it pursuant to Directive 77/187/EEC.[65] The question arose whether she had pleaded a ground of annullability of her dismissal.

Held: The Supreme Court of the Netherlands ignored the issues of invoking annullability and the limitation limit by means of harmonious interpretation of the relevant article. It held that the provision on annullability did not apply where a transfer of a company falls under Directive 77/187/EEC, Article 4(1) of which provides that such a transfer does not constitute a ground for dismissal. The employee was therefore considered to be still employed despite the (intended) dismissal, because the dismissal was null.

Judgment: 3.4 … With regard to this provision [Article 9(2) of the Extraordinary Labour Relations Decree], the question arises whether it is applicable in a case where the employment is terminated due to the company being transferred and because of the fact that it is transferred to another company which is not willing or not able to continue the employment. This question must be answered in the negative. Pursuant to Article 4(1) of Directive 77/187/EEC on the approximation of the laws of the Member States relating to the safeguarding of employees' rights, in the event of transfers of undertakings, businesses or parts of businesses, the transfer of a company is not a valid ground for termination. It follows from the CJ decision of 15 June 1998 [C-101/87 *Bork*] that this means that the employee must be regarded as still employed by the undertaking on the date of the transfer, notwithstanding the termination. It is clear that this entails that no further action is required, such as invoking the annullabillity of the termination. As the intention of Dutch legislation on this subject is to implement the framework of the directive into Dutch law, it must be assumed that Article 9(2) of the Extraordinary Labour Relations Decree does not rule out that the annullability of the termination of an employment relationship due to the undertaking being transferred does not have to be invoked to have effect, so that the limitation period mentioned above does not come into play.

Notes:

(1) When it interprets national measures implementing Directive 77/187/EEC,[66] the Supreme Court of the Netherlands attaches great value to the intention of the legislature to give full effect to the system set up by this Directive.[67]

(2) Moreover, the judgment shows how harmonious interpretation can serve as a technique to support a restrictive interpretation of the scope of national law. According to Dutch law, the interested party has to invoke the national statutory provision within six months in order to annul the termination. The expiry of this period cannot be raised by the court of its own motion. However, by means of a restrictive interpretation of this statutory provision (or rather a generous interpretation of Directive 77/187/EEC), it was held to be inapplicable, and therefore the dismissal was not annullable, but null and void. Accordingly, there was no time limit during which the employee should have raised the invalidity of the termination. As opposed to annullability, which the interested party must invoke to have effect, nullity has the automatic effect that an act is null and void.

---

[65] Council Directive 77/187/EEC (n 26).
[66] [1977] OJ L61/26 (see n 26).
[67] Hartkamp 2016 no 185.

Hoge Raad der Nederlanden (Supreme Court of the Netherlands),
13 September 1991[68]   **6.11 (NL)**

Dekker v Stichting Vormingscentrum voor Jong Volwassenen Plus

DISAPPLICATION OF FAULT REQUIREMENT

Disadvantages of being pregnant

Any breach of the prohibition of discrimination suffices to incur liability, without the possibility to rely on domestic law justifications

Facts: Dekker applied for a job, but she was refused by VJV because of her pregnancy, as VJV feared that it would not be able to bear the financial consequences of the pregnancy. Dekker claimed damages. The question arose whether VJV was at fault and, if so, whether it could rely on any ground of justification.

Held: The refusal to enter into an employment agreement because of her pregnancy constituted an infringement of the principle of equal treatment. Every infringement of the prohibition of discrimination sufficed to incur full liability. It was not possible to rely on any ground of justification.

Judgment: It follows from the judgment of the CJ that in these circumstances VJV has acted contrary to the principle of equal treatment as established in Articles 2(1) and 3(1) of Council Directive 76/207/EEC of 9 February 1976 on the implementation of the principle of equal treatment for men and women as regards access to employment, vocational training and promotion, and working conditions.

It also follows from this judgment that any infringement of the principle of equal treatment laid down in the directive is sufficient to make the employer fully liable and that the grounds of exemption provided by Dutch law cannot be invoked.

This means that VJV has acted contrary to Article 1637ij of the Civil Code, introduced by the Act on the equal treatment of men and women, which aims to bring Dutch law into line with the directive, and that it must bear the consequences of its unlawful actions, irrespective of the question whether any fault can be attributed to it.

Notes:

(1) This decision was rendered after a preliminary ruling by the CJ. In its judgment, the CJ ruled that 'when the sanction chosen by the Member State is contained within the rules governing an employer's civil liability, any breach of the prohibition of discrimination must, in itself, be sufficient to make the employer liable, without there being any possibility' of invoking the grounds of exemption provided by national law'.[69] The CJ therefore concluded that the Directive 'requires that, where a Member State opts for a sanction forming part of the rules on civil liability, any infringement of the prohibition of discrimination suffices in itself to make the person guilty of it fully liable, and no regard may be had to the grounds of exemption envisaged by national law'.[70]

---

[68] Supreme Court of the Netherlands 13 September 1995 *NJ* 1992, 225 annotated by PA Stein ECLI:NL: HR1991ZC0328 *Dekker v Stichting Vormingscentrum voor Jong Volwassenen Plus.*
[69] CJ 8 November 1990 Case C-177/88 *Elisabeth Johanna Pacifica Dekker v Stichting Vormingscentrum voor Jong Volwassenen (VJV-Centrum) Plus* [1990] I-03941 ECLI:EU:C:1990:383, para 25.
[70] ibid, para 26.

(2) This case can be considered as a rigorous example of harmonious interpretation,[71] although some might call it a disapplication of national law that is contrary to a directive.

(3) Article 6:162 of the Dutch Civil Code requires a fault of the tortfeasor in order for him to be held liable for damages. In this case, the court of first instance accepted the justifications put forward by the defendant. In its preliminary ruling, the CJ held that any infringement of the prohibition of discrimination suffices in itself to make the person guilty of it fully liable and that the national court may have no regard to any ground of exemption envisaged by national law. This interpretation is necessary to maintain the real deterrent effect of the provisions.[72] In line with this decision, the Supreme Court of the Netherlands ruled that the grounds of exemption under Dutch law could not be relied upon.

Hoge Raad der Nederlanden (Supreme Court of the Netherlands),
13 September 2013[73]   **6.12 (NL)**

Heesakkers v Voets

HARMONIOUS INTERPRETATION LEADS TO *EX OFFICIO* APPLICATION

Renovation of Dutch case law

Interpreted in conformity with the Unfair Contract Terms Directive, a Dutch court must raise Article 6:233 of the Dutch Civil Code ex officio

Facts: A private home owner (Heesakkers) instructed a contractor, Voets, to renovate his house. The general terms and conditions provided for a monthly interest at the rate of two per cent in case of late payment. A dispute arose about part of the main sum, in which the courts (including the appeal court) adjudicated in favour of Voets. In cassation, Heesakkers complained that the appeal court had not investigated *ex officio* whether the clause about two per cent interest was binding on him.

Held: As Dutch law must be interpreted in conformity with the Unfair Contract Terms Directive,[74] Dutch courts were under an obligation to apply the assessment of Article 6:233 of the Dutch Civil Code *ex officio.*

Judgment: 3.7.1. Directive 93/13 is not directly applicable in the Dutch legal system. Harmonious interpretation of Dutch law entails, however, that the Dutch court is obliged pursuant to Article 6:233 of the Civil Code to make the assessment mentioned above of its own motion when Directive 93/13 entails this obligation.

3.7.2. In this connection, it is important that Article 6(1) of Directive 93/13 obliges Member States to find an unfair term not binding. The CJ has interpreted this provision as meaning that a national court which has established that a term in a contract between a seller and a consumer is unfair, must automatically exclude the application of that clause in its entirety with regard to the consumer (CJ 30 May 2013, C-488/11 *Asbeek Brusse en De Man Garabito*, para. 55–60).

---

[71] In that sense Hartkamp 2016 no 186.
[72] CJ *Dekker* (n 70) paras 23–26.
[73] Supreme Court of the Netherlands 13 September 2013 *NJ* 2014, 274 annotated by HB Krans ECLI:NL:HR: 2013:691 *Heesakkers v Voets.*
[74] Council Directive 93/13/EEC of 5 April 1993 on unfair terms in consumer contracts [1993] OJ L095/29.

3.7.3. For Dutch law, the foregoing means that when the court has established that a term is unfair within the meaning of Directive 93/13, it is obliged to annul that term.

Notes:

(1) Before this judgment, the Supreme Court of the Netherlands was hesitant to apply the case law of the CJ on the *ex officio* application of consumer protection rules. This aspect is discussed in detail in Chapter 7 on the *ex officio* application of EU law by national courts.

(2) The Supreme Court confirmed that the Unfair Contract Terms Directive is not directly applicable in the Dutch legal system (in horizontal situations). However, an interpretation in conformity with the Directive obliges a national court to make the assessment referred to in Article 6:233 of the Dutch Civil Code (annullability of unfair contract terms) of its own motion, where the Directive so requires.

Sąd Najwyższy (Polish Supreme Court),
19 November 2010[75]   **6.13 (PL)**

AS and SS v ASB Sp j

DAMAGES FOR NON-MATERIAL LOSS

Curse of the pharaohs

Consumers can obtain damages for non-material loss due to improper performance of a package travel contract

Facts: A couple booked a holiday in Egypt with a travel agency. The holiday did not go according to their expectations. They were accommodated in a different hotel of a lower category in a room for employees. After they had complained, they were moved to a four-person room which they had to share with another couple. It was only during the last three days of their two-week holiday that they stayed in a double room in a different hotel. The issue arose whether the couple, relying on the interpretation by the CJ of Directive 90/314/EEC[76] in *Leitner*, could claim compensation for non-material damage caused by the improper performance of the package travel contract.

Held: Although compensation for non-material damage can generally only be claimed on the basis of a statutory provision, the Polish Supreme Court allowed the claim for damages.

Judgment: The non-material nature of damage for 'ruined holidays' is beyond all doubt ... The recognition that such damage has a non-material nature leads to the problem resulting in the legal issue under consideration of what could be the basis for liability of the organizer of a package holiday. This problem occurs because the prevailing view on Polish

---

[75] Polish Supreme Court 19 November 2010 *OSNC* 2011 no 4 item 41 *AS and SS v ASB Sp j*.
[76] Council Directive 90/314 of 13 June 1990 on package travel, package holidays and package tours [1990] OJ L158/159.

contract law is that under Article 157(3) of the Rules on Contract Law,[77] compensation for non-material damage (compensation for pain and suffering) can only be claimed in the cases designated by law … When considering the legal issue, however, the Regional Court also referred to provisions concerning the provision of tourist services and looked for a possible basis for liability for non-material damage due to 'ruined holidays' in Article 11a of the Tourist Services Act of 29 August 1997 …

Axiological arguments and arguments arising from [EU] law and the case law of the Court of Justice of the European Union also militate in favour of a search for an effective legal basis for liability on such grounds … [In *Leitner*] the CJ considered that the absence of a specification in Article 5 of the Directive 90/314 of the kinds of damages to be compensated implies that the term 'damage' is to be construed broadly, which is supported by a non-normative interpretation of package contract …

Under these circumstances, in view of the ruling of the Court of Justice in [*Leitner*] that Article 5 of the Directive 90/314 is to be interpreted to mean that the term damage includes non-material damage caused by 'ruined holidays', Article 11a of the TSA, which transposes Article 5 of the directive into the Polish legal system, has to be interpreted in the same way. Such an interpretation allows for a solution under national law which is consistent with the directive.

Notes:

(1) The case turned on the interpretation of Article 11a of the Polish Tourist Services Act, which was adopted in order to implement Directive 90/314/EEC.[78] That Article provides for liability of organisers of package travel for damages caused to the consumer as a result of non-performance or improper performance of the contract. The question was whether this included compensation for non-material damage. It is important to note that the Polish Civil Code of 1964 does not provide for such compensation.

(2) In *Leitner*, the CJ was asked to interpret the Directive in a similar case and it ruled that Article 5 of the Directive is to be interpreted to mean that in principle it confers on consumers a right to compensation for non-material damage resulting from the non-performance or improper performance of the services constituting a package holiday.[79] The Supreme Court followed this reasoning, with further references to CJ case law. By interpreting the term 'damage' to mean that it includes 'non-material damage', the Supreme Court arrived at a conclusion that is consistent with the Directive.

(3) Interestingly, the Polish Supreme Court also referred to Article 9:501(2) of the Principles of European Contract Law and Article 7.4.2 of the UNIDROIT Principles of International Commercial Contracts as inspirational sources, which both include non-material loss in the damage to be compensated in case of non-performance.

---

[77] Regulation of the President of the Republic Poland of 27 October 1933 DzU no 82 item 598 with amendments. It was in force until the end of 1964.

[78] See n 77.

[79] CJ 12 March 2002 Case C-168/00 *Simone Leitner v TUI Deutschland GmbH & Co KG* [2002] I-02631 ECLI:EU:C:2002:163, para 24.

Bundesgerichtshof (Federal Supreme Court of Germany),
26 November 2008[80] **6.14 (GERM)**

Quelle AG v Bundesverband der Verbraucherzentralen und Verbraucherverbände

HARMONIOUS INTERPRETATION LEADS TO TELEOLOGICAL
REDUCTION OF NATIONAL LAW PROVISIONS

'Eigener Herd ist Goldes wert'

The principle of harmonious interpretation requires national courts to go beyond inter-pretation sensu stricto *and to develop national law in conformity with the provisions of a directive where necessary and possible*

Facts: In August 2002, Quelle delivered a 'stove-set' to a consumer for her private use. Because the appli-ance was not in conformity with the contract and its reparation was not possible, the consumer returned the appliance to Quelle, which replaced it with a new appliance. However, Quelle required the consumer to pay compensation for the benefit she had obtained from using the appliance initially delivered.

The Bundesverband, acting as the consumer's authorised representative, demanded reimbursement to her of that amount. In addition, it applied for an order prohibiting Quelle, in cases where goods not in conformity with the contract of sale ('goods lacking conformity) are replaced, from invoicing consumers for the use of those goods.

Held: The Court of First Instance granted the claim for reimbursement, but dismissed the arguments for seek-ing an order directing Quelle not to invoice customers for the use of goods lacking conformity. The appeals brought against that judgment were dismissed. The Federal Supreme Court of Germany referred a question on the interpretation of Article 3(3) and (4) of the Consumer Sales Directive to the CJ. Following the decision of the CJ,[81] the Federal Supreme Court of Germany held that the consumer was entitled to a replacement free of charge.

Judgment: 19. National courts are bound by this interpretation [by the CJ in C-404/06 *Quelle*] …

20. a) However, this duty of harmonious interpretation cannot, in the present case, take place in the way of a narrow interpretation of the law, namely judicial construction within the wording of the law … which is limited by the meaning of the words …

21. b) The principle of harmonious interpretation, which is moulded by the case-law of the CJ, requires more of the national courts than just interpretation in the narrow sense. When the CJ used the term 'interpretation', it was not referring to the distinction, com-monly made in the German legal system but not in other European legal systems, between interpretation (in a narrow sense) and judicial development. The limitation formulated by the CJ that harmonious interpretation cannot serve as a *contra legem* interpretation of national law … does not refer to the limits of the literal wording. The concept of judging *contra legem* must rather be understood functionally; it refers to the area where judicial development is inadmissible under national techniques … The principle of harmonious interpretation therefore also requires judicial development of national law where this is necessary and possible … From this follows the duty of harmonious judicial development by means of a teleological reduction of §439(4) BGB to a content that is compatible with Article 3 of the Directive.

---

[80] Federal Supreme Court of Germany 26 November 2008 VIII ZR 200/05 *BGHZ* 179, 27 *Quelle v Bun-desverband der Verbraucherzentralen und Verbraucherverbände.*

[81] CJ 17 April 2008 Case C-404/06 *Quelle AG v Bundesverband der Verbraucherzentralen und Ver-braucherverbände* [2008] I-02685 ECLI:EU:C:2008:231.

Notes:

(1) Under German law, the concept of 'interpretation' (*Auslegung*) is usually under-stood in a narrow sense, looking for the meaning of a legal provision on the basis of its wording. An interpretation that goes beyond the mere wording of a provision is called *Rechtsfortbildung* (judicial development). The duty of harmonious interpretation requires more than just interpreting legal provisions in a narrow sense, and comprises an obliga-tion to construe national law in conformity with a directive, where this is necessary and possible.[82] This judgment is the first in which the Federal Supreme Court of Germany has expressly ruled that the duty of harmonious interpretation also requires German national courts to develop the law in conformity with a directive.

(2) In this controversial judgment, the Federal Supreme Court of Germany tried to find a compromise between the duty to interpret national law in conformity with the Consumer Sales Directive and the principle according to which such harmonious inter-pretation should not go beyond the clear wording of provisions of national law.

(3) According to German law (in particular, §§439(4), 346(1) and 346(2) BGB), a seller had a right to compensation for the use the consumer had had of a product when it proved to be defective. This right was expressly intended by the legislature. However, in its preliminary ruling, the CJ found that this compensation was contrary to Article 3 of Directive 1999/44/EC, which provides that the consumer may require the seller to repair or replace the defective goods free of charge.

(4) The reasoning of the Federal Supreme Court of Germany contains three steps. First, the Court considered that German law allows for a compensation which is contrary to the Directive. Second, it raised the question whether this breach of the Directive could be overcome by interpretation (*Auslegung*) of national law in conformity with the Direc-tive and held that this was not possible, taking into consideration the clear wording of the BGB. Third, it held that a solution in conformity with the Directive was possible, viz by judicial development (*Rechtsfortbildung*) of the relevant provisions in conformity with the Directive. It was able to do so by means of judicial development using a teleological reduction (*Rechtsfortbildung im Wege der teleologischen Reduktion*) of §439(4) BGB.[83].

(5) Such a legal development is possible where there is a hidden lacuna in national law in the sense of an unintended oversight of the legislature (*eine verdeckte Regelungslücke im Sinne einer planwidrigen Unvollständigkeit des Gesetzes*). According to the Federal Supreme Court, such a lacuna existed because §439(4) BGB, which provided for the compensation, did not provide for an exception for cases within the scope of the Direc-tive. This lacuna in the law was held to be contrary to the legal framework as intended by the legislature since it had expressly stated its intention to create rules that were in conformity with the Directive. Had the legislature known that the award of compensation was contrary to the Directive, it would not have drafted §439(4) BGB in the same way.

(6) According to the Federal Supreme Court, such judicial development is not con-trary to the constitutional principle that the judiciary is bound by the law. The case law

---

[82] Gebauer 2010 130; Roth 2010 130.

[83] C Höpfner, 'Anmerkung zum Urteil des EuGH vom 26.11.2008, Az.: VIII 200/05 Kein Wertersatz für die Nutzung mangelhafter Ware bei Ersatzlieferung' (2009) 20 *EuZW* 159–60.

of the Federal Constitutional Court of Germany does allow the judiciary to fill lacunae in national law through judicial development. The Federal Supreme Court admitted that courts should not resort to judicial development to change clear choices of the legislature according to a court's own policy choices. In this case, however, it was clear from the intention of the legislature that there was a lacuna in the legal rules which needed to be filled. This position has been proven right, as §474(2) BGB (now §474(5) BGB) has been amended to this effect.

(7) The Federal Supreme Court argued that its interpretation did not entail according direct horizontal effect to Article 3 of Directive 1999/44/EC. It held that it had confined itself to judicial development in conformity with the Directive through teleological reduction where this was possible and necessary within national law.

(8) It is worth mentioning that the Federal Supreme Court initially took a different stance in its referring decision. In its decision of 16 August 2006, it saw no possibility to correct the inadequate regulation by way of interpretation (*Auslegung*). The clear wording and the unequivocal will of the legislature, as expressed in the parliamentary preparatory documents, were considered to militate against such an interpretation.[84] In its decision of 26 November 2008, the Federal Supreme Court was able to deviate from this previous decision by referring to the intention of the legislature to correctly implement the Directive. Because the CJ ruled that a compensation was contrary to the Directive, the Federal Supreme Court could develop the law in the way the legislature would have enacted it if it had known that providing such compensation was contrary to the Directive.[85]

Bundesgerichtshof (Federal Supreme Court of Germany),
21 December 2011[86]   **6.15 (GERM)**

Weber

HARMONIOUS INTERPRETATION LEADS TO JUDICIAL DEVELOPMENT

The consumer's new tiles

The principle of harmonious interpretation requires national courts to go beyond interpretation sensu stricto and to develop national law in conformity with the provisions of a directive where necessary and possible

Facts: A consumer bought polished tiles from a professional seller for €1,300. When two-thirds of the tiles had been laid, the consumer noticed a shading on the tiles. The seller rejected his complaint. An expert concluded that the shading could not be removed and that the only possible remedy was the complete replacement of the tiles, the cost of which was estimated at €5,800. The first instance court awarded €270 as a price reduction. The appeal court ordered the seller to deliver new tiles and to pay the consumer €2,100 for removal of the tiles already installed. The seller took the case to the Federal Supreme Court of Germany. The two remaining

---

[84] Federal Supreme Court of Germany 16 August 2006 VIII ZR 200/05 no 12.
[85] See F Faust, 'Nutzungsentschädigung bei Ersatzlieferung, discussion of BGH 16 November 2008' (2009) 49 *JuS* 276.
[86] Federal Supreme Court of Germany 21 December 2011 VIII ZR 70/08 *BGHZ* 192, 148 *Weber*.

issues were whether the seller, when delivering the new tiles, was required to remove and replace the ones already installed and, if so, whether the seller could refuse if doing so would be disproportionate. The Federal Supreme Court ruled that the seller was not obliged to replace the tiles already laid, but acknowledged that the Consumer Sales Directive might require otherwise and referred two questions to the CJ.

The CJ held that the seller was obliged to either himself remove the installed goods and install replacement goods or bear the cost of removal of the installed goods and installation of the replacement goods. Furthermore, where replacing the goods not in conformity was the only remedy possible, the seller had no right to refuse to do so on the ground that replacement imposed costs on him which were disproportionate with regard to: (a) the value of the goods would there have been no lack of conformity; and (b) the significance of the lack of conformity.

Held: The Federal Supreme Court interpreted its national law in conformity with the Consumer Sales Directive and ruled that 'delivery of a good without defects' includes the removal of a defective good and the reinstallation of a conforming good. The right of the seller to refuse a remedy because of disproportionate costs does not exist where only one remedy is available or where the seller refuses the other available remedy.

Judgment: 31 a) Judicial development by means of teleological reduction requires a hidden regulative lacuna in the sense of an unintended oversight of the legislature contrary to the legal framework … This condition is satisfied.

32. aa) It follows from the preparatory documents that the legislature wanted to establish the exception of disproportionality in conformity with the directive. However, the legislature understood Article 3(3) of the directive to mean that it included the absolute disproportionality exception …

33. bb) The understanding underlying the drafting of §439(3) BGB that Article 3(3) of the directive included the absolute disproportionality exception is, however, incorrect, as the CJ has established in a binding ruling. Article 3(3) of the directive only allows the consumer's right to reimbursement of the cost of removing the defective goods and installing the replacement goods to be limited to payment by the seller of a proportionate amount, but does not allow the consumer's right to replacement as the only remedy possible to be completely excluded on the ground of disproportionality of the costs of removal and installation. The regulation of §439(3) BGB is therefore contrary to the basic intention of the Act Modernizing the Law of Obligations, which was intended to implement the Consumer Sales Directive correctly before 31 December 2001.

Notes:

(1) This judgment demonstrates another application of harmonious interpretation through judicial development by reducing the scope of application.

(2) To resort to judicial development, there must be a hidden regulative lacuna in the sense of an unintended oversight of the legislature contrary to the legal framework. In *Quelle*, the Federal Supreme Court of Germany founded this finding on the intention of the legislature expressed during the implementation process of the Consumer Sales Directive. The *Weber* judgment contains a significant step forward in that it already finds judicial development possible when the concrete regulative intention is contrary to the general intention of the legislature when implementing a directive. This enlarges the scope for judicial development in conformity with directives.[87]

---

[87] See F Faust, 'Kaufrecht: Richtlinienkonforme Auslegung und Rechtsfortbildung' (2012) 52 *JuS* (456) 459.

(3) On 17 October 2012, the Federal Supreme Court ruled that this interpretation is limited to cases within the scope of the Directive. This judgment will be discussed in detail under section VII.A.

Cour de Cassation, chambre commerciale (Court of Cassation, Commercial Division), 13 July 2010[88]   **6.16 (FR)**

Free & SFR v France Télécom, Orange sports et Ligue nationale de football

BOLD HARMONIOUS INTERPRETATION

A combined offer you cannot refuse

The general prohibition on combined offers in national law, which is precluded by the Unfair Commercial Practices Directive, can be interpreted in conformity with that Directive to mean that it only prohibits combined offers which are unfair under the general prohibition of unfair commercial practices

Facts: France Télécom had acquired the broadcasting rights of the football matches of the French Ligue 1. In order to broadcast these matches on its dedicated sports channel, it had restricted access to this channel to those of its customers who had opted for its multi-services offer, *triple play*, combining telephone, internet and television. Several rival internet providers considered this combined offer an unfair commercial practice. Whereas the Commercial Court of Paris allowed the claim, the Court of Appeal of Paris refused it.

Held: The French Court of Cassation rejected the appeal in cassation (the combined offer thus remains possible). Interpreting the prohibition on combined offers in the light of the CJ decisions in *VTB-VAB* and *Galatea*, it ruled that the Court of Appeal could take into account the circumstances of the case to assess whether the combined offer was an unfair commercial practice.

Judgment: The decision reiterates the obligation which is binding on all the authorities of Member States ... to achieve the result envisaged by the directives and their duty under [now Article 4(3) TEU], to take all appropriate measures, whether general or particular, to ensure the fulfilment of that obligation. The decision then mentions that with the judgment of 23 April 2009 (C-261/07 and C-299/07), ... the CJ has ruled with binding force that Directive 2005/29/EC ... must be interpreted as precluding national legislation which, with certain exceptions, and without taking account of the specific circumstances, imposes a general prohibition of combined offers made by a vendor to a consumer. Having mentioned that Article L. 122-1 of the Consumer Code prohibits such combined offers without taking account of specific circumstances, the Court of Appeal, without having to undertake the ineffective assessment envisaged by the fourth objection ... inferred that it had to apply the Article according to the criteria set out in the directive in order to assess the unfair nature of a commercial practice. The Court of Appeal, without resorting to direct application of the directive by means of substitution and without violating the principle of contradiction, rightly assessed whether the criteria were satisfied in this case. Therefore, the ground of appeal is unfounded.

---

[88] French Court of Cassation Commercial Division 13 July 2010 no 09-15304 and no 09-66970 *Bulletin* 2010 IV no 127 *Free & SFR v France Télécom, Orange sports et Ligue nationale de football*.

Notes:

(1) Pursuant to Article L 122-1 of the French Consumer Code (*Code de la consommation*), it is, inter alia, prohibited to make the sale of a product subject to the purchase of a minimum quantity or to the complementary purchase of another product or another service, and also to make the provision of a service subject to provision of another service or to the purchase of a product.[89] Article L 122-1 thus contains a per se prohibition of combined offers to a consumer.

(2) However, in the joined cases *VTB-VAB* and *Galatea*, the CJ has ruled that Directive 2005/29/EC[90] must be interpreted as precluding national legislation which, with certain exceptions, and without taking account of the specific circumstances of the case, imposes a general prohibition of combined offers made by a seller to a consumer.[91] Combined offers are not listed in Annex I to the Directive, which lists the commercial practices which are prohibited in all circumstances. Accordingly, combined offers have to be assessed on a case-by-case basis. The establishment of a presumption of unlawfulness of combined offers is therefore not in conformity with the Directive.[92] Since the Directive aims at maximum harmonisation, stricter national legislation is not admitted.

(3) After holding that Article L 122-1 of the Consumer Code is contrary to Directive 2005/29/EC, the Court of Appeal of Paris confirmed that it must do everything within its jurisdiction, taking into account the whole of national law, to ensure the full effectiveness of the Directive when applying Article L 122-1. The Court of Appeal therefore assessed *in concreto* whether the combined offer constituted an unfair commercial practice. In its assessment, the Court applied the general prohibition, under which a commercial practice is considered unfair if it is contrary to the requirements of professional diligence and materially distorts the economic behaviour of the average consumer, and concluded that there was no unfair commercial practice.

(4) The French Court of Cassation accepted this decision. In a forceful consideration, it approved the harmonious interpretation undertaken by the Court of Appeal. The French Court of Cassation was careful to highlight that this was neither a case of direct application of the Directive nor of an interpretation *contra legem*, and founded its decision on the requirement of harmonious interpretation.

(5) The decision is a clear example of the potency of harmonious interpretation and the decision borders on interpretation *contra legem*. In light of the case law of the CJ, the French Court of Cassation allowed a harmonious interpretation of Article L 122-1 of the Consumer Code, which entailed the incorporation of the general prohibition on unfair commercial practices (of Article 5 of the Directive or Article L 120-1 of the Consumer

---

[89] Art. L 122-1 *Code de la consommation*: 'Il est interdit de refuser à un consommateur la vente d'un produit ou la prestation d'un service, sauf motif légitime, et de subordonner la vente d'un produit à l'achat d'une quantité imposée ou à l'achat concomitant d'un autre produit ou d'un autre service ainsi que de subordonner la prestation d'un service à celle d'un autre service ou à l'achat d'un produit.'

[90] Directive 2005/29/EC of the European Parliament and of the Council of 11 May 2005 concerning unfair business-to-consumer commercial practices in the internal market and amending Council Directive 84/450/EEC, Directives 97/7/EC, 98/27/EC and 2002/65/EC of the European Parliament and of the Council and Regulation (EC) No 2006/2004 of the European Parliament and of the Council [2005] OJ L149/22.

[91] CJ 23 April 2009 Joined Cases C-261/07 and C-299/07 *VTB-VAB NV v Total Belgium NV and Galatea BVBA v Sanoma Magazines Belgium NV* [2009] I-02949 ECLI:EU:C:2009:244, para 68.

[92] See ibid, paras 59–61.

Code) into the specific prohibition of a combined offer. This could be seen as a teleological reduction of Article L 122-1 'till nought'.[93] One could argue that in doing so, the Court of Appeal effectively disapplied Article L 122-1 in favour of Article L 120-1.

(6) It is interesting to draw attention to the follow-up case law in Belgium after the *VTB-VAB* and *Galatea* rulings, which were issued after a preliminary request relating to the Belgian prohibition of combined offers made by the President of the Commercial Tribunal of Antwerp. In several decisions, the prohibition in Article 54 of the Act on Commercial Practices and Consumer Protection was disapplied and the combined offer was assessed *in concreto* to decide whether it was an unfair commercial practice.[94] In a case on a combined offer of publicity in a newspaper and on the website of that newspaper, the Court of Appeal of Brussels confirmed that Article 54 was contrary to the Directive and that it should apply the *VTB-VAB* and *Galatea*[95] decisions. The Court then proceeded to assess the fairness of the combined offer in conformity with the general unfairness rule of Article 5 of the Directive and held that the offer could not materially distort the economic behaviour of the average consumer.[96] In that case, the Court of Appeal seemed to disapply Article 54 altogether, without trying to interpret it in conformity with the Directive.

(7) The French legislature reacted by adding that the prohibition in Article L 122-1 only applies when the combined offer constitutes an unfair commercial practice within the meaning of Article L 120-1. The Belgian legislature responded in a similar way by enacting what is now Article VI.80 of the Code of Economic Law. Pursuant to that Article, combined offers are allowed provided they do not constitute an unfair commercial practice.

III.C LIMITS

III.C.i SOURCES: CJ CASE LAW

Although the duty of harmonious interpretation is very strong, it is nonetheless subject to certain limits. First of all, the national courts are obliged to interpret national law 'as far as possible' in conformity with a directive.[97] And the question whether national law is amenable to an interpretation in conformity with the directive depends on the flexibility of its provisions.[98] However, the obligation of harmonious interpretation cannot serve

---

[93] Against such a far-reaching teleological reduction: C-W Canaris, 'Gemeinsamkeiten zwischen verfassungs- und richtlinienkonformer Rechtsfindung' in *Wirtschaft im offenen Verfassungsstaat* (Munich, Verlag CH Beck, 2006) 58. According to this author, the Federal Supreme Court of Germany implicitly accepted this principle in the *Heininger* case (*cf* section III.C below), where it held that the harmonious interpretation of §5(2) of the Doorstep Selling Cancellation Act did not amount to a methodologically questionable stripping of meaning of that paragraph or derogation from it. According to some, this was the case: W-D Hochleitner, M Wolf and H Großerichter, 'Teleologische Reduktion auf Null?' (2002) 56 *WM* 534.

[94] See the references in H de Wulf, B Keirsbilck and E Terryn, 'Overzicht van rechtspraak. Handelsrecht en handelspraktijken 2003–2010' (2011) 48 *TPR* 1140 nos 286 ff.

[95] CJ *VTB-VAB and Galatea* (n 91).

[96] Court of Appeal Brussels 4 February 2010 *DCCR* 2011,191 annotated by F Longfils.

[97] CJ *Marleasing* (n 44) para 8.

[98] See Kapteyn 2008 530–31; Lenaerts and Van Nuffel 2011, para 22-088. In CJ 16 December 1993 Case C-334/07 *Teodoro Wagner Miret v Fondo de Garantía Salarial* [1993] I-06911 ECLI:EU:C:1993:945, para 22, the CJ held that 'the national provisions cannot be interpreted in a way which conforms with the directive'.

as a basis for interpreting national law *contra legem*.[99] This means that EU law does not require a national court to resort to a *contra legem* interpretation of its national law, but leaves the possibility of doing so to be resolved by national law.[100] Second, general principles of law may limit the scope of harmonious interpretation as well.[101] In *Kolpinghuis Nijmegen*, the CJ held that the principles of legal certainty and non-retroactivity preclude that a directive would 'of itself and independently of a law adopted for its implementation, have the effect of determining or aggravating the liability in criminal law of persons who act in contravention of the provisions of that directive'.[102] Third, in non-criminal cases, the obligation of harmonious interpretation is furthermore limited where such an interpretation would mean that obligations laid down in a non-implemented directive would be imposed on an individual.[103]

It is up to the national courts to determine whether the provisions of national law can be interpreted to achieve the result sought by the applicant. Where necessary, the national court may have to disapply conflicting rules of national law.[104] If the application of interpretative methods recognised by national law makes it possible to interpret a provision of national law in such a way as to avoid conflict with another rule of national law or to restrict the scope of that provision to that end by applying it only insofar as it does not conflict with that other rule, the national court is bound to use those methods in order to achieve the result sought by the directive.[105]

III.C.ii NATIONAL CASE LAW

Gerechtshof Amsterdam (Court of Appeal Amsterdam),
10 November 2009[106]   **6.17 (NL)**

NO HARMONIOUS INTERPRETATION *CONTRA LEGEM*

The mathematics of holidays

Although a national court has a strong obligation to interpret national law as much as possible in conformity with a directive, it cannot resort to contra legem *interpretation*

Facts: After two years of incapacity for work, an employee's employment contract was terminated. The employee sued his former employer for payment of compensation for unused holidays which he had built up during his period of incapacity. He alleged that pursuant to Article 7 of Directive 2003/88/EC, he was entitled to 40 days, whereas Dutch law only entitled him to 10 days.

---

[99] CJ 16 June 2005 Case C-105/03 *Criminal Proceedings v Maria Pupino* [2005] I-05285 ECLI:EU:C:2005:386, para 47; CJ *Adeneler* (n 41) para 110.

[100] Roth 2010 321.

[101] See Kapteyn 2008 530; Lenaerts and Van Nuffel 2010 para 22-088

[102] CJ 8 October 1987 Case C-80/86 *Criminal Proceedings v Kolpinghuis Nijmegen BV* [1987] I-03969 ECLI:EU:C:1997:431, para 13.

[103] CJ 26 September 1996 Case C-168/95 *Criminal Proceedings v Luciano Arcaro* [1996] I-04705 ECLI:EU:C:1996:363, para 42.

[104] Lenaerts and Van Nuffel 2011 para 22-089.

[105] CJ *Pfeiffer* (n 40) para 116.

[106] Court of Appeal Amsterdam 10 November 2009 *NJ* 2010, 466 annotated by MR Mok ECLI:NL:GHAMS:2009:BK4648.

Held: The claim was rejected as a directive is not directly applicable in a horizontal relationship and the obligation of harmonious interpretation cannot serve as the basis for interpreting national law *contra legem*.

Judgment: 3.9.3 … The correct implementation of this directive would indeed result in the right for the employee to payment of 40 days of holidays, as claimed by him, instead of 10 days. This means that the first sentence of Article 7:635(4) of the Civil Code is contrary to the directive.

3.9.4. An employee cannot rely directly on Article 7 of the directive, because in principle directives are only binding on the Member States. Pursuant to Article 249 EC Treaty [now Article 288 TFEU] a directive must first be implemented into national law. The basic rule is that only then an individual can claim the rights arising from the implementation of the directive. The CJ has in some circumstances accepted that individuals can derive claims against the government that arise from a directive which has not been implemented on time and/or not been implemented correctly (vertical direct effect), but it has not (yet) accepted direct effect between individuals (horizontal direct effect).

3.9.5. The national judge has a strong duty in a case like this to interpret the applicable national legislation as much as possible in conformity with the directive. The question thus arises whether the court can interpret Article 7:635(4), first sentence of the Civil Code … in conformity with the directive. For employees who do not perform their work because of illness, this sentence makes an express exception to the general rule of Article 7:634(1) of the Civil Code, which provides (in conformity with the purport of the directive) that employees are entitled to annual leave of at least four times the agreed weekly working hours. In the parliamentary history, express attention was given to the reason for this exception, namely to avoid a reservoir of unused leave and to control the costs of incapacity for work for businesses … In these circumstances, the Court considers that harmonious interpretation is not possible as this would result in an interpretation *contra legem*. Pursuant to the case-law of the CJ, the national courts are not obliged to apply interpretation *contra legem* (see CJ 16 June 2005, nr. C-105/03 (*Pupino*), para. 47). It is up to the legislature to bring its legislation into conformity with the directive.

3.9.6. The conclusion following from the foregoing is that the payment of the additional 30 days of holidays claimed by the employee cannot be awarded.

Bundesgerichtshof (Federal Supreme Court of Germany),
14 October 2003[107] **6.18 (GERM)**

H v. M

NO HARMONIOUS INTERPRETATION WHERE THE WORDING IS CLEAR

Flat luck

There is no need for harmonious interpretation where the wording of national law is clear

Facts: A consumer bought a flat using an agent. The agent held a power of agency authenticated by a notary. After the agent had concluded the contract, the consumer wanted to cancel the contract concluded with the agent. The purchasing price for the flat was financed by two consumer credit contracts, which the consumer wanted to cancel as well. The claimant (the consumer) claimed that the bank (respondent) should pay back the paid interests and part of the paid expenses.

---

[107] Federal Supreme Court of Germany 14 October 2003 XI ZR 134/02 *NJW* 2004, 154.

Held: The claim was dismissed by the court of first instance and the appeal court. The Federal Supreme Court of Germany allowed the appeal in cassation because the contract concluded with the agent and the power of attorney given to him were null and void (not because of the cancellation of the contract concluded with the agent and of the power of attorney given to him).

Judgment: b) Cancelling the power of agency authenticated by a notary granted to C [the agent] by the claimant and his wife, is precluded pursuant to the clear regulation of §1(2) no. 3 of the Doorstep Selling Cancellation Act. Even if this provision would go less far than the provisions of Council Directive 85/577/EEC of 20 December 1985 to protect the consumer in respect of contracts negotiated away from business premises, there is no room for harmonious interpretation, given the clear wording of the law … That is also the case when the power of attorney authenticated by a notary is null … In that case, the principal, in the absence of an effective power of attorney, does not need the protection of the Doorstep Selling Cancellation Act.

Notes:

(1) In this judgment, the Federal Supreme Court of Germany considered whether a consumer can cancel a consumer credit contract concluded by an agent acting on behalf of the consumer if the power of attorney was given away from the agent's business premises. Regardless of whether Directive 85/557/EEC[108] applied to the granting of the power of attorney by the consumer,[109] the Federal Supreme Court of Germany concluded that the consumer could not cancel this contract because he expressed his intention in the form of an authentic deed, drawn up by a notary. According to the former §1(2) of the Doorstep Selling Cancellation Act (*Haustürwiderrufsgesetz*), no right of cancellation exists when the declaration of will was made in the form of a notarial deed.

(2) In this judgment, the Federal Supreme Court of Germany followed the findings expressed in a previous judgment where it held that there is no room for interpreting §1(2) of the Doorstep Selling Cancellation Act in conformity with Directive 85/557/EEC because of the clear wording of this provision.[110]

Bundesgerichtshof (Federal Supreme Court of Germany),
9 April 2002[111]　　　　　　　　**6.19 (GERM)**

Heininger v Bayerische Hypo- und Vereinsbank AG

HARMONIOUS INTERPRETATION

Heininger

The Federal Supreme Court of Germany allows harmonious interpretation and refuses to accept the arguments raised against it

Facts: A couple took out a loan in order to finance the purchase of a flat, which they bought after a real estate agent paid several visits to their home. Repayment of the loan was secured by a land charge (*Grundschuld*).

---

[108] Council Directive 85/557/EEC of 20 December 1985 to protect the consumer in respect of contracts negotiated away for business premises [1985] OJ L373/31. The Doorstep Selling Directive was repealed as of 13 June 2014 by Directive 2011/83/EU of 25 October 2011 on consumer rights [2011] OJ L304/64.

[109] This question was not settled in the judgment.

[110] Federal Supreme Court of Germany 29 April 2003 XI ZR 201/02 *ZIP* 2003, 1692.

[111] Federal Supreme Court of Germany 9 April 2002 XI ZR 91/99 *BGHZ* 150, 248 *Heininger v Bayerische Hypo- und Vereinsbank AG*.

385

The loan agreement was concluded on the premises of the bank, where they were not informed about their rights of cancellation. Five years later, the couple cancelled the loan agreement and sought repayment of parts of the loan and interest paid to the bank.

Held: The claims were dismissed by the District Court and the Higher Regional Court of Munich, which held that neither the Doorstep Selling Cancellation Act[112] nor the Act on Consumer Credit[113] provided for a right of cancellation in the present case. The Federal Supreme Court of Germany referred several questions regarding the relationship between the Doorstep Selling Directive and the Consumer Credit Directive to the CJ. The Federal Supreme Court then followed the decision of the CJ,[114] in which it held that the consumer had a right of cancellation.

Judgment: 2. Pursuant to the preliminary ruling of the CJ, the principle of harmonious interpretation requires that to the extent there is room for interpretation, the applicable national rules must be interpreted to mean that a consumer who has concluded a loan contract falling within the scope of the Doorstep Selling Directive, has a right of cancellation pursuant to Article 5 of the directive.

Notes:

(1) In this case, a question rose about the relationship between Directive 85/557/EEC and Directive 2008/48/EC and their respective implementations into German law. According to German law, (§5(2) of the Doorstep Selling Cancellation Act), that Act was not applicable to contracts which fell both within the scope of the Doorstep Selling Cancellation Act and the Consumer Credit Act (*Verbraucherkreditgesetz*).[115] In such cases, only the Consumer Credit Act was applicable and that Act did not provide for a right of cancellation for loans secured by security rights on immovables. The CJ ruled that this was contrary to the Doorstep Selling Directive, which gives the consumer a right of cancellation when he has not been sufficiently informed before concluding the contract. Through the harmonious interpretation of §5(2) of the Doorstep Selling Cancellation Act, the Federal Supreme Court of Germany held that the consumer was entitled to cancel the loan agreement.

(2) This judgment of Federal Supreme Court is interesting because it considers various arguments which were raised against the harmonious interpretation of §5(2) of the Doorstep Selling Cancellation Act.

(3) First of all, harmonious interpretation is not rendered impossible by the wording of the legal provisions. The Federal Supreme Court interprets §5(2) of the Doorstep Selling Cancellation Act to mean that it does not exclude the applicability of this Act (and its right of cancellation) when the Consumer Credit Act does not provide for a

---

[112] German Official Gazette I 30 June 2000 955–956 (*Haustürwiderrufsgesetz*).

[113] German Official Gazette I 30 June 2000 940–945 (*Verbraucherkreditgesetz*).

[114] CJ 13 December 2001 Case C- 481/99 *Georg Heininger and Helga Heininger v Bayerische Hypo- und Vereinsbank AG* [2001] I-09945 ECLI:EU:C:2001:684.

[115] §5(2) *Haustürwiderrufsgesetz*: 'Erfüllt ein Geschäft im Sinne des §1 Abs. 1 zugleich die Voraussetzungen eines Geschäfts nach dem Verbraucherkreditgesetz, nach §11 des Gesetzes über den Vertrieb ausländischer Investmentanteile und über die Besteuerung der Erträge aus ausländischen Investmentanteilen, nach §23 des Gesetzes über Kapitalanlagegesellschaften oder nach §4 des Gesetzes zum Schutz der Teilnehmer am Fernunterricht, so sind nur die Vorschriften dieser Gesetze anzuwenden.'

comparable protection. This is the case for loans to consumers secured by security rights on immovables. Second, the intention of the legislature does not prevent such an interpretation either. The Federal Supreme Court held that the legislature cannot be presumed to have taken breach of the Doorstep Selling Directive into account.[116] Third, legal certainty does not pose a problem either, as the interpretation of the provision was already intensely debated before the decision of the CJ. Fourth, harmonious interpretation does not run counter to the coherent system of German law, nor does it deprive the provision of its meaning. Fifth, harmonious interpretation is not a disguised direct horizontal effect of the directive. It is still interpretation, which is possible within the jurisdiction of the Federal Supreme Court.

(4) This case furthermore illustrates the issues raised by voluntary harmonisation and will be further discussed in section VII.A below.

Cour de Cassation, 1^{ière} chambre civile (Court of Cassation,
First Civil Chamber), 12 May 2011[117]   **6.20 (FR)**

SAIF, USOPAV & SCEI v Maia Films

'HARMONIOUS INTERPRETATION' BY ACCEPTING A
NON-IMPLEMENTED DIRECTIVE EXCEPTION

Être et avoir

The Cour de Cassation directly relies on an exception which was optional in the directive and was not implemented into French law

Facts: In the movie *Être et Avoir*, a documentary about life at a rural school, educational drawings hanging on the classroom wall are shown several times. These drawings were protected by copyright and the copyright holders sued the producers of the movie for infringement.

Held: The Court of Appeal refused to allow the claim for damages as the drawings only appeared incidentally in the movie, thus applying the theory of incidental appearance. The Court of Cassation rejected the appeal against that judgment, even though France had chosen not to implement the optional exception for incidental inclusion of a work in other material provided for in Article 5(3)(i) of Directive 2001/29/EC.

Judgment: But whereas the judgment points out that where the illustrations of which Mr. X is the author figure in the documentary movie in question and in the DVD bonus, the camera merely sweeps over them and just gives fleeting glimpses, that they are more frequently in the background with the individual students and the teacher in prominent position, that they are at no time presented while being used by the teacher and form part of the scenery of which they constitute a usual element, appearing in short sequences but never being represented for themselves; that it was precisely from these facts that the Court of Appeal inferred that such a presentation of the work in question was incidental to the subject treated in a documentary presentation of the life and the relations between teacher and children in one single class in the countryside, in such a way that it should

---

[116] See, eg, CJ *Wagner Miret* (n 98) para 20.
[117] French Court of Cassation Civil Chamber 12 May 2012 no 08-20651 *Bulletin* 2011 I no 87 *SAIF, USOPAV & SCEI v Maia Films.*

be considered as an incidental inclusion of a work, which constitutes a limitation on the monopoly of the author, in the sense of Directive 2001/29/EC of 22 May 2001, which, according to the preparatory documents, the legislature intended to implement in view of current French law; from which it follows that all parts of the ground for cassation are unfounded.

Notes:

(1) Article 5 of Directive 2001/29/EC contains a list of exceptions and limitations to the exclusive rights of the copyright holder.[118] The content of this list is mostly optional and the French legislature has not taken over all exceptions and limitations in Article L 122-5 of the French Code of Intellectual Property. It is relevant for this case that the legislature did not transpose Article 5(3)(i), which allows incidental inclusion of a work or other subject matter in other material, into Article L 122-5.

(2) The French Court of Cassation nevertheless applied this exception in a curious harmonious interpretation of the Directive. It referred to the preparatory documents of the implementation of the Directive and stressed the intention of the legislature to implement the Directive in view of current French law. Before the Directive had been implemented, French case law accepted an exception for incidental inclusion. By referring to the intention of the legislature, the Court of Cassation presented the silence of the legislature (and the non-transposition of Article 5(3)(i) of the Directive) as a tacit intention to maintain this exception, which is also included in the Directive.

(3) Although the decision might seem fair, the Court of Cassation ruled as if the legislature had adopted the exception. The decision fills a lacuna, but it remains uncertain whether or not this void was intended by the legislature.[119] The decision seems to put into question the policy choices made by the French legislature when implementing the Directive, since amendments to this effect proposed by members of the *National Assembly* were rejected when the Directive was implemented.

IV. HARMONIOUS INTERPRETATION NOT IMPOSED BY EU LAW: INTERPRETATION OF OPEN-ENDED PRINCIPLES OF NATIONAL PRIVATE LAW

A directive can have indirect horizontal effect in the sense that it can influence (legal) relationships between individuals through the interpretation of open-ended concepts of national private law, such as good faith, reasonableness and fairness, and abuse of rights.[120]

---

[118] Directive 2001/29/EC of the European Parliament and of the Council of 22 May 2001 on the harmonisation of certain aspects of copyright and related rights in the information society [2001] OJ L167/10.

[119] C Castets-Renard, 'Etre et avoir... et apparaître accessoirement! Ou comment limiter le monopole de l'auteur' (2011) *D* 1875.

[120] See Hartkamp 2016 no 158; Ch 1 sections II.B.ii and II.C.iv.

Arbeidsrechtbank Brussel (Employment Tribunal Brussels),
2 December 2005[121]   **6.21 (BE)**

VP v Royal Belgian Football Association

INDIRECT EFFECT OF A NON-DISCRIMINATION DIRECTIVE
THROUGH THE PROHIBITION OF ABUSE OF RIGHTS

Finished whistling I

Application of a directive using the concept of abuse of rights

Facts: VP was a referee and had an employment contract with the Royal Belgian Football Association. In accordance with the policy of the Association, this contract was terminated when VP reached the age of 45. VP claimed damages.

Held: The claimant's claim was upheld as the discriminatory practice constituted abuse of the Association's right to unilaterally terminate the employment contract.

Judgment: Both parties to an employment contract have the right to terminate the contract by a unilateral declaration of will, ie by giving notice, if it concerns a contract concluded for an indefinite period. This way of unilateral termination implies that all parties have the right to give notice. It is a contractual right, which must be exercised in good faith. It is therefore possible to abuse the right to give notice ...

An employer is prohibited from discriminating when giving notice. Pursuant to the Framework Directive it is prohibited to discriminate on the grounds of age. Belgian law must be interpreted in conformity with the directive, also during the implementation period of the directive, which means that there can be no discrimination on the grounds of age when giving notice ...

The tribunal finds that it is clear that the defendant pursued the dismissal because of the age limit of 45 years reached by the claimant. This dismissal constitutes discrimination on the grounds of age.

One can accept that working as a professional referee requires an adequate physical condition. Such a condition can, however, be assessed objectively by specific tests. Using an age limit is therefore unnecessarily discriminating and has no legitimate purpose which is objectively and reasonably justified.

Notes:

(1) Directive 2000/78/EC prohibits, inter alia, discrimination on the grounds of age.[122] This Directive should in principle have been implemented into national law by 2 December 2003 at the latest, with a possibility of extension of the period until 2 December 2006 (see Article 18 of the Directive) as far as it concerned discrimination on the grounds of age and disability. Belgium implemented the Directive by an Act of 25 February 2003 that was not yet applicable to the case.[123]

---

[121] Employment Tribunal Brussels 2 December 2005 *Sociaalrechtelijke Kronieken* 2008 vol 1 48-51 *VP v Royal Belgian Football Association*.
[122] Council Directive 2000/78/EC of 27 November 2000 establishing a general framework for equal treatment in employment and occupation [2000] OJ L303/16.
[123] Belgian Official Gazette 17 March 2003 no 89 12844–12851.

(2) The Employment Tribunal Brussels confirmed the obligation for the national courts to interpret national law as far as possible in the light of the wording and the purpose of the Directive. The Employment Tribunal (wrongly) went further than the CJ required in *Adeneler*[124] by holding that this obligation would exist even before the period for implementing the Directive had expired.

(3) Although the Employment Tribunal founded its argumentation on the obligation of harmonious interpretation, it also included traces of another technique to achieve indirect effect: application of a directive through open-ended concepts of national private law. The Employment Tribunal creatively applied the related principle of good faith and the prohibition of abuse of rights. On the basis of those principles, which preclude a person from exercising a right in a manner which exceeds the normal exercise of that right by a prudent and careful person, the Employment Tribunal found that the prohibition of discrimination on the grounds of age as provided for in the Directive was applicable. The Employment Tribunal held that the Football Association had abused its right to unilaterally terminate the employment contract by exercising it in a discriminatory manner.

(4) The Employment Tribunal not only applied the prohibition of discrimination as laid down by the Directive and the Act, but even discussed the potential justifications for differential treatment. According to the Employment Tribunal, the policy of the Football Association was unnecessarily discriminatory and therefore served no legitimate aim which could objectively and reasonably justify it.

(5) The appeal against this decision, which was successful, is discussed below in section V.B.

(6) The prohibition of abuse of rights under EU law is further discussed in section III in Chapter 5.

V. REVIEW OF NATIONAL LAW AGAINST EU LAW: EXCEPTIONALLY, DISAPPLICATION OF NATIONAL LAW WHICH CONFLICTS WITH EU LAW

V.A INTRODUCTION

The principle of supremacy of EU law implies that directive provisions, regardless of whether they are directly effective or not, enjoy precedence over conflicting rules of national law. National courts must assess 'whether the competent national authorities, in exercising the choice which is left to them as to the form and the methods for implementing the directive, have kept within the limits as to their discretion set out in the directive'.[125] The same obligation applies to public authorities.[126]

---

[124] CJ *Adeneler* (n 41).

[125] CJ 1 February 1977 Case C-51/76 *Verbond van Nederlandse Ondernemingen v Inspecteur der Invoerrechten en Accijnzen* [1977] I-00113 ECLI:EU:C:1977:12, para 24.

[126] CJ 22 June 1989 Case C-103/88 *Fratelli Costanzo SpA v Comune di Milano* [1989] I-01839 ECLI:EU:C:1989:256, para 33.

The obligation to review national law in the light of the relevant directive arises irrespective of whether or not the national law concerned was adopted to implement the directive. It covers all rules governing the application of the directive in the national legal system, including rules which were applicable before the directive was adopted.[127] In principle, however, the obligation to review only arises after the deadline for implementing the directive has expired.[128]

In principle, in a horizontal relationship, parties cannot rely on a directive in order to disapply national provisions which conflict with the directive. EU law does not require the national courts to disapply conflicting rules of national law where an individual invokes provisions of an unimplemented or incorrectly implemented directive against another individual. See section II.B above and Chapter 1.[129] However, exceptions are possible, so that one of the parties to the case can be subject to a legal liability or a disadvantage to which it would not have been subject had the conflicting national law been applied.[130] In the *CIA Security v Securitel* case, a provision of Belgian law was held to be non-binding as it was adopted contrary to a duty of notification imposed by a notification directive.[131] In *Unilever v Central Food*, a private law effect was clearly noticeable. A buyer refused payment of a consignment of olive oil on the grounds that the oil did not satisfy an Italian labelling regulation. The CJ ruled that the regulation was inapplicable because it infringed the procedures to be followed pursuant to the aforementioned directive (although in this case the regulation had been notified, Italy had not observed the standstill period). As a result, the goods were found to conform to the contract and the buyer was bound to pay.

V.B REVIEW AGAINST GENERAL PRINCIPLES OF EU LAW UNDERLYING DIRECTIVE PROVISIONS

The absence of horizontal effect of directive provisions discussed in section II.B above calls for further comment. In some cases, the national courts do not apply secondary EU law, ie, the provisions of the relevant directive, but rather apply primary EU law, ie, the general principle underlying those directive provisions. In its controversial decision in *Mangold*,[132] the CJ ruled that the principle of non-discrimination on the grounds of age must be regarded as a general principle of EU law which requires national courts to

---

[127] CJ 29 November 1078 Case C-21/78 *Knud Oluf Delkvist v Anklagemyndigheden* [1978] I-02327 ECLI:EU:C:1978:213, paras 13–16.

[128] See Lenaerts and Van Nuffel 2011 para 22-090.

[129] See Craig and De Búrca 2015 216; Lenaerts and Van Nuffel 2011 para 22-091.
In this interpretation, this constitutes an exception to the rule set out in section II.B that a directive cannot be invoked in a horizontal relationship to set aside conflicting national provisions.

[130] Craig and De Búrca 2015 216. See, eg, CJ 30 April 1996 Case C-194/94 *CIA Security International v Signalson and Securitel* [1996] I-02201 ECLI:EU:C:1996:172, paras 32–55; CJ 26 September 2000 Case C-443/98 *Unilever Italia SpA v Central Food SpA* [2000] I-07535 ECLI:EU:C:2000:496, paras 45–51.

[131] Directive 83/189/EEC subsequently superseded by Directive 98/34/EC, supplemented by Directive 98/48/EC.

[132] CJ *Mangold* (n 7) paras 74–78.

disapply any contrary provision of national law falling within the scope of EU law.[133] Reliance on this principle, which is given expression in Directive 2000/78/EC, in a horizontal relationship was not conditional upon the expiry of the period allowed the Member States for transposing that Directive.[134] In a horizontal relationship, individuals can thus invoke a general principle of law against a conflicting provision of national law falling within the scope of EU law.[135] In *Kücukdeveci*, the CJ confirmed and clarified the core of the *Mangold* decision.[136] It is not the Directive that has an indirect horizontal effect, but rather the general principle that has direct effect. The CJ effectively ruled that 'it is the general principle of EU law prohibiting all discrimination on grounds of age, as given expression in Directive 2000/78, which must be the basis of the examination of whether EU law precludes national legislation such as that at issue in the main proceedings'.[137] In *AMS*, the CJ ruled against direct effect of Article 27 of the Charter (the right of workers to information and consultation). The CJ distinguished that case from *Kücükdeveci* because the principle of non-discrimination on the grounds of age was sufficient in itself to confer on individuals an individual right which they may invoke as such, whereas Article 27 of the Charter must be given more specific expression in EU law or national law to be fully effective.[138]

Arbeidshof Brussel (Employment Court Brussels),
11 April 2008[139]   **6.22 (BE)**

Royal Belgian Football Association v VP

REFUSAL TO APPLY A DIRECTIVE THROUGH A GENERAL
PRINCIPLE OF NON-DISCRIMINATION ON THE GROUNDS OF AGE

Finished whistling II

A general principle of non-discrimination on the grounds of age cannot be invoked in a horizontal relationship

Facts: VP was a referee and had an employment contract with the Royal Belgian Football Association. In accordance with the policy of the Association, this contract was terminated in 2002 because VP had reached age of 45. VP claimed damages.

Held: In contrast to the Employment Tribunal, the Employment Court dismissed the claim.

---

[133] See on review against the general principle of non-discrimination and the controversy caused by *Mangold* also Ch 5 section II.B.

[134] CJ *Mangold* (n 7) para 76.

[135] Craig and De Búrca 2015 220; Hartkamp 2016 no 144. Criticizes this possibility: Hartley 2010 239–240.

[136] Craig and De Búrca 2015 934.

[137] CJ 19 January 2010 Case C-555/07 *Kücükdevci v Swedex & Co* [2010] I-00365 ECLI:EU:C:2010:21, para 27.

[138] CJ 15 January 2014 Case C-176/12 *Association de Médiation Sociale v Union locale des syndicats (CGT), Hichem Laboubi et al* nyr ECLI:EU:C:2014:2, paras 44–48.

[139] Employment Court Brussels 11 April 2008 *Sociaalrechtelijke Kronieken* 2009 vol 2 102–06 *Royal Belgian Football Association v VP.*

Judgment: The court of first instance held that the law regarding dismissal must nevertheless be interpreted in conformity with the directive, so that a dismissal may not lead to discrimination on grounds of age.

The court of first instance did not indicate, however, which provision of Belgian law regarding dismissal it held to imply discrimination on grounds of age …

But by finding on the basis of harmonious interpretation that the dismissal of Mr V. was contrary to the prohibition of discrimination on grounds of age, the court of first instance applied a directive not yet implemented at the time in a horizontal situation, since it did not refer to any provision of Belgian law on the basis of which it considered discrimination on grounds of age to have been institutionalised.

Directives generally do not aim at determining horizontal relationships and this is certainly not the case here, since Articles 16 and 18 of the directive expressly order the Member States to take the necessary measures before 2 December 2003, extendible if necessary.

In his opinion the Advocate General nevertheless refers to the CJ judgment in *Mangold* …

There are doubts in legal doctrine whether these considerations lead to the result that the prohibition of discrimination on grounds of age is directly applicable in horizontal relationships …

… that the *Mangold* judgment did not decide on the horizontal direct effect; indeed the Court did not have to give a decision on this issue, because in *Mangold* the CJ was requested to interpret a German legal standard and consequently the case was about vertical effect; it is for the national courts, moreover, to decide on the concrete application …

The Advocate General [Mazak in *Palacios de la Villa*, C-411/05] further argued for great caution in inferring the existence of a specific prohibition of discrimination on grounds of age from the general principle of equality (see point 94) and stated that the CJ had not done so either with respect to other grounds of discrimination, such as discrimination on grounds of sexual orientation, because in these fields it is left to the [EU] legislature and the Member States to take appropriate measures (see point 95) …

As Advocate General J. Mazak indicated, the Court [in *Mangold*] did not give any decision whatsoever on the issue of horizontal direct effect …

The Employment Court therefore holds that the *Mangold* judgment does not support the argument that a prohibition of discrimination on the grounds of age in horizontal relationships can be inferred from the general principle of [EU] law …

It was explained above that the dismissal of Mr V was indeed based on his age, but that at the time of the dismissal Framework Directive 2000/78 had not yet been implemented into Belgian law, so that the finding of abuse of the right to give notice cannot be founded on this basis alone.

Notes:

(1) This case concerns the appeal from the judgment of the Employment Tribunal of Brussels of 2 December 2005, discussed above in section IV.

(2) This decision, given after *Mangold* but before *Kücükdeveci*, reflects the controversy which the CJ caused with its *Mangold* decision.

(3) At the time when the employment contract was terminated, the time limit for implementing Directive 2000/78/EC into national law had not yet expired and the Belgian law implementing the Directive was not yet in force. As a result, the claim for damages of the retired referee was dismissed, although the Employment Court Brussels admitted that

the dismissal was discriminatory. The Employment Court stressed that a directive is not intended to determine horizontal relationships and referred to the criticism to which the *Mangold* decision had gave rise, and distinguished it from that case. Whereas in *Mangold* the conflict arose between national legislation and a general principle of law, this case deals with the effect of that principle on a horizontal relationship. The Employment Court concluded that the *Mangold* decision did not support the argument that a prohibition of discrimination on the grounds of age in horizontal relationships can be inferred from a general principle of EU law. Furthermore, the Employment Court rather easily brushed off the argument based on the (Belgian law) prohibition on abuse of rights.

(4) The Employment Court wrongly found that the Employment Tribunal had directly applied the Directive in a horizontal situation. The Tribunal did, however, apply the general principle that precludes age discrimination and that underlies the Directive (as well as national Belgian law) by using the prohibition of abuse of rights. It coloured the open norm of the prohibition of abuse of rights with the general principle of non-discrimination.

Sąd Najwyższy (Polish Supreme Court),
16 February 2012[140]   **6.23 (PL)**

TK v R Bank Polska SA

APPLICATION OF A DIRECTIVE THROUGH THE GENERAL PRINCIPLE OF EQUAL TREATMENT

Pre-contractual information duties

There is a general principle of law providing for pre-contractual information duties

Facts: Poland had failed to implement Directive 2004/39/EC on markets in financial instruments[141] in due time. Since 2006, the claimant had been entering into derivative and forward transactions with a bank. In September 2008, a currency option contract was concluded between the parties. In this case, the claimant sought: (a) a declaration that the contract he had concluded with a bank was null; and (b) restitution of undue performance, or alternatively, compensation or termination of the contract.

Held: The Polish Supreme Court considered the possibility of directly applying provisions of Directive 2004/39/EC and the issue of the provision of proper information on the risks related to the currency option contract concluded between the claimant and the bank.

Judgment: The Court concurs with the position of both courts that the provisions of Directive 2004/39/EC cannot be applied in this case … The Directive had not been implemented into the Polish legal system at the time the contract was concluded between the parties, nor at the time of the conclusion of subsequent transactions. However, as the Regional Court correctly pointed out, the essential objectives of as yet unimplemented European directives are a proper model for interpreting Polish law. Thus, it is irrelevant that the provisions of the Directive of 2004 have no binding force for the defendant bank

---

[140] Polish Supreme Court 16 February 2012 Case IV CSK 225/11 *OSNC* 2012 no 9 item 105 *TK v R Bank Polska SA*.

[141] Directive 2004/39/EC of the European Parliament and of the Council of 21 April 2004 on markets in financial instruments amending Council Directives 85/611/EEC and 93/6/EEC and Directive 2000/12/EC of the European Parliament and of the Council and repealing Council Directive 93/22/EEC [2004] OJ L145/44.

(formal aspect of binding force). It is important that the provisions of the directive ... are a model for banks performing 'financial forward transactions', including transactions falling outside the specific legal regime for so-called investment firms (Article 70(3) of the Act of 25 July 2005). This is justified by the aforementioned similar nature of the transactions governed these two these legal regimes ... It would be difficult to rationally explain a situation where similar forward transactions, of a similar legal structure, performed by professionals acting on the financial services market, are treated differently from the point of view of information provision standards applicable in the period preceding the formation of a contract.

In other words, an information provision standard which is identical or closely similar to the one that underpins the relevant provisions of the Directive of 2004 should apply to banks that perform 'financial forward transactions' within the meaning of Article 5(2)(4) and (7) of the Banking Law Act, even if in 2008 there was no basis to apply the provisions of the Directive directly to the contract between the parties.

Notes:

(1) The Polish Supreme Court noted in this judgment that Directive 2004/39/EC on markets in financial instruments did not govern horizontal relationships between private parties, as the Member State had failed in its obligation to transpose the Directive.

(2) The Financial Instruments Act[142] was not applicable in this case. However, the Supreme Court reasoned that the principle of equal treatment required that a bank must provide information to a client according to a standard of information duties similar to the standard applying to investment firms. The Supreme Court ruled in this judgment that pre-contractual information duties may arise from the law on banking, from codes of conduct containing good banking practices or from the general principles of fairness in contracting. The problem is that at the time when the contract was concluded, neither the Banking Act of 1997[143] nor the Civil Code contained any provision imposing a duty on a bank to provide pre-contractual information to a client (apart from the pre-contractual information duties in consumer credit contracts). Such a general obligation does not exist in Polish civil law.

VI. STATE LIABILITY FOR DAMAGES

VI.A SOURCES

VI.A.i CJ CASE LAW

The question of state liability for incorrect or late implementation of a directive is important since provisions of a directive are not accorded direct horizontal effect.[144] In its older case law, the CJ held that if damage was caused through an infringement of EU law, the

---

[142] Act of 25 July 2005 on financial instruments, consolidated text DzU 2014 item 94.
[143] The Banking Act of 29 August 1997, consolidated text DzU 2015 item 128 as amended.
[144] Prechal 2005 271.

state was liable to the injured party for the consequences under the national legislation on state liability.[145] However, the national laws on this subject differ significantly from each other and often impose strict conditions on state liability.[146]

Since the *Francovich* judgment,[147] it is clear that liability for loss or damage caused by a breach of EU law constitutes a general principle of EU law. According to the CJ, such liability is inherent in the system of the Treaty.[148] This is founded on two arguments:[149] the EU's own legal order, and the requirement for the courts to ensure the full effectiveness of EU law and the protection of the EU rights of individuals. An additional argument can be found in Article 4(3) TEU, which requires Member States to take all appropriate measures to ensure the fulfilment of EU obligations.[150] The CJ consolidated its case law in subsequent cases. In *Brasserie du Pêcheur*,[151] it confirmed that the principle of state liability applies not only to the non-implementation of directives, but also to all breaches of EU law. Furthermore, it made clear that a judgment under Article 258 TFEU was not a preliminary condition for liability. The direct effect of the breached provisions does not preclude state liability either. Moreover, the CJ held that a state will be liable irrespective of which organ of the state is responsible for the breach and regardless of the national division of powers between constitutional authorities, even where the national legislature was responsible for the breach in question.[152]

It is now clear that an individual may obtain redress for loss or damage sustained as the result of the non-transposition of a directive by bringing a claim against the Member State. Where national law cannot be interpreted in conformity with a directive, the Member State concerned is obliged to make good the loss and damage sustained as a result of the failure to implement the directive in their respect.[153] This is also the case where an individual cannot rely on the direct effect of provisions of a directive because they are invoked against another individual,[154] or where the directive provisions do not satisfy the substantive requirements for direct effect.[155]

The potential sources for state liability are not restricted to actions or omissions to act in the part of the legislature or the government. Incorrect decisions of the judiciary can lead to state liability too. In *Köbler*, the CJ established that the principle of state liability is 'also applicable where the alleged infringement stems from a decision

---

[145] CJ 22 January 1976 Case C-60/75 *Carmine Antonio Russo v Azienda di Stato per gli interventi sul mercato agricolo (AIMA)* [1976] I-00045 ECLI:EU:C:1976:9.

[146] Kapteyn 2008 556; Prechal 2005 274.

[147] CJ 19 November 1991 Joined Cases C-6/90–C-9/90 *Andrea Francovich and Danila Bonifaci et al v Italian Republic* [1991] I-05357 ECLI:EU:C:1991:428, para 37.

[148] ibid, paras 31–35.

[149] Hartley 2010 249–50; Kapteyn 2008 556; Lenaerts and Van Nuffel 2011, para 21-014; Prechal 2005 274.

[150] CJ *Francovich* (n 147) para 36.

[151] CJ 5 March 1996 Joined Cases C-46/93 and C-48/93 *Brasserie du Pêcheur SA v Bundesrepublik Deutschland and The Queen v Secretary of State for Transport ex parte Factortame Ltd et al* [1996] I-01029 ECLI:EU:C:1996:79.

[152] Hartley 2010 250; Prechal 2005 277; Kapteyn 2008 557–58; Lenaerts and Van Nuffel 2011 para 21-014.

[153] CJ *Wagner Miret* (n 98) para 22.

[154] CJ *Faccini Dori* (n 16) para 27.

[155] See Lenaerts and Van Nuffel 2011 para 22-092.

of a court adjudicating at last instance'. In that case, however, state liability will only arise in an 'exceptional case where the court has manifestly infringed the applicable law'.[156] This qualification puts a significant limit to the scope of state liability caused by the judiciary.[157] Member States cannot, however, limit such liability solely to cases of intentional fault or serious misconduct of the court 'if such a limitation were to lead to exclusion of the liability of the Member State concerned in other cases where a manifest infringement of the applicable law was committed'.[158]

VI.A.ii NATIONAL CASE LAW

Hof van Cassatie België (Belgian Court of Cassation),
28 September 2001[159]　　　　　　　　　　**6.24 (BE)**

Belgian State v SH and FA

STATE LIABILITY FOR A BELATEDLY IMPLEMENTED DIRECTIVE

Passing on the bill

The Belgian state incurs liability for not implementing Directive 86/653/EEC, as this renders it impossible for a commercial agent to receive from its former principal the indemnity provided for by Article 17 of that Directive

Facts: SH concluded a commercial agency contract with the company VM, which became insolvent. The contract was terminated in 1994. In 1995, SH sued VM for payment of an indemnity, as provided for by Article 17 of Directive 86/653.[160] This claim failed, as the Belgian Act implementing Directive 86/653 was not yet into force, although it should have been. Therefore, SH sued the Belgian state for payment of damages and interest.

Held: The Court of Appeal of Liège and the Belgian Court of Cassation both upheld the agent's claim.

Judgment: Whereas the court considers that 'before the act of 13 April 1995 concerning the contract of commercial agency entered into force, no rule or principle of law allowed the award under Belgian law of an indemnity for loss of clients or an indemnity to a self-employed commercial agent who has brought his principal new clients or who has significantly increased the volume of business with existing customers ...'; that it is not possible, not even by a broad interpretation of internal law in the light of the European directive, to create non-existent law without any legal basis in internal law.

　　Whereas the court by these considerations legally justifies its decision to declare the claim of the first defendant against his principal unfounded and therefore to order the claimant in cassation [the Belgian state] to pay damages under Article 1382 of the Civil Code to the first defendant.

---

[156] CJ 30 September 2003 Case C-224/01 *Gerhard Köbler v Republik Österreich* [2003] I-10239 ECLI:EU:C:2003:513, paras 59 and 53. See also CJ 13 June 2006 Case C-173/03 *Traghetti del Mediterraneo SpA v Repubblica italiana* [2006] I-05177 ECLI:EU:C:2006:391, para 32.

[157] Hartley 2010 253–54.

[158] CJ *Traghetti del Mediterraneo* (n 156) para 46.

[159] Belgian Court of Cassation 28 September 2001 *Pas* 2001 vol 9–10 1534 *Belgian State v SH and FA*.

[160] Directive 86/653/EEC of the Council of 18 December 1986 on the coordination of the laws of the Member States relating to self-employed commercial agents [1986] OJ L382/17.

Notes:

(1) According to its Article 22, all Member States, except Ireland, the UK and Italy, had to implement Directive 86/653/EEC into national law by 1 January 1990, and its provisions had to be applicable to contracts in operation by 1 January 1994 at the latest. The Belgian legislature, however, belatedly implemented the Directive by an Act of 13 April 1995, which entered into force on 12 June 1995.[161]

(2) Pursuant to Article 17 of Directive 86/653/EEC, Member States must take the necessary measures to ensure that the commercial agent is, after the termination of the agency contract, indemnified or compensated for damage. It was only after the Act of 13 April 1995 entered into force that Belgian law provided for indemnification for commercial agents upon the termination of the agency contract.

(3) The Belgian Court of Cassation first referred to the obligation for national courts to interpret national law, as far as possible, in the light of the wording and the aim of the Directive. Next, the Court of Cassation approved the argumentation of the Court of Appeal, which held that such an interpretation of internal law, however broad, would not allow the creation of a non-existing right that had no legal basis in internal law.[162] The Court of Cassation then held that in such a case, the Belgian state incurred extra-contractual liability on the basis of Article 1382 of the Belgian Civil Code.

(4) The case is apparently an application of the *Francovich* case law, even though that case law is not expressly mentioned. Where a Member State has failed to implement a directive on time, it can incur liability when the harmonious interpretation of that directive is not possible.

VI.B CONDITIONS

VI.B.i SOURCES: CJ CASE LAW

In *Francovich*, the CJ not only established the EU principle of state liability, but also laid down the conditions under which Member States are bound under EU law to make good loss or damage suffered by individuals as a result of a failure to transpose a directive.[163] It elaborated upon those conditions in subsequent cases.[164]

First of all, the legal rule infringed must be intended to confer rights on individuals. It is irrelevant whether or not the provision has direct effect.[165] Second, the breach must be

---

[161] Belgian Official Gazette 2 June 1995.
[162] This was confirmed by the Belgian Court of Cassation in a decision of 24 January 2003 *Pas* 2003 vol 1 188 *HF v Belgian State*.
[163] CJ *Francovich et al* (n 147) paras 39–41.
[164] Kapteyn 2008 556–64; Hartley 2010 250–55; Prechal 2005 283–91; and recently CH Sieburgh, 'EU Law and Non-contractual Liability of the Union, Member States and Individuals' in Hartkamp/Sieburgh/Keus/Kortmann/Wissink (eds) 2014 465, 489 ff.
[165] CJ *Brasserie du Pêcheur and Factortame III* (n 151) paras 18–23.

sufficiently serious. This is the case where the Member State has manifestly and gravely disregarded the limits of its discretion.[166] Where a Member State fails to take any of the measures necessary to achieve the result prescribed by a directive within the period it lays down, that Member State manifestly and gravely disregards the limits of its discretion.[167] Where a directive is incorrectly implemented, the breach is sufficiently serious when the Member State manifestly and gravely disregarded the limits on the exercise of its discretion.[168] Where the Member State in question was not called upon to make any legislative choices and had only considerably reduced, or even no discretion at all, the mere infringement of EU law may be sufficient to establish the existence of a sufficiently serious breach.[169] Where a directive leaves a certain degree of discretion to the Member States, the national court hearing a claim for reparation must take account of all the factors which characterise the situation put before it to determine whether a Member State has manifestly and gravely disregarded the limits to its discretion.[170] As a result, where a Member State has incorrectly implemented a provision which is capable of bearing several interpretations on which neither the CJ nor the Commission has given a ruling, it will not have committed a sufficiently serious breach.[171] It is important to note that Member State liability does not depend on a prior finding by the CJ of an infringement of EU law attributable to the state, or on the existence of intentional fault or negligence on the part of the organ of the state to which the infringement is attributable.[172] Finally, there must be a direct causal link between the breach of the Member State's obligation and the loss or damage sustained by the injured parties. This is largely a question of fact, which must be assessed by the national court in the light of the facts of the case. However, it is ultimately for the CJ to indicate its main elements, as causality is one of the EU law conditions for Member State liability.[173] Where these conditions are met, no other conditions need to be taken into consideration.

---

[166] ibid, para 55; and CJ 17 April 2007 Case C-470/03 *AGM-COSMET Srl v Suomen valtio and Tarmo Lehtinen* [2007] I-02749 ECLI:EU:C:2007:213, para 80.

[167] CJ 8 October 1996 Joined Cases C-178/94 C-179/94 C-188/94 C-189/94 and C-190/94 *Erich Dillenkofer Christian Erdmann Hans-Jürgen Schulte Anke Heuer Werner Ursula and Trosten Knor v Bundesrepublik Deutschland* [1996] I-04845 ECLI:EU:C:1996:375, para 26.

[168] CJ 26 Marsh 1996 Case C-392/93 *The Queen v HM Treasury ex parte British Telecommunications plc* [1996] ECLI:EU:C:1996:131, paras 39–45.

[169] CJ 23 May 1996 Case C-5/94 *The Queen v Ministry of Agriculture, Fisheries and Food ex parte Hedley Lomas (Ireland) Ltd* [1996] I-02553 ECLI:EU:C:1996:205, para 28.

[170] It must take into account the clarity and precision of the rule breached, the measure of discretion left by that rule to the national or EU authorities, whether the infringement and the damage caused was intentional or involuntary, whether any error of law was excusable or inexcusable, the fact that the position taken by an EU institution may have contributed towards the omission, and the adoption or retention of national measures or practices contrary to EU law. See CJ *Francovich et al* (n 147) para 56; and CJ 25 January 2007 Case C-278/05 *Carol Marilyn Robins et al v Secretary of State for Work and Pensions* [2007] I-01053 ECLI:EU:C:2007:476, paras 76–77.

[171] CJ *British Telecommunications* (n 168) paras 42–46.

[172] CJ *Dillenkofer et al* (n 167) paras 37–38.

[173] See Prechal 2005 277; Lenaerts and Van Nuffel 2011 para 22-093.

Sąd Apelacyjny (Court of Appeal Warsaw), 9 November 2011[174]   **6.25 (PL)**

X v State Treasury of the Republic of Poland

NO STATE LIABILITY BECAUSE NO CAUSAL LINK

Pre-contractual information duties

A claim for damages is refused because of the lack of causal relationship between the non-implementation and the damage

Facts: Poland had failed to implement in due time the following directives: Directive 2004/39/EC of the European Parliament and of the Council of 21 April 2004 on markets in financial instruments[175] and Commission Directive 2006/73/EC of 10 August 2006 implementing Directive 2004/39/EC.[176]

The claimant, a limited liability company, argued that the failure to implement the Directives in time resulted in a reduction of the scope of protection of clients of investment firms and the lack of sufficient information on the nature and risk of the services provided.

Held: The Court of First Instance dismissed the claim for damages, while the Court of Appeal of Warsaw dismissed the appeal of the claimant.

Judgment: The rules on Member State liability for breach of EU Law as developed in the case law of the CJ constitute one of the elements of the acquis …

The amendment of 17 June 2004 to the Civil Code[177] and some other statutes … which came into force on 1 September 2004, supplemented Article 417(1). Article 417(1) §1 of the Civil Code provides that if the damage has been inflicted by a normative act, one may claim compensation after it has been recognized in an appropriate procedure that this act is contrary to the Constitution, a ratified international treaty or a statute. Article 417(1) §4 of the Civil Code provides that if the damage has been inflicted by the failure to issue a normative act where the law provides for a duty to issue it, a court of law hearing the case for compensation of the damage may find that failure to issue that act is contrary to the law. The latter provision enacts liability for damages for so-called legislative negligence …

In this situation the question arose whether there was a causal link between the legislative negligence consisting in the delayed implementation of Directives 2004/39/EC and 2006/73/EC and the damage suffered by the claimant. In the view of the Court of Appeal there is no such link, and therefore, despite the fact that the other requirements for liability for damages of the State Treasury are met, the claim cannot be awarded …

In case of liability for omission to act, the causal link between omission and damage can only exist in cases where taking the required action could, in the ordinary course of events, prevent infliction of damage.

---

[174] Court of Appeal Warsaw Case I ACa 386/11 Lex (database) 1164703.

[175] [2004] OJ L145/44 (see n 143).

[176] Commission Directive 2006/73/EC of 10 August 2006 implementing Directive 2004/39/EC of the European Parliament and of the Council as regards organisational requirements and operating conditions for investment firms and defined terms for the purposes of that Directive [2004] OJ L241/26.

[177] The Polish Civil Code was adopted on 23 April 1964. See the consolidated text DzU 2014 item 121 as amended.

... In fact it is altogether difficult to speak about the existence of a causal link between the omission to act of the State Treasury in implementing Directives 2004/39/EC and 2006/73/EC and the damage suffered by the claimant. Although these directives confer a number of rights on investors and impose specific obligations on investment firms, they have not at the same time introduced any prohibitions on concluding financial transactions, including CIRIS type transactions. Nor do they have any influence on rules and means of clearing financial transactions. The adoption of a contrary position would have to lead to unlimited liability of the State Treasury for every transaction in the financial market that resulted in a loss for investors in the period between the deadline for implementation and the date of their actual transposition into national law. In the view of the Court of Appeal such a broad scope of liability of the State Treasury would exceed the framework of causal link within the meaning of Article 361§1 of the Civil Code.

Notes:

(1) According to the Court of Appeal of Warsaw, a comparison between the requirements for liability in damages in EU law and the requirements for liability in damages for legislative negligence in Polish law demonstrates that in this regard, national law is less restrictive than EU law. First of all, the Polish legislature did not introduce a requirement that the breach of law must be sufficiently serious, but merely requires that the unlawfulness results from the failure to issue a normative act, whose issuance was prescribed by law.

(2) It must be underlined that the Polish Civil Code does not require any fault on the part of the state treasury if the damage was suffered because of the way in which it exercised public authority.[178] This is strict liability. In *Brasserie du Pêcheur*, where the CJ held that state liability is not conditional upon a fault (intentional or negligent) of the organ of the state responsible for the breach, it nonetheless indicated that certain objective and subjective factors connected with the concept of fault under a national legal system may be relevant for determining whether or not a given breach of European law is serious.[179]

(3) The CJ requires a direct causal link between the breach of an obligation by the state and the damage sustained by the injured parties. The CJ does not define the term 'direct causal link'. In its judgment, the Court of Appeal of Warsaw did not consider whether an adequate causal link as required by the Civil Code between the damage and the omission to implement Directives 2004/39/EC and 2006/73/EC would meet the prerequisite of direct causal link in the case law of the CJ.

(4) The judgment of the Court of Appeal of Warsaw was confirmed by the Polish Supreme Court.[180] Referring to CJ cases, the Supreme Court ruled that Polish civil law did not set less favourable prerequisites for State liability for omission to implement directives than those arising from the case law of the CJ. The Supreme Court underlined that the scope of the information duties under Polish law and Directives 2004/39/EC and

---

[178] See art 77(1) of the 1997 Polish Constitution, according to which everyone may demand compensation for any harm done to them by any action of an organ of public authority contrary to law.

[179] CJ *Brasserie du Pêcheur and Factortame III* (n 151) paras 75–80.

[180] See judgment of the Polish Supreme Court of 19 June 2013 I CSK 392/12 OSN ZD 2014 C item 58.

2006/73/EC was not wide and that the claimant had not proven that non-implementation had caused the damage suffered in settling the transaction concluded with the bank. This meant that there was no causal link between the non-implementation of the Directives into Polish law and the damage sustained by the claimant.

VI.C CONSEQUENCES: REPARATION OF DAMAGES

Where the three conditions for state liability are satisfied, EU law gives rise to a right on the part of individuals to obtain reparation. However, it is on the basis of national tort law that the state must make reparation for the consequences of the loss and damage caused.[181] It is thus for the national legal order to determine against which authority the claim has to be made and to designate the judicial authority competent to determine disputes relating to compensation for damage.[182] However, the substantive and procedural conditions for reparation of loss and damage laid down by the national law of the Member States must not be less favourable than those relating to similar domestic claims and must not be so framed as to make it virtually impossible or excessively difficult to obtain reparation.[183]

Corte di Cassazione, Sezioni Unite (Italian Court of Cassation,
United Section), 17 April 2009[184]   **6.26 (IT)**

Ministero dell'università e della ricerca scientifica v Caggia

THE OBLIGATION TO AWARD DAMAGES FOR STATE LIABILITY IS AN *EX LEGE* OBLIGATION

Doctor please

The claim for damages in case of non-implementation of a directive is founded on breach of an ex lege *obligation by the Italian state*

Facts: A doctor was not paid the salary to which he was entitled as a specialist because the Italian state did not implement Directive 75/362/EEC on the mutual recognition of diplomas in medicine.[185] In this connection, the issue of the statutory limitation period for that claim for damages arose.

Held: The Supreme Court rejected the claim raised by the *Ministero dell'Università*, ruling that the liability of the State for damages based on a failure to implement a directive arises from the breach of an *ex lege* obligation to which the ten-year limitation period provided for contractual liability applies.

---

[181] CJ *Francovich et al* (n 147) paras 41–42.

[182] CJ *Köbler* (n 156) paras 44–50.

[183] CJ *Francovich et al* [1991], para 43.

[184] Italian Court of Cassation, United Section 17 April 2009 no 4197 *Ministero dell'Università e della ricerca scientific v Caggia, Corriere giuridico* 2009, 1345.

[185] Council Directive 75/362/EEC of 16 June 1975 concerning the mutual recognition of diplomas, certificates and other evidence of formal qualifications in medicine, including measures to facilitate the effective exercise of the right of establishment and freedom to provide services [1975] OJ L167/1.

Judgment: Given the autonomous and distinct nature of the two legal systems, European and national, legislative action may be characterized as illegal from an [EU] point of view, but not from the national point of view, according to fundamental principles clearly following from the Constitution itself …

It follows that for the law to be in conformity with [EU] law, it should ensure fair compensation for damage suffered by an individual caused by the fact that as a result of the breach of [EU] law he was not entitled to a right …

4.9 In conclusion, to achieve the result required by [EU] law by the means available under national law, the injured party must be allowed to claim damages suffered as a result of a so-called unlawful act of the legislature …

4.10 It follows that the claim of C., which arose when the damage occurred, is subject to the general limitation period (ten years) because the claim is aimed at the fulfilment of an obligation (being an indemnity obligation) imposed by law and is therefore held to fall within the scope of contractual liability'.

Notes:

(1) This decision sheds light on the nature of claims for damages arising from the non-implementation of a directive under Italian law. Although some earlier cases tended towards tortious liability, the Italian Court of Cassation in this decision held that this type of claim is based on contractual liability of the state for breach of an *ex lege* obligation. The legal nature of this state liability has the result that the statutory limitation period for contractual claims for damages is applicable (10 years, as opposed to five years, which is the limitation period for tortious liability). In itself, this case law is not contrary to EU law, as it is for the Member States' national law to lay down the relevant rules.

(2) In 2011 a provision was introduced to put an end to the debate. The statutory limitation period applicable to state liability claims is now determined by reference to the relevant provisions on tortious liability. It is therefore five years (Article 4, para 43, legge n. 183/2011).

VII. SPILLOVER EFFECTS OF DIRECTIVES

So far, this chapter has concerned itself with problems related to the incorrect or late implementation of directives into national law. Equally interesting, however, are the so-called spillover effects of directives, occurring where directive provisions are applied outside the directive's scope, in other (non-harmonised) areas of national law. Most common is the situation where a national legislature adjusts its national law beyond what is required by the directive.[186] Such 'spontaneous implementation' should be distinguished from the adoption of further-reaching measures, eg, expanding the level of protection provided for by a directive, but without enlarging the scope of protection beyond what is required by the directive.[187]

---

[186] Hartkamp 2016 no 154; Loos 2007 515–31. In Germany, this phenomenon is known as *'überschießende Umsetzung'*; see Habersack and Mayer 2010 335.
[187] Hartkamp 2016 no 154; Habersack and Mayer 2010 342–43.

The issue of spillover effects is closely related to the dynamics of private law harmonisation in the EU. Directives are usually limited in scope, being aimed at solving specific issues or eliminating disturbances to the internal market. This pointillist[188] nature of EU harmonisation is due to the limited transfer of competences to the EU, the necessity for every EU instrument to have a legal basis in EU Treaty law, and the principles of proportionality and subsidiarity.[189] As a result, the nature of directives not only tends to be specific rather than general, but coordination between different directives themselves is often lacking.[190] Consequently, EU harmonisation produces a dual harmonising and de-harmonizing effect. Positively, it leads to increasing uniformity between (certain areas of) the national laws of the Member States. The dark side of such harmonisation is that it leads to the fragmentation and incoherence of the national legal orders. The national laws of the Member States come to be composed of (at least) two sets of rules: those affected by EU harmonisation and those which remain unaffected.[191] Metaphorically speaking, an increasing number of European islands are appearing in the wide sea of Member State law.[192] The introduction of new rules through the implementation of a directive thus produces a certain amount of irritation and disturbance in the existing national legal orders. It raises many questions as to the role that the new rules play within the national legal order and the functioning of the legal system as a whole.[193] This poses a challenge to the legislature, the judiciary and legal doctrine.

When Member States have to implement a directive into their national legal orders, it is in the first place up to the legislature to cope with the potential dark side of harmonisation. There are roughly speaking two potential strategies.[194] The first is to simply implement the directive without having regard to other (non-harmonised) areas of national law. This means that the legislature accepts the fragmentation and irritation which the implementation causes to national law. The second is more challenging and cumbersome. It involves the adjustment and a new coordination of existing national law, even where this is not required by the directive, in order to maintain the coherence of national

---

[188] Hommelhoff, 'Zivilrecht under dem Einfluß europäischer Rechtsangleichung' (1992) 192 *AcP* 71, 102; H Kötz, 'Rechtsangleichung—Nutzen, Kosten, Methoden, Ziele'(1986) 50 *RabelsZ* 5; W-H Roth, 'Transposing 'Pointillist' EC Guidelines into Systematic National Codes: Problems and Consequences' (2002) 10(6) *ERPL* 6 761.

[189] Habersack and Mayer 2010 336–37; Van Gerven 2011 489–90.

[190] S Leible, 'The Approach to European Law in Domestic Legislation' (2003) 4(12) *German Law Journal* 1256–57; O Remien, 'Über den Stil des Europäischen Privatrechts' (1996) 60 *RabelsZ* 9. The ambitious objective of the Consumer Rights Directive proposal was to coordinate the existing consumer protection directives and replace minimum harmonisation by maximum harmonisation. This proposal met with considerable criticism and its scope was considerably reduced (Directive 2011/83 on consumer rights only repeals and amends the Doorstep Selling Directive and the Distance Selling Directive). One of the main criticisms was that as long as general contract law is not sufficiently harmonised, full harmonisation of consumer contract law remains an illusion: ME Storme, 'Editorial: Consumer Rights Proposals and Draft CFR' (2010) 18(1) *ERPL* 1–3.

[191] Van Gerven 2011 489–90.

[192] F Rittner, 'Das Gemeinschaftsprivatrecht und die europäische Integration' (1995) 50 *JZ* 851. See also: Loos 2007 521; R Schulze, 'European Private Law and Existing EC Law' (2005) 13(1) *ERPL* 4. Similarly, see O Remien, 'Über den Stil des Europäischen Privatrechts'(1996) 60 *RabelsZ* 8.

[193] Loos 2007 521.

[194] Roth (n 188) 770–72.

law. In this case, the legislature not only implements the provisions of the directive into national law, but also changes other rules of national law in order to make the provisions of a directive fit in more coherently.[195] In such cases, the national legislature can use the implementation as an opportunity to reconsider the content of national law and change outdated concepts. Mostly, however, national legislatures tend to opt for the first strategy and accept the incoherence it creates.[196]

In the latter case, the judiciary can still play an important role in bringing coherence in the national law where the implementation of a directive has distorted it. This can happen by means of an interpretation *per analogiam*, whereby rules and principles of EU law are applied to a part of private law which has not been harmonised yet in order to eliminate unwanted inconsistencies between the harmonised and non-harmonised parts of private law.[197] There is no EU law requirement for the national courts to interpret national rules which do not fall within the scope of a particular directive in accordance with that directive.[198] From the perspective of EU law, such interpretation remains entirely voluntary. It depends on several factors whether national courts will resort to such voluntary interpretation, including the willingness of a court to do so and the extent to which the provision of national law concerned is amenable to such interpretation.[199] Although there may not be an EU duty to interpret non-harmonised national law in conformity with a directive, such a duty may nevertheless arise from national (constitutional) law.[200]

VII.A VOLUNTARY BROADER IMPLEMENTATION

Entwurf eines Gesetzes zur Modernisierung
des Schuldrechts[201]   **6.27 (GERM)**

The modernization of the law of obligations is necessary at this point in time, because the directives mentioned above[202] oblige changes in parts of the Civil Code, which needed change anyway, and because isolated implementation of the directives would to an unacceptable extent enhance the structural deficits of the current law of obligations. It should also counter the increasing placement of important legal provisions outside the Civil Code and the related fragmentation of the law, and integrate consumer contract law into the Civil Code.

---

[195] Habersack and Mayer 2010 335; J Koch, 'Die Einheit der nationalen Rechtsordnung und die europäische Privatrechtsangleichung' (2006) 61(6) *JZ* 279.

[196] For the Netherlands, see Loos 2007 526 ff. For Belgium, see W van Gerven, 'Verkokering van het privaatrecht' (1991) 28 *TPR* 1021; S Stijns and I Samoy, 'Le nouveau droit de la vente: la transposition en droit belge de la Directive européenne sur la vente des biens de consommation' (2003) *TBBR* 2.

[197] Loos 2007 527; Van Gerven 2011 492.

[198] CJ 7 November 1989 Case C-125/88 *HFM Nijman* [1989] I-03533 ECLI:EU:C:1989:401.

[199] Loos 2007 527.

[200] *cf* section VII.B below.

[201] Deutscher Bundestag Drucksache 14/6040 2.

[202] Reference is made to Directive 1999/44/EC ([1999] OJ L171/12 (see n 63)) on certain aspects of the sale of consumer goods and associated guarantees, and to Directive 2000/35/EC of the European Parliament and the Council of 29 June 2000 on combating late payment in commercial transactions and Directive 2000/31/EC [2000] OJ L178/1 on electronic commerce.

In German law, there are many illustrations of the spillover effect of directives resulting from harmonization of national law outside the directives' scope. The German legislature has eg expanded the protection of the Doorstep Selling Directive to cases where a contract was not actually concluded in a doorstep situation, but where such a situation played a role in the contract being concluded. The most illustrative application of such spontaneous implementation, however, is the enactment by the German legislature of the Act on the Modernization of the Law of Obligations,[203] which came into force on 1 January 2002. Its main objectives were to integrate all contract law (including consumer contract law) into the Civil Code and to modernize the general contract law regime. In doing so, the German legislature broadly implemented various directives, and specifically the Consumer Sales Directive in order to establish a more coherent general contract law system. For example, it integrated the provisions of that directive into Germany's general contract law and sales law.[204]

One of the major questions entailed by such a broad harmonization of national law is how these provisions should be interpreted. More precisely, should such a provision be given a uniform interpretation ('*einheitliche Auslegung*') whether or not the matter falls within the scope of the directive, or would differentiated interpretation ('*gespaltene Auslegung*') be permitted? In other words, can the same provision be interpreted differently depending on whether or not the situation falls within the scope of the directive? There is no such duty of uniform interpretation in EU law, nor is there in national law.[205] It depends on the (national) criteria that determine interpretation. The difference between harmonious interpretation within and outside the scope of the directive is relevant here. Whereas the former has priority over all other national methods of interpretation, this is not so in the latter case, where an overall assessment is necessary and where no criterion takes priority.[206] To mark this difference terminologically, German doctrine calls the interpretation of non-harmonized national law in conformity with a directive 'quasi-harmonious interpretation' or 'directive-oriented' interpretation ('*quasi-richtlinienkonforme*' or '*richtlinienorientierte*' *Auslegung*).[207]

Most scholars attach great importance to the historical intention of the legislature as a basis for a presumption in favour of uniform interpretation of national law.[208] This intention is reflected in the creation of a uniform provision and would only allow differentiated interpretation in exceptional cases. Such a presumption would exist in particular where the legislature expressly refers to the directive and/or the case-law of the CJ. But even in the absence of such references there is a systematic argument which militates in favour of uniform interpretation. This argument loses force, however, where the legislature has introduced special rules for other issues within the scope of the directive. Where the non-harmonized part of national law concerns different interests than the directive (eg consumer protection), differentiated interpretation can be appropriate as well. This is the case where the legislature

---

[203] German Official Gazette 29 November 2001 3138 (*Gesetz zur Modernisierung des Schuldrechts*).

[204] S Grundmann and S Uhlig, 'German Contract Law—Nearly a Decade after the Fundamental Reform in the Schuldrechtsmodernisierung' (2011) 7(3) *ERCL* 78; B Gsell, 'Kaufrechtsrichtlinie und Schuldrechtsmodernisierung' (2001) 56 *JZ* 65; Koch (n 195).

[205] For a thorough discussion, see Habersack and Mayer 2010 347–55.

[206] Gebauer 2010 124; Habersack and Mayer 2010 355.

[207] Habersack and Mayer 2010 355–56.

[208] Gebauer 2010 124; Habersack and Mayer 2010 357; Koch (n 195).

has implemented directives providing consumer protection through national norms which are applicable to both B2B and B2C situations. The CJ will interpret such rules from the perspective of consumer protection only.[209] Although not decisive in itself, there is some force in the argument for uniform interpretation that differentiated interpretation will render the application of a norm more difficult and leads to other demarcation issues.[210]

The two following cases demonstrate the arguments for and against uniform interpretation, respectively.

Bundesgerichtshof (Supreme Court of Germany), 9 April 2002[211]   **6.28 (GERM)**

Heininger v Bayerische Hypo- und Vereinsbank AG

NO DIFFERENTIATED INTERPRETATION (*GESPALTENE AUSLEGUNG*)

Heininger, doorstep to uniform interpretation

The harmonious interpretation of §5(2) of the Doorstep Selling Cancellation Act also applies to cases within the scope of that Act, but outside the scope of the Doorstep Selling Directive

Facts: A couple took out a loan in order to finance the purchase of a flat, which they bought after a real estate agent paid several visits to their home. Repayment of the loan was secured by a land charge (*Grundschuld*). The loan agreement was concluded on the premises of the bank, where they were not informed about their rights of cancellation. Five years later, the couple cancelled the loan agreement and sought repayment of parts of the loan and interest paid to the bank.

Held: The claims were dismissed by the District Court and the Higher Regional Court of Munich, which held that neither the Doorstep Selling Cancellation Act[212] nor the Act on Consumer Credit[213] provided for a right of cancellation in the present case. The Federal Supreme Court of Germany referred several questions regarding the relationship between the Doorstep Selling Directive[214] and the Consumer Credit Directive to the CJ. The Federal Supreme Court followed the decision of the CJ,[215] in which it held that the consumer had a right of cancellation. However, the Federal Supreme Court even went further than it had to under EU law and ruled that the interpretation of the CJ was also valid for cases which were outside the scope of the Doorstep Selling Directive, but within the scope of the German implementation of it. The right of cancellation exists for all credit agreements which are doorstep contracts under the Doorstep Selling Cancellation Act, even when they fall outside the scope of the directive.

Judgment: ... Having regard to the spontaneous implementation into German law of the directive, this has the result that the loan contract indeed satisfies the criteria of a doorstep contract within the meaning of the Doorstep Selling Cancellation Act, yet does not fall within the scope of the Doorstep Selling Directive ...

---

[209] Habersack and Mayer 2010 359; H. Sprau, 'Einleitung' in *Palandt Bürgerliches Gesetzbuch*, Munich, Beck, 2011 no 44.

[210] Habersack and Mayer 2010 356–57.

[211] Federal Supreme Court of Germany 9 April 2009 XI ZR 91/99 *BGHZ* 150, 248 *Heiniger v Bayerische Hypo- und Vereinsbank AG*. Other aspects of this case were discussed above in section III.C.ii.

[212] *Haustürwiderrufsgesetz* (see n 113).

[213] *Verbraucherkreditgesetz* (see n 114).

[214] [1985] OJ L372/31 (see n 15). The Doorstep Selling Directive was repealed as of 13 June 2014 by Directive 2011/83/EU of 25 October 2011.

[215] CJ *Heininger* (n 114).

The scope of the Doorstep Selling Directive, which by comparison is narrower than the scope of the Doorstep Selling Cancellation Act, does not justify a different interpretation of §5(2) of the Doorstep Selling Cancellation Act. Rather, harmonious interpretation expands its applicability to contracts which, while not falling within the scope of the directive, do satisfy the national-law criteria of a doorstep selling contract. Differentiated interpretation, as advocated by a part of legal doctrine ... according to which harmonious interpretation should remain limited to cases falling within the scope of the directive, is not convincing ... It is contrary to the equal treatment of different doorstep situations which is necessitated by German law ...

Moreover, differentiated interpretation is contrary to the meaning and purpose of §1 (in its old version) Doorstep Selling Cancellation Act. This §1 requires equal treatment of all agreements made in a doorstep situation itself or under the influence of a doorstep situation. Differentiated interpretation would frustrate this legislative purpose. The German legislature did not allow scope for such interpretation. With its decision to give a wider definition of the concept of doorstep selling contract than the Doorstep Selling Directive requires, it has in fact given expression to its intention to consider customers in all situations covered by §1 (in its old version) Doorstep Selling Cancellation Act equally worthy of protection, irrespective of whether or not they fall within the scope of the directive.

Notes:

(1) The first part of this case has already been discussed in section III.C.ii above.

(2) The German definition of the concept of doorstep contract is broader than the definition given to it in Directive 85/577/EEC. The Directive is only applicable to contracts which are concluded in the home or the working place of the consumer, whereas the German Doorstep Selling Cancellation Act is already applicable where pre-contractual negotiations took place away from the trader's premises.

(3) According to the Federal Supreme Court of Germany, the interpretation given by the CJ in its *Heininger* judgment (the consumer has a right of cancellation) is also applicable to such contracts when they fall within the scope of the Doorstep Selling Cancellation Act, even if the Directive is not applicable to them.

(4) This could be called second-degree spontaneous harmonisation. The German legislature first chose to implement Directive 85/577/EEC beyond what was strictly required and broadened the scope of the right of cancellation. Next, the Federal Supreme Court ruled that the interpretation, given by the CJ, also applied to situations not falling within the scope of the Directive, without there being any EU law obligation for such harmonious interpretation.

(5) The issue which the Federal Supreme Court had to resolve, was a consequence of the fact that the legislature implemented the Doorstep Selling Directive more widely than was required by the Directive. As a result, the question arose whether the interpretation given to §5(2) of the Doorstep Selling Cancellation Act was to be the same for all situations, within or outside the scope of the Directive. Many scholars argued in favour of differentiated interpretation (*gespaltene Auslegung*).[216] They argued that this paragraph

---

[216] eg, M Habersack and C Mayer, 'Der Widerruf von Haustürgeschäften nach der "Heininger"-Entscheidung' (2002) *WM* vol 56 257–58; A Piekenbrock and G Schulze, 'Die Grenzen richtlinienkonformer Auslegung—autonomes Richterrecht oder horizontale Direktwirkung' (2002) *WM* 527–528.

should be interpreted differently depending on whether or not the situation falls within the scope of the Directive.

(6) The Federal Supreme Court refused to adopt a differentiated interpretation. It ruled that such interpretation would go against the equal treatment of different doorstep situations intended by German law. According to the Federal Supreme Court, the German legislature has demonstrated, by implementing the Directive more broadly, that it wanted to give equal treatment to all doorstep situations, whether or not they fell within the scope of the Directive. The Federal Supreme Court added that a differentiated interpretation would lead to many practical issues, thus making it necessary to assess in each individual case whether it fell within the scope of the Directive or not.

Bundesgerichtshof (Supreme Court of Germany),
17 October 2012[217] **6.29 (GERM)**

DIFFERENTIATED INTERPRETATION *(GESPALTENE AUSLEGUNG)*

The (artificial) grass is always greener …

The requirement to take away the defective goods and install replacement goods in case of non-conformity is not applicable in B2B or C2C situations

Facts: Two enterprises concluded a contract for the delivery of granulation to repair an artificial turf. After installation, the material delivered appeared defective. The supplier put replacement materials at the buyer's disposal, but refused to take away the defective granulation and put in the replacement materials. Referring to the Federal Supreme Court's decision in *Weber*, the buyer brought proceedings against the supplier.

Held: The Federal Supreme Court of Germany held that its case law (and that of the CJ), according to which a seller is required to take away the defective goods and install the replacement goods in case of non-conformity, is only applicable to situations within the scope of the Consumer Sales Directive, ie, between a seller and a consumer. It is not applicable to sales contracts between enterprises or between consumers.

Judgment: 17. b) The court has not yet given any decision on the interpretation of §439(1), alternative 2, BGB outside the field of consumer sales …

18. aa) The obligation of harmonious interpretation following from the obligation to implement a directive laid down in Article 288(3) TFEU and the EU principle of good faith of Article 4(3) TEU, is not applicable here. It is limited to the scope of the directive. The provisions of the directive and the judgment of the CJ only pertain to consumer sales and not to other sales contracts.

19. The harmonious interpretation of §439(1), alternative 2, BGB undertaken by the Court in its decision of 21 December 2011 [*Weber* case] does not go beyond the directive itself, and is therefore likewise limited to consumer sales …

20. bb) Harmonious interpretation can, however, also be relevant to national law outside the scope of a directive, when there has been spontaneous implementation of a directive into national law [reference to the *Heininger* case]. In that case no duty arises from EU law to harmoniously interpret law which does not fall under the directive. Such

---

[217] Federal Supreme Court of Germany 17 October 2012 VIII ZR 226/11 *BGHZ* 195, 135.

a duty can, however, follow from national law, ie, from an intention of the national legislature to such effect.

21. This is a case of transposition beyond the requirements of the directive. The legislature did not implement the provisions of EU law on supplementary performance as part of the special provisions on consumer sales (§474 ff BGB), but introduced them into the provisions of §433 ff BGB which are applicable to all sales contracts.

22. A further requirement for harmonious interpretation of §439(1) alternative 2, BGB beyond the field of consumer sales is, as mentioned above, that the will to expand the obligation to deliver replacement goods as referred to in the decision of the CJ corresponds with the will of the legislature ... This cannot be presumed. When the legislature spontaneously implemented the provisions of EU law on supplementary performance, it proceeded on the basis of a different understanding of the directive than the CJ. The preparatory documents for the Reform of the Law of Obligations show that the legislature did not intend such a far-reaching expansion of the obligation of replacement as established by the CJ, and that it therefore would not have wanted it to apply to sales law as a whole. This justifies limiting harmonious interpretation of §439(1) alternative 2, BGB—as well as teleological reduction of §439(4) BGB [reference to the *Quelle* case] to consumer sales and not expanding it to other contracts which do not fall within the scope of the directive.

23. To this extent there is a substantial difference from the decision of the Federal Supreme Court of 9 April 2002 [*Heininger* case], ... Expanding harmonious interpretation beyond the field of consumer sales to include the wider field of contracts between businesses or between consumers, which is the subject of the present case, was not the intention of that decision either ...

27. The legislature did indeed intend to create uniform rules for all sales contracts when it transposed the provisions of the directive on supplementary performance into §439 BGB. This intention was, however, founded on the explained incorrect understanding of the scope of the obligation of supplementary performance when replacing defective goods by conforming goods. There is therefore no indication that the legislature would have uniformly regulated the obligation of supplementary performance under §439(1) alternative 2, BGB with respect to all sales contracts, if it had been aware of the CJ's subsequent interpretation of the directive. Rather, it must be assumed that the legislature would have limited the implementation of the provisions of the directive regarding the obligation of supplementary performance to consumer sales, if it had already known at the time that the CJ would assign a meaning to supplementary performance going beyond repeating the obligations of the seller and expanding it into a contract for services ... A Harmonious interpretation of §439(1) alternative 2, BGB beyond the field of consumer sales into the wide field of sales contracts between businesses or between consumers must therefore be rejected.

Notes:

(1) In its *Weber* judgment (discussed in section III.B.ii above), the Federal Supreme Court of Germany, following the CJ, had held that a consumer who had a good installed which turned out to be defective was entitled to removal of the defective good and the installation of the replacement good. As the German legislature had implemented the Consumer Sales Directive more broadly than the Consumer Sales Directive required, the question arose whether the decision in *Weber* was valid between enterprises as well.

(2) In the *Weber* case, contrary to the decision in *Heininger* discussed above, in which the Federal Supreme Court refused a differentiated interpretation, it adopted such an interpretation. In other words, §439 BGB on the remedies of a buyer in case of non-conformity is interpreted differently (and gets a narrower meaning) when it is applied outside the scope of Directive 1999/44/EC, ie, between enterprises or between consumers. In that case, 'delivery of a conforming good' does not include the removal of a defective good and reinstallation of a conforming good. In other words, the case law on B2C contracts is not expanded to apply to B2B or C2C situations.

(3) The Federal Supreme Court made it clear that in *Weber*, it only ruled on the interpretation of §439 BGB for consumer sales. It then confirmed that the (EU) duty to interpret national provisions in conformity with a directive is limited by the scope of that directive. This is not the end of the matter. A duty to interpret national provisions falling outside the scope of a directive in conformity with that directive can still arise out of national law, eg, from the intention of the legislature.[218] According to the Federal Supreme Court, when the German legislature implemented Directive 1999/44/EC beyond its scope, it had a different understanding of the remedies than the CJ. Referring to the preparatory documents, it ruled that the legislature did not have in mind an extension of the remedies available to the buyer in the way done by the CJ. It could therefore not have had the intention to introduce such broad remedies into its general sales law. For the Federal Supreme Court, this is the decisive distinction between *Heininger* and the present case. In the former, consumer protection was only expanded to cover some other situations which the German legislature had intended to treat equally as doorstep situations. According to the Federal Supreme Court, the important expansion of consumer protection cannot be expanded to B2B or C2C situations. While it is true that the German legislature, when implementing Directive 1999/44/EC, sought to create a coherent scheme for all sales contracts, it did so under an incorrect understanding of the scope and the content of the remedies in case of non-conformity. Had the legislature known how widely the CJ would interpret these remedies, it would have limited those provisions to consumer sales.

(4) The criterion of the intention of the legislature is to some extent controversial. According to some, the criterion of the hypothetical intention of the legislature is absolutely adequate. One commentator has put it like this: 'The more surprising the interpretation of a provision of a directive by the CJ is, the stronger is the argument against a hypothetical intention of the legislature to create a uniform scheme.'[219]

---

[218] This is sometimes called 'directive-oriented interpretation', as opposed to 'directive-conform interpretation: see, eg, S Lorenz, 'Aus- und Wiedereinbaukosten bei der kaufrechtlichen Nacherfüllung zwischen Unternehmern' (2013) 66 *NJW* 207–09.

[219] ibid 208–09.

VII.B MANDATORY BROADER IMPLEMENTATION THROUGH THE (NATIONAL) PRINCIPLE OF EQUALITY

A Belgian case offers a clear illustration of the interaction between the content of a directive (and its implementation) and the national legal order as a whole. It illustrates how national constitutional principles can oblige the legislature to implement the rules of a directive beyond the limited scope of that directive. In this case, the interaction comprised five stages: the implementation of the Late Payment Directive, a judgment of the Constitutional Court of Belgium, the enactment of the Act on the Recovery of Legal Fees, another judgment of the Constitutional Court and a drastic solution.

The Late Payment Directive is part of the policy of the EC to protect small and medium-sized enterprises (SMEs) against late payments. The European Commission had established that one-quarter of all insolvencies were caused by late payment and that SMEs were especially vulnerable. The Directive therefore establishes a period of 30 days within which a debtor must pay its debt. When there is no payment, interest becomes payable at a high rate. Furthermore, the creditor is entitled to claim reasonable compensation from the debtor for all relevant recovery costs.

Article 3(1)(e) of the Late Payment Directive
2000[220]   **6.30 (EU)**

[U]nless the debtor is not responsible for the delay, the creditor shall be entitled to claim reasonable compensation from the debtor for all relevant recovery costs incurred through the latter's late payment. Such recovery costs shall respect the principles of transparency and proportionality as regards the debt in question. Member States may, while respecting the principles referred to above, fix maximum amounts as regards the recovery costs for different levels of debt.

Article 6 of the Belgian Act on Late Payment
2002 (original version)[221]   **6.31 (BE)**

Moreover, unless the parties have otherwise agreed with regard to Article 7, when the debtor has not made payment within the agreed term of payment or, in the absence of such agreement, within the payment term established in Article 4, the creditor is entitled to reasonable compensation for all relevant recovery costs incurred through the late payment without prejudice to his right to compensation for legal costs pursuant to the Judicial Code. The application of this Article precludes awarding the sums set by Article 1018(1), 6° and 1022 of the Judicial Code.

---

[220] Directive 2000/35/EC of the European Parliament and the Council of 29 June 2000 on combating late payment in commercial transactions [2000] OJ L200/35. This Directive was recast by Directive 2011/7/EU of the European Parliament and of the Council of 16 February 2011 on combating late payment in commercial transactions [2011] OJ L48/1.
[221] Belgian Official Gazette 7 Augustus 2002 (Act of 2 August 2002 on combating late payment in commercial transactions).

These recovery costs shall satisfy the principles of transparency and shall be proportionate to the relevant debt.

The King will set maximum amounts as regards the recovery costs for different levels of debt.

The Belgian legislature implemented the Late Payment Directive through the Late Payment Act. The choice for an independent law, instead of introducing the relevant rules into the Civil Code and the Judicial Code, was deplored in legal doctrine.[222] Moreover, questions were already raised during the parliamentary preparations for the Act and in legal doctrine[223] about the constitutionality of the way in which the Belgian legislature intended to implement the Directive. In particular, Article 6 of the Act, taken almost verbatim from Article 3(1)(e) of the Directive, caused a lot of concern. At issue was the discrimination it introduced between those creditors outside and those within the scope of the Act. Only the latter were entitled to compensation for all judicial and extra-judicial recovery costs. This was due to the traditional opinion in Belgian law, which is hostile to the recovery of legal fees. In principle, each party pays its own lawyer. In 2007, a Justice of the Peace referred the issue to the Belgian Constitutional Court, which ruled that the situation was unconstitutional.

Grondwettelijk Hof België (Constitutional Court of Belgium),
17 January 2007[224]   **6.32 (BE)**

nv Lebelco v Coolen

SPILLOVER EFFECT AS A RESULT OF THE CONSTITUTIONAL PRINCIPLE OF EQUALITY

Money makes (a lawyer's) world go round

The absence of a statutory scheme on the recovery of legal costs and fees for citizens outside the scope of the Late Payment Act is contrary to the constitutional principle of equality—yet the source of this discrimination is not the Act itself, but rather the absence of a general statutory scheme, which has to be created by the legislature

Facts: In a dispute between an enterprise and an individual relating to rent in arrears and the termination of the rental contract, the question arose whether the lessor could claim compensation for fees payable to its lawyer. The Late Payment Act, which provides for such a rule, was not applicable. The Justice of the Peace referred several questions to the Constitutional Court as to whether this was constitutional.

Held: The absence of a statutory scheme on the recovery of legal costs and fees for citizens outside the scope of the Late Payment Act was contrary to Articles 10 and 11 of the Belgium Constitution (the principle of equality and non discrimination). The source of this discrimination is not the Act itself, but the absence of a general statutory scheme, which has to be created by the legislature.

---

[222] eg, V Sagaert and I Samoy, 'De wet van 2 augustus 2002 betreffende de bestrijding van de betalingsachterstand bij handelstransacties. Een verwittigd wanbetaler is er twee waard' (2002–03) 45 *RW* 334.

[223] *Parl St* Kamer 2001-02 no 1827/5 16; ME Storme, 'De wet van 2 augustus 2002 inzake betalingsachterstand en de discriminatie inzake de verhaalbaarheid van advocatenkosten' (2003) 40 *TPR* 1077.

[224] Constitutional Court of Belgium 17 January 2007 *RGAR* 2007 no 2 14222 annotated by F Glansdorff *nv Lebelco v Coolen.*

Judgment: B.4.1 The Act of 2 August 2002 on combating late payment in commercial transactions provides for a special regulation on payment of compensation for commercial transactions …

B.4.3. The aforementioned Act of 2 August 2012 is however not applicable to the case pending before the judge *a quo* …

B.5. There is therefore a difference in treatment between citizens who enter into commercial transactions within the meaning of the Act of 2 August 2002 and citizens entering into transactions who do not fall within the scope of that act. The former can rely on a legal arrangement as regards the recovery of legal costs and fees, whereas this is not the case for the second category. The preliminary questions aim to obtain a ruling from the Court whether this difference in treatment is contrary to Articles 10 and 11 of the Constitution.

B.6. The Act of 2 August 2002 on combating late payment in commercial transactions aims to implement Directive 2000/35/EC of the European Parliament and the Council of 29 June 2000 on combating late payment in commercial transactions … The ratio legis of the directive is that late payment in commercial transactions and specifically the different regulation of its consequences in the Member States of the European Union, constitutes an obstacle to the proper functioning of the internal market and particularly affects small and medium-sized enterprises …

B.7. The difference in treatment in question does not arise from the Act of 2 August 2002, of which the scope is in effect perfectly in conformity with the purpose it pursues, but rather stems from the fact that, since the judgment of the Court of cassation of 2 September 2004, the legislature has not provided in a more general manner for the recovery of legal costs and fees.

B.8. As in the judgments nos. 57/2006 and 95/2006, the Court considers that it is up to the legislature to appreciate in which manner and to what extent the recovery of legal fees and costs must be organized.

B.9. It follows from the foregoing that the difference in treatment forming the issue of the preliminary questions is discriminatory, but that this discrimination does not stem from the Act of 2 August 2002 on combating late payment in commercial transactions, but from the absence of a general scheme, which only the legislature can provide, with regard to the Articles 10 and 11 of the Constitution.

Notes:

(1) In this case, the Constitutional Court of Belgium assessed the limited scope of the Act on Late Payment in the light of the principles of equality and non-discrimination (Articles 10 and 11 of the Belgian Constitution).

(2) The Constitutional Court held that there is a difference in treatment between citizens falling within and outside the scope of the Late Payment Act. Only the former are entitled to the recovery of legal fees and costs; the latter are not. The source of this difference is not the Act itself, whose scope is in conformity with its *ratio legis*, but rather stems from the fact that the legislature has not provided for a general scheme for the recovery of legal fees and costs. The Constitutional Court ruled that this difference in treatment was discriminatory and therefore in breach of Articles 10 and 11 of the Belgian Constitution in conjunction with Article 6 of the ECHR. However, the source of the discrimination does not lie in the Late Payment Act itself, but rather in the absence of a general scheme, which only the legislature can provide.

(3) In an earlier decision, the Constitutional Court had already had to deal with the question whether the limited scope of a directive could justify a difference in treatment.[225] At issue was the constitutionality of the Belgian deposit-guarantee scheme, which was limited to deposits in a currency of the EU. This limitation was permitted by Article 7(2) of Directive 94/19/EC on deposit-guarantee schemes.[226] The government argued that the Constitutional Court lacked competence on the grounds of the supremacy of EU law, since the Directive permitted the limitation. The Constitutional Court, however, ruled that it was nonetheless competent to assess the constitutionality of a provision of law permitted by a directive. Furthermore, when the nature of the exception is optional, the Constitutional Court can assess how the legislature had used its discretion. In this earlier case, however, the Constitutional Court held that the difference in treatment was justified by objective criteria and did not have disproportionate consequences. The case already made it clear that the Constitutional Court would assess the implementation of directives and that the limited scope of a directive does not constitute a justification for introducing unconstitutional discrimination. The national legislature must also obey the constitutional principles of equality and non-discrimination when implementing a directive.[227]

The legislature took the clear hint of the Constitutional Court. Only a few months later, it passed the Act on the Recovery of Legal Fees.[228] This act introduced a new Article 1022 into the Judicial Code. This Article entitles the winning party to a lump sum compensation for legal costs and fees. The precise amounts are established by Royal Decree, taking into account the nature and the importance of the case. The court may, however, modify the compensation, taking into account the financial resources of the losing party, the complexity of the case, contractually stipulated compensations and the manifestly unjust nature of the situation.

This was not the end of the matter. The 2007 Act did not alter the regime of the Late Payment Act. As a result, there were still two different regimes in existence. Under the Late Payment Act, the court has much wider discretion in awarding compensation for legal fees, and the applicable criteria diverge significantly. Pursuant to Article 6 of the Late Payment Act, such compensation must be reasonable, transparent, proportionate to the claim and relevant. Pursuant to Article 6 *in fine*, the maximum amount of such compensation would be established by Royal Decree. However, this Royal Decree was never enacted. This had the curious consequence that some courts looked to the Royal Decree relating to the 2007 Act for inspiration to decide what was reasonable compensation. In other words, courts that had to apply the national law implementing a directive based their judgments on national rules which were themselves enacted because of the limited scope of the implementation of a directive in national law.

This difference in treatment was brought before the Constitutional Court. In a judgment of 2008, it ruled that the difference was not discriminatory. The Constitutional Court

---

[225] Constitutional Court of Belgium 20 September 2001 *BFR* 2001/IV 249 ff annotated by M Tison.

[226] Directive 94/19/EC of the European Parliament and of the Council of 30 May 1994 on deposit-guarantee schemes [1994] OJ L135/5.

[227] ME Storme, 'De wet van 2 augustus 2002 inzake betalingsachterstand en de discriminatie inzake de verhaalbaarheid van advocatenkosten' (2003) 3 *TPR* 1084.

[228] Belgian Official Gazette 31 May 2007 no 161 29541-29543 (Act of 21 April 2007 on the Recovery of Legal Fees and Costs Related to the Assistance of a Lawyer).

held that the legislature could create another general scheme adjusted to the diversity of litigation and that it was not bound to simply copy the rules of Article 6 of the Late Payment Act. Nevertheless, the Constitutional Court added that it would be desirable that the differences between the two regimes (the Late Payment Act versus the Act on the Recovery of Legal Fees) would not be too great. It also called to mind that it is for the government to enact the Royal Decree mentioned in Article 6 of the Late Payment Act. Instead of aligning the two regimes and enacting the Royal Decree, the legislature chose to eliminate the difference by simply repealing Article 6 of the Late Payment Act altogether. However, this abrogation has not yet entered into force. This raises the question whether the current situation is still in conformity with the Late Payment Directive. Pursuant to the Directive, a creditor is entitled to recover all relevant costs and not to a mere lump sum compensation.

VIII. CONCLUSION

This chapter has dealt with the private law effects of directives. The focus was not on the correct transposition of directives into the different national legal systems, and the details of specific private law directives were not discussed. The first part of the chapter dealt with the legal techniques available to the national courts to ensure the effectiveness of directives, even when their provisions have not been implemented correctly or not in time.

National case law first of all confirms the established case law of the CJ according to which provisions of a directive cannot be invoked by individuals in a horizontal relationship.[229] This remains a lacuna in the framework of judicial protection created by the EU and threatens to undermine the effectiveness of those provisions. Therefore, the CJ has nevertheless accepted various exceptions or nuances to this strict principle. An interesting, but not uncontroversial, nuance is that the concept of 'Member State' is given a broad interpretation.[230] This allows national courts to construe a case as a case between an individual and a Member State, ie, a vertical relationship. This has the result that the individual can directly rely on the provisions of a directive which has not been implemented correctly or not in time. This transformation of a case which at first glance seems to involve a horizontal relationship into a case concerning a vertical relationship is a powerful technique to ensure the effectiveness of a directive.

An extremely potent technique, and probably the one that is used most frequently, is the principle of harmonious interpretation. National courts are obliged to interpret national law as far as possible in conformity with the provisions of a directive. In the *Von Colson* case, this technique allowed the national court to award compensation amounting to the positive interest, where German law expressly only allowed compensation

---

[229] eg Italian Court of Cassation 5 April 2005 (n 25); Court of Appeal Antwerp 1 March 2010 (n 62); Supreme Court of the Netherlands 13 September 2013 (n 73); and Court of Appeal Amsterdam 10 November 2009 (n 106).

[230] eg, Polish Supreme Court 13 March 2008 about an independent public health care unit (n 33).

for 'Vertrauensschaden'.[231] The court took the ground that the principle of harmonious interpretation trumped the ordinary national methods of interpretation of the law. This technique also allowed the Polish Supreme Court to award damages for non-pecuniary loss in a case concerning a package travel contract, where this was not possible under national law.[232] It allowed the Supreme Court of the Netherlands to rule that the courts had a duty to *ex officio* annul unreasonable contract clauses, where Dutch law seemed to require the invocation of nullity or a claim for annulment by the consumer.[233]

The duty of harmonious interpretation has a large scope. It invites and challenges national courts to be creative in order to grant the protection which the directive is aimed at providing. This creativity can go very far, especially when open norms are applicable, since these are more readily amenable to harmonious interpretation. The Belgian cases on the belated implementation of Directive 1999/44/EC constitute excellent examples of this. The concept of a 'short period' in the Civil Code was interpreted in conformity with Article 5(2) of that Directive, so that it could not be less than two years.[234] However, some Belgian courts went further and ventured into the boundaries of harmonious interpretation by also ruling that hidden defects becoming apparent within six months after delivery should, in the absence of proof to the contrary, be considered to have been present at the moment of delivery.[235] In those cases, the courts seem to have allowed the horizontal direct effect of Article 5(3) of the Directive. In some cases, the national courts expressly attached importance to the fact that the legislature, when it implemented the Directive, had the intention of giving full effect to the system set up by the Directive.[236] The German case law on harmonious interpretation clearly demonstrates the creative and innovative force which this principle enshrines, forcing national courts to go further than mere interpretation in the light of a directive. The courts must also, where possible, develop the law in conformity with directives. They can do so through teleological reduction when the legislative framework appears to be incomplete in a way which is contrary to the legislative scheme. According to the German Supreme Court, this is not contrary to the constitutional principle that the judiciary is bound by the law.[237] In some cases, national courts go to great lengths to conform to EU law (and CJ case law). In one of the cases discussed, the French Court of Cassation resorted to a teleological reduction of its national law in such a way that it could be considered to have effectively disapplied a national provision that was contrary to a directive.[238]

Harmonious interpretation is not always imposed by EU law—it can also be voluntary. This happens mainly through the application of open-ended concepts of national law, which can then be concretised or 'coloured' in function of directives. In a Belgian

---

[231] Employment Tribunal Hamm 6 September 1984 (n 46).
[232] Polish Supreme Court 19 November 2010 (n 75).
[233] Supreme Court of the Netherlands 13 September 2013 (n 73).
[234] Court of Appeal Mons 30 May 2005 (n 60); Court of Appeal Antwerp 1 March 2010 (n 62).
[235] Court of Appeal Liège 10 October 2007 (n 61); Court of Appeal Antwerp 1 March 2010 (n 62).
[236] Supreme Court of the Netherlands 29 December 1995 (n 64); Federal Supreme Court of Germany 26 November 2008 (n 80).
[237] Eg Federal Supreme Court of Germany 26 November 2008 (n 80); Federal Supreme Court of Germany 21 December 2011 (n 86).
[238] French Court of Cassation 13 July 2010 (n 88).

case, a creative tribunal applied the prohibition of abuse of rights to sanction a discriminatory dismissal.[239]

The application of the principle of harmonious interpretation is subject to limitations. Although national courts are under a strong obligation to interpret their national law in conformity with a directive, they are not bound to resort to a *contra legem* interpretation of national law.[240] This applies even more forcefully where such harmonious interpretation would clearly go against the express intention of the legislature. It is in the first place for the legislature to bring its legislation into line with directives.[241]

A technique which cannot always be clearly distinguished from harmonious interpretation is the technique of reviewing, and possibly disapplying, national law in the light of a directive or of other instruments of EU law, eg, a general principle of EU law. Such disapplication can indirectly influence legal relationships between individuals.

In a Belgian case, however, the application of the principle of non-discrimination on the grounds of age was refused in a horizontal relationship.[242]

When all other techniques fail, individuals who did not receive the protection to which they were entitled according to a directive which had not been implemented correctly or not in time can claim damages from the Member State for the loss caused thereby. This obviously involves a vertical relationship between an individual and a Member State. For example, where a former commercial agent was not entitled to compensation because Belgium had implemented the relevant directive belatedly, his claim against the Belgian state was accepted.[243]

The last part of this chapter dealt with the spillover effects of directives. These effects embrace all forms of influence which are exercised by directives beyond their scope. A national legislature can, eg, choose to implement a directive more broadly than the directive requires. This option was taken by the German legislature when it modernised the law of obligations in 2001. One of the main questions arising in this situation is whether the national provisions which are based on the directive but are outside its scope should nevertheless be interpreted in conformity with that directive (and its interpretation by the CJEU). The principle of coherence and the clear intention of the legislature that certain situations be given equal treatment militate in favour of uniform interpretation.[244] However, in cases where the interpretation given to a directive by the CJ clearly departs from its interpretation by the national legislature, an argument can be made in favour of restricting that interpretation to the scope of the directive. This is especially the case where the national legislature has implemented a consumer protection directive so as to include all contracts. The specific consumer protection rationale underlying the CJ case law may not be readily applicable to a B2B or C2C relationship. The Federal Supreme Court of Germany therefore refused to expand the interpretation given by the CJ in the *Weber* case to cover a B2B contract.[245]

---

[239] Employment Tribunal Brussels 2 December 2005 (n 121).
[240] Federal Supreme Court of Germany 14 October 2003 (n 107).
[241] Court of Appeal Amsterdam 10 November 2009 (n 106).
[242] Employment Court Brussels 11 April 2008 (n 139).
[243] Belgian Court of Cassation 28 September 2001 (n 159).
[244] Federal Supreme Court of Germany 9 April 2002 (n 111).
[245] Federal Supreme Court of Germany 17 October 2012 (n 217).

In other cases, national general principles of law or constitutional principles of equality and non-discrimination may require a certain regulation to be applied beyond the limited scope of a directive. In such cases, it is not EU law, but rather national law which fuels a spillover effect. The saga on recovery of legal fees in Belgium provides a textbook example. When the Late Payment Act only provided for the recovery of legal fees for commercial transactions, the absence of a more general scheme was held to constitute unconstitutional discrimination.[246] Ultimately, the Belgian legislature had to take action to end this unconstitutional situation.

FURTHER READING

P Craig, Directives: Direct Effect, Indirect Effect and the Construction of National Legislation' (1997) 22(6) *EL Rev* 519–38.

P Craig, 'The Legal Effects of Directives: Policy, Rules and Exceptions' (2009) 34(3) *EL Rev* 339–77.

Craig and De Búrca 2015, 1198.

Dashwood/Dougan/Rodger/Spaventa/Wyatt 2011.

M Domańska, *Implementacja dyrektyw unijnych przez sądy krajowe* (Warsaw, Wolters Kluwer Business, 2014).

M Gebauer and T Wiedmann (eds), *Zivilrecht under europäischem Einfluss* (Stuttgart, Richard Boorberg, 2010).

Gebauer 2010 111–39.

Habersack and Mayer 2010 334–65.

Hartkamp 2016.

Hartley 2010.

P Kapteyn, A McDonnell, K Mortelmans, C Timmermans and L Geelhoed (eds), *The Law of the European Union and the European Communities* (Alphen aan den Rijn, Kluwer Law International, 2008) 1406.

Kapteyn 2008 511–74.

A Kunkiel-Kryńska, *Metody harmonizacji prawa konsumenckiego w Unii Europejskiej I ich wpływ na procesy implementacyjne w państwach członkowskich* (Warsaw, Wolters Kluwer Business, 2013).

B Kurcz, *Dyrektywy Wspólnoty Europejskiej I ich implementacja do prawa krajowego*, Serie Monografie Zakamyca (Kraków, Zakamycze, 2004).

Lenaerts and Van Nuffel 2011.

M Lenz, 'Horizontal What? Back to Basics' (2000) 25(5) *EL Rev* 509–22.

L Mance, 'The interface between National and European Law' (2013) 38 *EL Rev* 437–56.

Prechal 2005 349.

S Prechal, 'Remedies after *Marshall*' (2009) *CMLR* 451–73.

S Prechal, 'Member State Liability and Direct Effect: What's the Difference after All?' (2006) 17 *EBLR* 299–316.

Roth 2010 308–33.

CH Sieburgh, 'EU Law and Non-contractual Liability of the Union, Member States and Individuals' in Hartkamp/Sieburgh/Keus/Kortmann/Wissink (eds) 2014 465–542.

---

[246] Constitutional Court of Belgium 17 January 2007 (n 224).

W van Gerven, 'A Common Law for Europe: The Future Meeting the Past?'(2001) 4 *ERPL* 485–503.

W van Gerven, 'The Horizontal Effect of Directive Provisions Revisited: The Reality of Catchwords' in D Curtin and T Heukels (eds), *Institutional Dynamics of European Integration, Essays in Honour of Henry G. Schermers Volume II* (Dordrecht, Martinus Nijhoff, 1994) 335–54.

7

APPLICATION OF PRIMARY AND SECONDARY EU LAW
ON THE NATIONAL COURTS' OWN MOTION

*Balázs Fekete and Anna Maria Mancaleoni**

I. GENERAL APPROACH

Whether national courts are allowed to raise points of law of their own motion is a procedural question that is strongly linked to direct (horizontal) effect. The reason why it becomes relevant in this context is that the functioning in actual practice of rules having direct effect depends, amongst other things, on the national courts' *ex officio* competences.

The study of this problem is relevant for substantive private law, too. *Ex officio* application of a given EU law provision may lead to the nullity or unenforceability of contracts under national laws; therefore, it may seriously influence private interests.

I.A THE EU LAW CONTEXT

The CJEU has a long-lasting and consistent case law touching upon certain dimensions of national procedural regimes in which it regularly refers to national procedural autonomy. This concept in the first place reflects the recognition that national procedural regimes are inherently diverse and in the second place that their approximation or harmonisation is simply unnecessary at this stage of integration. So, the structure of the judiciary and procedures remains fundamentally in the hands of the Member States. From an institutional perspective, this approach implies that the Member States remain free to determine which courts or tribunals are competent to deal with EU law-related claims.

This does not mean, however, that the EU legal order should not establish certain requirements which these regimes must satisfy in order to fully ensure the primacy of EU law. Many landmark rulings of the CJ stress that national procedural regimes must always respect the principles of effectiveness and equivalence since the protection of rights derived from EU law requires it.

---

[*] Co-author Anna Maria Mancaleoni was assisted by Margharita Colangelo.

In *Rewe*,[1] the CJ held that 'in the absence of [EU] rules on this subject, it is for the domestic legal system of each Member State to designate the courts having jurisdiction and to determine the procedural conditions governing actions at law'[2] that protect rights emanating from EU law. However, national procedural provisions may neither establish less favourable conditions for EU law-related claims than for similar domestic ones, nor render the exercise of rights arising from EU law 'virtually impossible or excessively difficult'.[3] The most important consequence of this approach is that national procedural provisions that infringe the principles of effectiveness and equivalence may not be applied because they impede the effective application of EU law.

The national courts' option to raise points of law of their own motion should be regarded as part of this broader and rather sophisticated context, too. Should national courts have any special powers or even obligations to raise points of EU law of their own motion when they are dealing with cases comprising EU law elements? How does the CJ regard the diversity of national civil procedures when dealing with cases in which national rules restricting the *ex officio* application of legal rules endanger the effectiveness of EU law?

I.B THE STRUCTURE OF THIS CHAPTER

The following parts of this chapter discuss various aspects of the *ex officio* application of EU law. Section II seeks to map the issue in the context of EU law; it discusses the general case law of the CJ, the field of competition law and the broader area of consumer contracts directives. National case law relating to the *ex officio* application of primary and secondary EU law is analysed in section III. Lastly, some scholarly and comparative conclusions are drawn in section IV.

II. SOURCES OF EU LAW

The *ex officio* application of primary and secondary EU law is a multi-faceted issue. For a proper understanding, various specific manifestations of *ex officio* application have to be analysed in detail.[4] This chapter is devoted to three of them: the so-called *Van Schijndel*[5]

---

[1] CJ 16 December 1976 Case C-33/76 *Rewe Centralfinanz eG and Rewe Central AG v Landwirtschaftskammer für das Saarland* [1976] I-1989 ECLI:EU:C:1976:188.

[2] ibid.

[3] CJ 16 February 1980 Case C-68/79 *Hans Just I/S v Danish Ministry for Fiscal Affairs* [1980] I-00501 ECLI:EU:C:1980:57, para 25; CJ 9 November 1983 Case C-199/82 *Amministrazione delle Finanze dello Stato v SpA San Giorgio* [1983] I-03595 ECLI:EU:C:1983:318, paras 12 and 14.

[4] Hartkamp 2016 nos 124 ff; HJ Snijders, 'New Developments in National Rules or *ex Officio* Raising of Points of Community Law by National Courts' in Hartkamp/Sieburgh/Keus/Kortmann/Wissink (eds) 2014 p 96-116; Hartkamp 2014 467 ff; J Chorus, 'Le relevé d'office de moyens de droit et de fait: l'application de règles du droit européen par le juge national. Étude de droit compare et d'histoire de droit' in L Vacca (ed), *Scienza giuridica interpretazione e sviluppo del diritto europeo. Convegno ARTISTEC Roma 9–11 giugno 2011* (Naples, Jovene Editore, 2013) 123–65.

[5] CJ 14 December 1995 Joined Cases C-430/93–C-431/93 *Jeroen van Schijndel and Johannes Nicolaas Cornelis van Veen v Stichting Pensioenfonds voor Fysiotherapeuten* [1995] I-04705 ECLI:EU:C:1995:441.

case law; certain implications of Article 101 TFEU; and the impact of Directive 93/13/EEC[6] on unfair terms in consumer contracts and of other consumer contracts directives.

II.A THE *VAN SCHIJNDEL* LINE OF CASE LAW

In the early 1970s, the CJ had already accepted the existence of power of the national courts to request preliminary rulings of their own motion, irrespective of both the actual procedural rules and the parties' intents.[7] It did so in the *Reinmühlen*[8] decision, in which it established a brand new power, an 'unfettered right' for the national courts to refer problems for a preliminary ruling whenever they deem it necessary, irrespective of the national civil procedural rules or constitutional provisions. EU law lifted restrictions created by national procedural laws.

Almost two decades later, the question whether national courts have a general power to raise points of EU law when the parties do not explicitly refer to them came to the forefront in the *Verholen*[9] case. It made its appearance in the context of the effectiveness of secondary anti-discrimination and social security legislation. When answering the question whether a national court may apply certain provisions of a social security directive even though the applicants have not invoked them, the CJ recognised a general power of the courts to apply directives of their own motion. It pointed out that '[EU] law does not preclude a national court from examining of its own motion whether national rules are in conformity with the precise and unconditional provisions of a directive, the period for whose implementation has elapsed, where the individual has not relied on that directive before the national court'.[10]

It should be pointed out that this wording suggests that national courts only have this power with regard to the unconditional provisions of directives. However, it would be rather illogical to exclude other sources of EU law (ie, founding Treaties, regulations and decisions). It is more likely that the CJ restricted its ruling to directives because the Dutch court raised the question in the context of a case concerning a directive. However, the validity of this ruling should be extended to other sources of EU law since any other solution would endanger the uniform application of EU law.[11] Another relevant question is whether the *ex officio* application of EU law is merely optional or an obligation for the national courts. In its judgment, the CJ merely ruled that EU law does not preclude national courts from examining of their own motion the conformity of national rules

---

[6] Council Directive 93/12/EEC of the European Communities of 5 April 1993 on unfair terms in consumer contracts [1993] OJ L095/29.

[7] *cf* CJ 16 February 1974 Case C-166/73 *Reinmühlen-Düsseldorf v Einfuhr- und Vorratsstelle für Getreide und Futtermittel* [1974] I-00033 ECLI:EU:C:1974:3.

[8] ibid.

[9] CJ 11 July 1991 Joined Cases C-87/90–C-89/90 *A Verholen et al v Sociale Verzekeringsbank Amsterdam* [1991] I-03756 ECLI:EU:C:1991:314.

[10] ibid.

[11] *cf* AG Darmon Opinion 29 May 1991 in Joined Cases C-87/90–C-89/90 *A Verholen et al v Sociale Verzekeringsbank Amsterdam* [1991] I-03757 ECLI:EU:C:1991:223, para 19. AG Darmon argues that the primacy of community law 'cannot be left to the discretion of national courts without the risk of its uniform application being seriously compromised'.

with unconditional rules of directives. The CJ did not impose a general obligation on national courts to apply EU law provisions of their own motion—it solely established the possibility.

In conclusion, the *Verholen*[12] case confirmed the power of national courts to raise EU law provisions of their own motion and to review the relevant national rules for conformity with them where necessary in a given case.

In a further step, the CJ established a framework for handling cases in which national procedural law prohibits the *ex officio* application of law. In its *Van Schijndel*[13] judgment, which concerns the *ex officio* application of EU law provisions by national courts, the CJ distinguished three different approaches. First, applying the criterion of equivalence, it ruled that where national courts are obliged of their own motion to raise points of national law in national cases, they have to do the same in cases touching upon EU law issues. Examples are public policy considerations, third-party interests or essential procedural requirements. Second, if national procedural law provides for the possibility of the *ex officio* application of certain national rules, the national courts are obliged to do so in EU law-related cases. Here, the CJ went further and ruled that the 'may is must' rule must be applied in order to provide broader legal protection for rights emanating from EU law.[14] Third, in order to solve the problem of national procedural provisions that explicitly prohibit the *ex officio* raising of points of national law, the CJ established the following test, usually referred to as the 'test of effectiveness'.[15] The test pays attention to three elements: the role of the given rule in the national procedure; the stage of the procedure; and the special features of the procedure.[16] If the national general prohibition on *ex officio* raising points of law fails to pass this test, EU law precludes its application.

---

[12] ibid.

[13] CJ *Van Schijndel* (n 5).

[14] The CJ explicitly upheld this approach in its subsequent case law. *cf* CJ 24 October 1996 Case C-72/95 *Aannemersbedrijf PK Kraaijeveld BV v Gedeputeerde Staten van Zuid-Holland* [1996] I-05403 ECLI:EU:C:1996:404, paras 57–58. Moreover, it also further refined it, since in the *Van der Weerd* case (CJ 7 June 2007 Joined Cases C-222/05–C-225/05 *J van der Weerd et al v Minister van Landbouw, Natuur en Voedselkwaliteit* [2007] I-04233 ECLI:EU:C:2007:318, paras 31 and 41), it emphasised that if the parties had had a genuine opportunity to plead a rule of EU law before the national court, the EU legal order, particularly the principle of effectiveness, did not impose a duty on the national courts to raise of their own motion a rule of law which is not a matter of public policy.

[15] T Heukels, 'Joined Cases C-430/93 and C-431/93, and C-312/93. Case Comment' (1996) 33(2) *CMLR* 337–53, at 347. In a more general context, Prechal 1998 690–699 speaks of 'procedural rule of reason', but she definitely used this term in a broader sense, since she approached the problem from the justification perspective, while the court focused on the functional assessment of the conflicting rule and the given national procedure (the role of the rule, the progress and the features of the procedure). Thus, Heukels' 'test of effectiveness' seems to be a more appropriate denomination.

[16] CJ *Van Schijndel* (n 5); CJ 14 December 1998 Case C-312/93 *Peterbroeck, Van Campenhout & Cie SCS v Belgium State* [1995] I-04599 ECLI:EU:C:1995:347, para 14.

II.B *EX OFFICIO* APPLICATION OF EU LAW
IN RELATION TO ARTICLE 101 TFEU

Article 101 TFEU   **7.1 (EU)**

1. The following shall be prohibited as incompatible with the internal market: all agreements between undertakings, decisions by associations of undertakings and concerted practices which may affect trade between Member States and which have as their object or effect the prevention, restriction or distortion of competition within the internal market …

2. Any agreements or decisions prohibited pursuant to this Article shall be automatically void …

Article 101 TFEU was discussed in detail in Chapter 2. In the present chapter, it will only be taken into consideration in relation to the obligation for the national courts to apply the provisions of their own motion. In *Manfredi*,[17] the CJ argued for the first time that '[now Articles 101 and 102 TFEU] are a matter of public policy which must be automatically applied by national courts' (*Manfredi* para 31). Subsequently, the same concept was restated in *T-Mobile*:[18] '[Now Article 101 TFEU], first, produces direct effects in relations between individuals, creating rights for the persons concerned which the national courts must safeguard and, second, is a matter of public policy, essential for the accomplishment of the tasks entrusted to the [EU], which must be automatically applied by national courts' (*T-Mobile* para 49).[19] Therefore, the *ex officio* application of Article 101 is justified by the paramount importance of this provision within EU public policy.

Manfredi and *T-Mobile* should be considered in juxtaposition to *Van Schijndel*,[20] since the latter, too, dealt with the *ex officio* application of Article 101 TFEU. In *Van Schijndel*, the CJ held that the obligation for the national courts to apply a legal ground based on Article 101 TFEU did not exist when this would imply going beyond the ambit of the claim or the defence and abandoning the principle of judicial passivity as recognised by the internal law. On the contrary, *Manfredi* and *T-Mobile*, in which the CJ ruled that Article 101 TFEU must be automatically applied by the court, do not envisage any limitation to the *ex officio* application of the Article and they seem to imply that the national court has to apply the Article even beyond the ambit of the claim or the defence as submitted by the parties.

Nevertheless, the different rulings in these judgments are not in contradiction, as they refer to different situations. In *Van Schijndel*, the *ex officio* application of Article 101

---

[17] CJ 13 July 2006 Joined Cases C-295/04–C-298/04 *Manfredi et al v Lloyd Adriatico Assicurazioni SpA et al* [2006] I-06619 ECLI:EU:C:2006:461.

[18] CJ 4 June 2009 Case C-8/08 *T-Mobile Netherlands BV, KPN Mobile NV, Orange Nederland NV and Vodafone Libertel NV v Raad van bestuur van de Nederlandse Mededingingsautoriteit* [2009] I-04529 ECLI:EU:C:2009:343.

[19] Some scholars asserted that *Manfredi* ((n 17) para 31) is an obiter and 'a slip of the pen' and should not be interpreted in the sense that art 101 is a public policy provision for the purpose of the *ex officio* application. See Snijders (n 4). This position is difficult to maintain, particularly because the CJ reiterated the statement in CJ *T-Mobile* (n 18). See Hartkamp 2016 no 127.

[20] CJ *Van Schijndel* (n 5).

[21] Hartkamp 2014 470–71; Hartkamp 2016 nos 124–27.

TFEU would have entailed an obligation for the national Court of Appeal to examine the claim on a different basis from the basis alleged by the claimant.[21] In *Manfredi* and *T-Mobile*, the issue was the nullity of a legal act pursuant to Article 101(2) TFEU. In this case, the *ex officio* application by the national court concerned a rule imposing nullity even if this meant going beyond the ambit of the claim or the defence. In this respect, the position taken by the CJ reflects the laws of a number of Member States that accept that nullity can be established by the court even if it has not been invoked by the parties to the litigation.[22]

As regards the characteristics and the regulation of the nullity pursuant to Article 101 TFEU, see section II.A in Chapter 2. Here it suffices to remark that the nullity *ex* Article 101(2) TFEU is an absolute nullity[23] (unlike the sanction imposed on terms in consumer contracts that are unfair pursuant to Article 6 of Directive 93/13/EEC;[24] see section II.C.i below).

II.C *EX OFFICIO* APPLICATION IN RELATION TO CONSUMER CONTRACT DIRECTIVES

II.C.i DIRECTIVE 93/13/EEC ON UNFAIR TERMS IN CONSUMER CONTRACTS

There have been a considerable number of CJ judgments on the power and obligation of national courts to intervene *ex officio* in consumer contract cases. The reason lies in the protective aim of the EU rules in combination with the restrictive attitude towards the *ex officio* application of legal grounds in a number of Member State jurisdictions. The predominant part of these judgments concerns Directive 93/13/EEC on unfair terms in consumer contracts.

Council Directive 93/13/EEC of 5 April 1993   **7.2 (EU)**

Article 6

1. Member States shall lay down that unfair terms used in a contract concluded with a consumer by a seller or supplier shall, as provided for under their national law, not be binding on the consumer and that the contract shall continue to bind the parties upon those terms if it is capable of continuing in existence without the unfair terms ...

---

[22] Therefore, 'the case of enforceability of contracts essentially is not covered by *Van Schijndel'*; see Hartkamp 2014 471.

[23] See section II.A.iii in Ch 2 and in particular the reference to CJ 20 September 2001 Case C-453/99 *Courage v Crehan* [2001] I-06297 ECLI:EU:C:2001:465, para 22: 'That principle of automatic nullity can be relied on by anyone, and the courts are bound by it once the conditions for the application of [now Article 101(1) TFEU] are met ... Since the nullity referred to in [now Article 101(2) TFEU] is absolute, an agreement which is null and void by virtue of this provision has no effect as between the contracting parties and cannot be set up against third parties'; this paragraph has been reproduced almost word for word in CJ *Manfredi* (n 17).

[24] [1993] OJ L095/29 (n 6).

Article 7

1. Member States shall ensure that, in the interests of consumers and of competitors, adequate and effective means exist to prevent the continued use of unfair terms in contracts concluded with consumers by sellers or suppliers ...

In many cases, the question of the powers of the national court to intervene of its own motion and assess the unfairness of contractual clauses arose in relation to territorial jurisdiction clauses (*Océano*,[25] *Pannon*,[26] *Pénzügyi*)[27] and arbitration clauses (*Mostaza Claro*,[28] *Asturcom*,[29] *Pohotovost'*).[30] Such clauses can easily cause a significant imbalance between the consumer and the seller or supplier, as they affect the consumer's right to take part in the proceedings and for this reason pertain to the very core of consumer protection. Furthermore, the unfair nature of these terms can usually be ascertained without further investigation. The 'consumer-friendly' attitude developed by the CJ in relation to those clauses has also been maintained by it when it deals with other types of clauses such as penalty clauses[31] and interest on late payment clauses.[32]

In some cases, the question arose in the context of special proceedings (eg, arbitration proceedings: *Mostaza Claro*, *Asturcom*, *Pohotovost*; order for payment: *Banco Español de Crédito*;[33] mortgage enforcement proceedings: *Banco Popular Español*)[34] as opposed to regular court proceedings, or in the context of appeal proceedings (*Asbeek Brusse*,[35] *Jőrős*).[36] Distinguishing between types of proceedings is important. It must always be taken into consideration that 'each case which raises the question whether a national procedural provision renders application of [EU] law impossible or excessively difficult must be analysed by reference to the role of that provision in the procedure, its progress and its special features, viewed as a whole, before the various national instances' (*Van Schijndel* para 19). Furthermore, caution is advised in drawing too far-reaching conclusions from a specific CJ decision and applying them to other cases, as cases on *ex officio* application differ widely.[37]

---

[25] CJ 27 June 2000 Joined Cases C-240/98–C-244/98 *Océano Grupo Editorial SA v Roció Murciano Quintero and Salvat Editores SA José M Sánchez Alcón Prades, José Luis Copano Badillo, Mohammed Berroane and Emilio Viñas Feliú* [2000] I-04941 ECLI:EU:C:2000:346.

[26] CJ 4 June 2009 Case C-243/08 *Pannon GSM Zrt v Erzsébet Sustikné Győrfi* [2009] I-04713 ECLI:EU:C:2009:350.

[27] CJ 9 November 2010 Case C-137/08 *VB Pénzügyi Lízing Zrt. v Ferenc Schneider* [2010] I-10847 ECLI:EU:C:2010:659.

[28] CJ 26 October 2006 Case C-168/05 *Elisa María Mostaza Claro v Centro Móvil Milenium SL* [2006] I-10421 ECLI:EU:C:2006:675.

[29] CJ 6 October 2009 Case C-40/08 *Asturcom Telecomunicaciones SL v Cristina Rodríguez Nogueira* [2009] I-09579 ECLI:EU:C:2009:615.

[30] CJ 27 February 2014 Case C-470/12 *Pohotovosť sro v Miroslav Vašuta* ECLI:EU:C:2014:101.

[31] CJ 30 May 2013 Case C-488/11 *Dirk Frederik Asbeek Brusse and Katarına de Man Garabıto v Jahani BV* ECLI:EU:C:2013:341.

[32] CJ 14 June 2012 Case C-618/10 *Banco Español de Crédito SA v Joaquín Calderón Camino* ECLI:EU:C:2012:349.

[33] ibid.

[34] CJ 14 November 2013 Joined Cases C-537/12 and C-116/13 *Banco Popular Español SA v Maria Teodolinda Rivas Quichimbo and Wilmar Edgar Cun Pérez and Banco de Valencia SA v Joaquín Valldeperas Tortosa and María Ángeles Miret Jaume* ECLI:EU:C:2013:759.

[35] CJ *Asbeek Brusse* (n 31).

[36] CJ 30 May 2013 Case C-397/11 *Erika Jőrős v Aegon Magyarország Hitel Zrt* ECLI:EU:C:2013:340.

[37] Hartkamp 2014 482.

The leading case with regard to the power and obligation of the national courts to intervene of their own motion is the judgment in *Océano*,[38] in which the CJ found that Directive 93/13/EEC on unfair terms in consumer contracts allowed the judge *ex officio* to evaluate the unfairness of a territorial competence clause: 'The requirement for an interpretation in conformity with the Directive requires the national court, in particular, to favour the interpretation that would allow it to decline of its own motion the jurisdiction conferred on it by virtue of an unfair term.' The reasoning is focused on the weakness of consumers vis-a-vis the seller and on the need to make the protection provided by the directive effective. When referring to the *status* of the rules at issue, the CJ does not make use of any given category or formula, such as 'public policy' or 'mandatory' rules (see below), but directly stresses the need to make the protection effective, having regard to the *rationale* of Articles 6 and 7 of Directive 93/13/EEC. *Océano* does not find that the national court is under an obligation to decline jurisdiction of its own motion, but it holds that a court must be able to do so. The existence of an obligation in this respect has been clearly established by subsequent judgments (*Mostaza Claro, Pannon*).[39]

Shortly afterwards, a similar approach was taken in *Cofidis*,[40] in which the CJ ruled that Directive 93/13/EEC precludes the application of a national provision which prohibits the national court, on expiry of a limitation period, from finding, of its own motion or following a plea raised by the consumer, that a term of the contract is unfair. The CJ referred to both the effectiveness of the protection conferred by Articles 6 and 7 of Directive 93/13 (*Cofidis* paras 32–35 referring to *Océano*) and the principle of procedural autonomy.

Whereas in *Océano*, the CJ gave a ruling only in relation to the court's option to intervene of its own motion, in *Mostaza Claro*,[41] it made it clear for the first time that the court had an obligation to assess whether the clause was unfair. In this case, the consumer had not contested the validity of the arbitration clause at issue during the arbitration proceedings and then sought annulment of the award before the national court on the ground that the clause was unfair. According to the Spanish rules applicable to the main proceedings, any claim on the invalidity of the arbitration agreement must be raised at the same time as the parties make their original submissions.[42] The CJ, referring to *Océano* and *Cofidis*, restated that 'the nature and importance of the public interest underlying the protection which the Directive confers on consumers justify, moreover, the national court being required to assess of its own motion whether a contractual term is unfair, compensating in this way for the imbalance which exists between the consumer and the seller or supplier'.[43]

Following *Mostaza Claro*, the CJ dealt with the *ex officio* question in the context of consumer arbitration proceedings in *Asturcom*[44] and *Pohotovosť*.[45] In *Asturcom*, it

---

[38] CJ *Océano* (n 25).
[39] CJ *Mostaza Claro* (n 28); CJ *Pannon* (n 26).
[40] CJ 21 November 2002 Case C-473/00 *Cofidis v Jean-Louis Fredout* [2002] I-10875 ECLI:EU:C:2002:705.
[41] CJ *Mostaza Claro* (n 28).
[42] Furthermore, according to Spanish law, an arbitration award can only be annulled on some specific grounds, including the case in which it infringes 'public policy': *cf* CJ 1 June 1999 Case-126/97 *Eco Swiss China Time Ltd v Benetton International NV* [1999] I-03055 ECLI:EU:C:1999:296, in which art 101 TFEU was at stake: see section II.A.ii in Ch 2.
[43] CJ *Mostaza Claro* (n 28) para 38.
[44] CJ *Asturcom* (n 29).
[45] CJ *Pohotovosť* (n 30).

ruled that Directive 93/13/EEC must be interpreted as meaning that a national court or tribunal hearing an action for enforcement of an arbitration award—which has become final and was made in the absence of the consumer—is required to assess of its own motion whether the arbitration clause is unfair, 'in so far as, under national rules of procedure, it can carry out such an assessment in similar actions of a domestic nature'. The judgment is therefore based on the principle of equivalence.[46] The CJ followed the same line of reasoning in *Pohotovost'*, which concerned, inter alia, the *ex officio* annulment of an arbitration award issued without the participation of the consumer, on the ground that the credit agreement contract at issue contained an unfair penalty clause.

It is noticeable that the CJ does not qualify the relevant rules that must be applied of the court's own motion as rules of 'public policy', but in terms of rules protecting the 'public interest'. This approach becomes evident particularly in *Asbeek Brusse*,[47] an appeal judgment in a case where the unfairness of a penalty clause was raised only in appeal proceedings. The CJ did not state that the rules at issue were 'public policy rules', but considered that they had an 'equal standing to national rules which rank, within the domestic legal system, as rules of public policy' (*Asbeek Brusse*, para 44). In substance, the CJ implied that the rules of Directive 93/13/EEC may be applied *ex officio* even if they are not qualified as 'public policy' rules, since they protect the 'public interest' and this public interest requires that the national courts must be able to intervene *ex officio* (effectiveness). Furthermore, where a national court has a special power in case of a violation of a national public policy rule, it must also exercise that power when dealing with problems related to this directive (equivalence).[48]

One line of cases decided by the CJ concerns the *ex officio* power of the court in relation to the *examination* necessary for the purpose of assessing whether a contractual term is unfair. After ruling that the national court has to examine of its own motion whether a clause is unfair where it has available the legal and factual elements necessary for that task (*Pannon*, para 32),[49] the CJ went a step further in *Pénzügyi*[50] by stating that the *ex officio* obligation also requires the court to act of its own motion in order to establish facts to find out whether the directive is applicable.[51] Both *Pannon* and *Pénzügyi* were about a territorial jurisdiction clause, but the same line of reasoning may be extended to cover all other contractual terms.[52] The subsequent judgment in *Faber*[53] further quali-

---

[46] See Schebesta 2010 847 ff; and Ebers 2010 823 ff, focusing on the relationship between effectiveness and equivalence and on the difficulty in defining public policy.

[47] CJ *Asbeek Brusse* (n 31).

[48] Furthermore, the use of the different categories to be considered at the national and EU levels for the purpose of *ex officio* application may be connected to the problem of the consequences following the *ex officio* assessment whether the contract clause is unfair under art 6 of the Directive. See CJ *Asbeek Brusse* (n 31) para 11.

[49] CJ *Pannon* (n 26).

[50] CJ *Pénzügyi* (n 27) para 56.

[51] In the words of the CJ in *Pénzügyi* (ibid), the national court 'must investigate of its own motion whether a term conferring exclusive territorial jurisdiction in a contract concluded between a seller or supplier and a consumer, which is the subject of a dispute before it, falls within the scope of Directive 93/13 and, if it does, assess of its own motion whether such a term is unfair' (the operative part).

[52] Hartkamp 2014 479.

[53] CJ 4 June 2015 Case C-497/13 *Froukje Faber v Autobedrijf Hazet Ochten BV* ECLI:EU:C:2015:357.

fied the requirement that the national courts must act of their own motion by ruling that the principle of effectiveness requires the national court to determine of its own motion whether the purchaser may be classified as a consumer, not only 'as soon as the court has at its disposal the matters of law and fact that are necessary for that purpose', but also when the court 'may have them at its disposal simply by making a request for clarification' (*Faber*, para 46 and operative part).

In assessing the unfairness of a contractual clause, the national court must also observe the principle of *audi et alteram partem*, which, 'as a general rule, requires the national court which has found of its own motion that a contractual term is unfair to inform the parties to the dispute of that fact and to invite each of them to set out its views on that matter, with the opportunity to challenge the views of the other party, in accordance with the formal requirements laid down in that regard by the national rules of procedure' (*Banif*,[54] *Asbeek Brusse*).[55]

Where the national court considers a contractual term to be unfair, it must not apply it, unless the consumer, after having been informed by the court, opposes the disapplication (see *Pannon*, paras 33 and 35). It follows that the sanction provided for by the national law implementing Article 6 of Directive 93/13/EEC[56] cannot be conceived in terms of 'absolute' nullity, since then the consumer would not be allowed to oppose disapplication. This is a clear distinction from rules that have a public policy character (on Article 101 TFEU, see section II.B above). Moreover, in subsequent judgments, the CJ has made it clear that the consequences of the fact that a contract clause is unfair must be determined on the basis of the domestic law, subject to the conditions laid down by the CJ itself with regard to different types of contractual clauses and depending on the applicable national rules (*Banco Español de Crédito, Banif, Pannon, Jőrös, Asbeek Brusse, Kásler*).[57]

II.C.ii THE OTHER CONSUMER CONTRACTS DIRECTIVES

A trend can be observed towards an increase in the application to other consumer directives of the principles developed in relation to Directive 93/13/EEC. The CJ has recognised the existence of an obligation for the national courts *ex officio* to raise provisions of directives on consumer protection, such as Directive 87/102/ECC[58] on consumer credit (*Rampion*), Directive 85/577/EEC[59] on contracts negotiated away from business

---

[54] CJ 21 February 2013 Case C-472/11 *Banif Plus Bank Zrt v Csaba Csipai and Viktória Csipai* ECLI:EU:C:2013:88.

[55] CJ *Asbeek Brusse* (n 31).

[56] On the implementation of art 6 of Directive 93/13 into the Member States, see H Schülte-Nölke, C Twigg-Flesner and M Ebers (eds), *EC Consumer Law Compendium: The Consumer Acquis and its Transposition in the Member States* (Munich, Sellier European Law Publishers, 2008) 197–261. See also: www.eu-consumer-law.org/consumerstudy_part2c_en.pdf.

[57] CJ 30 April 2014 Case C-26/13 *Árpád Kásler, Hajnalka Káslerné Rábai v OTP Jelzálogbank Zrt* ECLI:EU:C:2014.282.

[58] Council Directive 87/102/EC of 22 December 1986 for the approximation of laws, regulations and administrative provisions of the Member States concerning credit [1986] OJ L042/48.

[59] Council Directive 85/557/EEC of 20 December 1985 to protect the consumer in respect of contracts negotiated away for business premises [1985] OJ L373/31.

premises (*Eva Martín*) and Directive 99/44/EC[60] on consumer sales and associated guarantees (*Duarte, Faber*). In all these cases, the emphasis is on the need to ensure the protection conferred by the relevant directive (the principle of effectiveness).

In *Rampion*,[61] the CJ held, by analogy with the case law on Directive 93/13/EEC, that Directive 87/102/ECC on consumer credit (repealed by Directive 2008/48/EC)[62] must be interpreted so as to allow the national courts to apply of their own motion the provisions transposing Article 11(2) of the Directive (establishing a link between the contract for the supply of the good or service and the financial contract in order to allow the consumer, subject to certain conditions, to pursue remedies against the creditor in case of non-performance by the supplier). To justify making the relevant provisions *ex officio* applicable, the CJ emphasised the 'dual aim' of Directive 87/102/EEC: the Directive 'was adopted with the dual aim of ensuring both the creation of a common consumer credit market (third to fifth recitals) and the protection of consumers who avail themselves of such credit (sixth, seventh and ninth recitals)' (*Rampion*, para 59). Following the opinion of AG Mengozzi,[63] the CJ itself placed the case in the context of the French legal system, from which the question referred originated (para 58). The case law of the French Court of Cassation used to regard the rules relating to consumer credit as falling within the category of the *règles d'ordre public de protection*, adopted in the interest of a particular category of persons and which may be relied upon only by persons belonging to that category (as opposed to the *règles d'ordre public de direction* adopted in the general interest and which the court may raise of its own motion).[64]

In *Eva Martín*,[65] concerning the interpretation of Directive 85/577/EEC on contracts negotiated away from business premises (which was repealed by Directive 2011/83/EU on consumer rights), the Spanish appeal judge requested a ruling on the question whether Article 4 of the Directive—according to which 'Member States shall ensure that their national legislation lays down appropriate consumer protection measures in cases where the information referred to in this Article is not supplied'—allows a national court to raise, of its own motion, an infringement of that provision and to declare a contract void on the ground that the consumer was not informed of his right of cancellation. The CJ held that Article 4 of Directive 85/577/EEC does not preclude a national court from declaring, of its own motion, the nullity of the contract, as provided by the national rule implementing Article 4 of Directive 85/577/EEC. This conclusion is based on the 'public interest' underlying the protection conferred by the Directive (*Eva Martín*, paras 21 and 28) and on the consequent need to ensure its effectiveness (*Eva Martín*, para 27). The 'public interest' pursued by the Directive justifies the derogation from the general rule

[60] Directive 1999/44/EC of the European Parliament and the Council of 25 May 1999 on certain aspects of the sale of consumer goods and associated guarantees [1999] OJ L171/21.

[61] CJ 4 October 2007 Case C-429/05 *Max Rampion and Marie-Jeanne Godard, née Rampion v Franfinance SA and K par K SAS* [2007]I-08017 ECLI:EU:C:2007:575.

[62] Directive 2008/48/EC of the European Parliament and the Council of 23 April 2008 on credit agreements of consumers and repealing Council Directive 87/102/EEC [2008] OJ L133/66.

[63] AG Mengozzi Opinion 29 March 2007 in Case C-429/05 *Max Rampion and Marie-Jeanne Godard, née Rampion v Franfiance SA and K par K SAS* [2007] I-08017 ECLI:EU:C:2007:199.

[64] Following the CJ case law, French law was modified: see section III.B.i below (case 7.6 (FR)).

[65] CJ 17 December 2009 Case C-227/08 *Eva Martín Martín v EDP Editores SL* [2009] I-11939 ECLI:EU:C:2009:792.

according to which the national court is not allowed to act on its own motion when this would mean going beyond the claim as submitted by the parties (see *Eva Martín*, para 20, referring to *Van Schijndel*, para 19).[66]

In *Duarte*,[67] concerning the interpretation of Directive 99/44/EC on consumer sales and associated guarantees, the question referred was whether the national court could of its own motion grant an appropriate price reduction where the consumer was only seeking rescission of the contract in the legal proceedings and such rescission was not available because the lack of conformity was minor. The preliminary ruling reference took place in the context of Spanish procedural law, according to which—as described by the referring court—the consumer cannot modify the claim during the proceedings, or appeal the decision while seeking price reduction, or start new proceedings after the claim for rescission was rejected, as the decision on rescission is also regarded as final (*res judicata*) in relation to the latter action (the claim for rescission also covering the claim on price reduction). The CJ did not give a direct answer to the question as worded by the referring national court and did not state whether the national court must or may of its own motion grant price reduction: the essential point for the CJ was that the effectiveness of the remedy for which the Directive provided (price reduction) must be guaranteed. The national court, for example, could interpret domestic law in conformity with the Directive so that it allowed the consumer to refine his initial claim to include price reduction or so that price reduction was excluded from the *res judicata*, thereby allowing the consumer to potentially bring a fresh action (as suggested by the AG). The question whether the court could *ex officio* grant a remedy beyond the limit of the claim would be considered only as the *extrema ratio*.

In *Faber*,[68] the CJ extended the line of reasoning with regard to the Directive 93/13/EEC on unfair terms to Directive 99/44/EC on certain aspects of the sale of consumer goods and associated guarantees. In this case, a Dutch Court of Appeal referred several questions to the CJ, asking in particular—as regards the power of the court to act of its own motion—whether it was required to examine of its own motion whether the purchaser might be classified as a consumer, even though the file contained insufficient information for this purpose and the examination would take place in the context of appeal proceedings.

As to the court's power to examine of its own motion, the CJ ruled that a national court before which an action has been brought relating to a contract that may be covered by

---

[66] CJ *Van Schijndel* (n 5) para 19: 'That limitation is justified by the principle that, in a civil suit, it is for the parties to take the initiative, the court being able to act of its own motion only in exceptional cases where the public interest requires its intervention.' Interesting is the Opinion by AG Trstenjak of 7 March 2009 in Case C-227/08 *Eva Martín v EDP Editores SL* [2009] I-11939 ECLI:EU:C:2009:295, paras 83 and 84. After regarding the existence in the Member States of different systems of nullity (absolute/relative; annulment), it considers whether the absolute nullity is the appropriate answer, as the case law on Directive 93/13/EEC cannot be transposed to the facts at issue (absolute nullity would imply the nullity of the entire contract, whereas according to art 6 of Directive 93/13/EEC, the remaining part of the contract may remain valid if that is possible after the unfair term is struck down). According to the AG, there is no need to categorise the relevant rule of Directive 85/577/EEC as a public policy rule, as it is sufficient to invoke its protective aim.

[67] CJ 3 October 2013 Case C-32/12 *Soledad Duarte Hueros v Autociba SA e Automóviles Citroën España SA* ECLI:EU:C:2013:637.

[68] CJ *Faber* (n 53).

the Directive 99/44/EC is required to determine of its own motion whether the purchaser may be classified as a consumer. This obligation exists not only 'as soon as that court has at its disposal the matters of law and of fact that are necessary for that purpose', but also when it 'may have them at its disposal simply by making a request for clarification' (*Faber*, para 46 and operative part). The CJ stated that in the light of the principle of procedural autonomy, it is for the national court, for the purposes of identifying the rules applicable to the dispute, to assign the legal classification to facts and acts on which the parties rely in support of their claim, if necessary by requiring the parties to provide details. Consequently, the same process has to be carried out by the national court for determining whether EU law is applicable (the principle of equivalence). Nevertheless, referring to the case law relating to Directive 93/13/EEC (*Faber*, para 42), the CJ ruled that the obligation to carry out this process also arises from the principle of effectiveness: the national rules at issue in the main proceedings would not meet the principle of effectiveness, as they would make the protection afforded by Directive 99/44/EC excessively difficult (*Faber*, para 45).

Furthermore, the CJ held that Article 5(3) of Directive 99/44/EC—pursuant to which the seller 'must be liable to the consumer for any lack of conformity which exists at the time the goods were delivered'—must be regarded as a provision of equal standing to a national rule which ranks, within the domestic legal system, as a rule of public policy and that the national court must of its own motion apply any provision which transposes it into domestic law. Therefore, just as in *Asbeek Brusse* (see section II.C.i above), the CJ did not classify the rule at issue as a rule of public policy, but made it *ex officio* applicable on the ground of equivalence.

The CJ, in answer to a specific question raised by the referring court, stated expressly that the question whether or not the consumer is assisted by a lawyer has no bearing on the interpretation of EU law (*Faber*, para 47, with reference to *Rampion*, para 65).

III. NATIONAL CASES

III.A COMPARATIVE BACKGROUND

The question whether courts may raise a new point of law not included in the parties' claims or defences has no uniform solution in the national civil procedures of the EU. Apart from the nature of the specific point of law at hand, each national solution is dependent on both the role of the courts and the principles of civil procedure, with special regard to the basic principle that a court is bound by the parties' claims (eg, 'Dispositionsmaxime'). Before discussing the national cases in detail, a brief comparative introduction to various national procedural solutions seems to be necessary.

The first dividing line should be drawn between common law and continental law jurisdictions. In the UK, the problem of the *ex officio* application of law does not exist in a practical sense. Because of the historical formation of the role of common law judges, the *ex officio* application of legal points not submitted by the parties is handled in a different way compared to the continental systems. In essence, as Lord Diplock explained in *Bremer Vulkan v South India Shipping*, 'the court had jurisdiction to grant an injunction for the enforcement or protection of legal or equitable right when it was just or convenient to do so'.[69] This also implies, for example and as Whittaker emphasises, that 'where a contract is on its face illegal the court will not enforce it, whether the illegality is pleaded or not',[70] which means that the courts must of their own motion examine whether a contract is illegal. In other words, in common law, the question whether courts may raise new points of law is determined by the priority of protecting rights. This approach enables the courts to grant the injunctions they deem necessary in the given case on any legal basis, independent of the parties' claims. In sum, if it is necessary for the protection of a given right, the courts may of their own motion raise new points of law not submitted by the parties.

When discussing continental law, a basic procedural question has to be touched upon first. Rules of civil procedure usually provide for a well-defined possibility for courts to raise either basic and general procedural requirements[71] or points of public order[72] autonomously, that is, without examining whether or not the parties relied on these points of law or not. Thus, when courts have to deal with legal issues of a fundamental procedural, public policy or public interest nature, they generally have the power to raise these points of their own motion. This feature of national civil procedure regimes was also recognised by the CJ in *Van Schijndel*, where it required national courts to raise EU law provisions if the same courts must of their own motion raise similar provisions of national law.[73]

The second dividing line has to do with differences between the continental legal systems. Two models can be identified. In the first, the principle of judicial passivity and the binding nature of the parties' claim play a crucial role; there are, however, several exceptions to this general principle. It is the model used, for example, in Italy, Hungary and Switzerland. The second model is based on a general power of the courts to apply legal grounds *ex officio*; however, they may only do so under strict conditions with special regard to the requirements of fair trial. The civil procedures of France, Germany, Belgium and Austria follow this approach.

In the first model, one can always find a general procedural provision emphasising the party-driven nature of civil proceedings. The Italian Civil Code of Procedure provides, for instance, that the 'court shall decide upon all the claims and within its limits'[74] and the Hungarian Code provides, in the same vein, that courts are generally bound by the parties' claims and submissions.[75] Alternatively, a procedural code may require the courts not to award more or to award less than, or different from that which the parties

---

[69] *Bremer Vulkan Schiffbau und Maschinenfabrik* v *South India Shipping Corporation Ltd* [1981] AC 909, 980.

[70] S Whittaker, 'Who Determines What Civil Courts Decide? Private Rights, Public Policy and EU Law' in D Leczykiewicz and S Weatherill (eds), *The Involvement of EU Law in Private Relationships* (Oxford, Hart Publishing, 2013) 96.

[71] See, eg, art 139(3) ZPO, which provides that the court must call the parties' attention to those points, mostly prerequisites to suit, that may be raised by the court's own motion.

[72] See, eg, art 3:40(1) Dutch Civil Code.

[73] CJ *Van Schijndel* (n 5) para 13.

[74] Italian Code of Civil Procedure (*Codice di procedura civile*), art 112.

[75] Hungarian Code of Civil Procedure (1952. *évi III. törvény a polgári perrendtartásról*), art 3(2).

have requested, as is the case in Swiss civil procedure.[76] All in all, courts in jurisdictions that follow this model must strictly respect both the scope of the claims and the parties' will in general.

However, these legal systems have harmonising mechanisms in order to soften the rigidity of the general prohibition. These exceptions can be broad or narrow and can be grouped around various patterns. First, some of them explicitly authorise the courts to deviate from the general rule in special cases. Typical examples are child issues in family law or matrimonial law.[77] A second set of exceptions arises from the case law of the national courts. In Hungarian law, for example, the courts are not bound by the parties' claims when deciding about the type of damages to award.[78] Finally, courts may exempt themselves from the general prohibition by taking an interpretative approach. The Italian Code of Civil Procedure allows the courts to interpret claims according to their legal substance, and not therefore according to their precise formulation.[79] This means that the legal content of a claim has to be determined by its substance, not by its literal wording.

The second model represents an alternative view. The starting point is the same, namely the principle of party autonomy. In this model, however, one can always find a provision expressly granting the courts power to apply the law *ex officio* subject to strict procedural safeguards. This means that the legislator has solved the *ex officio* issue in a general sense. The French Code of Civil Procedure provides that the courts can base their decision on a point raised of its own motion, but they must first invite the parties to comment on the matter ('principe de la contradiction').[80] In German law, the legislator formulated this rule in a different way, but the underlying logic is very similar. Article 139(2) of the German Code of Civil Procedure (ZPO) warns the courts that they can only base their decisions 'on a point of fact and law which a party has apparently overlooked or considered insignificant'[81] if they call the parties' attention to this point and invite them to comment thereon. Moreover, German courts have the same obligation if they intend to assess a certain legal or factual point in a way that is fundamentally different from the assessment by the parties.[82] This approach is subject to the restriction that the subject matter of a case (the 'goal of the case') may not be altered in this way.[83]

In conclusion, there are in fact three distinct basic approaches to the *ex officio* application of law in civil procedure in the legal systems of the EU. The English approach places

---

[76] Swiss Procedure Code, art 58(1).

[77] These points can be found in Swiss and Hungarian law.

[78] *cf* 1/2014 PJE Határozat (uniformity decision) with reference to an earlier opinion of the Supreme Court (Legfelsőbb Bíróság PK 44).

[79] In Italy, case law created this exception; see eg Cass it. Labour Division 11 January 2011 no 455. *cf* S Grossi and MC Pagni, *Commentary on the Italian Code of Civil Procedure* (New York, Oxford University Press, 2015) 158–59. In Hungarian law, the legislator made it explicit in the second sentence of art 3(2) of the Hungarian Code of Civil Procedure.

[80] NCPC, art 16(3). For an English translation see N Brooke (ed), *The French Code of Civil Procedure in English* (Oxford, Oxford University Press, 2008) 4.

[81] For the English translation, see PL Murray and RH Stürner, *German Civil Justice* (Durham, NC, Carolina Academic Press, 2015) 168.

[82] ZPO, art 139(2), second sentence.

[83] Murray and Stürner (n 81) 172.

particular emphasis on the protection of rights and on making procedural principles secondary to this aim. On the continent, certain procedural regimes are based on the principle of judicial passivity, while others provide for a general power of *ex officio* application subject to strict procedural safeguards. Even though the diversity is apparent, there is a common point in all of them: the courts are always allowed either broad or narrow leeway to base their decisions on points of law raised of their own motion. However this may be, EU law may require the national courts to find a possibility for the *ex officio* application in its national procedural law.

III.B NATIONAL CASE LAW: MAJOR PATTERNS

The national cases are classified by the following criterion: decisions in which the reference to EU law was decisive (section III.B.i), and decisions in which both national and EU law played a considerable role (section III.B.ii). A third type of situation occurred in a case dealt with under section III.B.iii, in which the national court on questionable grounds did not refer a question to the CJ for a preliminary ruling.

III.B.i DECISIVE REFERENCES TO EU LAW

This section considers five cases from various jurisdictions: Dutch, Belgian, French and Spanish. Four of these cases have in common that the court was faced with the legal problem of *ex officio* classifying certain contractual terms in the light of EU law, mostly Directive 93/13/EEC. In doing so, the courts referred extensively to both primary or secondary EU law and the case law of the CJ. Since most Member States—Italy being an exception—did not, in their implementation of Directive 93/13/EEC, explicitly provide for the possibility of *ex officio* examination whether contract clauses are unfair, the equivalent rule was based on CJ case law. In certain cases—the Dutch and the French—national courts even had to overstep the former practice of supreme courts in order to ensure the conformity of their decisions with EU law. There is also a Belgian case in which the national court applied Article 101 TFEU of its own motion.

Hoge Raad der Nederlanden (Supreme Court of The Netherlands), 13 September 2013[84]   **7.3 (NL)**

Heesakkers v Voets

UNFAIR TERMS AND EX OFFICIO APPLICATION

Two per cent overdue rate

The lower court has to examine of its own motion whether or not Directive 93/13/EEC applies to an agreement and whether a given term is unfair

Facts: The respondent undertook to refurbish the home of the applicant. Within the terms of the service contract, there was an article providing that in the event of overdue payment, the applicant had to pay interest

---

[84] HR 13 September 2013 *NJ* 2014, 274 ECLI:NL:HR2013:691 *Heesakkers v Voets*.

at a rate of two per cent per month. A dispute arose and the respondent claimed an amount increased by the contractually stipulated rate of two per cent per month. The main legal issue was whether the court should have assessed of its own motion whether the disputed contractual term was binding pursuant to Article 6 of Directive 93/13/EEC.

Held: The Court of Appeal should have raised the presumption that the term at issue might be an unfair term and it should have examined of its own motion in order to assess whether or not the term was unfair.

Judgment: Furthermore in CJ 9 November 2010, C-137/08 ECLI:NL:XX:2010:BO5516, *NJ* 2011/41 (*VB Pénzügyi Lízing*) the Court of Justice held in relation to Directive 93/13:

> Thus, in the exercise of the functions incumbent upon it under the provisions of the Directive, the national court must ascertain whether a contractual term which is the subject of the dispute before it falls within the scope of that Directive. If it does, that court must assess that term, if necessary, of its own motion, in the light of the requirements of consumer protection laid down by that Directive …

The national court is therefore required to assess of its own motion whether a contractual term falls within the scope of Directive 93/13, and if it does, the national court must assess whether or not this term is unfair, if the court has access to the necessary required information, both factual and legal …

According to Court of Justice case law, such assessment regards rules which are equivalent to national rules of public policy. In CJ 30 May 2013, C-488/11 (*Asbeek Brusse and De Man Garabito*), the Court of Justice held:

> It follows that, where the national court has the power, under internal procedural rules, to examine of its own motion the validity of a legal measure in the light of national rules of public policy, which, according to the information provided in the order for reference, is the case in the Netherlands judicial system for a court ruling in appeal proceedings, it must also exercise that power for the purpose of assessing of its own motion, in the light of the criteria laid down in the directive, whether a contractual term coming within the scope of that directive may be unfair …

The foregoing implies for Dutch law that the Court of Appeal is required to assess of its own motion whether a contractual term is unfair according to the criteria of Directive 93/13, also if this means that the Court of Appeal has to go beyond the limits set by the grounds of appeal. Under the Dutch law on appeal procedure the national court must in principle apply public policy rules also beyond the limits set by the grounds of appeal, with the provision that the national court must respect the ambit of the parties' legal dispute. The national court is therefore not required to make this assessment when the parties did not appeal the award or the rejection of the relevant claim, in which case a court of appeal is not competent to give a decision on that claim.

Directive 93/13 is not directly applicable in the Dutch legal system. Harmonious interpretation of Dutch law entails, however, that the Dutch court is obliged pursuant to Article 6:233 of the Civil Code to make the assessment mentioned above of its own motion when Directive 93/13 entails this obligation.

In this connection, it is important that Article 6(1) of Directive 93/13 obliges Member States to find an unfair term not binding. The CJ has interpreted this provision as meaning that a national court which has established that a term in a contract between a seller and a consumer is unfair, must automatically exclude the application of that clause in its entirety with regard to the consumer (CJ 30 May 2013, C-488/11 Asbeek Brusse en De Man Garabito paragraphs 55–60).

437

For Dutch law, the foregoing means that when the court has established that a term is unfair within the meaning of Directive 93/13, it is obliged to annul that term.

By way of exception, the considerations set out in paragraphs 3.5.1–3.7.3 do not apply if the consumer opposes the non-application of a contractual term which the court holds to be unfair (CJ 30 May 2013, C-488/11 (*Asbeek Brusse and De Man Garabito*), paragraph 49).

With regard to the obligation of *ex officio* assessment, the Supreme Court finds the following. If the court has the necessary factual and legal information to suspect that an agreement falls within the scope of Directive 93/13 and contains a clause which is unfair within the above meaning, it should examine the matter, even if the claim or the defence have not been based on allegations aimed at such examination. This applies in both the first instance and the appeal, the latter with due regard to the above considerations. If not all the relevant facts have been established, the court will have to take the necessary measures of inquiry to ensure the full effect of Directive 93/13, both as regards the applicability of the directive, as the possible unfairness of the clause. The court must respect the principle of hearing both parties. It must give the parties the opportunity to express their views on the matter and, if necessary, to adjust their allegations accordingly.

The court will also have to perform this assessment of its own motion in default proceedings, in that case on the basis of Article 139 Dutch Civil Procedure Code (*Wetboek van Burgerlijke Rechtsvordering*), since the directive involves law that is equivalent to national public policy rules (see: CJ 14 June 2012, C-618/10, ECLI:NL:XX:2012:BW9433, NJ 2012/512 (*Banco Español de Crédito*) paragraph 48). The assessment must be done on the basis of the writ of summons. In that case, too, the court will have to take the necessary measures of inquiry to ensure the full effect of Directive 93/13. And in that case too, moreover, the court must observe the principle of *audi et alteram partem* and give the claimant an opportunity to make further comments and, if necessary, to adjust his arguments.

With regard to the cassation proceedings the foregoing considerations mean that a complaint that the lower court has failed to make the assessment referred to above will be successful, if it is incomprehensible that the facts that emerged in the proceedings did not give the court cause for the suspicion referred to above.

Against the background of the above considerations the complaints are successful. The facts stated in the complaints are such that they should have given the court cause for the presumption that the agreement for services at issue falls within the scope of Directive 93/13, that no negotiations as meant in Article 3(1) Directive have taken place about the term in question, that the term is not a core term within the meaning of Article 4(2) Directive, and that the term is unfair within the meaning of the Directive, also having regard to the amount of the contractual interest of two per cent per month, which is well above the statutory interest rate of Article 119 Book 6 Dutch Civil Code and above the commercial interest rate of Article 119a of Book 6 Dutch Civil Code. Consequently, although the claimant has not contested the stipulated rate, the national court should have examined of its own motion whether or not Directive 93/13 applies to the agreement between the parties and whether the term on which the [defendant's] claim for interest is based is unfair within the meaning of the Directive.

Notes:

(1) An excerpt of this decision is also reported in section III.C.ii in Chapter 6 (case 6.12 (NL)). It is a landmark judgment, as the Supreme Court of the Netherlands—unlike

the lower courts[85]—had previously been hesitant to follow the case law of the CJ. It was uncertain on which provision of national law the power of the courts to intervene *ex officio* could be based (whether Article 6:233 sub a,[86] Article 6:248(2)[87] or Article 3:40(2) of the Dutch Civil Code[88]).[89] The Supreme Court of the Netherlands interpreted Article 6:233 of the Dutch Civil Code, concerning general contract terms, in conformity with the Directive and held that the Court of Appeal should have assessed of its own motion whether the contract clause was unfair. In doing so, it referred extensively to CJ case law (*Pénzügyi, Banco Español de Crédito, Asbeek Brusse*). The Supreme Court not only ruled that there is an obligation for the lower court to intervene of its own motion, but also that the lower court must examine of its own motion both whether a term falls within the scope of Directive 93/13/EEC (*Pénzügyi*) and whether the term is unfair. The Dutch Supreme Court thus accorded a wide scope to the obligation to examine, even beyond what the CJ itself required in *Pénzügyi*. Moreover, the Supreme Court ruled that if the court finds that a clause is unfair, it must annul it unless the consumer opposes the non-application of the clause (*Pannon*).

(2) The fact that rules of consumer law have to be applied *ex officio* does not mean that the rules have a public policy nature (see section II.C.ii above). The CJ has ruled in ordinary first instance proceedings that they must be applied *ex officio* because of the public interest pursued by consumer directives. In other procedures, the CJ reviewed the issue on a case-by-case basis against the principles of effectiveness and equivalence. The latter principle plays a role in the present case, as in *Asbeek Brusse* and *Faber* (see section II.C.ii above). In conformity with the CJ decision in *Asbeek Brusse*, the Supreme Court stated in the decision quoted above that the EU rules at issue also apply in appeal proceedings, as Article 6 has to be considered as having equal standing to the national rules of public policy which, as explained by the referring court (the Amsterdam Court of Appeal), have to be applied *ex officio* in appeal proceedings also beyond the limits set by the grounds of appeal (the principle of equivalence). In cassation, parties may therefore

---

[85] See, eg, District Court of Arnhem 27 April 2009 *NJF* 2009,337 ECLI:NL:RBARN:2009:BJ1729, referring to CJ *Océano* (n 25) and CJ *Mostaza Claro* (n 28).

[86] BW, art 6:233: 'A stipulation in general conditions may be annulled: a) if it is unreasonably onerous to the other party, taking into consideration the nature and the further content of the contract, the manner in which the conditions have arisen, the mutually apparent interests of the parties and the other circumstances of the case; or b) if the user has not afforded the other party a reasonable opportunity to take cognizance of the general conditions.'

[87] BW, art 6:248: '1. An agreement not only has the legal effects agreed upon by the parties, but also those which, according to the nature of the agreement, apply by virtue of law, usage (common practice) or the standards of reasonableness and fairness.

2. A rule that is binding upon the parties as a result of the contract does not apply to the extent that, in the given circumstances, this would be unacceptable according to the standards of reasonableness and fairness.'

[88] BW, art 3:40(2): 'Violation of a mandatory statutory provision leads to nullity of the juridical act; if, however, the provision is intended solely for the protection of one of the parties to a multilateral juridical act, it leads to nullification only; in both cases this applies to the extent that it does not follow otherwise from the purport of the provision.'

[89] Another problem that has arisen is how to make the sanction on unfairness pursuant to internal law (in particular the 'annulment' provided by art 6:233 BW) compatible with art 6 of Directive 93/13/EEC, as interpreted by the CJ. See Hartkamp 2016 nos 188 and 252.

raise the complaint that the lower court has failed to carry out the examination of its own motion if the nature of relevant facts before the court is such that the court should have presumed that the directive might be applicable. The question of the *status* of the rules on consumer contracts—whether merely mandatory or of public policy—has been a significant issue particularly in Dutch law, which traditionally allows *ex officio* application only for public policy rules, not for mandatory rules (irrespective of whether or not they 'only' have a protective purpose). The question has also been raised in the context of competition law: see section II.B above and section III.B.ii (case 7.11 (NL)) below.

Hof van Beroep Gent (Court of Appeal of Gent),
4 January 2012[90]   **7.4 (BE)**

Sint Lucas v DSD

UNFAIR TERMS

Hospital invoice

The court is obliged to examine whether a contract term is unfair if the necessary legal and factual elements are available

Facts: A hospital sought payment due under a liquidated damages clause and a default interest clause included in the contract. The first instance court had *ex officio* raised the issue whether these clauses were in conformity with consumer law legislation.

Held: EU law requires the national court to assess of its own motion whether a contractual clause is unfair where it has available to it the legal and factual elements necessary for that task. If it considers such a term to be unfair, it must not apply it, except if the consumer opposes the non-application (*Pannon Gsm* and *VB Pénzügyi Lizing*).

Judgment: Articles 74, 17 WMPC—formerly Articles 32, 15 WHPC—is not a public policy rule. The prohibition contained in that provision protects private interests and does not concern essential interests of society. This does not, however, prevent the court from assessing of its own motion whether the clauses in a contract between a seller or enterprise and a consumer are in accordance with the relevant provisions and by doing so the court does not infringe the 'principe dispositive'. The court seized of the action is required to ensure the effectiveness of the protection which the Directive is intended to provide. Consequently, the role thus attributed by [EU] law to the national courts in this area is not limited to the mere power to rule on the possible unfairness of a contractual term, but also comprises the obligation to examine that issue of its own motion where it has available to it the legal and factual elements necessary for that task. When it considers such a term to be unfair, it must not apply it, except if the consumer opposes that non-application (reference the *Pannon Gsm* and *VB Pénzügyi Lizing*) ...
    ... The aim of the Directive is to ensure that unfair terms used in contracts concluded between a seller and a consumer are not binding on the consumer and that the contract will continue to bind the parties upon those terms if it is capable of continuing in existence

---

[90] Court of Appeal of Ghent 4 January 2012 *NJW* 2012,255 *VZW Algemeen Ziekenhuis St. Lucas and Volkskliniek v DSD.*

without the unfair term (Art. 6(1) Directive 93/13). That aim would not be achieved if the consumer were obliged to raise the unfairness of a contractual term himself. Effective protection of the consumer can only be attained if the national court acknowledges that it has power to evaluate terms of this kind of its own motion. The protection which the Directive confers on consumers thus extends to cases in which a consumer who has concluded a contract with a seller or supplier that contains an unfair term, fails to raise the unfair nature of the term (reference to *Cofidis*).

Notes:

(1) The decision serves as a typical example of the impact of CJ case law on Belgian law with regard to the *ex officio* assessment of the unfairness of contractual clauses in consumer contracts. On this issue, a convergence of results has been reached following both internal case law and the case law of the CJ. In a landmark decision of 2005, the Belgian Court of Cassation[91] ruled that the court is obliged to give a different qualification to facts and to raise different grounds when this possibility arises out of the facts 'spécialement invoqués' (expressly alleged) in the debate; if the facts have not been expressly alleged (they are only 'adventices'), the court merely has the option to exercise this power. The court must in any case respect the right to defence, that is, it has to inform the parties when it re-qualifies facts and must give them the opportunity to express their views on the matter.

(2) However, in light of the decision of the Belgian Court of Cassation and of CJ case law, the opposition between mandatory rules ('normes impératives') and public policy rules ('normes d'ordre public')—the former pertaining to the protection of private interests and the latter to fundamental values of society—has definitely been blurred. Previously, it was deemed that the courts could only *ex officio* raise the unfairness of a contractual clause by implying that consumer protection rules had to be characterised as *ordre publique* rules.[92] In the aforementioned decision, the Court of Appeal made it clear that the court is required to act of its own motion whether or not the consumer contract rules at issue are qualified as public policy rules.

---

[91] Belgian Court of Cassation 14 February 2005 *JLMB* 2005,856.

[92] See C Delforge,'Clauses abusives, office du juge et renunciation' (2008) 3 *JLMB* 93 ff with a comment to Court of Appeal of Liège (3th Chamber), 6 February 2006 in which decision the court first considered that the clauses at issue might be unfair and then opened the debate on the issue of unfairness. On the position that rules on unfair terms are rules of public policy, see Justice de paix de Charleroi (3ᵉ canton) 4 July 2008 *JLMB* 2008 p 1658; Justice de paix de Charleroi (3ᵉ canton) 25 October 2006 *JLMB* 2007 p 199 obs. P Wéry.

Audiencia Provincial de Madrid (Court of Appeal),
4 March 2013[93]   **7.5 (ES)**

El Corte Inglés, EFC, SA

UNFAIR TERMS

Order for payment procedure (*Banco Español de Crédito*)

The Spanish rules regarding the order for payment procedure must be interpreted in conformity with Directive 93/13/EEC and the case law of the CJ. Consequently, the court is allowed to assess whether a contractual clause is unfair at the first stage of the procedure

Facts: The claimant based his application for an order for payment on a consumer credit contract. The court considered that the contract contained an unfair term, but according to the Spanish rules it would not be allowed to assess the unfairness issue of its own motion.

Held: The Court of Appeal reversed the decision, stating that in light of the CJ judgment in *Banco Español de Crédito*, Spanish law can be interpreted to the effect that the court may assess whether or not a contractual clause is unfair at the first stage of the order for payment procedure.

Judgment: Therefore if one assumes, contrary to the position previously taken by the Court of Appeal of Barcelona in its reference for a preliminary ruling, that the court may assess of its own motion whether contractual terms stipulated to the detriment the consumer are unfair during the first stage of the Spanish order for payment procedure in which it decides on admissibility, the problem will cease to exist as a result of the consequences if the terms are declared unfair and therefore void … We interpret the national regulation on order for payment procedure in the light of the literal wording and the aim of Directive 93/13, as required by the judgment of 27 June 2010, *Murciano Quintero-*; and we preserve the Spanish rules regarding the order for payment procedure, whose stability would otherwise be seriously compromised while also taking into consideration that a different position would affect the application of EC Regulation CE 1896/2006 of 12 December 2006 creating a European order for payment procedure.

The judgment of 14 June 2012 is the outcome of the approach taken by the [Court of Appeal of Barcelona] to the Spanish rules regarding the order for payment procedure in its reference of the question to the CJ and cannot be considered more than that and, moreover, it cannot constitute a limit to the interpretation of the Spanish order for payment procedure in conformity with Directive 93/13/EEC of the Council of 5 April 1993 and with the CJ case law.

SIXTH.-In light of the foregoing, according to the criterion established by this *Audiencia Provincial*, in its broadest composition [*pleno*], the appeal must be allowed and the decision appealed must be annulled, in order to allow the *a quo* court to assess *ex officio* the unfairness of contractual clauses in the credit contract causing a detriment to the consumer and to declare them null and void with the consequences this will have according to the court for the contract and for the order for payment procedure.

Notes:

(1) The main issue decided by the Spanish Court of Appeal was whether the courts may assess in the context of an order for payment procedure whether a contractual clause

---

[93] Court of Appeal of Madrid 4 March 2013 no 906, 2012.

is unfair. Due to the importance of the issue, the Court of Appeal decided it sitting in full court ('pleno': 53 judges, of whom only five wrote a dissenting opinion). In its decision, the Spanish Court of Appeal extensively refers to the case law of the CJ relating to the *ex officio* assessment of the unfairness of contractual clauses which is an illustration of the line of reasoning and the style that characterise the Spanish decisions dealing with this issue.[94]

(2) Spanish legislation does not empower courts before which an application for an order for payment has been brought to find, of their own motion and *in limine litis*, that unfair contract terms are void. This means that the lawfulness of such terms can be assessed in the ordinary judicial procedure, which will only be initiated if the debtor lodges an objection to the application. It follows that if the debtor does not lodge an objection, the protection afforded by Directive 93/13/EEC cannot be enforced. Following a reference for a preliminary ruling made by a Spanish court, the CJ ruled in *Banco Español de Crédito* that Directive 93/13/EEC must be interpreted as precluding national legislation which, in cases where the consumer concerned has not lodged an objection, does not allow the court before which an application for an order for payment has been brought to assess of its own motion, *in limine litis* or at any other stage during the proceedings, whether a contractual term is unfair—even though it already has the legal and factual elements necessary for that task available to it. In the case discussed above, the Spanish first instance court, following the CJ ruling, had rejected the application made by the claimant on the grounds that the Spanish law on the order for payment procedure did not allow the court to assess whether the contractual clause was unfair. The decision of the Court of Appeal of Madrid discussed above gives a different interpretation of the national law in the light of *Banco Español de Crédito*,[95] which, unlike the interpretation by the first instance court, takes credit for ensuring the functioning of the Spanish order for payment procedure whilst making it compatible with EU law.

(3) The Spanish legislation implementing Directive 93/13/EC (*Ley 7/1998, de 13 de abril, sobre condiciones generales de la contratación*) does not specify whether the *nullidad* of the unfair terms can be declared *ex officio*, but only states that the consumer can claim such nullity under the general rules on nullity of contracts (Article 9). Recent national judgments on this matter have followed the CJ case law.

(4) When evaluating the impact of EU case law on the Spanish rules on consumer contracts, it must be mentioned that important legislative changes have been introduced in internal law following the CJ judgment in *Aziz*.[96] The reform (*Ley 1/2013 de 14 de*

---

[94] See in particular Supreme Court of Spain Section Civil 9 May 2013 no 241, 2013 concerning injunctions for the protection of consumer interests: this decision, even if incidentally, dedicates many paragraphs to the role of the courts in the assessment of the unfairness of the contractual clauses, with extensive references to CJ case law (paras 110–30); AP Castellón, sec 3, 24 July 2013.

[95] CJ *Banco Español de Crédito* (n 32).

[96] CJ 14 March 2013 C-415/11 *Mohamed Aziz v Caixa d'Estalvis de Catalunya, Tarragona i Manresa (Catalunyacaixa)* [2013] ECLI:EU:C:2013:164: Directive 93/13/EEC precludes legislation of a Member State which, while not providing in mortgage enforcement proceedings for grounds of objection based on the unfairness of a contractual term on which the right to seek enforcement is based, does not allow the court before which declaratory proceedings have been brought to grant interim relief, including, in particular, the staying of those enforcement proceedings, where the grant of such relief is necessary to guarantee the full effectiveness of its final decision.

Mayo, de medidas para reforzar la protección a los deudores hipotecarios, reestructuración de deuda y alquiler social) has amended the Spanish Code of Civil Procedure (*Ley de Enjuiciamiento Civil* (LEC)) in order to allow the courts, either on a party's request or *ex officio*, to assess the unfairness of contractual terms during the enforcement proceedings.[97] The Mortgage Law (*Ley Hipotecaria*) was amended too, to the effect that the notary must stay the extra-judicial auction when he has knowledge from the parties that the unfair terms of the mortgage credit contract at issue have been challenged before the civil court.[98]

Tribunal d'instance de Roubaix (First Instance Court),
16 October 2003[99]   **7.6 (FR)**

Soficino v époux D.

TWO YEAR PRESCRIPTION PERIOD (DÉLAI DE FORCLUSION)

In honor of Cofidis

The court may assess whether a term in a consumer contract is unfair even if the two-year prescription period provided for by Article L-311-37 of the code de la consommation has elapsed

Facts: The creditor claimed payment of principal, interest and costs due by the debtor under a consumer credit contract.

Held: On the basis of the CJ judgment in *Cofidis*, the tribunal may *ex officio* assess whether the clause is unfair even if the two-year prescription period provided for by internal law has expired.

Judgment: On the power of the court *ex officio* to raise the unfairness of a clause in a credit contract.

It is laid down by law that the court of first instance may raise the unfairness of a contractual clause included in a credit contract, either *ex officio* or following a defence raised by the consumer, even when the time limit [*délai de forclusion*] provided for by Article L-311-37 of the French Consumer Code has elapsed, in order to achieve the aim pursued by [Article] 6 of Directive 93/13/CEE of the Council on unfair terms in consumer contracts and to ensure that unfair clauses are not binding on the consumer (CJ, 21 November 2002, COFIDIS …).

One should bear in mind in this context that the solution envisaged by the CJEU is binding on all the national jurisdictions (Cass. ch.mixte, 24 mai 1975, Jacques Vabre, AJDA 1975, 567, note J. Boulouis et CJEU 9 mars 1978, Simmenthal, 106/77, Rec. p. 629) and that consequently the limits on the power of the courts to intervene *ex officio* in the field of consumer credit, as previously established by the *Cour de cassation* (Civ 1ère, 15 fév. 2000, Bull. civ. 1 no 49; 10 juin. 2002, Bull. civ. 1 no 195) no longer exist.

In the case under consideration, the contract concluded between the parties on the 18th of June 2001, is a consumer credit contract to which the public policy rules of the

---

[97] See LEC, arts 552, 557, 561 as amended.
[98] *Ley Hipotecaria, Texto Refundido según Decreto de 8 de febrero de 1946*, art 129(2)(f) as amended.
[99] TI Roubaix 16 October 2003 *SA Soficino v époux D.*

French Consumer Code apply. Even though the two year prescription period [*délai de forclusion*] had expired on the 19th of June 2003, the first instance court could assess the unfairness of the clauses in the consumer credit contract by its provisional judgment [*par jugement avant dire droit*] rendered on 3 July 2003 properly and in accordance with Articles 12 and 16 of *NCPC* [new code of civil procedure] since the parties had had the opportunity to discuss the unfairness issue and it was irrelevant that the contract clause at issue was stipulated before the MURCEF law of 12 December 2001, since this solution is based on the wording of Article L. 311-37 of the French Consumer Code interpreted in the light of Directive 93/13/EC.

Notes:

(1) The decision discussed above is one of numerous cases in which the courts did not follow the case law of the French Court of Cassation as developed from 2002 to 2009.[100] This case law did not allow the courts *ex officio* to raise the issue of violation of consumer contract rules, a problem which was perceived as relevant above all in the field of consumer credit, from which the major part of this case law originates. In 2009, the French Court of Cassation[101] changed its position by recognising that the *ordre public* provisions of the French Consumer Code (*Code de la consommation*) can be applied *ex officio*, in so doing substantially aligning with the view expressed by the lower courts deciding on factual issues and the CJ.

(2) Article 141-4 of the French Consumer Code currently provides the following: 'The court may raise of its own motion all the provisions of the code in disputes stemming from its application. After having heard the parties, the court of its own motion disapplies a clause whose abusive character results from the elements of the debate.' The first sentence was introduced by the *loi n° 2008-3* (*Loi Chatel*) in order to put an end to the case law of the French Court of Cassation as developed until 2009. The provision does not provide for an obligation, but only for an optional power. The second sentence was introduced by the *loi n° 2014-344* to adapt the *ex officio* rule to CJ case law and especially to the judgment in *Rampion* (see section II.C.ii above). Previously, it was maintained that the aim of consumer protection rules was to protect the interest of a specific individual or group (rules of *ordre public de protection*), which had the consequence that the courts were not allowed to raise the infringement of these rules *ex officio*. It may be noted that Article L 141-4(1), which provides that the courts may *ex officio* apply the rules of the Consumer Code, does not refer to *ordre public* provisions only (and therefore does not distinguish between *ordre public de protection* and *ordre public de direction*).

---

[100] See also: TI Vienne 19 October 2001 *CCC* 2001,21 (preliminary reference to the CJ); TI Niort 15 May 2002 *CCC* 2002, 21; TI Saintes 16 November 2005 *CCC* 2006 comm 37 note G Raymond (CJ *Rampion* (n 61)). See G Poissonnier, 'Mode d'emploi du relevé d'office en droit de la consommation' (2009) 5 *CCC* Étude 5; G Paisant, 'L'obligation de relever d'office du juge national' (2009) 42 *JCP G* 33–37; S Moracchini-Zeidenberg, 'Le rélevé d'office en droit de la consommation interne et communautaire' (2013) 7 *CCC* Étude 9.

[101] French Court of Cassation First Civil Chamber 22 January 2009 no 05–20.176 *Bull.* 2009, I, n° 9; *CCC* 2009 no. 86 note G Raymond.

(3) The possibility of an *ex officio* application of legal grounds based on EU law has never been questioned by the French Court of Cassation.[102] The general principle of the power of the courts to decide of their own motion can be inferred from Article 12 of the Code of Civil Procedure (*Code de procédure civile* (CPC)), which provides that it is for the courts to apply the rules that are applicable to the case.[103] It is generally recognised that the courts can of their own motion apply the nullity of a legal act, on the condition that the nullity has its basis in facts that have come to light in the debate and that the principle of the right to defence is respected. According to some opinions, the courts are obliged to apply the nullity *ex officio*.[104]

Hof van Beroep Brussel (Court of Appeal Brussels),
10 October 2008[105]   **7.7 (BE)**

Bima NV v Sodrepe NV

NULLITY OF ARTICLE 101 TFEU

Breweries waste

An agreement falling under Article 101 TFEU is automatically void and cannot be invoked by the parties as a basis for their claim

Facts: The claimant Bima was a firm that bought waste from breweries and sold it in the form of animal feed to farmers. Sodrepe worked for Bima as a collector of the waste and signed an agreement with Bima under which it engaged in the 'beer waste' trade in both Belgium and the Netherlands. Subsequently, Bima discovered out that Sodrepe had been engaging in anti-competitive practices. It suspended payment to Sodrepe for its collecting activities and sued Sodrepe, claiming compensation for damage suffered as a result of Sodrepe's anti-competitive practices.

Held: The agreement between Bima and Sodrepe was contrary to what is now Article 101 TFEU and therefore void, with the consequence that no claim based on that contract could be brought.

Judgment: The contract between Bima and Sodrepe—which includes the preamble mentioned as well as the management contract—is an agreement that could negatively affect trade between Member States and which has as its object or effect the prevention, restriction or distortion of competition within the [internal] market, and more specifically is an agreement that fixes purchase and selling prices, controls production, divides the markets, and consequently is *ab initio* void within the meaning of [now Article 101 TFEU] ...

---

[102] See Cour de Cassation, Rapport Annuel 2006, La Cour de cassation et la construction juridique européenne, La documentation Française, 142.

[103] The debate ensuing from the interpretation of this article also refers to the distinction between 'moyens de pur droit' and 'moyens mélangés de fait et de droit': in the former, the court has an obligation to intervene *ex officio*, while in the latter, this is optional. The Court of Cassation cannot apply of its own motion a *moyen mélangé de fait et de droit*, as it is not a court that decides on the facts. See J Normand, 'Principes directeurs du procès—Office du juge—Fondement des pretentions litigieuses' *Jurisclasseur Procédure civile* Fasc. no 152 1995.

[104] Y Picod, *Nullité, Rép. Civ. Dalloz* March 2013 no 35 p 9.

[105] Court of Appeal Brussels 10 October 2008 *TBH* 2009, 5 *Bima NV v Sodrepe NV*.

This nullity has the result that Bima cannot found any claims on alleged breach of contract (and specifically not termination of the contract against Sodrepe ...) and that Sodrepe, too, cannot found any claims on alleged breach of contract by Bima (and specifically not a claim for payment of outstanding and invoiced honoraria on the one hand, and payment of a conventional termination fee on the other hand).

Notes:

(1) The Court of Appeal Brussels applied Article 101 TFEU *ex officio* and declared the contract void. In Belgian law, the competition rules are considered public policy rules, regardless of whether they have their origin in internal law or in EU law.[106] In the context of this debate, see also *Brouwerij Haacht*, which also refers to *Van Schijndel*.[107]

(2) The general rule in Belgian law is that the courts can apply the nullity of a legal act of their own motion. Parties can make a procedural agreement to limit the object of the claim and to bind the court to pronouncing only on a specific point of law or fact, but, so the Belgian Court of Cassation has ruled, this agreement cannot prevent the court from applying rules of public policy.[108]

III.B.ii REFERENCES TO BOTH NATIONAL LAW AND EU LAW

Most of these cases illustrate the different ways in which EU law sources make their appearance in decisions of the national courts. In the various jurisdictions—Hungarian, Polish, Italian and Dutch—the problems that arose in specific cases could be properly solved on the basis of national provisions (relevant Codes and Acts). However, the courts at the same time decided to refer to EU law of their own motion, mostly to case law of the CJ. In most of these cases, the references are extensive and aimed mainly at giving a broader perspective to judicial argumentation. In this way, the references to EU law strengthen the argumentation in the obiter parts of the judgments.

---

[106] X Taton, 'L'office du juge et la nullité en droit de la concurrence' (2009) 5 *RDC* 492–93.

[107] Belgian Court of Cassation 15 May 2009 no C.08.0029.N *Brouwerij Haacht NV v BM*. Some doubts have arisen as to the meaning of this decision. See X Taton, N Franchoo, T Baeten and S Rooms, 'Chronique de jurisprudence (2004–2010)—Overzicht van rechtspraak (2004–2010). Les actions civiles pour infraction au droit de la concurrence—Private handhaving van het mededingingsrecht' (2013) 1 *RDC* 42–43, 23–25 (the rationale of the decision may be linked to the lack of proof of the conditions of exemption and then the decision may not be interpreted to the effect that art 101(3), unlike art. 101(1) TFEU, cannot be applied *ex officio*).

[108] Belgian Court of Cassation 28 September 2012 no C.12.0049.N *Renders Maria and Renders-Wilmsen v Westerdal*.

Fővárosi Ítélőtábla (Hungarian Regional Court of Appeal),
14 February 2014[109]   **7.8 (HU)**

UNFAIR TERMS

Mortgage debt in Swiss francs

National courts shall secure the conformity of national law with EU law by interpretation; consequently, Directive 93/13/EEC has to be taken into account when dealing with a consumer contract

Facts: One of two applicants borrowed just under €100,000 from a financial service provider, and the second applicant agreed to mortgage his house to secure repayment of this loan. Due to a delay in payment, the lender terminated the loan agreement and wanted to validate the mortgage debt, yet not at the price agreed in the contract, but at a much lower amount provided by an independent expert appointed unilaterally by the lender. Furthermore, the lender wanted to take possession of the house within five days. Both the right to appoint an independent expert to reconsider the value of the house and the five-day deadline to take possession were provided for by various articles of the loan agreement. The applicants challenged these articles as well as several others on various grounds, including their questionable fairness.

Held: The Regional Court of Appeal partially accepted the claims of the applicants. Referring to Directive 93/13/EEC, it took the ground that it might have the option of setting aside certain national rules in order to guarantee the coherence between EU law and national law. On the basis of a provision of the Hungarian Civil Code and Article 3(1) of the Directive, it declared that the disputed provisions of the loan agreement caused a significant imbalance between the parties, which it therefore held to be clearly unfair. In sum, the Regional Court of Appeal set aside these provisions (the other parts of the loan agreement were declared binding).

Judgment: When analysing the agreements in this case one must start from the fact that these agreements are to be classified as consumer contracts containing provisions not negotiated individually. On the basis of the declaration of the first respondent Article 7 of the agreement, which provides that an option to purchase the house constitutes a security for the loan, can be regarded as a general term. Consequently, Directive 93/13/EEC on unfair terms in consumer contracts (hereafter: Directive) must be taken into account in deciding this dispute …

The main aim of this Directive, so its preamble shows, is to create a regulatory framework that provides uniform protection against unfair terms and unambiguously defines consumer rights in the field of consumer protection, which has great relevance in the Member States of the European Union. The Member States may only adopt or retain provisions that are stricter than those of the Directive to ensure a maximum degree of protection for consumers (Article 8).

The national courts have an obligation arising from the substance of the Directive and the case law of the CJ to examine the conformity of national law with [EU] law in cases requiring the application of [EU] law. If necessary, national courts must ensure conformity by either harmoniously interpreting or setting aside the relevant national provisions. The fact that the national legislator has declared its intention to harmonize national law and [EU] law does not exempt the courts from this obligation. On the contrary, the examination of conformity is based on this intention. Thus, because of the primacy of [EU] law (see *Costa-Enel* C-6/64) provisions of national law are to be applied in conformity with both the Directive and those decisions of the CJ that interpret the Directive even following its successful implementation …

---

[109] Hungarian Regional Court of Appeal 14 February 2014 Pf.5. 21. 599/2013/6 nyr.

The Regional Court of Appeal finds that Article 7 of the contract offers the respondent a unilateral option to change the purchase price and this will be declared unfair pursuant to both Article 209(1) of the Civil Code and Article 3(1) of the Directive. This article of the contract is unfair since it is unfoundedly and unilaterally detrimental to the obligor in that it goes against the requirements of *bona fide* and fairness; furthermore, it also makes the relationship of the parties unbalanced. In examining the unfairness of this article the Regional Court of Appeal also refers to the operative part of the judgment of the CJ in C-415/11 *Aziz* which states that significant imbalance to the detriment of the consumer—as mentioned in Article 3(1) of the Directive—exists if a contract term puts the consumer into a situation which is a less favourable legal situation than that provided for by the national law. It must be examined whether the imbalance was caused by disregard of the requirement of *bona fide* during the contract-making process. The main question is whether the party making the contract with a consumer in a fair and equitable process could also have expected acceptance of the term in question if it had been negotiated individually. The Court concludes that the article at issue created significant imbalance in the relationship of the parties since it makes it possible for the obligee to unilaterally influence the purchase price in its favour; changing the purchase price, however, should only be possible by mutual agreement of the parties; and it can also be held that reasonably speaking a consumer will not accept such a contract term if negotiated individually. Therefore, Article 7 of the contract is unfair and does not bind the first applicant.

The Regional Court of Appeal also finds that Article 5.3 and 5.4 of the loan contract are invalid.

Notes:

(1) The decision of the Hungarian Regional Court of Appeal is not focused on the possibility for the courts to apply *ex officio* a legal ground not invoked by the parties, but it is nevertheless relevant to this issue, since the court interpreted national law in the light of Article 3(1) of Directive 93/13/EC on unfair terms in consumer contracts and in the light of related case law *(Aziz)*[110] in order to reach the conclusion that the term at issue was unfair (harmonious interpretation). The Hungarian courts may be expected to follow the CJ case law on the obligation of *ex officio* application as well.

(2) This judgment may shed light on an important general development in Hungarian civil justice. Although the case could be properly solved on the basis of national law, the court felt it necessary when it decided the case on the merits to turn to EU law of its own motion, namely to Directive 93/13/EEC. This argumentation strategy is intended to strengthen the authority of the decision and also indicates that over the past decade, judges have become increasingly familiar with EU law in general.[111]

---

[110] CJ *Aziz* (n 96).

[111] For a detailed analysis and discussion of the Hungarian courts' application of EU law provisions, see A Osztovits (ed), *A magyar bírósági gyakorlat az előzetes döntéshozatali eljárások kezdeményezésének tükrében 2004–2014* (Budapest, HVG-Orac Journal Publisher, 2014).

Sąd Najwyższy (Polish Supreme Court),
19 April 2007[112]   **7.9 (PL)**

Centrum Leasingu i Finansow v Aleksandra P

PROOF OF UNFAIRNESS

Expensive car

The court must of its own motion assess the value of the car and therefore the unfairness of the contractual clause providing for transfer of title to the car

Facts: In April 2001, the parties negotiated a sales contract for the sale of an Alfa Romeo car and a related consumer credit contract. As a security for the loan, the parties also concluded a contract providing for the transfer of title from the defendant—*Aleksandra P*—to the claimant—*Centrum Leasingu i Finansów.* In December 2001, the claimant terminated the consumer credit contract and claimed restitution of the car. The car was returned in 2002, and in 2003, the claimant sold it for 27,000 PLN. The claimant claimed payment of the difference between the amount of the loan and the (lower) proceeds of the sale of the car. The Regional Court dismissed the claim, while the Appellate Court awarded the amount claimed, holding that the burden of proof as to the value of the car was on the defendant (the defendant had submitted an expert's opinion, which showed that at the time of its restitution, the car was worth 52,000 PLN; however, she did not file a motion for admission to provide evidence by expert witness testimony and a mere expert's opinion did not constitute evidence in the case).

Held: The Supreme Court set aside the ruling and ordered the court deciding on the merits to take evidence as to the value of the car and to assess whether the terms of the contract providing for the transfer of title as security for the creditor were unfair.

Judgment: If therefore the case falls under the rules of the Civil Code relating to standardised consumer contracts, the court of first instance and the court of second instance must of their own motion apply these rules to a dispute between the entrepreneur and the consumer … for instance rules concerning interpretation of ambiguous terms of standard contracts and constituting a basis for the incidental ex officio examination of terms of standard contracts from the perspective of unfairness. An opinion expressed in academic legal literature that the courts lack this power … is misconceived. The legal position presented above, according to which courts apply substantive law of their own motion, including rules of the Civil Code concerning standard contracts used in legal relationships involving consumers, is in harmony with the view expressed in the Judgment of the [CJ] of 27 June 2000 in … *Océano* …, C-240/98 and C-241–244/98 ([2000] ECR I-4941). In this judgment, the Court of Justice accepted the power of a court seized of a case to ex officio declare a contract term unfair (see also Resolution of a panel of seven judges of the Supreme Court of 31 March 2004, III CZP 110/03, OSNP 2004, No. 9, item 133, and Resolution of the Supreme Court of 13 July 2006, III SZP 3/06, OSNP 2007, No. 1–2, item 35).

    …
    The court may also, however, of its own motion admit as evidence facts covered by the allegations of the defendant. This follows from article 232 2nd sentence of the Code of Civil Procedure (hereinafter: C.C.P.). With the exception of evidence falling under an explicit statutory prohibition (for example prohibitions following from Article 247 and 259 C.C.P.), the aforementioned possibility covers all evidence, including evidence by

---

[112] Polish Supreme Court 19 April 2007 *OSNC* 2008 no A item 25.

expert witness testimony; it is not restricted either by provisions establishing a so-called time-barring of evidence (see particularly Article 495(3) C.C.P.). In exceptional, special cases where this is justified by the circumstances, the courts may even be obliged to apply the second sentence of Article 232 C.C.P., in which case failure of the court of second instance to comply with this obligation may constitute a basis for an appeal in cassation [the Supreme Court referred to its previous case law].

That is what happened in this case. One must agree with the allegation made in the appeal in cassation that the Court of Appeal had violated Article 232 2nd sentence in conjunction with Article 278(1) C.C.P. by failing of its own motion to allow evidence by expert witness testimony of the value of the car at the moment of its surrender to the claimant, taking into consideration its condition, market prices of comparable cars and selling possibilities at that time. In a case like this where the defendant, relying on a privately obtained expert opinion, disputed the amount of the claim against her and argued that the value of the car had been arbitrarily fixed at a much lower sum than the market price and where the Court of Appeal had doubts about this claim even though the claimant had not submitted evidence to the contrary, the obligation of the court of its own motion to allow evidence by expert witness testimony on the matter did not only arise from the status of the defendant (a consumer), but also from the fact that the disputed sale of the car was made in connection with its transfer for security purposes ... The satisfaction of a creditor by way of enforcement proceedings protects not only the interests of other creditors but also the interest of the owner of the good serving as collateral—in particular the owner's interest in obtaining a high price. A creditor's means to obtain satisfaction provided for in a contract of title transfer for security purposes do not include comparable guarantees of the aforementioned interests, including the interest of the transferor ... because of the aforementioned doubts the courts should in particular closely examine the provisions in a contract of title transfer for security purposes that relate to the creditor's means of obtaining satisfaction and their enforcement. In fact, such examination serves as a minimum requirement for obtaining leave to enforce transfer of title for security purposes in a legal system. Especially when the transferor contests the appropriateness of the creditor's obtaining satisfaction by selling the good transferred, the court should of its own motion allow evidence by expert witness testimony of this fact, even though the burden of proof rests on the transferor—as in the present case—if the evidence presented so far is insufficient for the court to make a firm decision on the matter and if the failure of the transferor to submit a motion for such evidence may be considered excusable under the circumstances of the case. In this case the absence of such a motion in the appellate proceedings may be considered excusable since the first instance judgment was in the defendant's favour and she could assume that her first instance allegations based on a privately obtained expert opinion would also be sufficient in the appellate proceedings.

Notes:

In the above case, the Polish Supreme Court interpreted national law in conformity with CJ case law (*Océano*) in order to reinforce the argument that the court is allowed to apply legislation on unfair terms of its own motion. Furthermore, it ordered the lower court deciding on the merits to take evidence—by hearing an expert witness—as to the value of the car in order to enable it to assess whether the price obtained for the car was too low compared to its value and the creditor might therefore have abused his right. This latter decision is based on national law, as (pursuant to Article 232, second sentence of the Polish Code on Civil Procedure) the Court is allowed to take evidence of its own motion.

Tribunale di Genova (First Instance Court of Genova),
14 February 2013[113]   **7.10 (IT)**

SR v P SPA

UNFAIR TERMS

Luxury furniture

The court must of its own motion assess the unfairness of terms in consumer contracts

Facts: Following an opposition lodged by the consumer in an order for payment procedure, the fairness of several contract clauses in a consumer credit contract for the sale of furniture was at issue.

Held: The First Instance Court was obliged to assess on the basis of the CJ case law relating to Directive 93/13/EEC whether the contractual terms are unfair.

Judgment: When assessing the unfairness of the terms at issue, one must first of all bear in mind that the system of consumer protection was introduced by the European Directive 93/13 and that it is based on the idea that the consumer is in a weak position vis-à-vis the seller or supplier, as regards both his bargaining power and his level of knowledge and this leads to the consumer agreeing to terms drawn up in advance by the seller or supplier without being able to influence the content of the terms (CJ judgments 27 June 2000, *Océano* C-240/98 to C-244/98 … para 25; 26 October 2006, *Mostaza Claro* C-168/05 … para 25, and 6 October 2009, *Asturcom* C-40/08, … para 29).

Because of this position of weakness, Article 6(1) of the directive provides that unfair terms shall not be binding on consumers.

It follows from CJ case law that Article 6 is a mandatory provision aiming to replace the formal balance between rights and obligations reciprocally arising from the contract by a substantive balance, in order to re-establish equality between the parties (*Mostaza Claro* para 36; *Asturcom* para 30; 9 November 2010, *VB Pénzügyi Lízing* C-137/08 … para 47, and 15 March 2012, *Pereničová en Pereníč* C-453/10, para 28).

The CJ has underlined on several occasions that in order to ensure the effectiveness of the protection afforded by Directive 93/13, the imbalance between the consumer and the seller or supplier may only be corrected by positive action unconnected with the actual parties to the contract (see *Océano* para 27; *Mostaza Claro* para 26; *Asturcom* para 31, and *VB Pénzügyi Lízing* para 48 …).

On the basis of these principles the CJ has ruled that the national courts are required to assess of their own motion the contractual terms falling within the scope of Directive 93/13, thus compensating for the imbalance existing between the consumer and the seller or supplier (see to this effect, judgments *Mostaza Claro* para 38; *Pannon, Asturcom* para 32, and *VB Pénzügyi Lízing* para 49). Consequently, the role thus attributed by [EU] law to the national courts in this area is not limited to the mere power to rule on the

---

[113] *Nuova giur civ comm* 2013 I 1059; http://www.ilcaso.it/giurisprudenza/archivio/8973.pdf. See also Cass it Section II 21 March 2014 no 6748, *Nuova giur civ comm* 2014 I 727 ff, referring as well to the CJ case law relating to the *ex officio* assessment of unfairness.

possible unfairness of contractual terms, but also comprises the obligation to examine this issue of their own motion where it has available to it the legal and factual elements necessary for that task (see *Pannon* para 32).

Notes:

(1) In the above decision, the national court declared the nullity of several terms in a consumer credit contract. It should be noted that the court refered extensively to CJ case law to find that there is an obligation for the national court to assess of its own motion the unfairness of contractual clauses in consumer contracts even if the question of unfairness was explicitly raised by the consumer on the basis of national rules. Furthermore, it can be observed that pursuant to the Italian legislation implementing Directive 93/13/EEC, the sanction on unfairness provided by the national law is labelled in terms of 'nullità di protezione' (protective nullity; Article 36(3) of the Consumer Code (*Codice del Consumo*)). This is a peculiarity of the Italian rules on unfair terms as compared to the rules applying in other EU Member States: the contract is void and it is specified that the courts may *ex officio* apply the nullity, subject to the condition, however, that this application is not detrimental for the consumer. Since 1996, Italy has therefore, unlike most Member States, introduced a pattern of rules into its national legislation implementing Directive 93/13/EEC that is similar to that which has subsequently been developed by the CJ.[114]

(2) References to the case law of the CJ in general and especially to *Pannon* are made in a complex breakthrough decision of the United Section of the Italian Court of Cassation dealing with the question of the *ex officio* application of the nullity of a claim based on other grounds (in particular on annulment, termination or other grounds for nullity), and with the related issue of *res judicata*. In its rulings on the issues submitted to it, the Italian Court of Cassation laid down a general framework encompassing all the types of nullity for which the legal system provided, including 'nullità di protezione' under the rules on unfair terms in consumer contracts as well as the other types of nullity introduced into the legal system in recent times ('nullità speciali'), which constitute derogations from the notion of nullity as originally conceived. As the rules on these types of nullity were not always clear or complete, the problem of determining which rules apply had arisen, including the option or the obligation of the court to intervene of its own motion when the nullity is 'protective' and relative. In particular, the Italian Court of Cassation made clear that all the types of nullity, including protective nullity, are aimed at protecting a general interest and therefore may or must be applied *ex officio*. The references to the case law of the CJ serve to reinforce and enlarge the power and the duty of the national court to intervene of its own motion. The judgment in *Pannon* serves to demonstrate that there is no incompatibility between the *ex officio* application of nullity pursuant to the rules on unfair terms in consumer contracts (unless the consumer opposes the non-application of the unfair terms) and the fact that the nullity has a protective

---

[114] It is a matter of debate whether the same rules can be applied in other cases in which legislation provides for the sanction of nullity in relation to contracts between professionals or undertakings in which one is weaker than the other without further specifying the characteristics of the nullity.

function. According to the Italian Court of Cassation, the same line of reasoning must be extended to the other cases of protective and relative nullity provided by the legal system, even in the absence of a specific provision regarding the power of the courts to intervene of their own motion.[115]

(3) The power of the court to raise grounds based on EU law *ex officio* is generally recognised and several decisions—even though they concern vertical relationships—refer to the relevant CJ judgments, particularly in relation to cassation proceedings (*Van Schijndel, Peterbroek*).[116]

Hoge Raad der Nederlanden (Supreme Court of the Netherlands),
3 December 2004[117]   **7.11 (NL)**

Vreugdenhil v BVH

ANTI-COMPETITIVE AGREEMENTS

Spanish flowers

The nullity of a legal act that is contrary to EU competition law must be applied by the Court of Appeal of its own motion

Facts: Vreugdenhil and BVH concluded an agreement for the handling of Spanish flowers (*Dianthus*) for BVH. Article 1 of the agreement provided: 'Vreugdenhil shall handle the Dianthus flowers which are delivered ... from Spain to [BVH].' *Vreugdenhil* found out that another company handled part of the Spanish flowers for BVH. It claimed damages from BVH for breach of contract, alleging that the contractual provision (Article 1) entailed an exclusive right to handle *all* Dianthus flowers from Spain. BVH argued that it could not oblige its suppliers to have their Dianthus flowers handled by Vreugdenhil; the contractual obligation vis-a-vis *Vreugdenhil* only applied to cases in which the suppliers instructed BVH to handle the flowers.

Held: Assuming that Vreugdenhil's interpretation of Article 1 of the contract was correct, the Court of Appeal *ex officio* declared the contract partially void. The Supreme Court confirmed the judgment of the Court of Appeal.

Judgment: The Court of Appeal took the ground—rightly not challenged in cassation—that, insofar as necessary, it must *ex officio* establish the nullity of the contractual clause if the allegations made by the parties do not imply reliance on such nullity.

Notes:

(1) The issue of the *ex officio* application and status of competition law rules has been controversial particularly in Dutch law, as is also demonstrated by two seminal CJ

---

[115] Cass it Section United 12 December 2014 no 26242.

[116] Cass it Section V 9 June 2000 *Ministero delle Finanze v L. Piemonte* no 7909; Cass it Section V 10 December 2002 no 17564; Cass it Section III 5 December 2003 no 18642; Cass it Section V 16 July 2004 no 13225; Cass it Section II 15 March 2010 no 6231. There are also judgments of the administrative jurisdiction referring to *Van Schijndel* (n 5): see, eg, Council of State (*Consiglio di stato*) Section V 5 December 2002 no 6657.

[117] HR 3 December 2004 *NJ* 2005,118 ECLI:NL:HR:2004:AR0285 *Vreugdenhill v BVH*.

judgments regarding those fields, *Van Schijndel* and *Eco Swiss*,[118] which originated from a reference made by a Dutch court.[119] The problem arose on the one hand from the fact that under Dutch internal law, the courts may *ex officio* apply public policy rules even beyond the ambit of the contentions of the parties, while the *ex officio* application of mandatory rules not relating to public policy (even if the rule entails absolute nullity) is not allowed. On the other hand, the qualification of both national and EU competition rules as public policy rules, and hence the power (or duty) of the courts to apply such rules of their own motion, is subject to debate. The above decision preceded the CJ's decision in *Manfredi* and found that nullity of Article 101 TFEU must be applied *ex officio*.[120]

(2) According to an academic opinion[121] along the lines of the above decision, the courts should also have the power to declare a legal act null and void of their own motion if the violated rule is a mandatory rule entailing absolute nullity even if it does not concern public order. This is not, however, the prevailing view and the contrary opinion is supported by a decision of the Supreme Court of the Netherlands restricting the obligation of the court to intervene of its own motion with regard to rules of public policy by declaring that Article 6 of the Dutch Competition Act (*Mededingingswet*) (the national provision equivalent to Article 101 TFEU) is not a provision of public policy and, as a consequence, may not be applied *ex officio*.[122]

(3) Interestingly, in a (vertical) case outside the field of competition law, the Supreme Court of the Netherlands did not apply the traditional national criterion based on the rule at issue being classified in terms of public policy, but endorsed the CJ line of reasoning by directly referring to the ranking of the interest protected by the EU rule. Reviewing compatibility with EU law of a national measure connected with EC Decision 2000/766[123] (concerning certain protection measures with regard to transmissible spongiform encephalopathies and the feeding of animal protein), in particular the measure's date of entry into force prior to the EC decision, it ruled that the EU interest at stake

---

[118] CJ *Eco Swiss China* (n 42), concerning the *ex officio* application of a national rule requiring the court to annul an arbitral award violating EU competition law (see section II.A.ii in Ch 2). A similar problem was dealt with by the CJ in the two Spanish cases *Mostaza Claro* (n 28) and *Asturcom* (n 29) concerning the power of the national court to annul an arbitral award and to deny enforcement of a final arbitral award, respectively, on the ground that the arbitration clause was unfair. See section II.C.i above.

[119] Nevertheless, and interestingly, neither the CJ nor AG Jacobs paid much attention to the issue of the classification of the Dutch competition rules as rules of public policy in the procedure before the CJEU. See S Prechal and N Shelkopylas, 'National Procedures, Public Policy and EC Law: From van Schijndel to Eco Swiss and Beyond' (2004) 12 *ERPL* 596.

[120] For a description of the Dutch procedural framework, see J Chorus, 'Le relevé d'office de moyens de droit et de fait: l'application de règles du droit européen par le juge nationale: étude de droit compare et d'histoire de droit' in L Vacca (ed), *Scienza giuridica e interpretazione e sviluppo del diritto europeo. Convegno ARTISTEC Roma 9-11 giogno 2011* (Naples, Jovene Editore, 2013) 139–45.

[121] Hartkamp 2016 no 128.

[122] HR 16 January 2009 *NJ* 2009,54 ECLI:NL:HR:2009:BG3582 *De gemeente Heerlen v Whizz Croissanterie*. See Hartkamp 2016 nos 127–28.

[123] Council Decision of the Council of the European Union of 4 December 2000 on concerning certain protection measures with regard to transmissible spongiform encephalopathies and the feeling of animal protein [2000] OJ L306/32.

was not of such fundamental importance as to require the Court of Appeal to apply EU law of its own motion.[124]

III.B.iii MISCELLANEOUS

The last case is from the UK and it presents a different attitude to EU law. Here, the judges of the Supreme Court were reluctant to refer a question regarding the national legislation implementing Directive 93/13/EEC to the CJ for preliminary ruling.

UK Supreme Court, 25 November 2009[125]   **7.12 (UK)**

The Office of Fair Trading v Abbey National plc et al

ACTE CLAIRE

Application of construction

There is no need to refer the question of the definition of 'core terms' to the CJ for a preliminary ruling, as the matter is acte claire

Facts: The appellants were seven of the largest banks in the UK and one building society. The issue was whether the contractual term providing for the fees charged to the banks' customers for unauthorised overdrafts might be considered unfair or whether it had to be excluded from assessment of fairness on the basis of regulation 6(2) of the Unfair Terms in Consumer Contracts Regulations implementing Directive 93/13/EEC, insofar as this term is a 'core term'.

Held: Both the High Court and the Court of Appeal unanimously held that the term was not a core term and that it could therefore be assessed for fairness. The UK Supreme Court reversed the Court of Appeal's decision, holding that the term at issue could not be assessed for fairness by the Office of Fair Trading or the courts, since overdraft fees relate to a bank's remuneration and therefore fall under regulation 6(2) of the Unfair Terms in Consumer Contracts Regulations. The Supreme Court unanimously denied any reference for a preliminary ruling to the CJ.

Judgment: Lord Walker: If (as I understand to be the case) the Court is unanimous that the appeal should be allowed, then in my opinion we should treat the point as *acte clair*, and decide against making a reference. It may seem paradoxical for a court of last resort to conclude that a point is clear when it is differing from the carefully-considered judgments of the very experienced judges who have ruled on it in lower courts. But sometimes a court of last resort does conclude, without any disrespect, that the lower courts were clearly wrong, and in my respectful opinion this is such a case.

Even if some or all of the Court feel that the point is not *acte clair*, I would still propose that we ought not to incur the delay involved in a reference under [now Article 279 TFEU], since a decision on the correct construction of Article 4(2) of the Directive is not essential for the determination of this appeal. The correct construction of Article 4(2) is a question of [EU] law, but the application of the Article, properly construed, to the facts is a question for national law. Even if the Court of Appeal was not clearly wrong on the issue of

---

[124] HR 11 September 2009 *NJ* 2010, 369 ECLI:NL:HR:2009:BI7145 *Cagemax Holland BV v De Staat der Nederlanden, Ministerie van Landbouw, Natuur en Voedselkwaliteit.*

[125] *The Office of Fair Trading v Abbey National plc et al* [2009] UKSC 6.

construction, it was in my respectful opinion clearly wrong in applying its construction to the facts. In other circumstances it might be regarded as rather unprincipled to take that means of avoiding an important issue of [EU] law, but in the special circumstances of this case I would regard it as the lesser of two evils. There is a strong public interest in resolving the matter without further delay.

...

Lord Phillips: I have not found this an easy case and I do not find the resolution of the narrow issue before the court to be *acte clair*. I agree, however, that it would not be appropriate to refer the issue to the [CJEU] under Article 234. I do not believe any challenge to the fairness of the Relevant Terms has been made on the basis that they cause the overall package of remuneration paid by those in debit to be excessive having regard to the package of services received in exchange. In these circumstances the basis on which I have answered the narrow issue would seem to render that issue academic. It may be that, if and when the OFT challenges the fairness of the Relevant Terms, issues will be raised that ought to be referred to Luxembourg. That stage has not yet been reached.

...

Lord Mance: However, if one takes a different view on whether the position is *acte clair*, there remains the question of relevance. Eliminating the Court of Appeal's clear error in introducing as part of the test whether the relevant term had been 'directly negotiated', and assuming that the Court of Appeal was generally right in adopting as a test whether the term was 'not ... ancillary to the main bargain', the question would be whether the Court was right to treat the terms of the package contracts relating to the Relevant Charges as ancillary terms, rather than as part of the agreed price or remuneration in exchange for which the banks undertook to provide their whole package of services. That question would involve the application of the Directive and Regulations, which is, as I have said, a matter for domestic, not [EU], law ...

In these circumstances, it would be unnecessary to make a reference, even if the view were to be taken that the meaning of price and remuneration in Article 4(2) of the Directive is not *acte clair*.

Notes:

(1) This decision has great importance for the banking sector, since the clause under consideration is commonly used in contractual practice and since the decision was given in an action brought by the Office of Fair Trading under regulation 6(2) of the Unfair Terms in Consumer Contracts Regulations, on the basis of Article 7(2) of Directive 93/13/EEC, and therefore concerned all contracts concluded by the bank. The issue of classifying a specific contractual clause as a core term under Article 4 of Directive 93/13/EEC is particularly crucial in the case of bank, credit, insurance and investment contracts, which may contain clauses that are difficult to define as 'core' or 'ancillary' due to the complexity of the transaction as a whole.[126] Nevertheless, and although the first instance court and the appeal court took an opposite stand, all the judges of the Supreme

---

[126] The CJ rendered a significant decision on the interpretation of art 4 of Directive 93/13 in *Kásler* (n 57) concerning both the definition of 'core terms' and the notion of transparency, while also dealing with the *ex officio* issue.

Court agreed that reference was not required, a position they based on various and over-lapping considerations: the matter is *acte claire*; reference would cause delay; and lack of relevance.

(2) Without discussing the merits of the matter, this reluctance of the Supreme Court to refer the case to the CJ[127] can be set against the more proactive approach shown by other national courts, in particular, the Spanish courts, which do not seem to hesitate to seek guidance from the CJ when they are in doubt as to the interpretation of EU law or to follow the CJ rulings. The possibility of referring the question regarding the unfair terms regulations to the CJ was also considered, though less extensively, in *Director General of Fair Trading v First National Bank*,[128] in which Lord Bingham excluded the need for a preliminary ruling as the language was, in his opinion, 'clear and not reasonably capable of differing interpretations' (para 17). The UK Court of Appeal referred to the CJ some questions relating to the interpretation of the *Unfair Commercial Practices Directive* (Directive 2005/29 EC)[129] in the *Purely Creative* case.[130]

IV. CONCLUSION AND COMPARATIVE REMARKS

1. In *Van Schijndel*, the CJ accepted that the courts may in principle raise points of EU law of their own motion.

2. Subsequent case law dealing with the *ex officio* application of grounds based on EU law has been focused mainly on the field of consumer contracts. In this context, the procedural autonomy of Member States—however it may be interpreted[131]—has been remarkably limited, as the CJ tends to tilt the balance towards effectiveness. This finds expression in the leading cases of *Océano* and *Mostaza Claro* and in a series of subsequent cases. The principle of equivalence plays a role as well. This principle is applied when the national procedural rules that limit the possibilities for the courts to intervene of their own motion are not applied in ordinary first instance proceedings, but in other procedures and when the national law offers a general point of reference for *ex officio* application in those procedures, eg, procedures for the enforcement of a final arbitration award (*Asturcom, Pohotovost'*) or appeal proceedings (*Asbeek Brusse, Faber*). In these cases, the CJ seems to take a more deferential approach to the national procedural systems.[132]

---

[127] The same reluctance can be inferred from the UK Supreme Court decision in *Stott v Thomas Cook Tour Operations Ltd* [2014] UKSC 15. See J Prassl, 'Montreal Convention Exclusivity and EU Passenger Rights: "Exposing Grave Injustice"'(2014) 130 *LQR* 538 ff.

[128] *Director General of Fair Trading v First National Bank* [2001] UKHL 52.

[129] Directive 2005/29/EC of the European Union Parliament and the Council of 11 May 2005 concerning unfair business-to-consumer commercial practices in the internal market and amending Council Directive 84/450/EEC, Directives 97/7/EC, 98/27/EC and 2002/65/EC of the European Parliament and of the Council and Regulation (EC) No 2006/2004 of the European Parliament and of the Council [2005] OJ L149/22.

[130] CJ 18 October 2012 C-428/11 *Purely Creative Ltd et al v Office of Fair Trading* ECLI:EU:C:2012:651.

[131] Prechal 1998 682, which includes further references to the debate.

[132] However, it seems that the principle of equivalence has been interpreted by the CJEU beyond its traditional understanding, in the direction of a greater interference with the national procedural rules, by the elaboration of an autonomous conception of (European) public policy prevailing over the domestic categorisations. See Ebers 2010 857; Schebesta 2010 857.

3. The trend observed in the context of consumer contracts can be described as incremental. The rules introduced by the CJ with respect to specific cases tend to be extended to other cases. In particular, where Directive 93/13/EEC is concerned, the rules introduced with respect to jurisdiction clauses have been applied to all contractual clauses falling under the Directive. The line of reasoning developed in relation to Directive 93/13/EEC has also been applied in relation to Directive 87/102/EEC, Directive 85/577/EEC and Directive 99/44/EC. There seems to be room for further extension, particularly regarding the obligation for the national courts to examine of their own motion, since the CJ has provided only limited guidance on this point.

4. Furthermore, there has been an increase in the number of rules that are recognised by the CJ as rules of public policy or as equivalent to rules which the national legal systems qualify as public policy rules: Articles 101 and 102 TFEU, Article 6 of Directive 93/13/EC, Article 11(2) of Directive 87/102/EEC, Article 4 of Directive 85/577/EEC and Article 5(3) if Directive 99/44/EC.[133] This has resulted in broader opportunities for EU law to influence the traditional course of national civil procedures.

5. Six grounds can be identified in the discussion on the *ex officio* application of EU law provisions by the national courts. There is no conceptual connection between these six grounds, but occasional overlaps may occur depending on the specific context. These grounds are the following:

1. The first ground is any express provision of law requiring the courts to automatically apply a rule of EU law …
2. The second ground is an interpretation given by the Court of Justice to a rule of (written or unwritten) EU law to the effect that the rule must be automatically applied …
3. The third ground is a provision or judicial interpretation from which it can be deduced that a rule of EU law is a rule of public policy …
4. and (5) The fourth and the fifth grounds are the well-known principles of (4) effectiveness and (5) equivalence …
5. The principle of equivalence is further tightened by what is known as the 'may as must' rule: if the national courts may apply a rule of national law of their own motion, they must of their own motion apply the corresponding rule of EU law.[134]

It may be concluded that EU law provisions have certainly pierced the veil of national civil procedures at many points, so that primary and secondary EU law currently has a much wider scope for influencing private relationships in Member States than was the case in the first decades of European integration.

6. Since the most significant examples of the *ex officio* application of EU law are found in the fields of competition law and consumer contracts, it is difficult to present a general assessment. However, some considerations and conclusions can be formulated. In some legal systems, such as that of the Netherlands, the power of the courts to raise

---

[133] For the debate on the classification of national and EU law as public policy rules and its implications, see in particular Ebers 2010 823 ff; Schebesta 2010 847 ff; Prechal and Shelkopylas (n 119) 589 ff; T Corthaut, *EU Ordre Public* (Alphen aan den Rijn, Kluwer Law International, 2012) 200 ff.
[134] Hartkamp 2016 no 130; Hartkamp 2014 483–84.

points of law of their own motion is subject to stricter requirements and is made dependent on the characterization of the rule at issue as a rule of public policy, i.e. a rule of the strictest mandatory character. On the contrary, in other legal systems such as those in Italy and Spain, this characterisation does not play a role in the *ex officio* application of points of law. This distinction has been blurred in the field of consumer contracts, due to the impact of the case law of CJ. As a result, the Dutch national courts have recognised the existence of an obligation to raise *ex officio* the unfairness of contractual terms in consumer contracts.

7. In France, the case law of the CJ likewise forced the French Court of Cassation to change its previous approach and it also led to subsequent legislative reform, to the effect that the distinction between *ordre public de protection* and *ordre public de direction* ceased to hamper the *ex officio* assessment of unfairness in consumer cases. In Spain, too, the case law of the CJ has been invoked by national courts as a legal foundation for their *ex officio* assessment, likewise leading to legislative reforms in specific sectors of consumer law. In Italy, the influence of EU law has gone beyond the fields covered by the EU directives, leading to significant changes in the traditional concept of nullity in general. Some other national courts—such as the Dutch and the Polish Supreme Courts— have recognised the obligation of *ex officio* examining factual elements of a case for the purpose of assessing the unfairness of consumer contract clauses in general, whereas so far the CJ has only had occasion to issue rulings on a court's power to examine whether a contract falls within the scope of application of a directive (*Pénzügyi* and *Faber*). This is a significant development, since in the matter of distributing proof between the parties and the court, the national legal systems generally apply the principle that it is for the parties to furnish facts, while the duty of a court to investigate elements of fact of its own motion is conceived as an exception to the rule.

8. There is one more development that can be mentioned. National courts refer to the case law of the CJ by way of illustration of their reasoning. Even though a case can be decided solely on the basis of national law, some courts include references to relevant primary and secondary EU law provisions and to CJ case law.

FURTHER READING

F Castillo de la Torre, 'Le relevé d'office par la juridiction communautaire' (2005) 41(3–4) *CDE* 397–401.

J Chorus, 'Le relevé d'office de moyens de droit et de fait: l'application de règles du droit européen par le juge nationale: étude de droit compare et d'histoire de droit' in L Vacca (ed), *Scienza giuridica e interpretazione e Sviluppo del diritto europeo. Convegno ARTISTEC Roma 9–11 giogno 2011* (Naples, Jovene Editore, 2013).

T Corthaut, *EU Ordre Public* (Alphen aan den Rhijn, Kluwer International, 2012) 200–51.

M Ebers 'ECJ (First Chamber) 6 October 2009, Case C-40/08, Asturcom Telecomunicaciones SL v. Cristina Rodríguez Nogueira. From Océano to Asturcom: Mandatory Consumer Law, *Ex Officio* Application of European Union Law and Res Judicata' (2010) *ERPL* vol 18 no 4 p 823–846.

B Fekete, 'Raising Points of Law on the Courts' Own Motion? Two Models of European Legal Thinking' (2014) 21(4) *MJ* 652–75

AS Hartkamp, '*Ex officio* Application in Case of Unenforceable Contracts or Contract Clauses: EU Law and National Laws Confronted' in L Gullifer and S Vogenauer *English and European Perspectives on Contract and Commercial Law*, Essays in Honour of Hugh Beale (Oxford, Hart Publishing, 2014) p 467–484.

T Heukels, 'Joined Cases C-430/93 and C-431/93, and C-312/93, Case Comment' (1996) 33(2) *CMLR* 337–53.

S Prechal, 'Community Law in National Courts: The Lessons from Van Schijndel' (1998) 35(3) *CMLR* 681–706.

S Prechal and N Shelkopylas, 'National Procedures, Public Policy and EC Law: From van Schijndel to Eco Swiss and Beyond' (2010) *ELRP* 589–611.

H Schebesta, 'Does the National Court Know European Law? A Note on *Ex Officio* Application after Asturcom' (2010) *ERPL* vol 18 no 4 p 847–880.

M Storme (ed), *Rapprochement du Droit Judiciaire de l'Union européenne—Approximation of Judiciary Law in the European Union* (Dordrecht, Kluwer & Martinus Nijhof, 1994).

V Trstenjak, 'Procedural Aspects of European Consumer Protection Law and the Case Law of the CJEU' (2013) 21(2) *ERPL* 451–78.

S Whittaker, 'Who Determines What Civil Courts Decide? Private Rights, Public Policy and EU Law' in D Leczykiewicz and S Weatherill (eds), *The Involvement of EU Law in Private Relationships* (Oxford, Hart Publishing, 2013).

INDEX